Learning Disabilities: Concepts and Characteristics

second edition

Gerald Wallace
University of Virginia

James A. McLoughlin
University of Kentucky

Charles E. Merrill Publishing Company
A Bell & Howell Company
Columbus   Toronto   London   Sydney

for our children

**Christopher and T.J. Wallace
Sean and Timothy McLoughlin**

Published by
Charles E. Merrill Publishing Company
A Bell & Howell Company
Columbus, Ohio 43216

This book was set in Helvetica and Avant Garde.
The production editor was Linda Hillis Bayma.
The cover was prepared by Will Chenoweth.

Photos on pp. 3, 23, 77, 349 by Celia Drake; pp. 366, 369, 385, 387, 483 from *Resource Teaching,* Charles E. Merrill Publishing Co., 1978; pp. 357, 389 courtesy of The University of Southern California; p. 47 and all photos appearing in chapters 5-10 by Tom Hutchinson; photos in chapters 12-14 by Lee Edgington.

Library of Congress Catalog Card Number: 78-78261

International Standard Book Number: 0-675-08263-3
1 2 3 4 5 6 7 8 9 10/ 85 84 83 82 81 80 79
Printed in the United States of America

The purpose of this book is to acquaint readers with concepts of learning disabilities and to describe observable characteristics of learning disabled children. This book is intended to serve as a basic text for introductory courses in learning disabilities and as an overview for professionals in service who want to know more about this rapidly growing field.

The second edition of this book is significantly different from the first edition in many aspects. The recent national effort to define learning disabilities and the continuing controversy concerning certain testing and teaching procedures have contributed to our discussion regarding the concept of learning disabilities. The Education of All Handicapped Children Act, P.L. 94–142, helped to reshape our focus in all chapters, particularly in our discussion of diagnosis, educational provisions, and parent involvement. New case studies and profiles are included in this edition in order to illustrate more fully the various types of learning disabilities. New chapters on adolescents and adults and current issues in learning disabilities are also reflective of recent emphases in this field.

The plan of this book is to provide readers with the basic information and foundational skills for understanding and working with learning disabled children. We believe that this information and these skills are critical prerequisites for selecting and implementing effective remedial stategies for those children. To that end, the chapters are organized to focus on three major kinds of information: what the concept of learning disabilities involves, how to recognize learning deficits in children, and how to explore effective solutions for their difficulties.

Part one serves to ground the reader in the major ideas upon which the concept of learning disabilities has been built. Forged from many philosophies and fields, LD continues to function as a viable educational perspective in learning. As we survey historical directions and current influences in the field, we make note of professional efforts to synthesize earlier and more recent practices, especially in the area of educational assessment. We also point out, where relevant, some of the more questionable aspects of the LD concept.

Part two contains the major emphasis of this book and, we believe, the most immediately useful material for present or prospective workers in this field. Six chapters, each focusing on a different problem area, describe the characteristics of learning disabled children in terms of *practical classroom behaviors*. Each chapter lists *specific* academic tasks and social skills, detailing the problems LD children have with each. In addition, each chapter discusses levels of severity of these learning problems and lists an array of informal techniques and standardized tests for diagnosing problems. Each of these chapters concludes with a discussion of available programs and sources for teaching materials and procedures that have been successfully used in remediation.

Part three discusses the possible future solutions for reducing the causes and improving the remediation of learning disabilities. Various educational provisions, the LD specialist, and parents of the learning disabled are discussed as essential resources for delivering services to the LD student. Special needs during the early childhood years, and at the adolescent and adult levels, are also described in this part of the book.

The reader will find a specific educational point of view espoused throughout the book, a viewpoint developed out of our own experiences of teaching learning disabled children and our activities in training teachers in this field. In addition, the *in-perspective* sections of many chapters contain our own conclusions about major needs and possible new directions in the field. It is our sincere hope that our readers will find this material beneficial in helping learning disabled individuals.

Gerald Wallace
James McLoughlin

ACKNOWLEDGEMENTS

We would like to express our appreciation to a number of people who have provided us with support throughout the completion of this book. Professor Don Deshler of the University of Kansas, Steve Larsen of the University of Texas at Austin, Rena Lewis of San Diego State University, and Fred West of Jefferson County Schools in Louisville, Kentucky offered many useful suggestions and material. Jo-Ann McFadden, Jim Patton, Cindy Patterson, and Vicky Perkins, graduate students at the University of Virginia, helped with library research, references, and the index. We appreciate the children and adults who appeared in the photographs taken by Lee Edgington and Tom Hutchinson. Our thanks are also extended to Sharron Hall and Suzanne Haggard who helped type the manuscript. Finally, the loving encouragement and unique support of our wives, Marti and Jo-Ann, are deeply appreciated.

CONTENTS

part one

A Conceptual Basis for Learning Disabilities

Children with difficulties in learning have been the concern of specialists from many different disciplines for a number of years. Educational, psychological, and medical services for the mentally retarded, emotionally disturbed, and children with sensory handicaps have long been offered through various schools, agencies, and organizations.

The field of education, in particular, has greatly contributed to a more thorough understanding of children with mental, physical, and emotional handicaps by organizing many different *special education* programs for handicapped children. Special schools, self-contained special classes, and, more recently, resource rooms have been the major special education offerings.

Since the 1960s, children with "learning disabilities" have been the focus of both educational and psychological concern. Learning disabilities constitute a recent addition to special education. This field emerged as a self-conscious discipline during the early 1960s. The term is used to describe a particular group of exceptional children experiencing certain specific learning disabilities. The term is *not* intended as a generic classification for all children with learning problems. It does not include learning problems that are primarily due to other handicapping conditions. Children who are mentally retarded or blind, for example, may have learning problems; however, the primary handicap is other than a learning one.

Due to the relatively recent origin of this field, there are many definitions, approaches, and techniques that describe the child with learning disabilities. Part one of this book is intended to provide you with a conceptual basis for further study in this area. Chapter 1 introduces the dimensions of learning disabilities, including the multidisciplinary nature of this area of study. Chapter 2 outlines the historical development of the learning disabilities concept. Definitions of learning disabilities are discussed in this chapter. Chapter 3 surveys the educational, environmental, psychological, and physiological factors causing learning disabilities. Chapter 4 provides an overview of how learning disabilities are diagnosed. The Individual Education Plan (IEP) serves as a focus in this chapter. The in-perspective section at the conclusion of most chapters highlights our personal perspectives on the topic.

1
Dimensions of
Learning Disabilities

PREVIEW

It has been suggested that learning disabilities represents one of the largest, and perhaps most controversial, categories in special education (Larsen, 1976). The implementation of a full range of public school programs for LD children and youth and the establishment of professional organizations, journals, and certification standards reflect this growth in public interest. In addition, 47 states now mention the category of learning disabilities in their administrative guidelines.

The specific dimensions that characterize LD individuals serve as a focus for this introductory chapter. Learning disabled students, by definition, do differ from other children encountered by teachers in their classrooms. Learning disabilities describes a *specific* population of handicapped children. The term should not be used as a broad, inclusive term for all children experiencing learning problems. Our discussion of the Public Law (P.L.) 94-142 definition of learning disabilities, along with specific details of how the LD individual differs from other students, should provide a basic introduction to this topic. The prevalence of learning disabilities among the school-age population is also summarized.

Our discussion of the interdisciplinary nature of learning disabilities outlines the perceived roles and contributions of specialists from the various disciplines interacting with LD children and youth. Without question, we believe that the LD specialist should be primarily responsible for coordinating any efforts of contributing professionals. It is our opinion that the LD specialist is indispensable in planning, initiating, and maintaining the educational program for learning disabled students.

Profile

Jason, age 13, received special instruction from a teacher of learning disabled children for 4 years. During his first year in a self-contained learning disabilities classroom, Jason was described as academically impoverished and extremely disruptive. On the playground, he would climb trees, basketball poles, and fences. He played only by himself. In the classroom, he would not attend to any one activity for a reasonable amount of time. School records indicated a superior intelligence; however, Jason exhibited meager math and reading skills. His reading vocabulary was limited to approximately 10 words.

Jason went home at noon during that first year in the special class. The teacher reported that neither she nor Jason could survive any longer than half a day. The teacher's morning hours during that year were spent in attempting to teach Jason how to read by a multisensory approach and in reviewing math skills. By the end of his first year in the learning disabilities class, Jason learned to discriminate individual sounds and identify most sounds with the corresponding symbol. He could also add and subtract number combinations up to 10. Jason's superior art ability and his keen interest and skill in playing checkers became the main reinforcers for the completion of various assignments.

During his second year in the learning disabilities class, Jason continued to increase in word recognition skills. He combined letters that were placed on cubes into words. His sight word vocabulary also increased to the extent that he was able to read a number of first-grade-level books. Jason also became very interested in math as he progressed in this subject. During the beginning of his second year of special help, Jason's pediatrician also prescribed a medication that helped increase his concentration and decrease his hyperactivity. He was attending the learning disabilities class for the full day by the end of his second year in the program.

By the middle of his third year, Jason received regular class math instruction. He learned successfully in a large class for the first time in his school career. Jason also continued to make satisfactory reading progress. He could decode words well and comprehend stories at the second-grade reading level.

Jason's fourth year in the learning disabilities class was his last year in the program because his parents moved out of state. By the time he moved, Jason had progressed to spending all afternoon in a regular classroom. His math skills were near grade level, and his achievement in reading was at approximately the third-grade level. Jason was beginning to exhibit some confidence in his ability just prior to his move. He continued, however, to require supportive help in reading, written expression, and various study skills. Jason's learning disabilities were far from completely remediated. His teacher recommended continued special education services in junior high school.

The plight of the child with learning disabilities is exemplified by the case of Jason. Prior to the early 1960s, there were few public school services available for children with learning disabilities. However, in the short time since then, the field of education has witnessed a nationwide surge of interest in these children. Classes for the LD child are found in school districts throughout this country. Colleges and universities have also reacted to this interest in the learning disabilities field by implementing programs for training teachers in this area.

Although the proportion of all handicapped students receiving an education has seen a steady rise, the National Advisory Committee on the Handicapped reported that 45% of all handicapped students were not being served during the 1975-76 school year. It is even more astonishing to note that only 13% of the learning disabled were being served during this same time period.

These figures were pointed out by the United States Congress in forming the Education for All Handicapped Children Act of 1975. This legislation, known as P.L. 94-142, has been called a bill of rights for the handicapped. According to Ballard (1977), the law has four major purposes:

- Guarantee the availability of special education programming to handicapped children and youth who require it.
- Assure fairness and appropriateness in decision making about providing special education to handicapped children and youth.
- Establish clear management and auditing requirements and procedures regarding special education at all levels of government.
- Financially assist the efforts of state and local government through the use of federal funds. (p. 1)

The National Advisory Committee on the Handicapped points out that P.L. 94-142 gives national approval to the proposition that handicapped children have a right to an education geared to their needs and aspirations. The law actually opens the way for schools to broaden their horizons by giving equal consideration to those students with handicaps.

Of course, children not achieving at a level commensurate with their intellectual capabilities have been the concern of educators for years. In his historical perspective on the education of the learning disabled, Wiederholt (1974) points out that the roots of scientific and philosophical interest in the LD student are probably as old as these disciplines themselves. However, the extent of the current interest in handicapped children, as reflected by P.L. 94-142, and more specifically the extent of the current interest in learning disabilities, is both unique and unparalleled in the history of educational services to exceptional individuals.

Since this chapter is designed to serve as an overview of the LD field, many of the dimensions discussed here will be more fully developed in subsequent chapters. The parameters described in this chapter merely serve as an introduction to this area of special education.

SPECIFIC DIMENSIONS

What Is a Learning Disability?

The term *learning disabilities* refers to a *specific* group of handicapped children and youth. The definition in the Education for All Handicapped Children Act is as follows:

Specific learning disability means a disorder in one or more of the basic psychological processes involved in understanding or in using language, spoken or written, which may manifest itself in an imperfect ability to listen, think, speak, read, write, spell, or to do mathematical calculations. The term includes such conditions as perceptual handicaps, brain injury, minimal brain disfunction, dyslexia, and developmental aphasia. The term does not include children who have learning problems which are primarily the result of visual, hearing, or motor handicaps, of mental retardation, or of environmental, cultural, or economic disadvantage. (Section 5(b) (4) of P.L. 94-142)

Although the definition will be further discussed in some depth in chapter 2, we believe it is important to point out at the onset that the term *learning disabilities* is not synonymous with terms such as *remedial reader* or *slow learner.* This definition deals specifically with children and youth who have very *severe* and *specific* learning disabilities. The learning disabled student will need special education that Ames (1977) believes "should involve practices that are unique, uncommon, of unusual quality and that, in particular, supplement the organizational and instructional procedures used with the majority of children" (p. 8). The LD specialist usually assumes instructional responsibility for re-mediating a child's specific learning disability. This specialist works with the child individually or in small groups and also assists with regular class placement and adjustment.

In contrast, there is a broader group of children in our schools with learning problems who are not considered to be a part of this definition. These children need to be differentiated from the *specific* learning disabled. Kirk (1978) points out that the broader group of students with learning problems can often be handled through consulting teachers, the education of regular teachers, or modifications of the elementary school curriculum, whereas the specific LD child will usually require intensive remedial assistance. Similarly, Ames (1977) believes that students with mild learning problems can often remain in the main-stream of education with an adapted curriculum, but special educational provisions will usually be necessary for the student with specific learning disabilities.

In sum, we believe it is necessary to reiterate that all learning problems are not necessarily within the scope of the P.L. 94-142 definition of specific learning disabilities.

How Does the LD Student Differ from Other Individuals?

As compared to more visible handicaps, such as orthopedic problems and sensory deficits, the LD student has often been referred to as an individual with an "invisible handicap." The LD child usually appears normal in every respect except for the fact that his or her learning difficulties limit progress in school. In describing this problem, Anderson (1970) refers to learning disabilities as a "hidden handicap."

> It is not apparent in the physical appearance of the young person. He may have a robust body, good eyes, sound ears, and a normal intelligence. He has a disability of function, however, which is just as real as a crippled leg. (p. 1)

Chronological age, grade level, a multitude of specific academic disabilities, different modes of learning, and underachievement are some of the most important dimensions that must be considered in diagnosing a learning disability.

Chronological Age and Grade Level

Learning disabled children can be found at all ages and grade levels. A large number of these youngsters are identified during the late primary and early intermediate grades, when independent achievement in basic school subjects is expected. Children who have academic difficulties at these grade levels are often readily identified and subsequently diagnosed. In addition, the current educational emphasis upon early recognition of LD children has increased the number of these children identified at the kindergarten and first-grade levels. Some of the difficulties associated with the early recognition of learning disabilities are discussed in chapter 12.

Educational provisions for LD adolescents are not as prevalent as elementary grade provisions for LD children, and the actual number of adolescents who have learning disabilities is unknown at the present time (Hammill, 1978). There are, however, many adolescents whose learning disabilities have only recently been diagnosed, and others who will continue to require the help begun in elementary school (Anderson, 1970).

Services for the learning disabled have also recently been initiated at post-secondary levels. Many college-age individuals with learning disabilities are provided with personalized programs of instruction. Fortunately, a number of colleges and universities have recognized the significant differences among learning styles that are found in the learning disabled, even at the post-high school level. Some of the problems associated with LD adolescents and adults are discussed in chapter 13.

Individuals with learning disabilities are found at each succeeding chronological age and at every grade level from kindergarten through college. The preponderance of these children at the elementary level is primarily due to the interest in and emphasis on identification and remediation at this level. The successful remediation of many LD children also correspondingly reduces the actual number of cases at higher grade levels. Even fewer numbers of LD children might be found in higher grade levels in the future, as more schools increase their emphasis upon early identification and remediation. Chapter 11 further delineates the variety of educational provisions for learning disabled children.

Types of Learning Disabilities

The basis of homogeneity for LD children is their *disability in learning.* It is only when we begin to categorize the specific types of learning disabilities that differences among these children show up.

The characteristics of the learning disabled child vary widely. Many of these children encounter difficulties in one specific area (e.g., arithmetic), while others experience problems with a number of academic subjects. Difficulties are primarily divided among many school-related tasks, including listening, thinking, talking, reading, writing, spelling, and arithmetic. Part two of this book outlines many of the specific characteristics of learning disabilities in school-related subjects. However, even within each of these areas, many learning disabled children will be markedly different. Children with written language problems, for example, vary from the child who is unable to hold a writing implement properly to the older LD child who has difficulties in expressing his thoughts in writing. For example, Chuck's work, as shown in figure 1-1, indicates a number of written language problems.

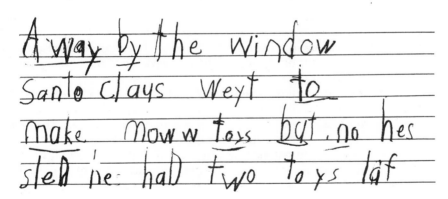

Figure 1-1
Example of a Nine-Year-Old Boy's Written Language

The complexity of the learning disability will often be dependent upon the chronological age of the child. Younger LD children exhibit difficulties that are often easily recognized. As the child matures, the once-clear difficulties pervade other academic areas and often become very complex.

Learning disabled children often have problems which permeate a number of academic areas. Achievement in many school tasks will be affected, for example, by various auditory difficulties. In addition to the problems the child may have in learning phonics, this youngster might also have difficulty in following directions, in completing assignments, or in expressing himself or herself verbally. The interference from auditory difficulties might therefore extend over a number of academic subject areas.

Learning disabilities are not similar among all LD children. Each youngster exhibits difficulties that are unique to him or her. Wallace and Kauffman (1978) have noted that not all children are hampered by identical deficiencies. In addition to extending across academic tasks, learning problems are complicated by varying degrees of difficulty, by the age of the child, and by the child's attitude toward his disabilities (pp. 8-9).

Mode of Learning

The LD child's approach to learning may differ markedly from that of the child who learns without any difficulties. Many learning disabled children will require new ways to learn concepts or particular skills that they were unable to learn in the conventional fashion. The preferred modality for learning has been frequently mentioned in regard to LD students. Tarver and Dawson (1978) point out that a student's strengths and weaknesses have often been related to sensory modality capabilities, resulting in the notion of auditory learners, visual learners, and so forth. However, their review of research finds very little empirical support for the validity of the modality strength concept. This particular topic is discussed further in chapter 10.

An integrated approach to learning which emphasizes kinesthetic and tactile stimulations along with visual and auditory presentations is also frequently suggested for some LD children (Luria, 1970). The VAKT (visual-auditory-kinesthetic-tactile) approach often utilizes the tracing of letters and words in reading or the tracing or numerals in arithmetic.

Multisensory stimulation is but one teaching adjustment that might be implemented because of a child's unique learning style. A study carrel where a child is not distracted by extraneous stimuli and is able to concentrate upon the task at hand is another example. Smaller classes, specialized equipment, unusual teaching materials, and shorter school days are other adjustments that have been successfully utilized in response to an LD child's specific style of learning.

All of these adjustments help to teach the learning disabled child in a more efficient fashion. Many LD children learn differently. Consequently, alternative approaches to instruction are often a necessary part of any program of remediation. Part two of this book outlines many alternative instructional programs for the child with learning disabilities.

Underachievement

One of the major criteria for the classification of children as LD is their underachievement. The learning disabled child's underachievement must be considered in terms of capacity, or ability for learning, in contrast to underachievement due to mental retardation or sensory deficits (Bryant, 1972).

Underachievement is most often defined in terms of 1 or 2 years behind grade level for children of normal intelligence. However, *discrepancy* may also be used to define underachievement. With this method, it is necessary to determine a child's *present* level of achievement and his or her own *potential* for learning. A certain amount of discrepancy between the two ratings is then judged to be significant.

The discrepancy method of determining underachievement has been used with only a limited degree of success. Determining a child's potential for learning has been beset with the problems involved in assessing intellectual capacity, including test selection, fairness to various minority groups, and the accuracy of the IQ concept. The amount of discrepancy between potential and actual level of achievement is another factor that must be considered. Johnson and Myklebust (1967) caution that this approach has some inherent problems. The second grader with a 1-year discrepancy in achievement is certainly in much greater difficulty than the ninth-grade youngster with a 1-year discrepancy. The use of a discrepancy score for determining underachievement is further discussed in chapters 2 and 4.

Attempts to determine the basis for underachievement have not been particularly helpful. However, motivational factors, inappropriate teaching, and a specific disability in learning certain skills all seem related to the extent of underachievement for some students.

What Is the Prevalence of Learning Disabilities?

The task of determining the prevalence of certain groups of people within a given population is usually handled by agencies of the federal or state government. Prevalence figures are studied for a number of different reasons. For the purposes of our discussion, note that these figures usually provide guidelines for planning and funding educational programs on the local, state, and national levels. National and state prevalence figures provide local school officials with some idea of the actual number of learning disabled children, for example, within their individual school districts. On the other hand, many national prevalence figures cannot be easily applied to local school districts because of the tremendous differences among towns and cities across the country. Extreme caution must be exercised in applying national figures to local jurisdictions. School districts must realize that a 12% figure quoted nationally, for example, might be totally inappropriate when applied locally.

The determination of the prevalence of any type of child is usually beset by difficulties with the criteria, techniques, and instruments used to identify that particular group (Bruininks, Glaman, & Clark, 1971; Kass & Myklebust, 1969). Estimating the prevalence of LD children has been no exception. The growing number of programs and the many misconceptions of learning disabilities have certainly contributed to the confusion in estimating realistic prevalence data.

A number of writers have suggested that the lack of a precise definition of children with learning disabilities is the major reason for the lack of definitive prevalence rates in the area (Payne, Kauffman, Brown, & DeMott, 1974). Other studies have pointed out that few current prevalence estimates of children with learning disabilities are supported by findings from empirical studies (Bruininks et al., 1971).

The variety of prevalence rates is illustrated in the estimates listed in table 1-1. Comparison between these estimates is certainly not suggested since each estimate is based upon a somewhat different definition of learning disabilities or a different group of children. The Meier (1971) prevalence estimate is based upon an investigation that studied more than 3,000 second-grade children in 110 regular classes randomly selected from eight Rocky Mountain states. The Bryant (1972) figures, in contrast, are based upon a review of 21 different surveys of school populations.

The actual number of LD children will probably continue to remain unclear and somewhat confusing until identification procedures are clarified and more objective research is conducted. In the meantime, professionals in this field must continue to work at the challenge of further clarification of specific learning disabilities.

INTERDISCIPLINARY NATURE OF LEARNING DISABILITIES

The complex and varied nature of learning disabilities has attracted individuals from widely different backgrounds. The interdisciplinary nature of this field is reflected in the settings—schools, hospitals, mental health clinics, diagnostic centers, and private clinics—in which learning disabled children are served. Furthermore, professionals from education, speech and language, psychology, and medicine have all contributed to the identification, diagnosis, and remediation of specific learning disabilities. In the following section, the roles and contributions of specialists from each of these disciplines will be discussed.

Education

The field of education is primarily concerned with teaching people. Teachers consequently emerge as *the* most important professional

Table 1-1
Prevalence of Learning Disabilities

study	estimated percentage
National Advisory Committee on Handicapped Children (1968)	1-3%
Kass and Myklebust (1969)	3-5
Meier (1971)	15
Bryant (1972)	3-28
Kirk and Elkins (1975)	2.5

working with the LD child, since this child's problem is *a learning* disability. Education serves the learning disabled child through a variety of specialties.

Learning Disabilities Specialists

Many school districts presently employ individuals whose primary responsibility is that of serving children with learning disabilities. These teachers, most often trained through special education departments, are commonly labeled according to the administrative provisions for LD children within an individual school district. Consequently, the titles *resource room teacher* or *special class teacher* are actually by-products of the programs in specific school districts. However, Larsen (1976) maintains that the responsibility of the LD specialist in the school is to plan, initiate, and maintain educational programs for children and youth who have been labeled learning disabled. Frequently, it is the LD specialist's responsibility to deal with some or all of the following questions:

- Of the frequently large number of referred pupils, which ones will be identified and eventually labeled as learning disabled?
- What diagnostic and remedial strategies offer the best hope in assisting the child to receive a quality education?
- Would it be more efficient to establish a resource room consulting teacher program, or self-contained class?
- Are other specially trained personnel available in cases where relatively unique problems exist? (Larsen, 1976, p. 38)

Regular Classroom Teachers

The role of regular classroom teachers has been described as increasingly more important in the remediation process (MacMillan & Becker, 1977). The current emphasis on mainstreaming LD students into regular classrooms has certainly contributed to this importance. Regular classroom teachers are additionally being requested to help both identify and assess those children who might be *potentially* learning disabled. The skills that are required of the classroom teacher to adequately identify, assess, and remediate some learning disabled children are being taught through inservice meetings and workshops. In some few cases, preservice training programs are offered to elementary education majors. The role of the regular classroom teacher is defined by both increased awareness and responsibility. It is based upon the current emphasis in special education on actively involving the regular classroom teacher with learning disability specialists and with the learning disabled individual himself.

Physical Education Teachers

Some learning disabled children have difficulties in the area of gross motor skills, balance, and coordination. The physical education teacher who provides a special program of remediation serves as a vital part of the educational team working with the child. A number of physical education teachers have incorporated *adaptive physical education classes* into their schedules to accommodate the needs of these children. The child is usually provided with an individually prescribed program of remediation during these sessions. The skills that are gained often help to increase the child's self-confidence, besides teaching some important physical skills.

Remedial Reading Teachers

The majority of children who are classified as learning disabled have as their most obvious symptom difficulty in learning to read (Abrams, 1976; Kirk & Elkins, 1975). Moreover, since the onset of remedial reading services in public schools, teachers in this area have been concerned with learners disabled in reading. It is therefore not surprising to note the continued interest in the LD student by remedial reading teachers.

Some remedial reading teachers have recently been denied the opportunity of working with disabled students due to various misunderstandings, faulty certification regulations, discriminating funding, and the problem of territorial rights (Sartain, 1976). The confusion and misunderstandings that emerge from the overlapping efforts of professionals are not easily resolved. Nonetheless, we believe a cooperative effort among educators is absolutely essential if we are to consider the best interest of all LD students.

Speech and Language

The field of speech and language pathology has many interests in and concerns with learning disabled children. Typically, these professionals are most concerned with articulatory deficits, voice quality, and the acquisition of both receptive and expressive language. An audiologist is the specialist interested in the normal and abnormal aspects of hearing.

The relationship between language and learning (Chomsky, 1968; Skinner, 1957) has been investigated with some intensity during the past few years. The academic difficulties that often correspond to many language deficits are but one indication of the very close relationship between these two areas. Progress in reading, in written expression, and even in certain quantitative processes will be hampered by a child's inability either to understand or to use spoken language.

Speech and language clinicians have only recently become aware of the considerable number of LD children who have language problems. Close working relationships between learning disability specialists and speech and language clinicians are slowly developing. These relationships are crucial in terms of remedial methods, ongoing research, and cooperative in-school efforts for the learning disabled child.

Psychology

The major contributions of people in the field of psychology to learning disabilities have been primarily within the areas of diagnostic assessment, observation, and therapeutic counseling. In terms of specific occupational roles, school psychologists and guidance counselors have made important contributions in helping the LD child.

School Psychologists

In contrast to clinical psychologists, most school psychologists work primarily in educational settings. One of their major roles is the psychological evaluation of children suspected of being learning disabled. Individual assessments most often include measures of intellectual functioning, behavioral observations, and specific psychological indices of particular learning problems. The educational implications of psychological evaluations are usually shared with classroom teachers, learning disability specialists, and the child's parents.

School psychologists also serve as an important resource to other school personnel. Many have successfully attempted to emphasize the educational aspects of their role and to place their psychometric or testing tasks in better perspective. Consequently, large numbers of classroom teachers are now being provided with pertinent suggestions for managing various types of behavior problems in the classroom.

Guidance Counselors

The school psychologist in many school districts is supported by guidance counselors. These professionals are also basically trained in a psychological perspective. Guidance counselors typically engage in both individual and group counseling. The emotional health of the learning disabled child is the primary focus of their concern. In addition to serving the child in learning disabilities by directly counseling him or her, many guidance counselors work indirectly by offering management suggestions to classroom teachers.

Guidance counselors also serve as the liaison between the home and the school. Problems of a personal nature that are directly attributable to the home situation are often explored by the guidance counselor. Many parent groups that meet to discuss the commonality of problems that they share as parents of LD children have been initiated or led by guidance counselors (McWhirter & Cabanski, 1972). Some counselors also have private practices to provide therapeutic counseling to either the child with learning disabilities, his or her parents, or both.

Medicine

Various medical specialists (pediatricians, neurologists, ophthalmologists, psychiatrists, otologists, endocrinologists, biochemists, and nurses) help in both preventing learning disabilities and in determining possible organic causes. The following discussion briefly outlines the individual roles of some of the more important medical specialists who deal with LD children.

Pediatricians

The medical specialty of pediatrics is primarily concerned with the diagnosis, treatment, and prevention of childhood diseases. The pediatrician is often the first professional to recognize an abnormality in the child's development because he or she sees a child from an early age over a long period of time. Parents who are concerned about a child's slowness in developing motor skills, for example, or about delayed acquisition of language will often first consult with a pediatrician. Even in later school years, pediatricians often counsel parents who are upset over a child's behavior or academic difficulties.

It has only been in the past few years that pediatricians as a group have recognized the important role they should serve in regard to learning disabled children (Garrard, 1973). Medical schools have recently begun to teach the characteristics of LD children. Many pediatricians who have become knowledgeable in this area have volunteered to educate other physicians. Seminars on learning disabilities are becoming commonplace at medical society meetings. In short, the last few years have witnessed a tremendous increase in both the awareness and management of learning disabilities within the field of pediatrics. Pediatricians are recognizing their responsibility in both the recognition and prevention of learning disabilities.

Neurology is the branch of medicine that deals with the nervous system and its diseases. The neurologist is the individual who is most often consulted when it is suspected that the disability might have an organically related cause. Neurologists usually study a child's medical history, examine his or her reactions and reflexes, and often give a brain wave test, or electroencephalogram (EEG), to measure the electrical activity of the brain. The neurologist may prescribe tranquilizers and other drugs following the examination.

The physician who specializes in the eye and related diseases is called an ophthalmologist. Many children with learning disabilities, especially those in the area of reading, are given eye examinations as part of a complete battery of diagnostic tests. Ophthalmologists, however, rarely detect any eye disease that would cause the learning disability. Wagner (1971) further suggests that even when glasses are prescribed, the child will not necessarily read better, even though he or she may see better.

The confusion in regard to the role of the ophthalmologist with the LD child is probably due to the early emphasis that was placed upon visual perceptual factors. Ophthalmologists were mistakenly consulted if a child was suspected to have a problem in this area. However, visual perceptual disturbances are due to cognitive or psychological dysfunctions, and not to the organic ocular difficulties with which the ophthalmologist is concerned.

Psychiatry is the branch of medicine that treats mental and neurotic disorders and the pathologic changes associated with them. A psychiatrist is the physician who deals with the emotional problems that often appear as a secondary reaction to the specific learning disability. Lack of academic success for a child with average or above-average intellectual capacity and the corresponding frustrations are often manifested in various types of social-emotional problems. Some types of personality disorders are also associated with learning disabilities (Gottesman, Belmont, & Kaminer, 1975).

In addition to the help that some psychiatrists provide for LD children through individual or group therapy, a number of parents are also counseled. Many parents require therapeutic help to accept the child's problem or to overcome the feelings of guilt, denial, or anger that sometimes accompany the initial diagnosis of their child.

The psychiatric help that many children receive often enables them to participate more fully in various programs of remediation. The psychiatric counseling, in other words, seems to prepare the learning disabled child to cope with academic frustrations. Psychiatrists are just beginning to explore various other types of therapeutic interventions (e.g., drug therapy) available for the child with learning disabilities. The effectiveness of additional alternatives such as drug therapy will hopefully be more fully understood in the years ahead (Nichol, 1974).

Other Professions

Social Workers

Professionals in the field of social work have been active members of many interdisciplinary teams that evaluate learning disabled children. Social workers usually interview the parents of the child during the diagnostic work-up. They gather pertinent home and family information, along with any other developmental information that might relate to the child's learning disability. The social worker may also be an agent to implement needed changes in the home environment.

Optometrists

An optometrist is basically concerned with measurement of the eye's refractive powers. He or she also fits glasses to correct ocular defects. Optometry is not a medical specialty, and the optometrist is not a medical doctor. Optometrists can prescribe eye exercises or eye training procedures for some learning disabled children. However, many writers (Benton, 1973) seriously question the specific value of optometric treatment for LD children and youth. No impartial research is available to document the validity of eye exercises. Consequently, it is our belief that such training programs are unnecessary for LD students.

Occupational Therapists, Physical Therapists, and Recreational Therapists

Some severely learning disabled children who are evaluated and treated through mental health or hospital clinics are often prescribed various therapies as part of their programs of remediation. Occupational, physical, or recreational therapy might be suggested depending on the age of the child, the severity of the learning disability, and the availability of such services.

INTERDISCIPLINARY APPROACHES: IN PERSPECTIVE

The usefulness and relevance of a interdisciplinary approach to learning disabilities have recently been questioned by a number of workers in this field. The reasons for all learning disabled children being evaluated by professionals from a wide variety of disciplines, the use of drug therapy with some children, and optometric training have all come under attack during the past few years. Some question the applicability of many diagnostic results, while others suggest that there is little educational relevance in eye exercises.

There seems to be little wisdom in having all learning disabled children evaluated by a team of 8 to 10 professionals from different disciplines over a period of days. Likewise, there seems to be little reason to place *all* children with learning disabilities on tranquilizers (Sprague & Sleator, 1973) or under the care of an optometrist. The usefulness of these procedures to the child, the parent, and to the individual professional must be seriously considered in each case.

In addition to these concerns, disputes have also arisen as to which professional groups are best qualified to instruct the LD child. Larsen (1976) refers to this as the *territorial rights* issue. The problems associated with this issue are naturally both varied and complex. Nonetheless, we believe that Larsen speaks clearly to providing a solution for this problem when he suggests that "the person with the demonstrated skills corresponding to the needs of the pupil will take responsibility for carying out an appropriate educational plan" (p. 507).

It is our belief that all children with learning disabilities must be individually judged. Some children, for example, will not need an ophthalmological examination or a psychiatric evaluation. However, we believe that *all children will probably require some sort of educational intervention.* Learning disabilities specialists should serve a central role in working with the LD student. Many educational findings have direct applicability to both actual classroom procedures and the remediation of certain specific learning disabilities. In contrast, some interdisciplinary evaluations or procedures have little direct effect on the amelioration of learning disabilities.

Education is *the most important component* in the learning disability process when the nature of interdisciplinary approaches is placed in proper perspective, though the contribution of other professions to the growth of this field must not be overlooked. On the contrary, we believe that many important advances in this field are due to the mutual cooperation among different disciplines. The nature of their responsibilities, however, dictates the very important role to be assumed by the learning disabilities specialist.

SUMMARY

This chapter has presented an overview of the dimensions of learning disabilities. The heterogeneity of learning disabled children was demonstrated in a discussion of chronological age and grade level differences, specific disability variability, different modes of learning, and under-achievement. The confusion regarding the prevalence of learning disabilities was also explained. Finally, the interdisciplinary nature of learning disabilities was discussed, and the roles of various professionals in education, speech and language, psychology, medicine, and ancillary fields were reviewed.

SUGGESTED ACTIVITIES

1. Write what you consider to be a good definition of learning disabilities, and list some characteristics which might be observed in LD students. Save your definition and list of characteristics for future comparison with chapter discussions in this book.

2. Attend a local or state Division for Children with Learning Disabilities (DCLD) meeting or an Association for Children with Learning Disabilities (ACLD) meeting.

3. Become familiar with the following journals:
   Learning Disabilities Quarterly
   (official journal of DCLD)
   1920 Association Drive
   Reston, Va. 22070
   Journal of Learning Disabilities
   101 E. Ontario Street
   Chicago, Ill. 60611
   Academic Therapy Quarterly
   P.O. Box 899
   San Rafael, Calif. 94901

4. Arrange a visit to a local educational facility for learning disabled students. Choose one particular child to observe and write up a report of your observations.

5. To what extent are the various disciplines discussed in this chapter involved in the learning disabilities program in your own geographical region?

6. Ask various individuals to define learning disabled and note the variations among responses.

7. The National Information Center for the Handicapped will provide information concerning handicapped children to parents and professionals. Write to
   Closer Look
   P.O. Box 1492
   Washington, D.C. 20013

8. Arrange to visit a local pediatrician. Ask the pediatrician to outline his or her role with the learning disabled.

References

Abrams, J.C. More on interdisciplinary cooperation. *Journal of Learning Disabilities,* 1976, *9,* 603-604.

Ames, L.B. Learning disabilities: Time to check our roadmaps? *Journal of Learning Disabilities,* 1977, *10,* 328-330.

Anderson, L.E. (Ed.). *Helping the adolescent with the hidden handicap.* Los Angeles: California Association for Neurologically Handicapped Children, 1970.

Ballard, J. *Public law 94-142 and section 504—Understanding what they are and are not.* Reston, Va: Council for Exceptional Children, 1977.

Benton, C. Comment: The eye and learning disabilities. *Journal of Learning Disabilities,* 1973, *6,* 335-337.

Bruininks, R.H., Glaman, G.H., & Clark, C.R. *Prevalence of learning disabilities: Findings, issues, and recommendations.* Washington, D.C.: Department of Health, Education, and Welfare, U.S. Office of Education, Project No. 332189, 1971.

Bryant, N.D. Subject variables: Definition, incidence, characteristics, and correlates. In N.D. Bryant & C.E. Kass (Eds.), *Leadership training institute in learning disabilities* (Vol. 1). Washington, D.C.: U.S. Office of Education, Bureau of Education for the Handicapped, 1972.

Chomsky, N.A. *Language and mind.* New York: Harcourt Brace Jovanovich, 1968.

Garrard, S. Role of a pediatrician in the management of learning disorders. *Pediatric Clinics of North America,* 1973, 20, 737-754.

Gottesman, R., Belmont, I., & Kaminer, R. Admission and follow-up status of reading disabled children referred to a medical clinic. *Journal of Learning Disabilities,* 1975, *8,* 642-650.

Hammill, D.D. Adolescents with specific learning disabilities: Definition, identification, and incidence. In L. Mann, L. Goodman, & J.L. Wiederholt (Eds.), *Teaching the learning-disabled adolescent.* Boston: Houghton Mifflin, 1978.

Johnson, D.J., & Myklebust, H.R. *Learning disabilities: Educational principles and practices.* New York: Grune & Stratton, 1967.

Kass, C., & Myklebust, H. Learning disabilities: An educational definition. *Journal of Learning Disabilities,* 1969, *2,* 377-379.

Kirk, S.A. An interview with Samuel Kirk. *Academic Therapy,* 1978, *13,* 617-620.

Kirk, S.A., & Elkins, J. Characteristics of children enrolled in the child service demonstration centers. *Journal of Learning Disabilities,* 1975, *8,* 630-637.

Larsen, S.C. The learning disabilities specialist: Role and responsibilities. *Journal of Learning Disabilities,* 1976, *9,* 498-508.

Luria, A.R. The functional organizations of the brain. *Scientific American,* 1970, *222,* 66-78.

MacMillan, D.L., & Becker, L.D. Mainstreaming the mildly handicapped learner. In R. Kneedler & S.G. Tarver (Eds.), *Changing perspectives in special education.* Columbus, Ohio: Charles E. Merrill, 1977.

McWhirter, J., & Cabanski, C. Influencing the child: A program for parents. *Elementary School Guidance and Counseling,* 1972, *7,* 26-31.

Meier, J.H. Prevalence and characteristics of learning disabilities found in second grade children. *Journal of Learning Disabilities,* 1971, *4,* 6-21.

National Advisory Committee on Handicapped Children. *Special education for handicapped children.* First Annual Report. Washington, D.C.: U.S. Department of Health, Education, and Welfare, January 31, 1968.

Nichol, H. Children with learning disabilities referred to psychiatrists: A follow-up study. *Journal of Learning Disabilities,* 1974, *7,* 118-122.

Payne, J.S., Kauffman, J.M., Brown, G.B., & DeMott, R.M. *Exceptional children in focus.* Columbus, Ohio: Charles E. Merrill, 1974.

Sartain, H. Instruction of disabled learners: A reading perspective. *Journal of Learning Disabilities,* 1976, *9,* 489-497.

Skinner, B.F. *Verbal behavior.* New York: Appleton-Century-Crofts, 1957.

Sprague, R.L., & Sleator, E. Effects of psychophramacologic agents on learning disorders. In H. Grossman (Ed.), *The pediatric clinics of North America,* 1973, *20,* 719-736.

Tarver, S.G., & Dawson, M.M. Modality of preference and the teaching of reading: A review. *Journal of Learning Disabilities,* 1978, *11,* 17-29.

Wagner, R.F. *Dyslexia and your child.* New York: Harper & Row, 1971.

Wallace, G., & Kauffman, J.M. *Teaching children with learning problems* (2nd ed.). Columbus, Ohio: Charles E. Merrill, 1978.

Wiederholt, J.L. Historical perspectives on the education of the learning disabled. In J. Mann & D.A. Sabatino (Eds.), *The second review of special education.* Philadelphia: JSE Press, 1974.

The Concept of Learning Disabilities

PREVIEW

There *is* something called a learning disability. We listen with chagrin to claims that a learning disability is better defined by saying what it is *not*. In this chapter we will discuss the LD definition in P.L. 94-142 and other LD definitions. Four basic aspects of the LD concept will be used to analyze these definitions: (1) establishing a discrepancy between what an LD child should but cannot do; (2) knowing what a learning disability appears as; (3) ruling out other considerations; and (4) focusing upon possible explanations.

Learning disabilities as a concept has been shaped by many historical factors. This heterogeneity of input may explain both the confusion and vitality in the field. What is more evident to us is the definite direction in which the concept of LD is going and must go.

> Specific learning disability means a disorder in one or more of the basic psychological processes involved in understanding or in using language, spoken or written, which disorder may manifest itself in imperfect ability to listen, think, speak, read, write, spell, or do mathematical calculations. The term includes such conditions as perceptual handicaps, brain injury, minimal brain dysfunction, dyslexia, and developmental aphasia. The term does not include children who have learning problems which are primarily the result of visual, hearing, or motor handicaps, of mental retardation, of emotional disturbance, or environmental, cultural, or economic disadvantage. (Section 5(b) (4) of P.L. 94-142)

The definition just given is the result of an extensive effort to establish an operational definition of learning disabilities. As we shall see, the definition produced from input by professionals and others in the field is essentially a definition developed in 1968 by the National Advisory Committee on Handicapped Children (NACHC). This NACHC definition has been used by most states to direct services for children with learning disabilities (Gillespie, Miller, & Fielder, 1975).

The present state of the concept of learning disabilities and services for LD children is well characterized by the recent effort to define learning disabilities in P.L. 94-142. Few professionals were satisfied with the end result, but were willing to accept a least restrictive definition. The search for a definition to label a form of service conflicted with the goal of serving LD children. Every effort to become specific, for example, to develop a formula to establish the presence of LD, was frustrated by the weaknesses of measurement techniques.

Nonetheless, learning disability professionals agree upon many critical factors. The common experiences of persons who have worked with

LD children have created certain dimensions to our understanding of what a learning disability is.

DIMENSIONS OF THE DISABILITY

There are many definitions of specific learning disabilities. Table 2-1 contains representative conceptualizations, with the P.L. 94-142 definition being the most popular. The authors of these definitions and others have the same intent, that is, to define learning disabilities in such a way as to organize the necessary services.

There are four basic dimensions across definitions: (1) a discrepancy between the expected performance and actual performance of a child; (2) behavioral manifestations or indications in academic and language areas of strengths and weaknesses in learning; (3) integrities or absence of other complications such as deafness; and (4) the focus or primary explanation for the learning problem. Considerable similarity exists among definitions in terms of the descriptions of manifestations and integrities. Though every definition does not explicitly include the discrepancy dimension, it is fairly well accepted and implied in practice.

It is also evident, however, that definitions emphasize and focus on different explanations for learning disabilities. As we shall discuss later, the shifts in philosophy about learning disabilities have directed attention upon developmental problems, neurological dysfunctions, psychological processes, language problems, and task/environmental factors. Certain themes have persisted throughout the brief history of learning disabilities, as evidenced by the recent perceptual and perceptual-motor definition of Wepman, Cruickshank, Deutsch, Morency, and Strother (1975). Also, we can note the emergence of a totally different emphasis in the form of definitions following the principles of applied behavioral analysis (Lovitt, 1977, 1978).

Discrepancy Between Expected and Actual Achievement

Learning disabled children are first identified as underachievers (see chap. 1). The underachievement is usually manifested in disorders of listening, thinking, talking, reading, writing, spelling, or arithmetic. This consideration is closely related to the integrity of intellectual development, since children with learning disabilities have average or above average intellectual ability. In spite of this potential, these children are encountering severe learning problems, either hindering early learning or resulting in academic underachievement when they are older.

The discrepancy between expected and actual achievement is usually evaluated in terms of the child's chronological age, mental age, and actual level of classroom achievement. Standardized achievement tests

Table 2-1
Dimensions of Learning Disabilities Definitions

	discrepancy	manifestation	focus	Integrities (or exclusion)
Gallagher (1966, p. 28)	Children with developmental imbalances are those who reveal a *developmental disparity.*		In psychological processes related to education of such a degree (often four years or more) as to require the instructional programming of developmental tasks appropriate to the nature and level of the deviant developmental process.	
Johnson and Myklebust (1967)			We refer to children as having a psychoneurological learning disability, meaning that behavior has been disturbed as a result of a dysfunction of the brain and that the problem is one of altered processes, not of a generalized incapacity to learn.	
Kass and Myklebust (1969)	Children with learning disabilities generally demonstrate a discrepancy between expected and actual achievement.	In one or more areas, such as spoken, read, or written language, mathematics, and spatial orientation.	Learning disabilities refers to one or more significant deficits in essential learning processes (perception, integration, and expression, either verbal or nonverbal).	The learning disability referred to is not *primarily* the result of sensory, motor, intellectual, or emotional handicap or lack of opportunity to learn.

P.L. 94-142, Section 5 (b) (4) (1975)	Involved in understanding or in using language, spoken or written, which disorder may manifest itself in imperfect ability to listen, think, speak, write, read, spell, or do math calcuulations. Such disorders include such conditions as perceptual handicaps, brain injury, minimal brain dysfunction, dyslexia, and developmental aphasia.	The term "children with specific learning disabilities" means those children who have a disorder in one or more of the basic psychological processes.	Such a term does not include children who have learning problems which are primarily the result of visual, hearing, or motor handicaps, of mental retardation, of emotional disturbance, environmental, cultural, or economic disadvantage.
Wepman et al. (1975, p. 306)	Specific learning disability refers to those children of any age who demonstrate a substantial deficiency in a particular aspect of academic achievement.	Because of perceptual or perceptual-motor handicaps, regardless of etiology or other contributing factors. The term *perceptual* as used here relates to those mental (neurological) processes through which the child acquires his basic alphabets of sounds and forms.	

Table 2-1 (*cont.*)

	discrepancy	manifestation	focus	integrities (or exclusion)
State of Washington (Laws of Washington State, 1975)	Learning/language disability is a performance deficit in one or more of the processes involved in understanding and/or using spoken or written language wherein there exists a measurable discrepancy between academic potential and actual performance.	This performance deficit may manifest itself in impaired ability to attend to task, to conceptualize, to speak or communicate clearly, to read with comprehension, to write legibly and with meaning, to spell accurately, and to perform mathematical calculations, including those involving reading.	The presence of a learning/language disability in children with near average, average, or above average intelligence is indicated by signicant performance deficits in language achievement and/or basic educational skills as measured by norm-referenced standardized testing and/or progressive within-individual assessment methods.	

and individual intelligence tests are relied upon to establish the discrepancy. The observations of regular classroom teachers should also play an important part in determining the significance of a discrepancy.

Johnson and Myklebust (1967) suggest that 1 or 2 years below the expected level of achievement has been the most common criterion for determining the significance of a discrepancy. They also point out that the practice has "serious limitations because one year below expectancy at eight years of age is not comparable to one year below expectancy at sixteen years of age or, for that matter, at three or four years of age" (p. 18).

Recent efforts to conceptualize an operational definition and formula for documenting this discrepancy have been thwarted by a number of factors (Lloyd, Sabatino, Miller, & Miller, 1977; Sulzbacher & Kenowitz, 1977). The formula, *Chronological Age (IQ/300 + 0.17) - 2.5 = Severe Discrepancy Level,* did not account for preschool LD children. A 50% level of discrepancy was proposed for LD placement; neither differences across disability areas nor grade levels were permitted. Finally, the proposed formula was questioned because of its use of intelligence and achievement test scores as true scores; measurement error would create imprecision.

Manifestations of Learning Disabilities

Most learning disabilities are indicated by disorders of listening, thinking, language, reading, writing, spelling, and arithmetic. The substance of the concept is embedded in these learning areas. Disorders in these achievement skills initially draw attention to the child and ultimately provide the basis for subsequent remedial programs.

Children with specific learning disabilities do not have underachievement in every area. For example, a child may have a disability in reading and not in arithmetic. Formal and informal tests help to delineate specific strengths and weaknesses of a child. Knowledge of the sequence of skills in each area of learning also permits greater specificity in describing the learning disability.

Learning disabilities may be manifested within a particular area of achievement, for example, reading. It is necessary to also identify the specific established and deficient skills in reading such as consonant sounds, vowels, and so forth. The same kind of assessment is required in language, arithmetic, and other areas of achievement.

The final level of indication of a learning disability is dependent upon the kind of explanation used for LD. As we will discuss later, one may use neurological, psychological, language, or behavioral descriptions of the learning disability. As with each achievement area, an analysis of strengths and weaknesses permits a better understanding of the definition of the learning problem. A mere statement of reading grade level, intelligence quotient, and so forth, is not sufficient to describe a specific learning disability.

Furthermore, the definition of learning disabilities as the mere identification of underachievement or lack of learning readiness is not educationally useful. The older learning disabled child is often 2 or more years behind in academic abilities, but the primary grade child might be experiencing severe problems in even getting started. Underachievement may be produced by factors other than a learning disability (Wallace & Kauffman, 1978). Lack of motivation on the part of the child and inappropriate educational planning are often causes and must be accounted for in identifying LD children.

Integrities

In addition to their potential for achievement, LD children are not *primarily* hindered by other handicapping conditions, such as visual, hearing, or motor handicaps, emotional disturbances, or environmental disadvantages. In other words, it is important to determine that these children can in fact see and hear normally, are not severely deprived of motor ability, and have had the benefit of a normal home and school environment for learning basic skills. Thus many handicapped children have been arbitrarily excluded from most learning disabilities definitions. The deaf child with problems in learning, for example, will presumably still be deaf after his learning difficulties have been remediated. The learning disabled child, on the other hand, is primarily encountering a disability in learning, which can potentially be remediated.

Nonetheless, the exclusion clause has caused considerable controversy in the field (Hammill, 1972). This dimension is motivated by two factors: (1) to supply services to a certain group of children who have not been given attention through another category; and (2) to satisfy the theoretical assumption that severe academic underachievement and difficulty exist in the absence of more apparent conditions, for example, poor education. This dimension of the definition has obvious sociological and cultural implications. Specifically, there is a danger that we erroneously conclude that deprived children or children with other kinds of disabilities cannot have learning disabilities. This aspect of the LD definition is primarily designed to insure services for children not served under other arrangements, for example, for the deaf or the deprived.

Focus

As noted in table 2-1, most definitions of learning disability focus upon psychological dysfunctions as the precipitating factors involved in the discrepancy. Efforts to pinpoint specific physical or neurological factors causing learning disabilities have not proven very fruitful thus far (Myklebust & Boshe, 1969). Consequently, the psychological processes of understanding and using spoken and written language have been primarily considered in defining a learning disability. These psychological processes are generally described as perception, integration, and expression, both verbal and nonverbal (Kass & Myklebust, 1969).

The role of language in learning disabilities has always been a curiosity to professionals; its exact relationship to and impact upon reading and other disabilities have been receiving increasing attention. Chapter 5 will focus on language and learning disabilities.

Probably the third most interesting explanation and/or description of learning disabilities is being generated from principles of applied behavioral analysis. While the above two emphases that is, psychological processes and language, primarily stress intrachild variables, the behavioral approach focuses attention upon extrachild variables such as the task. It is necessary to understand these three different, though related, bases for explaining learning disabilities in order to understand fully the specific learning disability in reading, arithmetic, or written language.

Psychological Process Focus

Efforts to specify psychological process for purposes of diagnosis and remediation rely upon a variety of conceptualizations or models. Johnson and Myklebust (1967) approach learning disabilities from a psychoneurological perspective. They describe the following psychological processes: (1) sensation, (2) perception, (3) imagery, (4) symbolization, and (5) conceptualization. Their psychoneurological perspective explains academic disorders in terms of these processes and accompanying visual, auditory, and motor modalities.

Chalfant and Scheffelin (1969) use an information-processing model to explain the role of psychological processes in connection with academic disorders: "Auditory, visual, and haptic stimuli (or sensory information) are transmitted to the central processing mechanism (brain) where they are analyzed, integrated, and stored. The behavioral response of the subject serves as an additional input source (feedback) for correcting or adjusting further behavioral responses" (p. 3).

Kirk and Kirk (1971) conceptualize learning disabilities in the context of a psycholinguistic model that involves three types of learning disabilities: (1) academic disorders, (2) nonsymbolic disorders, and (3) symbolic disorders. These three kinds of learning disabilities may often overlap. The academic disabilities commonly involve reading, writing, and arithmetic. The nonsymbolic disabilities involve the ability to recognize, integrate, and use sense impressions. The linguistic or symbolic disabilities involve the ability to understand and/or express visual and auditory symbols meaningfully.

Chalfant and King (1976) have defined psychological approaches in an attempt to operationalize a LD definition. Admitting that "there were few standardized tests for quantifying process dysfunctions," they define the following processes: (1) attention (selective narrowing and focusing on the relevant stimuli in a situation); (2) discrimination (detection of differences in stimuli); (3) memory (recognition or recall of what has been learned or retained); (4) sensory integration (simultaneous functioning of two or more sensory systems); (5) concept formation (development of a specific response to a class of stimuli); and (6) problem solving (act in which prior experience is used to reorganize the components of a problem situation to achieve a designated objective). Chalfant and King (1976) provide a list of questions to study these psychological processes.

These explanations of psychological processes have a number of points in common. First, the learner must be able to receive, integrate, and do something with information which he takes in. Second, all modalities (vision, hearing, touch, etc.) must be considered important factors in learning, either on an individual basis or combined. Third, each model recognizes that psychological processes overlap, are on-going, and are not unitary functions.

Fourth, the effort is made to distinguish between processing information in a meaningful or nonmeaningful way; in a symbolic or nonsymbolic way; and in a verbal or nonverbal way. These three distinctions describe the differences between levels of learning, such as between perception and conceptualization, and between modalities. The models from which the descriptions are generated often reflect the connection of psychological process with neurological function (Johnson & Myklebust, 1967), with language (Kirk & Kirk, 1971), and with information processing (Chalfant & Scheffelin, 1969).

Finally, these descriptions of the psychological processes generally include an explanation of their effects on academic learning. Thus the particular ramifications of a visual perceptual problem on reading, for example, or an auditory memory problem on following directions, are often described.

One of the major disagreements in the LD field centers around this focus on psychological processes. Although this focus has been the traditional view since the 1968 definition by the National Advisory Committee on Handicapped Children, the past 10 years have witnessed serious questions about the theoretical and technical usefulness of this approach. Much of the controversy surrounding the drafting of the P.L. 94-142 definition of LD was a result of the critics of the tests and methodologies based on this emphasis. The validity of perceptual tests has been debated by Larsen, Rogers and Sowell (1976) and McCarthy (1976). Newcomer and Hammill (1975), Minskoff (1975), and Hammill and Larsen (1978) have examined psycholinguistic factors. This controversy will be explained in detail in chapters 5 and 10.

Although each model or conceptualization of this focus on psychological processes has its own unique flavor, let us summarize by identifying and briefly defining some of the more prevalent terms used

(Chalfant & King, 1976; Chalfant & Scheffelin, 1969; Johnson & Myklebust, 1967; Kirk & Kirk, 1971).

1. *Attention* is the ability to concentrate on a task long enough to localize and receive the essential features of the stimuli. If a child does not look at the page, he will be unable to read. Attention is both active and passive.

2. *Perception* is the ability to organize stimuli in a useful way (Johnson & Myklebust, 1967). It can be thought of as a change or transduction of sensory information into electrical or neurological impulses.

   A child who hears oral directions must perceptually organize the auditory stimuli in the correct order. This function does not necessarily require that the child grasp the meaning or significance of the verbal symbols or sounds; merely that he can organize the stimuli as he hears them.

3. *Discrimination* is the ability to establish a difference between two stimuli on the basis of certain traits. A child who confuses *m* and *n* is not distinguishing the peculiar traits of each letter as he views them.

4. *Sequencing* ability enables you to arrange phenomena in a correct order. Children without sequencing ability cannot follow directions, write a dictated arithmetic problem, or correctly sound out a word.

5. *Memory* is the ability to recall newly learned (short-term) or stored (long-term) information (Chalfant & King, 1976). A child may be unable to read a word which has been recently taught. He may not recall his address, how to write his name, or the product of a multiplication problem. Disorders of memory presuppose that the child has learned the information at one time.

6. *Symbolization,* a representational type of processing, is the ability to not only organize phenomena in a fashion consistent with how you heard or saw it, but also to attach meaning to stimuli. This ability particularly refers to how you process symbols in oral and written language. A child might be able to sound out a word on a page, but couldn't tell you what it means.

7. *Synthesis* and *analysis* are dual functions that allow an individual to compose the necessary elements of a phenomenon and subsequently to break up that phenomenon. A child with a synthesis problem cannot blend the elements of a word. An analysis problem may prevent a child from identifying the root part of a word.

8. *Conceptualization* is the ability to group a number of phenomena on the basis of attributes or significant traits (Bruner, Goodnow, & Austin, 1956). Instruction in reading often takes the form of teaching a particular word and then associating other similar words with it (*at, cat, mat, fat,* etc.).

This focus on psychological processes has generated an abundance of assessment devices and materials. They will be described and discussed later in the chapters on perceptual-motor and language problems.

Language Focus

Language dysfunctions have been considered related to or even the cause of learning disabilities. Lack of success and satisfaction with using pschological processes to explain learning disabilities has encouraged many professionals to consider linguistic constructs (Newcomer & Hammill, 1975). Indeed, proponents of psychological explanations have frequently incorporated linguistic considerations into their models (Myers & Hammill, 1976).

However, with advances in language assessment and remediation, clearer connections between language disabilities and learning disabilities are evident (Wiig & Semel, 1976). The primary process components are receptive, inner, and expressive language disabilities. The primary structural components are phonology, morphology, syntax, and semantics. As Wallace and Larsen (1978) point out, language serves as an essential prerequisite and companion to all phases of academic achievement.

Behavioral Focus

As the definition used by the state of Washington indicates (see table 2-1), considerable emphasis is being placed upon describing and explaining learning disabilities in measurable and observable terms. Another application of behavioral psychology is evident in the use of Gagné's types of learning and conditions for learning. Rather than analyzing the child, a task upon which a child fails is analyzed to determine the type of learning involved and whether the correct conditions were provided. These types of learning are signal learning, stimulus-response learning, motor chaining, verbal chaining, discrimination learning, concept learning, rule learning, and problem solving (Gagné, 1970).

The learning disabilities of children can be better understood by examining the tasks upon which they fail with these concepts. Using Gagné's guidelines for conditions for learning, one can modify the task accordingly.

The behavioral approach focuses attention on the environment, task, teacher behavior, and so forth. The interaction of child, teacher, and task can become the focal point for examination when one tries to describe and/or explain a learning disability in different academic and language areas (Worell & Nelson, 1974).

Therefore, the concept of learning disabilities can be understood by virtue of these four dimensions—discrepancy between expected and actual performance, behavioral indicators, integrities, and primary focus. While these aspects of the definition outline its key features, its development has been punctuated by a number of historical forces. These historical influences shaped many of the past and present practices and contribute to current controversies.

HISTORICAL INFLUENCES

Wiederholt (1974) and Hallahan and Cruickshank (1973) have chronicled the stages of development and figures connected with learning disabilities. After genesis in medical research and terminology, the field of learning disabilities was shaped by progress in assessing psychological factors. Roots of LD can be clearly seen in work with the retarded and perceptually handicapped. Development of school-based programs has accompanied the infusion of LD with information from reading and language fields. Two persistent forces in the formation of LD services, as we presently know them, have been governmental and private support.

Sensory Education

Itard, Seguin, and Montessori (Ball, 1971) stressed the need to train the senses of mentally retarded and academically underachieving youngsters. Their early efforts drew attention to not only the functions of vision and hearing in learning, but also to perceptual aspects. The focus upon psychological processes in definitions of learning disabilities indicates this influence, as do many of our present instructional strategies.

Factors of Intelligence

Following Binet's creation of the first individual intelligence test, there have been efforts to conceptualize factors of intelligence in a measurable and educationally meaningful fashion. The developments of Thurstone's model of primary mental abilities (1938) and Guilford's structure of intelligence (1967) have inspired many efforts to test one or more psychological processes presumably underlying learning disabilities. An adequate definition demands diagnostic instruments to assess psychological processes, which of themselves have become the focus of many definitions. Because of the desire to go beyond diagnostic tests used only for placement or classification, some measurement devices have been developed to give clues for remediation.

Assessment of intelligence is also intimately involved in the concept of LD since intelligence testing is used to establish the discrepancy between expected and actual achievement required for placement.

Generally, cut-off scores on individual intelligence tests are used to include children in LD services. Obviously, recent dissatisfaction with intelligence testing for educational decision making has affected the present status of the concept of LD.

Mental Retardation

Trends in the area of mental retardation have contributed significantly to the concept and definition of learning disabilities (Hallahan & Cruickshank, 1973). A subtype of the mentally retarded, the *exogenous* or brain-injured retarded, demonstrate certain learning characteristics (perceptual disorders, perseveration, etc.) which have been called the *Strauss syndrome* (Stevens & Birch, 1957). The experiences of Strauss and Lehtinen (1947) with these brain-injured children, many of whom demonstrate learning characteristics similar to those of the learning disabled population, have had an impact on screening, diagnostic, and instructional strategies for LD children.

The nature versus nurture controversy concerning the causes of mental retardation (McCandless, 1965) inspired many educators to teach exceptional children not only basic skills but also learning abilities themselves. Those who attempted to "educate intelligence" invariably began to conceptualize it as a composite of types of learning and learning styles. Consequently, Kirk (1964) and others devised programs, particularly at the preschool level, directed toward specific learning problems of the retarded. Jastak's (1949) interest in the significance of irregularities in the retarded child's development of various abilities contributed to the effort to identify intraindividual strengths and weaknesses.

This change from a focus on the individual child's ability in comparison to other children to the intraindividual differences has profoundly influenced the education of the retarded and the learning disabled as well (Kirk & Kirk, 1971). The realization that a child may develop different learning skills at different rates has led to individualized assessment and instructional strategies. Some professionals have attempted to remediate deficient skill areas with the intention of improving overall performance.

Recent changes in the field of mental retardation have affected learning disabilities. The American Association of Mental Deficiency has suggested the use of at least two standard deviations in making placements of children in services for the retarded (Kirk, 1976). Since placement in LD and EMR services had been partially based on a performance above and below *one* standard deviation respectively from the mean on an intelligence test, it is obvious that the field of LD must decide its role in serving this disenfranchised population. Indeed many professionals have begun to emphasize the conceptual and historical links between the fields of learning disabilities and mental retardation. Serious questions have arisen about the supposed intellectual normalcy of children presently served under the LD label (Kirk & Elkins, 1975).

The Brain Damaged

The concept of learning disabilities has been influenced by individuals with neurological and psychoneurological perspectives of learning. Strauss and Lehtinen's (1947) work with brain-injured children led to the conceptualization of learning disabilities as a type of minimal brain injury. As mentioned in chapter 1, a neurological examination has been and is often a part of the diagnosis for learning disabilities. Myklebust's early work with Johnson (Johnson & Myklebust, 1967) and his research project with Boshe (Myklebust & Boshe, 1969) used a psychoneurological perspective. See table 2-1 for the Johnson and Myklebust (1967) definition. In addition, Orton (1937) examined the notion of cerebral dominance and its connection with learning abilities of children. His influence inspired the Gillingham and Stillman (1966) remediation program for LD children. Many of the traditional perceptual and perceptual-motor procedures grew out of this orientation. See chapter 10 for a discussion of the present status of this approach.

Reed (1972) has noted evidence of a blending between neurological and psychological perspectives of childhood learning disabilities. This joint effort in exploring brain-behavior relationships undoubtedly will have an impact on the concept of learning disabilities.

Reading Disabilities

A large number of children with learning disabilities have specific problems in reading. Professionals in the area of reading have contributed to diagnostic testing and remedial programs. Conditions labeled *strephosymbolia* (Orton, 1937), *developmental dyslexia* (Critchley, 1964), and *dyslexia* (Myklebust & Johnson, 1962) have been used to describe severe reading problems with or without neurological correlates. However, the reading problems of LD children are one aspect of their overall learning problems. Indeed, some children may have disabilities in other areas and not in reading, though such cases are in the minority. Reading, understandably, serves as a common denominator for success in other academic areas (Smith, 1974). Kirk and Elkins (1975) found a primary emphasis on reading disabilities in model LD programs around the country.

Language

Many of the diagnostic and remedial procedures common to the area of asphasia (severe difficulty in understanding and using language) have found their way into the concept of learning disabilities (Bateman, 1964). Oral language often needs remediation in and of itself, but also because of its connection with reading, arithmetic, and other disabilities

(Johnson & Myklebust, 1967). Wallace and Larsen (1978) describe many ways to assess the role of language in learning disabilities. Vogel (1974, 1977) and Wiig and Semel (1976) describe the growing application of language research to the explanation of learning disabilities.

Assessment

The development of the field of learning disabilities has been accompanied by and has even stimulated a proliferation of psychological and educational assessment techniques. LD specialists have incorporated many psychoeducational assessment activities into their roles.

Recent attacks on neurological, intelligence, perceptual, and psycholinguistic testing have cut at the traditional structure of the concept of learning disabilities. Alternative and/or additional approaches have been found in criterion-referenced assessment, task analysis, progressive measurement, and applied behavioral analysis (Wallace & Larsen, 1978). Since the concept of learning disabilities suggests more than only underachievement in academic skills, its clarity relies upon accurate and valid measurement of many factors. The credibility, usefulness, and validity of learning disabilities are closely associated with the status of educational and other kinds of measurement.

Governmental and Private Support

Initial impetus for the concept for learning disabilities came from professionals and parents wishing to obtain services for children with severe learning problems (Kirk, 1976). Given parental support through the Association for Children with Learning Disabilities, this interest quickly translated into legislative commitment from the federal government in the form of a series of provisions. Beginning with obscure inclusion under provisions for "other health impaired" in 1964, services for LD children received formal support under P.L. 91-230 in 1969. Successive mention in P.L. 93-380 in 1974 and P.L. 94-142 in 1975 has maintained encouragement from the federal level to the efforts of states in training teachers, developing model programs, and performing research.

In the short time since Congress passed the bill specifically titled "Children with Specific Learning Disabilities Act," a cooling in the federal ardor for the concept of LD has become evident. Massive financial support for LD teacher training and model LD centers has dwindled. Unprecedented pressure for an operationalized LD definition was evident, including an effort to curtail LD services to 2% of the school age population.

While the future of LD services continues to rely on federal sustenance, provisions of P.L. 94-142 indicate that the real support for the concept of LD rests at the state and local education levels. By 1980, federal monies for LD programs will be channeled directly to local school systems. Success of LD programs will depend on support from local administrators, teachers, and parents. The cooperative effort of the official parent (Association for Children with Learning Disabilities) and professional (Division for Children with Learning Disabilities in the Council for Exceptional Children) organizations will be imperative to safeguard implementation of the laws.

These historical influences have not been orderly or coordinated. The full impact of any contributing influence on the concept of LD has been determined by the professional synthesis available and by chance. Nonetheless, learning disabilities as a viable educational construct has undergone profound changes in a short period of time.

DIRECTIONAL INFLUENCES

The concept of learning disabilities has definitely shifted from a neurological-medical model to one of educational relevancy. Factors emphasized in the course of this directional change were (1) neurological, (2) perceptual, (3) psychoeducational, (4) language, (5) behavioral, and (6) categorical.

The early learning disability definitions had a definite neurological flavor. (See table 2-1.) The concept involved minimal brain damage, which is a condition exhibiting characteristics similar to brain injury but not necessarily accompanied by evidence of brain injury (Clements, 1966). Educators had difficulty identifying with this medical model and argued for a more relev nt one because:

a. Evidence of neurological problems was often difficult to establish.
b. A diagnosis of minimal brain damage was often tenuous and not very enlightening for instructional purposes.
c. It introduced a vocabulary foreign to many educators.

Another directional change was the waning interest in perceptual and perceptual-motor impairments. Formerly, many diagnostic and remedial programs focused upon only the perceptual components of the learning disability. In some states, such as New Jersey and Kentucky, the definition of *learning disabilities* was synonymous with that of *perceptual handicap and neurological impairment.*

This emphasis was short-lived for a number of reasons. First, the emphasis on visual and motor perception in diagnosis and remediation often excluded auditory perception as a consideration. This narrow emphasis prevented the necessary integration of visual, auditory, and other areas of perception. In addition, attention was shifted to other aspects of learning such as memory and conceptualization. Perceptual training did not substantially increase achievement in reading, arithmetic, etc. (See chapter 10.) Furthermore, the perceptual skills that were developed, for example, walking a balance beam, were not always necessary skills for academic success. Finally, and most importantly, interest has turned to the associated language and academic problems that learning disabled children encounter.

A third factor in the shift was the attempt to blend the psychoeducational and psycholinguistic models to learning theory, language, and basic skills (reading, arithmetic, etc.). Current screening and diagnostic strategies that contribute to educational planning now encompass many associated disabilities.

Fourth, language assessment and remediation are quickly becoming integral parts of LD methodology. Always present in the concept of learning disability, language components have come into more precise focus recently. This emphasis is considered by many as an alternative, or at least addition, to process approaches (Newcomer & Hammill, 1975).

A fifth change is due to the far-reaching applications of behavioral psychology. Behavioral strategies for screening, gathering baseline data, programming instruction, modifying behavior, and evaluating the efficacy of teaching strategies are replacing many of the diagnostic and remedial strategies presently in use with LD children. The consequences for many of the perceptual, psycholinguistic, and psychoeducational diagnostic and remedial models are actually still developing. The application of principles of applied behavioral analysis is significantly altering the assessment and programming procedures in learning disabilities (Lovitt, 1977). Wallace and Larsen (1978) suggest the use of an ecological assessment that views LD children and their learning environment as a system rather than as discrete and separately functioning entities.

The recent efforts to reconceptualize all categories of exceptionality (Blackhurst, McLoughlin, & Price, 1977) and increasing concern over the underachievement of many children precipitated a final directional change, a broader, noncategorical concept of learning disabilities.

Many professionals view the concept of *learning problems* as more realistically suited to the needs of children having academic difficulties (Wallace & Kauffman, 1978). The realization that the diagnostic and remedial strategies developed for children with learning disabilities are appropriate for most children with special needs has led to a movement toward noncategorization. Many individuals have concluded that many distinctions between problems are probably useless in diagnosis and remediation of children with *mild* learning handicaps. Hallahan and Kauffman (1976) have suggested the use of the term *learning disabilities* "to refer to learning problems found in children who have traditionally been classified as mildly handicapped whether it be emotionally disturbed, mildly retarded, or learning disabled" (p. 28).

THE CONCEPT OF LEARNING DISABILITIES: IN PERSPECTIVE

We strongly believe that learning disabilities describes a *specific* population of handicapped children and adolescents. We are not referring to every student who has a special need or problem in learning. As you read the profile of Jason in chapter 1, you must have felt that you knew or have heard of children like him. LD children are distinctive in many ways, but particularly in their need to be evaluated individually. We realize that there are real problems in generalizing from a small group of children to many children. It seems to us, however, that the reverse position is equally untenable, that is, to ignore obvious similarities and needs.

Learning disabilities are *specific*, not generalized, learning deficits. They are also *severe* problems, not temporary or situational lapses in performance. We consider *specificity* and *severity* two keys in understanding learning disabilities. It is the responsibility of state and local educators to serve the most severely learning disabled students.

Finally, we have and will continue to make the point that learning disabilities is primarily an educational concern. Our definition procedures and staff should reflect this orientation. We will indicate in our forthcoming discussion of the causes and diagnosis of learning disabilities how to maintain this educational perspective. At the same time, however, learning disabilities must remain the common meeting ground for many different professionals interested in the LD child.

SUMMARY

In this chapter, we have analyzed the definition of learning disabilities across four dimensions: discrepancy, manifestation, focus, and integrity. The historical influences that shaped our present concept of LD were discussed. Finally, we identified the direction in which the concept of LD seems to be moving.

SUGGESTED ACTIVITIES

1. Ask some of your friends and colleagues, especially those not involved with education, to define learning disabilities. Note the variety of responses.
2. Obtain a copy of P.L. 94-142. Read specifically Section 121a.532(e) and 121a.540.
3. What are the definitional requirements used in your school district to identify a child as learning disabled?

4. Obtain a copy of your state guidelines. Decide to what degree they are operationalized, that is, that you are told how to document the requirements.

5. Read the article by Gillespie et al. (1975) and Mercer et al. (1976). Compare your state definition of LD to the definitions in other states.

6. Look at the topics of articles published in the *Learning Disabilities Quarterly, Journal of Learning Disabilities,* or *Academic Therapy Quarterly.* Try to identify the orientation of the authors toward LD.

7. Discuss why learning disabilities is more open to criticism than any other handicapping condition.

8. Discuss whether the LD child possesses a learning disability or is the victim of his environment.

References

Ball, T.S., *Itard, Sequin and Kephart*. Columbus, Ohio: Charles E. Merrill, 1971.

Bateman, B. Learning disabilities—Yesterday, today and tomorrow. *Exceptional Children*, 1964, *31*, 167-177.

Blackhurst, A.E., McLoughlin, J.A., & Price, L. Issues in the development of programs to prepare teachers of children with learning and behavior disorders. *Journal of Behavioral Disorders*, 1977, *2*, 157-168.

Bruner, J., Goodnow, J., & Austin, G. *A study of thinking*. New York: Wiley, 1956.

Bryant, N.D. Subject variables: Definition, incidence, characteristics, and correlates. In N.D. Bryant & C. Kass (Eds.), *Final report: LTI in learning disabilities* (Vol. I). U.S.O.E. Grant No. OEG-0-71-4425-604, Project No. 127145. Tucson: University of Arizona, 1972.

Chalfant, J.C., & King, F.S. An approach to operationalizing the definition of learning disabilities. *Journal of Learning Disabilities*, 1976, *9*, 228-243.

Chalfant, J., & Scheffelin, M. *Central processing dysfunctions in children: A review of research* (NINDS Monograph No. 9). Bethesda, Md.: U.S. Department of Health, Education and Welfare, 1969.

Clements, S.D. *Minimal brain dysfunction in children* (NINDS Monograph No. 3, U.S. Public Health Service Publication No. 1415). Washington, D.C.: U.S. Government Printing Office, 1966.

Critchley, M. *Developmental dyslexia*. Springfield, Ill.: Charles C Thomas, 1964.

Gagné, R.M. *The conditions of learning* (2nd ed.). New York: Holt, Rinehart & Winston, 1970.

Gallagher, J. Children with developmental imbalances: A psychoeducational definition. In W. Cruickshank (Ed.), *The teacher of brain-injured children: A discussion of bases of competency*. Syracuse, N.Y.: Syracuse University Press, 1966.

Gillespie, P.H., Miller, T., & Fielder, V. Legislative definitions of learning disabilities: Roadblocks to effective service. *Journal of Learning Disabilities*, 1975, *8*, 660-666.

Gillingham, A., & Stillman, B. *Remedial training for children with specific learning disability in reading, spelling and penmanship* (7th ed.). Cambridge, Mass.: Educators Publishing Service, 1966.

Guilford, J.P. *The nature of human intelligence*. New York: McGraw-Hill, 1967.

Hallahan, D., & Cruickshank, W. *Psychoeducational foundations of learning disabilities*. Englewood Cliffs, N.J.: Prentice-Hall, 1973.

Hallahan, D.P., & Kauffman, J.M. *Introduction to learning disabilities.* Englewood Cliffs, N.J.: Prentice-Hall, 1976.

Hammill, D.D. Learning disabilities: A problem in definition. *Prise Reporter.* Pennsylvania Resources and Information Center for Special Education, No. 4, 1972.

Hammill, D.D., & Larsen, S.C. The effectiveness of psycholinguistic training: A reaffirmation of position. *Exceptional Children,* 1978, *44,* 402-417.

Jastak, J. A rigorous critique of feeblemindedness. *Journal of Abnormal Social Psychology,* 1949, *44,* 367-378.

Johnson, D., & Myklebust, H. *Learning disabilities: Educational principles and practices.* New York: Grune & Stratton, 1967.

Kass, C., & Myklebust, H. Learning disabilities: An educational definition. *Journal of Learning Disabilities,* 1969, *2,* 377-379.

Kirk, S.A. *Early education of the mentally retarded: An experimental study.* Urbana: University of Illinois Press, 1958.

Kirk, S.A. Research in education. In H.A. Stevens & R. Herber (Eds.), *Mental retardation: A review of research.* Chicago: University of Chicago Press, 1964.

Kirk, S.A. Personal perspectives. In J.M. Kauffman & D.P. Hallahan (Eds.), *Teaching children with learning disabilities.* Columbus, Ohio: Charles E. Merrill, 1976.

Kirk, S., & Elkins, J. Characteristics of children enrolled in the Child Service Demonstration Center. *Journal of Learning Disabilities,* 1975, *10,* 630-637.

Kirk, S.A., & Kirk, W.D. *Psycholinguistic learning disabilities: Diagnosis and remediation.* Chicago: University of Illinois Press, 1971.

Larsen, S.C., Rogers, D., & Sowell, V. The use of selected perceptual tests in differentiating between normal and learning disabled children. *Journal of Learning Disabilities,* 1976, *9,* 85-90.

Laws of Washington State: Rules and Regulations for Special Education. Chapter 392-145, Washington Administrative Code, 1975.

Lloyd, J., Sabatino, D., Miller, T., & Miller, S. Proposed federal guidelines: Some open questions. *Journal of Learning Disabilities,* 1977, *10,* 69-71.

Lovitt, T.C. *In spite of my resistance . . . I've learned from children.* Columbus, Ohio: Charles E. Merrill, 1977.

Lovitt, T. The learning disabled. In N. Haring (Ed.), *Behavior of exceptional children* (2nd ed.). Columbus, Ohio: Charles E. Merrill, 1978.

McCandless, B.R. Relation of environmental factors to intellectual functioning. In H.A. Stevens & R. Herber (Eds.), *Mental retardation.* Chicago: University of Chicago Press, 1965.

McCarthy, J.J. Rebuttal. The validity of perceptual tests—The debate continues. *Journal of Learning Disabilities,* 1976, *9,* 332-337.

Mercer, C.D., Forgnone, C., & Wolking, W.D. Definitions of learning disabilities used in the United States. *Journal of Learning Disabilities,* 1976, *9,* 376-386.

Minskoff, E. Research on psycholinguistic training: Critique and guidelines. *Exceptional Children,* 1975, *42,* 136-144.

Myers, P., & Hammill, D. *Methods for learning disorders* (2nd ed.). New York: Wiley, 1976.

Myklebust, H., & Boshe, B. *Final report: Minimal brain damage in children.* U.S. Public Health Service Contract 108-65-142. Evanston, Ill.: Northwestern University Publications, 1969.

Myklebust, H., & Johnson, D. Dyslexia in children. *Exceptional Children,* 1962, *29,* 14-25.

National Advisory Committee on Handicapped Children. *Special education for handicapped children.* First Annual Report. Washington, D.C.: U.S. Department of Health, Education and Welfare, January 31, 1968.

Newcomer, P., & Hammill, D. *Psycholinguistics in the schools.* Columbus, Ohio: Charles E. Merrill, 1975.

Orton, S.R. *Reading, writing and speech problems in children.* New York: Norton, 1937.

Reed, H. Brain-behavior relationships and learning disabilities. In N.D. Bryant & C. Kass (Eds.), *Final report: LTI in learning disabilities* (Vol. II). U.S.O.E. Grant No. OEG-0-71-4425-604, Project No. 127145. Tucson: University of Arizona, 1972.

Smith, R. *Clinical teaching: Methods of instruction for the retarded* (2nd ed.). New York: McGraw-Hill, 1974.

Stevens, G.D., & Birch, J.W. A proposal for clarification of the terminology used to describe brain-injured children. *Exceptional Children,* 1957, *23,* 346-349.

Strauss, A., & Lehtinen, L. *Psychopathology and education of the brain-injured child.* New York: Grune & Stratton, 1947.

Sulzbacher, S., & Kenowitz, L. At last, a definition of learning disabilities we can live with. *Journal of Learning Disabilities,* 1977, *10,* 67-96.

Thurstone, I.L. Primary mental abilities. *Psychometric Monographs.* Chicago: University of Chicago Press, 1938.

Vogel, S.A. Syntactic abilities in normal and dyslexic children. *Journal of Learning Disabilities,* 1974, *7,* 103-109.

Vogel, S.A. Morphological ability in normal and dyslexic children. *Journal of Learning Disabilities,* 1977, *10,* 35-43.

Wallace, G., & Kauffman, J.M. *Teaching children with learning problems* (2nd ed.). Columbus, Ohio: Charles E. Merrill, 1978.

Wallace, G., & Larsen, S. *Educational assessment of learning problems: Testing for teaching.* Boston: Allyn & Bacon, 1978.

Wepman, J.M., Cruickshank, W.M., Deutsch, C.P., Morency, A., & Strother, C.R. Learning disabilities. In N. Hobbs (Ed.), *Issues in the classification of children* (Vol. 1). San Francisco: Jossey-Bass, 1975.

Wiederholt, L. Historical perspectives on the education of the learning disabled. In L. Mann & D. Sabatino (Eds.), *The second review of special education,* Philadelphia: JSE Press, 1974.

Wiig, E.H., & Semel, E.M. *Language disabilities in children and adolescents.* Columbus, Ohio: Charles E. Merrill, 1976.

Worell, J., & Nelson, C.M. *Managing instructional procedures.* New York: McGraw-Hill, 1974.

Etiology of Learning Disabilities

PREVIEW

We have discussed the major aspects of the concept and definition of learning disabilities. We focused upon psychological, linguistic, environmental, and other factors which seemed to explain learning disabilities in academic subjects.

In this chapter we will discuss a broad array of possible causes and explanations of learning disabilities. Certain educational factors may cause the LD child's difficulties. The environment provides another broad category of possible causes. Psychological factors, when well defined, can also assist in understanding learning disabilities. We will finally consider physiological conditions and events that may precipitate the development of learning disabilities.

INTRODUCTION

The causes of learning disabilities have proven to be fairly elusive. Some of the difficulties with our present concept of learning disabilities reflect our inability to pinpoint exactly the causes of the learning problems that we observe. The study of any problem or condition is at a rather sophisticated level of development when the causes of the condition have been identified. Needless to say, the study of learning disabilities has not yet arrived at that level (Bryant, 1972). If it had, the concept of learning disabilities would be much more clearly defined than it is, and there would be fewer problems in using the concept.

There are several reasons why the study of the causes of learning disabilities is still at an early stage. First, since learning disabilities is primarily an educational problem, we often make etiology a secondary concern. The educator is certainly better trained and equipped to deal with the many observable academic behaviors such as poor reading, arithmetic, or language skills than to explore possible causes of learning disabilities. In fact, the impact of behavioral psychology and technology occupies more interest than any other perspective on child learning and even decreases the need and appropriateness of examining underlying causes (Dunn, 1968).

Teachers instinctively seek educationally relevant information. Our present knowledge of the causes of learning disabilities, however, does not supply this kind of information. The few strategies that seem physiologically motivated (drug therapy, megavitamins, etc.) are identified more with the medical profession than the educational field. The use of teaching strategies borrowed from techniques used for brain-injured mentally retarded children (Strauss & Lehtinen, 1947) or aphasic children (McGinnis, 1963) and other similarly motivated teaching activities (Cruickshank, 1961; Frostig & Horne, 1964; Kephart, 1971) seem more indicative of educators' desperate search for new ideas than any conviction about the etiology with which they work.

Most of the potential for practical implications from the study of the causes of learning disabilities lies in the area of prevention (e.g., parent counseling concerning the Rh factor, maternal nutrition, and general health). Consequently, the classroom teacher of LD children will probably not be the primary agent for these efforts. Nonetheless, there are other factors contributing to learning disabilities that are less physiological or neurological in nature. Poor sensory and language stimulation or inappropriate teaching strategies, for example, more properly fall within the educational realm. The teacher is more likely to become interested in these factors, which often call for an early educational effort.

The educational attitude toward etiology may also reflect an aversion to factors that might inappropriately dampen the expectations for some children. Of course, knowledge or concern about the causes of problems may not always affect the amount and kind of instruction offered by a teacher. However, the educational literature is replete with examples of and warnings about teachers' unconscious and unwitting use of information such as intelligence test quotients or family background in not meeting actual instructional needs of children (Rosenthal & Jacobson, 1968). Etiology poses a similar threat for teachers.

Study of the causes of learning disabilities usually involves the use of medical terminology and models. Unfortunately many of these terms are unknown to teachers. In addition, the complexity and ambiguity of research findings leave many teachers with more questions about possible causes (e.g., birth complications, heredity) than definitive answers.

The educational orientation toward etiology does not mean that we do not often talk about causes of learning disabilities. Some samples of statements might include the following:

> "He can't read *because* he doesn't know how to sound blend."
> "It's an *emotional* block."
> "If he could only *remember* the rules, he could read."
> "It's a *perceptual* problem."
> "Have you noticed how many *boys* have these problems?"
> "The report indicated quite a few problems at *birth*."
> "If it is a question of information processing, then we must consider the developmental status of the *brain and central nervous system*."

It is obvious that consciously or unconsciously we are at least skirting the issue of causality. Depending upon our concept of learning disabilities and our primary professional orientation (e.g., medical, psychological, educational), we might consider a particular factor in contexts other than causality (Bryant, 1972). For example, when we pinpoint a sound-blending deficit, we are, in fact, describing the specific learning disability in reading, rather than identifying the cause. Perceptual disorders are often considered *signs,* or *symptoms,* of learning disabilities. An *associated* factor, perhaps even a resulting one, might be various emotional and social behavioral problems. A memory disorder may be more accurately called a major *contributive* cause of learning disabilities in spoken and written language.

Birth complications and various childhood diseases are often considered to have many specific and general effects on learning abilities. It is well-known that the development of the physiological bases for learning (the brain, central nervous system, sensory organs, etc.) are affected in many different ways by such factors as anoxia and rubella. However, the ambiguity of their roles as specific causes of learning disabilities, the tenuousness of their relationship to actual learning deficits, and the educator's usual inability to do anything about them often relegates such factors to a lower priority of educational concern.

Our discussion of etiological factors takes an educational perspective. We will first consider those factors (e.g., poor education, psychological functions) that are most pertinent to educational diagnosis and intervention. Then, factors which are more commonly considered etiological are discussed. We must caution, however, that these latter concerns represent medical and neuropsychological perspectives that usually call for preventive diagnosis and intervention in contexts other than the classroom.

CAUSATIVE FACTORS

Learning disabilities of children are usually considered perplexing discrepancies between some well-developed abilities and other poorly developed learning skills (e.g., good verbal language, poor reading skills, inappropriate social behaviors). These discrepancies are particularly difficult to understand since the children seem to have the necessary aptitudes, sensory abilities, and environmental backgrounds to enjoy successful learning.

We generally distinguish between the descriptive *manifestations* of learning disabilities (e.g., poor reading achievement, lack of computational skills, faulty expressive verbal abilities) and underlying *psychological* and *physiological factors* (conceptualization, genetic or neurological handicaps) of the learning disability (Bryant, 1972).

It is lamentably true that inadequate and inappropriate teaching may be a consideration in many learning disabilities (Bruner, 1971; Cohen, 1971). A number of children with learning disabilities seem never to have been taught. Some teachers have not developed the necessary skills to teach basic school subjects. Surveys of the phonic knowledge of teachers responsible for reading instruction, for example, have revealed serious flaws in their backgrounds (Lerner & List, 1970).

Besides the unfortunate possibility that teachers have not taught the LD child, teachers may be equally culpable in allowing their expectations for the young learner to be inappropriately affected (Rosenthal & Jacobson, 1968). Teacher expectations, often based upon extraneous information, may be either too high or too low. Knowledge of family background, information from cumulative folders or informal sources such as intelligence quotients, medical histories, and comments of former teachers, and difficulties in managing unruly behavior sometimes cause teachers to limit their instruction of and expectations for some children.

We must also consider the possibility that some LD children may not have developed necessary prerequisite skills for their level of instruction. The problem of *inadequate instruction* can often be reduced to a question of the amount of emphasis and the time spent on necessary subskills. Some children may have been moved along too quickly, with their readiness skills neglected. Often, there are not enough opportunities to respond verbally, to learn skills sequentially, and to learn to use visual and auditory cues in many classrooms. *Educators can learn much about the needs of learning disability children and the factors compounding, perhaps even causing, their problems by examining the curricula and teaching strategies used for these children.* Poor instructional programming and design, lack of motivating activities, and inappropriate teaching practices must be considered causes of childhood learning disorders.

Education is also responsible for the rather narrow *curricular content.* Instructions in social skills, physical and motor learning, and oral language abilities are often relegated to secondary roles in curricula. Although we specifically teach reading, writing, and spelling skills, we often do not offer structured instruction in talking, in interacting with other people, and in using our bodies in a purposeful fashion. Some children with learning disabilities have pronounced needs in these areas. It is definitely possible that their present learning problems may at least be compounded by the lack of specific instruction.

Finally, learning disabilities can be caused by the use of *inappropriate methods, materials, and curriculum.* Many reading series, for example, do not provide for cultural diversity. Some children have a difficult time identifying with and reading material that is unlike their natural environment. Motivation and self-concept can both be adversely affected by this problem and can complicate learning disabilities. Lovitt (1977) has identified many procedures that have been documented as useful.

How a child learns or how he may be compensating for specific kinds of learning disabilities is frequently overlooked in teaching. Consequently, some methods and materials may not respond to a child's disorders in understanding, associating, and using information he is learning. Underlying the acquisition of any basic skill (reading, speaking, writing, etc.) are a myriad of factors that can seriously affect learning. Lack of prerequisite skills, problems in remembering, and difficulty in conceptualization dictate many educational considerations. Consequently, teachers may be arranging learning tasks without having adequate knowledge of how much such factors are complicating the child's learning ability.

Environmental Factors

There are many environmental factors that can compound and perhaps even cause learning disabilities. The features of a child's environment that we will discuss may have been present throughout his development or may have had a more temporary, though equally devastating, effect upon his psychological and physiological bases for learning. We will focus on the effects of these environmental factors upon classroom behaviors. Some of these factors will be discussed later in the physiological and neurological context, since a number of them also play a major role in the development of a sound neurological basis for learning.

Maslow (1954) has fully outlined the needs of every learner for environmental support in learning. Each learner demands some basic physical and emotional features in his surroundings to facilitate the successful acquisition of basic skills. The learning disabilities of a child may be caused, or certainly contributed to, by the absence or quality of these factors.

Nutrition, Health, and Safety

Inadequate nutrition can affect the immediate learning ability of a child in a classroom. Poor motivation, attention, and application to the task at hand can be caused by something as basic as hunger. One way to help solve this problem is to supply dietary supplements through special projects such as Head Start or school lunch programs. Concern about the amount and kind of children's nutritional intake has led to increased interest in megavitamins and other aspects of the child's diet (Cott, 1972; Wunderlich, 1973).

Feingold (1976) has focused attention upon the behavioral effects of food additives, especially synthetic colors and flavors. He believes that through dietary control a child's hyperactivity may be modified; other kinds of coordination and learning problems may also improve. Feingold (1976) uses the Kaiser-Permanente (K-P) Diet with hyperactive children. The diet eliminates all artificial food colors and flavors as well as foods with natural salicylates or preservatives (see table 3-1).

However, the reported etiology and treatment are controversial (Feingold, 1977; Spring & Sandoval, 1976; Wender, 1977).

> The present authors believe that it is plausible that food additives may contribute to hyperactivity in some children, and that the K-P diet may help some hyperactive children function better. Whether this is *true,* however, is still an open question. It may be that only a small number of hyperactive children, if any, are helped by the diet. It may also be that other treatments, separately or in conjunction with the K-P diet, will be more successful than the diet alone. (Spring & Sandoval, 1976, p. 568)

Other areas of concern in regard to nutrition are maternal diet during pregnancy and the quantity and quality of a child's food intake. We will discuss these areas in respect to the development of the central nervous system in a later section.

Of no less importance is the general health of the child. Chronic colds, respiratory problems, and allergies may be involved in learning disorders. The clinical observations of such factors in LD cases have been outlined by Cook (1974).

Children's physical safety can be another cause for learning disabilities. Reports of falls, brain injury, head traumas, and so on, appear in clinical records of these children. The effects of these events are sometimes difficult to ascertain. Nevertheless, inadequate provisions for children at home, on the playground, and at school can contribute to physical, if not educational, disabilities.

Sensory Stimulation

The developing child requires the input of his senses both to learn about his environment and himself. Perhaps more importantly, the child needs this experience to learn *how to learn..*

It is usually assumed that most LD children have adequate sensory abilities. We exclude the possibility that a child's sensory organs and peripheral nervous system are damaged (Johnson & Myklebust, 1967). The distinction is usually made between acuity and perception. We must realize that there are subtleties involved in basic seeing and hearing that escape casual screening efforts. Even after having the best correction available (lenses, surgery, hearing devices, etc.), the child does not always experience learning improvement. The recent criticism of the

Table 3-1
The Kaiser-Permanente (K-P) Diet

Omit the following, as indicated:

I. Foods containing natural salicylates

Almonds	Mint flavors
Apples (cider & cider vinegars)	Nectarines
Apricots	Oranges
Blackberries	Peaches
Cherries	Plums or prunes
Cloves	Raspberries
Cucumbers and pickles	Strawberries
Currants	All tea
Gooseberries	Tomatoes
Grapes or raisins (wine & wine vinegars)	Oil of wintergreen

The salicylate-containing foods may be restored following 4 to 6 weeks of favorable response provided no history of aspirin sensitivity exists in the family.

II. All foods that contain artificial colors and flavors

III. Miscellaneous items

All aspirin-containing compounds
All medications with artificial colors and flavors
Toothpaste and toothpowder (substitute salt and soda or unscented Neutrogena® soap)
All perfumes

Note: Check all labels of food items and drugs for artificial coloring and flavoring. Since permissible foods without artificial colors and flavors vary from region to region, it is not practical to compile a list of permissible foods. Each individual must learn to read the ingredients on the label. When added colors and flavors are specified, the item is prohibited. If in doubt, the food should not be used. Instead, it is advisable to prepare the substitute at home from scratch.

From "Hyperkinesis and Learning Disabilities Linked to the Ingestion of Artificial Food Colors and Flavors" by B.F. Feingold, *Journal of Learning Disabilities*, 1976, 9, 554. Copyright 1976 by Professional Press, Inc. Reprinted by special permission of Professional Press, Inc.

validity and educational relevancy of the concept of perception makes the significance of sensory screening even greater than before.

The second aspect of the question of sensory stimulation involves the amount and kind of sensory stimulation for the LD child. The authors have become increasingly aware of the lack of such stimulation in institutional settings for the retarded (Kirk, 1964) and in economically deprived sectors of our society. Some children undergo prolonged periods during which they do not experience a sufficient variety of activities, including sensory, linguistic, and cognitive activities. Piaget (1952), Kephart (1971), and others have indicated the tremendous need for early experiences in these areas. The cumulative effects upon later learning can be even more serious if the child has physiological disorders.

Language Stimulation

Language is a particularly crucial aspect of a child's environment because of its role in thinking and in learning other skills. The learning disabilities of a child may be the result of inadequate models in early development. We find many children in our schools who have not received the necessary amount and kind of linguistic activities for good verbal language abilities.

Differential language stimulation and experience have been associated with social class membership (Bernstein, 1961) and ethnicity (Baratz & Shuy, 1969). The use of nonstandard English dialects, however, need not adversely affect academic achievement. We need only to structure educational curricula and methods with an appreciation of the validity and integrity of other language forms. Children's lack of adequate experience in language in certain economic and social class areas has encouraged many educators to supply more enriching language experiences. Although learning disabilities respect no social class or ethnic boundaries, it seems that the academic problems of some children can be further complicated by various forms of language deprivation and diversity.

As mentioned in chapter 2, language disorders may be at the root of many learning disabilities in reading, arithmetic, and written language. Research is quickly accumulating that LD children have particular problems in understanding and using syntactic structures (Semel & Wiig, 1975; Vogel, 1974), use of morphological markers such as tense and plurals (Wiig, Semel, & Crouse, 1973; Vogel, 1977), and semantic production abilities (Wiig & Semel, 1975). Bryan and Bryan (1978) consider language problems as the cause of the LD child's interpersonal difficulties. We discuss language disabilities in detail in chapter 5.

Emotional and Social Development

Many children with learning disabilities are anxious, insecure, impulsive, and unruly. Such behaviors may be related to a lack of natural security, consistency, love, warmth, and acceptance in the home and school. The psychological, and perhaps even physiological, bases for learning can be adversely affected if a child is subjected to a prolonged or critical period of emotional deprivation. Some LD children are victims of a generally unstable home life, perhaps being subjected to physical and emotional abuse. Many coping and compensating behaviors that interfere with learning may result. Furthermore, many of these children do not approach learning with self-confidence and enthusiasm.

There are also many LD children who do not appreciate the value of education. Some children do not learn the potential usefulness of developing basic skills. The problem may be a function of the value system of a child's parents, or the low priority on academic skills within certain segments of our society. As is the case so often in this chapter, there are many implications for parent training and involvement in the prevention of learning disabilities. Parent participation will be discussed in chapter 14.

Psychological Factors

Children with learning disabilities may exhibit disorders in basic psychological functions such as perception, recall, and conceptualization. Some learning disabled children cannot, for example, understand directions, remember material recently taught, organize a meaningful thought, or perhaps write a proper sentence. Some diagnostic and educational practices are based on the hypothesis that such psychological disabilities are the cause of, or at least contributors to, interferences in learning (Kirk, McCarthy, & Kirk, 1968; Roach & Kephart, 1966).

If one assumes that the LD child is engaged in information processing, then we consider disorders in understanding, associating, and expressing information as adversely affecting the child's ability to learn to talk and read. Visual, auditory, tactile, and kinesthetic information may not be processed appropriately. More importantly, it may not be processed in an integrated fashion (Chalfant & King, 1976; Chalfant & Schefflin, 1969).

Besides giving attention to the psychological processes, some professionals also note the presence of different kinds of learning deficits: poor visual or auditory perception and discrimination, slow understanding and interpretation of concepts, poor organizing and generalizing ability, inability to express concepts, minimal motor and verbal skills, poor short-term memory, and poor closure (Kirk & Kirk, 1971). These behaviors are often considered correlates or symptoms of some underlying minimal brain dysfunction or neurological problem in LD children.

Considerable controversy surrounds the definition, measurement, and educational significance of these psychological processes. Efforts to explain learning disabilities on the bases of perceptual, processing, and psycholinguistic factors are being critically reviewed (Bryan & Bryan, 1978; Hammill, 1976; Wallace & Larsen, 1978). We discuss these issues in chapters 10 and 15.

Keogh (1977) feels that previous research placed too much emphasis on child-referenced dimensions. Intelligence and similar kinds of tests were used to measure individual differences; however, they did not consider the interaction of LD children and their programs. This form of analysis is being represented by research on *cognitive styles.*

> Although cognitive-style theorists agree as to qualitative aspects of the constructs, there are some differences in emphasis and content which reflect different conceptualizations. Kogan (1971), for example, in adapting an earlier analysis by Messick (1970) describes nine cognitive styles: field independence vs. field dependence; scanning; breadth of categorization; conceptualizing styles; cognitive complexity vs. simplicity; reflectiveness vs. impulsivity; leveling vs. sharpening; constructive vs. flexible control; and tolerance for incongruous or unrealistic experiences. Kogan also added a dimension of risk taking vs. cautiousness as having educational implications. (Keogh, 1977, p. 322)

Epstein, Hallahan, and Kauffman (1975) have reviewed the most highly researched cognitive style, that is, the reflectivity-impulsivity dimension. Many LD children demonstrate impulsive behavior, including difficulty in inhibiting motor movements, distractibility, and inattention. The academic and social learning disabilities of children may not be caused by lack of ability or knowledge. A partial cause may be an impulsive cognitive tempo or disposition in performing tasks or answering questions.

Impulsivity is also related to a commonly mentioned factor in learning disabilities, hyperactivity. Keogh (1971) has described three hypotheses about hyperactivity. First, hyperactivity may be associated with a neurological impairment. Second, the nature and extent of motor activity may interfere with the accurate assimilation of information. Third, the hyperactive child may react too impulsively to a task or problem.

Block (1977) laments the recurring assumption of most hypotheses about hyperactivity; that is, the problem is within the child or his immediate surroundings. A cultural etiological view focuses upon the many changes in our society. Factors needing attention are changes in family life, eating habits, chemical pollutants, and other features of cultural tempo.

This ecological perspective has been suggested by many professionals in the field of learning disabilities (Wallace & Larsen, 1978). Psychological factors underlying these severe academic and language disabilities must be examined in a broader context. Peer and teacher relations, classroom climate, scholastic motivation, and so forth, must be considered when we wish to explain a child's learning disability.

This orientation toward understanding and measuring psychological factors is well represented in applied behavioral analysis. Learning is an interactional phenomenon. Gagné (1970) has drawn attention to the conditions necessary for certain kinds of learning. The questions "Why doesn't the child learn?" or "How does the child learn?" are reworded into "What must the child learn?" and "Are the conditions (stimulus, reinforcement, and so forth) appropriate?" (Haring & Schiefelbusch, 1976; Lovitt, 1977).

Physiological Factors

Brain injury, overt or minimal, and damage to the central nervous system are considered by many as primary and basic causes of learning disabilities (Hallahan & Cruickshank, 1973; Myklebust, 1964; Strauss & Lehtinen, 1947). The neuropsychological orientation reflects the historical genesis of the concept of neurological disorders in children (Bryant, 1972).

The question of whether some LD children have suffered insults to their brain and central nervous system involves two aspects:

1. The events and conditions that seem typically to cause serious damage to the physiological and neurological bases for learning.
2. Our present ability to establish any relationship between minimal brain dysfunction and the learning disability behaviors observed in the classroom.

Various events and conditions in the development of children with learning disabilities have been studied for their roles as causal agents. Let us initially review these factors before we consider evidence for the hypothesis that learning disabilities may result from some kind of brain injury or central nervous system dysfunction.

Genetic Factors

There is some evidence that learning disabilities may occur more frequently in particular families. Hallgren (1950) reported a genetic study of 276 children and their families. Of these children, 116 were diagnosed as having reading, spelling, and writing difficulties, which he labeled "dyslexia." Of the families of dyslexics, 88% had other family members with learning disabilities. The analysis showed a high probability that specific dyslexia is a genetic disorder, and Hallgren suggested that it follows an autosomal dominant pattern of inheritance (i.e., not a sex-linked factor).

Studies of twins have similarly demonstrated evidence of genetic etiology. According to Hermann (1959), in one study of 12 pairs of identical twins, all 12 sets showed both children classified as dyslexic. In another study of 33 pairs of fraternal twins, only 11 sets showed both children having dyslexia. In the other 22 cases, only one of each pair was classified as dyslexic. On the basis of these studies and other information, Hermann concluded that this type of learning disability seems inherited. Walker and Cole (1965), Wolf (1967), Delker (1971), and Silver (1971a) have also found familial patterns in connection with learning disabilities.

When evidence for genetic factors has been found, there has been some difference of opinion about the nature of the genetic factor; it has been said to be a recessive rather than dominant trait (Ingram, 1965; Orton, 1937), a polygenetic factor (Bannatyne, 1971), and a dominant sex-influenced trait (Lennenberg, 1967). Stafford (1972) has suggested that, in general, there is an underlying hereditary component for a proficiency in quantitative reasoning that fits the sex-linked recessive model fairly well. He points out, however, as have others (Kirk, 1964; Dobzhansky, 1955), that while genetic factors may decide a *range* of potential ability, it is environmental factors (home life, choice of school, adequacy of teaching, proper attitude, and family support, etc.) that ultimately decide varying degrees of achievement in quantitative reasoning. Certain correlates of learning disorders are also found in non-hereditary genetic defects caused by sex-chromosome aberrations. Turner's syndrome (one x and no other sex chromosome) (Alexander, Walker, & Money, 1964) and Kleinfelter's syndrome (an extra x) (Money, 1964) are examples of nonhereditary genetic defects from a sex-chromosome problem.

Bryant (1972) concluded from his review of the literature that "the presence of familial patterns, as opposed to family environmental influences, still does not imply that a given case of learning disability is a result of genetic factors, but only that genetic factors seem to operate in a large number of cases" (p. 58). The interaction of environment and heredity, plus the difficulties of research methodology, make deriving any conclusion very difficult.

Biochemical Factors

Various metabolic disorders have been suggested as causes of learning disabilities. However, while certain metabolic defects (phenylketonuria and galactosemia) are known to cause mental retardation, the evidence that such disorders cause learning disabilities is only suggestive (Bryant, 1972). Some of the biochemical factors mentioned in connection with learning disorders are hypoglycemia (Cott, 1972; Green & Perlman, 1971), an imbalance of acetylcholinesterose (Smith & Carrigan, 1959), hypothyroidism (Money & Lewis, 1964). Rossi (1972) has associated a deficiency of GABA, an inhibitory chemical transducer which is genetically transmitted, with various kinds of learning difficulties. Silver (1971b) particularly focused upon norepinephrine as a key neurochemical in its association with the ascending reticular activating system and the limbic system.

The use of psychotropic drugs has become prevalent in learning disabilities. Sprague and Speery (1974) found evidence of the use of many kinds of medication with learning disabled, retarded and emotionally disturbed children. (See table 3-2 for a list of drugs used in pediatric psychopharmocology.) Of all of these medications, Ritalin and

Table 3-2

List of Generic Names, Trade Names, Drug Classification, and Manufacturers

generic name	trade name	classification	manufacturers
amitriptyline	Elavil	antidepressant	Merck, Sharp, & Dohme
amphetamine	Benzedrine	stimulant	Smith, Kline, & French
carbamazepin	Tegretol	antidepressant	Geigy
chlordiazepoxide	Librium	antianxiety	Roche
chlorpromazine	Largactil	antipsychotic	Rhome-Poulenc
	Thorazine	antipsychotic	Smith, Kline, & French
chlorprothixene	Taractan	antianxiety	Roche
deanol	Deaner	stimulant	Riker
desoxyephedrine	Desoxyne	stimulant	Abbott
dextroamphetamine	Dexedrine	stimulant	Smith, Kline, & French
diazepam	Valium	antianxiety	Roche
diphenylhydantoin	Dilantin	anticonvulsant	Parke-Davis
dixyrazine	Esucos	antipsychotic	Union Chimiques Belge
haloperidol	Haldol	antipsychotic	McNeil
imipramine	Trofranil	antidepressant	Smith, Kline, & French
levoamphetamine	Cydril	stimulant	Tutag
magnesium pemoline	Cylert	stimulant	Abbott
methophenazine	Frenelon	antipsychotic	Medimpex
methylphenidate	Ritalin	stimulant	CIBA
perphenazine-amitriptyline	Trilafon	antipsychotic	Schering
phenobarbital	Phenobarbital	anticonvulsant	Lilly
promethazine	Phenergan	antipsychotic	Wyeth
propericiazine	Neuleptil	antipsychotic	Rhome-Poulenc
reserpine	Serpasil	antipsychotic	CIBA
secobarbital	Seconal	sedative	Lilly
thioridazine	Mellaril	antipsychotic	Sandoz
trifluperazine	Stelazine	antipsychotic	Smith, Kline, & French

Dexedrine are most frequently mentioned in connection with LD children.

They concluded that "drugs can alleviate certain behavior problems, can improve social behavior in school, and can improve learning performance under some conditions" (p. 36). However, they note the small amount of attention given to the combined effects of medication and special education programs.

Whalen and Henker (1976) suggest that drugs have very specific effects under specific conditions. That is, medication may help the child control impulsive, inattentive, aggressive, and other kinds of behavior. However, significant overall improvements in problem solving, reasoning, nonrote learning or actual school achievement have not been documented. Furthermore, it seems difficult to generalize the results from one situation to another and to predict the appropriate choice and dosage of drug(s) for a specific child.

Adelman and Compas (1977) criticize studies which support the use of medication because of methodological problems that preclude generalization of results. Specifically, children in these studies may represent a selected group and demonstrate a variety of behavior problems. Second, the reliability and validity of measures of progress are questionable. Of particular interest to the educator is the problem of identifying relevant behaviors and substantiating their relationship to classroom and home situations. The tasks used in these studies are not truly representative of the learning tasks faced by LD children.

For these reasons and others, Adelman and Compas (1977) seriously question even the qualified support for psychotropic procedures. They see no satisfactory research supporting the use of stimulants to improve academic or behavior problems at school or at home.

Although such high educational criteria are not usually maintained in these procedures, the practices will continue. Consequently, the prevalent position in LD today is to establish appropriate guidelines. Also, there is a need to clarify the role of the LD teacher and parents in regard to drug therapy.

Neisworth, Kurtz, Rose, and Madle (1976) suggest minimal standards for drug therapy. They are responding to the shortcomings in the administration, monitoring, and evaluation of such procedures.

1. Translate the diagnosis and impressions of teachers, parents and others into observable, objective school and home behaviors.
2. Collect baseline information about the pinpointed behaviors in the natural environment, that is, the classroom or school.
3. Supplement the clinical diagnosis and initial data with other information as the treatment is used. Thus a child's target behavior (e.g., in-seat behavior or task completion) will be compared to that of other children in the class to substantiate the need for medication.
4. Maintain data on the target behavior after the therapy has begun. Necessary adjustments can be made decisively. Comparison of later data to initial information will establish the effectiveness of the procedure. The more typical subjectivity and confusion of present practices can be avoided.

Sprague and Sleator (1973) have described their use of the Conner's Abbreviated Teacher Rating Scale (see figure 3-1).

> The teacher is instructed to observe the child for some period of time (typically either 1 week or 4 weeks), remember these observations, and then fill out the form at the end of the period, basing her ratings on that child for that period. There are 10 questions, each of which can be marked as either applying not at all (0), just a little (1), pretty much (2), or very much (3). The total score is then averaged, and a mean score is obtained. (p. 20)

```
CONNERS' ABBREVIATED TEACHER RATING SCALE
Child's Name _____

                    TEACHER'S OBSERVATIONS

Information Obtained _____ By _____
                    Month    Day    Year
```

	Degree of Activity			
Observation	Not at all 0	Just a Little 1	Pretty much 2	Very much 3
1. Restless or overactive				
2. Excitable, impulsive				
3. Disturbs other children				
4. Fails to finish things he starts, short attention span				
5. Constantly fidgeting				
6. Inattentive, easily distracted				
7. Demands must be met immediately—easily frustrated				
8. Cries often and easily				
9. Mood changes quickly and drastically				
10. Temper outbursts, explosive and unpredictable behavior				

OTHER OBSERVATIONS OF TEACHER (Use reverse side if more space is required.)

_____

_____

_____

_____

_____

Figure 3-1
Conner's Abbreviated Teacher Rating Scale

From "Effects of Psychopharmacologic Agents on Learning Disorders" by R. Sprague and E. Sleator, *Pediatric Clinics of North America*, 1973, 20, 726. Copyright 1973 by Saunders Co. Reprinted by permission.

Scranton, Hajicek and Wolcott (1978) have described how a classroom teacher and physician can work together. The teacher gave two LD children the following tasks representative of classroom procedures: listening comprehension, letter calling, digit span, writing, and counting. These objective and easily gathered data were shared with the physician to monitor the children's progress under medication.

Pre-, Peri-, and Postnatal Factors

The learning disabilities of some children may be the result of prenatal, perinatal, and immediate postnatal problems. Kawi and Pasamanick (1959) and Pasamanick and Knoblock (1960) found that children with reading difficulties were more often products of pregnancies with complications (such as toxemia, bleeding, and prematurity) than children without reading problems. Low birth weight has also been significantly related to problems in development and later learning. Pasamanick and Knoblock (1973) mention the following factors in association with prenatal neurological damage and later learning problems:

1. Maternal-fetal blood type incompatabilities (Rh factor)
2. Maternal endocrine disorders (hypothroidism, diabetes, etc.)
3. Radiation
4. Maternal age, reproductive readiness, and efficiency
5. Drugs
6. Rubella
7. Anoxia
8. Maternal cigarette smoking
9. Prematurity
10. Accidents

There seems to be ample evidence that prenatal factors such as maternal health, diet, and life-style must be considered as potential causes of learning disabilities. Wallace (1972) reported the results of a longitudinal study of 55,908 pregnant women and their children (Niswander & Gordon, 1972) that identified neurological problems in the children of:

1. Older mothers (30 years and over)
2. Mothers who are single or separated from their husbands
3. Mothers with less education
4. Mothers with increasing parity
5. Mothers with such conditions as bronchial asthmatic attacks, diabetes, infection of kidney and bladder, mental retardation, and neurologic or neuromuscular diseases
6. Mothers with labor and delivery abnormalities such as breech presentation, very short duration of labor, hydramnios, placenta praevia, and premature rupture of membranes
7. Low birth weight

Postnatal factors also can affect the developing child adversely. Head injuries can result in brain injury (Pasamanick & Knoblock, 1973; Wallace, 1972). Lead poisoning can also cause neurological damage (Walzer & Richmond, 1973). In a follow-up study of 425 children in Chicago who were treated for lead poisoning, 39% had some kind of neurological damage, 54% had recurrent seizures, 38% were mentally retarded, and 13% had cerebral palsy (Wallace, 1972).

Nutritional deficits are also a possible cause of learning disabilities (Cott, 1972; Hallahan & Cruickshank, 1973; Winick, 1968). Cravioto, DeLicardie, and Birch (1966) have reported developmental delays in intersensory integration with protein-calorie malnutrition. Malnutrition may directly and indirectly affect the development of the central nervous system (Cravioto, 1973) and may also modify the growth and bio-chemical maturation of the brain. The relationship of brain weight and total body weight may be distorted, and even conditioned responses in children may be affected. Indirect effects might be the loss of learning time, interference during critical periods of learning, and apathy to social stimuli.

Presently the relationship between malnutrition, particularly protein-calorie malnutrition, and learning disabilities is merely hypothesized from its association with mental retardation (Hallahan & Cruickshank, 1973). The task has been complicated by the economic and socio-cultural variables usually associated with malnutrition.

Deprivation of sensory stimulation may also affect the adequate development of neurological and psychological bases of learning (Hallahan & Cruickshank, 1973). The basis for drawing this conclusion includes studies of the effects of some institutional settings (Dennis, 1960) and animal studies (Cragg, 1967; Valverde, 1967).

As mentioned earlier, considerable attention has been given the chemicals added to food as well as some natural agents. Feingold (1976, 1977) claims a causal relationship between these agents and hyper-activity. The hypothesis is still under study.

All of the factors associated with pre-, peri-, and postnatal periods in a child's development may have specific, or more likely, generalized and cumulative effects. Their obvious interactional relationship makes it rather difficult to ascribe the cause of learning disabilities to any one of them.

Maturational Lag

Bender (1968), deHirsch, Jansky, and Langford (1965), and Silver and Hagin (1960) suggest that the apparent immaturity of some LD children may be related to a lag in the maturation of some central nervous system components. This immaturity, however, does not necessarily imply a structural deficiency, loss, or even a limitation of potential (Bateman, 1966). Bryant (1972) suggests that a maturational lag may be the result of complications during pregnancy, early trauma, infection, or poor nutrition. He also observes that children with learning disabilities due to a maturational lag may partly overcome this difficulty as they grow older.

Ames (1977) feels strongly that LD children are simply victims of being academically overplaced in school. That is, they are too immature to do the tasks set for them and consequently fail. Others may not be as intelligent or as bright as presumed by current testing procedures. Better screening techniques are necessary.

Minimal Brain Dysfunction

The relationship of brain damage and central nervous system dysfunction to learning disabilities is actually a tenable hypothesis. Many of the physiological factors we have mentioned could have specific or cumulative effects on learning.

Clements (1966) reported the 10 characteristics most frequently associated with minimal brain damage (in order of their frequency): hyperactivity, perceptual-motor impairments, emotional liability, general coordination deficits, disorders of attention (short attention span, distractibility, and perseveration), impulsivity, disorders of memory and thinking, specific learning disabilities (reading, arithmetic, writing, and spelling), disorders of speech and hearing, and equivocal neurological signs and electroencephalographic irregularities. These behaviors are considered the signs and symptoms most often associated with some form of minimal brain dysfunction in children with learning disabilities. The work of Strauss and Lehtinen (1947) also affirms many of these characteristics.

Myklebust and Boshe (1969) included various neurological examinations in a comparative study of 627 children with learning disabilities (including both borderline and severe problems) and children with normal achievement. The results of their effort to identify behaviors indicative of some type of neurological problem are fairly representative of our present ability to diagnose and establish a causal relationship between learning disabilities and brain injury. The results of the EEG study were not highly definitive, though some children with less severe deficits demonstrated EEG abnormalities. Children with nonverbal disturbances had abnormal EEGs more often than the children who achieved normally. Pediatric neurological examinations did not yield any profile of neurological disorders. However, more children with nonverbal learning disabilities were classified as "abnormal" neurologically. The learning disability children exhibited many more signs of neurological disturbance than the contrasting group. The borderline group manifested more soft (suggestive) neurological signs, and the severely learning disabled group exhibited more hard (obvious) neurological signs. The authors conclude from the study that there is a relationship between neurological disturbance and deficiencies in learning.

Orton (1928) associated lack of cerebral dominance with dyslexia. Areas of the brain that have been implicated are the angular gyrus, the parietal lobes, the parietal occipital lobes, and other (Bateman, 1966).

There is significant difference of opinion as to whether we can accurately justify the conclusion of some kind of brain injury or central nervous dysfunction in children with learning disabilities. Birch and Bortner (1968) highlight some of the questions about our ability to define and diagnose brain injury and the usefulness of the concept for intervention. Adams (1973) argues that there is no consistent, systematic body of knowledge about the clinical neuropsychology of children with learning disorders. He questions the practice of making inferences from adult patients to children with learning disorders. The use of such correlates as hyperactivity, visual perceptual functions, right-left discrimination, and spatial orientation, for example, to substantiate cerebral dysfunctions in children with learning disabilities seems highly questionable.

There are also differences of opinion about the accuracy and usefulness of EEGs in the diagnosis of brain injury in children with learning disabilities (Hughes, 1971; Page-El & Grossman, 1973; Sedgwick, 1968; Tymchuk, Knights, & Hinton, 1970). Hughes (1971) indicates significant results in the use of the EEG to separate underachievers from achievers. He also suggests that the EEG may be utilized to predict learning disorders and to identify the children more likely to benefit from psychoeducational therapy. However, Page-El and Grossman (1973) do not share this enthusiasm. Tymchuk, Knights, and Hinton (1970) also caution that an abnormality in the EEG of a child with learning problems should not be given great emphasis, unless it is combined with other significant neurological information.

Much attention has previously been given cortical dysfunctions in children. Frank and Levinson (1973) have noted a cerebellar-vestibular dysfunction in 112 of 115 dyslexic children. The children had been selected and referred because of poor or refractory response to reading instruction. This cerebellar-vestibular dysfunction manifested itself by difficulty in tandem walking, articulatory speech disorders, hypotonia, and various dysmetric, or past-pointing disturbances during finger-to-nose, heel-to-toe, writing, and drawing activities, as well as during ocular fixation and scanning testing. The authors hypothesized that cerebellar-vestibular dysfunctions are involved in disorders of ocular fixation, sequential scanning of letters and words, and scrambling of letters and words.

DeQuiros (1976) has described diagnostic procedures to identify these vestibular disorders early. The battery is called a neurolabyrinthine examination. Furthermore, Ayres (1978) has taken this form of emphasis a step further by relating the sensorimotor aspects of these problems to language development; she also suggests remedial procedures.

It seems that any conclusions about organicity (brain damage) in children with learning disabilities are very tentative at best. Many questions about the concept of childhood brain injury and neurological involvement and the medical and educational implications of such involvement are still under investigation.

CONCLUSIONS

The interaction of all factors that might cause learning disabilities must be considered (Walzer & Richmond, 1973). Biological, psychological, and sociocultural factors have a cumulative effect upon learning disabled children.

Considerations of the many causes of learning disabilities are usually marked by the complexity and tenuousness of our present knowledge. McCarthy (1972), however, concisely summarized the current state of affairs in this area.

> What can the responsible educator say when the parent asks what has caused the learning disability in my child? This is one of the most important and significant questions that parents ask, "Why is my child this way?" They ask it in a variety of ways but it is the question underlying much of their anxiety. Right now, with most of these children, when a person asks why, what caused it, the most reasonable and accurate response for the educator at this point in the development of knowledge, must be both equivocal and open-ended.
>
> As far as I can see, we probably have six causes of nonlearning in children. First, genetic variations in the function of the central nervous system. Second, chemical or physical trauma or infection in utero, as in the case of rubella, blood incompatibilities, ingestion of drugs by the mother, and so forth. Third, trauma during the birth process. Fourth, trauma after birth, including damage to the central nervous system due to chemical or metabolic trauma or infections during childhood (encephalitis, meningitis, galactosemia, and all the other things that happen). Fifth, delayed maturation of some of the functions of the nervous system perhaps due to inadequate sensory stimulation and resulting biochemical imbalances. And then sixth, none of the above. I think every one of us has to throw that in if we're going to be realistic and accurate. Teachers need to know that they should not hesitate to say they don't know. Too often teachers feel that someone else knows all the answers and they don't, so they are embarrassed to say "I don't know." (pp. 162-63)

ETIOLOGY: IN PERSPECTIVE

Current attitudes in LD discourage needless curiosity and infatuation with questions about the causes of LD. We can be expending our energy much more profitably examining the variables obviously connected with a child's failure. An ecological perspective of etiology is definitely the most useful.

However, as we indicated earlier, learning disabilities is a multidisciplinary concept by virtue of history and practice. We feel a responsibility to maintain open communication with professionals in other fields who serve LD children. Current research on the use of drug, food, and vitamin therapies are only a few examples of areas in which we must maintain an active interest.

Indeed, as Neisworth et al. (1976) and Scranton et al. (1978) suggest, LD teachers have a particular responsibility to participate intelligently in the use of drug therapy with LD children. We feel strongly that professionals in LD should encourage parents and regular classroom teachers to use behavioral, curricular, and other forms of environmental intervention *before* drug therapy. However, given the adoption of such a procedure, LD teachers should provide useful feedback to the physician and parents.

Fortunately, the general assumption that all LD children are brain damaged has been disregarded. The terminology is disappearing from our vocabulary. More slowly are we abandoning a medical perspective of the learning problems of these children. As we discussed in chapter 2, it makes a great deal of difference whether you focus upon the central nervous system or the environmental system of the LD child. It decides what diagnostic procedures you use and what remediation techniques seem appropriate.

Finally, it seems to us that the area of etiology holds the greatest promise for prevention. Many of the variables we have discussed represent vital information to get to teachers, parents, physicians, and others responsible for the physical, psychological, and social development of children. Adequate prenatal and postnatal care, language stimulation, and appropriate educational procedures, among others, are areas in which our society should devote its energy.

SUMMARY

We have discussed the etiology of learning disabilities from an educational perspective. Inappropriate teaching and materials were discussed as possible educational factors in learning disabilities. The effect of various environmental influences, including nutrition, sensory and language stimulation, and emotional development, were also discussed. The impact of various psychological disorders on etiology was reviewed. Finally, the genetic, biochemical, prenatal, perinatal, postnatal, maturational, and neurological aspects of learning disabilities were briefly outlined.

SUGGESTED ACTIVITIES

1. Interview a parent with an LD child. Discuss the child's learning difficulties and the implications for the family, school, and so forth. Later, identify what the parent said about the reasons for the learning disability.

2. Examine recent issues of popular magazines (*Good Housekeeping, Redbook, Women's Day, Family Circle*). Identify the common assumptions about the causes of LD.

3. Interview a pediatrician about drug therapy. Find out the types of cases with which he or she uses drugs. What kinds of drugs are popular? What effects do they have? Are parents and teachers asked for systematic feedback?

4. Interview a school official (i.e., principal, director of special education, etc.) about school policies on drug therapy. Find out who administers medication in the school and the role of the teacher.

5. Examine foods in a local market that are not acceptable according to Feingold's diet. Ask a teacher to find out how many of her students eat the items. Note any relationship to various behaviors exhibited in the classroom.

6. Compare the etiological factors mentioned here to those causes commonly reported for mental retardation and emotional disturbance.

7. Organize a parent group of individuals whose children are on medication. Discuss the procedures for administration and monitoring the drugs in the school. Are the parents involved systematically?

8. Discuss the question: Is there anything wrong with the LD child's brain or nervous system? If so, what can be done about it?

References

Adams, J. Clinical neuropsychology and the study of learning disorders. *Pediatric Clinics of North America,* 1973, *20,* 587-598.

Adelman, H.S., & Compas, B.E. Stimulant drugs and learning problems. *Journal of Special Education,* 1977, *11,* 377-416.

Alexander, D., Walker, H., & Money, J. Studies in direction sense: I. Turner's syndrome. *Archives of General Psychiatry,* 1964, *10,* 337-339.

Ames, L.B. Learning disabilities: Time to check our roadmaps? *Journal of Learning Disabilities,* 1977, *10,* 328-330.

Ayres, J.A. Learning disabilities and the vestibular system. *Journal of Learning Disabilities,* 1978, *11,* 18-29.

Bannatyne, A.D. *Language, reading and learning disabilities.* Springfield, Ill.: Charles C Thomas, 1971.

Baratz, J.C., & Shuy, R.D. (Eds.). *Teaching black children to read.* Washington, D.C.: Center for Applied Linguistics, 1969.

Bateman, B. Learning disorders. *Review of Educational Research,* 1966, *36,* 93-119.

Bender, L. Neuropsychiatric disturbances. In A.H. Keeney & V.T. Keeney (Eds.), *Dyslexia.* St. Louis: Mosby, 1968.

Bernstein, B. Language and social class. *British Journal of Sociology,* 1961, *11,* 271-276.

Birch, H., & Bortner, M. Brain damage: An educational category? In M. Bortner (Ed.), *Evaluation and education of children with brain damage.* Springfield, Ill.: Charles C Thomas, 1968.

Block, G.H. Hyperactivity: A cultural perspective. *Journal of Learning Disabilities,* 1977, *10,* 236-240.

Bruner, E. Teaching disorders. In B. Bateman (Ed.), *Learning disorders* (Vol. 4). Seattle: Special Child Publications, 1971.

Bryan, T., & Bryan, J. *Understanding learning disabilities* (2nd ed.). Sherman Oaks, Calif.: Alfred Publishing, 1978.

Bryant, N.D. Subject variables: Definition, incidence characteristics and correlates. In N.D. Bryant & C. Kass (Eds.), *Final report: LTI in learning disabilities* (Vol. 1). U.S.O.E. Grant No. OEG-0-71-4425-604, Project No. 127145. Tucson: University of Arizona, 1972.

Chalfant, J.C., & King, F.S. An approach to operationalizing the definition of learning disabilities. *Journal of Learning Disabilities,* 1976, *9,* 228-243.

Chalfant, J.C., & Scheffelin, M.A. *Central processing dysfunctions in children: A review of research* (NINDS Monograph No. 9). Bethesda, Md.: U.S. Department of Health, Education and Welfare, 1969.

Clements, S.D. *Minimal brain dysfunction in children* (NINDS Monograph No. 3, U.S. Publication No. 1415). Washington, D.C.: U.S. Government Printing Office, 1966.

Cohen, A.S. Dyspedagogia as a cause of reading retardation: Definition and treatment. In B. Bateman (Ed.), *Learning disorders.* Seattle: Special Child Publications, 1971.

Cook, W. Letters to the editor: Allergy, nutrition and hyperactivity. *Journal of Learning Disabilities,* 1974, *7,* 68.

Cott, A. Megavitamins: The orthomolecular approach to behavioral disorders and learning disabilities. *Academic Therapy,* 1972, *7,* 245-257.

Cragg, B.G. Changes in visual cortex on first exposure of rats to light. *Nature,* 1967, 251-255.

Cravioto, J. Nurtitional deprivation and psychobiological development in children. In S. Sapir & A. Nitzburg (Eds.), *Children with learning problems.* New York: Brunner/Mazel, 1973.

Cravioto, J., DeLicardie, E.R., & Birch, H.G. Nutrition, growth and neurointegrative development: An experimental and ecologic study. *Pediatrics,* 1966, *38,* 319.

Cruickshank, W. *A teaching method for brain-injured and hyperactive children.* Syracuse, N.Y.: Syracuse University Press, 1961.

deHirsch, K., Jansky, J., & Langford, W.S. *The prediction of reading, spelling, and writing disabilities in children: A preliminary study.* New York: Columbia University, 1965.

deQuiros, J.B. Diagnosis of vestibular disorders in the learning disabled. *Journal of Learning Disabilities,* 1976, *9,* 39-47.

Delker, L.L. *The role of heredity in reading disability.* Glassboro, N.J.: Graduate Division of Glassboro State College, 1971.

Dennis, W. Causes of retardation among institutional children: Iran. *Journal of Genetic Psychology,* 1960, *96,* 47-59.

Dobzhansky, T. *Evolution, genetics, and man.* New York: Wiley, 1955.

Dunn, L. Minimal brain dysfunction: A dilemma for educators. In H.C. Haywood (Ed.), *Brain damage in school age children.* Washington, D.C.: Council for Exceptional Children, 1968.

Epstein, M.H., Hallahan, D.P., & Kauffman, J.M. Implications of the reflectivity—impulsivity dimension for special education. *Journal of Special Education,* 1975, *9,* 11-26.

Feingold, B.F. Hyperkinesis and learning disabilities linked to the ingestion of artificial food colors and flavors. *Journal of Learning Disabilities,* 1976, *9,* 551-559.

Feingold, B.F. Letter to the editor. *Journal of Learning Disabilities,* 1977, *10,* 122-124.

Frank, J., & Levinson, H. Dysmetic dyslexia and dyspraxia. *Journal of the American Academy of Child Psychiatry,* 1973, *12,* 690-701.

Frostig, M., & Horne, D. *The Frostig program for the development of visual perception.* Chicago: Follett, 1964.

Gagné, R.M. *The conditions of learning* (2nd ed.). New York: Holt, Rinehart & Winston, 1970.

Green, O.C., & Perlman, S.M. Endrocrinology and disorders of learning. In H. Myklebust (Ed.), *Progress in learning disabilities* (Vol. II). New York: Grune & Stratton, 1971.

Hallahan, D., & Cruickshank, W. *Psychoeducational foundations of learning disabilities.* Englewood Cliffs, N.J.: Prentice-Hall, 1973.

Hallgren, B. Specific dyslexia ('congenital word blindness'): A clinical and genetic study. *Acta Psychiatrica et Neurologica,* 1950, *65,* 1-279.

Hammill, D.D. Defining learning disabilities for programmatic purposes. *Academic Therapy,* 1976, *12,* 29-37.

Haring, N.G., & Schiefelbusch, R.L. *Teaching special children.* New York: McGraw-Hill, 1976.

Hermann, K. *Reading disability: A medical study of word-blindness and related handicaps.* Springfield, Ill.: Charles C Thomas, 1959.

Hughes, J.R. Electroencephalography and learning disabilities. In H.R. Myklebust (Ed.), *Progress in learning disabilities* (Vol. II). New York: Grune & Stratton, 1971.

Ingram, T.S. Specific learning difficulties in childhood. *Public Health,* 1965, *79,* 70-80.

Johnson, D., & Myklebust, H. *Learning disabilities: Educational principles and practices.* New York: Grune & Stratton, 1967.

Kawi, A.A., & Pasamanick, B. Prenatal and perinatal factors in the development of childhood reading disorders. *Monograph of Social Research in Child Development,* 1959, *24,* 14.

Keogh, B.K. Hyperactivity and learning disorders: Review and speculation. *Exceptional Children,* 1971, *38,* 101-110.

Keogh, B.K. Research on cognitive styles. In R.D. Kneedler & S.G. Tarver (Eds.), *Changing perspectives in special education.* Columbus, Ohio: Charles E. Merrill, 1977.

Kephart, N. *The slow learner in the classroom* (2nd ed.). Columbus, Ohio: Charles E. Merrill, 1971.

Kirk, S.A. Research in education. In H.A. Stevens & R. Heber (Eds.), *Mental retardation: A review of research.* Chicago: University of Chicago Press, 1964.

Kirk, S.A., & Kirk, W.D. *Psycholinguistic learning disabilities* (Rev. ed.). Urbana: University of Illinois Press, 1971.

Kirk, S., McCarthy, J.J., & Kirk, W.D. *Illinois Test of Psycholinguistic Abilities* (Rev. ed.). Urbana: University of Illinois Press, 1968.

Kogan, N. Educational implications of cognitive styles. In G. Lesser (Ed.), *Psychology and educational practices.* Chicago: Scott Foresman, 1971.

Lennenberg, E.H. *Biological foundation of language.* New York: Wiley, 1967.

Lerner, J., & List, L. The phonics knowledge of prospective teachers, experienced teachers, and elementary pupils. *Illinois School Research,* 1970, *7,* 39-42.

Lovitt, T.C. *In spite of my resistance . . . I've learned from children.* Columbus, Ohio: Charles E. Merrill, 1977.

McCarthy, J. Input lecture by Jeanne McCarthy. In N.D. Bryant & C. Kass (Eds.), *Final report: LTI in learning disabilities* (Vol. II). U.S.O.E. Grant No. OEG-0-71-4425-604, Project No. 127145. Tucson: University of Arizona, 1972.

McGinnis, M. *Aphasic children.* Washington, D.C.: Volta Bureau, 1963.

Maslow, A. *Motivation and personality.* New York: Harper & Row, 1954.

Messick, S. The criteria problem in the evaluation of instruction: Assessing possible, not just intended, outcomes. In M.C. Wittrock & D.E. Wiley (Eds.), *The evaluation of instruction: Issues and problems.* New York: Holt, Rinehart & Winston, 1970.

Money, J. Two cytogenetics syndromes-psychological comparisons: Intelligence and specific factor quotients. *Journal of Psychiatric Research,* 1964, 2, 223-231.

Money, J., & Lewis, V. Longitudinal study of intelligence quotient in treated congenital hypothyroidism. In M. Cameron & M. O'Connor (Eds.), *Brain-thyroid relationships.* CIBA Foundation, study group No. 18. Boston: Little, Brown, 1964.

Mykelbust, H.R. Learning disorders: Psychoneurological disturbances in childhood. *Rehabilitation Literature,* 1964, 25, 354-360.

Myklebust, H., & Boshe, B. *Final reports: Minimal brain damage in children.* U.S. Public Health Service Contract 108-65-142. Evanston, Ill.: Northwestern University Publications, 1969.

Neisworth, J.T., Kurtz, D., Ross, A., & Madle, R. Naturalistic assessment of neurological diagnoses and pharmacological intervention. *Journal of Learning Disabilities,* 1976, 9, 149-152.

Niswander, K.R., & Gordon, M. *The collaborative perinatal study: The women and their pregnancies.* National Institute of Neurological Diseases and Stroke. Philadelphia: Saunders, 1972.

Orton, S.T. Specific reading disability—Strephosymbolia. *Journal of the American Medical Association,* 1928, 90, 1095-1099.

Orton, S.T. *Reading, writing, and speech problems in children.* New York: Norton, 1937.

Page-E1, E., & Grossman, H. Neurologic appraisal in learning disorders. *Pediatric Clinics of North America,* 1973, 20, 599-605.

Pasamanick, B., & Knoblock, H. Brain damage and reproductive casualty. *American Journal of Orthopsychiatry,* 1960, 30, 229-305.

Pasamanick, B., & Knoblock, H. The epidemiology of reproductive casualty. In S. Sapir & A. Nitzburg (Eds.), *Children with learning problems.* New York: Brunner/Mazel, 1973.

Piaget, J. *The origins of intelligence in children.* New York: International University Press, 1952.

Roach, E.G., & Kephart, N.C. *Purdue Perceptual-Motor Survey.* Columbus, Ohio: Charles E. Merrill, 1966.

Rosenthal, R., & Jacobson, L. *Pygmalion in the classroom: Teacher expectations and pupils' intellectual development.* New York: Holt, Rinehart & Winston, 1968.

Rossi, A. Genetics of learning disabilities. *Journal of Learning Disabilities,* 1972, *5,* 489-496.

Scranton, T.R., Hajicek, J.O., & Wolcott, G.J. The physician and teacher as team: Assessing the effects of medication. *Journal of Learning Disabilities,* 1978, *11,* 205-209.

Sedgwick, R. The examination of higher cerebral functions in children. In J. Hellmuth (Ed.), *Learning disorders* (Vol. III). Seattle: Special Child Publications, 1968.

Semel, E.M., & Wiig, E.H. Comprehension of syntactic structures and critical verbal elements by children with learning disabilities. *Journal of Learning Disabilities,* 1975, *8,* 46-52.

Silver, L. Familial patterns in children with neurologically based learning disabilities. *Journal of Learning Disabilities,* 1971, *4,* 349-358. (a)

Silver, L. A proposed view on the etiology of the neurological learning disability syndrome. *Journal of Learning Disabilities,* 1971, *4,* 123-132. (b)

Silver, L., & Hagin, R. Specific reading disability, delineation of the syndrome and relationship to cerebral dominance. *Comprehensive Psychiatry,* 1960, *1,* 126-134.

Smith, D.E., & Carrigan, P. *The nature of reading disability.* New York: Harcourt Brace Jovanovich, 1959.

Sprague, R., & Sleator, E. Effects of psychopharmacologic agents on learning disorders. *Pediatric Clinics of North America,* 1973, *20,* 710-736.

Sprague, R.L., & Speery, J.B. Psychotropic drugs and handicapped children. In L. Mann & D. Sabatino (Eds.), *The second review of special education.* Philadelphia: JSE Press, 1974.

Spring, C., & Sandoval, J. Food additives and hyperkinesis: A critical evaluation of the evidence. *Journal of Learning Disabilities,* 1976, *9,* 560-569.

Stafford, D. Hereditary and environmental components of quantative reasoning. *Review of Educational Research,* 1972, *42,* 183-201.

Strauss, A.A., & Lehtinen, L. *Psychopathology and education of the brain-injured child.* New York: Grune & Stratton, 1947.

Tymchuck, A., Knights, R., & Hinton, G. The behavioral significance of differing EEG abnormalities in children with learning and/or behavior problems. *Journal of Learning Disabilities,* 1970, *3,* 547-552.

Valverde, F. Apical dendrite spines of the visual cortex and light deprivation in the mouse. *Experimental Brain Research,* 1967, *3,* 337-352.

Vogel, S.A. Syntactic abilities in normal and dyslexic children. *Journal of Learning Disabilities,* 1974, *7,* 103-109.

Vogel, S.A. Morphological ability in normal and dyslexic children. *Journal of Learning Disabilities.* 1977, *10,* 35-43.

Walker, L., & Cole, E. Familial patterns of expression and specific reading disability: Part I, prevalence, distribution and persistence. *Bulletin of the Orton Society,* 1965, *15,* 12-25.

Wallace, G., & Larsen, S. *Educational assessment of learning problems: Testing for teaching.* Boston: Allyn & Bacon, 1978.

Wallace, H. *The epidemiology of developmental disabilities.* Paper presented at the meeting of United Cerebral Palsy of Kentucky, October 1972.

Walzer, S., & Richmond, J. The epidemiology of learning disorders. *Pediatric Clinics of North America,* 1973, *20,* 719-736.

Wender, E. Food additives and hyperkinesis. *American Journal of Diseases of Children,* 1977, *131,* 1204-1206.

Whalen, C.K., & Henker, B. Psychostimulants and children: A review and analysis. *Psychological Bulletin,* 1976, *83,* 1113-1130.

Wiig, E.M., & Semel, E.M. Productive language abilities in learning disabled adolescents. *Journal of Learning Disabilities,* 1975, *8,* 578-588.

Wiig, E.M., Semel, E.M., & Crouse, M.A.B. The use of English morphology by high-risk and learning disabled children. *Journal of Learning Disabilities,* 1973, *6,* 457-465.

Winick, M. Changes in nuceleic acid and protein content of the human brain during growth. *Pediatric Research,* 1968, *2,* 325-355.

Wolf, C. An experimental investigation of specific language disability. *Bulletin of the Orton Society,* 1967, *17,* 32-39.

Wunderlich, R.C. Treatment of the hyperactive child. *Academic Therapy,* 1973, *8,* 375-390.

Diagnostic Strategies for Learning Disabilities

PREVIEW

Educational assessment is the basis for accurate decision making in learning disabilities. It is important to conceptualize diagnosis as an integral part of educational planning. We will consider the definition, role, purpose, form, and focus of diagnosis in order to provide a suitable orientation.

We consider the Individual Education Plan (IEP) as one of the most exciting aspects of the services offered through P.L. 94-142. The provisions and formats of IEPs are the end products of valid and reliable assessment procedures. We will track the relationship of assessment and IEP development through four ongoing and interactive phases or stages: identification and referral, bi-level assessment, educational planning, and evaluation. In the process, we will indicate ways in which different forms of assessment procedures can benefit the LD child.

Profiles

Richard is a 5-year-old enrolled for the past 3 months in a kindergarten program. He is inattentive and very active at school. His teacher worries about his inability to perform various verbal and perceptual-motor activities. She reports that he bothers other children.

By the end of the first grade Della has not learned any basic skills in reading, arithmetic, or handwriting. She cannot follow directions or work by herself. Della is quiet and does not bother any of her classmates.

Tom is a fifth grader who repeated third grade. Friendly and talkative, he is well liked by his teacher and fellow students. He is interested in sports and does well on the playground. His teacher is impressed by his verbal abilities, never finding him without something to say. Tom's problem is that he cannot read.

These children are candidates for what has been commonly called the *diagnostic process*. These sketches demonstrate that a child with a learning problem may be identified as a potential LD case at any point in his or her educational career. However, proper diagnostic procedures are necessary to understand the learning disability adequately and to guide appropriate educational planning. P.L. 94-142 guarantees that these children will receive an accurate and meaningful assessment. The provisions of this law set forth the appropriate procedures to be followed.

ORIENTATION TO EDUCATIONAL DIAGNOSIS

Definition

Educational diagnosis is the asking of educationally relevant questions about a child's learning behavior for the purpose of instruction. The learning behaviors of children with educational disabilities usually stimulate *questions* to be answered (Gardner, 1977). They also direct our choice of devices for gathering information to answer questions. As mentioned in chapter 1, the indiscriminate use of lengthy, numerous and/or tangential test batteries is to be avoided.

An LD diagnostician seeks information that is *educationally relevant* and pertinent to the learning disabilities in understanding and using spoken and written language and in other areas. The educational relevancy of diagnosis cannot be overly stressed. Furthermore, the questions that are asked must be *realistic* questions. However, the skills of available diagnosticians, the state of knowledge in certain areas (e.g., causes of learning disabilities), and the likelihood that we have the resources to deal with certain problems (e.g., changing the past or present home life of a LD child) may dictate that some questions are not very realistic to ask at the present time.

The focus of educational diagnosis is obviously *the learning behavior* of the child. The perception of learning disabilities will differ among various diagnosticians. Consequently, the professional orientation of the diagnostician will influence how educational problems are perceived, how the type of diagnostic test is chosen, and how resultant data are interpreted. The learning disabilities teacher, however, must always use procedures that reflect relevancy and suitable reliability and validity for educational matters.

Educational diagnosis is intended to *produce useful instructional ideas.* In practical terms, specific objectives for instruction and the methods and materials to accomplish the objectives should be gleaned from the diagnosis. Otherwise, the diagnosis has been futile.

Educational diagnosis should be performed in the context of the school. This setting dictates certain criteria for educational relevance. Schools also demand that diagnosis should relate to ongoing programs of instruction. Most of all, schools focus upon objectives that other settings do not. One objective, of course, is to supply educational services to *all* children with learning disabilities. Part of these services should certainly include appropriate diagnostic services.

General Role of Diagnosis

P.L. 94-142 is quite explicit in its demands for an accurate and reliable assessment as part of its various provisions. Diagnostic activities fulfill requirements for identification and "child-find" activities, for placement procedures, for program development, and for evaluation of the program.

The diagnosis of learning disabilities is part of the total process involving the development of the Individual Educational Plan. Hudson and Graham (1978) have outlined the procedural aspects of the process, as noted in figure 4-1.

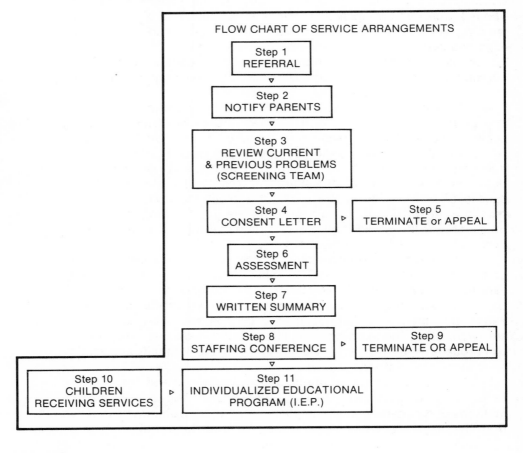

Figure 4-1

Steps in the Individual Education Plan Process

From "An Approach to Operationalizing the IEP" by F. Hudson and S. Graham, *Learning Disability Quarterly*, 1978, *1*, 14. Copyright 1978 by Learning Disability Quarterly. Reprinted by permission.

After a referral by a teacher or parent (Step 1), special education personnel and parents are informed of the school concern (Step 2). If a preliminary examination of the child's past and current records suggests the need for further study (Step 3), the parents are asked for written consent (Step 4). Parents have the right to appeal throughout this process.

With parental consent (Step 5), an assessment team performs the necessary testing (Step 6) and writes a summary report (Step 7). The assessment team, parents, and other involved parties participate in a staffing to arrive at a decision about service arrangements (Step 8). Given parental agreement and the need, a team develops an in-depth instructional IEP (Step 11) for new students. In the case of current students (Step 10), an IEP must be developed prior to October 1 of the new school year.

The process cannot be performed effectively without the use of suitable forms of assessment. Some diagnostic procedures are used in the referral and screening processes; however, assessment figures most heavily in Steps 6 and 11, when LD placement and LD programming are documented. The reason is that the IEP requires these two kinds of documentation, that is, data to justify the decision to offer LD services and data to describe the specifics of the plan. In practical terms, the IEP indicates global, annual goals and specific objectives. First, the global, annual goals are created for placement decisions; certain diagnostic procedures facilitate the development of this aspect of the IEP. Second, the IEP offers specific behavioral objectives for each global goal; these are different diagnostic procedures used to develop these specific objectives.

Purposes of Diagnosis

There are many reasons for educational diagnosis (Salvia & Ysseldyke, 1978). Diagnostic findings have been used, and required in some cases, to define children as learning disabled and to justify their placement in LD classes. This use of diagnosis has been motivated by administrative considerations and frequently criticized, because the need for guidance in actual instruction has not usually been met.

The second major purpose and use of educational diagnosis is to establish instructional objectives based upon diagnostic results. LD diagnosticians or other educational specialists designate appropriate teaching methods and materials for the accomplishment of specific goals. At this point a particular delivery system is identified as appropriate for the child (e.g., a resource room, self-contained setting, consultant services). See chapter 11 for more detailed descriptions of these settings.

The third reason for assessment is to evaluate the implementation and effects of a program. Data are maintained on many factors to monitor the results of an approach or program.

Types of Diagnosis

The form that diagnosis takes may be one or more of the following: formal standardized tests, informal tests, observations, task analyses, criterion-referenced tests, and case histories and interviews (Wallace & Larsen, 1978). Formal standardized tests are the most frequently used because of explicitness of directions and the availability of norms and comparative information. These tests are generally used to establish present levels of functioning for IEPs. They may be the group intelligence and achievement tests given in regular classrooms. Individually administered academic, language, and other kinds of tests can also be used to pinpoint strengths and weaknesses. See table 4-1 for a list of individual standardized tests.

Informal tests or probes are teacher-made devices to measure attainment of a particular skill or subset of skills. An advantage of this approach is the high level of teacher involvement.

Observational techniques are very popular today. This type of assessment includes time-sampling techniques, event sampling, and rating scales and checklists (Wallace & Larsen, 1978). Critics of the standardized test approach strongly encourage this form of data collection (Lovitt, 1978).

Task analysis is also a commonly suggested form of assessment. Given a particular task, the teacher breaks the task into small steps and teaches the subtasks sequentially. This form of diagnosis places the focus on the task and makes no assumptions about the child.

Criterion-referenced testing is playing a very instrumental part in IEP development. In contrast to tests that yield merely normative and general information, this approach offers the identification of specific skill deficits and the degree of deficits. The acceptable level of performance is a criterion, not a normative standard.

Case histories and *interviews* also gather important information. Case histories can pinpoint significant factors that explain or at least better describe the learning disabilities (Bryan & Bryan, 1978). Interviews of children and adult informants can also supplement other forms of data (Johnson & Morasky, 1977; Pasanella & Volkmor, 1977).

Content and Diagnosis

Diagnosis of learning disabilities frequently consists of a battery of assessment techniques similar to those previously mentioned. Typically, the requirements of an IEP require measures of intelligence, achieve-

Table 4-1
Commonly Used Individual Diagnostic Tests

psychological	achievement	reading	arithmetic	spoken language	written language	perceptual / perceptual-motor
Detroit Tests of Learning Aptitude (Baker & Leland, 1955)	Wide Range Achievement Test (Jastak & Jastak, 1965)	Botel Reading Inventory (Botel, 1966)	Diagnostic Tests and Self-Help in Arithmetic (Brueckner, 1955)	Carrow Elicited Language Inventory (Carrow, 1974)	Gates-Russell Spelling Diagnostic Tests (Gates & Russell, 1940)	Bender Visual-Motor Gestalt Test for Children (Bender, 1962)
Illinois Test of Psycholinguistic Abilities (Rev. ed.) (Kirk, McCarthy, & Kirk, 1968 rev. 1974)	Peabody Individual Achievement Test (Dunn & Markwardt, 1970)	Durrell Analysis of Reading Difficulty (Durrell, 1955)	Key Math Diagnostic Arithmetic Test (Connolly, Natchman, & Pritchett, 1973)	Houston Test for Language Development (Crabtree, 1963)	Picture Story Language Test (Myklebust, 1965)	Frostig Developmental Tests of Visual Perception (Frostig, Lefever, & Whittlesey, 1964)
Wechsler Intelligence Scale for Children (Wechsler, rev. 1974)		Gates-McKillop Reading Diagnostic Test (Gates & McKillop, 1962)	Stanford Diagnostic Arithmetic Test (Beatty, Madden, & Gardner, 1966)	Illinois Test of Psycholinguistic Abilities (Kirk, McCarthy, & Kirk, 1968)	Sequential Tests of Educational Progress (Seashore, 1963)	Goodenough-Harris Drawing Test (Goodenough & Harris, 1963)
		Gilmore Oral Reading Test (Gilmore, 1951)		Mecham Verbal Language Development Scale (Mecham, 1959)	Test of Written Language (Hammill & Larsen, 1978)	Lincoln-Oseretsky Motor Development Scale (Sloan, 1965)
		Gray Oral Reading Test (Gray, 1963)		Northwestern Syntax Screening Test (Lee, 1969)	Test of Written Spelling (Larsen & Hammill, 1976)	Motor-Free Visual Perception Test (Colarusso & Hammill, 1972)
		Monroe Reading Aptitude Tests (Monroe, 1935)		Peabody Picture Vocabulary Test (Dunn, 1959)		Purdue Perceptual-Motor Survey (Roach & Kephart, 1966)
		Roswell-Chall Diagnostic Test of Word-Analysis (Roswell & Chall, 1959)		Test of Auditory Comprehension (Carrow, 1973)		Wepman Auditory Discrimination Test (Wepman, 1958)
		Spache Diagnostic Reading Scales (Spache, 1963)		Test of Language Development (Newcomer & Hammill, 1977)		
		Woodcock Reading Mastery Tests (Woodcock, 1974)				

ment, specific skills, environmental conditions, and so forth. The particular content of a diagnosis is determined by the child's problems, the professional's orientation, and the particular model of assessment being followed.

Lerner (1976) suggests that diagnosis usually includes the following steps:

1. Determine whether the child has a learning disability.
2. Measure the child's present achievement in basic skills.
3. Analyze how the child learns.
4. Explore why he is not learning.
5. Gather and interpret data into a diagnostic summary or hypothesis about the child.
6. Develop objectives and plans for teaching.

Other diagnostic designs are suggested by Bateman (1965), Smith (1969), and Lovitt (1978). Diagnostic paradigms are discussed by Wallace and Larsen (1978).

The content of diagnosis is also affected by the context or setting in which it occurs. Clinical settings permit investigation of many areas that a school setting would not have personnel or facilities to explore. For example, the physical health, neurological status, diet, and family history are matters that require rather sophisticated and well-developed diagnostic services.

Although the public school setting may not be able to provide a full clinical diagnosis, schools have incorporated the psychoeducational or diagnostic-prescriptive models of diagnosis. The contents of these plans stress educationally relevant and educationally suggestive diagnosis. The public schools need diagnostic answers that are economical, brief, and useful. The recent ready acceptance and application of various forms of observational and behavioral technology in diagnosis provide evidence of these needs.

Focus of Diagnosis

As indicated earlier in our definition of diagnosis, it is important to ask the right questions in assessment. Early diagnostic models in learning disabilities have focused exclusively on the child. Consequently, extensive effort was spent on looking for the cause, or underlying factors.

There is a shift away from such an extreme focus on the LD child. There is general disillusionment with the tests and programs based on the concept that hypothetical in-child disorders are the site of the problem.

The alternative is to recognize the child's learning disability as a product of the child's interaction with the learning environment (task) and the teacher. Furthermore, the focus of diagnosis must be upon observable, measurable, and educationally significant factors.

Nothing can maximize this kind of focus more than the appropriate and ethical implementation of the requirements of the IEP. As we shall see in the next section, the development of the total educational plan of the LD child demands a wide variety of diagnostic approaches.

INDIVIDUAL EDUCATIONAL PLAN

The Individual Educational Plan as a written document must contain certain features to satisfy requirements of P.L. 94-142. According to Turnbull, Strickland, and Hammer (1978b), the required components are:

1. The student's current level of educational performance;
2. Annual goals the student is expected to accomplish by the end of each school year;
3. Short-term objectives stated in behavioral terms outlining intermediate steps to reach annual goals;
4. Date the services will be initiated and terminated;
5. Documentation of the extent to which the student will be included in the regular education program;
6. Special education services needed by the student; and
7. Evaluation criteria and procedures to be used for determining mastery of goals and objectives on at least an annual basis. (p. 68)

Each of these components is based upon accurate and reliable assessment procedures for learning disabilities. Both Turnbull et al. (1978a, 1978b) and Hudson and Graham (1978) explain and illustrate these components and the process of development.

Pasanella and Volkmor (1977) depicted the development of the written IEP graphically (see figure 4-2). The identification (1) and referral phases (2) attempt to pinpoint children with a high probability of having learning disabilities. Through a cooperative effort with parents and other school personnel, the LD teacher examines records, submitted checklists, and other forms of information to establish whether a particular child's learning difficulties are sufficiently severe to merit further consideration.

The subsequent in-depth assessment (3) of all salient factors leads to the development of an IEP (4) with both broad annual goals and appropriate specific objectives. This assessment phase is, for all practical purposes, bi-level. The first level of assessment establishes the existence of a learning disability according to state requirements for LD placement. Broad annual goals must be established for any such placement.

The second level of assessment specifies the skill deficits and attendant objectives for teaching those skills. The IEP also contains mention of the methods and materials to be used.

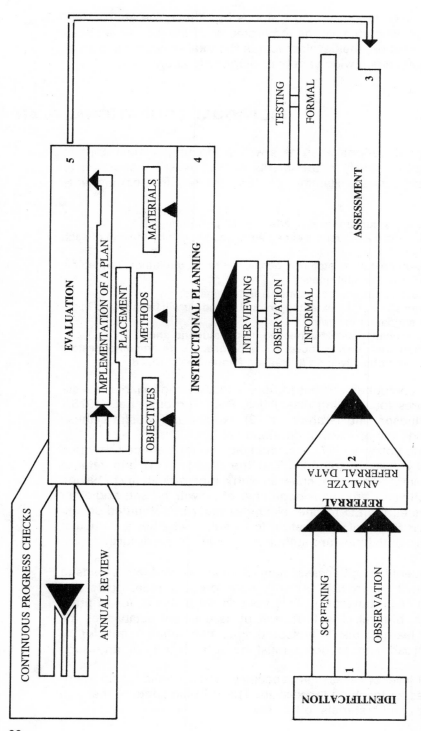

Figure 4-2
Stages of the IEP Process

Finally, during and subsequent to the implementation of the plan, various evaluation techniques (5) are used to guarantee data for the required annual reviews. Each of the phases of this process will now be discussed in relationship to learning disabilities.

Identification and Referral

This phase is extremely important. A regular classroom teacher should know the common characteristics of children with learning disabilities, be able to eliminate or deal with obvious factors in underachievement (such as sensory problems and reprogramming needs), report specific skill strengths and weaknesses of students, and describe present educational strategies (such as the type of reading program). Efficient, useful referrals come from an informed staff. The responsibilities of appropriate school personnel in helping to educate teachers in this regard are certainly a large part of making this process work.

The usual context for the identification phase takes one of three forms:

1. A school system beginning its learning disability program institutes a screening program.
2. A school system with an ongoing program seeks referrals from its teachers.
3. Some local diagnostic-clinical facility may take referrals from school systems or individual parents.

The typical pattern of referral and identification in a school system involves a regular classroom teacher composing a description of a student. These profiles are usually sketchy and often require more specific information. As will be discussed in chapter 14, parents are also involved in the process.

Pasanella and Volkmor (1977) note five recommended features of a teacher referral. First, the child's problem should be stated clearly and precisely. Second, a child's strengths should be mentioned as well as his or her deficits. Third, teachers should avoid making guesses at the causes of the problems, in preference to clearly describing the problem.

Fourth, supportive documentation should be provided, such as test scores and previously used methods and materials. Finally, all accurate identifying information should be supplied, that is, name, birth, date, grade, and so forth. See Pasanella and Volkmor (1977) and Wiederholt, Hammill, and Brown (1978) for examples of referral forms. A number of important referral concerns are now briefly outlined and discussed.

Underachievement or Poor Development

As discussed in chapter 1, excessive underachievement or poor development in a particular skill area is an initial cause of concern for parents and teachers. The areas of concern for the school-age child are generally reading, arithmetic, and writing. Behavior problems in the classroom (e.g., inattention and incompleteness of tasks) are also frequently mentioned. What makes these concerns about the underachievement of LD children particularly noticeable is the apparent absence of obvious reasons for poor skill development.

Parental and teacher concern is raised by poor performances of children on daily tasks, group achievement tests, and informal nonschool activities. This persistent and severe pattern of difficulty parallels average and above average performances in other areas.

Checking the Obvious

There are a number of factors affecting most children that should be examined before any further investigation of a child is begun.

1. *Seeing and hearing ability.* A teacher can check a child's cumulative folder for the results of standard school screening tests. These gross screening devices for vision and hearing do not identify all possible sensory problems. If the child has performed poorly on these screening devices or if there is any doubt about his or her ability based upon observation, the child should be referred for further examination.
2. *Motor impairment.* Usually, observation and a medical history of the child can establish whether the child is orthopedically or physically handicapped.
3. *Emotional problems.* Observation, home and school history, and clinical diagnosis can establish whether a child is suffering from a primary emotional problem. Although emotionally disturbed children may also have learning problems and require educational provisions similar to those for the LD child, an effort should be made at this point to rule out this compounding factor.
4. *Environmental factors.* Language models, emotional security, and general stimulating experiences should be checked by observation. Interviews with parents and others who know the home situation are also helpful.

The educational experience of the child is another area to check. Sometimes a child is encountering learning problems because of poor attention, motivation, or programming of instruction. Teachers should attempt to use behavior management techniques, to reprogram tasks that might be too complex, and to examine basic skill sequences for skills requiring more instruction. Many obvious features of underachievement can be dealt with successfully by an informed classroom teacher. These factors comprise the exclusionary clause of the definition of learning disabilities (see chap. 2). That is, a child who is served under LD services may not have as the *primary* disability any of the above four areas.

Behaviors of Concern

The behavior that motivated the teacher's concern should be described as specifically as possible. The learning disability specialist can direct the formal and informal analysis to these points. These behaviors usually are the "manifestations" of learning disabilities.

Teachers can be provided with informal checklists or formal screening devices to identify children with learning disabilities. Many school systems create their own checklists containing well-known characteristics of learning disabilities that are evaluated on a scale from mild to severe. These checklists often contain, in modified forms, these characteristics noted by Clements (1966):

1. Hyperactivity,
2. Perceptual-motor impairment,
3. Emotional problems,
4. General orientation defects,
5. Disorders of attention (e.g. short attention span, distractibility),
6. Impulsivity,
7. Disorders of memory and thinking,
8. Specific learning disabilities in reading, arithmetic, writing, and spelling,
9. Disorders of speech and hearing.

Another alternative for documenting or describing learning characteristics is the use of informal, nonstandardized devices, such as Valett's (1969) screening checklist for his remedial program or the Slingerland (1964) screening test. These instruments have suggestions for remedial work supplied by each author. A teacher can usually initiate remediation while further analytic work is being done, which is a feature teachers particularly like.

A third alternative is the use of standardized screening devices, such as the Pupil Rating Scale (Myklebust, 1971) and the Meeting Street School Screening Test (Hainsworth & Siqueland, 1969). The Myklebust scale covers five behavioral categories—auditory comprehension, spoken language, orientation, behavior, and motor. The teacher judges a student on each item using a scale. The normative group consisted of third and fourth grade students.

The Meeting Street School Screening Test is intended for children in kindergarten and first grade. This test covers visual-perceptual-motor, language, and body awareness-control. Each item is administered individually to the child. A cutoff mark and profile indicate children with "high-risk" probability of learning disabilities.

A criterion-referenced approach to early screening is the Basic School Skills Inventory (Goodman & Hammill, 1975). The child is given tasks identified by teachers as critical entry skills for first grade. A criterion for mastery is used to judge evidence of a learning disability in academic readiness for reading, arithmetic, oral language, and other areas.

A less test-oriented approach is based upon principles of applied behavioral analysis (Lovitt, 1978). Given specific behaviors reported by teachers and parents, the children are observed over a short period of time in the setting in which they are having problems (Magliocca, Rinaldi, Crew, & Kunzelman, 1977). Samplings of critical behaviors are proving to be reliable and efficient ways to identify LD children. Kunzelman (1970) and others use precision measurement techniques for screening as well as program design and evaluation.

Given a small group of children referred for further assessment, the next phase of the IEP process is assessment. As we shall see in the next two sections, assessment is performed on two levels.

Assessment—Level One

As mentioned earlier, the assessment process is typically twofold: (1) to establish the need for LD services based on state guidelines for identification and (2) to specify the objectives for actual instruction. The two levels of assessment parallel the requirements of the IEP process. First, data upon which to decide the need and extent of need for services are required. Later, if necessary, the LD teacher must perform additional assessments to plan a program. As we have discussed earlier, the elements of the LD definition must be documented for placement, i.e., the present achievement level, the expected achievement level, the degree of discrepancy, and any related factors.

Present Achievement Levels

It is necessary to document the degree of underachievement in basic skill areas. The level of achievement is of interest at this particular point. *Group* achievement test scores are usually found in a child's cumulative folder. Global achievement tests are administered regularly in most school districts. These tests usually include sections in reading, arithmetic, and spelling. The group achievement tests should not be confused with the *individually* administered achievement tests mentioned in table 4-1. Group achievement tests, such as the California Achievement Test (Tiegs & Clark, 1970) or Stanford Achievement Test (Madden,

Gardner, Rudman, Karlsen, & Merwin, 1973), are of initial use in referrals and screening. Group achievement test data may be adversely affected by the reading problems, poor motivation, and inattention of the LD child.

Therefore, *individual* achievement batteries, like the Peabody Individual Achievement Test (Dunn & Markwardt, 1970), are much more useful and reliable for establishing the LD child's present level of functioning. In addition to the kind of administration, such batteries offer special provisions for the child's disability.

A child's daily performance in the classroom and elsewhere is also considered. Samples of class work, performances on informal tests, and observations of the child in the situation substantiate and elaborate upon the results of formal assessment.

Expected Achievement Levels

Actual achievement levels are different from the *expected* achievement levels of the learning disabled child. The potential achievement level is usually measured in terms of observations and performance on an intelligence test.

The same problems that we have with group *achievement* testing affect the reliability of group *intelligence* test scores. Reading ability and motivation are among the variables influencing a child's performance. Consequently, individual intelligence measures are preferred by most educators. The Wechsler Intelligence Scale for Children-Revised (Wechsler, 1974), commonly referred to as the WISC-R is an individual intelligence test that measures both verbal and nonverbal abilities. This feature makes the WISC-R a preferred intelligence test for LD children.

Generally, the LD child's performance on the WISC-R or on another measure is within the normal range of measured intelligence. In most states, the LD child must score at least 85 on the WISC-R and 84 on the Stanford-Binet Intelligence Scale, i.e., above one standard deviation from the mean score of 100. However, criticism of the use of intelligence tests to establish entry into LD services has stimulated much flexibility in test score interpretation in individual cases.

The prevailing mood in the academic community is against the use of measures of intelligence or expectation in the form of formal tests. The preference today is to gather baseline data on specific behaviors in the form of timed samples of performance. Graphs are plotted for each behavior, with notations on the effects of educational interventions (Cohen & Martin, 1971; Lovitt, 1978). This alternative strategy basically replaces a consideration of expected performance and potential with a consideration of documented performance rates under various educational strategies and contingencies. The impact of more informal, individual, and observational definitions of learning disabilities will be discussed later in this chapter.

Discrepancy between Expected and Actual Achievement

Information obtained from the present and expected achievement levels is used to determine the existence of a *significant discrepancy.* Achievement and intelligence scores are usually converted to one similar scale in terms of years and months. Kirk and Kirk (1971) display the data used for determining the existence of a significant discrepancy in reading ability:

Chronological Age	8-4
Mental Age	8-2
Arithmetic Computational Age	7-8
Reading Age	6-3

In this case we have a discrepancy between chronological age, mental age, and arithmetic achievement age on the one hand, and level of reading on the other hand. It is assumed here that the child has attended school with fair regularity, has had adequate teaching for two years, and has still not learned to read. (p. 55)

Myklebust (1968) uses a "learning quotient" to quantify the degree of discrepancy. He averages three factors in computing expected ability or "expectancy age." That is, he divides the total of the following factors by three:

1. Mental age, computed from the WISC's verbal or nonverbal score.
2. Grade age, computed by adding the grade and 5.2.
3. Chronological age.

This expectancy age (EA) is divided into an achievement age (AA); the achievement age is computed by adding the achievement grade level and 5.2. Thus:

$$\text{LQ (Learning quotient)} = \frac{AA}{EE} \times 100$$

A learning quotient may be computed for as many achievement areas as desired (reading, arithmetic, etc.). Myklebust (1968) suggests that a learning quotient of 89 or below is one criterion for identifying a specific learning disability.

Kirk and Kirk (1971) determine whether "a specific learning disability exists by the amount of discrepancy between the capacity to perform and the actual development or achievement in reading, talking, listening, thinking, perceiving, etc." (p. 55).

Recent efforts to conceptualize a formula for the definition of learning disabilities failed (Lloyd, Sabatino, Miller, & Miller, 1977; Sulzbacher & Kenowitz, 1977) (see chap. 2). Some professionals are using as much as a 50% level of discrepancy between actual achievement and expected achievement for placement in LD services. The goal is to identify only the most severely involved LD children.

The identification and referral phase is completed when a child has been described as having a learning disability in one or more of the basic school-related areas. The judgment is based upon the documented discrepancy between expected and actual achievement in the presence of the integrities mentioned earlier. The degree of discrepancy must be such to distinguish the LD child's profile of abilities and disabilities from other cases of mild underachievement.

Focus

In traditional paradigms of LD diagnosis, some evidence of underlying factors or a diagnostic hypothesis must also be established. This basis is developed by giving some of the psychological, perceptual, and perceptual-motor tests mentioned in table 4-1. If the LD child performs below the standard on one or more of these tests or parts of these tests, then processing, perceptual, and/or attentional deficits are established as underlying factors involved in the severe learning disability.

As mentioned in chapter 2, severe criticism of these tests and attendant programs has resulted in a significant shift in diagnostic procedures for most LD professionals. The more current practices include the use of language assessment or applied behavioral analysis, as exemplified by the LD definition used in the State of Washington (see table 2-1). One or more of the language screening tests mentioned in table 4-1 may be used to identify factors in language ability affecting the academic underachievement. In this procedure, the LD child's severe learning problems are described as language-related, either verbal or nonverbal.

In behavioral procedures, frequency counts of troublesome behaviors are kept over a short period of time. The result is documentation of consistently low performance under existing instructional procedures and other conditions. Compared to other well-developed skills, these skill areas are significantly deficit.

The end products of the first level of assessment are the necessary IEP features to establish data for LD placement. Supporting test data are available, and strengths and weaknesses are delineated. Annual long-term goals are stated, with an indication of the likely personnel to accomplish them. Given the above information, the extent of LD services and evaluation plan are also described.

As Hudson and Graham (1978) and Turnbull et al. (1978a, 1978b) state, a more specific level of assessment and planning is necessary to establish the other features of the IEP process.

Assessment—Level Two

The information gathered so far may satisfy IEP requirements for indications of present levels of functioning, strengths and weaknesses, and global goals. What is also necessary is the in-depth analysis of the learning disability areas so that objectives can be identified. Various disability areas, such as reading or arithmetic, are studied intensively. Factors related to severe academic and language disabilities are also examined.

Because children with learning disabilities will vary markedly on both the type and severity of the learning disability (see chap. 1), it is important to consider guidelines in choosing various informal and formal diagnostic instruments (Salvia & Ysseldyke, 1978).

1. The prior goals of the IEP, such as reading recognition or language expression, should be concentrated on.
2. Observations of the child in the classroom setting usually give balance to test score interpretations.
3. Consider both the *assets* and the *deficits* of each child on an intraindividual basis.
4. Use procedures that lead to instructional objectives.

In addition to the information accumulated in the preceding phases, specific assessments are performed upon the following areas: (1) academics, (2) skills, (3) task components, (4) language, (5) environmental factors, and (6) possible correlates.

Assessment of Academic Levels

All of the different kinds of assessment techniques mentioned earlier can be used to assess academic problems. Individual standardized tests, such as the Peabody Individual Achievement Test (Dunn & Markwardt, 1970), supply global scores in basic subject areas. Reading achievement can be probed more specifically by the Woodcock Reading Mastery Tests (Woodcock, 1974). The Key Math Diagnostic Arithmetic Test (Connolly et al., 1973), the Test of Language Development (Newcomer & Hammill, 1977), and the Test of Written Language (Hammill & Larsen, 1978) indicate strengths and weaknesses in their respective areas.

This level of assessment further documents the requirements of IEPs for strengths and weaknesses. By analyzing academic areas in these individual batteries, one can note patterns and relationships.

Assessment of Academic Skills

Criterion-referenced tests, scopes and sequences of skills, and informal tests pinpoint the exact skills present and absent in a child's repertoire (Pasanella & Volkmor, 1977; Wallace & Larsen, 1978). The criterion-referenced test, such as the Wisconsin Design Tests of Reading Skill Development (Kamm, Miles, Van Blaricom, Harris, & Stewart, 1972), identifies the reading skill performance in recognition and comprehension at different instructional levels. An LD teacher can determine whether the LD child reached criterion or not.

These skill deficits become target behaviors for instruction and are used as the short-term objectives for the IEPs. Generally, the initial IEP generated by the committee has enough data to satisfy requirements for placement; however, the full IEP must contain short-term objectives for each broad annual goal.

Another approach to identifying these IEP short-term objectives is the use of *scope and sequences of skills.* Many programs contain these lists, and some companies provide lists of objectives for areas like arithmetic and reading (Pasanella & Volkmor, 1977). Distar (Englemann & Bruner, 1969) has such a scope and sequence of skills in reading, math, and language. System FORE (Bell, 1972) contains lists of skills in reading, math, and language, as well as informal tests for each skill and references to materials.

The Instructional Based Appraisal System or IBAS (Meyen, Gault, & Howard, 1976) is a system for developing IEPs. It contains a cluster bank of goals and specific objectives for reading, arithmetic, and language. Stephens, Hartman, and Lucas (1978) have developed a similar system and have added teaching activities. Obviously, this trend toward skill assessment and accompanying retrieval systems makes the development of IEPs much easier.

Teachers also use *informal checklists* and *self-made tests* to good advantage (Mann & Suiter, 1974). Much useful information is gathered regularly by teachers who use tests based on the content and skills regularly called for in the classroom. Wallace and Larsen (1978), Pasanella and Volkmor (1977), and Mann and Suiter (1974) describe many such procedures.

Assessment of Task Components

Tasks with which children have had difficulty are also analyzed. One particular approach frequently used is *error analysis* (Smith, 1969). Close examination of reading, arithmetic, and other kinds of verbal and written products may reveal patterns of mistakes.

Task analysis is another form of assessment that blends in directly with requirements of the IEP. A given task is broken down into elemental steps and arranged in a sequence. The steps become the needed objectives.

This kind of assessment places a focus not on the child, but on the task. A frequent criticism of diagnosis is undue stress on the LD child's characteristics and not upon an equally plausible factor in severe underachievement, the task.

Assessment of Language Factors

Considerable attention has been given to the role of language in learning disabilities (Vogel, 1975; Wiig & Semel, 1976). As the relevancy of neurological and process testing has been questioned, renewed interest in the impact of language deficits is evident (Wallace & Larsen,

1978). Both oral and written language disorders can adversely affect a child's learning ability.

Formal and informal measures of phonology, linguistic structure (i.e., morphology and syntax), and semantics are available (Wallace & Larsen, 1978; Salvia & Ysseldyke, 1978). Language disabilities will be discussed in chapters 5 and 7.

The outcome of this kind of language analysis is twofold. First, specific objectives in language areas can be identified for remediation. An LD child who performs below criterion on the Test of Language Development (Newcomer & Hammill, 1977) and the Test of Written Language (Hammill & Larsen, 1978) would require more in-depth assessment in the deficient global areas.

Second, the primary academic disabilities in reading or arithmetic may have some troublesome language components. A language assessment can serve to better explain and describe disabilities in other areas.

Assessment of the Environment

Wallace and Larsen (1978) have identified many techniques to assess the learning environment. The school and classroom climate, teacher-child interaction, peer relationships, for example, represent critical factors in describing children's learning disabilities.

This kind of ecological analysis also represents a philosophical and procedural preference to examining the learning disability as a dynamic phenomenon. A learning disability does not reside in the child but rather is a product of a total life experience in the school and elsewhere. It must be assessed accordingly.

Assessment of Other Correlates

Considerable question has been raised recently about the reliability, validity, and educational relevancy of various forms of assessment. Neurological bases for learning disabilities have not been sufficiently substantiated to require that kind of assessment for every child suspected of having a learning disability (Bryan & Bryan, 1978).

Tests of auditory, visual, and motor perception have been criticized for their conceptual and technical bases (Hammill & Larsen, 1974; Hammill & Wiederholt, 1972; Salvia & Ysseldyke, 1978). Similar controversy also surrounds the assessment of possible correlates (Hammill & Larsen, 1974, 1978; Newcomer & Hammill, 1975).

At the present time, assessment and subsequent remediation of these processing types of constructs do not seem warranted. Educational purposes seem better served by attention to emphases previously mentioned.

Educational Planning

The total IEP must indicate objectives, materials, and methods for each annual goal. These objectives may be in any area, including basic skills, self-concept, vocational, and career development, and so forth. Pasanella and Volkmor (1977) indicate that the following factors must be present for each area of goals:

> (1) instructional objectives directly related to the child's need areas; (2) learning tasks sequentially arranged and designed to enable the student to master each objective; (3) descriptions of methods and techniques for presenting the learning tasks to the student; (4) descriptions of appropriate instructional materials; and (5) recommendations of environmental conditions which will maximize achievement of the learner objectives. (pp. 152-153)

Goals and Objectives

Hudson and Graham (1978) indicate that the goals for remediation that have been derived from assessment should be prioritized. They suggest the use of the following six principles:

1. Focus on the reason for referral.
2. Examine the student's present level of performance and note general areas in which progress is inadequate.
3. Examine the student's present level of performance and note areas of strength.
4. Determine what critical areas each team member considers to be educational priorities.
5. Examine each critical area with regard to the student's age, grade, rate of learning, amount of learning, likes, dislikes, strengths, weaknesses, abilities, etc.
6. Determine the prerequisite skills necessary to obtain more advanced skills in each critical area (p. 18).

Using the strategies described earlier (e.g., scope and sequence charts), the LD teacher establishes broad *annual goals.* An example of an *annual goal* is: "The student will be able to sound out initial consonants in words." Like all goals and objectives, annual goals should be in appropriate behavioral terms, i.e., observable and measurable.

The *specific objectives* for each goal must be identified and sequenced. Two examples of specific objectives for the previously mentioned goal would ·be: (1) Given a list of words with initial consonant sounds /b/, /d/, /f/, and /h/, the student will decode them with 90% accuracy; or (2) Given a list of words with initial consonant sounds /k/, /m/, /n/, /p/, and /q/, the student will decode them with 90% accuracy.

These objectives can be identified by using published retrieval systems (Meyen, Gault, & Howard, 1976; Stephens, Hartman, & Lucas,

1978) and by other strategies mentioned previously. Skill assessment, task analysis, and criterion-referenced assessment yield these specific objectives or close approximations. The severity of an LD child's disability and response to a particular level of presentation of a task will dictate the specificity and minuteness of instructional objectives.

Activities

For each objective, appropriate activities must be designed. The LD teacher chooses activities that are identical to or closely approximate the desired outcomes. For example, here is an objective: "Given a list of words with the following initial consonants /b/, /c/, /d/, and /f/, the student will decode them with 90% accuracy." It would be inappropriate to give the LD child an exercise of underlining the short vowels in a list of words to accomplish this objective.

We do not mean that activities for a given objective must be drill or rote. Cueing, game formats, and other techniques can be used to create effective and interesting activities. Wallace and Kauffman (1978) describe many interesting activities that can be used in LD remediation.

Learning disabilities in reading and other areas may also require a rigorous sequence of activities for effective remediation. *Delta: A Design for Word Attack Growth* (Morsink, 1977), a structured approach to teaching decoding skills, contains such a sequenced format.

Methods and Materials

Given a specific direction for remediation, the LD teacher must choose the kinds of methods and materials to support the needed activities and objective accomplishment. It is not wise to choose a material or method before deciding what kinds of exercises would help the LD child attain his or her goals.

Many materials and programs, however, have comprehensive and well-developed structures encompassing many objectives. LD teachers who know their materials and programs can develop their IEPs more quickly because they can interface learner needs and program features. Part two of this text contains descriptions of many programs and materials.

Some programming materials offer suggestions for materials and objectives. *System FORE* (Bell, 1972) is one such retrieval system, as is the *Behavior Resource Guide* (Cawley, 1973).

The choice of methods and materials must be guided by other considerations than instructional objectives. Bleil (1975), Brown (1975), and others have identified critical factors in the selection and purchase of materials and programs.

Teacher Behavior

The direct role of the LD teacher must be calculated in the development of the IEP. Pasanella and Volkmor (1977) and others have noted the following critical behaviors for the effective teacher: (1) uses a variety of materials, (2) stresses direct instruction, (3) uses reward systems, (4) requests student responses to indicate learning, (5) fades prompts and cues appropriately, (6) involves parents in instruction, and (7) teaches to mastery and criterion levels.

Wallace and Kauffman (1978) and the Division for Children with Learning Disabilities (DCLD) have identified competencies for effective teaching. They will be discussed in chapter 11.

Environmental Conditions

As Meyen et al. (1976) indicate, physical and other environmental factors must be arranged. Carrels, audiovisual equipment, and other materials facilitate instruction. The development of behavior management programs, use of a particular approach, such as the Fernald method (Fernald, 1943) and so forth, also serve to structure the necessary learning environment.

Delivery of Service

The final IEP format must include some additional features: the date and length of services, individuals responsible for the services, and the extent of time outside the regular classroom. Throughout the IEP assessment and planning phase, the LD teacher works with parents, regular classroom teachers, and support personnel. Goals and objectives are developed cooperatively and in the order in which they will be accomplished.

The last feature of the IEP is an evaluation system. Assessment procedures must be used to monitor the implementation and effectiveness of the IEP plan.

Evaluation

Hudson and Graham (1978) have indicated the need to monitor the development and implementation of the IEP for LD children. Data collection serves two functions: (1) to document achievement of annual goals and short-term objectives and (2) to provide information to modify the IEP.

Many of the previously mentioned techniques can be used for evaluation. There are two types of evaluation—formative and summative.

Formative evaluation involves informal and formal measures of whether a child has accomplished the planned behavioral objectives. Daily progress is often plotted on graphs or in some other fashion (Lovitt, 1977). Formative evaluation information is useful in modifying daily educational strategies.

Summative evaluation, on the other hand, typically involves pretest and posttest strategies. Pretest information is usually composed of the test results gathered in the identification and assessment phases of the IEP development. Alternate forms of the same tests and/or other tests make up posttest information. The successful completion of the long-term goals is usually determined by comparing the pretest and posttest data.

Wiederholt, Hammill, and Brown (1978) suggest a format for total program evaluation. This assessment of the components of the program would be evaluated by administrators, teachers, parents, students, and other involved parties. The critical areas to examine include:

1. Physical environment.
2. Curriculum.
3. Time allocated for specific activities.
4. Factors that relate to the resource pupils (e.g., screening).
5. Personnel involved in the resource effort (e.g., the school psychologist).
6. Planning/monitoring (e.g., formats of the IEP).
7. Record keeping.
8. Materials used in the program.
9. Public relations activities.

The adequacy of the development process of the IEP and appropriateness of the actual product should be specifically evaluated. Hudson and Graham (1978) describe a questionnaire to be given parents about the IEP process. The evaluation form included such questions as:

"Were you notified that your child was referred for special education prior to your invitation to attend the staffing conference?";
"Were the team members knowledgeable of your child's academic status?";
"Did you feel comfortable attending the staffing conferences?";
"Are you satisfied with the decision made at the staffing conference?" (pp. 26-27)

A regular evaluation of procedures for developing the IEP for an LD child will permit modifications. It is important to obtain input from all involved parties.

Pasanella and Volkmor (1977) encourage an examination of the IEP itself. They suggest an analysis to answer these questions:

1. Are specific academic strengths identified?
2. Are learning strengths identified?
3. Are learning weaknesses identified?

4. Are student interests identified and incorporated?
5. Are the best probable reinforcers identified?
6. Is there a choice of instructional materials appropriate to the student's age, sex, learning problem, learning style?
7. Is there a choice of instructional materials suited to student's regular classroom instructional program?
8. Are objectives clearly stated and do they include evaluative criteria?
9. Are teaching procedures detailed and clearly understandable? (p. 195)

They also describe formats for total program evaluation by the regular faculty, administrators, and others.

Jones, Gottlieb, Guskin, and Yoshida (1978) have reviewed the major considerations in program evaluation of LD children in resource rooms in the mainstream. They stress the need to consider the nature and quality of instruction in terms of the match of instructional activities to stated goals. This focus for evaluation of regular classroom and LD resource rooms seems paramount.

> The authors believe, given the current state of knowledge about relationships between instructional achievements and academic and social growth in populations of exceptional children, that IEP's can be evaluated only for their content appropriateness (face validity); that is, the assessment of experienced teachers about what is likely to work and what is not likely to work (with sensitivity to the need to monitor instructional activities constantly and to modify programs when changes are appropriate) seems to reflect the state of the art with respect to the evaluation of IEP's. (p. 598)

ASSESSMENT: IN PERSPECTIVE

Logan (1977) has noted that we make three basic assumptions about educational assessment. First, we may think we understand and use the terms and concepts of the process well. Second, we may feel we possess adequate (i.e., valid and reliable) instrumentation. Third, we may imagine that we have considered all the ramifications of the assessment process for all groups and situations.

We do not think that anyone in learning disabilities with a modicum of sense would make such assumptions. As Larsen (1977) points out, the major shortcomings in our field are precisely in these areas. We expend inordinate amounts of time in educationally irrelevant formal evaluation. Particularly critical to LD diagnosis is the practice of assessing poorly defined psychological constructs that we presume underlie the severe academic and language disabilities. The companion error to an excessive child-focus approach is to ignore significant environmental factors that are causing and maintaining academic and social problems.

The area of diagnosis of learning disabilities is essentially caught up in the process of narrowing a gap. The gap is one which exists between assessment and teaching. As Lovitt (1977) points out: "When we take time to diagnose precisely the exact nature of a child's problems, subsequent teaching can be simple" (p. 21).

There seems a wise shift away from formal standardized assessment to more informal measures. Criterion-referenced assessment, applied behavioral analysis, and so forth, maximize educational direction (Fedner & Duffy, 1978).

The requirements of P.L. 94-142 for a complete IEP for each LD child should guarantee greater educational relevancy in assessment procedures. The role of the LD teacher on assessment teams is imperative to maintain this focus (Wallace & Larsen, 1978). As the one who will exercise the leadership role in educational planning and implementation, the LD teacher's participation in the IEP process is imperative.

SUMMARY

In this chapter we reviewed the nature, scope, and formats of diagnostic procedures. Given a discussion of the requirements of P.L. 94-142 for assessment activities, we described the main features of the IEP. Finally, we traced the development of the IEP for an LD child through four critical phases: identification and referral, bi-level assessment, educational planning, and evaluation.

SUGGESTED ACTIVITIES

1. Interview an LD teacher about his or her diagnostic activities and about working relationships with other diagnosticians.

2. Review one of the tests mentioned in table 4-1. Examine its purposes, reliability and validity, format and instructions, and implications for designing an IEP.

3. Examine local and state practices in designing IEPs. Are all components present? How do different school systems comply with P.L. 94-142?

4. Make a list of questions that you imagine an LD teacher might ask about a child. Given the kinds of assessment procedures mentioned in this chapter, choose an appropriate assessment procedure.

5. Interview a school psychologist, pediatrician, counselor, or other kind of diagnostician. Ask them about their procedures for assessing learning disabilities.

6. Make a list of specific skill deficits for reading, arithmetic, and other areas of learning disability. Refer to part two in this text and/or observations of children's errors.

7. What diagnostic procedures are used to make placement and pro-gramming decisions for LD children in your district? Outline the steps and necessary assessment procedures.

8. Examine recent criticism of process and perceptual testing. Decide what professional posture you would assume on the use of such diagnostic tests. Is the definition of LD changed by discontinuing this form of assessment?

References

Baker, H.J., & Leland, B. *Detroit Tests of Learning Aptitude.* Indianapolis: Bobbs-Merrill, 1955.

Bateman, B. An educator's view of a diagnostic approach to learning disorders. In J. Hellmuth (Ed.), *Learning disorders* (Vol. I). Seattle, Wash.: Special Child Publications, 1965.

Beatty, L., Madden, R., & Gardner, E. *Stanford Diagnostic Arithmetic Test.* New York: Harcourt Brace Jovanovich, 1966.

Bell, B.A. (Coordinator). *System FORE.* Los Angeles: Foreworks, 1972.

Bender, L. *The Bender Visual-Motor Gestalt Test for Children.* Los Angeles: Western Psychological Services, 1962.

Bleil, G.B. Evaluating instructional materials. *Journal of Learning Disabilities,* 1975, *8,* 12-24.

Botel, M. *Botel Reading Inventory.* Chicago: Follett, 1966.

Brown, V. A basic Q-sheet for analyzing and comparing curriculum materials and proposals. *Journal of Learning Disabilities,* 1975, *8,* 407-476.

Brueckner, L. *Diagnostic Tests and Self-Help in Arithmetic.* Monterey, Calif.: California Test Bureau, McGraw-Hill, 1955.

Bryan, T., & Bryan, J. *Understanding learning disabilities* (2nd ed.). Sherman Oaks, Calif.: Alfred, 1978.

Carrow, E. *Test of Auditory Comprehension of Language.* Austin, Tex.: Learning Concepts, 1973.

Carrow, E. *Carrow Elicited Language Inventory.* Austin, Tex.: Learning Concepts, 1974.

Cawley, J.F. *Behavior resource guide.* Wallingford, Conn.: Educational Sciences, 1973.

Clements, S.D. Minimal brain dysfunction in children (NINDS Monograph No. 3, U.S. Public Health Service Bulletin No. 1415). Washington, D.C.: U.S. Government Printing Office, 1966.

Cohen, M., & Martin, G. Applying precision teaching to academic assessment. *Teaching Exceptional Children,* 1971, *3,* 120-128.

Colarusso, R., & Hammill, D. *Motor-Free Visual Perception Test.* San Rafael, Calif.: Academic Therapy Publications, 1972.

Connolly, A., Natchman, W., & Pritchett, E. *Key Math Diagnostic Arithmetic Test.* Circle Pines, Minn.: American Guidance Service, 1973.

Crabtree, M. *Houston Test for Language Development.* Houston: Houston Test, 1963.

Dunn, L.M. *Peabody Picture Vocabulary Test.* Minneapolis: American Guidance Service, 1959.

Dunn, L.M., & Markwardt, F.C. *Peabody Individual Achievement Test.* Circle Pines, Minn.: American Guidance Service, 1970.

Durrell, D.D. *Durrell Analysis of Reading Difficulty.* New York: Harcourt Brace Jovanovich, 1955.

Engelmann, S., & Bruner, E.C. *Distar: An instructional system.* Chicago: Science Research Associates, 1969.

Fedner, M., & Duffey, J. Educational diagnosis with instructional use. *Exceptional Children,* 1978, *44,* 246-253.

Fernald, G. *Remedial techniques in basic school subjects.* New York: McGraw-Hill, 1943.

Frostig, M., Lefever, D.W., & Whittlesey, J.R. *The Marianne Frostig Developmental Test of Visual Perception.* Palo Alto, Calif.: Consulting Psychologists Press, 1964.

Gardner, W. *Learning and behavior characteristics of exceptional children and youth.* Boston: Allyn & Bacon, 1977.

Gates, A.I., & McKillop, A.S. *Gates-McKillop Reading Diagnostic Test.* New York: Bureau of Publications, Teachers College, Columbia University, 1962.

Gates, A.I., & Russell, D.H. *Gates-Russell Spelling Diagnostic Test.* New York: Columbia University Press, 1940.

Gilmore, J.V. *Gilmore Oral Reading Test.* New York: Harcourt Brace Jovanovich, 1951.

Goodenough, F., & Harris, D. *Goodenough-Harris Drawing Test.* New York: Harcourt Brace Jovanovich, 1963.

Goodman, L., & Hammill, D. *Basic School Skills Inventory.* Chicago: Follett, 1975.

Gray, W.S. *Gray Oral Reading Test.* Indianapolis: Bobbs-Merrill, 1963.

Hainsworth, P., & Siqueland, M. *Early Identification of Children with Learning Disabilities: The Meeting Street School Screening Test.* Providence: Crippled Children and Adults of Rhode Island, 1969.

Hammill, D., & Larsen, S. The effectiveness of psycholinguistic training. *Exceptional Children,* 1974, *41,* 5-15.

Hammill, D., & Larsen, S. *Test of Written Language.* Austin: Services for Professional Educators, 1978.

Hammill, D.D., & Larsen, S.C. The effectiveness of psycholinguistics training: A reaffirmation of position. *Exceptional Children,* 1978, *44,* 402-418.

Hammill, D.D., & Wiederholt, J.L. Review of the Frostig visual perception test and the related training program. In L. Mann & D. Sabatino (Eds.), *The first review of special education* (Vol. 1). Philadelphia: JSE Press, Grune & Stratton, 1972.

Hudson, F., & Graham, S. An approach to operationalizing the IEP. *Learning Disability Quarterly,* 1978, *1,* 13-32.

Jastak, J.F., & Jastak, S.R. *The Wide Range Achievement Test* (Rev. ed.). Wilmington, Del.: Guidance Associates, 1965.

Johnson, D., & Myklebust, H. *Learning disabilities: Educational principles and practices.* New York: Grune & Stratton, 1967.

Johnson, M., & Kress, R. *Informal reading inventories.* Newark, Del.: International Reading Association, 1965.

Johnson, S., & Morasky, R. *Learning disabilities.* Boston: Allyn & Bacon, 1977.

Jones, R.L., Gottlieb, J., Guskin, S., & Yoshida, R.K. Evaluating mainstreaming programs: Models, coveats, considerations, and guidelines. *Exceptional Children,* 1978, *44,* 588-601.

Kamm, K., Miles, P.J., Van Blaricom, V.L., Harris, M.L., & Stewart, D.M. *Wisconsin Design Tests of Reading Skill Development.* Minneapolis: National Computer Systems, 1972.

Kirk, S.A., McCarthy, J., & Kirk, W.D. *Illinois Test of Psycholinguistic Abilities* (Rev. ed.). Urbana, Ill.: University of Illinois Press, 1968.

Kirk, S.A., & Kirk, W.D. *Psycholinguistic learning disabilities: Diagnosis and remediation.* Urbana, Ill.: University of Illinois Press, 1971.

Kunzelman, H.P. (Ed.). *Precision teaching.* Seattle: Special Child Publications, 1970.

Larsen, S. The educational evaluation of handicapped students. In R.D. Kneedler & S.G. Tarver (Eds.), *Changing perspectives in special education.* Columbus, Ohio: Charles E. Merrill, 1977.

Larsen, S., & Hammill, D. *Test of Written Spelling.* San Rafael, Calif.: Academic Therapy Publications, 1976.

Lee, L. *The Northwestern Syntax Screening Test.* Evanston, Ill.: Northwestern University Press, 1969.

Lerner, J. *Children with learning disabilities* (2nd ed.). Boston: Houghton Mifflin, 1976.

Lloyd, J., Sabatino, D., Miller, T., & Miller, S. Proposed federal guidelines: Some open questions. *Journal of Learning Disabilities,* 1977, *10,* 69-71.

Logan, D. Diagnosis: Current and changing considerations. In R.D. Kneedler & S.G. Tarver (Eds.), *Changing perspectives in special education.* Columbus, Ohio: Charles E. Merrill, 1977.

Lovitt, T. *In spite of my resistance . . . I've learned from children.* Columbus, Ohio: Charles E. Merrill, 1977.

Lovitt, T. The learning disabled. In N. Haring (Ed.), *Behavior of exceptional children* (2nd ed.). Columbus, Ohio: Charles E. Merrill, 1978.

Madden, R., Gardner, E.R., Rudman, H.C., Karlsen, B., & Merwin, J.C. *Stanford Achievement Test.* New York: Harcourt Brace Jovanovich, 1973.

Magliocca, L., Rinaldi, R., Crew, J., & Kunzelman, H. Early identification of handicapped children through a frequency sampling technique. *Exceptional Children,* 1977, *43,* 414-423.

Mann, P.H., & Suiter, P. *Handbook in diagnostic teaching.* Boston: Allyn & Bacon, 1974.

Mecham, M.J. *Verbal Language Development Scale.* Minneapolis: American Guidance Service, 1959.

Meyen, E.L., Gault, S., & Howard, C. *Instructional based appraisal system.* Bellevue, Wash.: Edmark Associates, 1976.

Monroe, M. *Monroe Reading Aptitude Test.* Boston: Houghton Mifflin, 1935.

Morsink, C. *Delta: A design for word attack growth.* Minneapolis, Minn.: National Computer Systems, 1977.

Myklebust, H. *Picture Story Language Test: The Development and Disorders of Written Language* (Vol. I). New York: Grune & Stratton, 1965.

Myklebust, H. Learning disabilities: Definition and overview. In H. Myklebust (Ed.), *Progress in learning disabilities* (Vol. I). New York: Grune & Stratton, 1968.

Myklebust, H. *Pupil Rating Scale: Screening for Learning Disabilities.* New York: Grune & Stratton, 1971.

Newcomer, P., & Hammill, D.D. *Psycholinguistics in the schools.* Columbus, Ohio: Charles E. Merrill, 1975.

Newcomer, P., & Hammill D.D. *The Test of Language Development.* Austin, Tex.: Empiric Press, 1977.

Pasanella, A., & Volkmor, C. *Coming back . . . or never leaving.* Columbus, Ohio: Charles E. Merrill, 1977.

Roach, E., & Kephart, N. *The Purdue Perceptual-Motor Survey.* Columbus, Ohio: Charles E. Merrill, 1966.

Roswell, F., & Chall, J. *Roswell-Chall Diagnostic Test of Word-Analysis Skills.* New York: Essay Press, 1959.

Salvia, J., & Ysseldyke, J. *Assessment in special and remedial education.* Boston: Houghton Mifflin, 1978.

Seashore, H. *Sequential Tests of Educational Progress.* Princeton, N.J.: Cooperative Test Division, Educational Testing Service, 1963.

Slingerland, B. *Screening Tests for Identifying Children with Specific Language Disability.* Cambridge, Mass.: Educator Publishing Service, 1964.

Sloan, W. *Lincoln-Oseretsky Motor Developmental Scale.* Los Angeles: Western Psychological Services, 1965.

Smith, R.M. *Teacher diagnosis of educational difficulties.* Columbus, Ohio: Charles E. Merrill, 1969.

Spache, G.D. *Diagnostic Reading Scales.* Monterey, Calif.: California Test Bureau, 1963.

Stephens, T.M., Hartman, A.C., & Lucas, V.H. *Teaching children basic skills.* Columbus, Ohio: Charles E. Merrill, 1978.

Sulzbacher, S., & Kenowitz, L. At last, a definition of learning disabilities we can live with. *Journal of Learning Disabilities,* 1977, *10,* 67-69.

Tiegs, E.W., & Clark, W.W. *California Achievement Test.* Monterey, Calif.: CTB/McGraw-Hill, 1970.

Turnbull, A., Strickland, B., & Hammer, S. The individualized education program—Part 1: Procedural guidelines. *Journal of Learning Disabilities,* 1978, *11,* 40-46. (a)

Turnbull, A., Strickland, B., & Hammer, S. The individualized education program—Part 2: Translating law into practice. *Journal of Learning Disabilities,* 1978, *11* 67-72. (b)

Valett, R. *Valett Developmental Survey of Basic Learning Abilities.* Palo Alto, Calif.: Fearon, 1969.

Vogel, S.A. *Syntactic abilities in normal and dyslexic children.* Baltimore: University Park Press, 1975.

Wallace, G., & Kauffman, J. *Teaching children with learning problems* (2nd ed.). Columbus, Ohio: Charles E. Merrill, 1978.

Wallace, G., & Larsen, S. *Educational assessment of learning problems: Testing for teaching.* Boston: Allyn & Bacon, 1978.

Wechsler, D. *Weschler Intelligence Scale for Children* (Rev. ed.). New York: Psychological Corp., 1974.

Wepman, J. *Auditory Discrimination Test.* Chicago: Language Research Associates, 1958.

Wiederholt, J.L., Hammill, D.D., & Brown, V. *The resource teacher.* Boston: Allyn & Bacon, 1978.

Wiig, E.H., & Semel, E.M. *Language disabilities in children and adolescents.* Columbus, Ohio: Charles E. Merrill, 1976.

Woodcock, R. *Woodcock Reading Mastery Tests.* Circle Pines, Minn.: American Guidance Service, 1974.

Characteristics of Learning Disabilities

Children with learning disabilities exhibit a wide variety of different characteristics. Most difficulties are in the school-related tasks of listening, thinking, talking, reading, writing, spelling, and arithmetic. However, the specific types of each deficit and the differing degrees of difficulty extend the variations found within this group of children.

The most prevalent types of learning disabilities are discussed in part two of this book. For each chapter in this section, component subskills are described, assessment procedures delineated, and programs of remediation summarized.

An introductory statement in each chapter classifies the topic under discussion. Many of the chapters note the developmental skill sequence. Practical examples of subskill deficiencies are included whenever possible. Informal techniques and standardized tests are discussed in the assessment section. Similarly, programs of remediation are outlined for developing skills in each area.

We will discuss the characteristics of LD children under the headings of spoken language, reading, written language, arithmetic, social-emotional, and perceptual-motor problems. Some overlap may be noted among these areas since the categories have been arbitrarily grouped for discussion purposes. Some LD children may exhibit difficulties in only one of the areas discussed while others may experience learning disabilities in many of these academic areas.

5

Spoken Language Problems

PREVIEW

Language is both a fascinating and complicated process that is a uniquely human accomplishment. The acquisition of language usually follows an ordered sequence of well-defined steps. Remarkably, by age 4, the child's linguistic system is essentially that of the adults in his surroundings (Eisenson, 1972). By any account, this must be considered a truly remarkable feat to be accomplished in the relatively brief period of 48 months.

We believe that our introductory discussion of normal language development will provide the reader with a solid basis for understanding the relationship of language to learning and the problems associated with language encountered by many LD children and youth. The nature of language is considered by describing three major theories of language acquisition. The components of language and the various developmental language stages are also summarized in this section.

Specific language learning disabilities are discussed under the headings of inner language, receptive language, and expressive language. Skill deficiencies in each of these areas are described in this section.

Because the degree of competency that a child develops in spoken language skills will influence later academic achievement, a teacher should be prepared to appraise components of spoken language to determine if deficiencies in this area are contributing to academic failure (Wallace & Larsen, 1978). Consequently, our assessment section describes both informal, teacher-made instruments and published tests.

The general principles of language remediation and descriptions of commercial language kits discussed in the final section of this chapter are intended to provide the reader with an overview of various instructional approaches for language development and remediation. More complete information may be obtained by consulting the original sources of these programs.

Spoken language deficits, similar to those experienced by Todd, account for an exceedingly large proportion of children with learning disabilities (McGrady, 1968). The difficulties encountered by LD children in this area have been recognized by many writers as closely associated with other academic disabilities (Irwin & Marge, 1972; Skinner, 1957).

Most workers in this field view language development in the broader context of acquiring skills in listening, speaking, reading, and writing. Children seem to learn language skills by following this hierarchical development. Each successive skill is built upon a firm foundation of

Todd is an alert and even-tempered child. His cooperative spirit and high motivation have always been assets to his personality. As an only child in a closely knit family, Todd has experienced a relatively secure and pleasant family environment for most of his 8 1/2 years of life. However, Todd's growth in verbal communication has been slow.

Todd's major obstacle to successful academic achievement is his inappropriate recall of words and sentences. For example, he often says "nabana" for "banana," "racamoni" for "macaroni," and "tikchen," for "kitchen." He also asks, "What this is?" instead of "What is this?" and is unaware of his inappropriate word order. In reading class, his teacher reports that when Todd is asked to recall the meaning of a short oral paragraph that has just been read to him, he cannot remember the names of characters or the sequence of events. On occasion, he will answer a question pertaining to the story, but his response will be limited to two- or three-word combinations. For instance, if asked, "What happened to Sam when he fell off his bike?" Todd would answer, "hurt knee."

Todd is able to read on a third-grade level. Most verbal experience requirements, however, are too taxing and frustrating for his participation. Todd attempts to avoid as many verbal communication situations as possible.

At the present time, Todd is enrolled in a regular third-grade class with a 30-minute daily tutorial program. Unfortunately, there is insufficient coordination between his classroom teacher and the LD specialist. It is apparent that the daily disappointments and frustrations he experiences in this situation are contributing to an already damaged self-concept.

preceding abilities. It is usually expected, for example, that a child will acquire adequate listening skills prior to developing the expressive skill of speaking. Figure 5-1 illustrates the developmental hierarchy which leads to language proficiency. In this chapter, the parameters of spoken language problems will be discussed. Problems associated with reading and written language disorders will be discussed in later chapters.

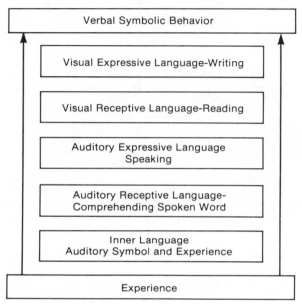

Figure 5-1
Developmental Hierarchy of an Individual's Language System
From *The Psychology of Deafness* (2nd ed.) by H.R. Myklebust. New York: Grune & Stratton, 1964. Copyright 1964 by Grune & Stratton. Reprinted by permission.

THE NATURE OF LANGUAGE

What Is Language?

Language is a system of verbal symbols used for human communication. The verbal symbols we use are commonly called words. Language is a system uniquely human and very different from the communication systems used by other forms of life (Wardhaugh, 1972). According to McGrady (1968), language is the thing which makes man unique among all species. The communicative aspects of language permit each individual to participate in many different situations. Wood (1969) describes a number of the opportunities.

It is through language that we can express our feelings, discuss an idea, or present a point of view. Through language we can share our experiences with others by describing for them things we have seen, places we have been, or people we have met. Through language we can speak or write about an object without the necessity of having the object present and we can understand an abstract idea with which we have had no personal experience. (p. 3)

Individuals from many different disciplines, including audiology, education, linguistics, medicine, psychology, and speech pathology, have studied language. Cooperation between professionals in psychology and linguistics led to the development of another area of study, *psycholinguistics,* which is concerned with the interrelationships of psychological and linguistic behavior (Hodges & Rudorf, 1972). Some of the basic concepts and terms developed and studied by all these professionals are discussed in the following sections.

Theories of Language Acquisition

The complexity and diversification of language behavior have attracted the attention of scholars from many different disciplines and have influenced a number of theories and concepts concerning the nature of language acquisition. Three major theorists who present different explanations of language acquisition are Skinner (1957), Chomsky (1965), and Lenneberg (1967).

The behaviorist model proposed by Skinner views language acquisition as a process of reinforced imitative behavior. Skinner (1957) uses the term *verbal behavior* to account for the phenomenon known as language. He believes that language is a learned behavior that may be observed. The environment plays an important role in Skinner's model. Language is both defined and increased in complexity through the reinforcement offered by individuals in the child's environment through listening, commenting, and so forth. In other words, Skinner believes that a child's verbal behavior is shaped by the verbal community in which he lives. Berry (1969) notes that in a normal family environment these spontaneous reinforcers are always present.

A baby's copy of an intonational pattern of the mother is reinforced instantly by her expression of delight or her action in picking up and cuddling the baby. The copy may be a remote facsimile, but in the beginning any verbal behavior that is part of the final pattern will be immediately reinforced. As speech develops, only closer approximations or matches of the speech in the baby's environment will be rewarded. With systematically applied rewards, the child tends to repeat the word or phrase. (p. 115)

The frequency, arrangement, and withholding of reinforcement are important variables in learning verbal behavior. The systematic and immediate application of rewards is most often recommended by Skinner in order for children to acquire language.

Chomsky (1957), a renowned linguistic scholar, views language quite differently. His theory of language is based on the premise that language competence is an innate competency. Chomsky is concerned with the system of rules within an individual by which communication is both interpreted and produced. He believes a child has innate linguistic *universals* that allow him to build a theory of grammar, which in turn help him to comprehend and produce an infinite number of sentences. Chomsky believes that these universal dimensions of grammar vary little from language to language, and that individuals from all cultures have a common process for generating linguistic messages. In the process of developing language, the child knows or deduces rules for producing language which allow him to form, use, and understand sentences that he has never heard before. The system of rules allows the child to generate the underlying meaning and transform it into a surface struc-ture that is syntactically correct. Chomsky contends this aspect of language provides the most critical support for his theory.

The language model proposed by Lenneberg (1964, 1967), is based upon the belief that language has a biological basis. He asserts that language is learned by the child as the brain matures both neurolog-ically and chemically. Lenneberg does not emphasize environmental variables in his thoery. He believes that environment has little effect on language development, except for providing the child with raw material to be utilized in communication. Language is derived from cognitive processes that are unique to humans and that involve the categorization and extraction of similarities from the environment. Thus, the child creates his own language by using the raw materials provided by his environment. Yet, language from child to child is similar because cognitive processes are similar due to our common neurological organi-zation developed through genetic transmission.

Since his theory regards language development as being regulated by a unique maturation process, Lenneberg suggests that there is a critical decade for language to develop. He believes that the optimal period for primary language development is approximately 2-12 years. Before this time, the brain is too immature and undergoing too rapid changes in structural, chemical, and neurophysiological states for language learn-ing to take place. Lenneberg notes that once the brain is fully matured (at age 12) primary language acquisition is difficult.

These three theorists would probably not disagree that a child acquires language in a certain order: babbling, talking, echolalia, and so forth. However, they would disagree on *how* the child acquires these developmental milestones (Beers, 1973). Although each man proceeds from very different theoretical frameworks, we believe they each offer unique ideas to the concept of language acquisition.

Language Components

Language is composed of many interrelated factors. The major dimensions of language as viewed by linguists, who scientifically study language, are discussed in this section. These factors are *phonology, morphology, syntax,* and *semantics.*

Phonology

Phonology is the first element studied in modern linguistics. Phonology is concerned with the *phonemes,* or speech sounds, of a language. The child learning any language must first learn the phonemes of the language. Wallace and Larsen (1978) point out that, in and of themselves, phonemes have no meaning. The phonemes become meaningful when they conform to standards of accepted usage within a language. For example, the phonemes /f/ and /s/ are essentially meaningless by themselves; however, they alter the meaning of a word when they are interchanged, such as in *fat* and *sat.* The phonemic elements within a word are also important for a child learning to read. *Phonics* is the method of teaching reading in which the key units taught to children are letter-sound correspondences (Hodges & Rudorf, 1972).

Morphology

Morphology is the study of the smallest units of meaning in a language, the *morphemes.* A morpheme may be a complete word by itself, such as *car,* or it may be a unit of speech that has no meaning by itself, but contributes to the meaning of words, such as /s/ sound added to *car* to produce the plural form *cars* (Hodges & Rudorf, 1972). Consequently, the word *cars* is composed of two distinct morphemes or meaning units—the concept of a car and the concept of plurality.

According to Myers and Hammill (1976), morphemic analysis is also concerned with the grammatical markers used in language to note such concepts as *plurality,* marked by *s* for regular nouns; *verb tense,* marked by *ed, ing,* and so forth; and *person,* marked by such devices as the *s* at the end of regular verbs like *run.*

Syntax

Syntax refers to the arrangement of words into meaningful sequences. The major areas of syntactical concern are the *order* and relationship of the elements within a sentence. For example, the sentence, "Will you come with me?" implies a question that changes in meaning when the word order is altered to "You will come with me." Obviously, some children learn very quickly that the ordering of words within a sentence will be crucial to meaning. Individuals who encounter difficulty in syntactical development usually exhibit difficulties in both comprehending and using language.

Semantics

Semantics refers to the ability to obtain meaning from words, sentences, and other linguistic entities. Semantics has received considerably less attention when compared to other components of language. Myers and Hammill (1976) believe that the most cogent reason for the neglect of research in this area is the lack of a clear framework for semantic analysis. They allude to the irony of this situation since meaning is the single most important factor in language.

Irwin, Moore, and Rampp (1972) point out that semantics is actually concerned with the linguistic elements, and with how language is used. Hammill and Bartel (1978) further suggest that until a child understands, at least in rudimentary form, the nature of some objects and events in his environment, he has no referents for a system of meaning, and hence is incapable of learning language.

Developmental Language Stages

Dale (1976) notes that the major developmental stages through which a child progresses in acquiring linguistic competency have been the topic of intense study for 50 years. We believe that a general overview of these stages will provide a basis for studying children with language disturbances.

The child's first attempt to use vocal mechanisms is the *birth cry* (Lerner, 1976). Usually, the birth cry provides the attending physician with some assurance that all is well. Eisenson (1972) points out that during the second and third month cooing, gurgling, squealing, and sounds that approximate consonants and vowellike sounds become part of the infant's vocalizations.

An important stage in prelingual speech development is *babbling*, which typically occurs between 3 and 6 months of age. This stage is characterized by vocal play during which identifiable sounds such as /ae/, /k/, /m/, and /b/ are produced (Wallace & Larsen, 1978). The infant also shows increased awareness of persons in his or her environment during this stage. It has been noted by Lerner (1976) that some children with language disorders are reported by parents not to have engaged in babbling activities.

Around 6 to 8 months of age, most children begin to repeat or imitate intentionally their own random sounds. This is called *lalling*. Some of the repeated syllables which may be heard often are *da-da, ga-ga,* and *ma-ma* (Eisenson, 1972).

At about 8 or 9 months of age, *echolalia* usually begins with most normal children. At this stage, the child purposefully imitates sounds made in the environment but does not associate any meaning with them.

Around the age of 1 year, most children begin to say single words with meaning. The first words are usually reduplicated syllables such as *dada* or *mama* (Eisenson, 1972). Two- and three-word sentences *(Daddy go, Mommy eat,* etc.) usually follow around 18 months of age. By age 2, most children have vocabularies of 50 to 100 words or more. However, Eisenson notes that the most distinctive achievement is not in vocabulary growth but in the ability to combine words into phrase-sentences.

The vocabulary growth is proportionally greater at 30 months then at any other period of the child's life, and by age 3 children can understand thousands of words and have a productive vocabulary that may reach or exceed 1,000 words (Eisenson, 1972).

By the time most children enter school, their linguistic systems are essentially that of the adults in their environment, except for articulation. The average length of spoken sentences consists of approximately 4.5 words at this age, and spoken language proficiency becomes highly correlated with other elements of the language arts.

Many children with specific learning disabilities do not follow the normal developmental stages in language acquisition. The speed and efficiency with which many normal children learn language is not always characteristic of the LD child. Some of the specific difficulties encountered by these children in spoken language are discussed in the next section.

LANGUAGE AND LEARNING DISABILITIES

The term *aphasia* has been used to describe children with various types of auditory language disturbances. We have chosen instead to discuss these problems under the heading of "spoken language problems." The difficulties discussed in this section include deficits with *inner language, receptive language,* and *expressive language.*

Inner Language

Most people who work with language agree that inner language disturbances are probably the most debilitating of all language disorders. Inner language refers to internalized language, or the language which one uses to communicate with oneself (Goldstein, 1948). Inner language has also been referred to as "inner speech" (Vygotsky, 1962).

Disturbances in inner language are not as well understood as the difficulties that children experience in receptive and expressive language, nor is it altogether clear *how* inner language deficits affect other areas of learning.

The various types of inner language disorders have not been well delineated. However, the process is believed to involve the establishment of verbal imagery for words and concepts. The ability to assimilate experiences (Lerner, 1976) is also involved in inner language development.

Children with difficulties in this area are unable to attach meaning to specific words. The word *train,* for example, may have no meaning to a child, even though he is able to hear the word spoken and auditorially express the word himself. Part of the difficulty seems due to the child's inability to transform any experiences with the word or concept into verbal symbols. However, the neurological reasons why some children do not assimilate experiences are not completely known at the present time. In addition, very little information is available on remediating inner language disturbances. The problem is one which certainly requires further study and research.

Auditory Receptive Language

Auditory receptive language is the ability to understand verbal language. Children with deficits in this area usually hear what is said but they are unable to comprehend the meaning of it. According to Chalfant and Scheffelin (1969), the acquisition of receptive language involves a number of interrelated tasks.

> The child first attends to vocally produced sound units, then must discriminate between them. A reciprocal association is formed between the sound unit and an experience. This association allows the child to interpret the vocal sound unit as a meaningful language signal which is stored for retrieval at a future time. The child improves his receptive language by analyzing more complex signals and by increasing the speed and accuracy of interpretations. Finally, with sufficient practice the child can shift attention from the vocal language signal to the meaning carried by the signal sequence. Thus, he will be able to respond appropriately to verbal commands, instructions, explanations, and questions. (p. 77)

Receptive language difficulties have been labeled *word deafness, receptive aphasia, sensory aphasia,* and *auditory verbal agnosia* (Orton, 1937; Goldstein, 1948; Wepman, 1951; Myklebust, 1954; McGinnis, 1963). However, the degree of disturbance among these children will vary according to a number of different dimensions. Typically, children with receptive difficulties will have problems associating names with objects, be unable to name objects, have poor recall of names, and have some difficulty in interpreting environmental language (McGinnis, 1963). *Echolalia,* the repetition of words and sentences without meaning, is also associated with receptive language disorders among some school-age children.

The major subskills of receptive language with which LD children have difficulties are described in the following section.

Perceiving Speech Sounds

A common problem is the inability to understand, localize, and attend to various speech sounds. The adequacy of this skill is basic to the understanding of all spoken language. If a child does not perceive isolated speech sounds such as /m/, /s/, or /v/ it seems fair to assume that he or she will also have difficulties with words and sentences.

Perceiving speech sounds is dependent upon the child being *aware* of sounds in general. Some children give no observable indications that they are aware of sounds. Johnson and Myklebust (1967) suggest that it is important to begin training by making children aware of sound.

Once awareness is established, the child must also be able to localize sounds. This skill is particularly dependent upon *attending* to sounds and the immediate environment. Distractible, hyperactive, and other children with short attention spans are often unable to localize sounds because of their short periods of concentration.

Discrimination among various speech sounds is a higher level skill subject to adequate awareness, localization, and attention. Learning disabled children with these difficulties usually have problems in differentiating between two sounds or choosing a word which begins with a particular sound in a list of words read to them.

Understanding Words

The skill of understanding various words used in our language is closely associated with perceiving speech sounds. Children typically progress from understanding this skill to comprehending both concrete and abstract words. In this regard, Johnson and Myklebust (1967) caution that children should have had the experience with which a given word is to be associated before it is taught. Otherwise, the word might be meaningless to the child.

The different types of words which must be learned by most children have been listed by Lerner (1976). She mentions the names of objects, the names of actions, the names of qualities, and the names of abstract concepts among the various kinds of words that must be learned. A suggested hierarchy of difficulty for adjective comprehension is presented in table 5-1.

Children with receptive language problems usually find concrete words easier to learn, since these words are most often associated with their daily experiences. The words *school, chair,* and *man* will probably be easier for most children to learn than words such as *with, the,* and *who.* These words are more abstract and require in-depth experiences for complete understanding.

Finally, it is important to note that many words in our language have multiple meanings (*can, run,* etc.) and are confusing to children. Similarly, *homonyms,* which are words that sound alike but are spelled differently, are a source of difficulty for many LD children (see table 5-2). Words must therefore be associated with the many experiences with which they are associated. Johnson and Myklebust (1967) believe that many words must be taught as concepts and not simply as auditory-motor associations.

Table 5-1

Suggested Hierarchy of Difficulty for Adjective Comprehension by LD children

aspect	adjectives
1. Color	red, blue, green
2. Size	big, small, large
3. Size-Color	big red, small blue, large green
4. Shape	round, square, oblong
5. Size-Color-Shape	big red round, small yellow square, large green oblong
6. Length	long, short
7. Height	tall, short
8. Width	wide, narrow, thin
9. Age	old, young, new
10. Taste	sweet, sour, bitter
11. Smell	sweet, pungent, stale
12. Attractiveness	pretty, ugly, beautiful
13. Speed	fast, slow
14. Temperature	hot, cold, tepid
15. Quality	rough, smooth, hard
16. Affect	happy, sad, angry
17. Distance	near, far, distant
18. Comparatives-Superlatives	bigger, hotter, nearer biggest, hottest, nearest

From *Language Disabilities in Children and Adolescents* by E.H. Wiig and E.M. Semel. Columbus, Ohio: Charles E. Merrill, 1976. Copyright 1976 by Bell & Howell. Reprinted by permission.

Understanding Syntactical and Grammatical Structure

In addition to comprehending words and their meanings, children must also understand how words are grouped together to form phrases, sentences, paragraphs, and other meaningful units. An understanding of simple rules of grammar and syntax is usually necessary for comprehending the most basic sentence.

Some LD children have difficulties in this area because they have learned many words in isolation, rather than in the context of sentences. These children are consequently confused when the word is used in conjunction with other words in a sentence.

The amount of language that is used in a sentence may also be troublesome for some children. Sometimes adults use too many words in talking with young children. Johnson and Myklebust (1967) point out that reducing the carrier phrase (the length of the statement) will usually aid auditory comprehension. They provide the example of a 5-year-old boy who could not complete the word meaning subtests on a reading readiness test when instructions were given normally, "Mark the _____ ." However, he responded correctly when the isolated words *battle* or *carrot* were said by the teacher.

Table 5-2
Difficult Homonyms

do	dew	sail	sale
dear	deer	hair	hare
way	weigh	made	maid
hall	haul	one	won
pair	pare	poor	pour
beat	beet	red	read
know	no	ring	wring
to two	too	would	wood
knew	new	whole	hole
mail	male	tail	tale
road	rode	steal	steel
wait	weight		

From *Principles and Practices of Teaching Reading* (4th ed.) by A.W. Heilman. Columbus, Ohio: Charles E. Merrill, 1977. Copyright 1977 by Bell & Howell. Reprinted by permission.

Syntactical and grammatical aspects of language are seldom taught directly to young children. Nevertheless, these aspects have been demonstrated to be particularly confusing to many children, and they are crucial to adequate language development. These areas of language must be further researched and developed before we fully understand the implications for LD children.

Following Directions

The ability to follow directions is a skill closely related to understanding words and sentences. Children who have trouble with this skill usually do not comprehend various words, are bombarded with too much language, or cannot relate what they hear to the subsequent motor or cognitive skills necessary to complete the directive. One boy, for example, did not understand the word *outline,* so he was unable to complete the teacher's direction "to outline all the circles" on a worksheet. Another child could not "take a left at the next corridor" because he had not mastered left-right discrimination. In all cases, the reasons for not following directions should be determined in order to remediate the problem effectively. Many different factors affect achievement in this area. Therefore, the *precise* nature of the difficulty should be carefully delineated.

Auditory Expressive Language

The inability to use spoken language as a means of communication is usually categorized as an expressive language disorder. Children with disturbances in this area typically hear what is said to them. They do not have problems in understanding language for communicating with others. However, Wood (1969) suggests that it is unusual for a child to have a problem which is exclusively receptive or entirely expressive. In other words, both processes are interdependent.

Chalfant and Scheffelin (1969) have also described a task analysis for acquiring expressive language.

> First, the child must possess the need to communicate, and make the decision to send the message. Second, he must formulate the message by retrieving and sequencing the appropriate language signals. The third stage consists of organizing the vocal-motor sequences for producing that vocal-language signal. Simple vocal language signals are combined to form more complex vocal-language signals. In time, the child gradually increases the accuracy, length, number, and types of automatic production. Finally, the child shifts attention from the mechanical aspects of sound production to the content of the message to be sent. This enables him to produce appropriate verbal instruction, commands, explorations, descriptions, and questions. (p. 77)

Auditory expressive language disorders in children have also been classified as *expressive,* or *motor aphasia* (McGinnis, 1963) and *congenital oral (articulatory) apraxia* (Eisenson, 1972). The degrees of this disability vary in the same way as receptive language disorders. Bryant (1972) notes that these children may be unable to reauditorize (retrieve) words for spontaneous usage. Others might have difficulty in planning or organizing words and phrases to express an idea. In severe cases, the child might be unable to imitate sounds or execute the motor patterns for speaking.

The most common types of auditory expressive language problems are discussed in this section.

Expressing Speech Sounds

The inability to move various parts of the body when the power of movement is intact is referred to as *apraxia* (Johnson & Myklebust, 1967). Some LD children with language difficulties are unable to execute particular motor patterns to produce various speech sounds. The problems encountered by these children usually involve "making the transition from one phoneme to another, repeating a series of words or phrases, reproducing melodies, or changing the order of word sequences" (Chalfant & Scheffelin, 1969, p. 87).

Since children's difficulties in expressing speech sounds are considered to be articulatory, and not perceptual or cognitive in nature (Eisenson, 1972), the teaching activities for remediating the problems are often provided by speech clinicians, rather than LD teachers. In fact, Myers and Hammill (1976) point out that most of the public school speech and language clinician's caseload is composed of children with a variety of articulation problems.

Formulating Words and Sentences

A sizable number of children with expressive language disorders are able to express isolated words and phrases but unable to organize their thoughts in the correct form for communication. These children tend to omit words, add inappropriate words, use incorrect grammar, and distort the order of words and phrases (Johnson & Myklebust, 1967)

These children tend to use very simple sentences. They merely string together isolated words and phrases. Often, their sentences include just one or two words. Farrald and Schamber (1973) note that "this form of sentence structuring is typically utilized by the child functioning at the 'naming' level; that is, the child who merely enumerates objects or events when asked to interpret a picture" (pp. 344-345). Table 5-3 presents a dialogue with a child experiencing difficulties with the linguistic dimension of language.

The grammatical errors most frequently noted among children with expressive language disorders include the use of plurals, verb tenses, and prepositions. "She were running," "It be me," and "The cat like milk" are typical.

Table 5-3
Dialogue with Frank, a 6-Year-Old with a Language Disorder

(Frank walked into the clinician's
office)

	hi/doing
I'm typing	help ↑
No, thank you, I'm all through/ I have to teach now	
	teach ↑
Yes	where
Over in that white building	
	Oh/
(Pointing to pencil sharpener)	that
You know/what's it for?	
	pencil/sharp
Right, it's a pencil sharpener	
(Walking out door)	bye

Frank communicates well but generally with only one- and two-word utterances.

From *Language Development and Language Disorders* by L. Bloom and M. Lahey. New York: John Wiley & Sons, 1978. Copyright by John Wiley & Sons. Reprinted by permission.

The inability to acquire syntax is most often characterized by incorrect word order, such as "Me with you go" for "You go with me," and "Something I want to drink" for "I want something to drink." These difficulties can cause misinterpretations of the child's meaning.

Word Selection

According to Johnson and Myklebust (1967), a number of children with auditory expressive difficulties cannot remember or retrieve certain words for spontaneous usage. This difficulty is essentially a word-finding difficulty, and it seems to affect all parts of speech. Often these children have the most difficulty with words which have the greatest consequence to meaning in a sentence. Johnson and Myklebust (1967) call this a *reauditorization* problem. They suggest that children usually adapt to this particular problem in a number of different ways. Some children wait and delay their responses until the desired word comes to mind. However, other children attempt to convey the intended meaning through synonyms, gestures, or actually defining the word. In all cases, however, the child usually finds communication a difficult process; some children even attempt to avoid auditory communication entirely.

SPOKEN LANGUAGE ASSESSMENT

The primary tasks of the evaluator in regard to assessing a student's language ability have been clearly outlined by Kleffner (1973).

1. Establish whether or not a language disorder exists, since that will determine the *type* of remedial effort to be made.
2. Describe the child's current levels of language ability, since that will establish the linguistic *content* of the remedial effort and also serve as the basis against which to measure the results of remediation.
3. Identify problems such as hearing impairment, poor motor function, or physical disabilities which might have pertinent generalized influences on remedial *procedures*. (p. 20)

We have found these guidelines to be very helpful in appraising the language abilities of LD students. Some of the tests and techniques utilized in this area are discussed in the assessment section of this chapter. It is important to note that the extensive research and study in investigating language acquisition has increasingly been reflected in the actual number of evaluation instruments available to assess spoken language deficits. We have chosen to summarize a limited number of the more widely used informal techniques and published tests.

In general, Todd's severe deficits in formulation and syntax have hampered his abilities to express himself verbally. No motoric or articulatory disabilities have been evidenced. An examination by an audiologist and otologist found that Todd has no hearing impairment.

During an informal language sample, Todd's teacher observed the difficulty he encountered in formulating and organizing words according to correct language structures. He tended to distort word order, omit words, and use incorrect verb tenses. For example, Todd said:

> Tomorrow picnicic for class. 'Big Mac!' You can come, We go to park for eating hot dogs. No McDonald's for if want.

In addition to his difficulty in retaining linguistic patterns, Todd also experiences some difficulty in remembering the correct order of syllables within words (e.g., racamoni for macaroni, picnicic for picnic, etc.)

Todd was administered The Test of Language Development (Newcomer & Hammill, 1977), among a variety of both formal and informal appraisal techniques, and his performance revealed receptive and expressive syntactical difficulties, along with some difficulty in giving oral definitions to common words (expressive semantics).

A series of classroom observations by the LD specialist confirmed the standardized test results. The specialist noted that Todd experienced difficulty in understanding each of the following words: *underline, outline, complete, draw,* and *finish.* Todd also exhibited some problems in naming pictures of various vehicles and household appliances.

Informal Techniques

Using various informal procedures for evaluating children with language disturbances has been widely recommended (Berry, 1969; Wood, 1969). It has also been suggested that informal techniques will provide information concerning a child's language skills that might be difficult to obtain from standardized tests (Spradlin, 1967). Two types of informal procedures are discussed in this section.

Case History

A case history of the child with a language disturbance is often recommended since data pertinent to the problem is usually obtained. Otto, McMenemy, and Smith (1973) note that, in some cases, home factors may be contributing to the child's difficulty, while in other cases resources in the home may be useful in overcoming the problem.

Case history information may be obtained from interviews with the child's parents or other adult informants, written completion of case history forms, or interviews with the child. Various forms for case histories are provided by Berry (1969) and Wallace and Larsen (1978). The latter authors recommend the following as important questions to be asked while the case history is being completed:

- When did the child speak his or her first words?
- Does the child have a history of upper respiratory infections that caused hearing problems?
- Were there severe emotional upsets in the home during the first few years of the child's life?
- Do siblings also evidence language problems?
- Has the child's language problem been evaluated previously?
- When did the parents notice, if at all, that something was wrong?
- Were there long periods in the child's life during which no language was used?
- At what level is the child's social relationship with peers, siblings, and parents? (p. 263)

Language Samples

The careful observation of children in various speaking and nonspeaking situations is often very helpful. In obtaining a *language sample* it is important not to make clinical judgments based upon isolated behaviors. A language sample should be considered only one part of the total assessment procedure. As Strang (1969) notes, observations made by a teacher may tell more about the teacher than about the child. She cautions that a teacher may be influenced by various beliefs, by his or her interest in the child, and by subtle expectancies of a child's success or failure.

The creative use of such stimulus materials as toys, picture books, fruit, musical instruments, and small animals has been recommended for eliciting language samples from children (Wallace & Larsen, 1978). Children should never be forced to speak. In situations where the child is hesitant in speaking, teachers might need to spend some time in building effective relationships with the child before he or she feels comfortable enough to speak.

The Developmental Sentence Analysis (DSA) (Lee, 1974) is a published procedure in which an analysis is made of a child's language sample. DSA is actually a method for evaluating a student's use of standard English grammatical rules. We recommend it as a very comprehensive and complete method for evaluating language structure.

The method consists of two separate procedures, Developmental Sentence Types (DST) and Developmental Sentence Scoring (DSS). DST involves collecting 100 presentence phrases (subject or predicate missing) which are analyzed to indicate if grammatical structure is developing in an orderly manner before basic sentences emerge. The DSS, on the other hand, scores 50 complete sentences obtained from the child and analyzed according to various grammatical structures (personal pronouns, conjunctions, etc.) Scoring tables are included for children between the ages of 2 years and 6 years 11 months.

Additional methods for eliciting language samples are provided by Menyuk (1969) and Wallace and Larsen (1978).

Published Tests

There are many different types of published language tests currently available. Some of these tests are considered to be comprehensive tests of language ability, while others measure only specific components of linguistic performance. In addition, some published tests appraise various correlates of language functioning, such as cognition and motor ability. Many of the published language tests presently available require specialized clinical training for proper administration and interpretation. Some of the more widely used tests are summarized in table 5-4.

REMEDIATING SPOKEN LANGUAGE PROBLEMS

According to Marge (1972), there are three general approaches to language training. The *phonetic approach* is the traditional program utilized by speech and language clinicians. This approach emphasizes the correct formation of speech sounds with a gradual progression to syllables, words, phrases, and sentences.

The second approach emphasizes the *development of perceptual skills and concept formation.* The focus of this approach is on developing a meaningful experiential background for the child. Perceptual and conceptual growth are viewed as by-products of enriching experiences.

The *grammatical approach* seeks to improve the child's grammar, which is viewed as the most important aspect of language development.

Table 5-4
Published Language Tests

name (author of test)	aspect of language measured	target population	purported purpose	comments
Assessment of Children's Language Comprehension (Foster, Giddan, & Stark, 1973)	Ability of children to identify pictures containing 1, 2, 3, or 4 verbal elements	Preschool through elementary	"To define receptive language difficulty in children and to indicate guidelines for correction"	Available in group or individual form. No expressive ability in children required. Reliability and validity not reported. Not a complete test of language comprehension, as title states (no testing of syntactic comprehension), but useful for measuring number of verbal information bits child can integrate concurrently.
Carrow Elicited Language Inventory (Carrow-Woolfolk, 1974)	Expressive language in elicited situation (emphasis on syntax)	Ages 3 to 8	To assess a child's productive control of grammar	52 stimulus sentences and phrases are used to elicit responses. Child's responses are taped, require phonemic transcription. Analysis system covers 12 grammatical categories and 5 error types. Provides for in-depth analysis of child's errors on verbs.
Developmental Sentence Analysis (Lee, 1974)	Expressive syntax in spontaneous speech	Ages 2 to 7	To evaluate the grammatical structure of child's spontaneous speech	100 different intelligible spontaneous utterances are taped and analyzed according to length and type. Basic assumption: increasing length a measure of increasing grammatical complexity. Score is weighted for presence of

Table 5-4 (cont.)

indefinite pronoun or noun modifiers, personal pronouns, main verbs, secondary verbs, negatives, conjunctions, interrogative reversals, and wh- questions. Elements that normally occur later are given greater weight. Interjudge reliability = .94; split-half reliability = .73. Valid data supportive.

Test	Content	Age	Purpose	Comments
Goldman-Fristoe Test of Articulation (Goldman & Fristoe, 1969)	Articulation	Above age 2	To assess child's ability to produce speech sounds	Attractively illustrated. Well standardized. Takes about 30 minutes to administer. Measures speech sound production in initial, medial, and final positions in words and sentences.
Houston Test of Language Development (Crabtree, 1963)	A variety of expressive and receptive language and language-related tasks	6 months to 6 years	To assess child's developmental language	Standardization is incomplete. Test has two parts—Part I is a checklist for parent or teacher to check items at the age they were first observed in the child. Part II measures syntactical complexity, intonation, vocabulary, comprehension, and self-identity.
Illinois Test of Psycholinguistic Abilities (Kirk, McCarthy, & Kirk, 1968)	Correlates of language such as duplicating a sequence of geometric designs, also vocabulary and expression	Ages 2 to 7	To identify the psycholinguistic abilities and disabilities of children	Based on a model that separates various skills into expressive, receptive, and organizing aspects, and into representational and automatic levels. Relationship of various subtests to language itself not well established. Overall reliability satisfactory; some

Table 5-4 (cont.)

name (author of test)	aspect of language measured	target population	purported purpose	comments
Language Comprehension Tests (Bellugi-Klima, 1973)	Selected aspects of language comprehension	Preschool	To test comprehension of linguistic constructions	Child is asked to manipulate real objects in response to examiners' instructions at three levels: (1) active sentences, singular/plural nouns, possessives; (2) negative/affirmative, singular/ plural verbs, inflections, adjectival modifications; (3) negative affixes, reflexivization, comparatives, passives, embedded sentences. Items are exemplary rather than comprehensive. Test lends itself well to diagnostic teaching.
Miller-Yoder Test of Grammatical Competence, Experimental Edition (Miller & Yoder, 1972)	Syntactic comprehension	Ages 3 to 6	To assess a child's grammatical comprehension	42 stimulus sentence pairs spoken by examiner; child points to appropriate picture on plate. Untimed. Not standardized. Internal reliability = .93. Lexical items representative of 5-year-olds. Measures active passive, prepositions, possessives, negative affixes, pronouns, singular/ plural nouns and verbs, verbal inflections, adjectival modifications, reflexivizations.

There is also text above the first row on the right side: subtest reliabilities too low for diagnosis of individuals. Validity issues unresolved.

Table 5-4 (*cont.*)

Northwestern Syntax Screening Test (Lee, 1966)	Syntactic expression and comprehension	Ages 4 to 8; standard English speakers	To screen children on the basis of receptive and expressive syntactic usage	20 receptive items are measured by child indicating which of four pictures is appropriate for sentence. 20 expressive items are similar, except child repeats stimulus sentences as he points. Age norms are presented for small standardization sample. No reliability or validity data reported.
Parsons Language Scales (Spradlin, 1963)	Expressive aspects of language, vocal and nonvocal; comprehension	Children with severe mental handicaps	To sample language behavior according to Skinnerian outline	Considerable use with very low-functioning children. Seven subtests including vocal and nonvocal. Standardized on mentally retarded children. Overall reliability is satisfactory; subtests too highly correlated to be used diagnostically. Does not measure syntax.
Peabody Picture Vocabulary Test (Dunn, 1965)	Receptive vocabulary of standard English	Mental ages 2 to adult	To derive an IQ score	Test is untimed and well standardized. Child points to appropriate picture on plate in response to stimulus word spoken by examiner. May be given by teacher; takes 10-20 minutes.
Slingerland Screening Tests for Identifying Children with Specific Language Disability (Slingerland, 1970)	Correlates of language such as memory of geometric forms	Children in the early grades	To detect deficits in one or more areas on which receptive and expressive written language is based	Consists of three sets of tests, each with nine subtests—eight for group administration, one for individual. Wall charts, test booklets, and cards are the simulus materials. Tasks

Table 5-4 (cont.)

name (author of test)	aspect of language measured	target population	purported purpose	comments
				include copying from a model (both written and oral), matching, kinesthetic-motor acts, sound discrimination, sentence completion, among others. No reliability or validity data are presented.
Templin-Darley Tests of Articulation (Templin & Darley, 1960)	Articulation	Ages 3 to 8	Screening or diagnosis of articulation	Sound elements tested include 25 consonant blends, 12 vowels, and 6 diphthongs. Child utters sounds in isolation, in words, and in a sentence. Short form (50 items) may be used for screening; all 176 items for diagnosis.
Test for Auditory Comprehension of Language (Carrow-Woolfolk, 1973)	Auditory comprehension of vocabulary, morphology, syntax	Ages 3 to 6	To measure receptive language in English or Spanish	Test consists of 101 pictorial stimuli plates of three drawings each. One of the drawings is the correct representation, one is the reverse of the stimulus sentence, and the other serves as a distractor. Test is individually administered, with child pointing to appropriate drawing. Provides indication of child's proficiency in vocabulary, morphology, syntax. English and Spanish versions field-tested on native speakers of each language.

Table 5-4 *(cont.)*

Test of Language Development (TOLD) (Newcomer & Hammill, 1977)	Receptive and expressive aspects of vocabulary, syntax, and phonology	Ages 4 to 9	To give indication of child's overall strengths and weaknesses in each are tapped.	Test is short and easy to administer. Five principal subtests measure receptive and expressive aspects of vocabulary and grammar. Two supplemental subtests measure articulation and speech sound discrimination. Test subtests correlate with criterion tests, with *r*'s mostly in .70's. Subtests generally internally consistent and stable.
Utah Test of Language Development (UTLD) (Mecham, Jex, & Jones, 1967)	Expressive and receptive language, aspects of conceptual development	Ages 1.6 to 14.5	To derive an overall picture of a child's language development as compared with his peers	Test consists of two sections—one an informant-interview section based on the Vineland Social Maturity Scale. the other a direct test requiring the child to perform such things as repeat digits, recite a story, reproduce geometric forms. Yield score in form of language age. Internal reliabilities high.
Vocabulary Comprehension Scale (Bangs, 1975)	Assesses child's ability to follow instructions involving use of various lexical and function words	Ages 2 to 6 language disabled	To provide information on comprehension of pronouns, words of position, quality, size, and quantity	Attractive kit in shape of house. Has manipulative items such as cars, balls. Instructions to child in form of games—Garage, Tea Party, Buttons, Miscellaneous. Standardized on culturally diverse middle-income population in Texas.

From *Teaching Children with Learning and Behavior Problems* (2nd ed.) by D.D. Hammill and N.R. Bartel. Boston: Allyn & Bacon, 1978. Copyright 1978 by Allyn & Bacon. Reprinted by permission.

The primary educational goal for Todd was to develop a correct, natural, spontaneous flow of language (Johnson & Myklebust, 1967). To provide him with some structure and practice in general grammar and syntax, the Fokes Sentence Builder (Fokes, 1976) was used with Todd for a short period each day. He was encouraged to use the Sentence Builder in formulating and interpreting sentences, and in creating sentences and stories about various pictures and experiences.

Todd's teacher also introduced a picture file that was used to develop phrases and sentences. Sentences were built from one or two words. In these cases, nouns or verbs were often given as introductory clues. Another instructional activity which Todd enjoyed was reassembling sentences into the proper sequence after they had been cut apart into words and phrases.

Todd's regular class teacher and the LD specialist developed a coordinated language arts program which integrated spoken and written language activities with various reading assignments. Many of the sentences generated from pictures and the Sentence Builder were expanded into language experience stories. Stories were often recorded on audio tape by Todd and usually copied for additional practice. One of Todd's recent stories was:

> During summer, we go to San Francisco. I like the cable cars on hills. We go to Golden Gate Park to ride my bicycle.

This approach is based on Chomsky's model of language development (summarized earlier in this chapter). Children are taught basic sentence patterns and transformations of these patterns.

In addition to these three general approaches to language learning, a number of diversified programs have also been developed. The works of McGinnis (1963), Bereiter and Engelmann (1966), and Johnson and Myklebust (1967) are particularly noteworthy in this regard.

Psycholinguistic Programs

Recently, a number of authors have developed psycholinguistic training systems based upon the clinical model of the Illinois Test of Psycholinguistic Abilities (Kirk, McCarthy, & Kirk, 1968). This model attributes language acquisition skills to the following psychological functions: (a) two levels of mental organization, including representational (meaningful) and automatic (nonmeaningful); (b) three representational processes: reception, association, and expression; and two automatic mental processes: memory and closure; and (c) two sensory channels, auditory-vocal and visual-motor.

Programs designed to remedy psycholinguistic disorders have been seriously questioned by a number of writers (Hammill & Larsen, 1974; Newcomer & Hammill, 1976). According to Myers and Hammill (1976), many of these writers fear that

> such approaches tend to "fractionalize" the child, that is, to view him as a collection of isolated malfunctions rather than as a unitary, complex, and interrelated individual; tend to encourage "off task" teaching, for example, to train a child in "visual sequential memory" in the hope that it will generalize to reading or at least make the child more ready for reading; and are based on inadequate or unsubstantiated theoretical assumptions. (p. 252)

Before teachers make decisions regarding the usage of these teaching procedures, we sincerely recommend that they become familiar with the positions of professionals both advocating and criticizing these approaches. We suggest the works by Hammill and Larsen (1974) as appropriate readings regarding the effectiveness of psycholinguistic teaching procedures.

Remedial Guidelines

We have found it helpful to consider a number of teaching guidelines in planning and evaluating instructional activities for children and youth with language problems. The suggestions offered by Wood (1969) are particularly timely and practical in this regard. In general terms, she suggests the following:

- Work with the child at his own level of speech and language, rather than by using words suggested by methods and word lists.
- Allow the child to say what he is attempting to say by not being too specific or demanding.
- Translate gestures into simple concrete words.
- Allow the child to show you what he means if he is unable to express his ideas verbally.
- Always give a child the feeling that you are interested in what he is attempting to say.
- Attempt to eliminate gestures which substitute for understanding verbal commands.
- Work from the concrete to the abstract.
- Capitalize on the child's strengths.
- Utilize manipulative objects initially in working with a child who has limited speech.
- Use stimuli natural to each child's own environment.
- Keep careful records of a child's progress. (pp. 51-52)

Many of these teaching suggestions should be kept in mind when utilizing any of the commercially available language programs which are described here.

DISTAR Language I, II, III (Engelmann & Osborn, 1970, 1973, 1975). This highly structured and organized program was developed to teach language concepts and skills to educationally disadvantaged children with conceptual problems. Daily lesson plans provide the teacher with explicit directions for implementing the precise techniques. The program is based upon small sequential steps with continual repetition, feedback, and reinforcement.

Language I focuses on the language of instruction and takes a child from the identification of familiar objects to the description and classification of those objects. Children are also taught concepts for logical reasoning such as *before-after, some,* and *only.*

Language analysis is emphasized in Language II through work in opposites, synonyms, analogies, and questioning skills. Lessons in Language II also involve classification, function, absurdity, and problem solving.

The major focus of Language III is on the analysis of both spoken and written sentences. The skills developed in this program are designed to lay a foundation for communication skills, particularly written communication (Engelmann & Osborn, 1973). The specific topics covered in Language III are listed in table 5-5.

The teaching materials include a teacher's guide, spiral-bound presentation books, storybooks, color books, and take-home exercises for the students that reinforce concepts taught in the daily lessons and evaluate the skills acquired.

Fokes Sentence Builder (Fokes, 1976). This program provides a systematic approach to sentence construction through the ordering of five

Table 5-5 *DISTAR Language III Topical Sequence*

sentence structure processing

Making Up Sentences
  Subject Given
  Simple Subject Given
  Verb Given
Sentence Transformations
  Statement to Question
  Question to Statement
  Moving Words in the Predicate
  Simple Sentence Patterns
Verb Transformations
  1-Word/2-Word Verbs
  Present/Past and Past/Present Time
  Present/Past/Future Time
New Language (Abstract Sentence Patterns)

mechanics and usage

Word Practice
Punctuation
  Endmarks
  Comma
    To replace conjunction in series
    in quotations
    After introductory predicate modifier
    In compounding 2 simple sentences
  Quotation Marks
Capitalization
  Beginning of Sentence
  Pronoun I
  Names of People
  Names of Days of Week
  Names of Months of Year
Contractions
Singular/Plural Forms of Nouns and Verbs
Subject-Verb Agreement
Abbreviations
Possessive Form of Names
Vowel Sounds
Consonant Sounds

writing

Writing Stories about Pictures
  Description
    1 sentence, copy model
  Description and Interpretation
    2 sentences, copy model
    2 sentences, independent
    4 sentences, independent
  Sequence
    2 sentences—action before scene in
      picture
    4 sentences—action before scene in
      picture, scene in picture
    Story to tell what happened before scene
      in picture, what is happening,
      what will happen next
  Sequence and Dialogue
Constructing Dialogue (Quotation Marks)
Writing Exact Descriptions
Completing Stories

information analysis

Modifiers
  In the Subject
  In the Predicate
  In Subject or Predicate
Sentence and Paragraph Comprehension
  Sentence
  Paragraph
  Selecting Summary Sentence
Redundant Information
Pre-deduction Skills
  Identifying True-False Statements
  Identifying True-False-Maybe Statements

information processing

Common Objects-Parts, Materials, and
    Function (Information)
Classification
Following Directions
Synonyms and Opposites
Definitions
  Recognizing Object Defined
  Identifying Key Words in Definition
  Constructing Definitions
  Writing Definitions
Analogies
  Completing Analogies
  Applying the Rule for an Analogy
  Analogous Patterns (New Language)
  Inductive Reasoning (Discovering and
    Following a Rule)
Modifiers in Subject and Predicate
Descriptions
  Writing Exact Descriptions
Deductions (Formal)

sentence structure analysis

Sentence/Nonsentence Discrimination
  Statements
  Questions
  Commands
Simple Sentence Patterns
  Statement/Question Discrimination
  Statement/Question/Command
    Discrimination
Subject Identification
  Complete Subject
    In statements
    In questions
    In commands
  Simple Subject
Predicate Identification
  Complete Predicate
  Simple Predicate (Verb)
  Verb Time
    Present Time
    Past Time
    Future Time

From Distar® Language III, by S. Engelmann and J. Osborn.© 1973, Science Research Associates, Inc.
Reprinted by permission of the publisher.

grammatical categories: WHO and WHAT (subject and direct object), IS DOING (verb), WHICH (adjective), and WHERE (prepositional phrase). The *Fokes Sentence Builder* (FSB) was originally developed for use with children whose language development is delayed, but it can also be used with children whose language development is normal.

Fokes (1976) points out that each category is designated by a colored box containing pictures representative of items within the word class. Children learn the items represented in each box and arrange them in specific order. Grammatical rules underlying a variety of sentences are consequently learned by each student. Figure 5-2 shows a lesson using sentences with *ing* verbs and WHERE.

	WHO	IS DOING	WHAT	WHERE
1				

Figure 5-2
Sample of Fokes Sentence Builder

From *Fokes Sentence Builder* by J. Fokes. New York: Teaching Resources Corp., 1976. Copyright 1976 by Teaching Resources Corp. Reprinted by permission.

The FSB is essentially an adaptation of the Fitzgerald Key which was a method to guide deaf and hard-of-hearing students in the acquisition of written language. The program is both highly structured and multisensory. The *visual* display of the boxes and the *auditory* stimulus of the spoken sentences are combined with the *manipulated* activity of arranging the boxes and selecting pictures to form sentences. No known research is available documenting the effectiveness of this program for LD children and youth.

Peabody Language Development Kits (Dunn & Smith, 1965, 1966, 1967; Dunn, Horton, & Smith, 1968). Each of the four Peabody Language Development Kits (PLDK) consists of a series of lessons and a wide range of materials. Each kit helps to stimulate receptive, associative, and expressive linguistic and intellectual processes. The kits may be used with preschool through primary grade children. No reading or writing is involved in the program. The philosophy of the PLDK is that language time should be a daily interlude from conventional school work. Thus, the teacher is strongly encouraged to make the lessons a game and as a time for more talk and activity than is usually allowed. The authors also recommend the following guidelines:

- PLDK are intended to be part of the total language arts program.
- The materials should supplement, but not replace, regular daily activities in the classroom.
- Atmosphere should allow for spontaneity in speech since this is primarily a talking time for the children.
- The lessons have been planned to provide repetition, so teachers should stress overlearning.
- Even minimal performance should be reinforced with liberal praise by the teacher.
- The 30 to 45 minute lessons should be taught at the same time each day. (Dunn & Smith, 1965, pp. ix-x)

Detailed lesson plans provide the teacher with directions of daily sessions with the PLDK. No specialized training in language and intellectual development is required to present the lessons. Figure 5-3 shows a daily lesson from Level 1, the kit most appropriate for children who are intellectually 4½ to 6½ years of age. The available research to date on the PLDK has been inconclusive.

SUMMARY

Spoken language problems among LD children and youth were discussed in this chapter. The introductory language section included a summary of three theories of language acquisition, a description of various language components, and a discussion of developmental language stages. Inner language, receptive language, and expressive language problems were also described. Informal assessment techniques and published language tests were summarized. General principles of language remediation were outlined, along with a description of some widely used commercial language tests.

SUGGESTED ACTIVITIES

1. Arrange to visit a speech and language clinican in your local school district. Discuss his or her role and responsibilities in working with LD students.

2. Obtain a copy of a published spoken language test listed in table 5-4. Review the test and arrange to observe the test being administered and scored by a trained examiner.

3. Arrange to visit a group of language handicapped children. Note the various types of receptive and expressive language difficulties being encountered by these students.

DAILY LESSON No. 88

MATERIALS — **Puppets** (optional)

---

1. **LISTENING — IDENTIFICATION TIME** I want you to listen for the name of an animal. When you hear the name of an animal, clap your hands.

(Example: knocks, fox) Pause after each word.

how	now	cow	allow	
tony	pony	tony	pony	
peep	keep	sheet	sheep	sleep
tear	bear	fair	near	
fear	tear	deer	near	deer
dish	nish	fish	lish	fish
ham	slam	lamb	tam	ram
habit	labbit	rabbit	nabbit	rabbit
horse	force	course	horse	source
sale	whale	pail	nail	whale

This activity may also be done for individual children.

2. **SPEED-UP TIME** We are going to play a speed-up game. You will have to hurry. You will have only 30 seconds or thirty counts to do what I tell you. Call on individuals to name as many of the following as they can in thirty seconds.

boys' names	drinks	things to do at school
girls' names	foods	things to draw with
animals	colors	things to ride on or in

Optional: Have one child count to 30 while the other names.

3. **ACTIVITY TIME** Play: Simon, Telsie, or Peabo Says. In this case Simon always Says. The children are to do what Simon says if it makes sense, and to keep their hands at their sides when it is "silly." All children stand. Make up possible and silly statements about "fly," "swim," "walk," "run," etc.

Examples:

Birds fly.	Whales walk.
Fish fly.	Robins fly.
Fish run.	Dogs fly.
Fish swim.	Fish walk.

Figure 5-3

Sample of Daily Lesson—Peabody Language Development Kit

From *Peabody Language Development Kit, Level 1* by L. M. Dunn and James O. Smith. Circle Pines, Minn.: American Guidance Service, 1965. Copyright 1965 by American Guidance Service. Reprinted by permission.

4. Locate copies of any two of the published language kits discussed in this chapter. Compare the content of each program and consider the appropriateness of each program for various spoken language problems.

5. After reading the original sources, discuss the strengths and weaknesses of each language acquisition theory discussed in this chapter.

6. Develop an informal checklist that might be used by kindergarten teachers in evaluating the language skills of 5-year-old children.

7. Discuss the available instructional alternatives for secondary-level students still encountering spoken language problems.

8. Describe the characteristics of an instructional program that integrates all facets of the language arts—listening, speaking, reading, and writing.

References

Bangs, T. *Vocabulary Comprehension Scale.* Austin, Tex.: Learning Concepts, 1975.

Beers, C.S. *A comparison of three major theories of language acquisition.* Unpublished manuscript, 1973. (Available from Dept. of Special Education, University of Virginia, Charlottesville, Va.).

Bellugi-Klima, U. Language comprehension tests. In C. Lavatelli (Ed.), *Language training in early childhood education.* Champaign-Urbana, Ill.: University of Illinois, 1973.

Bereiter, C., & Englemann, S. *Teaching disadvantaged children in the preschool.* Englewood Cliffs, N.J.: Prentice-Hall, 1966.

Berry, M.F. *Language disorders of children: The basis and diagnoses.* New York: Appleton-Century-Crofts, 1969.

Bloom, L., & Lahey, M. *Language development and language disorders.* New York: Wiley, 1978.

Bryant, N.D. Subject variables: Definition, incidence, characteristics, and correlates. In N.D. Bryant & C. Kass (Eds.), *Final Report: LTI in learning disabilities* (Vol. 1). (U.S.O.E. Grant No. OEG-0-71-4425-604, Project N. 127145). Tucson: University of Arizona, 1972.

Carrow-Woolfolk, E. *Test for Auditory Comprehension of Language.* Austin, Tex.: Learning Concepts, 1973.

Carrow-Woolfolk, E. *Carrow Elicited Language Inventory.* Austin, Tex.: Learning Concepts, 1974.

Chalfant, J., & Scheffelin, M. Central processing dysfunctions in children (NINDS Monograph No. 9). Bethesda, Md.: U.S. Department of Health, Education and Welfare, 1969.

Chomsky, N. *Syntactic structure.* The Hague: Mouton Press, 1957.

Chomsky, N. *Aspects of a theory of syntax.* Cambridge, Mass.: MIT Press, 1965.

Crabtree, M. *The Houston Test of Language Development.* Houston: Houston Test Co., 1963.

Dale, P.S. *Language development.* New York: Holt, Rinehart & Winston, 1976.

Dunn, L.M. *Peabody Picture Vocabulary Test.* Circle Pines, Minn.: American Guidance Service, 1965.

Dunn, L. Horton, R., & Smith, J. *Peabody language development kit: Level P.* Circle Pines, Minn.: American Guidance Service, 1968.

Dunn, L., & Smith, J. (Eds.). *Peabody language development kit: Level number 1.* Circle Pines, Minn.: American Guidance Service, 1965.

Dunn, L., & Smith, J. (Eds.). *Peabody language development kit: Level number 2.* Circle Pines, Minn.: American Guidance Service, 1966.

Dunn, L., & Smith, J. (Eds.). *Peabody language development kit: Level number 3.* Circle Pines, Minn.: American Guidance Service, 1967.

Eisenson, J. *Aphasia in children.* New York: Harper & Row, 1972.

Engelmann, S., & Osborn, J. *DISTAR.* Chicago: Science Research Associates, 1970, 1973, 1975.

Farrald, R., & Schamber, R. *A diagnostic and prescriptive technique.* Sioux Falls, S.D.: ADAPT Press, 1973.

Fokes, J. *Fokes sentence builder.* New York: Teaching Resources Corp., 1976.

Foster, R., Giddan, J.J., & Stark, J. *Assessment of Children's Language Comprehension Test.* Palo Alto, Calif.: Consulting Psychologists Press, 1973.

Goldman, R., & Fristoe, M. *Goldman-Fristoe Test of Articulation.* Circle Pines, Minn.: American Guidance Service, 1969.

Goldstein, K. *Language and language disturbances.* New York: Grune & Stratton, 1948.

Hammill, D.D., & Bartel, N.R. *Teaching children with learning and behavior problems* (2nd ed.). Boston: Allyn & Bacon, 1978.

Hammill, D.D., & Larsen, S.C. The effectiveness of psycholinguistic training. *Exceptional Children,* 1974, *41,* 5-15.

Heilman, A.W. *Principles and practices of teaching reading* (4th ed.). Columbus, Ohio: Charles E. Merrill, 1977.

Hodges, R., & Rudorf, H. *Language and learning to read.* Boston: Houghton Mifflin, 1972.

Irwin, J., & Marge, M. *Principles of childhood language disabilities.* New York: Appleton-Century-Crofts, 1972.

Irwin, J., Moore, J., & Rampp, D. Nonmedical diagnosis and evaluation. In J. Irwin & M. Marge (Eds.), *Principles of childhood language disabilities.* New York: Appleton-Century-Crofts, 1972.

Johnson, D., & Myklebust, H. *Learning disabilities: Educational principles and practices.* New York: Grune & Stratton, 1967.

Kirk, S., McCarthy, J., & Kirk, W. *Illinois Test of Psycholinguistic Abilities* (Rev. ed.). Urbana, Ill.: University of Illinois Press, 1968.

Kleffner, F.R. *Language disorders in children.* Indianapolis: Bobbs- Merrill, 1973.

Lee, L. Developmental sentence types: A method for comparing normal and deviant syntactic development. *Journal of Speech and Hearing Disorders,* 1966, *31,* 311-330.

Lee, L. *Developmental sentence analysis.* Evanston, Ill.: Northwestern University Press, 1974.

Lenneberg, E. *Biological foundations of language.* New York: Wiley, 1967.

Lenneberg, E. (Ed.). A biological perspective of language. In E. Lenneberg (Ed.), *New directions in the study of language.* Cambridge, Mass.: MIT Press, 1964.

Lerner, J. *Children with learning disabilities* (2nd ed.). Boston: Houghton Mifflin, 1976.

Marge, M. The general problems of management and corrective education. In J. Irwin & M. Marge (Eds.), *Principles of childhood language disabilities.* New York: Appleton-Century-Crofts, 1972.

McGinnis, M. *Aphasic children: Identification and education by the association method.* Washington, D.C.: Volta, 1963.

McGrady, H. Language pathology and learning disabilities. In H. Myklebust (Ed.), *Progress in learning disabilities.* New York: Grune & Stratton, 1968.

Mecham, M.J., Jex, J.L., & Jones, J.D. *Utah Test of Language Development.* Salt Lake City, Utah: Communication Research Associates, 1967.

Menyuk, P. *Sentences children use.* Cambridge, Mass.: MIT Press, 1969.

Miller, J., & Yoder, D. *Miller-Yoder Test of Grammatical Competence, Experimental Edition.* Madison, Wis.: University of Wisconsin Bookstore, 1972.

Myers, P., & Hammill, D.D. *Methods for learning disorders* (2nd ed.). New York: Wiley, 1976.

Myklebust, H.R. *Auditory disorders in children.* New York: Grune & Stratton, 1954.

Myklebust, H.R. *The psychology of deafness* (2nd ed.). New York: Grune & Stratton, 1964.

Newcomer, P.L., & Hammill, D.D. *Psycholinguistics in the schools.* Columbus, Ohio: Charles E. Merrill, 1976.

Newcomer, P., & Hammill, D.D. *Test of Language Development (TOLD).* Austin, Tex.: Empiric Press, 1977.

Orton, S. *Reading, writing, and speech problems in children.* New York: Norton, 1937.

Otto, W., McMenemy, R.A., & Smith, R.J. *Corrective and remedial teaching* (2nd ed.). Boston: Houghton Mifflin, 1973.

Skinner, B.F. *Verbal behavior.* New York: Appleton-Century-Crofts, 1957.

Slingerland, B.H. *Slingerland Screening Tests for Identifying Children with Specific Language Disability* (2nd ed.). Cambridge, Mass.: Educators Publishing Service, 1970.

Spraldin, J.E. Assessment of speech and language of retarded children: The Parsons Language Scales. *Journal of Speech and Hearing Disorders.* Monograph Supplement *10,* 1963, 8-31.

Spradlin, J. Procedures for evaluating processes associated with receptive and expressive language. In R. Schiefelbusch, R. Copeland, & J. Smith (Eds.), *Language and mental retardation.* New York: Holt, Rinehart & Winston, 1967.

Strang, R. *Diagnostic teaching of reading* (2nd ed.). New York: McGraw-Hill, 1969.

Templin, M.D., & Darley, F.L. *The Templin-Darley Tests of Articulation.* Iowa City, Iowa: Bureau of Educational Research and Service, State University of Iowa, 1960.

Vygotsky, L. *Thought and language.* Cambridge, Mass.: MIT Press, 1962.

Wallace, G., & Larsen, S.C. *Educational assessment of learning problems: Testing for teaching.* Boston: Allyn & Bacon, 1978.

Wardhaugh, R. The study of language. In R. Hodges & H. Rudorf (Eds.), *Language and learning to read.* Boston: Houghton Mifflin, 1972.

Wepman, J. *Recovery from aphasia.* New York: Ronald Press, 1951.

Wiig, E.H., & Semel, E.M. *Language disabilities in children and adolescents.* Columbus, Ohio: Charles E. Merrill, 1976.

Wood, N. *Verbal learning.* Belmont, Calif.: Fearon, 1969.

PREVIEW

Reading problems have been noted to be the most important single cause of school failure (Strang, 1969). Difficulties in reading actually serve as a common denominator for the lack of success in many other areas of the curriculum. In dealing with this vast area of study, we initially outline a number of developmental reading skills and stages that serve as a focus for understanding children and youth with specific reading disabilities. A special emphasis is placed on discussing the more important reading problems encountered by LD individuals. The behaviors described in this section of the chapter, under types of reading problems, are the behaviors most often exhibited by the learning disabled in actual classroom situations.

We believe that the most proficient assessment of the reading disabled should include a variety of appraisal techniques. Consequently, our assessment section includes a large number of both informal and formal approaches to reading diagnosis. Similarly, it is our belief that teachers should be able to handle any number of different reading problems by finding out what will work for individual children. We therefore discuss a variety of reading methods and materials available to teachers working with reading disabled children and youth. We strongly feel that there is no one best instructional material or method for children with reading difficulties. A versatile approach to assessment and instruction is basic to successful remediation.

Finally, we urge our readers to experiment with a number of the suggested activities listed at the conclusion of this chapter in order to increase their awareness and knowledge of the reading disabled.

READING AND LEARNING DISABILITIES

Scotty is one example of the estimated over 8 million children who have learning disabilities in reading (National Advisory Committee, 1969). Others have noted that 85% to 90% of all LD children have reading problems (Kaluger & Kolson, 1978), and that over 25% of the failures in the elementary grades are attributed to reading disabilities (Leary, 1965). Boys with reading problems outnumber girls with similar difficulties by the astonishing rate of 10 to 1 (deBoer, 1958).

Through history, children with reading disabilities have been classified according to a variety of terms. Orton (1937) used the term *strephosymbolia* to refer to the child with "twisted symbol" difficulty.

Scotty is a 9-year-old fourth grader who has experienced reading difficulties since his first year in school. He is the youngest of five children, none of whom have had reading problems. Scotty is considered to be a bright child who is easily distracted by other children and activities in his classroom. His teacher reports that it is "nearly impossible for Scotty to sit in his chair for longer than three minutes." Other children in the class also complain about Scotty's frequent pushing and shoving.

Individuals who know Scotty consider him to be a "Huck Finn" type of boy because of his great interest in the outdoors and his constant exploring for "secret trails and paths." Scotty's imagination is readily apparent from his vivid descriptions of after-school play at a local creek and in his backyard treehouse. He obviously delights in outdoor exploration and play.

Scotty's stories have always been an excellent record of his remarkable memory and imagination. During the second grade, he dictated the following story to his teacher.

All About the Orchard

The orchard had apples and there were thousands of apple trees. Some apple trees had so many apples, the weight of them took some of the branches down. That was good because we got to climb some of the trees and I got to climb the highest of everyone. Mrs. Wilk told me to get down. We rode the bus there and back. Some of the apples were rotten.

A special resource teacher, Mrs. O'Neill, works with Scotty for 30 minutes each school day. He has received this assistance for the past few months. Mrs. O'Neill has noted that Scotty can recognize individual letters and give the corresponding sound, but blending the sounds into words has been a consistently difficult task for him. He also has had some problems in remembering various sight words. Scotty's approximate reading level is the beginning second grade level.

As noted on page 162, Scotty continues to miscall over one-half of the Dolch Basic Sight Words. His continual problem with these sight words has hampered his progress in utilizing conventional basal readers and various library books.

Later, *alexia, word blindness,* and *minimal brain dysfunction* were used. Recently, the term *dyslexia* has been used to identify children with learning disabilities in reading. This term was originally proposed to denote those children with reading disturbances due to neurological involvement. However, it is currently being used in a variety of ways including, for example, the indication of a genetic cause for reading disturbance.

Many different methods, materials, techniques, and suspected causes have been studied and discussed since children with reading disabilities were first reported in the literature by Morgan (1896). Individuals from a wide variety of disciplines, including medicine and education, have contributed their expertise in attempting to better understand these children.

The medical field has concentrated its efforts on etiology. Consequently, physicians usually infer that some type of brain dysfunction is causing dyslexic patterns of behavior in a child.

On the other hand, many educators believe that reading disorders are due to a variety of other causes, not the least of which is poor or inappropriate instruction. Nonetheless, the major concern of many educators is simply to identify the deficient reading behaviors and consequently teach appropriate reading skills (Jordan, 1977).

DEVELOPMENTAL READING SKILLS

In recent years, the dominant approach to reading instruction has been that of teaching a set of specific reading skills (Erickson, 1978). The complex behavior called "reading" has been viewed as consisting of a number of separate and identifiable behaviors, or skills, which teachers can describe and around which they can organize instruction or evaluation.

Generally, most reading skills can be classified as either *word analysis skills* or *comprehension skills.* Word analysis skills are usually grouped into the categories of configuration, structural analysis, context clues, pictorial clues, and phonic analysis. The three levels of comprehension skills are most often classified as literal, interpretive, and critical. More detailed discussion of the sequential skills that comprise word analysis and comprehension is provided by Barrett (1972), Ekwall (1976), and Kaluger and Kolson (1978).

A number of writers have suggested that children gradually learn to read as they learn sequential skills and complete one stage of development and move into another. Each succeeding stage of reading development then builds on preceding stages. Among the available descriptions of reading stages, we have found the "cone" of reading development provided by Carrillo (1976) to be particularly valuable. The cone, as shown in figure 6-1, lists five stages of reading development

5. REFINEMENT

Development of flexibility of rate. Refinement of comprehension (emphasis on drawing conclusions, tone and mood, inferences, critical thinking and application). Learning prefixes, suffixes, multiple word meanings, technical vocabulary. Improving study skills, interests, and tastes.

4. WIDE READING

Locating and using references. Continuing improvement in rate of silent reading. Rapid growth in enjoyment of print. Expansion of vocabulary, comprehension skills (emphasis, main idea, sequence). Selection, evaluation, and organization of study-type materials. Review of phonic and structural analysis (extension to syllabication and accent). Large amount of independent reading.

3. RAPID DEVELOPMENT

Extension of sight vocabulary and word-analysis skills (including phonic and structural analysis, use of context clues). Start of work-type skills such as use of different parts of books and selective reading to locate information. Completion of major portion of phonic analysis, including vowels, digraphs, diphthongs, and variants. Beginnings of wider reading and content-field reading. Development of the ability to read more rapidly silently, but with fluency and ease in oral reading at the same time. True recreational reading begins for most children.

2. INITIAL READING

Continued development of auditory and visual perception, handling of books, listening to and using language better, concept and background improvement. Beginning of a sight vocabulary of instantly recognizable words for immediate reading and for building word-attack skills; learning letter names, auditory-visual perception of consonants, consonant blends and digraphs, double consonants, and phonograms; using context and picture clues to check meaning; reading aloud for variation in pitch, stress, and volume; indication of relationship between speech and print; using library; learning structural elements such as inflectional variants and plurals.

1. READINESS

Guided development of such basics as left-right progression and top-bottom approach to printed page; differentiation of colors; visual and auditory discrimination as preparation for both sight and sound attack on words; development of fuller verbal expression; listening skills; eye, hand, and motor coordination; awareness of words and their functions; following directions; understanding of story sequence. Aided adjustment to school by building positive experiences with books, by broadening concepts, and by increasing breadth and depth of experiential background.

Physical Development	Mental Maturity	Emotional Stability	Social Adjustment	Educational Situation

All aspects of heredity and environment, family, and neighborhood

Figure 6-1
Cone of Reading Development

From *Teaching Reading: A Handbook* by L. Carrillo. New York: St. Martin's Press, 1976. Copyright 1976 by St. Martin's Press, Inc. Reprinted by permission.

151

along with a brief description of specific skills included within each stage. The reading stages are discussed further in the following section.

Stage 1. Development of readiness for beginning reading. This stage serves as a foundational phase for subsequent growth in reading and it usually occurs from birth to age 6. Carrillo (1976) points out that maturation and learning from experience contribute to the development of the readiness skills required for reading success. Materials and teaching approaches tend to be quite informal at this stage, but gradually become more formalized as the child progresses.

Stage 2. Initial stage in learning to read. This period is usually characterized by instruction in sound-symbol relationships and in decoding words. The emphasis at this stage is most often on building a basic sight vocabulary, developing confidence in the reading situation, and beginning instruction in word analysis skills. It has been suggested by Lerner (1976) that the greatest number of reading innovations and changes have occurred at this stage.

Stage 3. Rapid development of reading skills. A thorough grounding in basic reading habits and skills is usually provided at this stage. Carrillo (1976) places major emphases on the extension of a sight vocabulary, improvement of reading comprehension, building competency in independent word analysis, building interest in reading, and encouraging the beginnings of wider reading in a variety of materials.

Stage 4. Wide reading stage. The emphasis in this stage, which typically occurs doing the intermediate grades, in on independent reading with continuing expansion of vocabulary, building further comprehension skills, and constant review of word analysis skills. This period is also marked by the usage of a wider range of reading methods and materials.

Stage 5. Refinement of reading. This stage, which most often occurs in junior and senior high school, is characterized by advanced comprehension and study skills, along with increased proficiency in reading for different purposes at varying rates.

Children and youth encountering reading disabilities may exhibit skill deficits during any of the aforementioned reading stages. Some of the most common reading disturbances among the learning disabled are discussed in the following section.

TYPES OF READING PROBLEMS

Visual Discrimination

Many children with reading disabilities are unable to discriminate visually among various letters or words. The child with difficulties in this area might be confused by letters with similar configurations (e.g., *h-n, i-j, v-w*). Other children with visual discrimination problems are unable to distinguish visually among words. The general configuration of some words might be difficult to differentiate, or difficulty in noting the differences between such pairs as *lap* and *lip* might be experienced.

The fine discriminations between many letters are indistinguishable to a number of reading disabled children. Some youngsters are unable to discriminate between the *n* and *m* until they are taught that the *m* has an additional hump. Similarly, the differences that distinguish the *n* and *h*, the *b* and *d*, and *i* and *j*, and the *w* and *v* must be learned by all children. Those who do not learn certainly experience many difficulties in learning how to read.

Chalfant and Scheffelin (1969) suggest that the beginning reader must also learn that some aspects of letters are not necessarily distinctive features. According to these authors:

> Size is not distinctive: An *A* can be a half-inch high, an inch high, or in the case of a billboard, four feet high; yet its signal is the same regardless of its size. Color is not distinctive, nor is material. The child must learn the distinguishing characteristics. (p. 93)

Visual discrimination difficulties may also be observed among younger children. The inability to match various sizes, shapes, or objects is indicative of discrimination problems. The emphasis upon such activities in readiness workbooks and in reading readiness tests serves as evidence of the importance these skills play in later academic success.

Auditory Discrimination

One of the major characteristics of children with auditory disturbances in reading is the inability to differentiate between phonemic sounds. The ability to distinguish similarities and differences among words is also closely associated with this skill.

Children with disturbances in this area would be unable, for example, to identify the word that began with the /s/ sound among a list of words read aloud. Similarly, the auditory differences between *beg* and *bag, pit* and *pet,* or *pin* and *pen* would be difficult for these children to distinguish. One of the most noteworthy characteristics of a child with auditory discrimination problems is his or her inability to tell whether two words read aloud are the same or different *(tank-sank, man-mat, car-can,* etc.). Most auditory tests assess this particular ability when evaluating a child's auditory discrimination skills (Jordan, 1977; Wepman, 1958).

Rhyming is another confusing activity for some children with auditory discrimination problems since it requires the ability to perceive auditory similarities among words. This is one of a number of auditory discrimination skills which may be evaluated during early school years. The young child who has some difficulty distinguishing among loud and soft sounds, animal sounds, and various vehicle sounds will probably later experience difficulty distinguishing, for example, /m/ from /n/ or /p/ from /d/.

The confusion that results from auditory discrimination disturbances differs among children. Some children experience difficulties with certain sounds (e.g., /b/, /t/, /s/), while other children have problems with only initial or final consonant sounds. Young children with auditory discrimination problems will probably have some difficulty learning to read. Spache and Spache (1977) report that skill in auditory discrimination was the best single predictor among a group of skills that were studied for predicting first-grade reading success. Heilman (1977) also indicates the importance of auditory discrimination in determining a child's success in learning to read.

Sound Blending

Sound blending is the ability to synthesize sounds into a complete word. Children with this difficulty are unable, for example, to blend /m/ /a/ /t/ into the word *mat*. The three phonemes of this word remain as separate sounds. According to Kirk and Kirk (1971) a child will encounter reading problems if sounds cannot be synthesized into words, even if the child knows all the sounds.

Difficulties in sound blending often occur when undue emphasis is placed upon speech sounds and when these sounds are learned in isolation. Some children have learned to separate speech sounds so distinctly that it is almost impossible for them to synthesize the sounds into a word. Other children who have auditory discrimination or auditory memory deficits find it difficult to blend word parts after having struggled with remembering and differentiating various isolated sounds.

Sound-blending activities for many reading disabled children will not resemble traditional instructional approaches. Jordan (1977) suggests a highly structured method emphasizing key word patterns and regular word forms. Bannatyne (1973) asserts that blending and other such basic skills should become fully automatic so the child can concentrate on the communication aspects rather than on the coding factors in the process. Emphases upon blending syllables, using words in a meaningful context, and some overlearning of important patterns seem to be the keys to remediating various sound-blending deficits.

Memory Skills

Children with memory disturbances experience difficulty in recalling information that has been learned. According to Chalfant and Scheffelin (1969), memory skills in reading include the ability to:

(1) Retain impressions or traces of visual and auditory stimuli;
(2) Make comparisons with past auditory and visual experiences; and
(3) Store and retrieve grapheme-phoneme correspondences. (p. 96)

The memory disturbances of many LD children are associated with various visual or auditory processes. Auditory memory problems, for example, may affect a child's ability to remember letter sounds and later blend these sounds into a word. On the other hand, a child with visual memory deficits may be unable to recognize specific letters and words.

The storage and retrieval components of memory are most applicable to the learning disability population. Children who are unable to recall the image of the letter *p,* for example, are encountering retrieval problems. The memory for this letter, however, is dependent upon adequate storage. Consequently, a major characteristic of remedial programs facilitates recall through multisensory presentations, repetitions, and varied materials.

The role of attention among memory problems has been noted by a number of writers (Johnson & Myklebust, 1967; Malmquist, 1958). Some have suggested that failure on many tasks may be due to attention deficits rather than to the lack of ability for the task (Harris & Sipay, 1975). The attention deficits of many LD children certainly seem to be associated with corresponding problems in remembering what is seen and heard. Similarly, the distractibility found among these children may account for many memory disturbances. Finally, the difficulties that some encounter in following directions may also be associated with these factors.

Sequential memory deficits must also be discussed as a component of the memory process. Many children have difficulty remembering the order of letters in words or the sequence of sounds within a word.

Visual sequential memory problems affect the *order* of letters in words and the *sequencing* of words within sentences. Scrambled words often result from this deficit (e.g., *chrai* for *chair, mlik* for *milk, jetkac* for *jacket).* Johnson and Myklebust (1967) point out that visual sequence problems are common among LD children and often persist longer than other reading deficits. Jordan (1977) suggests that visual sequencing problems have pervasive effects upon various academic areas, including reading.

The omission or distortion of speech sounds and syllables is a characteristic of the child with auditory sequential memory disturbances. The child who reads *member* for *remember* or *uitcase* for *suitcase* may have some difficulty in remembering initial consonants. Distortion of the sequence of sounds, on the other hand, may be the problem of the child who reads *terinest* for *interest* or *lowbe* for *below.*

Some learning disabled children consistently omit various sounds (e.g., /c/, /z/, /r/) Other children find the order of sounds confusing. Transposing final syllables to initial or medial positions is not unusual for these children. It is important for the teacher to note the frequency of particular errors, since the *order* of sounds and letters in words will become the focus of most corrective programs in sequential memory.

Letter and Word Reversals

A widely discussed characteristic of children with reading disabilities is the tendency of many children to read (or write) some letters and words backwards, rotated, or inverted. Single letters such as *b, d, p, q, n, u, m,* and *w* are often among the letter symbols which are read upside down and backwards. Learning disabled children are also observed reversing whole words (e.g., *saw* for *was),* parts of words (e.g., *tow* for *two),* and initial letters (e.g., *big* for *dig).* Table 6-1 lists some of the most commonly reversed words.

Table 6-1
Commonly Reversed Words

was	pin	no	pal	rats
step	tub	spot	on	nip
saw	trap	net	tip	lap
tap	rat	part	pot	star
pan	ten	tops	nap	pit
cop	but	pat	tar	pets

From *Principles and Practices of Teaching Reading* (4th ed.) by A.W. Heilman. Columbus, Ohio: Charles E. Merrill, 1977. Copyright 1977 by Bell & Howell. Reprinted by permission.

The inability to discriminate left from right is the reason most often given for reversals. Orientation confusion is actually fairly common among young children. It is not at all unusual for preschool and primary-age youngsters to reverse various letters as reading instruction is introduced. The difference among the LD population is the *intensity* and *duration* of reversals. The child with learning disabilities will probably reverse more letters and words over a longer period of time than younger children who reverse as part of a normal developmental process.

Careful initial instruction is crucial both to detecting and to correcting reversal problems. Preletter configurations and geometric shapes can be utilized to teach position and direction. Perceiving the details of forms and patterns is a highly recommended activity to correct orientation confusion.

Word Analysis Skills

One of the most important skills for learning to read adequately is the ability to analyze words effectively. Adequate word analysis skills are usually judged by the versatility of techniques utilized by the reader. Among the many word analysis techniques available, *phonics* is probably the most widely used technique. However, *structural analysis, configuration, picture clues, sight vocabulary,* and *contextual analysis* should also be used by the efficient reader.

Structural analysis refers to the identification of words by using word parts such as prefixes, suffixes, root words, and inflections. Configurative analysis identifies words by their length and shape. The context in which a word is used may also be helpful in the analysis of some unknown words.

Heilman (1976) believes that these word analysis approaches are not all of equal value in learning to read. Some methods (e.g., configuration) have only limited value, while other techniques (e.g., phonics) may be used over a period of time.

Many word analysis techniques are inappropriately used by the reading disabled child. Some children are unable to choose an analysis approach once an unknown word has been inspected. Brueckner and Bond (1955) advise that words should be analyzed only when a child is unable to recognize a word by sight. They emphasize the necessity of flexibility in word analysis, so that if one method does not work, other approaches may be utilized. Many reading disabled children rely exclusively upon one particular technique. The child who sounds out every unknown word, for example, must be taught to vary analysis approaches according to specific words. The simultaneous use of a variety of analysis techniques should be the goal for all reading disabled children.

Sight Words

Words which a reader can recognize instantly are referred to as *sight words.* Some words appear over and over again in basic reading material (e.g., *said, you, all).* The ability to recognize these words immediately facilitates early achievement in reading. Other words do not conform to common phonic generalizations (e.g., *should, were, eight)* and cannot be easily analyzed. Consequently, the child usually learns these words as whole words by sight. The Dolch Basic Sight Word List (Dolch, 1953) is a widely known list which was updated by Johnson (1971) to reflect currently used words. The revised list, as shown in table 6-2, is divided into five groups which represent words for the first five reading levels.

The child who is unable to recognize some words at sight will be severely limited in reading. Heilman (1977) also suggests that he or she may develop many unfortunate reading habits, perhaps including wild guessing, very slow reading, substituting words, and constantly losing the place. In addition, the child with an inadequate sight vocabulary will probably rely upon phonic analysis of words for many nonphonetic words.

Some reading disabled children have difficulty in learning sight words due to visual memory problems, which were discussed earlier in this

Table 6-2

Kucera-Francis List of Basic Sight Words

preprimer	primer	first	second	third
1. the	45. when	89. many	133. know	177. don't
2. of	46. who	90. before	134. while	178. does
3. and	47. will	91. must	135. last	179. got
4. to	48. more	92. through	136. might	180. united
5. a	49. no	93. back	137. us	181. left
6. in	50. if	94. years	138. great	182. number
7. that	51. out	95. where	139. old	183. course
8. is	52. so	96. much	140. year	184. war
9. was	53. said	97. your	141. off	185. until
10. he	54. what	98. may	142. come	186. always
11. for	55. up	99. well	143. since	187. away
12. it	56. its	100. down	144. against	188. something
13. with	57. about	101. should	145. go	189. fact
14. as	58. into	102. because	146. came	190. through
15. his	59. than	103. each	147. right	191. water
16. on	60. them	104. just	148. used	192. less
17. be	61. can	105. those	149. take	193. public
18. at	62. only	106. people	150. three	194. put
19. by	63. other	107. Mr.	151. states	195. thing
20. I	64. new	108. how	152. himself	196. almost
21. this	65. some	109. too	153. few	197. hand
22. had	66. could	110. little	154. house	198. enough
23. not	67. time	111. state	155. use	199. far
24. are	68. these	112. good	156. during	200. took
25. but	69. two	113. very	157. without	201. head
26. from	70. may	114. make	158. again	202. yet
27. or	71. then	115. would	159. place	203. government
28. have	72. do	116. still	160. American	204. system
29. an	73. first	117. own	161. around	205. better
30. they	74. any	118. see	162. however	206. set
31. which	75. my	119. men	163. home	207. told
32. one	76. now	120. work	164. small	208. nothing
33. you	77. such	121. long	165. found	209. night
34. were	78. like	122. get	166. Mrs.	210. end
35. her	79. our	123. here	167. thought	211. why
36. all	80. over	124. between	168. went	212. called
37. she	81. man	125. both	169. say	213. didn't
38. there	82. me	126. life	170. part	214. eyes
39. would	83. even	127. being	171. once	215. find
40. their	84. most	128. under	172. general	216. going
41. we	85. made	129. never	173. high	217. look
42. him	86. after	130. day	174. upon	218. asked
43. been	87. also	131. same	175. school	219. later
44. has	88. did	132. another	176. every	220. knew

From "The Dolch List Reexamined" by Dale D. Johnson, *The Reading Teacher*, 1971, *24*, 455-56. Copyright 1971 by the International Reading Association. Reprinted with permission of Dale D. Johnson and the International Reading Association.

chapter. Other children have problems because of the abstract nature of many sight words. There are very few associated clues to use in learning sight words. Little is left to the child to rely upon in remembering these words.

Sight words must be gradually and carefully introduced to the reading disabled child. It will be confusing to the child if too many words are introduced by the sight approach. Various approaches to analyzing words (e.g., phonics, structural analysis, configuration) need to be introduced and learned. Otherwise any growth in reading will be in jeopardy.

Literal Comprehension Skills

Many of the comprehension skill deficits that are observed among the reading disabled may be classified as *literal comprehension* difficulties. Gilliland (1978) refers to literal comprehension as recall of directly stated facts. Some of the skills involved in literal reading include noting specific facts and details, understanding words and paragraphs, recall-ing a sequence of events, following directions, skimming reading to locate specific information, and grasping the main idea.

Children with literal comprehension difficulties might find it difficult to locate or recall specific reading passages which describe a person, place, or thing. Reading for details or recalling particular facts to answer specific questions might also be frustrating.

Many literal comprehension difficulties arise from the inability to understand various words (Gillespie & Johnson, 1974). Some have even suggested that word meaning is the most important single factor accounting for variability in reading comprehension (Karlin, 1975). The difficulties that many reading disabled children encounter in word meanings are associated with repeated attempts to decode various words. The word analysis difficulties observed among these children affect their ability to derive meaning.

On the other hand, many children have difficulty differentiating various meanings of words (such as the multiple meanings of the word *can*). Selecting the literally correct meaning for particular passages is confusing to some children.

A limited experiential background will also affect vocabulary, or word meaning. Some children do not know word meanings because they have not been exposed to various experiences (e.g., books, people, places). Children must have had some experience with the concept which the words represent before they can relate to the words (Gillespie & Johnson, 1974).

Grasping the main idea is another literal comprehension problem. Many children are unable to separate the myriad of details in some reading passages from the central theme of the selection. The basic idea of the reading passage is lost. Sometimes undue emphasis upon facts and details will be associated with this problem. For other children, the length of a selection may influence whether they are able to grasp the main idea.

Not all children encounter the same literal comprehension difficulties. However, many of the problems that these children experience should signal the teacher that higher level comprehension skills will also be affected unless remedial procedures are implemented.

Interpretive Comprehension Skills

In contrast to literal skills, interpretive comprehension involves those skills which go beyond the printed page, including critical judgments. The ability to make inferences, predict outcomes, and form opinions are other kinds of interpretive comprehension skills.

The majority of interpretive abilities must be considered higher cognitive mental processes. Many learning disabled children have comprehension disturbances because of cognitive deficits. The difficulties that are experienced in these areas are frustrating to the child and teacher alike. Overcoming interpretive comprehension deficits actually involves remediation of various thinking skills.

The problems that many LD children encounter in the mechanical aspects of reading certainly preclude adequate literal comprehension, let alone interpretive comprehension. Some children have a difficult enough time merely reading a short passage. To ask interpretive comprehension questions of these children is what Jordan (1977) labels "particularly punitive." In addition, Spache and Spache (1977) indicate that the slow reading of these children focuses attention on word recognition and other mechanical aspects, with consequent loss of retention of the ideas being expressed.

Finally, it needs to be reiterated that many learning disabled children have deficits in the thinking process, and the essence of interpretive comprehension involves thinking skills. It is both logical and reasonable that these children will have some difficulty with the higher mental abilities of drawing conclusions, comparing ideas, inferring meanings, evaluating reading passages, and integrating new ideas with previous learnings.

Critical Reading Skills

Critical reading is a type of comprehension which involves critical and value judgments based on the attitudes and experiences of the reader (Spache & Spache, 1977). It is usually considered the highest level of comprehension when the reader analyzes and evaluates the reading material. Some skills included under critical reading include judging accuracy, drawing conclusions, distinguishing between fact and opinion, and evaluating the author's intentions and beliefs. Kaluger and Kolson (1978) suggest that the reader must engage the material in a dialogue at the critical reading level in which he compares the printed material with other material, or with the total conceptual background he possesses.

Critical reading is an area of growth that is often overlooked by many teachers of reading disabled children and youth. However, we believe that many of these students are confronted daily with situations requiring critical thinking and reading skills. Gillespie and Johnson (1974) note that judging the worth of a product for itself rather than by the claims made by advertisers, investigating sources of information, and differentiating fact and opinion are reasoning skills which aid social living.

The development of critical reading skills is dependent upon literal and interpretive comprehension, and difficulties with either of these skills will certainly affect the degree of critical reading growth. These skills can be developed by encouraging children to relate reading material to their own experiences and to evaluate the worth of various statements and stories (Gillespie & Johnson, 1974). Additional teaching suggestions for developing critical reading skills may be found in Spache and Spache (1977) and Durkin (1978).

READING ASSESSMENT

Instructionally relevant information for remediating a reading disturbance is usually gathered during the assessment phase of instruction. Many writers have noted that assessment in reading should lead directly to the formulation of remedial programs (Myers & Hammill, 1976; Wallace & Larsen, 1978). The close relationship of reading assessment to reading remediation is appropriate for the teacher informally assessing in the regular classroom, or the LD specialist dealing with more complex reading problems. Brueckner and Bond (1955) suggest that the difference between the two situations is one of degree and the extent to which various assessment techniques are utilized. The use of different assessment techniques will depend upon the specific difficulties the child encounters, the availability of specialized services, and the teacher's ability to use diagnostic tools (Wilson, 1977). However, both the classroom teacher and the LD specialist will need to have the same understanding of the child's reading problem.

Informal Techniques

One of the most important parts of the reading assessment will include the time spent *observing* the child reading both orally and silently

A large amount of assess-ment data on Scotty has accumulated over the years because of his long-term reading difficulties. During the second grade, Scotty was administered a Stanford-Binet Intelligence Test (Terman & Merrill, 1973) and his score placed him in the high average range of intelligence. His second grade teacher also ad-ministered an informal reading inventory (IRI) which showed Scotty to be

at the primer instructional level. He had great difficulty in recognizing various letters and words on the IRI and in responding to the comprehension questions following each reading passage.

Mrs. O'Neill, the resource teacher, recently administered the Woodcock Reading Mastery Tests (1974) to Scotty and obtained the following results:

subtests	reading grade level
Letter Identification	3.1
Word Identification	1.9
Word Attack	2.4
Word Comprehension	1.6
Passage Comprehension	2.6
Total Reading	2.3

All of the reading grade level scores, except letter identification, were below Scotty's present grade placement. The low word identification and word comprehension are indica-tive of his difficulty with sight words.

During an informal screening of Dolch Basic Sight Words, Scotty knew approximately 50% of the words. However, he continued to miscall many words after attempting to sound out words on a letter-by-letter basis. A number of incorrect sight words were actually wild guesses with little resemblance to the actual word; for example, he said *baby* for *what*, *maybe* for *now*.

(Strang, 1969). An analysis of observed reading skills will often provide answers to the following questions:

- what word analysis skills does the child utilize?
- how extensive is the child's sight vocabulary?
- what *consistent* word analysis errors are made by the child?
- does the child depend upon one analysis skill (e.g., sounding words out)?
- are particular words or parts of words consistently distorted or omitted?
- does the child read too fast, too slow, or word by word?
- are factual questions answered correctly?
- is the child able to answer comprehension questions requiring inferential and critical reading ability?

Many different opportunities to observe a child's reading are available throughout a school day. Silent and oral reading periods, class discussions, and oral and written reports, seatwork activities, and library reading can all serve as ideal observation situations. Strang (1969) believes that the systematic recording of observations through anecdotal records or checklists is both helpful and useful in planning remedial programs. Checklists and anecdotal record forms for this purpose have been developed by Spache and Spache (1977). Figure 6-2 provides an example of a checklist for recording information in regard to various reading skills.

Informal diagnostic reading procedures also include informal tests designed to provide information concerning *specific* reading skills. These objective tests usually measure skills that are directly related to classroom instruction. Consequently, many informal tests are constructed by teachers themselves.

The analysis of specific educational tasks for assessing various reading difficulties usually involves a sequence which includes the following five steps:

a. Specify clearly what outcome is to be evaluated.
b. Define the outcome in terms of observable behavior or characteristics of the learner.
c. Prepare test items or test situations by which the behavior or characteristics can most readily be evaluated.
d. Secure some kind of record of the behavior exhibited in the test or test situation.
e. Analyze the information secured and judge the significance of the findings. (Brueckner & Bond, 1955, p. 14)

Informal tests may be used to measure the effects of various instructional programs, to screen for general levels of achievement, to assess specific skills, and to supplement standardized reading tests. Numerous informal tests for evaluating reading skills are currently available (Ekwall, 1976; Guzak, 1972; Wallen, 1972; Wallace & Larsen, 1978). Table 6-3 illustrates two informal reading tests.

NAME _____

GRADE _____

TEACHER _____

SCHOOL _____

#	1st Check	2nd Check	3rd Check	Item	Category
1				Word-by-word reading	ORAL READING
2				Incorrect phrasing	
3				Poor pronunciation	
4				Omissions	
5				Repetitions	
6				Inversions or reversals	
7				Insertions	
8				Substitutions	
9				Basic sight words not known	
10				Sight vocabulary not up to grade level	
11				Guesses at words	
12				Consonant sounds not known	
13				Vowel sounds not known	
14				Blends, digraphs or diphthongs not known	
15				Lacks desirable structural analysis	
16				Unable to use context clues	
17				Contractions not known	
18				Fails to comprehend	ORAL SILENT DIFFICULTIES
19				Unaided recall scanty	
20				Response poorly organized	
21				Low rate of speed	SILENT READING
22				High rate at expense of accuracy	
23				Voicing-lip movement	
24				Inability to skim	
25				Inability to adjust reading rate to difficulty of material	
26				Written recall limited by spelling ability	OTHER RELATED ABILITIES
27				Undeveloped dictionary skill	
28				Inability to locate information	

D—Difficulty recognized
P—Pupil progressing
N—No longer has difficulty

The items listed above represent the most common difficulties encountered by pupils in the reading program. Following each numbered item are spaces for notation of that specific difficulty. This may be done at intervals of several months. One might use a check to indicate difficulty recognized or the following letters to represent an even more accurate appraisal:

Figure 6-2
Reading Assessment Checklist

From *Locating and Correcting Reading Difficulties* (2nd ed.) by E. E. Ekwall. Columbus, Ohio: Charles E. Merrill, 1977. Copyright 1977 by Bell & Howell. Reprinted by permission.

Table 6-3
Examples of Informal Reading Tests

Test 1

Objective: To assess knowledge of compound words.

Directions: Direct the child to list the two words found in each compound word.

1. baseball		6. into	
2. cowboy		7. downtown	
3. upstairs		8. playroom	
4. grandmother		9. something	
5. bedroom		10. classroom	

Test 2

Objective: To assess discrimination of the consonant *t*.

Directions: Show the child each pair of words. Pronounce the first word and ask the child to pronounce the second word (e.g., "That word is *can*. What is this word?").

1. can-tan		6. bank-tank	
2. fin-tin		7. den-ten	
3. mop-top		8. won-ton	
4. sip-tip		9. do-to	
5. foe-toe		10. car-tar	

Informal Reading Inventories

An informal reading inventory (IRI) is a series of sequentially graded reading paragraphs taken from one source. The IRI is widely used for informally determining a child's general reading level. An IRI differs from a standardized reading test by appraising a child's level of competence on a particular test without reference to other children. As described by Johnson and Kress (1965), the IRI may determine the *independent* level, the *instructional* level, the *frustration* level, and the *hearing comprehension* level.

At the *independent* level the child can read the selection with virtually no errors. Materials are usually read with 99% accuracy in word recognition. Reading comprehension is usually no less than 90%. The independent reading level is the level at which the child can do extensive supplementary reading for both recreation and information.

The level at which the child should be instructed and is able to make successful reading progress is the *instructional* level. Specifically, in terms of word recognition, the child should accurately perceive at least 95% of the words in the selection. The child should also comprehend 75% of the material. In general, the skills developed under teacher guidance at this level should prepare the child to read some material independently.

The *frustration* reading level is usually marked by comprehension of less than 50% of what is read and word recognition of 90% or less. The child is unable to handle reading materials at this level.

The highest level at which the child can satisfactorily understand materials when they are read to him is the *hearing comprehension* level. The child should be able to understand at least 75% of the material when it is read to him. This level of hearing comprehension indicates the vocabulary and language structure understood by the child.

An IRI has the advantage of being relatively easy to construct. Most inventories do not take very long to administer, nor is the procedure very expensive. Most importantly, however, the results may be readily applied to classroom instruction.

In addition to determining a child's reading level, an IRI may be used for detecting various word analysis and word recognition deficits or any number of comprehension skills. Gillespie and Johnson (1974) caution the teacher that the IRI does not measure all aspects of reading; and it should be used as just one measure of reading ability. One reading passage from an IRI, along with comprehensive questions, is illustrated in table 6-4. Other examples of IRIs are provided by May and Eliot (1978), Silvaroli (1973), Wallace and Larsen (1978), and Woods and Moe (1977).

Reading Miscue Analysis

An alternative approach for recording and analyzing oral reading errors (or *miscues)* is based upon the work of Goodman (1965). The emphasis in the approach is placed on an *analysis* of each specific miscue rather than on the number of errors made by the child. In other words, error analysis is considered qualitative rather than quantitative. Goodman and his colleagues believe that miscues are grammatical substitutions based on the syntactical and semantic information from the context and the redundancy of the language (Goodman, 1970). Miscues are seen as providing clues to the child's underlying language patterns.

The Reading Miscue Inventory (Goodman & Burke, 1972) analyzes errors according to graphic, syntactic, and semantic characteristics. Hammill and Bartel (1978) feel that by rating the relative proportion of miscues in each category, a teacher can form some idea of whether the child's difficulty is more of the word analysis type (mostly graphic miscues) or whether the child has linguistic or cognitive difficulty in forming hypotheses about the meaning of the material being read (mostly syntactic and semantic miscues).

Unfortunately, little research is available on the use of this technique with learning disabled children and youth. Miscue analysis nonetheless

Table 6-4
Sample Selection for an IRI

1st READER LEVEL

"Magic Doors"

Johnny's mother asked him to go
to the big new store at the corner.
His little brother Howie said,
"I want to go, too!: I want to go, too!
I'll be good."
So Johnny took his little brother
to the big new store.
There were two big doors.
One door had the word IN on it.
The other door had the word OUT.
Johnny and Howie went
to the IN door.
Whish!
The door opened all by itself!
Howie said, "Look at that!
It's Magic!"
"You are silly!" said Johnny.
"It isn't magic.
The new doors work by electricity."

Comprehension Questions

1. Who went somewhere? (Johnny & Howie)
2. Why did they go? (mother asked them)
3. Where did they go? (new store at the corner)
4. What was written on the doors? (IN, OUT)
5. What seemed like magic? (door opening by itself)
6. What was the magic really? (electricity)

holds great promise for both the assessment and remediation of reading problems among LD individuals.

Cloze Procedure

The cloze procedure is an informal technique used to obtain information about a child's reading level and comprehension. The procedure involves deleting every fifth word (starting with the second sentence) from a 100-250 word reading passage and replacing each word with a blank underline. Students are to then read the passage and attempt to fill in the blanks using the correct word according to the proper context of the sentence (Ekwall, 1976). The cloze procedure may be administered either individually or in groups. Children are asked to fill in the missing words during the group administration.

The cloze procedure has been widely utilized to evaluate a student's comprehension skills. However, Hafner (1965) also suggests that cloze errors can be examined for linguistic components, cognitive types, and reasoning skills. Guzak (1972) believes that the most appropriate usage of the technique is for upper-grade teachers in assessing the readability of a multitude of instructional materials and content area texts. Figure 6-3 provides an illustration of the cloze procedure.

Star Center

When summer came, Pam and the rest of the children on Grove Street played all day. Then one day Mr. (and) Mrs. Benton took Jim (and) Tim to Disneyland for (a) week.

Pam still had (Dan) and Jane and Linda (to) play with. But after (a) bit, Linda and Jane (went) to summer camp. So (Pam) played just with Dan. (Then) Dan went off to (visit) his grandmother, and Pam (was) left all alone.

Figure 6-3

Cloze Procedure

Adapted from *Take Flight,* Reader G, The Merrill Linguistic Reading Program by Mildred Rudolph, Richard Smith, and Rosemary Wilson. Columbus, Ohio: Charles E. Merrill, 1975. Copyright 1975, 1966 by Bell & Howell. Reprinted by permission.

Published Tests

Most traditional approaches to reading assessment involve some type of formal published test. Generally, the majority of diagnostic reading tests include subtests measuring word recognition, word analysis, comprehension, and related components of many general reading skills (e.g., auditory discrimination, visual memory). Most diagnostic reading tests are highly specialized and must be individually administered. Some of the more widely used published tests are briefly summarized in the following paragraphs.

Diagnostic Reading Scales (Spache, 1963). The Spache test is very similar in format to both the Gates and McKillop (1962) battery and the Durrell (1955) test. It includes 3 word recognition lists that assess word recognition and word analysis, 22 reading passages graded in difficulty, and 6 phonics tests, each measuring a specific skill. A child's reading level is obtained from the test. It also provides an evaluation of word recognition and analysis skills.

Durrell Analysis of Reading Difficulty (Durrell, 1955). This is a comprehensive series of individual subtests in oral and silent reading, listening comprehension, word recognition and word analysis, visual memory, auditory analysis, and learning rate. Additional tests are also available in phonic spelling of words, spelling, and handwriting. The battery may be used with nonreaders through the sixth-grade reading level.

Gates-McKillop Reading Diagnostic Tests (Gates & McKillop, 1962). This battery of tests is available in two forms. It is intended for usage with children severely disabled in reading and spelling. The complete battery includes subtests in oral reading, flash presentation of words, untimed presentation of words, flash presentation of phrases, knowledge of word parts, recognition of the visual form of sounds, and auditory blending. Supplementary tests are available in spelling, oral vocabulary, syllabication, and auditory discrimination.

Gray Oral Reading Test (Gray & Robinson, 1967). This test consists of 13 reading passages. Difficulty is increased in each passage by the range and diversity of vocabulary, length and complexity of sentences, and maturity of concepts. The total number of oral reading errors and the time in seconds the child uses to read each passage determine the grade equivalent in oral reading. All four forms of the test are similar in organization, length, and difficulty.

Woodcock Reading Mastery Tests (Woodcock, 1974). The five subtests which comprise this battery are intended to be individually administered to children in kindergarten through the twelfth grade. The subtests include letter identification, word identification, word attack, word comprehension, and passage comprehension. A composite index of a child's overall reading skill is provided, along with a specially designed *mastery scale,* which predicts a child's relative success with reading tasks at different levels of difficulty.

READING APPROACHES AND MATERIALS

The vast majority of reading materials used with the learning disabled are developmental reading approaches that have been individually adapted for children and youth handicapped in reading. The most popular of these reading approaches will be reviewed in the following section. A number of remedial approaches that have been specifically formulated for use with the reading disabled child will also be summarized.

Basal Reading Series

Basal reading series have been called the backbone of American reading instruction. Most basal series include a series of graded readers and accompanying teacher's manuals. Depending upon the program,

Due to Scotty's distractibility, a very structured program of remediation was implemented by both his regular class and resource room teachers. In order to hold his interest in a program that emphasized basic reading skills, a language experience approach (LEA) was implemented with Scotty. Teachers encouraged Scotty to write about his outdoor experiences. Some of the LEA stories are dictated to the teacher, while others are actually written by Scotty. At the same time, sight words have been selected from his stories and studied according to the Fernald VAKT word learning method. Words are placed on cards and filed in a file box once they have been mastered. A progress chart showing his daily, weekly, and monthly mastery of words has also been posted in order for Scotty to actually see what he has been learning.

A recent story written by Scotty is shown below.

Buter Biskits

On May 3rd we made buter and biskits. here is the resapee. first you wash the boal and the beter. then you mack sher you have the cream. Pour the craem into the boal. churn the craem. Wach for the buter to come. Drane the butermilk. Wash the buter. Sprikil salt on the buter. Taste it on the biskits.

In order to increase his interest in reading, a number of talking books have been used with Scotty. He enjoys listening to short, science-related stories, and his teachers have recently noticed that a number of the science facts have begun to appear in his LEA stories.

Scotty's teachers have found that relatively short lessons, followed by frequent breaks, have been the most successful. Both teachers feel that Scotty has shown increased progress since the structured LEA-based program was recently begun.

some series also include workbooks, charts, films, and other teaching aids. According to Spache and Spache (1977), approximately 95% to 98% of primary teachers and at least 80% of intermediate grade teachers in the United States use basal readers every school day.

Most basal series tended to be very much alike through the early 1960s. Since that time, many significant innovations have been incorporated into different series. Story settings now include apartment houses and trailer parks, among others, in addition to a variety of family backgrounds. More realism and stories of literary quality were added to basal readers. Most importantly, however, many basal series have emphasized word analysis techniques other than sight approaches. Phonic-based or linguistic-based series are now considered commonplace.

Basal readers have been widely used with LD children, but not without some criticism. Heilman (1977) particularly notes the dull, repetitive material in some basals, in addition to the little emphasis placed upon teaching letter-sound relationships in the early grades. Others have suggested that the approach might not provide for the individual differences among children with learning disabilities.

Many basal series can be effectively utilized with the exceptional child. The best use of basals seems to be in connection with other approaches that teach word analysis and word recognition skills. Basals should be carefully selected according to the child's interest level. Many learning disabled children will have been unsuccessfully exposed to basals before receiving remedial help. The child's attitude must certainly be taken into account in using various basals.

Language Experience Approach

The language experience approach (LEA) is not based upon a series of books. The oral and written expressions of children serve as the primary reading materials in this approach, since reading is considered to be a by-product of thinking and oral expression.

This approach differs from teacher to teacher, but generally a child's first stories are taken from his own drawings and paintings. The teacher usually writes down sentences and stories dictated by the child. As the child progresses, group stories are followed by individually written compositions. Formal instruction in word analysis skills is most often taught in small groups. Figure 6-4 illustrates a story written by a 6-year-old boy following a class visit to the local airport.

Lee and Allen (1963) point out that LEA is based upon the following principles:

- what a child thinks about he can talk about
- what he can talk about can be expressed in painting, writing, or some other form
- anything he writes can be read
- he can read what he writes and what other people write. (pp. 5-7)

The approach is often a very effective teaching tool for reading disabled children since it attempts to relate reading and other communication skills (listening, speaking, and writing) in an instructional program. The fact that each child is encouraged to proceed at his own pace is another major advantage of this approach. Reading disabled children are also interested in the story content of LEA, since the stories are made up of material of their choosing. We would also like to point out, however, that teacher organization and knowledge of the reading process are crucial to the success of LEA. Otherwise, sequential reading skills may not be learned. Teachers of learning disabled children cannot depend upon the incidental learning of important reading skills.

Programmed Reading

Programmed instruction in reading most often takes the form of workbooks. In most programs, the information is presented in a logical sequence of frames requiring some response from the child. Answers to questions are usually readily available so that the child may receive immediate feedback.

Most approaches to beginning reading instruction can be programmed. It is interesting, however, that the majority of presently

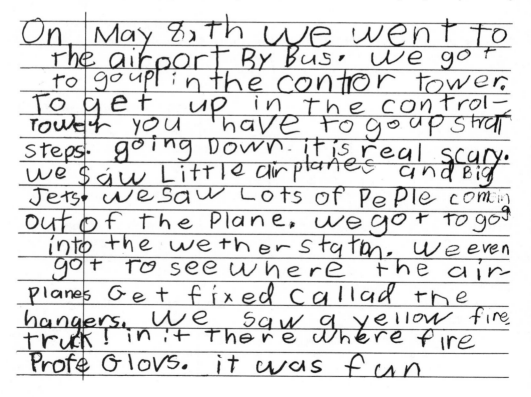

Figure 6-4
Language Experience Approach Story

available programs rely heavily upon a phonic-linguistic approach to reading. *Programmed Reading* (Buchanan, 1966) is a widely used programmed approach which incorporates many phonic and linguistic principles. A sample page from this program is shown in figure 6-5.

Figure 6-5
Programmed Reading Sample Page

From *Programmed Reading*, Book 2, revised edition. New York: McGraw Hill Book Co., 1968. Excerpted and reprinted by permission of Behavioral Research Laboratories, Inc.

Programmed reading materials offer a different format from the one to which most young readers are accustomed. This departure from tradition has proven to be motivating for many disabled readers. On the other hand, many LD children do not have the skills required to use self-pacing programmed formats. In addition, these children often require *direct instruction* of specific skills, which is a factor not usually included in programmed reading series.

Linguistics

Most linguists are primarily concerned with oral language. Since reading is part of the overall language process, some linguistic principles may be applied to the teaching of reading. The phonological part of linguistics, or the part most concerned with the phoneme-grapheme correspondence, usually forms the basis for the linguistic method of teaching reading.

Most linguistic approaches suggest that beginning reading words should essentially consist of three-letter words which follow a consonant-vowel-consonant (c-v-c) pattern containing only short vowels (e.g., *man, hit, pin*). The principle of minimal variation is employed in most linguistic approaches. Minimal variation words are alike except for one letter (*man, fan, can, tan,* etc.). Contrasting patterns are gradually introduced as the child progresses. Many linguistic series have no pictures or illustrations since it is felt that pictures encourage children to guess rather than recognize printed word forms. A story taken from a primary-level book in a linguistic series is illustrated in figure 6-6.

A BAD CAT

Dan had a bad cat.
The bad cat is Nat.
He had Dad's map.
Dad is sad.

Nat had Dan's cap.
Dan is mad.

Sad Dad!
Mad Dan!
Bad Nat!

Figure 6-6
Sample Page from a Linguistic Reader

From *I Can*, Reader A, The Merrill Linguistic Reading Program by Mildred Rudolph, Richard Smith, and Rosemary Wilson. Columbus, Ohio: Charles E. Merrill, 1975. Copyright 1975, 1966 by Bell & Howell. Reprinted by permission.

Learning words that are phonemically regular and then progressing to semiregular and irregular spellings has been an advantage for many learning disabled children. The frequent repetition of words to insure overlearning is another definite asset. However, the lack of initial emphasis on reading for meaning in linguistic readers has been a source of continuing controversy. Some commercially available linguistic reading materials are:

> *Let's Read.* Clarence L. Barnhart, Inc.
> *Linguistic Readers.* Harper & Row, Publishers
> *Merrill Linguistic Readers.* Charles E. Merrill Publishing Co.
> *Miami Linguistic Readers.* D.C. Heath Co.
> *SRA Basic Reading Series.* Science Research Associates
> *Structural Reading Series.* L.W. Singer

Phonics Approaches

The effectiveness of phonics instruction has been the center of controversy for many years. Matthes (1972) suggests that phonics "has either been condemned as a destructive method leading to slow, word-by-word readers who gain little comprehension from the printed page or a panacea for all the reading problems a child may encounter" (p. 44).

In actual practice, the content of phonics approaches differs from program to program. However, the methodology employed in phonics is usually either the *synthetic* or the *analytic* method. The synthetic approach to teaching phonics involves teaching isolated letter sounds that are synthesized or blended into words. This approach is most associated with phonics. In contrast, analytic phonics makes sound generalizations from words that have been learned as sight words. Phonics instruction is not introduced until the child has learned enough words to provide examples of letter-sound relationships (Matthes, 1972). A number of commercially available phonics programs are:

> *Conquests in Reading.* Webster Publishing Co.
> *New Phonics Skilltexts.* Charles E. Merrill Publishing Co.
> *Phonetic Keys to Reading.* Economy Co.
> *Phonics We Use.* Lyons & Carnahan
> *Phonovisual Method.* Phonovisual Products, Inc.
> *Remedial Reading Drills.* George Wahr Publishing Co.
> *Wordland Series.* Continental Press

Two phonic approaches widely used with LD children are the *Phonovisual Method* (Schoolfield & Timberlake, 1960) and the *Remedial Reading Drills* (Hegge, Kirk, & Kirk, 1955).

The *Phonovisual Method* is actually a supplementary phonics program that may be taught to an entire class. The method utilizes a synthetic phonics approach by introducing consonant and vowel sounds on wall charts that include pictures for each sound (e.g., *monkey* for /m/, *duck* for /d/). The charts serve as a means for the child to recognize the letter, the sound it signals, and the position of speech organs (lips, tongue, etc.) when the sound is produced. Writing is also included as a part of the program.

The *Remedial Reading Drills* were originally developed for use with mentally retarded children. The child learns to blend various letter sounds through lists of words emphasizing specific sounds. A multi-sensory approach is suggested throughout the program. The repetitious nature of the drills has been particularly helpful for the reading disabled child in providing for overlearning of sound-symbol relationships. The drill for the short /i/ is shown in figure 6-7.

New Alphabets

Some of the current reading approaches for beginning readers incorporate changes in the traditional 26-letter alphabet. Most changes have been made in order to assure a regular correspondence between sound and symbol and to eliminate multiple spellings of the same sound.

The *Initial Teaching Alphabet* (i.t.a.) is probably the best known of the new alphabets. The i.t.a. system includes a 44-character alphabet (see fig. 6-8) composed of 24 letters from the conventional Roman alphabet (*q* and *x* are eliminated) and 20 additional letters. Some of the new letters resemble Roman letters joined together. The system also uses lowercase letters and encourages the use of writing throughout the program. The child usually transfers to traditional orthography by the end of the first grade.

The system was actually proposed as a change in medium and not a change in method. It is important to note that i.t.a. is suggested for use in the beginning stages of reading. Consequently, the system has not been used extensively with reading disabled children. Most studies conclude that the approach is no more effective than other reading approaches (Woodcock, 1967).

Words in Color is a system for teaching beginning reading that makes uses of color to represent differing speech sounds. Each of 47 phonemes is assigned a different color. Wall charts are provided showing each sound and its color. Sounds are learned from the wall charts by drilling the sounds in isolation and blending them together. Children are also taught to write their own stories. There has not been much research to demonstrate that *Words in Color* offers any advantage for learning disabled children when compared to other reading approaches.

Individualized Reading

Individualized reading should be differentiated from individualized instruction. Basically, individualized reading is a specific approach to

Drill 4

i

s i t	f i t	h i t	b i t	k i t
h i m	r i m	d i m	J i m	T i m
s i p	r i p	n i p	l i p	d i p
w i n	t i n	s i n	f i n	b i n
f i g	r i g	p i g	b i g	d i g
h i d	l i d	d i d	k i d	m i d
r i b	f i b	b i b	f i b	r i b
m i x	s i x	f i x	s i x	m i x

h i t	h i m	h i d	h i p
s i n	s i t	s i p	s i x
r i b	r i m	r i p	r i g
t i n	T i m	t i p	t i n
l i d	l i p	l i t	l i p
p i g	p i n	p i t	p i g

s i t	h i m	f i t	r i m	h i t	d i m
s i p	w i n	r i p	t i n	h i p	s i n
r i d	h i d	r i g	h i t	r i m	h i p
m i d	d i g	b i n	d i p	p i t	l i p
f i n	b i g	k i d	f i b	s i x	r i b

tin	fib	pig	sin	bit	rip	pin	sip
jig	nip	him	hip	did	lip	dip	mix
hit	bin	hit	fin	fig	six	lip	hid
big	fit	dig	sit	mid	rig	rib	fix

Figure 6-7
Sample of the Remedial Reading Drills

teaching reading which includes self-selection of materials by pupils, self-paced reading, individual pupil conferences with the teacher, and emphasis on record keeping by teacher, pupil, or both (Heilman, 1977).

The reading of self-selected books at the child's own pace has been considered a key advantage of this approach. However, one of the often

Figure 6-8
Pitman's Initial Teaching Alphabet

Used with the permission of Initial Teaching Alphabet Publications, Inc., 6 East 43rd Street, New York, New York 10017.

cited dangers of an individualized program is insufficient skill development. According to Matthes (1972), the lack of systematic development of reading is a problem for children requiring sequential skills for unlocking new words. Heilman (1977) also suggests that the need for a wide variety of reading materials may be a problem for some schools.

The use of an individualized reading program may work for some children. Learning disabled children, however, often lack the necessary skills that seem to be required for self-pacing. Nonetheless, a number of studies have found more positive reading attitudes among children when an individualized approach was used (Meiselman, 1963; West, 1965).

Multisensory Reading Approaches

Multisensory approaches to reading instruction usually attempt to develop reading skills through auditory, visual, kinesthetic, and tactile stimulation. These approaches have received some attention in the field of learning disabilities due to the varied reading disturbances observed among these children.

The remedial method developed by Fernald (1943) has become almost synonymous with multisensory techniques. The Fernald approach essentially incorporates four stages whereby the child progresses from word recognition to extensive reading of books and other materials. Basically, this approach utilizes tracing as a method for learning whole words.

Stage one. The child selects a word he would like to learn, and the word is written or printed in large letters by the teacher. The child traces the word with his finger. He is instructed to say each syllable of the word as he traces it. The child repeats this process as often as necessary until he can write the word as a unit from memory. Next, the child is encouraged to incorporate the word into a story. The story is usually typed for the child by the teacher. Each new word that the child learns is placed on a card and alphabetically filed by the child in a file or box. These words are frequently utilized in stories.

Stage two. This stage is basically identical to stage one, except tracing is eliminated. The child learns words he has dictated and uses these words in stories. Stories usually increase in length during this stage.

Stage three. During this stage, words are no longer written on cards. The child learns words he has dictated and uses these words in stories. Stories usually increase in length during this stage.

Stage four. This is the stage where the child is encouraged to learn new words by generalizing from words he already knows. Children are instructed to survey a reading passage before reading and to learn information words.

The Gillingham-Stillman approach, sometimes called the Alphabetic Method, is also based upon a multisensory technique for learning specific reading skills. The approach was developed in conjunction with the research work of Orton (1937), who was interested in dyslexic children. This approach emphasizes individual letters. Children are taught letter sounds, visual symbols, and various linkages through tracing, copying, and writing particular letters. Phonetic drill cards and short stories are considered crucial parts of the program. Considerable emphasis is also placed on spelling, dictionary skills, syllabication, and rules.

Phonograms are introduced by the teacher through the following procedures:

   a. A small card with one letter printed on it is exposed to the student, and the *name* of the letter is spoken by the teacher. The name of the letter is repeated by the student. As soon as the name of the letter is mastered, the *sound* is made by the teacher and repeated by the student. The card is then exposed and the teacher asks, "What does this letter say?" The student is expected to give the sound.
   b. With the card not being exposed, the teacher makes the sound represented by the letter (phonogram) and says, "Tell me the

name of the letter that has this sound." The student is expected to give the name of the letter.

c. The letter is carefully made by the teacher and its form explained to the student. The letter is traced by the student on the teacher's lines, then copied, written from memory, and then written again without looking at the previously written letters. Finally, the teacher makes the sound and asks the student to "Write the letter that has this sound."

The Gillingham-Stillman approach is a highly structured technique that was developed as a remedial method. Kaluger and Kolson (1978) have pointed out, however, that the lack of emphasis on comprehension is a major disadvantage. The rigidity of the program and the phonics emphasis have also been mentioned as possible weaknesses of the technique (Gillespie & Johnson, 1974).

Other Reading Approaches

A number of methods used with reading disabled children cannot be classified according to any of the categories previously discussed. The *DISTAR* approach (Engelmann & Bruner, 1974) and the *Neurological Impress Method* (Heckelman, 1962), in particular, may be considered among the unique reading techniques.

The DISTAR reading program is a highly structured, fast-paced, and intensive program of instruction that emphasizes sequencing, left-right discrimination, and sound-symbol relationships. Children are taught sequencing skills through symbol-action games. Blending exercises are designed to teach both analytic and synthetic relationships of sounds and words. Children are taught to blend by the *say-it-fast* technique, while spelling words by sounds teaches the reverse procedure. Various *take-home* sheets are used to practice skills learned in school. Children also receive continuous positive reinforcement throughout the program. A sample page from the DISTAR reading program is illustrated in figure 6-9.

Very little published research evidence is presently available concerning the effectiveness of the DISTAR program. Nonetheless, teachers report that the program is highly effective in teaching many children to read. Kaluger and Kolson (1978) also report that the program is receiving some recognition and usage with children needing remedial work.

The SRA *Corrective Reading Program* (Engelmann, Becker, Carnine, Meyers, Becker, & Johnson, 1974), which is intended for students in grades 4 through 12, is another available program based upon the DISTAR concepts. Student contracts and program charts accompany this program.

STORY 113

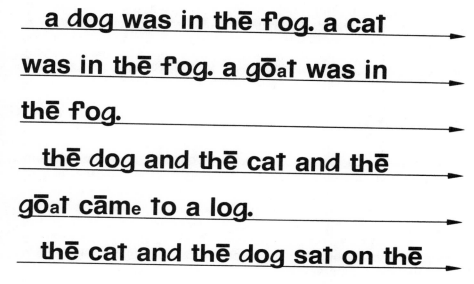

Figure 6-9
Sample Page—DISTAR Reading Program

From *Distar© Reading I: An Instructional System, 2nd edition—Storybook 1* by Siegfried Engelmann and Elaine C. Bruner.© 1974, 1969, Science Research Associates, Inc. Reprinted by permission of the publisher.

The Neurological Impress Method was originally developed for children who had not learned to read at a level commensurate with their ability. The approach is described by the author as

> a system of unison reading whereby the student and the teacher read aloud, simultaneously at a rapid rate. The disabled reader is placed slightly to the front of the teacher with the student and the teacher holding the book jointly. As the student and teacher read the materials in unison, the voice of the teacher is directed into the ear of the student at close range. (Heckelman, 1969, p. 178)

The child is also encouraged to slide his finger along the line, following the words as they are being spoken. One goal of the method is to cover as many pages of reading material as possible in the allotted reading time. Specific word analysis and comprehension skills are not taught at any time during the program. Very little research on this approach used with LD children has been reported in the literature.

SUMMARY

Learning disabilities in reading were discussed in this chapter. Some of the major word recognition, word analysis, and comprehension skill deficiencies were outlined and described. Informal diagnostic tech-niques, including the informal reading inventory and various informal tests, were summarized. A number of published reading tests were briefly described. The chapter concluded with a discussion of the major developmental and remedial reading methods currently being utilized with the learning disabled.

SUGGESTED ACTIVITIES

1. Observe various classes or groups of children in which different reading methods and materials are being utilized. Ask the teacher what he or she considers to be the advantages and disadvantages of each approach for particular children.

2. Have a child read a paragraph to you. Note any specific errors and ask the child to respond to questions based upon the content of the story. Analyze errors and responses in order to determine if a pattern of difficulty is apparent.

3. Observe children at each of the reading stages noted at the beginning of this chapter. Briefly outline skills that seem particularly vital to success at each stage.

4. Obtain a copy of a published reading test discussed in this chapter. Carefully examine the test and practice administering specific sub-tests to other adults or children. If possible, observe the test being administered by a trained examiner.

5. Arrange to visit a remedial reading teacher in your local school district. Discuss the role and responsibilities of this teacher in working with LD students. Note any similarities and differences when compared to the LD resource teacher.

6. Observe children who are experiencing specific reading difficulties with blending, visual discrimination, reversed errors, or memory skills. Discuss how these specific difficulties might affect the selec-tion and use of various reading materials.

7. What are the various methods and materials which are used to teach reading in your school district? Ask a teacher in your district to discuss the alternatives for children encountering difficulty with the presently utilized method(s).

8. Design a remedial program for Scotty, the reading disabled child described in this chapter. Be sure to consider the assessment data and the general information which was provided concerning Scotty.

References

Bannatyne, A. *Reading*. San Rafael, Calif.: Academic Therapy Publications, 1973.

Barrett, T.C. Taxonomy of reading comprehension. *Reading 360 Monograph*. Lexington, Mass.: Ginn, 1972.

Brueckner, L.S., & Bond, G.L. *The diagnosis and treatment of learning difficulties*. New York: Appleton-Century-Crofts, 1955.

Buchanan, C. *Programmed reading*. New York: McGraw-Hill, 1966.

Carrillo, L. *Teaching reading: A handbook*. New York: St. Martin's Press, 1976.

Chalfant, J.C., & Scheffelin, M.A. Central processing dysfunctions in children: A review of research (NINDS Monograph No. 9). Bethesda, Md.: U.S. Department of Health, Education, and Welfare, 1969.

deBoer, J.L. What does research reveal about reading and the high school student? *English Journal*, 1958, *47*, 271-281.

Dolch, E.W. *The Dolch basic sight word list*. Champaign, Ill.: Garrard, 1953.

Durkin, D. *Teaching them to read* (3rd ed.). Boston: Allyn & Bacon, 1978.

Durrell, D.D. *Durrell Analysis of Reading Difficulty*. New York: Harcourt Brace Jovanovich, 1955.

Ekwall, E.E. *Diagnosis and remediation of the disabled reader*. Boston: Allyn & Bacon, 1976.

Ekwall, E.E. *Locating and correcting reading difficulties* (2nd ed.). Columbus, Ohio: Charles E. Merrill, 1977.

Engelmann, S., Becker, W., Carnine, L., Meyers, L., Becker, J., & Johnson, G. *Corrective reading program*. Chicago: Science Research Associates, 1974.

Engelmann, S., & Bruner, E.C. *DISTAR: An instructional system*. Chicago: Science Research Associates, 1974.

Erickson, S.E. *Conference on studies in reading*. Washington, D.C.: National Institute of Education, U.S. Department of Health, Education, and Welfare, 1978.

Fernald, G.M. *Remedial techniques in basic school subjects*. New York: McGraw-Hill, 1943.

Gates, A.I., & McKillop. A.S. *Gates-McKillop Reading Diagnostic Tests*. New York: Bureau of Publications, Teachers College, Columbia University, 1962.

Gillespie, P.H., & Johnson, L. *Teaching reading to the mildly retarded child*. Columbus, Ohio: Charles E. Merrill, 1974.

Gilliland, H. *A practical guide to remedial reading* (2nd ed.). Columbus, Ohio: Charles E. Merrill, 1978.

Goodman, K. A linguistic study of cues and miscues in reading. *Elementary English Review,* 1965, *42,* 639-643.

Goodman, K. Reading: A psycholinguistic guessing game. In H. Singer & R. Ruddell (Eds.), *Theoretical models and processes of reading.* Newark, Del.: International Reading Association, 1970.

Goodman, Y.M., & Burke, C.I. *Reading miscue inventory: Manual procedure for diagnosis and remediation.* New York: Macmillan, 1972.

Gray, W.S., & Robinson, H.M. (Eds.). *Gray Oral Reading Test.* Indianapolis: Bobbs-Merrill, 1967.

Guzak, F.J. *Diagnostic reading instruction in the elementary school.* New York: Harper & Row, Publishers, 1972.

Hammill, D.D., & Bartel, N.R. *Teaching children with learning and behavior problems* (2nd ed.). Boston: Allyn & Bacon, 1978.

Hafner, L. Importance of cloze. In E.T. Thurstone & L.E. Hafner (Eds.), *The philosophical and social basis for reading 14th yearbook.* Milwaukee, Wis.: National Reading Conference, 1965.

Harris, A., & Sipay, E.R. *How to increase your reading ability* (6th ed.). New York: David McKay, 1975.

Heckelman, R.G. *A neurological impress method of reading instruction.* Merced, Calif.: Merced County Schools Office, 1962.

Heckelman, R.G. The neurological impress method of remedial reading instruction. *Academic Therapy,* 1969, *4,* 277-282.

Hegge, T.G., Kirk, S.A., & Kirk, W.D. *Remedial reading drills.* Ann Arbor, Mich.: George Wahr Publishing, 1955.

Heilman, A.W. *Phonics in proper perspective* (3rd ed.). Columbus, Ohio: Charles E. Merrill, 1976.

Heilman, A.W. *Principles and practices of teaching reading* (4th ed.). Columbus, Ohio: Charles E. Merrill, 1977.

Johnson, D.D. The Dolch list reexamined. *The Reading Teacher,* 1971, *24,* 455-456.

Johnson, D.J., & Myklebust, H.R. *Learning disabilities: Educational principles and practices.* New York: Grune & Stratton, 1967.

Johnson, M.S., & Kress, R.A. *Informal reading inventories.* Newark, Del.: International Reading Association, 1965.

Jordan, D.R. *Dyslexia in the classroom* (2nd ed.). Columbus, Ohio: Charles E. Merrill, 1977.

Kaluger, G., & Kolson, C.J. *Reading and learning disabilities* (2nd ed.). Columbus, Ohio: Charles E. Merrill, 1978.

Karlin, R. *Teaching elementary reading: Principles and strategies* (2nd ed.). New York: Harcourt Brace Jovanovich, 1975.

Kirk, S., & Kirk, W. *Psycholinguistic learning disabilities: Diagnosis and remediation.* Urbana, Ill.: University of Illinois Press, 1971.

Leary, B. Information please. *A monograph on reading,* No. 28. New York: Harper & Row, 1965.

Lee, D.M., & Allen, R.V. *Learning to read through experience* (2nd ed.). New York: Appleton-Century-Crofts, 1963.

Lerner, J. *Children with learning disabilities* (2nd ed.). Boston: Houghton Mifflin, 1976.

Malmquist, E. *Factors related to reading disabilities in the first grade of the elementary school.* Stockholm; Almquist and Wiksell, 1958.

Matthes, C. *How children are taught to read.* Lincoln, Nebr.: Professional Educators Publications, 1972.

May, F.B., & Eliot, S.B. *To help children read: Mastery performance modules for teachers in training* (2nd ed.). Columbus, Ohio: Charles E. Merrill, 1978.

Meiselman, M.S. *A comparison of two reading programs for retarded readers.* Unpublished doctoral dissertation, New York University, 1963.

Morgan, W.P. A case of congenital word-blindness. *British Medical Journal,* 1896, 2, 1387.

Myers, P., & Hammill, D.D. *Methods for learning disorders* (2nd ed.). New York: Wiley, 1976.

National Advisory Committee on Dyslexia and Related Reading Disorders. *Reading disorders in the United States.* Washington, D.C.: U.S. Department of Health, Education and Welfare, 1969.

Orton, S. *Reading, writing, and speech problems in children.* New York: Norton, 1937.

Schoolfield, L.D., & Timberlake, J.B. *The phonovisual method.* Washington, D.C.: Phonovisual Products, 1960.

Silvaroli, N.J. *Classroom reading inventory* (2nd ed.). Dubuque, Iowa: William C. Brown, 1973.

Spache, G.D. *Diagnostic Reading Scales.* Monterey, Calif.: California Test Bureau, 1963.

Spache, G.D., & Spache, E.B. *Reading in the elementary school.* Boston: Allyn & Bacon, 1969.

Spache, G.D. & Spache, E.B. *Reading in the elementary school* (4th ed.). Boston: Allyn & Bacon, 1977.

Strang, B. *Diagnostic teaching of reading* (2nd ed.). New York: McGraw-Hill, 1969.

Terman, L., & Merrill, M. *Stanford-Binet Intelligence Scale.* Boston: Houghton Mifflin, 1973.

Wallace, G., & Larsen, S. *Educational assessment of learning problems: Testing for teaching.* Boston: Allyn & Bacon, 1978.

Wallen, C.J. *Competency in teaching reading.* Chicago: Science Research Associates, 1972.

Wepman, J.M. *Auditory Discrimination Test.* Chicago: Joseph M. Wepman, 1958.

West, R. *Individualized reading instruction.* New York: Kennikat Press, 1965.

Wilson, R.M. *Diagnostic and remedial reading for classroom and clinic* (3rd ed.). Columbus, Ohio: Charles E. Merrill, 1977.

Woodcock, R. *The Peabody-Chicago-Detroit reading project—A report of second year results.* Nashville, Tenn.: George Peabody College, 1967.

Woodcock, R.W. *Woodcock Reading Mastery Tests.* Circle Pines, Minn.: American Guidance Service, 1974.

Woods, M.L., & Moe, A.J. *Analytical reading inventory.* Columbus, Ohio: Charles E. Merrill, 1977.

Written Language Problems

PREVIEW

The actual act of writing involves a number of very distinct skills, including the ability to keep one idea in mind, to formulate the idea in words, to plan the correct graphic form for each letter and word, to correctly manipulate the writing instrument, and to have sufficient visual and motor memory (Lerner, 1976). It is no wonder that many LD students intensely dislike written language activities and avoid them whenever possible.

The various types of skill deficiencies involved in handwriting, spelling, and written expression problems serve as a primary focus of this chapter. The most common disturbances in each of these areas are discussed and illustrated in terms of actual classroom behaviors of LD students.

Our assessment section emphasizes the variety of appraisal techniques that are available and utilized for evaluating written language problems. Handwriting scales, informal inventories, teacher-made tests, and various published tests are among the evaluative techniques discussed during this section of the chapter.

Our discussion of teaching techniques and instructional programs for developing written language skills reflects our basic belief that teaching programs should focus on the specific behaviors that teachers are attempting to develop. It is our opinion that children and youth need to be *directly* taught the specific skills they are lacking. Consequently, we list some very specific teaching systems for remediating written language disturbances.

We would also like to recommend the Suggested Activities found at the conclusion of this chapter. These activities provide you with a number of very different opportunities for learning more about the written language problems of LD students. We encourage you to experiment with these activities.

WRITTEN LANGUAGE AND LEARNING DISABILITIES

Written language is considered to be one of the highest forms of language. In the hierarchy of language abilities, it is the last to be learned. Abilities and experiences in listening, speaking, and reading usually precede the development of writing skills. Difficulties in any of these other language areas will certainly interfere with the acquisition of the written form of language (Johnson & Myklebust, 1967). Children

Marlene has difficulty in both writing and remembering various letters and words. She uses cursive and manuscript writing interchangeably. She also frequently confuses the two methods. During a recent assignment in which Marlene was asked to copy four short sentences from the chalkboard, she made 10 erasures and frequently referred to the chalkboard prior to writing many individual letters. These written language problems are compounded because Marlene is 13 years of age and in the eighth grade.

Marlene's height is equal to that of an average fifth grader, and her general maturity level is also more like that of a fifth grader than that of a junior high school student. Marlene remains very quiet in school, and socially she is virtually friendless.

Marlene has been sporadically provided with remedial help. She was initially referred for special remedial assistance during the fourth grade. At that time, she was classified as learning disabled by the district placement committee. She received

limited resource help for approximately two months before moving to a neighboring school district which did not provide educational services for students with learning disabilities until the past year. At the present time, Marlene is being seen by a resource teacher for one 45-minute period each school day.

Marlene's written language difficulties have also resulted in continued frustrations with other academic subjects. Her reading is marked by many mispronunciations and omissions. She will most often refrain from class discussions, and she usually avoids written assignments. Marlene's teacher has recommended that she be considered for placement in an all-day class for LD students. However, at the present time, the one self-contained class for learning disabled pupils in Marlene's school district has a waiting list of 14 students. The school district does not foresee adding another self-contained class for at least 2 years. Consequently, the resource room placement will probably be continued for some period of time.

with various reading problems, for example, invariably experience spelling disabilities. A number of other factors are also related to written language disorders, including spoken language disturbances, auditory blending problems, visual discrimination difficulties, word analysis deficits, speech articulation problems, and various instructional factors.

This list does not exhaust all the factors associated with written language problems, nor does it describe the entire group of contributing causes. However, the factors we have listed do indicate the exceedingly complex nature of written language and the number of skills required for success in this area. Table 7-1 outlines the sequential skills required in written language.

The three areas of written language in which disturbances occur most frequently are *handwriting, spelling,* and *written expression.*

TYPES OF WRITTEN LANGUAGE PROBLEMS

Handwriting

Handwriting has often been labeled the most concrete of all the basic academic skills. It differs from other communication skills in that a written record is provided. Handwriting deficits have been referred to as *visual-motor integration* problems (Johnson & Myklebust, 1967) and *dysgraphia* (Jordan, 1977). Table 7-2 (p. 192) lists the most common handwriting deficits.

In addition to poor motor skills, handwriting problems may be due to directionality confusion or even to various motivational difficulties. Some children with handwriting deficits are unable to hold a pencil properly, while others have problems in writing certain letters. Some of the more common handwriting disturbances are discussed in the following section. Figure 7-1 (p. 193) shows the handwriting of a 7-year-old boy who was asked to copy "Santa is coming" from the chalkboard.

Prewriting Skills

Many children are unable to use handwriting skills because they have not mastered a number of prewriting skills. An understanding of bodily relationships, such as *up, down, top,* and *bottom,* is included among the prerequisite skills for writing. The recognition and copying of different sizes and shapes, correct pencil grasp, paper position, and posture are other prewriting skills.

Many children have not developed sufficient fine motor coordination for adequate writing skill. Kimmell (1970) suggests that a number of LD children have not had the experience of handling, twisting, grasping, clutching, or squeezing objects in order to develop finer hand and finger

Table 7-1
Developmental Hierarchy of Writing Tasks

I.   Scribbling.
II. Tracing:
     (a) Connected letters or figures.
     (b) Disconnected letters or figures.
III. Copying:
     (a) From a model.
     (b) From memory.
     (c) Symbolic and nonsymbolic.
IV. Completion tasks:
     (a) Figure
     (b) Word completion—supply missing letters:
         1. Multiple-choice.
         2. Recall.
     (c) Sentence completion—supply missing word.
V.   Writing from dictation:
     (a) Writing from letters as they are spoken.
     (b) Writing words and sentences.
     (c) Supply missing word.
     (d) Supply missing sentence.
VI. Propositional writing.

From "Central Processing Dysfunction in Children: A Review of Research" by J.C. Chalfant and M.A. Scheffelin *NINDS Monograph* No. 9. Bethesda, Md.: U.S. Department of Health, Education and Welfare, 1969, p. 112.

muscles. The manipulation of pencils or crayons is consequently both frustrating and difficult for these children. Some hold the pencil too tightly, others not tightly enough. Some grasp the pencil with the entire fist, while others attempt to manipulate it with both hands. Many of these children must be sequentially taught how to grasp the pencil or crayon properly.

The inability to copy single geometric shapes is another prewriting deficit. Jordan (1977) points out that a frequently observed flaw in copying shapes is the tendency to draw "ears" at the corner of circles, squares, or triangles. Other children duplicate the shape incorrectly by omitting a stroke or by adding an extra stroke. The size of some shapes may be copied too small or too large. Unusual copying patterns (e.g., right to left) are also observed among some children. All of these behaviors provide early indicators that a child may have writing difficulties when presented with letters and words.

Paper position and body posture have also been mentioned as possible contributory causes of poor handwriting (Croutch, 1970; Johnson & Myklebust, 1967). The writing posture of some children is such that their heads are almost touching the paper. Often, the paper is

Table 7-2
Common Handwriting Errors

defect	causes
1. Too much slant	a. Writing arm too near body b. Thumb too stiff c. Point of nib too far from fingers d. Paper in wrong direction e. Stroke in wrong direction
2. Writing too straight	a. Arm too far from body b. Fingers too near nib c. Index finger alone guiding pen d. Incorrect position of paper
3. Writing too heavy	a. Pressing index finger too heavily b. Using wrong type of pen c. Penholder too small in diameter
4. Writing too light	a. Pen held too obliquely or too straight b. Eyelet of pen turned to side c. Penholder too large in diameter
5. Writing too angular	a. Thumb too stiff b. Penholder too lightly held c. Movement too slow
6. Writing too irregular	a. Movement lacks freedom b. Movement of hand too slow c. Pen gripping d. Incorrect or uncomfortable position
7. Spacing too wide	a. Pen progresses too fast to right b. Excessive, sweeping lateral movement

From *Educational Assessment of Learning Problems: Testing for Teaching* by G. Wallace and S.C. Larsen. Boston: Allyn & Bacon, 1978. Copyright 1978 by Allyn & Bacon. Reprinted by permission.

incorrectly positioned because of such poor writing posture. Some children slant the paper at an extreme angle, while others do not slant it enough. Croutch (1970) also suggests that oversized or undersized furniture may contribute to various handwriting problems. It is suggested that all of these problems be corrected during the prewriting stage before the child is introduced to extensive copying and writing.

Letter Formation

The formation of various letters causes difficulty for many learning disabled children. The addition, omission, or reversal of certain letter

Figure 7-1
Handwriting of 7-Year-Old Boy Asked to Copy "Santa is coming."

strokes seems particularly troublesome. The most commonly reversed letters include *b, d, p, q,* and *y.* The letters *u* and *n* are also very frequently inverted.

In general, letters are comprised of vertical, horizontal, or curved strokes. Children seem to have little difficulty with letters comprised entirely of vertical or horizontal strokes (e.g., *T, L, H, F).* Most difficulties seem to occur in those letters in which straight lines and curved lines are combined (e.g., *h, r, f, b).*

The basic strokes comprising most letters can be taught sequentially (Wallace & Kauffman, 1978). Children should be taught to combine the basic strokes of straight and curved lines once these have been learned. Larson (1970) believes that many letters are derived from other letters. She suggests that beginning letters should be taught before the derived letters. The letters *l, o, i, t,* and *c* are included among the beginning letters.

The size of various letters is an additional problem for many children. Lewis and Lewis (1965) found that incorrect size (either larger or smaller) was the most common type of manuscript error among a group of first-grade children. Letters which descend below the line (*p, j, y,* etc.) were often printed in the wrong size.

Many letter formation problems seem due to the child's lack of readiness in using various sizes and shapes. The use of prolonged drills and inappropriate materials (short pencils, unlined paper, etc.) is certainly another factor that must be considered.

Manuscript Writing

Most schools in this country initiate handwriting instruction with manuscript writing. Usually around the end of second grade or the beginning of third grade, children are taught cursive writing. There is still some controversy regarding the best approach for teaching writing to the child with learning disabilities. These arguments will be discussed later in this chapter. Many LD children do encounter difficulties with manuscript writing.

In addition to difficulties in forming letters, some children have problems in spacing manuscript letters. Words that are copied from the chalkboard are often irregularly spaced. Some children leave too much space between letters and words; others place some letters so close to other letters that words cannot be read.

A number of children have difficulty in remembering how to write certain letters. Their problem is sometimes due to the complexity of specific letters. Letters with simple strokes (e.g., *l, t, i)* are easier to remember than those with a number of different strokes (e.g., *b, m, k).* Closely related to this problem is the difficulty that some children have with differentiating the correct position of some letters (e.g., *p, c, f).* Many times letters are reversed because of left-right orientation problems or simply because the child cannot remember the correct position. In their study, Lewis and Lewis (1965) found the following, arranged in order of frequency:

1. The five most difficult letters (incorrect size) were the descenders: *q, g, p, y,* and *j.*
2. The letters *n, d, q,* and *y,* were most susceptible to unusual errors than were most letters.
3. The letter *m* was the most difficult of the nondescending letters.
4. Incorrect relationship of letter parts was greater in letters *k, R, M,* and *m* than in any other letter.
5. The most frequent error in the letter *U* was incorrect relationship of parts (partial omission).
6. Errors in the letter *a* were largely due to incorrect size and relationship of the large arc to the vertical line.
7. The inversion error occurred in *G.*
8. The easiest letters were *l, o, L, O,* and *H.*
9. Boys were more prone to errors than girls.
10. The next ten most difficult letters were: *R, d, Y, u, M, S, b, e, r,* and *Z.*

The early introduction of capital letters has been another problem for some children. Since most capital letters are not the larger versions of lowercase letters, it is necessary to learn two manuscript forms for each letter. Children with handwriting difficulties sometimes confuse lowercase and capital letters in writing, especially when the capital letters are taught before the child has mastered most lowercase letters.

Cursive Writing

In discussing cursive writing deficits, it is important to keep in mind one caution:

Cursive writing should not be taught to children who are still experiencing difficulties with manuscript writing. In all likelihood, children who exper- ience extreme difficulties with manuscript will also experience failure with cursive writing. (Wallace & Kauffman, 1978, p. 204)

Many cursive writing deficits are similar in form to manuscript writing disturbances. Consequently, Banas and Wills (1970) believe that the key to successful cursive writing is the establishment of an association between the printed and cursive word. The similarity between the two forms is often neglected in teaching a child to write. Some LD children therefore do not conceptualize or visualize cursive writing as the printed form that has been connected. The child thinks of cursive writing as an entirely new writing system.

The multiple-letter forms which are found in cursive writing are sometimes confusing to children. Some cursive letters change form according to placement in a word, and many capital cursive letters are totally unlike the lowercase form. A number of children have some difficulty remembering all these different forms, especially when they do not have a model to follow.

More specifically, Jordan (1977) suggests that many children have great difficulty remembering where to stop a sweeping or circular movement, how to swing back, and how to connect the lines of movement within complicated letter formations. He also points out that closed, circular movements (e.g., *o, a, d, e*) and letters requiring a change in direction of hand movement (e.g., *h, j, t, c*) are the most difficult cursive letters for some children to learn. Some of the most common cursive writing errors are shown in table 7-3 (p. 196).

The complex movements of cursive writing contribute to the difficulty of this writing style. In addition to the vertical, horizontal, and curved strokes found in manuscript writing, the mechanics of cursive writing require many intricate and precise movements that require fine motor coordination. The complex motor movements to write a word such as *people,* for example, can be very confusing to some children, especially if their fine motor dexterity is deficient.

In forming various cursive letters, many children experience diffi- culties with just one movement pattern. Some children have problems with many of the *ascender* letters *(b, k, l, t,* etc.), while others have difficulty with just the *descender* letters *(f, g, p, y,* etc.). Letters with similar movement patterns should be taught sequentially, just as each letter may be divided into steps and taught by joining the parts.

Finally, it must be reiterated that many children do not have the same ability to move freely from one printed form to another as other children. Johnson and Myklebust (1967) strongly suggest that writing disabled children be taught one form for both reading and writing and learn that one type thoroughly. We wholeheartedly endorse this suggestion.

Table 7-3
Cursive Writing Errors

errors	examples of errors
a like o	*O*
a like ci	*u*
d like cl	*l*
e closed	*l*
g like y	*y*
h like li	*h*
i with no dot	*l*
l like uncrossed t	*l*
m like w	*m*
r like s	*s*
r like n	*n*
t with cross above	*t*
5 like 3	*5*
6 like 0	*6*
7 like 9	*7*

From *Educational Assessment of Learning Problems: Testing for Teaching* by G. Wallace and S.C. Larsen. Boston: Allyn & Bacon, 1978. Copyright 1978 by Allyn & Bacon. Reprinted by permission.

Left-Handedness

The left-handed writer is accepted today as both normal and natural. There is now general agreement, unlike the past, that children should be allowed to write with the strongly preferred hand, be it left or right. Some particular problems of left-handed children, however, need to be briefly considered.

Many left-handers "hook" their hand as they write in order to see better what they have written and to avoid smudging. This problem is actually related to the slant of the paper. Otto, McMenemy, and Smith (1973) suggest that the left-hander is able to assume a natural and comfortable writing position once the paper is slanted opposite to the position used by right-handed writers.

Many of the difficulties experienced by left-handers seem caused by their use of procedures intended for right-handed individuals. In addition to paper and hand positioning, left-handers have some difficulty with the slant of their writing. The back slant often observed among the work of these children is somewhat natural because of the direction in which they make their letters. A severe back slant, however, is certain cause to suggest manuscript writing instead of cursive for some children. Finally, there is little support for the belief that left-handers write more slowly than right-handers. Figure 7-2 shows the alphabet as correctly written by a left-handed individual.

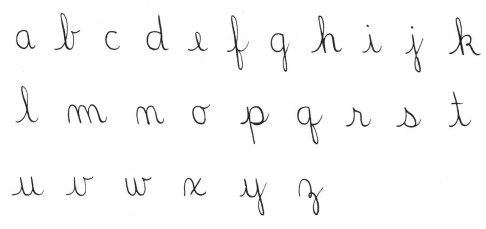

Figure 7-2
Left-hand Alphabet

From *A Writing Manual for Teaching the Left-handed* by M. D. Plunkett. Cambridge, Mass.: Educators Publishing Service, 1954. Copyright 1954 by Educators Publishing Service. Reprinted by permission.

Spelling

The ability to spell requires a number of complex and interrelated skills. Hunt, Hadsell, Hannum, and Johnson (1963) point out that, besides general intelligence, the four factors that affect the ability to spell English words are: (1) the ability to spell words that are phonetic; (2) the ability to spell words that involve roots, prefixes, suffixes, and the rules for combining; (3) the ability to look at a word and reproduce it later; and (4) the ability to spell the demons. Many of these skills are not apparent in the spelling ability of the student whose work is illustrated in figure 7-3 (p. 198).

Bryant (1972) and others indicate that spelling is frequently a more sensitive indicator of language disabilities than reading because there are fewer and less effective methods for compensation of spelling problems. An analysis of spelling errors indicates the numerous problems that might be exhibited in this area. Some of these deficits are listed in table 7-4 (p. 199) and discussed in the following section.

Phonics Ability

Spelling skill involves the ability to transpose sounds (phonemes) to letters (graphemes) accurately. Many learning disabled children have

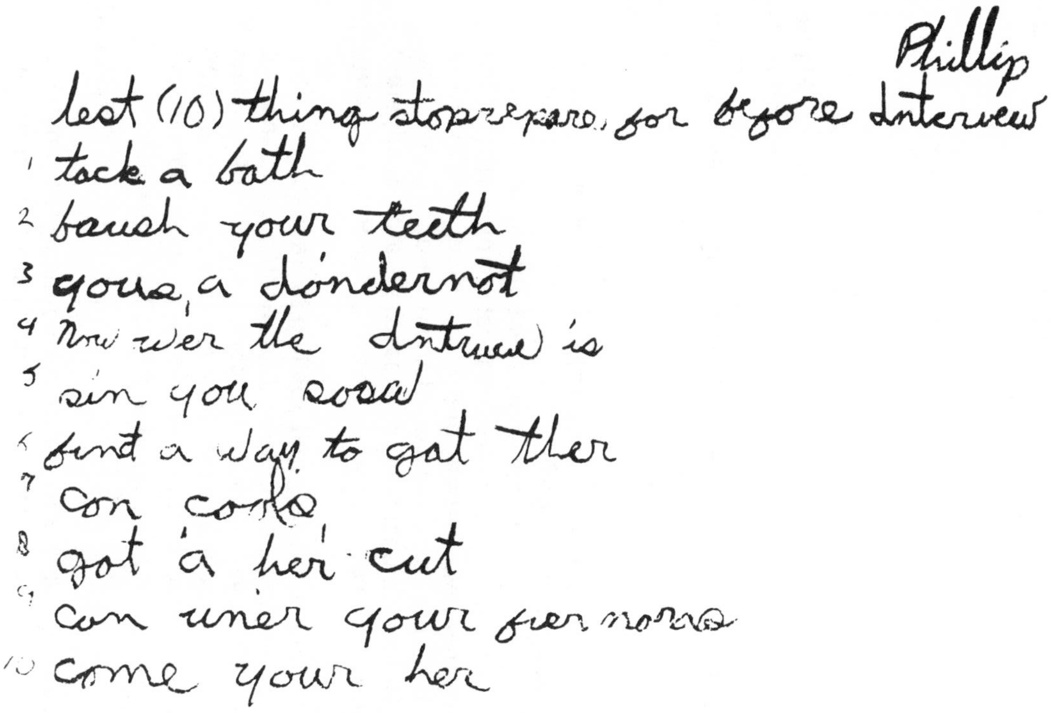

List of 10 things to prepare for before a job interview:

1. Take a bath
2. Brush your teeth
3. Use a deodorant
4. Know where the entrance is
5. Shine your shoes
6. Find a way to get there
7. Clean clothes
8. Get a haircut
9. Clean under your fingernails
10. Comb your hair

Correct version
_____

Phillip

lest (10) thing stopreperes. for begore Interview

1. tacke a bath
2. brush your teeth
3. youse a deoderrnt
4. knw zver the Intrveu) is
5. sin you scoes
6. find a way. to gat ther
7. Con cothe
8. got a her cut
9. Con uner your fier norns
10. Come your her

Spelling of an 18-year-old
LD boy.
_____

Figure 7-3

From *Learning Disabilities: Concepts and Characteristics* by G. Wallace and J. McLoughlin. Columbus, Ohio: Charles E. Merrill, 1975. Copyright 1975 by Bell & Howell. Reprinted by permission.

Table 7-4
Common Spelling Errors

error	example
Addition of unneeded letters	*dressses*
Omissions of needed letters	*hom* for *home*
Reflections of a child's mispronunciations	*pin* for *pen*
Reflections of dialectical speech patterns	*Cuber* for *Cuba*
Reversals of whole words	*eno* for *one*
Reversals of vowels	*braed* for *bread*
Reversals of consonant order	*lback* for *black*
Reversals of consonant or vowel directionality	*brithday* for *birthday*
Reversals of syllables	*telho* for *hotel*
Phonetic spelling of nonphonetic words or parts thereof	*cawt* for *caught*
Wrong association of a sound with a given set of letters, such as *u* has been learned as *ou* in *you*	
"Neographisms," such as letters put in which bear no discernible relationship with the word dictated	
Varying degrees and combinations of those or other possible patterns	

great difficulty in associating sounds with symbols. They cannot translate the sounds which they hear into letters and words. These children have difficulties in auditory memory, auditory discrimination, and the application of various phonic generalizations to spelling words.

A number of respected writers in this area have reported a significant difference in the auditory discrimination ability of good and poor spellers (Durrell, 1964; Russell, 1937). The child who incorrectly spells *cat* as *cad* or *sad* as *sat* will require remedial work in basic auditory discrimination skills in combination with the graphemic component of each sound. Brueckner and Bond (1955) suggest that the emphasis with poor spellers should *first* be to learn to associate sounds of single letters and their written symbols and *then* to proceed to letter and phonogram combinations.

Many children omit entire sound units from various words because of auditory discrimination difficulties. Jordan (1977) believes that the omission of sound units within multisyllablic words is one of the most significant indicators of a spelling disability. Examples of this difficulty include *rember* for *remember* or *somting* for *something*. In addition to eliminating various sound units from some words, other children add unnecessary sound units (e.g., *booker* for *book).*

Children who lack basic phonics ability usually do not have any dependable method to spell words and often rely on guessing. Four or five attempts to spell a word is not unusual. The child who guesses at various spellings is usually not any more sure he is correct on the last attempt than he was on his first try.

Finally, many LD children literally transform what they hear into the written form. The child who spells *exciting* as *icsiting* or *mystery* as *mistree* has not learned to apply phonic generalizations, nor has he or she probably been exposed to many nonphonetic words. These children will require some help in building adequate visual imagery for words.

Visual Memory

Many spelling difficulties are related to various visual memory deficits. A number of children are unable to retain the memory of either individual letters or the sequential order of letters in words.

The child who has trouble revisualizing letters in a word would make gross errors in spelling since he or she can recall very little visually about the word. On the other hand, the child who spells *girl* as *gril* or *mother* as *mohter* is probably experiencing some difficulty with visual *sequential* memory. In the latter case, most of the individual letters can be recalled. However, the correct order of the letters is not known.

Children with visual memory problems have difficulty in storing the visual image of a word for later visual recall. Johnson and Myklebust (1967) suggest that the primary teaching objective for children with these difficulties is to assist them in facilitating the revisualization of letters and words. The most successful approaches have been various tracing methods. The Fernald (1943) technique has probably been the most widely used tracing approach. The child is required to trace a word in this approach until he can produce it from memory and then write the word correctly in context. As the child progresses in recalling various words, the tracing stage is gradually eliminated. This approach is described in more detail later in this chapter.

Children with visual memory disturbances also experience some difficulty in recalling gross configurations of words. It would be difficult for this child to match configurations of specific words to actual words:

Examples

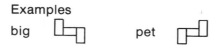

Mnemonic devices for remembering spelling patterns can be used by some children with spelling disabilities. Two illustrations of mnemonic aids are

1. *market* is *mark* with *et* at the end
2. *city* is *it* with a *c* at the beginning and a *y* at the end

Otto, McMenemy, and Smith (1973) recommend the use of mnemonic devices with spelling disabled children, but they caution that some mnemonic aids are more difficult to learn than the words themselves. Mnemonic devices are often very helpful in learning to spell the 100 most misspelled words listed in table 7-5.

Visual memory deficits are most often corrected through a simultaneous visual-auditory kinesthetic approach. There seems to be general agreement that the automatic recall and recognition of both letters and words is best strengthened through this multisensory technique.

Motor Memory

Fernald (1943) points out that in spelling the child must know every detail of the word form. It is not enough to merely recognize the word, as in reading. She describes the difference between reading and spelling as analogous to the difference between merely recognizing a person when you see him and paying enough attention to him to describe him in detail after he is gone.

Table 7-5
One Hundred Most Misspelled Words

again	dropped	looked	their
all right	every	many	then
always	February	money	there
an	first	morning	they
and	for	mother	they're
animals	friend	name	things
another	friends	named	thought
around	frightened	off	threw
asked	from	once	through
babies	getting	our	to
beautiful	going	people	together
because	happened	pretty	too
before	hear	received	tried
believe	heard	running	two
bought	here	said	until
came	him	school	very
caught	interesting	some	wanted
children	its	something	went
clothes	it's	sometime	were
coming	jumped	started	when
course	knew	stopped	where
cousin	know	surprise	with
decided	let's	swimming	woman
didn't	like	than	would
different	little	that's	you've

A number of LD children have problems with the additional skills required for adequate spelling. The ability to remember the sequential movement pattern of letters is one particular skill that many deficient spellers lack. These children often lack the ability to remember the kinesthetic "feel" of a word. The movements of the hand in writing certain words, for example, are totally forgotten by these children. The motor upsweep in writing the letter *t*, in contrast to writing the letter *c*, would be difficult for some children to describe.

Words may be recalled in a visual, auditory, or kinesthetic manner. Most people use all three methods at one time or another. The child with a spelling disability, however, is sometimes deficient in all three areas.

Written Expression

Many learning disabled children are unable to utilize the written form of language as an effective means of communication. Some are unable to transfer ideas to written communication, while others make grammar and syntax errors (Myklebust, 1965). The majority of children with written expression problems are referred for help after having been introduced to reading and spelling. Consequently, most written expression deficits are found predominately among young children beyond the second grade. It is not unusual for many of these children to be identified as late as secondary school because of the emphasis placed upon writing there.

Expression of Ideas

A major difficulty experienced by the child with written expression problems is the inability to organize thoughts into the proper form for written communication. Many children who can orally articulate their thoughts concisely are totally unable to communicate in a logical writing style.

Many researchers have suggested that there is a very strong relationship between oral language ability and experiences and the quality of written language. Some children are unable to express ideas in writing because they have had inadequate or limited experiential backgrounds. The child who has had many oral language experiences and opportunities to express, question, and respond to various ideas orally will probably be better equipped to communicate through writing. It should go without saying that the initial emphasis in the expression of ideas should be oral; the child should have abundant experiences about which to write.

Another group of LD children who are equally puzzling include those who have had extensive and appropriate input experiences but nevertheless are unable to communicate in writing. These children need positive and accepted writing experiences that emphasize specific concrete tasks. The quality of work required should be both minimal and very basic. Gradually, as the child increases in confidence, the structure and specificity may be reduced. The primary objective of the teacher should be one of developing children's confidence and satisfaction in their written expression. By accepting the first writings without question, a teacher helps build self-confidence.

Some children with written expression deficits are unable to categorize or classify ideas in the proper sequence. The written communication of these children is usually marked by gross disorganization. Units of thought are completely scrambled throughout paragraphs and even within sentences. These children should be required to reduce the amount of writing and to *gradually* build upon sequential ideas.

Many written expression deficits will not be quickly remediated, nor will some children ever learn to enjoy written communication. Disturbances of this type will be overcome only through an orderly remediation of sequential skill development.

Syntax and Grammar

Many children with written expression difficulties have trouble expressing their thoughts in the correct syntactical and grammatical order. This problem differs from the child who has limited ability to express himself in written language. The child with written syntax problems is able to express his thoughts in writing. However, numerous syntax and grammar errors totally distort his written output. Johnson and Myklebust (1967) consider some of the more frequent written syntax errors to be word omissions, distorted word order, incorrect verb and pronoun usage, incorrect word endings, and lack of punctuation. Many different syntax and grammar difficulties are illustrated in the example of one child's work in figure 7-4. Some words are out of order, other words are omitted, and no punctuation is used.

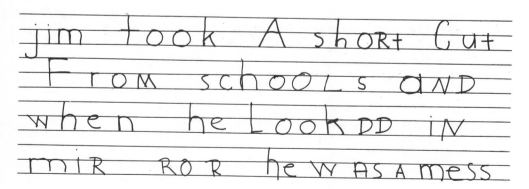

Figure 7-4
A Sample of an 8-Year-Old Child's Written Expression

The rules of grammar are also very confusing to many learning disabled children. The parts of speech, tenses, and the rules of usage are difficult to learn for the child with memory or conceptualization deficits. Various types of experiences are needed before many grammar principles can be internalized by the child. Cartwright (1969) cautions that it is not enough for a child to be able to recognize the correct statement of grammatical rules or to be able to pass a grammar test. The emphasis for the child with written language deficits must be on constant application, especially as it involves the abstractness of grammar and its related components.

Inadequate Vocabulary

The importance of vocabulary for adequate written expression is clearly outlined by Cartwright (1969). He states that "adequate written expression in any form, whether it is letter writing, a composition assignment, or an answer to an essay question, depends a great deal upon the variety of words known to the writer" (p. 99).

Some LD children have poor spoken and written language vocabularies because of the lack of various experiences (e.g., reading books, taking trips). Other children encounter difficulties in this area because of their impoverished oral language backgrounds. Children who are not given opportunities to listen to and use various oral language skills will probably have inadequate vocabularies. With all of these children it will be important to provide input experiences such as field trips and lively discussion periods. These activities will serve as stimulus to broaden vocabulary development and increase ideas for writing.

Mechanics of Writing

The remediation of written expression deficits usually emphasizes improvement in the written expression of ideas. Otto, McMenemy, and Smith (1973) suggest that considerably less attention should be given to the mechanics of writing (punctuation, capitalization, etc.). There is some evidence to suggest that too much emphasis on mechanics will interfere with the basic objectives of helping children improve their written expressions of ideas.

Nonetheless, many learning disabled children are unable to identify correctly or utilize commas, periods, or question marks. Punctuation symbols are often confused with each other or not used at all. The work of 10-year-old Donald in figure 7-5 serves as an illustration of these particular difficulties.

Some of the problems that these children have with punctuation seems due to the fact these marks are symbols, and many learning disabled children have symbolic disorders (Johnson & Myklebust, 1967). Other children encounter these difficulties because of inappro-

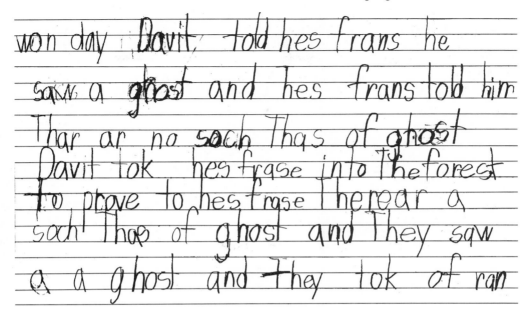

Figure 7-5
A Sample of a 10-Year-Old Boy's Written Expression

priate teaching methods which emphasize punctuation and capitalization rules rather than the practical function of these skills. Finally, excessive correction of the mechanical aspects of writing will probably be both discouraging and limiting to a child's improvement in the written expression of ideas.

WRITTEN LANGUAGE ASSESSMENT

Informal appraisal procedures are widely used in evaluating the written language skills of LD children and youth for a number of reasons. First, there are relatively few comprehensive standardized diagnostic batteries for assessing written language disorders. Chalfant and Scheffelin (1969), in reviewing the research, recommended the development of a diagnostic battery as one of the primary needs for working with disorders of written language. More importantly, Wallace and Larsen (1978) note that, at its most efficient level, the informal assessment should clearly outline the relevant skills which a student has or has not mastered, pinpoint patterns of errors, provide direction for systematic remedial instruction, and permit a nonsubjective measure to gain as the pupil moves from task to task.

An analysis of informal writing samples by Marlene's teacher indicates that there is very little consistency in Marlene's writing and spelling. She often omits the dots on *i*'s or crosses on the *t*. As mentioned, she frequently confuses manuscript and cursive writing.

An evaluation of Marlene's spelling skills also indicates her meager ability in this area. An example of her performance on an informal spelling test is shown below.

1. *laut* let		8. *unir* over
2. *live* live		9. *puyt* put
3. *mad* made		*taut* that
4. *meun* many		10. *teum* them
5. *ma* may		11. *teun* then
6. *now* new		12. *taue* they
7. *auu* now		13. *wllk* walk

The initial consonants for each of the fourteen words on this test were spelled correctly. Many final letters were also correct. Letters in the medial position were often incorrect. In addition, the formation of many cursive letters seemed to cause Marlene some difficulty. The *o*, *v*, and *w* were particularly troublesome.

Important Dates
1607 About 100 colonists founded Jamestown
1619 Virginia established the House of Burgesses
1620 The Pilgrims founded Plymouth Colony
1624 The Dutch established the settlement Netherlands

The Test of Written Spelling (Larsen & Hammill, 1976) was also administered to Marlene at chronological age 13-2 with the following results:

	predictable words	unpredictable words	total
Scores	18	4	22
Spelling Age	8-7	8-5	8-6
Spelling Quotient	65	63	64
Spelling Grade Equivalent	2.9	3.1	3.1

An informal analysis of this test indicated that Marlene was experiencing some of the same spelling difficulties noted by Marlene's teacher. Forming certain cursive letters continued to be a frustrating task for Marlene.

Among the variety of assessment procedures available for evaluating written language disturbances, Brueckner and Bond (1955) recommend the following:

1. Analysis of Written Work, Including Test Papers
   a. Legibility of handwriting
   b. Defects in letter forms, spacing, alignment, size
   c. Classification of errors in written work, letters or tests
   d. Range of vocabulary used
   e. Evidence of lack of knowledge of conventions or rules
2. Analysis of Oral Responses
   a. Comparison of errors in oral and written spelling
   b. Pronunciation of words spelled incorrectly
   c. Articulation and enunciation
   d. Slovenliness of speech
   e. Dialect and colloquial forms of speech
   f. Way of spelling words orally:
      1) Spells words as units
      2) Spells letter by letter
      3) Spells by graphs
      4) Spells by syllables
   g. Rhythmic patterns in oral spelling
   h. Blending ability
   i. Giving letters for sounds or sounds for letters
   j. Technique of word analysis used
   k. Quality and error made in oral reading
   l. Oral responses on tests or word analysis
   m. Analysis of pupil's comments as he states orally his thought process while studying new words
3. Interview with Pupil and Others
   a. Questioning pupil about methods of study
   b. Questioning pupil about spelling rules
   c. Questioning pupil about errors in convention
   d. Securing evidence as to attitude towards spelling
4. Questionnaire
   a. Applying checklist of methods of study
   b. Having pupil rank spelling according to interest
   c. Surveying use of written language
5. Free Observation in Course of Daily Work
   a. Securing evidence as to attitudes toward spelling
   b. Evidence of improvement in the study of new words
   c. Observing extent of use of dictionary
   d. Extent of error in regular written work
   e. Study habits and methods of work
   f. Social acceptability of the learner
   g. Evidences of emotional and social maladjustment
   h. Evidences of possible physical handicaps
6. Controlled Observation of Work on Set Tasks
   a. Looking up the meanings of given words in dictionary
   b. Giving pronunciation of words in dictionary

    c. Writing plural forms of derivations of given words
    d. Observing responses on informal tests
    e. Observing methods of studying selected words.[1]

Handwriting

Although the examination of several daily work writing samples serves as an excellent technique for focusing upon specific handwriting weaknesses, we usually recommend the use of a general *scale* to analyze a student's handwriting. The evaluation scales developed by Zaner-Bloser (1979) are among the most comprehensive and widely used scales currently available. The quality of a student's handwriting is determined by comparing the specimens to be evaluated with samples of established volume on grade level scales (Burns, 1974). The Zaner-Bloser Evaluation Scale provides five specimens of handwriting classified as *high, good, medium, fair,* and *poor* for each grade level. Samples for grade 2 are provided in figure 7-6 (p. 210).

    Additional suggestions for evaluating various aspects of handwriting, including letter formation, spacing, slant, line quality, letter size and alignment, and rate, are discussed in Burns (1974) and Wallace and Larsen (1978).

Spelling

Many assessment techniques are available for evaluating specific spelling difficulties. In general, the tests may be classified as either informal, teacher-made tests or published tests. We believe that the available informal techniques provide more usable instructional information regarding a student's specific spelling strengths and weaknesses then the available published spelling tests. A list of commonly used published tests is provided in table 7-6 (p. 211). These tests usually yield a general estimate of spelling ability. As mentioned, more in-depth diagnostic information is most often obtained from informal measures of spelling achievement.

    The Informal Spelling Inventory (ISI) is a widely used informal technique to determine a student's general spelling level and specific patterns of spelling errors. In this technique, the teacher selects a sample of words (usually 15-20) from each basal spelling book of a given spelling series. Words from each list are dictated to students until 6 words in a row are missed. A student's *achievement level* is determined by finding the highest level at which a score of 90% to 100% is obtained. The *teaching level* is the highest level at which a score of 75% to 89% is

1. From *The Diagnosis and Treatment of Learning Difficulties* by Leo J. Brueckner and Guy L. Bond,© 1955, pp. 369-370. Reprinted by permission of Prentice-Hall, Inc., Englewood Cliffs, New New Jersey.

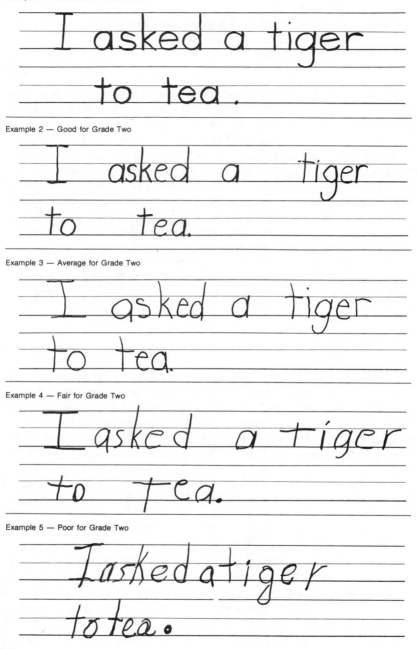

Example 1 — Excellent for Grade Two

Example 2 — Good for Grade Two

Example 3 — Average for Grade Two

Example 4 — Fair for Grade Two

Example 5 — Poor for Grade Two

Figure 7-6

Scale for Evaluating Manuscript Handwriting

From "Zaner-Bloser Evaluation Scale, Grade 2." Copyright 1979 by Zaner-Bloser. Reprinted by permission.

Table 7-6
Published Spelling Tests

test	content description	scores
Gates-Russell Spelling Diagnosis Test (Gates & Russell, 1940)	spelling words orally, word pronunciation, giving letters for sounds, spelling one syllable, spelling two syllables, word reversals, spelling attack, auditory discrimination, effectiveness of visual, auditory, kinesthetic, and combined areas of study	grade scores
Lincoln Diagnostic Spelling Test (Lincoln, 1955)	pronunciation, enunciation, and use of rules	percentile ranks
Test of Written Spelling (Larsen & Hammill, 1976)	dictated spelling lists of rule-governed words and spelling demons	spelling ages, grade equivalents, and spelling quotient

obtained. An analysis of errors also provides specific information concerning each student's spelling weaknesses.

The *cloze procedure* (discussed in chap. 6) is another informal technique which may be used to appraise specific spelling difficulties. Burns (1974) believes that the cloze procedure is particularly useful in the evaluation of a student's knowledge of spelling generalizations. For example, a student's performance on the following items would indicate his or her understanding of various homonyms:

1. The pla (n) (e) carried 200 passengers.
2. He carried the water in a pa(i) (l).
3. This is the third w(e) (e)k of the month.
4. Mother bought some new dresses at a clothing sa(l) (e).
5. The ma(i) (d) cleaned the room.
6. John was very w(e) (a)k during his illness.

The reading level of the sentence in the cloze procedure should be kept to a minimum in order to not penalize students with word analysis or comprehension difficulties. In addition, Wallace and Larsen (1978) suggest that if the word is not part of a student's oral language, it should not be used as a stimulus item on the cloze technique.

Written Expression

An analysis of several representative samples of a student's written work is probably the most effective and widely used procedure for appraising written expression. It is usually recommended that the following components be evaluated:

    a. *purpose*—main ideas unclear or missing, too broad, lacking in significance, or poorly stated.

    b. *content*—ideas unsupported, lack specifics, unrelated to the subject, or taken from another source.

    c. *organization*—introduction and conclusions poorly stated, ideas randomly presented, transition inappropriately used.

    d. *paragraphs*—paragraphs inadequately developed.

    e. *sentences*—sentences are fragmented, consist of dangling modifiers, lack variety, show problems with tense, subject-verb agreement, and pronoun-antecedent agreement.

    f. *word choice and usage*—vocabulary inappropriate, clichés, tone ineffective.

    g. *capitalization*—incorrectly used in titles, proper nouns, words for deity, etc.

    h. *punctuation*—italics, period, comma, exclamation point, quotes incorrectly used.

    i. *handwriting*—does not permit quick and easy reading in either manuscript or cursive style. (Wallace & Larsen, 1978, pp. 409-411)

Record keeping is absolutely essential for adequately evaluating each of the aforementioned written expression components. Burns (1974) points out that a review of the records will often reveal students encountering similar problems upon which succeeding language teaching could be based.

Among the few published tests of written language, the Picture Story Language Test (Myklebust, 1965) has been the only instrument widely used among LD students. This diagnostic instrument assesses the writing development of children ages 7 through 17. The child is presented with a picture about which he is asked to write a story. Scales are developed to measure length (productivity), correctness of expression (syntax), and content or meaning (abstract-concrete). Scores are determined for each of these areas and converted into age equivalents, percentiles, and stanines. Due to some question regarding the adequacy of the reliabilty and validity of this test (Anastasiow, 1972), it is usually recommended that it be used as an informal, observational scale of written language problems.

DEVELOPING WRITTEN LANGUAGE SKILLS

Handwriting

The goal of most remedial training in handwriting involves the correction of specific deficits. Consequently, the majority of remedial programs in this area have broken down the writing process into smaller steps and provided training exercises for each level. The procedures for training at various levels include *tracing* (Enstrom, 1966), *copying* (Birch & Lefford, 1967), *behavior modification* (Nichols, 1970), *typewriting* (Campbell, 1971), and other *kinesthetic methods*.

Tracing and Kinesthetic Methods

Bryant (1972) points out that since handwriting depends on the motor aspect of writing, a child cannot write until motor maturity has been attained. Consequently, many handwriting programs concentrate on motor patterns required for writing. Children are taught to draw designs in the air, trace geometric patterns, and trace sandpaper figures and letters. Templates and stencils are also used for kinesthetic and tactile stimulation.

Typewriting

The typewriter has been utilized for some LD children with severe handwriting disturbances; however, many children with handwriting problems do not have the eye-hand coordination or fine motor dexterity to learn typing. Other children find that typing reinforces both the visual image of words and their visual sequential memory. With some children, typing provides the only means of legible communication. We would caution the teacher to clearly consider the goals for teaching a child how to type. If typing is a long-range tool for the child's use in secondary school and college, we would advise teaching the skill correctly through use of a commercially available program, such as the one by Lloyd and Krevolin (1966).

Manuscript vs. Cursive Writing

A number of writers have pointed out persisting controversy over the type of writing that should be used with the LD child (Andersen, 1966; Johnson & Myklebust, 1967). Most American schools initiate writing instruction with manuscript. As mentioned earlier in this chapter, sometime around the end of second grade or beginning of third grade most children are taught cursive writing. Differences of opinion primarily involve whether to begin writing instruction with manuscript or cursive. Others question transferring to another writing style all together (Hildreth, 1963).

The study of Otto and Rarick (1969) suggests that the time of transition is of little consequence. The effect of four different transition times upon subsequent performance in handwriting, spelling, and reading was minimal. The *content* of the instructional program was more important than the time of transition.

Due to Marlene's serious language arts difficulties, her teacher implemented a program which integrated listening, speaking, reading, and writing. In order to build a background of experiences, opportunities were presented for viewing films, taking field trips, and listening to various speakers.

A visual-auditory-kinesthetic-tactile (VAKT) approach was implemented for spelling. Unknown words were copied and traced until each word could be written from memory. Known words were reviewed daily and used in experience stories which were written as part of the language arts approach. A linguistically based reading series was used as part of her reading instruction, and many of the words from these books were used as a part of the spelling program.

Marlene was encouraged to use manuscript writing until some of her other language arts skills improved. The programmed *Write and See* (Skinner, 1968) handwriting workbooks were also used with Marlene for a part of each school day.

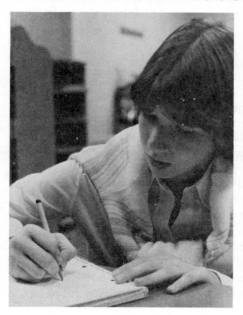

Marlene's progress is very slow. However, she expressed pleasure at the number of words which she had learned to spell and read since this approach was implemented. Marlene has also become more positive about school since some of her teachers permitted her to answer test questions orally and to use a tape recorder for reports.

Marlene has also attempted to complete various written language assignments which were required of other students in her class. These assignments are usually marked by many spelling and written expression errors. Nonetheless, Marlene is encouraged, and her positive attitude continues to help her overcome many of her difficulties.

The series of photographs on page 215

show Marlene using a VAKT approach in learning to spell an unknown word. The word was written correctly on paper by the teacher. Following the teacher's pronunciation of the word, time was allowed for Marlene to study the word. Marlene traced the word as many times as she thought was necessary in order to write the word from memory. The word was then written from memory and checked for accuracy. Marlene's teacher has found the VAKT technique to be an effective approach for remediating various spelling deficits.

Some who advocate teaching manuscript writing suggest that it is *less complex* as far as movements are concerned. Others argue that there is *less difficulty* in reading the printed page since all printed material is in manuscript type.

Those who advocate the use of cursive point out that there are *fewer spacing difficulties* with this form of writing because cursive letters are written as units. There are often *fewer reversal errors* with cursive writing because of its rhythmic flow. *Transference problems* are also eliminated when cursive writing is taught from the beginning of school.

Although many respected writers advocate the use of cursive writing with LD children (Strauss & Lehtinen, 1947), our experience suggests that it is generally advisable to utilize the same form of writing being used in the individual child's classroom. A child will be more confident if he is helped to succeed in the writing form used by his peers.

Commercial Programs

Many commercially available handwriting series are remarkably similar in format and approach (Chalfant & Scheffelin, 1969). Some programs which differ from the basic "look-trace-copy" method are briefly described here.

Handwriting with Write and See (Skinner, 1968). This program is designed to teach manuscript and cursive writing by use of specially prepared paper which turns a different color when a letter is incorrectly placed. The child progresses from the simple to the complex in a series of small steps. A fading technique is used to teach letter formation. The program allows for individual differences through self-pacing. Most importantly, the child is provided with instant feedback through the specially treated paper.

The program includes eight books. It is usually left to individual teachers to decide whether students should use books at grade level or proceed through the program at their own pace.

We feel that this is a highly successful program for LD children and youth. Handwriting becomes more interesting to the student, and each child learns to critically analyze his or her own handwriting with this program.

The Writing Road to Reading (Spalding & Spalding, 1962). This multisensory method teaches the elements of the English language by combining the teaching of speech, writing, spelling, and reading. Precise techniques for handwriting and accurate pronunciation are taught first in order to teach the 70 phonograms. Position and techniques for handwriting are introduced by the teacher, who gives general rules governing the letters. Letters are either *tall* or *short*. Manuscript letters involve only the six different strokes shown in figure 7.7. Manuscript letters are formed by using a clock, as shown in figure 7-8.

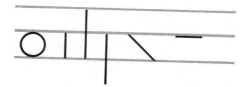

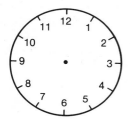

The Clock Face

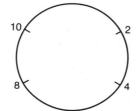

These are the four points
we use most often

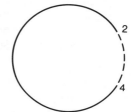

This shows how we use the
clock to write c (from 2 to 4)

Cursive writing is usually introduced in mid-second year when manuscript is perfected. Five connecting strokes are introduced as an adaptation of manuscript writing. The student is provided practice using these writing strokes at the chalkboard.

We have found the handwriting portion of this program to be highly successful with LD students. The structured sequence and the multisensory approach to teaching handwriting seem ideally suited to many children with written language problems.

Spelling

The remediation of spelling disabilities is often successful when the teacher uses an individualized approach. Isolation of the specific factors contributing to the problem will influence the type of remedial program which is finally selected. Brueckner and Bond (1955), however, outline a number of general principles to be followed in most remedial spelling cases.

1. A pretest should reveal to the pupil the words he does not know how to spell.
2. The pupil should focus his attention on the words or part of words he is unable to spell.
3. In presenting words, visualization should be the predominant procedure. Correct pronunciation and syllabication of words should be emphasized. The writing of the word in all cases should be included in word study.
4. Pupils should be encouraged to use any form or combination of types of imagery that will assist them to learn to spell, including visual, auditory, and kinesthetic imagery. It is very doubtful if there are dominant specific imagery types which can be the basis for deciding on methods of learning for all individuals.
5. Sensory impression should be accompanied by attempts to recall the spelling of words as an aid to temporary retention at the time of initial learning. Overlearning is also desirable.
6. Subsequently, distributed practice is necessary to insure retention of words learned, particularly in the case of slow learners. The amount and distribution of review needed will vary from learner to learner.
7. Tests by which the pupil can measure his progress are essential, since awareness of improvements is a valuable method of motivation. (p. 372)

Spelling and Linguistics

Typically, traditional spelling programs in American schools have selected irregular words or "frequency-of-use" words for spelling instruction. How frequently words were used in writing actually determined the core of spelling words for elementary school children.

Recently, research in the field of linguistics has indicated that English spelling is considerably more regular and consistent than previously assumed. The work of Hanna, Hanna, Hodges, and Rudorf (1966) is the primary research in this area. Computer technology was used in this work to predict the spelling of 17,000 commonly used words by using various rules. Of these words, approximately 50% were spelled without error, and 37% were spelled with only one error by the computer using the rules. These findings have had implications for traditional spelling programs. A number of writers, including the linguist Fries (1963), have argued that spelling words should be selected according to linguistic patterns (*an, man, fan, pan,* etc.). It is suggested by many linguists that the regularity of the English language can be ideally taught through the use of these various linguistic patterns.

The implications for children with spelling disabilities due to auditory discrimination problems, for example, should be apparent. These children should make greater progress in spelling when linguistic regularities and generalizations could be applied to spelling words. A number of studies (Hodges & Rudorf, 1966) seem to support this assumption.

Although the technique developed by Fernald (1943) has been largely utilized in remedial reading, the procedures have also been successful in ameliorating spelling disabilities. The Fernald approach is actually a multisensory technique which includes visual, auditory, kinesthetic, and tactile (VAKT) training. The following steps are recommended by Fernald for teaching spelling:

1. The word to be learned should be written on the blackboard or on paper by the teacher.
2. The teacher pronounces that word very clearly and distinctly. The children pronounce the word.
3. Time is allowed for each child to study the word.
4. When every child is sure of the word, the word is erased or covered and the child writes it from memory.
5. The paper should be turned over and the word written a second time.
6. Some arrangement should be made so that it is natural for the child to make frequent use, in his written expression, of the word he has learned.
7. Finally it is necessary that the child be allowed to get the correct form of the word at any time when he is doubtful of its spelling.
8. If spelling matches are desired, they should be written instead of oral. (pp. 199-201)

A number of commercial programs are available for teaching the child with spelling disabilities. These programs have usually been developed to teach spelling in sequential steps with specific objectives. The following programs are illustrative of remedial spelling programs.

A Spelling Workbook Series (Plunkett, 1960, 1961; Plunkett & Peck, 1960). This series includes four workbooks at the primary, intermediate, and secondary levels. The primary workbooks emphasize phonic elements of words in context. The intermediate workbook is aimed at children who have difficulty in the visual recall of words. The secondary-level workbook emphasizes rules and generalizations. All of the workbooks are intended to be corrective programs. Figure 7-9 shows a page from the primary workbook.

Spelling (Buchanan, 1967). This is a programmed basal course in spelling that employs a linguistic progression of sound-symbol associations. Words are taught as vocabulary items to minimize the need for reading skills. Although the series is planned for lesson presentations to an entire class, students may work independently, at their own pace, using a set of audio tapes that present the semantic and phonemic correlates for each grapheme.

$$\overline{e}$$

Here is a Magic Letter. We never hear it, but it tells the vowel before it to say its own name.
Read these words.

hat	-	hate	hid	-	hide
plan	-	plane	kit	-	kite
cap	-	cape	rip	-	ripe
mad	-	made	pin	-	pine
rob	-	robe	us	-	use
hop	-	hope	cut	-	cute
mop	-	mope	cub	-	cube
rod	-	rode	tub	-	tube

Copy these words.

lame _____	ate _____
tame _____	plane _____
take _____	grape _____
care _____	spade _____
bare _____	skate _____

Sentences for dictation.

Kip will <u>plan</u> a <u>plane</u> ride.
He will take his <u>cap</u> and <u>cape</u>.
Will he let <u>us</u> <u>use</u> his kite and rod?

Figure 7-9
Sample Page from A Spelling Workbook

From *A Spelling Workbook for Early Primary Corrective Work* by M.D. Plunkett and C.Z. Peck. Cambridge, Mass.: Educators Publishing Service, 1954. Copyright 1954 by Educators Publishing Service. Reprinted by permission.

The program is divided into eight levels, each represented by a 60-lesson workbook. The author suggests that students complete two workbooks per school year for the first four grades. Spelling lessons are given twice weekly in grade 1, and three times per week in grades 2-4.

The lesson format is identical for all levels. First, the teacher gives an oral chalkboard presentation of the second-symbol combinations or words for the day. Then the student completes the appropriate lesson pages in the workbook. It is suggested that each part of the lesson last approximately 30 minutes. The content for the entire program is listed in table 7-7.

Written Expression

Very little attention has been given to the systematic remediation of written expression deficits. Few commercial programs are available, and little has been written concerning remedial strategies for teaching written expression. Teachers often adapt traditional English and grammar programs for LD students. Some teachers combine instruction in reading, oral language, and spelling with activities in written expression. Objectives for developing the skill of writing ideas in meaningful and correct form can be included in experiential approaches.

Written expression is basically an extension of oral language development. The child who is deficient in oral language skills will first require help in this area. Writing skills can be gradually developed when an adequate oral language base is built.

Sufficient practice is essential to written language remediation. Otto, McMenemy, and Smith (1973) also caution that writing is basically a thinking process. Ideas must be clearly conceptualized in the mind of the writer to be clearly written and understood. Finally, it is important to reiterate a point made earlier in this chapter. Teachers should avoid

Table 7-7
Content for Spelling

level	grade	no. of words taught	no. of new sound -symbol relationships	grapheme/word characteristics
Introductory		8	a, m, n, o, c	
Book 1	1	168		consonants
Book 2	1		26, mastery in initial, medial, and final position; capital letters	short vowels; all but 4 consonants; one-syllable words with no more than 3 sounds or letters
Book 3	2	104	34; 2 long vowels, 7 digraphs, 25 consonant clusters	five-letter, one-syllable words
Book 4	2	103		
Book 5	3	121	32; blends and contractions	Six-letter, one-syllable words; read and define words before spelling them
Book 6	3	162		
Book 7	4	293	51; vowel digraphs, past tense, nasals	verb & syllabic 'es', 'er', 'ed' endings; two-syllable words
Book 8	4	397		
TOTAL:		1,348	148	

Compiled from *Spelling* by C. Buchanan. Palo Alto, Calif.: Behavioral Research Laboratories, 1967.

excessive correction of mechanical errors. Considerably more attention should be given to developing the written expression of ideas.

SUMMARY

In this chapter, we have discussed handwriting problems, spelling disabilities, and written expression difficulties. Various component problems in each of these three areas were described and illustrated. Informal assessment measures and published tests and scales for evaluating each of the written language deficits were concisely summarized. Instructional programs and a number of informal teaching techniques for developing skills in handwriting, spelling, and written expression were also outlined and discussed.

SUGGESTED ACTIVITIES

1. Compare a linguistically based speller with a frequency-of-use speller. Discuss the strengths and weaknesses of each approach for the LD student.
2. Locate a basal spelling series and construct an informal spelling inventory for grades 1-6. Administer the inventory to one child and analyze the student's spelling errors. Determine the achievement level and teaching level, as discussed in this chapter.
3. Obtain a story written by a child and evaluate the child's written expression according to the nine guidelines listed in this chapter.
4. Arrange to observe in a regular classroom in your local school district where children are learning cursive writing. Ask the teacher the instructional alternatives for children who encounter difficulty in learning this writing approach.
5. List some instructional activities that might be utilized with LD children and youth experiencing written expression problems.
6. Discuss your reactions to utilizing cursive writing with all LD students who experience handwriting difficulties.
7. Obtain a specimen copy of a published written language test discussed in this chapter. Review the test and arrange to observe the test being administered and scored by a trained examiner.
8. Discuss alternative instructional approaches for Marlene, the LD student discussed in this chapter. Be prepared to defend your choices based upon the available background information and assessment data.

References

Anastasiow, N. Review of the picture story language test. In O.K. Buros (Ed.), *Seventh mental measurement yearbook.* Highland Park, N.J.: Gryphon Press, 1972.

Andersen, D. Handwriting research: Movement and quality. In T.A. Horn (Ed.), *Research on handwriting and spelling.* Champaign, Ill.: National Council of Teachers of English, 1966.

Banas, N., & Wills, I.H. The vulnerable child and cursive writing. In J. Arena (Ed.), *Building handwriting skills in dyslexic children.* San Rafael, Calif.: Academic Therapy Publications, 1970.

Birch, H.G., & Lefford, A. Visual differentiation, intersensory integration, and voluntary motor control. *Monographs of Society for Research in Child Development,* 1967, *32* (2).

Brueckner, L.J., & Bond, G.L. *The diagnosis and treatment of learning difficulties.* New York: Appleton-Century-Crofts, 1955.

Bryant, N. Subject variables: Definition, incidence, characteristics, and correlates. In N.D. Bryant & C.E. Kass (Eds.), *Leadership training institute in learning disabilities* (Vol. 1). Washington, D.C.: United States Office of Education, Bureau of Education for the Handicapped, 1972.

Buchanan, C. *Spelling.* Palo Alto, Calif.: Behavioral Research Laboratories, 1967.

Burns, P.C. *Diagnostic teaching of the language arts.* Ikasca, Ill.: F.E. Peacock, 1974.

Campbell, D.D. *Typewriting compared with handwriting in teaching beginning reading to children with learning disorders.* Paper presented at Association for Children with Learning Disabilities International Conference, Chicago, March 1971.

Cartwright, G.P. Written expression and spelling. In R. M. Smith (Ed.), *Teacher diagnosis of educational difficulties.* Columbus, Ohio: Charles E. Merrill, 1969.

Chalfant, J.C., & Scheffelin, M.A. Central processing dysfunction in children: A review of research *(NINDS Monograph* No. 9). Bethesda, Md.: U.S. Department of Health, Education and Welfare, 1969.

Croutch, B. Handwriting and correct posture. In J.I. Arena (Ed.), *Building handwriting skills in dyslexic children.* San Rafael, Calif.: Academic Therapy Publications, 1970.

Durrell, D.D. Learning factors in beginning reading. In W.G. Cutts (Ed.), *Teaching young children to read* (Bulletin No. 19). Washington, D.C.: U.S. Department of Health, Education and Welfare, 1964.

Edgington, R. But he spelled it right this morning. In J.I. Arena (Ed.), *Building spelling skills in dyslexic children.* San Rafael, Calif.: Academic Therapy Publications, 1968.

Enstrom, A. Out of the classroom: Handwriting for the retarded. *Exceptional Children,* 1966, *32,* 385-388.

Fernald, G.M. *Remedial techniques in basic school subjects.* New York: McGraw-Hill, 1943.

Fries, C. *Linguistics and reading.* New York: Holt, Rinehart, & Winston, 1963.

Gates, A., & Russell, D. *Gates-Russell Spelling Diagnosis Test.* New York: Bureau of Publications, Teachers College, Columbia University, 1940.

Hanna, P.R., Hanna, J.S., Hodges, R.E. & Rudorf, E.H. *Phoneme-grapheme correspondences as cues to spelling improvement.* U.S. Department of Health, Education and Welfare. Washington, D.C.: U.S. Government Printing Office, 1966.

Hildreth, G. Simplified handwriting for today. *Journal of Educational Research,* 1963, *56,* 330-333.

Hodges, R.E., & Rudorf, H.E. Searching linguistics for cues for the teaching of spelling. In *Research on handwriting and spelling.* Champaign, Ill.: National Council for Teachers of English, 1966.

Hunt, B., Hadsell, A., Hannum, J., & Johnson, H.W. The elements of spelling ability. *Elementary School Journal,* 1963, *63,* 342-349.

Johnson, D.J., & Myklebust, H.R. *Learning disabilities: Educational principles and practices.* New York: Grune & Stratton, 1967.

Jordan, D.R. *Dyslexia in the classroom* (2nd ed.). Columbus, Ohio: Charles E. Merrill, 1977.

Kimmell, G.M. Handwriting readiness: Motor-coordinated practices. In J. Arena (Ed.), *Building handwriting skills in dyslexic children.* San Rafael, Calif.: Academic Therapy Publications, 1970.

Larsen, S.C., & Hammill, D.D. *Test of Written Spelling.* Austin, Tex.: Pro-Ed, 1976.

Lerner, J.W. *Children with learning disabilities* (2nd ed.). Boston: Houghton Mifflin, 1976.

Lewis, E.R., & Lewis, H.P. An analysis of errors in the formation of manuscript letters by first grade children. *American Educational Journal,* 1965, *2,* 25-35.

Lincoln, A.L. *Lincoln Diagnostic Spelling Test.* Princeton, N.J.: Educational Records Bureau, 1955.

Lloyd, A.C., & Krevolin, N. *You learn to type.* Manchester, Mo.: McGraw-Hill, 1966.

Myklebust, H.R. Picture Story Language Test: *The development and disorders of written language* (Vol. 1). New York: Grune & Stratton, 1965.

Nichols, S. Pupil motivation: A rewarding experience. *Maryland English Journal,* 1970, *8,* 3641.

Otto, W., McMenemy, R., & Smith, R. *Corrective and remedial teaching* (2nd ed.). Boston: Houghton Mifflin, 1973.

Otto, W., & Rarick, G.L. Effect of time of transition from manuscript to cursive writing upon subsequent performance in handwriting, reading and spelling. *Journal of Educational Research,* 1969, *62,* 211-216.

Plunkett, M. *A writing manual for teaching the left-handed.* Cambridge, Mass.: Educators Publishing Service, 1954.

Plunkett, M. *A spelling workbook for corrective drill for elementary grades.* Cambridge, Mass.: Educators Publishing Service, 1960.

Plunkett, M. *A spelling workbook emphasizing rules and generalizations for corrective drill.* Cambridge, Mass.: Educators Publishing Service, 1961.

Plunkett, M., & Peck, C. *A spelling workbook for early primary and corrective work.* Cambridge, Mass.: Educators Publishing Service, 1960.

Russell, D.H. *Characteristics of good and poor spellers.* New York: Bureau of Publications, Teachers College, Columbia University, 1937.

Skinner, B.F. *Handwriting with write and see.* Chicago: Lyons & Carnahan, 1968.

Spalding, R.B., & Spalding, W.T. *The writing road to reading.* New York: William Morrow, 1962.

Strauss, A., & Lehtinen, L. *Psychopathology and education of brain-injured children.* New York: Grune & Stratton, 1947.

Wallace, G., & Kauffman, J.M. *Teaching children with learning problems* (2nd ed.). Columbus, Ohio: Charles E. Merrill, 1978.

Wallace, G., & Larsen, S. *Educational assessment of learning problems: Testing for teaching.* Boston: Allyn & Bacon, 1978.

Zaner-Bloser. Evaluation Scale Grade 2. Columbus, Ohio: Zaner-Bloser, 1979.

Arithmetic Problems

PREVIEW

Although only minimal attention is given to arithmetic problems and remediation in the professional literature, large numbers of children and youth in our schools continue to experience failure in this area of the curriculum. Koppitz (1971) reported that 88% of the children referred to the LD program in her study were 1 to 3 years below the expected grade level in arithmetic computation. Similarly, Brenton and Gilmore (1976) pointed out that 52% of their LD population had educationally significant low scores in arithmetic.

In this chapter, we initially outline some of the reasons why we think arithmetic has been a neglected area of study. Possible causative factors and the association of arithmetic disabilities to other learning disabilities are also explored during the opening part of this chapter.

Our detailed discussion of the main types of arithmetic problems found among LD children and youth emphasizes the overlapping nature of arithmetic disabilities and the varying degrees of difficulty among each of these skill deficiencies.

The assessment section of this chapter outlines both informal and formal measures of arithmetic achievement. Basically, we believe it is important for the teacher to gather as much information as necessary to fully understand a student's arithmetic disabilities. The amount of data will obviously differ according to the specific difficulties encountered by each child.

Inappropriate or poor instruction is often mentioned as a major contributing cause of arithmetic disabilities; consequently, the instructional suggestions offered in this chapter are basic to the remediation of arithmetic problems. Finally, we believe the review of various arithmetic programs and materials at the end of this chapter offers the reader an introduction to the most appropriate remedial approaches for the LD student.

ARITHMETIC AND LEARNING DISABILITIES

Learning problems in arithmetic have not been as thoroughly studied and researched as other learning disabilities. Wallace and Larsen (1978) also note that the assessment and remediation of arithmetic problems have received very little attention in the professional literature. Otto, McMenemy, and Smith (1973) suggest that perhaps some of this neglect is due to the feeling among many teachers and parents that arithmetic is not as vital to academic success as are other areas of the curriculum.

Peggy Ann, 9 years old, has been in a self-contained LD class for the past two years. She is the second eldest of four children from a one-parent home. Peggy Ann is functioning at least two years below grade level in all academic areas, and she greatly lacks self-confidence. She is very concerned about obtaining the correct answer and will often ask "Is this right?" during various instructional activities.

Peggy Ann has a great deal of difficulty solving arithmetic problems of all types. She usually needs to use her fingers or other counters when adding, subtracting, or counting. She seems to understand the concept of place value, even though she often cannot correctly carry or borrow numbers. Peggy Ann does not know how to tell time nor count money, and the value of coins greater than a dime is a puzzle to her.

Peggy Ann's inability to tell time and know monetary values has become a source of great anxiety. She has begun to avoid many activities requiring skill in either area. Other children have also begun to taunt her when she requests assistance in telling time or in counting change. Math concepts known one day are often forgotten by Peggy Ann the following day. During these times, she will say "I know this," but still be unable to solve the particular arithmetic problem. She often becomes very frustrated during these instructional periods, and wild guesses are often given as answers to unknown problems. The inconsistency of Peggy Ann's performance is illustrated in the written responses she gave on the following worksheets:

34	21	73	18	66
+53	+36	+26	+11	+23
86	68	59	7	89

19	33	45	63	77
+17	+29	+26	+28	+18
2	52	27	81	89

The pervasive effects of a reading disorder or a language deficit have certainly received greater emphasis in the literature than the problems encountered by children with arithmetic disabilities.

Research in quantitative thinking has also lagged far behind empirical studies in other areas of the curriculum. Copeland (1970) points out that the work of Piaget on the thinking processes of children helped to set the stage for at least some research on how children learn mathematics. Nonetheless, there is still little known about faulty learning in mathematics, which seems to account for the lack of remedial textbooks and materials in mathematics.

Traditionally, the quantitative aspect of the elementary school curriculum was called *arithmetic*. Today, however, many schools label this part of the curriculum *mathematics* because of the influence of the so-called modern math programs. Lerner (1976) points out that the goal of the modern math program is to help the child develop an understanding of the basic structure of our number system rather than rote performance and rote learning of isolated skills and facts. The modern math emphasis is on teaching the *why*, as well as the *how*, of arithmetic. Nonetheless, the learning problems experienced by children exposed to modern math programs seem similar to the difficulties faced by individuals who have been taught by more traditional arithmetic programs (Lerner, 1976). The reasons for this are not entirely clear at this point due to the lack of research in this area; however, some possible explanations are now discussed.

Causative Factors

Difficulties in arithmetic, which have been also referred to as *dyscalculia* (Cohn, 1961), may be due to a number of reasons, some of which are briefly noted here.

Lack of Learning Readiness

Many children are unfortunately presented with concepts that are beyond their cognitive functioning. The lack of readiness for certain arithmetic skills has been seldom considered in arithmetic underachievement; however, children must exhibit some competency in a number of readiness skills before adequate achievement is demonstrated in other areas of the arithmetic curriculum. The ability to discriminate various sizes and shapes, for example, is certainly related to later numeral discrimination.

Poor Teaching

Inferior or inappropriate instruction is another factor that must be considered. The lack of sequential skill development and the use of inappropriate teaching materials for some children are prime examples of inadequate instruction. Many teachers, due to their lack of training, are not aware of the importance of sequential skills presentation. In addition, personalized programs of remediation for children with arithmetic problems are often overlooked. Insufficient training in teaching arithmetic skills seems obviously related to this particular problem.

Inappropriate Emphasis

The emphasis on rote learning of isolated skills and facts has proven to be disastrous for some learning disabled children. Newer math programs emphasizing the application and comprehension of various concepts and skills should prove to be more meaningful for many children with arithmetic deficits. Furthermore, the experiences with concrete materials that are offered in many modern math programs provide the LD youngster with an additional resource for understanding various arithmetic concepts.

Interest and Motivation

Because of previous failures, many children become very frustrated and discouraged when anything resembling arithmetic is presented to them. Learning disabled children who have rarely had any arithmetic success must be considered among this group. The attitude of the child is a very important consideration. Once a problem of this type is isolated, it is important to provide children with positive and successful arithmetic experiences. Otherwise, little success can be expected.

Age Differentiations

Children with arithmetic disabilities can be found at all age levels. Johnson and Myklebust (1976) report that case histories of these children often reveal many early nonverbal problems and that they rarely enjoy working with puzzles, blocks, or models at an early age. In the early primary grades, these are often the same children who have trouble in matching or sorting objects, understanding the language of arithmetic, or differentiating various sizes.

During elementary school, the child with arithmetic disabilities most often encounters difficulties with computational skills and related arithmetic processes. Although most problems in arithmetic are due to computational skill deficiencies (Otto, McMenemy, & Smith, 1973), arithmetic disabilities involve much more than computational difficulties (Bryant & Kass, 1972). Problems with measurements, decimals, fractions, and percentage, for example, need also to be considered during the elementary grades. Quantitative reasoning difficulty is an additional facet often identified during the elementary years.

The arithmetic difficulties noted among many secondary level young-sters are not necessarily different from the arithmetic deficits found among younger children. On the contrary, many children have problems in mathematics at this level because they have inadequate foundational skills basic to algebra and geometric principles. The arithmetic skill deficiencies of secondary LD students are very similar, for example, to the arithmetic deficits usually associated with elementary school chil-dren. The types of arithmetic disabilities discussed later in this chapter, consequently, must be considered in terms of the degree of severity, level of schooling, and age of the child.

Relationship to Other Disabilities

A number of writers have noted that many specific arithmetic deficits are related to other learning disabilities (Chalfant & Scheffelin, 1969; John-son & Myklebust, 1967; Kaliski, 1967). Various problems in memory, written language, spatial relationships, receptive language, left-right orientation, and reading should be thoroughly evaluated in terms of implications for arithmetic achievement and remediation.

Memory

Many important arithmetic skills are influenced by various memory disorders. The child who is unable to recall specific numbers or remember particular multiplication tables is certainly hindered in many arithmetic operations. Likewise, the child who cannot remember the shape of a 3 or 7 will encounter difficulties in recognizing these numerals. Johnson and Myklebust (1967) point out that rapid oral drills will be very frustrating for the child with auditory memory problems.

Written Language

Those children who have difficulties in learning to write letters and words will probably also have some difficulty in writing various num-bers. In addition, children with written language deficits will likely experience problems in aligning arithmetic examples correctly. Seat-work activities that require copying examples from a book or a chalk-board are devastating experiences for some children. Incorrect arith-metic answers are often due to the inaccurate alignment of numbers. The difficulty some children have in writing numbers is illustrated in figure 8-1.

Spatial Relationships

Bryant and Kass (1972) advise that spatial factors are a crucial part of arithmetic thinking. They point out that spatial orientation is essential to

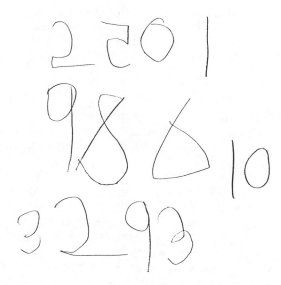

Figure 8-1
Numbers Written by a 7-Year-Old Boy

differentiating, for example, 9 from 6 and 21 from 12. Kaliski (1967) also emphasizes the importance of spatial relationships to arithmetic achievement by noting the difficulties that these children often encounter with such spatial relationships as *high-low, top-bottom,* and *beginning-end.*

Receptive Language

Although it has been suggested that many children with arithmetic disabilities have good spoken language ability, many LD children do have problems in understanding quantitative terms. The language of arithmetic often requires the child to attach additional meanings to words or terms that are already known. The terms *carry, empty set,* and *times* all convey quantitative meanings possibly different from the meanings for the words that were originally learned. In addition, Kaliski (1967) alerts the teacher of the learning disabled to be aware of the child who has great difficulty in using spoken language to express number concepts and processes.

Left-to-Right Orientation

Difficulty in left-right discrimination has been frequently mentioned as a detriment to arithmetic achievement. The following statement by Chalfant and Scheffelin (1969) summarizes the problems in this area.

While reading is conducted from left to right in the Western culture, addition, subtraction, and multiplication are calculated in the opposite direction, that is, from right to left. The fact that division is done from left to right only adds to the confusion. (p. 125)

Reading

Difficulties in the area of reading do not necessarily impede a child's progress in arithmetic; however, many specific reading skills are certainly related to quantitative processes. Deficits which cause a child to reverse, rotate, or invert letters will probably also affect numbers. Likewise, the visual discrimination problems which contribute to a child's inability to distinguish certain letters will certainly affect number recognition. Most importantly, the ability to read and analyze arithmetic story problems will be affected by various reading disorders. The reading disabled child will often be unable to solve arithmetic word problems because of word recognition difficulties. Reading comprehension problems can also contribute to the lack of reasoning ability evidenced by some children with arithmetic deficiencies.

TYPES OF ARITHMETIC PROBLEMS

Children with learning disabilities exhibit a number of different arithmetic deficits. The problems invariably overlap and appear with varying degrees of difficulty. Many of the following areas are troublesome for LD children.

Shape Discrimination

The ability to differentiate a circle from a square or a triangle is an example of a basic skill required for later success in many arithmetic processes. Some children are unable to perceive the differences among various shapes, and thus they may often incorrectly name them. Lerner (1976) cites the example of a square appearing as four unrelated lines to some children rather than as a connected square shape.

The discrimination of objects or shapes according to some common property is an ability that is often assumed in early quantitative work. A large part of the early curriculum in this area is based upon observations by the child. Workbooks and readiness programs for children at this level are filled with pages directing the child to place an X in all the squares or to count the circles on a particular page. Puzzles and pegboards requiring shape identification are also used extensively at this age level. Consequently, the child with shape discrimination difficulties will likely have had some early quantitative problems.

The young child's difficulties with shapes might also affect later recognition of specific numbers. Gross differentiations (e.g., distinguishing a 4 from a 2) prove difficult for some children, while other children incorrectly perceive finer discriminations (e.g., a 6 is confused with a 9).

Copying various shapes or numbers is a related area of difficulty for children with disturbances in visually recognizing shapes. We have previously discussed the written language difficulties that might affect various quantitative abilities. Difficulties in visual perception will also affect quantitative abilities. A child who cannot copy geometric shapes because of incorrect perception will have problems in performing various tasks.

Size Discrimination

Size relationships are very important in arithmetic concepts. If concrete-geometric concepts such as *big, small, long,* and *short,* and abstract numerical concepts such as *more* and *less* cannot be established, then the child might be unable to learn abstract number concepts (Kaliski, 1967). Any number of complex quantitative skills are based upon the ability to discriminate different sizes. Seriation of objects according to size is one particular skill required of many children in the early grades. Others include completing jigsaw puzzles, matching different size cubes to paper outlines, and fitting objects to certain holes or spaces. More advanced mathematical concepts such as estimating an area or perimeter also require some size discrimination.

Many children indicate problems in this area very early when they cannot identify the *biggest* box, the *longest* line, or the *smallest* circle. Other children with difficulties in discriminating sizes are unable to fit the correct size object into the right container or match a certain size block to a paper or space outline.

The ability to discriminate various sizes plays an important role in the child's later understanding that numbers also differ in size. The child who is unable to identify the *larger* circle might later be unable to identify the *larger* of two numbers. Similarly, choosing the group with *fewer* circles serves as a foundation for later work in understanding groups or sets.

Sets and Numbers

A set is a well-defined collection, or group, of objects. Peterson (1973) suggests that a collection of coins and a group of third graders are examples of a set. Everything that belongs to the set is an *element,* or member, of the set.

Sets have been used for many years to help children count. However, the language associated with this concept is new, and sometimes confusing, for the learning disabled child.

Many children are unable to understand the *concept* of a set. It is difficult for them to recognize, for example, the commonalities that distinguish a box of crayons, a bowl of apples, or a group of boys as three sets. Other LD children have problems in identifying certain sets. The classifying or grouping of objects into sets is still another problem experienced by some children.

The concept of number is actually basic to set theory since all equivalent sets share this concept. Many children are not able to discriminate among sets of varying size because the *number property* of sets is not understood. Many LD children, consequently, could not match the similar sets in figure 8-2 because they view set A as squares, set B as circles, set C as triangles, and set D as stars. The number property of each is completely misunderstood or overlooked.

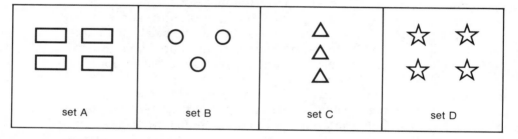

set A   set B   set C   set D

Figure 8-2

Naming the number property of a set (the last number or *cardinal* number) is also difficult for some learning disabled children. Counting problems, of course, complicate this difficulty. Associating three circles with the actual symbol 3 is another problem that certainly cannot be overlooked.

The terminology associated with set theory is particularly difficult for some children. *Equal sets, empty sets,* and *subsets* may be confusing terms that need to be illustrated in some detail before they are fully understood.

One-to-One Correspondence

Preschool and primary age children with potential learning problems often show some difficulty in understanding the concept of one-to-one relationships. This ability is considered crucial to the development of meaningful counting. Children with one-to-one correspondence problems do not understand that four cars, for example, would fill four vacant parking spaces. Neither would they understand the basic principle upon which the game of musical chairs is based. These children, of course, are often stymied by everyday classroom duties such as passing pencils, books, or papers to each child in a certain row or group.

The concept of number becomes confusing to the child with one-to-one correspondence difficulties because he is unable to attach numerical meaning to specific numbers. The numeral 5, for example, has no particular numerical meaning when compared with the numeral 3. The child with difficulties in this area often incorrectly counts any group of objects, such as the number of pegs in a design or the number of people in a picture. Assigning correct numbers to each object is very confusing to the young child with one-to-one correspondence difficulties.

Reisman (1978) suggests giving a child a basket of apples to count. If the child counts in either of the two ways shown in figure 8-3, he or she has not mastered the concept of one-to-one correspondence which Reisman believes is basic to any work with numbers.

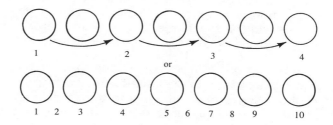

Figure 8-3

Counting

Counting is a fundamental quantitative skill by which the child determines the number of elements in a set. Bereiter and Engelmann (1966) suggest that counting is the first step in arithmetic training. Many children who are unable to count meaningfully are later hindered in the basic computational skills of addition and subtraction.

Children with counting difficulties often skip numbers when counting aloud (e.g., "1, 2, 3, 5, 6, 8, 9, 11"). Others learn to count correctly, but without the understanding that each number corresponds to a particular element in a set. They apparently do not grasp the concept that each number in the counting series is describing an element. Still others fail to comprehend that the final number refers to all the elements in the set. After counting *five* objects, this child will often incorrectly respond to the question, "How many did you count?"

The order of each element in a set is designated by an ordinal number (first, second, third, etc.). Children with difficulties in this area might be unable to tell the *fourth* chair in a row, *second* day of the week, or the *sixth* month of the year. This concept is somewhat more complicated than the cardinal system which names the number property of a set.

Some of the following extensions of counting listed by Bereiter (1968) also cause many LD children and youth extreme difficulty:

- counting perceptually dissimilar objects, such as pans or stones differing greatly in size, vases of differing shapes, or drawn figures differing in both size and shape.
- counting objects all visible at a glance but not touchable: trees or buildings at a distance, lights hanging from the ceiling, or panes on a window.
- counting objects one must move about to count: beds, doors, bookcases in a house, or benches in a park.
- counting the facets of a single object: sides of a cube, teeth in a gear, seams on a tire, corners on a stop sign, star, or a Christmas tree ornament.
- counting objects not simultaneously present: people who visited class, or animals seen on a nature walk.
- counting classes of objects: kinds of flowers in a garden, kinds of tropical fish in an aquarium, or brands of dog food in a grocery store.
- counting subclasses of objects: red beads in bead assortment, blue-eyed children in class, or hooved animals in a picture book. (pp. 15-16)

Counting difficulties may be due to a variety of problems. Johnson and Myklebust (1967) list one-to-one correspondence, maintaining the auditory series of numbers, and the association of a symbol with the quantity as three possible reasons. It should be noted that each of these possible causes requires the child to integrate a thought process with auditory and visual skills.

Auditory-Visual Association

Children with quantitative disabilities have been observed to have difficulty with associating the spoken word "six" with the written symbol 6 or even the written word *six*. These children have difficulties in relating what they see visually with what they know auditorially. Many times these children are unable to identify verbally the name of written numerals (e.g., 6, 3, 7, 4) which are presented to them or to write specific numbers from dictation. The problem for these children becomes one of associating the auditory and visual components of arithmetic.

The few opportunities that children have to associate spoken and written symbols certainly contribute to the intensity of this particular difficulty. For a large number of children, however, the problem involves a lack of understanding of the concept that spoken words ("six," "nine," etc.) also have written equivalents that might be represented as words (six, nine, etc.) or as symbols (6, 9, etc.). Some children additionally encounter problems with matching spoken or written symbols with a corresponding number of objects. Three crayons might be verbally identified as "two" and likewise written "2."

One of the major principles in our numeration system is positional patterns, or place value. Many children have trouble in attempting to understand that a value, based upon powers of ten, is assigned to each position in a numeral (e.g., 395). Further difficulty is often encountered by some children when they are taught that positional notation increases in value from *right* to *left*.

An understanding of the concept of place value is basic to many mathematical functions. Many learning disabled children do not grasp the idea that the same digit (e.g., 4) may denote different degrees of magnitude according to its place in the numeral (e.g., 47, 14, or 422). The child with a place value difficulty might not understand the reason that 47 is not just called a 4 and a 7. Nor would the child necessarily understand the significance involved in reversing 47 and 74, since place value is fundamental to this concept.

Successive progression in both addition and subtraction will also depend upon an understanding of place value. Some children are unable to complete arithmetic examples requiring *carrying* or *borrowing*. The child who adds 63 and 18, for example, and writes the answer as 711 is obviously not comprehending the concept of place value. Figure 8-4 is an example of 10-year-old Joan's work. Notice that Joan adds all digits, regardless of place value.

It is very difficult for some children to understand that our system of numbers makes it possible to convert a number unit to the next higher or smaller unit. The process of carrying and borrowing is, of course, based upon this important principle (Feingold, 1965). The sequential steps involved in regrouping numbers can also be very confusing. Consequently, a thorough understanding of place value is necessary for most

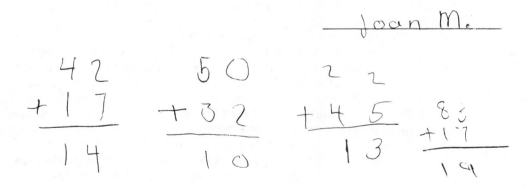

Figure 8-4
Example of Place Value Difficulty of a 10-Year-Old Girl

children to successfully complete these operations and other higher order mathematical processes, such as work with decimals.

Computational Skills

Some children have specific problems with the fundamental arithmetic processes of addition, subtraction, multiplication, and division. Many of these computational problems are due to difficulties with the foundation skills of one-to-one correspondence, counting, and set notation. Other computational deficits, however, may be due to particular problems encountered as the child progresses through each of these basic processes. Table 8-1 lists some of the most common computational errors and an analysis of each error. Reisman (1978) suggests that the table could also serve as an aid in appraising where a student is in need of reteaching.

The introduction of rote computational skills is certainly a major problem in this area. Many children cannot rely upon memory skills for various number combinations. Using tangible objects and practical situations is better for these children, in contrast to memorizing 30 to 50 different combinations.

The majority of computation problems exhibited by children with learning disabilities certainly seem related to the mode of presentation. The use of horizontal algorithms (e.g., $10 + 15 = \boxed{}$) instead of vertical algorithms $\left(\text{e.g., } \begin{array}{r} 10 \\ + \ 15 \end{array}\right)$ for example, will serve to be less confusing for some children with left-to-right difficulties. Furthermore, children usually better understand subtraction when it is introduced as the inverse operation of addition, multiplication as an extension of addition, and division as the inverse operation of multiplication, rather than when each of these operations is introduced as a totally new arithmetic process.

The interrelatedness of most quantitative skills is usually very apparent as children progress in arithmetic. The difficulties with regrouping are usually related to problems in understanding place value, just as division difficulties are often correlated with multiplication misunderstandings. The dependency of one skill upon another must be constantly demonstrated to the learning disabled child. Otherwise, unnecessary deficits will develop. Spencer and Smith (1969) suggest that some arithmetic skill deficiencies are caused by not mastering certain prerequisite skills. Consequently, all children with learning disabilities must be given ample opportunity to practice the application of specific arithmetic activities before being exposed to new skills and concepts.

Finally, the abstractness of adding, subtracting, multiplying, or dividing different numbers *requires* that most children with learning disabilities have a great deal of experience with concrete and manipulative materials. The use of tape recorders, number lines, and other ancillary aids may reinforce the understanding of certain concepts and skills.

Measurement

Measurement is an important area of mathematics, the most widely used area of applied mathematics in the elementary school curriculum (Virginia State Department of Education, 1970). The understanding of measurement certainly affects achievement in a wide variety of quantitative skills.

The process of measuring incorporates many of the concepts and ideas that we have previously discussed in this chapter. The idea that some objects are *taller, shorter, larger,* or *smaller* than other objects is one of the very first principles of measurement that might prove confusing to some children. The use of number lines and rulers, which involve principles of measurement, is an additional area of difficulty for many LD children.

As children progress in mathematical programs, they are introduced to different types of measurement, including liquid (teaspoon, cup, pint, etc.), time (day, month, year, etc.), length (inch, foot, yard, etc.), and metric. For many children, problems in this area seem to be related to the specific type of measurement. Some have difficulty in the actual measurement process (e.g., figuring the 3-inch mark on the ruler or measuring out a cup of milk), while others encounter difficulties *differentiating* a month from a year, decade, or century.

The introduction of perimeters, volume, and bar and circle graphs into intermediate-grade and secondary-level mathematics programs has added to the confusion for many children at these levels. Understanding the concept of volume is in itself a problem for some children. Others, however, encounter difficulty with more advanced skills, such as determining the value of a specific space.

Monetary Values

It is extremely difficult for some children to learn various coin and bill denominations. The actual *names* of the different denominations are often very confusing. Coins are consistently confused with other coins. Some learning disabled children, in addition, find it difficult to learn the different combinations of coins. Five pennies might sometimes equal a dime, for example, or two nickels might equal a quarter. Making change is very difficult for the child with this specific disability. In addition, the child with computational difficulties is also hindered when it comes to *adding* or *subtracting* various combinations of coins. The child who finds monetary values confusing will likely avoid situations involving

Table 8-1
Common Arithmetic Errors

Analysis	*Example*

1. Lacks mastery of basic addition facts.

$$\begin{array}{r} 3\;2 \\ +4\;3 \\ \hline 7\;4 \end{array}$$

2. Lacks mastery of basic subtraction facts.

$$\begin{array}{r} 3\;8 \\ -2\;5 \\ \hline 1\;2 \end{array}$$

3. Lacks mastery of basic multiplication facts.

$$\begin{array}{r} 3\;2 \\ \times\;\;3 \\ \hline 86 \end{array}$$

4. Lacks mastery of basic division facts.

$$35 \div 5 = 6$$

$$\begin{array}{r} 6\;\;\;\; \\ 9\overline{\smash)\;56} \\ -56 \\ \hline 0 \end{array}$$

5. Subtracts incorrectly within the division algorithm.

$$\begin{array}{r} 3)\;\;73\text{ rem }1 \\ 70) \\ 3\overline{\smash)230} \\ -21 \\ \hline 10 \leftarrow \\ -9 \\ \hline 1 \end{array}$$

6. Error in addition of partial product.

$$\begin{array}{r} 432 \\ \times 57 \\ \hline 3\;0\;24 \\ 21\;6\;0 \\ \hline 24\;0\;24 \end{array}$$

7. Does not complete addition:
   a. Does not write renamed number.

$$\begin{array}{r} 85 \\ +43 \\ \hline 28 \end{array}$$

   b. Leaves out numbers in column addition.

$$\begin{array}{r} 4 \\ 8 \\ 2 \leftarrow \\ +3 \\ \hline 15 \end{array}$$

8. Rewrites a numeral without computing.

$$
\begin{array}{r}
72 \\
+15 \\
\hline
\longrightarrow 77 \\
\longrightarrow 32 \\
\times \quad 3 \\
\hline
\longrightarrow 36
\end{array}
$$

9. Does not complete subtraction.

$$
\begin{array}{r}
582 \\
-\ 35 \\
\hline
47
\end{array}
$$

10. Does not complete division because of incompleted subtraction.

$$
\begin{array}{r}
1)\ \ 41 \\
40) \\
7\overline{)3\ 9\ 7} \\
-2\ 8\ 0 \\
\hline
7 \\
7 \\
\hline
\end{array}
$$

11. Fails to complete division; stops at first partial quotient.

$$
\begin{array}{r}
50 \\
7\overline{)\ 370} \\
350
\end{array}
$$

12. Fails to complete division; leaves remainder equal to or greater than divisor.

$$
\begin{array}{r}
80 \text{ rem } 9 \\
9\overline{)\ 729} \\
720 \\
\hline
9
\end{array}
$$

13. Does not complete multiplication within division algorithm.

$$
\begin{array}{r}
1)\ 201 \text{ rem } 3 \\
200) \\
3\overline{)\ 603} \\
600 \\
\hline
3
\end{array}
$$

14. Does not add by bridging endings—should think $5 + 9 = 14$, so $35 + 9 = 44$.

$$
\begin{array}{r}
35 \\
+9 \\
\hline
33
\end{array}
$$

15. Lacks additive identity concept in addition.

$$
\begin{array}{r}
35 \\
+20 \\
\hline
50
\end{array}
$$

Table 8-1 (*cont.*)

16. Confuses multiplicative identity within addition operation.

$$
\begin{array}{r}
71 \\
+13 \\
\hline
73
\end{array}
$$

17. Lacks additive identity concept in subtraction.

$$
\begin{array}{r}
43 \\
-20 \\
\hline
20
\end{array}
$$

18. Confuses role of zero in subtraction with role of zero in multiplication.

$$
\begin{array}{r}
37 \\
-20 \\
\hline
10
\end{array}
$$

19. Subtracts top digit from bottom digit whenever regrouping is involved with zero in minuend.

$$
\begin{array}{r}
30 \\
-18 \\
\hline
28
\end{array}
$$

20. Confuses role of zero in multiplication with multiplicative identity.

$$7 \times 0 = 7$$

21. Confuses place value of quotient by adding extra zero.

$$
\begin{array}{r}
20 \\
30\overline{)\,60}
\end{array}
$$

22. Omits zero in quotient.

$$
\begin{array}{r}
30 \text{ rem } 3 \\
4\overline{)\,1203} \\
1200 \\
\hline
3
\end{array}
$$

23. Lacks facility with addition algorithm:
    a. Adds units to units *and* tens;

$$
\begin{array}{r}
37 \\
+\ \ 2 \\
\hline
59
\end{array}
$$

    b. Adds tens to tens *and* hundreds;

$$
\begin{array}{r}
342 \\
+\ 36 \\
\hline
678
\end{array}
$$

    c. Adds units to tens *and* hundreds;

$$
\begin{array}{r}
132 \\
+\ \ 6 \\
\hline
798
\end{array}
$$

d. Is unable to add horizontally: $345 + 7 + 13 = 185$

Thinks: $3 + 7 + 1 = 11$; writes 1
$4 + 3 \qquad = 7 (+ 1 \text{ carried})$ 　　　　8
$5 \qquad\ \ = 5$ 　　　　　　　　　　　5
　　　　　　　　　　　　　　　　　　───
　　　　　　　　　　　　　　　　　185

May add zero to make sum
greater than largest addend: 1850.

24. Does not regroup units to tens.

$$\begin{array}{r} 37 \\ +\ 25 \\ \hline 52 \end{array}$$

25. Does not regroup tens to hundreds
(or hundreds to thousands).

$$\begin{array}{r} 973 \\ +862 \\ \hline 735 \end{array}$$

26. Regroups when unnecessary.

$$\begin{array}{r} 43 \\ +\ 24 \\ \hline 77 \end{array}$$

27. Writes regrouped tens digit in
units place, carries units digit
(writes the 1 and carries the 2
from "12").

$$\begin{array}{r} ② \\ 35 \\ +\ \ 7 \\ \hline 51 \end{array}$$

28. When there are fewer digits in
subtrahend:
a. subtracts units from units *and*
from tens (*and* hundreds);

$$\begin{array}{r} 783 \\ -2 \\ \hline 561 \end{array}$$

b. subtracts tens from tens *and*
hundreds.

$$\begin{array}{r} 783 \\ -\ 23 \\ \hline 560 \end{array}$$

29. Does not rename tens digit after
regrouping.

$$\begin{array}{r} 54 \\ -\ \ 9 \\ \hline 55 \end{array}$$

30. Does not rename hundreds digit
after regrouping.

$$\begin{array}{r} 532 \\ -181 \\ \hline 451 \end{array}$$

31. Does not rename hundreds or tens
when renaming units.

$$\begin{array}{r} 906 \\ -238 \\ \hline 778 \end{array}$$

Table 8-1 (*cont.*)

32. Does not rename tens when zero is in tens place, although hundreds are renamed.

$$\begin{array}{r} 803 \\ -478 \\ \hline 335 \end{array}$$

33. When there are two zeroes in minuend, renames hundreds twice but does not rename tens.

$$\begin{array}{r} 5 \\ \cancel{6}_{\,1\,1} \\ \cancel{7}00 \\ -326 \\ \hline 284 \end{array}$$

34. Decreases hundreds digit by one when unnecessary.

$$\begin{array}{r} 3\backslash 7\ 1 \\ -1\ |3\ 4 \\ \hline 1/3\ 7 \end{array}$$

35. Uses units place factor as addend.

$$\begin{array}{r} 32 \\ \times\ \ 4 \\ \hline 126 \end{array}$$

36. Adds regrouped number to tens but does not multiply.

$$\begin{array}{r} 35 \\ \times\ \ 7 \\ \hline 65* \end{array}$$

$$* \ 7 \times\ 5 = 35; \\ 30 + 30 = 60$$

37. Multiplies digits within one factor.

$$\begin{array}{r} 31 \\ \times\ \ 4 \\ \hline 34* \end{array}$$

$$* \ 4 \times\ 1 = \ 4; \\ 1 \times 30 = 30$$

38. Multiplies by only one number.

$$\begin{array}{r} 457 \\ \times\ 12 \\ \hline 914 \end{array}$$

39. "Carries" wrong number.

$$\begin{array}{r} 8 \\ 67 \\ \times\ 40 \\ \hline 3220 \end{array}$$

40. Does not multiply units times tens.

$$\begin{array}{r} 32 \\ \times\ 24 \\ \hline 648 \end{array}$$

41. Reverses divisor with dividend.

$$6\overline{)\,30}$$ with answer 2 *

    *   Thinks 6 ÷ 3 instead of 30 ÷ 6

42. Does not regroup; treats each
column as separate addition example.

$$\begin{array}{r} 23 \\ +\;\;8 \\ \hline 211 \end{array}$$

43. Subtracts smaller digit from
larger at all times to avoid
renaming.

$$\begin{array}{r} 273 \\ -639 \\ \hline 446 \end{array}$$

44. Does not add regrouped number.

$$\begin{array}{r} 37 \\ \times\;\;7 \\ \hline 219 \end{array}$$

45. Confuses place value in division:

    a. Considers thousands divided by
units as hundreds divided by units;

$$\begin{array}{r} 1) \\ 200)\;\;201 \\ 3\overline{)6003} \\ 6000 \\ \hline 3 \\ 3 \\ \hline \end{array}$$

    b. records partial quotient as tens
instead of units;

$$\begin{array}{r} 50) \\ 100)\;\;150 \\ 7\overline{)735} \\ -700 \\ \hline 35 \\ 35 \\ \hline \end{array}$$

    c. omits zero needed to show no
units in quotient.

$$\begin{array}{r} 2 \text{ rem } 1 \\ 3\overline{)61} \\ 6 \\ \hline 1 \end{array}$$

46. Ignores remainder because:
    a. does not complete subtraction;
    b. does not *see* need for further
       computation;
    c. does not know what to do with "2"
       if subtraction occurs, so does
       not compute further.

$$\begin{array}{r} 80 \\ 7\overline{)562} \\ 560 \\ \hline \end{array}$$

money. Collecting milk money for the teacher or going to the store for his or her parents might be frustrating and somewhat anxiety producing for this child.

Telling Time

Learning to tell time is one of the most difficult quantitative skills for some children. It is not unusual to see many adolescent LD children still struggling with this skill. Poor sequence of time coupled with the complexity of the clock's number system are mentioned by Peterson (1973) as possible contributing factors to poor time-telling skills.

A problem as basic as differentiating the hour hand from the minute hand limits growth in this area. Number identification difficulties also complicate the child's ability to distinguish different times (e.g., six o'clock from nine o'clock). In addition, the child who cannot count will probably have some difficulty in telling time because he will be unable to "count" the time from one hour to the next. The difference among various clocks, as noted in figure 8-5, is also very confusing to many LD children.

Additional confusion in learning to tell time will arise once some children are presented with half-hours, quarter-hours, and before and after the hour. The varying terminology for expressing 7:15—"fifteen after seven," "quarter after seven," for example—can be very confusing.

Finally, Peterson (1973) notes that it is not easy for some children to understand that the 24 hours in a day are indicated on the clock as two

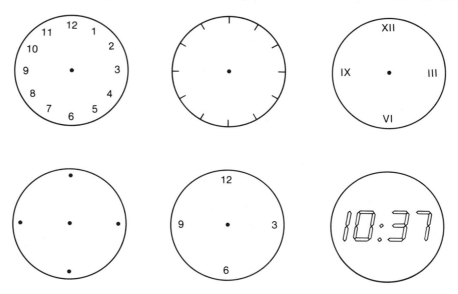

Figure 8-5

sets of 12. The fact that six o'clock occurs twice each day might consequently be very puzzling to some LD children.

Difficulty in understanding such quantitative concepts as *more* and *less*, *before* and *after*, or *big* and *little* is often an early indicator of later mathematical disabilities. Primary age children who show some difficulty in responding when asked what number comes *before* 3 might not understand the meaning of before. Similar difficulties are often encountered with other quantitative terms such as *fewer, small, large, more than, as many as,* and *fewer than.* Some commonly used quantitative terms are listed in table 8-2.

Some children have trouble with quantitative terms because of a receptive language difficulty. However, a large number of other learning disabled children do not understand the *quantitative* meaning of *less.* One obviously important consideration for the teacher of the LD child is

Table 8-2

Common Quantitative Terms

add	graph
algorithm	greater than
angle	increase
area	less than
associate property	measure
average	minus
cardinal number	multiply
circle	number
circumference	numerator
commutative property	one-to-one correspondence
counting	ordinal number
decimal	parallel
degree	percent
denominator	place value
diameter	plus
digit	product
distributive property	rectangle
divide	remainder
dividend	same as
divisor	set
equal	solution
equation	subtract
error	symbol
estimate	triangle
fraction	zero

to distinguish the more generalized receptive language deficits affecting mathematical achievement from the more specific deficit of understanding certain quantitative terms.

Operational signs are an additional quantitative language consideration causing confusion for some children. Johnson and Myklebust (1967) point out that a child is helpless in solving a problem unless he perceives the process sign and knows its meaning. Some children cannot differentiate a + from a ÷ ; others find it difficult to perceive particular symbols as a whole. The equal sign might be perceived by some children as two separate subtraction signs. The child with these difficulties is unable to solve very basic (e.g., 2 + 1 = 1 ☐) mathematical problems.

The introduction of modern math programs in many elementary schools has made necessary the use of some new symbols and vocabulary; however, a number of "older" words, such as *multiplier* and *borrowing,* have been deleted from many commercial math programs. Consequently, the overall increase in the total number of technical words and symbols is actually minimal (Virginia State Department of Education, 1970).

Terminology difficulties and problems in understanding operational signs are two of the quantitative language disabilities encountered by LD children. These specific difficulties also contribute to many of the other difficulties discussed under the types of arithmetic problems (e.g., measurement, problem-solving skills). Quantitative language disabilities seem to affect mathematical achievement at all levels, from preschool through secondary levels, more than most other specific disabilities discussed in this chapter.

Problem Solving

Some children with arithmetic disabilities encounter great difficulty solving word problems. The child with reading difficulties may be unable to read the word problem and consequently operationalize the number skills in the problem. In contrast to the reading disabled student handicapped in arithmetic, another group of children seem to experience problems in word problems due to the lack of analysis and reasoning skills. Chalfant and Scheffelin (1969) suggest that older children usually have the advantage of a more highly developed language system to rely upon in solving word problems. Large numbers of the learning disabled, however, are deficient in basic language skills. The abstractness of word problems and the lack of manipulative, concrete objects to use to solve these problems hinder the child with reasoning and analysis difficulties.

Determining what particular arithmetic process to use is a difficult part of solving word problems. The decision of whether to add or subtract is often a confusing puzzle. The sequence of steps utilized in solving story problems is also difficult for some children to both remember and apply. Trial and error is usually the method used because the child has no systematic or analytic approach to solving problems. The child may take two or three times longer to solve a problem because he or she uses a variety of incorrect operations before obtaining the correct answer.

Finally, too often word problems are set apart from practical and realistic applications, causing many children to be unnecessarily confused. Story problems should emphasize practical problems which make mathematical sense. Otherwise, we must question their use with any child.

ARITHMETIC ASSESSMENT

Informal Techniques

Many specific arithmetic deficits may be identified and analyzed by using a variety of informal assessment approaches. Spencer and Smith (1969) suggest that the following three procedures are ideally suited to informal arithmetic appraisal: examination of written assignments, oral questioning, and chalkboard work.

Written seatwork assignments actually serve as a series of informal tests. Ashlock (1976) has suggested that written work in arithmetic must not only be scored, it must be analyzed as well. An analysis of a student's performance following the completion of a written assignment will usually pinpoint specific difficulties the student is encountering with particular arithmetic concepts. A pattern of errors will often emerge after various written assignments are closely examined. Moran (1978) points out that arithmetic error patterns can occur in at least three major ways, singly or in combination:

a. *inadequate facts:* using a correct operation and a sound strategy, the student applies inaccurate addition, subtraction, or multiplication facts. This is probably the most frequent type of error.
b. *incorrect operation:* using accurate facts, the learner subtracts rather than adding or divides instead of multiplying.
c. *ineffective strategy:* using the proper operation and accurate facts, the learner applies steps out of sequence, skips steps, or applies a tactic which does not always result in a correct outcome. Errors in this category are considered more serious because they arise from misunderstanding of a misapplication of algorithms. (pp. 58-59)

Another component of informal arithmetic diagnosis involves asking the child to describe aloud the various procedures involved in solving a particular arithmetic operation (e.g., division of whole numbers). Interviews with children often reveal misunderstandings of basic arithmetic concepts or procedures. The teacher might ask the child to describe the

Peggy Ann has been administered a number of formal and informal arithmetic tests over the past few years. During the last academic year, the *Key Math Test* (Connally, Nachtman, & Pritchett, 1971) was administered to Peggy Ann with the following selected results:

subtest	grade equivalent
Numeration	3.4
Fractions	2.4
Geometry and Symbols	2.1
Addition	2.5
Subtraction	2.1
Mental Computation	2.9
Numerical Reasoning	4.4
Word Problems	1.3
Missing Elements	3.1
Money	2.5
Measurement	1.7
Time	1.7

A good deal of discrepancy is indicated by the scores on this particular test. Performance on numerical reasoning, numeration, and missing elements indicates that Peggy Ann has some understanding of mathematical reasoning. However, the depressed

scores on the various computational skills — word problems, measurement, and time — indicate difficulties in solving problems and in using scales of measurement.

Informal observations and seatwork activities also suggest that Peggy Ann leaves out basic steps in various addition and subtraction examples. Sometimes she does not regroup numbers when necessary, and other times she unnecessarily regroups certain numbers. In addition, Peggy Ann has some difficulty in keeping numbers in the correct columns. In the following subtraction problems, Peggy Ann again demonstrates the inconsistency of her errors. She correctly subtracts the first column in each of the first two examples, but then becomes confused in regrouping the tens column. Her confusion regarding regrouping is aptly illustrated in the third problem.

Examples of Peggy's work:

$$
\begin{array}{r}
5 \\
\cancel{7}5 \\
-28 \\
\hline
37
\end{array}
\qquad
\begin{array}{r}
4 \\
3\cancel{5} \\
-24 \\
\hline
10
\end{array}
$$

$$
\begin{array}{r}
4 \\
\cancel{6}8 \\
-39 \\
\hline
19
\end{array}
$$

steps in a specific problem where the child had some difficulty. Chalfant and Scheffelin (1969) suggest that the examiner should carefully analyze the various processes utilized by the child at this stage. Hammill and Bartel (1978) suggest the following guidelines for conducting an oral interview:

a. *Select one problem at a time.* The selected problem should be sequentially prior to others in a task analysis. For example, an addition problem should be cleared up prior to a multiplication difficulty.

b. *Begin with the easiest problem first.* This will give the student a sense of confidence.

c. *Tape or keep a written record of the interview.*

d. *The child simultaneously solves the problem in written form and "explains" what he is doing orally.*

e. *The child must be left free to solve the problem in his own way without a hint that he is doing something wrong.*

f. *Avoid hurrying the pupil.* The interview may last from 15 to 45 minutes. (pp. 118-119)

The use of the chalkboard as an informal assessment tool has the added advantage of allowing the teacher to survey a number of children simultaneously (Spencer & Smith, 1969). The teacher may also witness where the breakdown occurs in particular arithmetic operations.

It is very important for the teacher to record his or her observations during all of these informal techniques. The written record serves as a guide to further evaluations and programs of remediation.

Classroom observation is one of two components of informal diagnostic techniques. The other is informal testing. Many specific arithmetic deficits may be isolated through the use of well-constructed informal tests. Tests may be developed for any group of general skills or for very specific processes (e.g., multiplication of fractions). Examples of both types of informal tests are illustrated in figures 8-6 and 8-7.

Additional guidelines for constructing informal arithmetic tests are provided by Wallace and Kauffman (1978), Wallace and Larsen (1978), and Moran (1978).

Published Tests

A number of formal published tests are also available to appraise a student's specific skill strengths and weaknesses in arithmetic. One important aspect that should be considered in selecting such a test is the number of arithmetic subskills evaluated. Those tests which provide a profile of skills will be helpful in planning programs of remediation. Two types of published arithmetic tests—standardized achievement and diagnostic—will now be discussed.

Skill to be assessed	Examples of problems				
Number facts up to 10	8 − 5	9 − 2	7 − 4	8 − 6	6 − 4
Number facts above 10	11 − 8	17 − 9	17 − 8	13 − 7	12 − 4
No borrowing	38 − 5	79 − 8	57 − 3	68 − 8	95 − 3
With borrowing	40 − 7	63 − 9	56 − 7	70 − 4	21 − 6
Two numbers no borrowing	57 −37	68 −45	87 −24	88 −30	59 −36
Two numbers with borrowing	51 −18	72 −38	81 −29	73 −24	46 −28

Figure 8-6
Informal Subtraction Test

From "Arithmetic Skills" by E. F. Spencer and R. M. Smith. In R. M. Smith (Ed.), *Teacher Diagnosis of Educational Difficulties*. Columbus, Ohio: Charles E. Merrill, 1969. Copyright 1969 by Bell & Howell. Reprinted by permission.

Standardized Achievement Tests

Most published achievement tests consist of sections dealing with specific areas such as reading, arithmetic, and so forth. Intensive, in-depth assessment of arithmetic skills is not the purpose of these tests. They are intended to provide an overall measure of arithmetic achievement. Usually, a general instructional level is provided, along with class strengths and weaknesses in certain areas and skills. Some of the more commonly used achievement tests with arithmetic sections are listed in table 8-3.

Diagnostic Arithmetic Tests

The range of arithmetic skills assessed in diagnostic tests is broader and more specific than in achievement tests (Wallace & Larsen, 1978). Although most diagnostic arithmetic tests are individually administered, they do not require the formal administration training usually required of diagnostic reading tests (Smith, 1974). Generally, diagnostic arithmetic

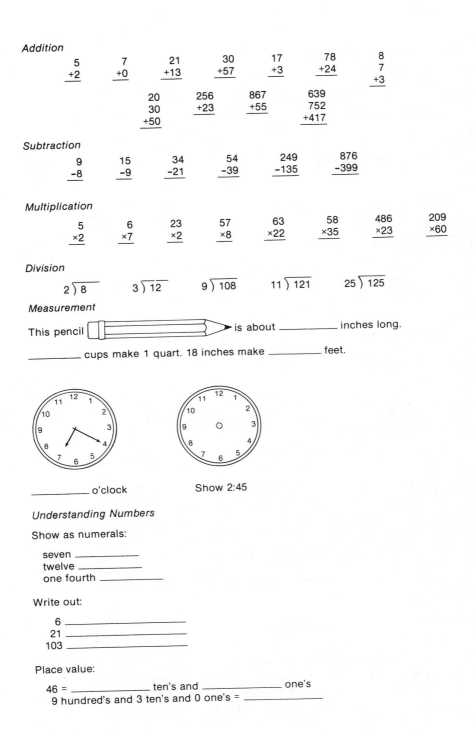

Addition

5	7	21	30	17	78	8
+2	+0	+13	+57	+3	+24	7
						+3

	20	256	867	639
	30	+23	+55	752
	+50			+417

Subtraction

9	15	34	54	249	876
-8	-9	-21	-39	-135	-399

Multiplication

5	6	23	57	63	58	486	209
×2	×7	×2	×8	×22	×35	×23	×60

Division

2) 8   3) 12   9) 108   11) 121   25) 125

Measurement

This pencil ➤ is about _____ inches long.

_____ cups make 1 quart. 18 inches make _____ feet.

_____ o'clock   Show 2:45

Understanding Numbers

Show as numerals:

seven _____
twelve _____
one fourth _____

Write out:

6 _____
21 _____
103 _____

Place value:

46 = _____ ten's and _____ one's
9 hundred's and 3 ten's and 0 one's = _____

Figure 8-7

Informal Arithmetic Survey Test

256

batteries include multiple subtests measuring basic arithmetic operations, decimals, fractions, and so forth. Administration of these tests is usually reserved for students experiencing severe arithmetic difficulties. Table 8-4 provides a brief summary of the five most common diagnostic arithmetic tests.

Table 8-3
Achievement Tests with Arithmetic Sections

name of test	grade level	arithmetic skills evaluated
California Achievement Test (Tiegs & Clark, 1963)	1-9	Basic computational skills and reasoning
Metropolitan Achievement Tests (Durost et al., 1971)	3-9	Concepts, problem solving, and computational skills
Peabody Individual Achievement Test (Dunn & Markwardt, 1970)	K-12	Matching skills through trigonometry concepts
SRA Achievement Series in Arithmetic (Thorpe, Lefever, & Naslund, 1964)	1-9	Computational skills, reasoning, and concepts
Wide Range Achievement Test (Jastak & Jastak, 1965)	Preschool and up	Counting, number symbols, oral problems, and written computations

Table 8-4
Diagnostic Arithmetic Tests

name of test	grade level	skills measured
Basic Educational Skills Inventory: Math (Adamson, Shrago, & VanEtten, 1972)	Elementary	Readiness skills, basic operations, decimals, fractions, time and money
Diagnostic Chart for Fundamental Processes in Arithmetic (Buswell & John, 1925)	2-8	Basic arithmetic operations with whole numbers
Diagnostic Tests and Self-Helps in Arithmetic (Brueckner, 1955)	3-8	Basic arithmetic operations, fractions, decimals, percent, and measurement
Key Math Diagnostic Arithmetic Test (Connolly, Nachtman, & Pritchett, 1971)	K-6	Basic arithmetic operations, fractions, numeration, word problems, money measurement, time, geometry, and symbols
Stanford Diagnostic Arithmetic Test (Beatty, Madden & Gardner, 1966)	2-8	Basic arithmetic operations, decimals, fractions, percent, and counting

In order to function in a regular math program, it was decided that Peggy Ann must first master basic addition and subtraction combinations. A precision teaching program was implemented where sheets of arithmetic facts were practiced and timed on a daily basis. It was felt that the constant review of various combinations was an added advantage of this program. A token

reinforcement system for completion of the practice sheets was also established. Earned tokens were converted to play money to teach various monetary values. She also learned to use the money when she "bought" items at the classroom store.

A programmed telling-time workbook was used with Peggy Ann in order to over-

come her difficulties in this area. The teacher also used schedules of TV programs to supplement the concepts introduced in the workbooks.

Special lined paper was used to help Peggy Ann write numbers in the correct columns, and connecting blocks were used to show the concept of regrouping. Using bundles of 10 sticks to illustrate place value concepts seemed to help her understanding in this area. Finally, the *Merrill Mathematics Skilltapes* (Spanga, 1977) were used as a supplement to the basic skills work introduced through the precision teaching program.

REMEDIATING ARITHMETIC PROBLEMS

As noted earlier in this chapter, the subject of remedial arithmetic instructional techniques has received less attention in the area of corrective teaching than any of the other basic skill subjects (Otto, McMenemy, & Smith, 1973). There is also a lack of definitive evidence that LD students would benefit as a group from instructional techniques different from those that are appropriate for *all* children (Haring & Bateman, 1977).

Otto, McMenemy, and Smith (1973) suggest that the following points are absolutely fundamental to remedial teaching in arithmetic:

a. *Enlist the cooperation of the child.* Teachers should capitalize on the fact that it is often easier for students to see the need for learning arithmetic than to see the need for learning other basic skills.
b. *Use efficient remedial procedures.* Writing down short-term achievable goals is a good practice for both the teacher and student.
c. *Use proven methods and materials.* Arithmetic is a sequential skill and new learnings cannot be attempted until all previous steps have been mastered. Visual and manipulative material should be used before confronting the student with abstractions.
d. *Investigate and correct related factors.* Emotional, physical, or environmental factors contributing to the arithmetic problem should also be corrected. (pp. 289-90)

Haring and Bateman (1977) suggest that proper instruction for the LD child, as well as every other child, consists of an appropriate amount of direct instruction necessary to learn the task, an appropriate amount of practice time required for mastery, and an appropriate kind of reinforcement necessary to develop and maintain the desired behavior. The need for employing task analysis to develop a hierarchy of skills which identifies prerequisite skills and terminal tasks within the instructional approach is often stressed (Capps & Hatfield, 1977; Dunlap & House, 1976; Spencer & Smith, 1969).

It was reported by Brummett (1978) that an increase in such learner-focused teaching was found in studies conducted by Freson (1975) and Warkentin (1975). Prospective teachers were taught mathematics through the use of manipulative materials. Observation of practical experiences revealed that these student teachers were more responsive to individual learner needs, had a more positive attitude toward mathematics as a whole, and used manipulative materials more often in teaching.

The arithmetic training suggestions outlined by Strauss and Lehtinen (1947) were certainly among the first techniques aimed at the remediation of arithmetic disturbances. The guidelines that were offered by these pioneer workers in learning disabilities still serve as reasonable remedial procedures in arithmetic. Many of these guidelines have been incorporated into a number of commercially available arithmetic pro-

Table 8-5
Math Textbooks Adaptable for LD Children

name (author)	components	content	method or approach	provisions for students with difficulties	special features
Holt School Mathematics	Student text Teacher text Cassettes Sound filmstrip Transparencies Jumbo screen Blocks and boxes Workbooks Drill masters Diagnostic tests Test masters Guide for individualizing	Sets, number operations and properties, problem solving numeration sentences, reasoning, probability and statistics, geometry, measurement, graphs, tables, scale drawings	"Guided discovery." Emphasis on getting students to discover patterns.	Suggestions for individualizing. Each lesson presented at three levels: *A*—minimal course with time for reinforcement and recycling; *B*—regular course; *C*—enriched course.	Strong problem-solving emphasis. Extra practice exercises provided.
Math Around Us	Teacher text Student text Punch-out materials Duplicating masters Test booklets Practice and activities book Optional: Geoboards, lab activities, metric booklets		Teaching strategy is to: 1. Motivate 2. Teach 3. Practice 4. Apply	Lesson notes in teacher's text have suggestions for "helping the low achiever" and "additional material for individualizing."	Built-in testing program. Emphasis on skills and applications. Extensive use of photographs "that bring the real world into the book."

260

Table 8-5 (*cont.*)

Ginn Elementary Mathematics (Scott, Immerzeel, and Wiederanders, 1972)	Pupil's book, Annotated teacher edition	Computation, functions, number systems, numeration, number theory, geometry, measurement, problem solving, probability and statistics, application	Steps to learning: 1. Image 2. Symbol 3. Organization 4. Generalization 5. Practice 6. Application	Plenty of opportunity for working with concrete materials. Each lesson has behavioral objectives and evaluation criterion.	Emphasis on math structure. Systematic variation of teaching strategy.
Modern School Mathematics (Duncan et al., 1970)	Teacher's book, Pupils' books	Numerals and numbers, sets, number sentences, mathematical operations, application, problem solving geometry, measurement, functions	Spiraled discovery approach	Three levels in "Assignment Guide" —for minimum, average, or maximum course of study. General suggestions for less-able students. Controlled reading level. Regular diagnostic chapter tests.	Emphasis on patterns and structures. Use of set language.

From *Teaching Children with Learning and Behavior Problems* (2nd ed.) by D.D. Hammill and N.R. Bartel. Boston: Allyn & Bacon,1978. Copyright 1978 by Allyn & Bacon. Reprinted by permission.

grams. The use of manipulative materials, repetition, and color are equally emphasized in many arithmetic programs used with LD children. Some of the more representative programs are briefly discussed in the following paragraphs. Table 8-5 also lists a number of regular mathematics materials which can be adapted for use with LD children and youth.

Cuisenaire Rods (Davidson, 1969). The Cuisenaire rods are designed to help children understand math concepts through the manipulation of 291 color-coded rods of varying length. Color and size characteristics are systematically associated with numbers. The names and sizes of representative Cuisenaire rods are shown in figure 8-8.

The rods are intended for use with students in grades K through 6, and they may be used individually or with an entire class. The rods are utilized for all basic arithmetic processes. Four stages are usually followed in introducing the rods: (1) independent exploration where the student is encouraged to play with the rods; (2) independent exploration and directed activities with the rods during which time relationships are observed without mathematical notation; (3) directed activities where mathematical notation is introduced, but number value is not assigned to the rods; and (4) directed activities where mathematical notation is extended and the rods are assigned number values.

Teachers of learning disabled children have found the rods to be especially useful in oral word problems, left-to-right discrimination, visual sequencing, and auditory and visual memory. In addition, the visual, tactile, and manipulative aspects of the rods have been particularly helpful to many LD children.

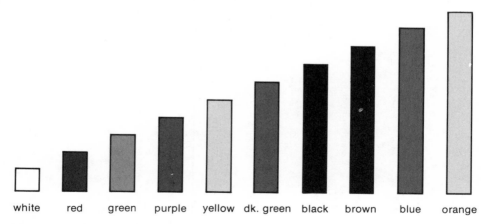

white   red   green   purple   yellow   dk. green   black   brown   blue   orange

Figure 8-8
Cuisenaire Rods

The above illustration is taken from *Using the Cuisenaire Rods—A Photo/Text Guide for Teachers* by Jessica Davidson. The name Cuisenaire and the color sequence of the rods are trademarks of the Cuisenaire Company of America, Inc.

DISTAR Arithmetic (Engelmann & Carnine, 1972). This is a beginning arithmetic program designed to provide a basic understanding of arithmetic and the skills necessary to solve and attack problems. The program consists of three consecutive parts that have been developed so that each skill is expanded and built into the next skill. Children are taught, for example, counting, symbol identification, the meaning of process signs, algebra addition, addition and subtraction story problems, and counting by various numbers.

A detailed teacher's guide provides instruction for organizing and implementing the program, including instruction for grouping, rules for effective teaching, and scope and sequence charts. Lesson format and cues for performance are well established so that each child knows what is expected. The program also includes workbooks for independent student work, and *take-homes* for each level that contain reteaching and reinforcement materials and the practice exercises for the lessons. The *take-homes* also serve as a motivating reward for student performance.

The carefully structured lessons are intended for presentation to small groups of children; however, instructional suggestions for teaching larger groups or an entire class are included. The program can be adapted for intermediate grade level LD students. The ordered nature of the program and the student's active participation leave very little room for confusion or misunderstanding in this program.

Merrill Mathematics Skilltapes (Sganga, 1977). This program consists of 40 audio cassette tapes which introduce 77 basic computational skills in sequential order. The addition, subtraction, multiplication, and division of whole numbers, fractions, and decimals are included among the topics. The 40 lessons are presented on separate cassettes with 15 to 18 minutes playing time on each side of each cassette. Student workbooks are also included for the entire program. The tapes have been successfully used with many learning disabled children.

Project MATH (Cawley et al., 1976). This very comprehensive curriculum was designed to present a mathematics instructional program to students through the sixth grade. The curriculum was developed over an 8-year period of research at the University of Connecticut. Cawley (1977) points out that the goal of the approach was to develop a means that would allow the nonreader to demonstrate proficiency in mathematics without being impeded by a lack of reading ability.

The program consists of a *Mathematics Concept Inventory* that was developed in order to screen and place the learner. The instructional program includes four kits which cover approximately 1½ grade levels. Each kit contains a *Multiple Option Curriculum* that provides the instructor with four alternatives for the learner to demonstrate proficiency. Six mathematical strands (geometry, patterns, sets, numbers and operations, measurement, and fractions) form the basis for the content. Verbal problem solving is treated from an informational processing perspective, and instructional activities are distinguished from those contained in the *Multiple Option Curriculum* (Cawley, 1977).

Project MATH also includes a series of mini units, called LABS, which last from periods of a few days to several weeks. The LABS are actually mathematically based activities that are used to structure experiences to facilitate the development of social skills and behaviors. Some of the topics include calculators, telephones, and metrics. Table 8-6 provides a listing of all Project MATH components by levels.

Structural Arithmetic (Stern, 1965). The goals of this program are intended to develop mathematical thinking and nurture an appreciation for its exactness and clarity. The program is based on work with different colored blocks and cubes having number properties. Insight into number relationships is achieved by having the child experiment with these concrete materials. Children also work out general principles that they apply to arithmetic operations. Students are expected to gain insight into an arithmetic procedure from each experiment. The experiments are carefully planned for each lesson described in the teacher's manual.

Structural Arithmetic is intended for children in kindergarten through third grade. The materials may be used with individuals as well as with groups of students. We feel that the program is ideally suited to the problems experienced by many LD children in arithmetic because of the number of manipulative materials, simplistic vocabulary, step-by-step organization, and the additional instructional activities provided for children experiencing particular problems.

SUMMARY

Arithmetic deficiencies in children and youth with learning disabilities were discussed in this chapter. A number of different causative factors were considered along with the relationship of arithmetic disabilities to other learning handicaps. Various types of arithmetic deficiencies were considered in some detail. Oral interviews and teacher-made tests were among the informal assessment techniques discussed. Standardized achievement tests with arithmetic sections and diagnostic arithmetic tests were also listed. A discussion of appropriate arithmetic instructional programs concluded the chapter.

SUGGESTED ACTIVITIES

1. Arrange to observe a group of children where manipulative arithmetic materials are in use. Discuss with the teacher and individual children what they think to be the relative advantages and disadvantages of utilizing manipulative materials.

Table 8-6
Components of Project MATH

	level I	level II	level III	level IV
I. Evaluation and Teaching				
Mathematics Concept Inventory	1	1	1	1
Learner profile	18	18	18	18
Class profile	1	1	1	1
II. Multiple Option Curriculum				
Instructional guides	358	420	420	325
Activity booklets	A, B, C	A, B, C	A, B, C	A, B, C
Supplemental activities				
Booklet for instructor	1	1	1	1
Manipulatives	192 blocks 400 chips	256 blocks 500 chips 3 geoboards 32 fractional pieces 8 rulers	3 geoboards 1 balance scale 8 rulers 32 fractional pieces	8 rulers 32 fractional pieces
III. Verbal Problem Solving				
Administrative guide	1	1	1	1
Story mats	18	20	—	—
Object cards	228	246	—	—
Line drawings	—	32		
Money cards	—	111		100
Problem cards			100	100
IV. LABS	1	1	30	60
V. Administrative Guide			1	1

From "Curriculum: One Perspective for Special Education" by J. Cawley. In R. Kneedler and S.G. Tarver (Eds.), *Changing Perspectives in Special Education*. Columbus, Ohio: Charles E. Merrill, 1977. Copyright 1977 by Bell & Howell. Reprinted by permission.

2. Locate a local or state guide to arithmetic instruction and determine the sequential arithmetic skills recommended for a particular grade level. Construct an informal test that would measure a student's skill strengths and weaknesses for the selected grade level.

3. Visit with a learning disabilities specialist and discuss the relationship of arithmetic problems to various other subject-area difficulties. Note any common areas of remediation.

4. Observe various classes in which modern math programs are being used with the students. Ask the teacher what he or she considers to be the primary problem with this approach for LD children.

5. Obtain a copy of a published arithmetic test discussed in this chapter. Review the test and arrange to observe the test being administered, scored, and interpreted by a trained examiner.

6. List some instructional activities that might be utilized with reading disabled children experiencing difficulties in solving word problems.

7. Arrange a role-playing situation in which you orally interview a student concerning the errors encountered on an arithmetic worksheet. Evaluate your performance in terms of instructional strengths and weaknesses.

8. Discuss the available instructional alternatives for secondary-level students still encountering basic computational problems.

References

Adamson, G., Shrago, M., & VanEtten, G. *Basic Educational Skills Inventory: Math* (Level A and Level B). Olathe, Kan.: Select Ed., 1972.

Ashlock, R.B. *Error patterns in computation: A semi-programmed approach* (2nd ed.). Columbus, Ohio: Charles E. Merrill, 1976.

Beatty, L.S., Madden, R., & Gardner, E. *Stanford Diagnostic Arithmetic Test.* New York: Harcourt Brace Jovanovich, 1966.

Bereiter, C. *Arithmetic and mathematics.* San Rafael, Calif.: Dimensions, 1968.

Bereiter, C., & Engelmann, S. *Teaching disadvantaged children in the preschool.* Englewood Cliffs, N.J.: Prentice-Hall, 1966.

Brenton, B.W., & Gilmore, D. An operational definition of learning disabilities (cognitive domain) using WISC full scale IQ and Peabody Individual Achievement Test scores. *Psychology in the Schools,* 1976, *13,* 427-432.

Brueckner, L.J. *Diagnostic Tests and Self-Helps in Arithmetic.* Los Angeles: California Test Bureau, 1955.

Brummett, D.S. *Arithmetic disabilities: Instructional aspects.* Unpublished manuscript, 1978. (Available from Department of Special Education, University of Virginia, Charlottesville, Va.)

Bryant, N.D., & Kass, C.E. *Leadership training institute in learning disabilities.* Vol. 1. Washington, D.C.: Office of Education, Bureau of Education for the Handicapped, 1972.

Buswell, G.T., & John, L. *Diagnostic Chart for Fundamental Processes in Arithmetic.* Indianapolis: Bobbs-Merrill, 1925.

Capps, L.S. & Hatfield, M.M. Mathematical concepts and skills. *Focus on Exceptional Children,* 1977, *8,* 1-8.

Cawley, J.F. Curriculum: One perspective for special education. In R.D. Kneedler & S.G. Tarver (Eds.), *Changing perspectives in special education.* Columbus, Ohio: Charles E. Merrill, 1977.

Cawley, J.F., Goodstein, H.A., Fitzmaurice, A.M., Lepore, A., Sedlak, R., & Althaus, V. *Project MATH.* Tulsa: Educational Programs Corp., 1976.

Chalfant, J.C., & Scheffelin, M.A. Central processing dysfunction in children: A review of research. (*NINDS Monograph* No. 9). Bethesda, Md.: U.S. Department of Health, Education and Welfare, 1969.

Cohn, Robert. Dyscalculia. *Archives of Neurology,* 1961, *4,* 301-307.

Connolly, A.J., Nachtman, W., & Pritchett, E.M. *Key Math Diagnostic Arithmetic Test.* Circle Pines, Minn.: American Guidance Service, 1971.

Copeland, R. *How children learn mathematics: Teaching implications of Piaget's research.* London: Macmillan, 1970.

Davidson, J. *Using the Cuisenaire rods.* New Rochelle, N.Y.: Cuisenaire, 1969.

Duncan, E.R., Copps, L.R., Dolciani, M.P., Quast, W.G., & Zweng, M.J. *Modern school mathematics: Structure and use K-6.* Boston: Houghton Mifflin, 1970.

Dunlap, W.P., & House, A.D. Why can't Johnny compute? *Journal of Learning Disabilities,* 1976, *4,* 210-214.

Dunn, L.M., & Markwardt, F.C. *Peabody Individual Achievement Test.* Circle Pines, Minn.: American Guidance Service, 1970.

Durost, W., Bixler, H., Wrightstone, W., Prescott, B., & Balow, I. *Metropolitan Achievement Tests.* New York: Harcourt Brace Jovanovich, 1971.

Engelmann, S., & Carnine, D. *DISTAR arithmetic.* Chicago: Science Research Associates, 1972.

Feingold, A. *Teaching arithmetic to slow learners and retarded.* New York: John Day, 1965.

Freson, K. The effects on preservice elementary teachers of learning mathematics and means of teaching mathematics through the active manipulation of materials. *Journal for Research in Mathematics Education,* 1975, *6,* 51-62.

Hammill, D.D., & Bartel, N.R. *Teaching children with learning and behavior problems* (2nd ed.). Boston: Allyn & Bacon, 1978.

Haring, N.G., & Bateman, B. *Teaching the learning disabled child.* Englewood Cliffs, N.J.: Prentice-Hall, 1977.

Jastak, J.F., & Jastak, S.R. *The Wide Range Achievement Test.* Wilmington, Del.: Guidance Associates, 1965.

Johnson, D.J., & Myklebust, H.R. *Learning disabilities: Educational principles and practices.* New York: Grune & Stratton, 1967.

Kaliski, L. Arithmetic and the brain-injured child. In E. Frierson & W. Barbe (Eds.), *Educating children with learning disabilities.* New York: Appleton - Century-Crofts, 1967.

Koppitz, E.M. *Children with learning disabilities: A five-year follow-up study.* New York: Grune & Stratton, 1971.

Lerner, J. *Children with learning disabilities* (2nd ed.). Boston: Houghton Mifflin, 1976.

Moran, M.R. *Assessment of the exceptional learner in the regular classroom.* Denver: Love Publishing, 1978.

Otto, W., McMenemy, R.A., & Smith, R.J. *Corrective and remedial teaching.* Boston: Houghton Mifflin, 1973.

Peterson, D. *Functional mathematics for the mentally retarded.* Columbus, Ohio: Charles E. Merrill, 1973.

Reisman, F. K. *A guide to the diagnostic teaching of arithmetic* (2nd ed.). Columbus, Ohio: Charles E. Merrill, 1978.

Scott, L., Immnerzeel, G., & Wiederanders, D. *Ginn elementary mathematics series.* Lexington, Mass.: Ginn, 1972.

Sganga, F.T. *Merrill mathematics skilltapes.* Columbus, Ohio: Charles E. Merrill, 1977.

Smith, R.M. *Clinical teaching: Methods of instruction for the retarded* (2nd ed.). New York: McGraw-Hill, 1974.

Spencer, E.F., & Smith, R.A. Arithmetic skills. In R.M. Smith (Ed.), *Teacher diagnosis of educational difficulties.* Columbus, Ohio: Charles E. Merrill, 1969.

Stern, C. *Structural arithmetic.* Boston: Houghton Mifflin, 1965.

Strauss, A., & Lehtinen, L. *Psychopathology and education of brain-injured children.* New York: Grune & Stratton, 1947.

Thorpe, L.P., Lefever, D.W., & Naslund, R.A. *SRA Achievement Series in Arithmetic.* Chicago: Science Research Associates, 1964.

Tiegs, E., & Clark, W. *California Achievement Test.* Monterey, Calif.: California Test Bureau, 1963.

Virginia State Department of Education, *Elementary Mathematics Guide K-7.* Richmond, Va.: Elementary Education Service, State Department of Education, 1970.

Wallace, G., & Kauffman, J.M. *Teaching children with learning problems* (2nd ed.) Columbus, Ohio: Charles E. Merrill, 1978.

Wallace, G., & Larsen, S.C. *Educational assessment of learning problems: Testing for teaching.* Boston: Allyn & Bacon, 1978.

Warkentin, G. The effect of mathematics instructing using manipulative models on attitude and achievement of prospective teachers. *Journal of Research in Mathematics Education,* 1975, *6,* 88-94.

Social-Emotional Problems

PREVIEW

Many children who are unable to learn in school become frustrated, anxious, depressed, and sometimes angry about their lack of academic achievement. In this chapter, we discuss the social-emotional problems that often accompany specific learning disabilities. Since mild behavioral disorders are frequently associated with LD problems, we believe it is important that educators have some knowledge in this area.

Our introductory section summarizes the most common social-emotional problems among LD students. The dimensions of disordered social-emotional behavior and a discussion of selected behavioral traits of the learning disabled serve as a focus for this section of the chapter.

It is generally suggested that social-emotional problems are most efficiently appraised in naturalistic environments where the student interacts with peers, parents, and teachers, among others. Consequently, the various evaluation techniques which we discuss in the assessment section of this chapter include a number of observational scales, checklists, and teacher-child interaction procedures. The basic principles of ecological assessment are also summarized in this section.

Although most social and emotional skills are learned as part of the everyday interaction of children with each other and with adults (Wallace & Kauffman, 1978), there are nonetheless a number of instructional procedures which are commonly used to develop social-emotional skills in LD children and youth. Various behavioral strategies, interpersonal techniques, and commercial programs useful to both teachers and students are presented in the final sections of this chapter. We also recommend the suggested activities as worthwhile aids for understanding the social-emotional problems of LD children and youth.

Liz's social-emotional problems are typical of similar disturbances among many LD children. According to Myers and Hammill (1976) and Lovitt (1978), social-emotional problems are common among children with learning disabilities. Some of the difficulties that have been typically observed among these children include extreme distractibility, short attention spans, hyperactivity, inadequate self-concept, withdrawal, personality problems, anxiety, and poor interpersonal relationships. Additional difficulties have been listed by Dupont (1975) and Kauffman (1977).

Many writers have suggested that psychological difficulties may cause certain learning problems among some children (Berkowitz & Rothman, 1960; Ephron, 1953). The large number of emotionally disturbed children with difficulties in learning provides some evidence for

Liz is a 15-year-old freshman in a large inner-city high school. She is functioning well below grade level in all academic areas. She cannot work independently, "hates" school, and rebels against all authority. Liz is very defensive. She uses abusive language with peers and adults. If her papers, pencils, or books are misplaced, she blames someone else for her carelessness. She seldom takes the responsibility for any of her inappropriate behaviors.

According to her parents, Liz has been in a state of perpetual motion since a very young age. They report that she seldom slept long enough to give them relief from her overt behaviors. As she grew older, Liz reacted impulsively to most situations regardless of the consequences. Her parents have tried numerous techniques — scolding, paddling, denying privileges, sending Liz to her room — in their attempts to correct her behavior. They feel that nothing seems effective.

Liz has been frequently referred for psychological evaluation in a school system where psychologists are backlogged with referrals. It was not until she was caught distributing drugs on the school grounds that her case was reviewed for possible evaluation.

As noted later in this chapter, Liz's parents have enlisted the services of a private clinical psychologist who has agreed to work with Liz on a weekly basis. Nonetheless, Liz refused to see the psychologist until she was threatened with expulsion from school.

this position (Bower, 1969). The opposite view was taken by some early workers in this field who felt that social-emotional problems resulted from a child's learning difficulties. Fernald (1943), for example, indicated that only a very small minority of the children with whom she worked had had emotional problems before the learning problem developed.

We believe that an exacting causal relationship between social-emotional problems and learning disabilities cannot be determined at the present time. The many interacting factors involved in both areas preclude any attempt to reach such a decision. Nonetheless, few would deny that social-emotional problems do exist among some LD children. Let's take a look at some of the more prevalent problems these children face.

TYPES OF SOCIAL-EMOTIONAL PROBLEMS

Dependency

A certain degree of independence usually emerges as most children develop and mature socially. Children often insist that they "can do it better themselves" as they grow older. Dependence upon other individuals is consequently decreased.

In contrast to the normally developing child, many LD children show excessive dependence upon parents, teachers, and other adults. The overdependence usually takes the form of requiring excessive assistance, reassurance, and help in most activities that the child is involved in (Blackham & Silberman, 1975).

According to Gardner (1978), children are taught to be excessively dependent by others in their environment. He suggests that dependency results from the difficulty that such children have doing things they see others doing or that the social environment requires of them. Adults and older siblings also have the tendency to provide too much assistance to some children when they are confronted with difficulties.

Young children entering school for the first time exhibit a number of behaviors associated with overdependence; however, most of these difficulties disappear during the first few months of school. But with some LD children, the dependency behaviors persist well into the primary and intermediate grades. The lack of academic success experienced by these children is certainly associated with this excessive need for assistance and reassurance. In this regard, it is crucial that overly dependent children acquire some degree of self-confidence. Providing the child with the particular successful, positive experiences that build his competence level is recommended. Gardner (1978) also provides a number of excellent suggestions for dealing with the dependent child. His behavior management program outlines successive steps for reducing this problem behavior.

Poor Self-Concept

Learning disabled children are frequently characterized as having negative or low self-concepts (Gardner, 1978; Wallace & Kauffman, 1978). These children often lack self-reliance and speak disparagingly of themselves. It is not unusual to find them feeling unable to accomplish anything correctly. Because of repeated academic failure, many LD children feel that they are "dumb," "stupid," "worthless," and simply unable to accomplish anything worthwhile.

Some children with poor self-concepts will refuse to complete assignments for fear of another failure. These children often appear to have completely given up. They are "convinced" of their inability to perform certain assignments. Other children with poor self-concepts exhibit undue concern over what other people think or feel because of their own lack of personal confidence.

According to Purkey (1970), there appears to be some relationship between self-concept and achievement. Fitts (1972) also asserts that children with positive self-concepts usually achieve more comfortably and effectively and are not easily threatened by unpleasant or difficult activities and individuals.

Finally, the results of a longitudinal government study (Sonstegard & Tseng, n.d.) indicated that feelings of self-worth consistently correlated with overall academic achievement among the variables designed to identify preschool children with learning problems.

Distractibility

Distractibility among LD children has historically been one of the most frequently mentioned characteristics (Strauss & Lehtinen, 1947). Early workers in this field associated this problem with various perceptual disorders.

The distractible LD child is unable to concentrate on any one activity for more than a few minutes, and he is easily distracted by irrelevant and inappropriate stimuli. The child finds it exceedingly difficult to focus his attention on a specific task, even when he is aware of the problem (Johnson & Myklebust, 1967).

The distractible nature of LD children in school may be noted in all areas of the curriculum. Myers and Hammill (1976) point out that complex or threatening activities may lead to daydreaming or mental blocking. Areas in which the child is experiencing some difficulty must be observed especially closely.

The review of 21 experimental studies of attention deficits in LD children by Tarver and Hallahan (1974) showed the LD students to be highly distractible when measures of distractibility were congruent with Cruickshank's definition of distractibility, the inability to filter out extraneous stimuli and focus selectively on the task.

In addition to the distractibility problems observed in school, Bryant (1972) reports that a substantial number of LD children seem to have attention problems in nonschool-related tasks, such as watching television.

Kagan's work (1965, 1966) on the concept of the reflectivity-impulsivity dimension—the degree to which the child reflects upon various alternatives in attempting to reach a decision—has some implications here. Some children impulsively select one alternative, while others reflect upon all available alternatives. Kagan believes that impulsive children do not care about making errors, since they offer answers quickly without considering accuracy. Recent studies have investigated the reflective-impulsive dimension in relationship to reading (Kagan, 1965), motor disturbances (Harrison & Nadelman, 1972), hyperactivity (Keogh, 1971), and perceptual functions (Keogh & McDonion, 1972).

Perseveration

Perseveration refers to the tendency on the part of some LD children to repeat a behavior continuously, especially when the behavior is no longer appropriate. Children who perseverate also have some difficulty in switching to another activity. Examples of perseveration include writing the same letter repeatedly (Blackham & Silberman, 1975), continuing to draw in circular motions after being requested to draw a circle (Strauss & Lehtinen, 1947), and covering an entire page with one color (Myers & Hammill, 1976). Verbal perseverations occur in the repetitions of words and phrases or in the difficulty some children have in shifting topics of conversations (Myers & Hammill, 1976).

Perseveration difficulties are closely associated with distractibility problems. Johnson and Myklebust (1967) suggest that, in perseveration problems, "normal monitoring of attention fails so it persists in a given direction without interruption" (p. 301). Consequently, perseveration disturbances are usually remediated by concentrating upon behaviors that allow the child to attend more closely to a particular task or activity.

Disruptive Behaviors

Many of the behaviors exhibited by LD children can be generically categorized as *disruptive*. These overly aggressive behaviors are usually of more concern to teachers than other types of socio-emotional problems because the behavior disrupts the learning process and order within a classroom, and the aggression usually cannot be ignored.

The disruptive behaviors exhibited in the classroom often involve altercations with other children, usually over some minor incident such as bumping or pushing. These precipitating factors become secondary once the child begins fighting or quarreling. It is not unusual for such disruption to occur during relatively quiet periods in the classroom when the teacher is working with individual children or small groups.

The disruptive behaviors of LD children are associated to a certain degree with the child's inability to perform a specific task. Some acting-out behaviors may result from a child's frustrations over the lack of academic success or reinforcement. The hypothesis offered by Dollard and his colleagues (1939) states that aggression is always a consequence of frustration. The frequency and intensity of frustration will also function to affect the type and amount of aggressive behavior.

Disruptive behaviors have been the concern of many investigations in this field (Lovaas et al., 1965; Sears, Maccoby, & Levin, 1957; Walters, 1964). Parent-child, teacher-child, and child-environment interactions have been hypothesized and studied. Recently, however, the emphasis has shifted to managing the behavior of disruptive children in the classroom (Wallace & Kauffman, 1978; Worell & Nelson, 1974.)

Withdrawal

In contrast to the overly aggressive and hyperactive child, some LD children can be characterized as lethargic, quiet, not given to much action, and the cause of little disturbance in class (Myers & Hammill, 1976). The withdrawal behavior exhibited by this kind of child frequently causes him to go unnoticed in regular classrooms.

These children frequently attempt as little contact as possible with both their peers and adults. Social interactions are completely avoided. These particular manifestations are distinguished from the generally shy or quiet child. Blackham & Silberman (1975) suggest that most children exhibit some withdrawal behavior at different developmental stages. The behavior only becomes maladaptive when it is used exclusively and when it prevents normal relationships from developing.

Withdrawal behavior may be due to a variety of factors. The inability to succeed at academic tasks and the memory of previous failures are among the primary reasons for withdrawal. Also, some children are inappropriately reinforced for remaining quiet.

Withdrawal behavior is usually corrected very gradually and in very small steps. Rice (1974) believes that considerable amounts of praise and support are necessary while gradually moving the child into various interpersonal relationships. Gardner (1978) points out that approximations of desired social behaviors should be reinforced and slowly shaped by the teacher.

Hyperactivity

Hyperactivity usually refers to excessive activity or mobility, and as such it has been most frequently considered a motor disturbance and not a social-emotional problem. Gardner (1978) points out that while it may be true that physical factors account for some of the excessive motor activity, it is also known that children learn some of these behaviors through inadvertent reinforcement by others.

Hyperactive behavior has also been labeled *hyperkinesis* in the literature. Children with these difficulties have been described as having perseveration difficulties, short attention spans, low frustration tolerance, motor difficulties, and disorganization problems.

Hyperactive children usually appear very restless and almost always in some type of motion. Keogh (1971) has stated that social and situational variables are important considerations in determining the level of hyperactivity. Many of the hyperactive behaviors are exhibited at inappropriate times.

The causes of hyperactivity are many and varied. Various biological causes have been suggested (Laufer, 1970), along with environmental factors (Chess, 1972), school experiences (Conners, 1966), and different types of allergies (Havard, 1973).

The problems associated with hyperactivity have been subjects of many different types of management systems. Among the approaches which have been attempted, behavior modification techniques, medications, directive teaching, and environmental adaptations have been the most successful with the learning disabled.

Finally, Bryant (1972) mentions that hyperactivity usually decreases with age. The obvious signs of hyperactivity become less noticeable, but disorders of attention, concentration, and distractibility may still be present.

Social Perception Problems

The ability to perceive oneself in relation to the behavior of other individuals, as well as to social situations, is called *social perception* (Johnson & Myklebust, 1967). The nature of social perception problems causes the child with these difficulties to be confused with the emotionally disturbed child or with the child who has a basic personality disorder.

Social perceptual deficits among LD children are most often apparent in their relationships with others in social situations. A lack of sensitivity for another individual's feelings is a common social perception deficit. The insensitivity toward another individual might be due to the LD child's inability to understand nonverbal communication clues, such as facial expressions, gestures, or general moods. Consequently, these children are often described as "socially immature." Interpersonal relationships with other individuals have frequently been described as both minimal and impaired (Baer, 1961).

Children with social perception problems are usually unable to assume personal or social responsibility. Younger children with these difficulties do not understand why they should share toys, nor are they able to participate in independent activities without constant support and direction. Parents of these children often report that their child fights with peers and has few friends with whom to play.

Older children with social perception difficulties are often described as having little or no self-control. They are viewed as rude and tactless due to their continually doing or saying the inappropriate thing (Lerner, 1976). These children have also been reported as unable to predict the consequences of their own and others' behavior in many different situations (Valett, 1967). This latter deficit poses significant dangers to both the child and other individuals if the disturbance is not remediated.

The insensitivity, irrational behavior, and poor social judgment of the child with social perception problems are not necessarily easy problems to correct in children; teaching appropriate behavior may be difficult. However, the social demands with which all children are faced require that social skills be taught to those children with disabilities in this area. Johnson and Myklebust (1967) suggest that social perception remediation requires working with practical situations. They also believe that nonverbal interactions must be verbalized and interpreted for the child.

Other Behaviors

In addition to these behaviors, a number of additional social-emotional problems among LD children are sometimes exhibited.

The *inconsistent behavior* of these children is mentioned as a difficult dimension to control. Related to this area is the *irritability* shown by some children. In addition, many signs of *insecurity* that are observed seem related to the lack of academic success.

Many *antisocial behaviors* are also exhibited by older LD children. The uses of *inappropriate vocabulary, lying,* and *stealing* are other maladaptive behaviors found among these children.

Finally, some children reveal *motivational deficits, temper tantrums,* and *low frustration tolerance.* Many of these problems require the use of specialized techniques, materials, and methods. Some of the assessment techniques used to evaluate the social-emotional problems of LD children and youth are discussed in the next section.

ASSESSMENT OF SOCIAL-EMOTIONAL PROBLEMS

Social-emotional problems are most efficiently appraised in natural environments. According to Adams (1964), some of the more pertinent settings include: (1) informal discussion periods, (2) self-directed student activities, (3) discussion of controversial issues, (4) social activities out of the classroom, (5) role playing and dramatic presentations, (6)

On the *Stanford-Binet Intelligence Test*, Liz's scores placed her in the high average range of intelligence. Nevertheless, her scores on the *Peabody Individual Achievement Test* in mathematics, reading recognition, reading comprehension, spelling, and general information placed her approximately at the fifth grade level. Informal observations by regular and special teachers have also verified her low academic achievement. Teachers report that Liz completes schoolwork hurriedly and without much success.

Class members also seem to view Liz in a negative manner. A recent sociogram showed no one choosing Liz in response to the question, "Who would you like to work with on the Civil War project?"

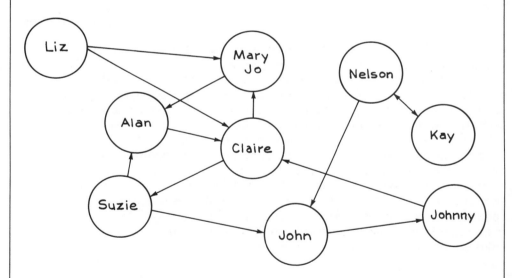

Liz was not chosen by anyone in her group. However, it is interesting to note that Claire and Mary Jo, the two students chosen by Liz, are bright and well-adjusted young women who seldom have any contact with Liz, either in school or in their neighborhood. Shortly after the administration of this sociogram, Liz initiated communication with Claire by asking her help on a class assignment. The teacher has continued to put them together on various projects with some success. Liz seems to welcome the opportunity of associating with a respected student in her class.

creative art periods, and (7) playground and recess periods. We believe that these situations will more likely provide the evaluator with a realistic estimate of a student's social-emotional behaviors. Various techniques for assessing these behaviors are now discussed.

Observational Techniques

The systematic observation of students can provide the teacher with valid and highly reliable information (Wallace & Larsen, 1978). Before actually observing a child, we have found it is usually helpful to conceptualize the child's behavior in terms of *excesses* and *deficits*. Wallace and Kauffman (1978) suggest that the following questions must be discussed in evaluating behavioral excesses:

- What does the child do that is maladaptive?
- How often does he do it under present conditions?
- What environmental events serve to maintain his behavior?
- How can I remove the events that support his undesirable behavior? (p.115)

Behavioral deficits, on the other hand, may be assessed by answering the following questions:

- What do I want the child to do?
- How often does he do it under present conditions?
- What approximations of what I want the child to do can I identify?
- What reinforcers for the child can I identify that are at my disposal?
- How can I provide reinforcers for successive approximations of what I want the child to do? (p. 115)

The observations which will help to answer these and other questions concerning a student's social-emotional behaviors should be systematically recorded. We believe that it is essential to record behavior immediately after it occurs and to record each instance of the behavior. It is also important to enter daily observations on a record form. A useful record form for nearly any behavior is shown in table 9-1.

The behavioral data which are obtained during various observations are usually plotted on some type of graph, as in figure 9-1, in order that the evaluator can "eyeball" the data and note behavioral trends or to see when the rate or duration of a behavior begins to increase or decrease (Brown, 1978).

A concise behavioral approach for evaluating LD children which also includes various observational techniques has been developed by Lovitt (1967). He outlines four essential steps in this procedure. During the first phase, a *baseline* of the child's performance is obtained. Baseline assessment is evaluating the child's behavior continuously over a period of time until a stable level of performance is determined.

The second step in this evaluation process involves assessing the behavioral components which maintain and modify behavior. Stimulus

Table 9-1
Behavioral Data Record Form

Behavior recorded: _____ Name of child: _____

day	date	behavior recorded from:	tot. time behavior recorded	# of behaviors observed	rate per min.	duration in min. and sec.	behavior recorded each ___ min. for ___ intervals	# of times behavior observed	% of intervals behavior observed	% of work completed	% of work correct	comments
1.		___ to ___										
2.		___ to ___										
3.		___ to ___										
4.		___ to ___										
5.		___ to ___										
6.		___ to ___										
7.		___ to ___										
8.		___ to ___										
9.		___ to ___										
10.		___ to ___										

(Continue in this manner)

From *Teaching Children with Learning Problems* (2nd ed.) by G. Wallace and J.M. Kauffman. Columbus, Ohio: Charles E. Merrill, 1978. Copyright 1978 by Bell & Howell. Reprinted by permission.

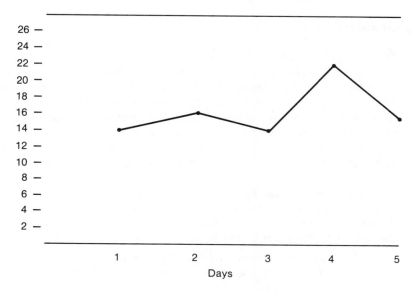

Figure 9-1
Number of Times Out-of-Seat for Keith

preference, response to the stimuli, the contingency system under which the child is operating, and the consequences of the child's behavior are evaluated during this phase.

The third part of the process involves the referring agent (teacher or parent) and the child. The adult is involved in the process to solicit cooperation in determining target behaviors for the child. Lovitt suggests that sometimes "the managerial and programming skills of the adult may be as incompetent as the compliance skills of the child" (1967, p. 237).

The final aspect of this process involves the generalizations of diagnostic information. The final result of the evaluation should include suggestions for the referring agent, usually the classroom teacher, which may be transmitted into programming procedures. The emphasis upon functional data is included during this part of the evaluation. The procedures outlined by Lovitt may be used equally well with other curriculum areas in addition to social-emotional problems.

Finally, Lister (1969) points out that the value of social-emotional observations should be based on

- the accuracy with which observations are made and recorded;
- the extent to which conditions under which observations occur are noted and considered in interpreting observational data;
- the degree to which observations focus on important aspects of the child's behavior; and
- the extent to which the child's behavior is not influenced by the observation procedures. (p. 184)

Ecological Assessment

Ecological assessment has become an increasingly common procedure during the past few years. This approach attempts to examine the child's functioning in the various environments in which the child operates. According to Wiederholt, Hammill, and Brown (1978), the major environments studied in most ecological assessments include the school, home, community, and peer interactions. The student's functioning in each of these areas has the potential to either positively or negatively influence his or her academic and social behavior (Wallace & Larsen, 1978).

Among the various approaches for organizing an ecological assessment, we have found the model formulated by Laten and Katz (1975) to be the most complete. They recommended five phases. A description of the activities for each phase is provided in the following outline.

I. Initial descriptions of the environment
   A. Engaging the environment for data collection on perceptions of the problem.
   B. Information is gathered from the particular setting(s) in which the problem is most noticeable.
   C. Information is gathered from the settings in which the problem is not noticeable.
II. Expectations
   A. Information is gathered about the expectations of the environments in which the child is experiencing problems.
   B. Information is gathered about the expectations of the environments in which the child is not having problems.
III. Behavioral descriptions
   A. Data is collected on the interactions and skills of the people involved in the problematic situations.
      1. present data
      2. historical data
      3. interactional analysis
      4. functional analysis
   B. Data collected on the interactions and skills of the people involved in successful situations.
      1. present data
      2. historical data
      3. interactional data
      4. functional analysis
   C. Assessment of the skills needed by the child to function successfully in different environments
IV. Data are summarized
V. Reasonable expectations are set for the child and for teachers in which the problem is most notable.

The diagnostic instruments utilized in conducting an ecological assessment will vary according to specific situations. The primary means of gathering ecological data is usually through the use of systematic observation, teacher-child interaction systems, checklists and rating scales, and sociometric techniques. We believe that ecological assessment techniques have tremendous potential for providing teachers of LD children and youth with a vast amount of instructionally useful information. More detailed procedures for conducting an ecological assessment are provided by Wallace and Larsen (1978).

Behavioral Checklists and Rating Scales

Checklists and rating scales are often used to organize and summarize the behavioral ratings of teachers and students. It has been noted that checklists and rating scales help to focus attention on specific behaviors (Cartwright & Cartwright, 1974). The basic difference between the checklist and rating scale is the *type* of judgment called for:

> A rating scale is designed to indicate the *degree* to which a characteristic is present or the *frequency* with which a behavior is observed, whereas the checklist determines the *presence* or *absence* of a particular characteristic or observation of that characteristic. (Wallace & Larsen, 1978, p. 112)

Although numerical ratings actually provide little information concerning appropriate intervention procedures, we have nonetheless found checklists and rating scales to be particularly helpful in estimating various strengths and weaknesses of students. Some of the more widely used published behavioral rating scales are summarized in table 9-2. Guidelines for constructing teacher-made checklists are provided by Wiederholt, Hammill, and Brown (1978). They suggest that checklists should cover at least three categories of behavior: *(a)* child behaviors, *(b)* teacher-child interactions, and *(c)* child-child interactions.

Teacher-Child Interaction Techniques

The amount and degree of teacher-child interaction are important variables which frequently are associated with an LD child's social-emotional problems. Many published instruments are available for measuring both the type and quality of teacher-child interactions. Some of these systems are listed in table 9-3. In addition, Bradfield and Criner (1973) have divised an informal procedure that provides the examiner with additional teacher-child interaction data.

We have found that the information which is obtained from these instruments concerning positive-negative interactions between the teacher and child is very important in both planning and implementing various instructional and management programs for the student. Other

Table 9-2
Published Behavioral Rating Scales

instrument	description
Fels Parent Behavior Scales (Fels Institute, 1949)	Parents are interviewed in regard to the child's home environment including sociability of the family, rapport with the child, and child-centeredness of the family
Walker Problem Checklist (Walker, 1970)	Scores are provided for identifying acting out, withdrawal, distractibility, disturbed peer relations, and maturity
Peterson-Quay Behavior Problem Checklist (Quay & Peterson, 1967)	Measures behaviors according to conduct disorders, personality disorders, inadequacy-immaturity, socialized delinquency, and autism
Behavior Rating Scales (Burks, 1968, 1969)	Teacher rates the child in twenty areas including anxiety, attention, withdrawal, and dependency
A Process for In-School Screening of Children with Emotional Handicaps (Bower & Lambert, 1962)	Social-emotional learning evaluated by teacher rating, self-rating, and peer rating

valuable data are also obtained on classroom atmosphere, teacher performance, teacher behaviors, and teaching style. We recommend the teacher-child interaction techniques as valuable additions to assessment procedures.

DEVELOPING SOCIAL-EMOTIONAL SKILLS

The development of healthy social and emotional skills was thought for years to be the exclusive task of psychiatrists, psychologists, psychotherapists, and other professionals with similar training. Teachers, however, have more recently been involved in the formal development of these skills.

In the process of attempting to teach LD children with social-emotional problems, many educators have utilized the principles of different psychological viewpoints and various commercial programs.

According to Frostig and Maslow (1973), these different psychological viewpoints concerning social-emotional problems are not necessarily contradictory. In fact, a number of similarities are noted among the approaches.

Table 9-3

Teacher-Child Interaction Systems

1. *Reichenberg-Hackett Teacher Behavior Observation System* (Reichenberg-Hackett, 1962)	Focuses upon nursery school teachers and pupils. Teacher-Behavior is coded according to five major categories.
2. *Teachers Practices Observation Record* (Brown, 1970)	Consists of 62 items grouped into seven categories. Requires little training of observers and possesses high reliability and validity.
3. *Connors-Eisenberg Observation System* (Connors & Eisenberg, 1966)	Is appropriate for use in nursery school and elementary grades. Yields three sets of scores that relate to "episodes," "activities," and "overall judgements."
4. *The Purdue Teacher Evaluation Scale* (Bentley & Starry, 1970)	Is designed to provide junior or senior high school teachers with an evaluation of their performance as seen through the eyes of students.
5. *Classroom Observational Scales* (Emmer, 1971)	Bases observations in 12 variables from "pupil attention" to "enthusiasm." Easily learned and administered.
6. *Flanders' System of Interaction Analysis* (Flanders, 1970)	Is intended to gather data on teacher behaviors that restrict or increase student freedom of action. Focuses upon categories of behavior.
7. *Nonverbal Interaction Analysis*	Provides a method of recording nonverbal behavior in classrooms. Designed to parallel the categories of verbal behavior in *Flanders' System of Interaction Analysis* (1970)
8. *Fuller Affective Interactions Records 33* (Fuller, 1969)	Assesses interpersonal behaviors of preservice teachers and their students. Utilizes five interpersonal dimensions.
9. *Teacher-Child Dyadic Interaction* (Brophy & Good, 1969)	Categories each teacher-student verbal interaction. Requires 20 hours of training to be used effectively. An excellent research tool.

From *Educational Assessment of Learning Problems: Testing for Teaching* by G. Wallace and S.C. Larsen. Boston: Allyn & Bacon, 1978. Copyright 1978 by Allyn & Bacon. Reprinted by permission.

The emphasis on observations of the child and analysis of these observations are apparent both in behavior modification and interpersonal education. Both of these approaches also stress the importance of a child's learning the relationship of his behavior to its consequences (Payne et al., 1974).

It is also suggested that the differences between the concepts are actually in the questions which are asked.

The emphasis of humanism is on the goals of education. The curriculum is considered important only so far as it is a means to achieve these goals.

A special education admissions committee has recommended that Liz be placed in a self-contained class for LD students at her high school. However, due to a waiting list, it will be approximately 6 months before Liz is actually placed in the class. In the meantime, Liz's parents have enlisted the services of a private clinical psychologist who has agreed to see Liz for weekly therapy sessions. The school counselor has also enrolled Liz in a weekly guidance group which meets at the local high school.

Liz's teachers met with the special education admissions committee, and a program of academic remediation was planned for the intermittent period until Liz is placed in the LD class. A very specific contingency contracting system was planned for Liz in order that appropriate academic and social behaviors would be rewarded. Liz's teachers felt that this technique would be easy to monitor and would also help Liz develop self-control and independent study skills. The clinical psychologist working with Liz concurred with these recommendations. Thus far, the approach has been successful. Liz has had increased contact with other students, and she seems happy with school.

> The emphasis of behaviorism is on the *how* of education—the methodology. (Frostig & Maslow, 1973, pp. 45-46)

It seems that both approaches for remediating social-emotional problems among LD children have merit. Each technique is essentially concerned with helping children overcome behaviors which interfere with personal productivity and learning. As such, both techniques offer alternatives for application to individual difficulties. A knowledge of each approach will help the teacher decide the most appropriate technique for individual children within a class.

Behavioral Strategies

Many approaches to educating children with social-emotional problems are derived from the work of various behavioral scientists (Hall, 1971; Lovitt, 1977; Skinner, 1953, 1971). Behavioral approaches to classroom management typically employ precise measurement techniques and emphasize the role of the teacher as the primary agent of positive behavior change in the classroom (Wallace & Kauffman, 1978). Some widely used behavioral strategies are now reviewed.

Behavior Modification

Of all the many different techniques that have been developed for changing behavior, behavior modification has probably generated more interest among educators and psychologists than any other behavior management technique. Some professionals have condemmed it as a very destructive procedure, while others view it as a panacea for managing children's behavior. According to Wallace and Kauffman (1978), behavior modification refers to any systematic arrangement of environmental events that produces a specific change in observable behavior.

Behavior modification procedures stress the importance of external and observable behaviors, rather than internal factors over which the teacher would have little control. Behavior modification seeks to modify an individual's behavior by concentrating upon the specific behaviors that are exhibited by the child, especially those which interfere with learning.

Reinforcement is central to the behavior modification process. A reinforcer is an event which controls behavior. Reinforcers can be positive (things a person will try to get or retain) or negative (things a person will try to avoid or escape) (Wallace & Kauffman, 1978). For example, the teacher who recognizes children who raise their hands is reinforcing this particular behavior. The likelihood that this behavior will increase in some children is quite good.

Punishment refers to withdrawing something pleasant (a positive reinforcer) or presenting something unpleasant (a negative reinforcer) after a behavior. Punishment has the effect of decreasing or weakening the behavior it follows. For example, if the teacher consistently and totally withdraws his attention from the child who "tattles" to the teacher, tattling behaviors will likely decrease.

The actual arrangements of reinforcers and punishment are usually governed by schedules of reinforcement. The two broad classes of reinforcement schedules are *continuous,* in which every response is reinforced, and *intermittent,* in which not all of the student's appropriate responses are reinforced (Wallace & Kauffman, 1978). An outline of the basic schedules of reinforcement is shown in table 9-4.

The differential reinforcement of successive approximations of a behavior is referred to as *shaping.* This approach involves arranging a sequence of ordered steps or tasks, reinforcing a behavior that the child already emits, and gradually increasing the requirement for reinforcement. The child who is to color within the lines, for example, must first hold the crayon and then color in large areas which gradually decrease in size until the desired area is colored. The successvie approximations of various area sizes will probably need to be adjusted according to individual learning styles.

A tremendous amount of research indicates that behavior modification techniques are very effective classroom management procedures (Lovitt, 1977; Wallace & Kauffman, 1978). We like this technique because it is easily understood and applied by teachers working with children and youth in the classroom.

Precision Teaching

Some very specific techniques for the measurement and analysis of behaviors were developed by Lindsley (1964). These techniques, known as precision teaching, have generated a considerable amount of research with LD students. The five characteristics of precision teaching listed by Lovitt (1978) include:

    a. The teacher or pupil must *pinpoint* each behavior of a child's program. If one goal is to increase a student's ability to read orally from a certain text, a situation would be arranged to deal directly with that behavior.

    b. An *aim* must be determined for each identified goal. In order to determine an aim, the teacher or pupil must decide the rate at which the selected behavior should occur and the date that criterion should be achieved. Lines of programs would then be drawn on a chart of that activity from the intersection of the current data and rate to the point the projected date and rate intersect.

    c. The teacher or pupil must *count* the number of times the behavior occurs. For reading orally, the pupil might be required to read from a basal reader for one minute. While the child does so, the teacher would count the number of correctly and incorrectly pronounced words.

Table 9-4

Schedules of Reinforcement

I. **Continuous Reinforcement**

Every time the behavior occurs, it is reinforced.

Example: Each time the child completes an arithmetic problem correctly he is given a point for his progress chart.

II. **Intermittent Reinforcement**

A. *Ratio Schedules*

Reinforcement is given for every *n*th behavior and depends on the number of behaviors the child performs regardless of time.

1. *Fixed Ratio*

A fixed number of behaviors must occur for each reinforcement.

Example: Every 10th sight word read correctly is rewarded with a piece of candy.

2. *Variable Ratio*

An average number of behaviors must occur for each reinforcement. The number of behaviors required varies around a mean.

Example: On the average, every 5th time the child raises his hand he is called on by the teacher. The actual number of times he raises his hand before being called on varies.

B. *Interval Schedules*

Reinforcement depends on the passage of time *and* the occurrence of a behavior.

1. *Fixed Interval*

A fixed amount of time must pass, after which the next appropriate behavior will be reinforced.

Example: Every 3 minutes during recess the teacher observes the child to see whether or not he is talking to another child. The next time he approaches another child and speaks to him, the teacher pats him on the shoulder and praises him for being friendly.

2. *Variable Interval*

A variable amount of time must pass, after which the next correct response will result in reinforcement. The amount of time required varies around a mean.

Example: On the average, every 5 minutes the teacher observes whether or not the child is writing another correct answer to the questions covering the geography lesson. When he answers the next question correctly, a smiling face is drawn on his paper. The actual number of minutes which elapse before the teacher checks the child's behavior varies.

From *Teaching Children with Learning Problems* (2nd ed.) by G. Wallace and J.M. Kauffman. Columbus, Ohio: Charles E. Merrill, 1978. Copyright 1978 by Bell & Howell. Reprinted by permission.

  d. The teacher or pupil should *chart* each day the number of times the pinpointed behavior occurred. In the oral reading example, two entries should be charted each day. One should reveal the number of correctly pronounced words and another the number of incorrectly pronounced words.

  e. The teacher and pupil should *evaluate* the performance of each charted behavior each day. If the correct rate is above and the incorrect rate below the corresponding progress lines, the current instructional technique should be continued. If, however, the progress is not satisfactory, an instructional change should be considered. (p. 175)

The 6-cycle chart which is commonly used in precision teaching to record and display changes in children's performance is shown in figure 9-2. The use of this chart allows teachers and pupils to pinpoint the outcome of various instructional procedures being utilized.

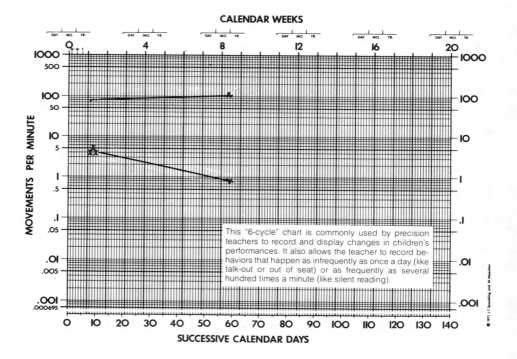

Figure 9-2
Sample of 6-Cycle Chart

From "The Learning Disabled" by T. C. Lovitt. In N. G. Haring (Ed.), *Behavior of Exceptional Children* (2nd ed.). Columbus, Ohio: Charles E. Merrill, 1978. Copyright 1978 by Bell & Howell. Reprinted by permission.

Token Economy

A token economy has been defined as a set of procedures for systematically using tokens to increase desired behavior (Walker & Buckley, 1974). A token reinforcer is an object (e.g., chips, tickets, stars, play money) which can be exchanged for items or activities of value. No matter how elaborate the economy systems established in LD classrooms, there are basic rules listed by Walker and Shea (1976) that usually apply to all token systems.

1. Select the target behavior.
2. Conceptualize and present the desired behavior to the child or group.
3. Select an appropriate token.
4. Establish rewards for which tokens can be exchanged.
5. Develop a reward menu and post it in the classroom.
6. Implement the token economy.
7. Provide immediate reinforcement for acceptable behavior.
8. Gradually change from a continuous to a variable schedule of reinforcement.
9. Provide time for children to change tokens for rewards.
10. Revise the reward menu frequently. (pp. 57-58)

It has been noted that token economies are often established in educational settings to help motivate individual students and to help children with academic and behavior problems learn more effectively (Walker & Shea, 1976). We recommend this procedure as another effective technique for managing the hard-to-teach child in the regular or special classroom.

Contracts

Contingency contracting is a behavioral strategy that arranges conditions so that the child gets to do something he or she wants to do after doing something the teacher wants the child to do. For example, the student will get 5 minutes of free time if he completes a specific workbook page. Contacts essentially seem to reward approximations of a desired behavior. Wiederholt, Hammill, & Brown (1978) suggest that teachers use contracts to specify "a task to be completed, a time limit for completing the task, how others are involved, the reward for completing the task, and the individuals responsible for recognizing the completion of the task" (p. 224).

Walker and Shea (1976) note that contracts might be either verbal or written. They feel that verbal contracts (e.g., "Mary, if you remain in your seat for 5 minutes, you may work in your coloring book ") are more useful to educators than written contracts, which tend to be more elaborate. Contracts can also be utilized by parents and other adults in managing children's behavior outside the school. An example of a written contract that may be used by teachers or parents is shown in figure 9-3.

Interpersonal Education

Programs of interpersonal education which seek to remediate a child's social-emotional skills have also been categorized as *humanistic education* (Bühler, 1969) and *psychoeducational approaches* (Payne et al., 1974).

According to Patterson (1973), the two most important aspects of interpersonal education include facilitating subject matter learning by

Date _____

CONTRACT

This is an agreement between _____
CHILD'S NAME

and _____ . The contract begins on
TEACHER'S NAME

_____ and ends on _____ . It will be
DATE   DATE

reviewed on _____ .
DATE

The terms of the agreement are:

Child will _____

_____

_____

_____

Teacher will _____

_____

_____

_____

If the child fulfills his part of the contract, he will receive the agreed-on reward from the teacher. However, if the child fails to fulfill his part of the contract, the rewards will be withheld.

Child's signature _____

Teacher's signature _____

Figure 9-3
Sample Contract

From *Behavior Modification: A Practical Approach for Education* by J. E. Walker and T. M. Shea. St. Louis: C. V. Mosby, 1976. Copyright 1976 by C. V. Mosby. Reprinted by permission.

teaching in a more human way, and "developing persons who understand themselves, who understand others, and who can relate to others" (p. x). This second aspect involves the nonintellectual, or affective, features of the child.

Interpersonal approaches to education stress the importance of the individual's feelings. A major goal of these approaches is to help a child feel good about himself and respect the dignity of other people.

Interpersonal education attempts to manage social-emotional difficulties in a variety of ways. Some techniques which have been used include *psychoeducational therapy* (Berkowitz & Rothman, 1960), *crisis teachers* (Morse, 1971), and various psychiatrically oriented programs. Patterson (1973) also notes that the British infant and junior schools are another recent humanistic development in education. We now turn our attention to another interpersonal approach, the Life Space Interview.

Life Space Interview

One technique suggested by Redl (1959) is the Life Space Interview (LSI), which is a cathartic technique in which a child's problems are discussed with a teacher immediately after some crisis situation. According to Wiederholt, Hammill, and Brown (1978), the LSI usually involves the following six steps when a crisis arises:

1. Each student involved in the situation gives his/her own impression of what has happened. The teacher listens and makes sure that each student is allowed to describe the situation as he/she perceives it without interruption.
2. Next, each student is questioned by the teacher in order to determine the actual cause of the disturbance.
3. Once the students have finished describing their individual perceptions of the problems and the teacher has helped determine the accuracy of their perceptions, the children must specify what can be done to resolve the situation. If a remedy is suggested that is agreeable to all of the persons involved, the LSI stops at this step.
4. If no agreeable remedy can be found, the teacher has to assume a more active role—the realities of the situation are defined and the consequences of behavior spelled out.
5. At this step, the teacher begins to make suggestions that might solve the problem.
6. The final step in the LSI process is the development of a plan that can be used should the problem arise again. Again, the students play a major role in deciding on the plan. (p. 221)

Redl (1976) suggests that the two major components of life space interviewing are *(a)* emotional first aid, and *(b)* clinical exploitation of life events.

Five subcategories are usually listed for emotional first aid:

1. *Drain-off of frustration acidity* attempts to reduce hostility caused by various disappointments and frustrations.

2. *Support of the management of panic, fury, and guilt* provides temporary aid for the child unable to effectively deal with feelings of anxiety, panic, shame, guilt, or fury.
3. *Communication maintenance in moments of relationship decay* is an attempt to keep communication flowing between child and adult during crisis periods.
4. *The regulation* of behavioral and social traffic emphasizes the importance of an authority figure applying appropriate rule-following behavior.
5. *Umpire services* is the need for an impartial adult for both intrachild and interchild conflicts.

When time is available at the moment of need and the situation is receptive to therapy, Redl offers five techniques of clinical exploitation:

1. *Reality rub-in* attempts to make the child aware of what really happened during a crisis situation.
2. *Symptom estrangement* helps the child let go of inappropriate behaviors.
3. *Massaging numb value areas* seeks to awaken appropriate values that may be dormant in the child.
4. *New-tool salesmanship* promotes new socially acceptable behaviors to replace unacceptable behaviors.
5. *Manipulation of the boundaries of the self* desensitizes the child to deviant behavior.

Reinert (1976) notes that teachers will probably spend more time and energy on emotional first aid rather than clinical exploitation. Despite the limitations of this approach for use in large classes, we have found the LSI to be an effective resource for dealing with various crises that occur in all classrooms.

Commercial Programs

It has been noted that most social and emotional skills are learned as part of the everyday interaction of children with each other and with adults (Wallace & Kauffman, 1978). Furthermore, the nature of social-emotional problems often requires that these maladaptive behaviors be corrected through ongoing programs of remediation in varied academic areas. Behavior modification approaches or interpersonal techniques are often applied as a child is involved, for example, in reading or arithmetic programs. Usually the teacher attempts to work on particularly troublesome behaviors throughout the school day. There are a few commercial programs specifically available for remediating social-emotional problems, but they are limited to 30-40 minute of use each day. Three widely used commercial programs are reviewed here.

Developing Understanding of Self and Others (DUSO) (Dinkmeyer, 1970, 1973). This program includes two kits, one for kindergarten and the lower primary grades, and the other for upper primary and fourth grade. The kits are designed to help children better understand social and emotional behavior. The DUSO kits include records or cassettes, posters, activity cards, puppets, discussion pictures, and a program manual. DUSO D-1, the kit for younger children, is organized around the themes of understanding and accepting self; understanding feelings; understanding others; understanding independence; understanding goals and purposeful behavior; understanding mastery, competence, and resourcefulness; understanding emotional maturity; and understanding choices and consequences. The kit for older children, DUSO D-2, includes the following units: developing self-awareness and a positive self-concept, understanding peers, growth from self-centeredness to social interest, personal responsibility, personal motivation, accomplishment, stress, and values.

The DUSO kits are structured so that teachers or counselors may use the program on a daily basis throughout the school year. The program makes extensive use of an inquiry, experiental, and discussion approach to learning, and numerous types of activities (role playing, puppeting, group discussion, music, etc.) are provided in pursuing various DUSO themes. Figure 9-4 shows the directions for a role-playing activity in DUSO D-2.

As an alternative, the author of the program suggests that the teacher may select activities from the total program to fit the specific needs of interests of various classes. In this regard, we have found the materials to be helpful in developing spoken language skills among LD children, even though the program focuses on the child's understanding of self and others.

The Social Learning Curriculum (Level 1) (Goldstein, 1974). Level 1 of the curriculum, which is marketed as an instructional kit, is a developmental program of activities designed to promote the social adjustment of various special students (mildly retarded, emotionally disturbed, and learning disabled). The primary goals of Level 1 are to teach children to think critically and act independently to such an extent that they can become socially and occupationally competent.

Level 1 is divided into curricular sections called phases that represent relevant teaching content. The 10 phases of Level 1 include perceiving individuality, recognizing the environment, recognizing interdependence, recognizing the body, recognizing and reacting to emotions, recognizing what the senses do, communicating with others, getting along with others, identifying helpers, and maintaining body functions. Each of these phases contains approximately 15 to 20 instructional lessons.

Components included in the Level 1 kit include phase books, spirit duplicating masters, stimulus pictures, a scope and sequence chart, and supplements for science, physical education, and mathematics. Each phase also includes a separate teacher's guide. Figure 9-5 shows a lesson from the phase on getting along with others.

Dentist

PURPOSE: To help children learn to develop patience.

PROCEDURE:

1. INTRODUCTION How many of you have been to the dentist lately? Sometimes we have to wait in the dentist's office for a long time, because emergency patients have come in ahead of us. Why is that? Elicit response. Dentists have to be very careful in their work and very patient. Why?

2. ENACTMENT Today we are going to divide into groups of six. There will be one receptionist, four regular patients, and one emergency case in each group. These people will be in the dentist's office. Some of them will have a great deal of patience, and others will have little or none. Who can tell me the difference between patience and patients? Write response on board.

   When you are in your groups, decide what kinds of people you will portray — for example, what you do for a living, your likes and dislikes, and whether you tend to be patient or impatient. Try to think of a way to work these characteristics into your scene. You will probably have to do more talking than ordinarily goes on in a dentist's office.

   Notice that each of you has some purpose for being in the office. Not everyone has a toothache. One is the receptionist, four have appointments, and one is an emergency.

   You will have ten minutes to plan and rehearse your scene.

   Divide into groups and allow time for planning. Enact scenes, discussing each enactment in turn.

3. DISCUSSION Once again, who were the people in the dentist's office? Why were they there?

   Which one seemed to have the most patience? How did you know that?

   Which one had the least patience? How could you tell? What seemed to be the cause of impatience? Did you feel you wanted to help that person?

   Ask person who behaved impatiently — How did you feel when you were being so impatient? Why did you think you should have special treatment?

   Ask audience — If you had been the dentist and had seen this group of people and could choose any one of them to work on first, who would you have chosen?

4. EXTENSION Go back to your group again and think of another situation in which people must exercise patience at home or in school. This time we will try to guess what the situation is from what the characters say and do in the scene. You will have five minutes to plan.

   Allow time for planning and enact scenes. Discuss each enactment in turn.

   Where were they that required patience? Why was patience important?

   Were they all equally patient?

   Who seemed to be the most patient? Who was the least patient?

   What happens to you when you get impatient?

Figure 9-4
Sample Activity Page from DUSO Kit

From *Developing Understanding of Self and Others* (D-2) by D. Dinkmeyer. Circle Pines, Minn.: American Guidance Service, 1973. Copyright 1973 by American Guidance Service. Reprinted by permission.

LESSON 6

BEING COOPERATIVE

LESSON OBJECTIVE The student should be able to describe ways in which he can be cooperative.

MATERIALS	PREPARATION
• Long jump rope	No preparation is needed.
• Broom, dustpan	
• Several books	

TEACHER INFORMATION

In order to reinforce the concept that cooperation is necessary, assign tasks throughout the school day that require the students to cooperate. When each task is completed, ask the students what might have happened if they had not cooperated. You may also want to assign one student a task for which he needs help, then have him enlist the cooperation of a classmate.

LESSON STRATEGIES

To introduce the concept of cooperation, ask the students to imagine they are in the following situation:

You are at the park with some friends. You want to play on the seesaw. You ask one of your friends if he would like to seesaw with you. He says "Yes." The two of you get on the seesaw. Then your friend decides he does not want to seesaw, so he leans back and will not let his end of the seesaw move off the ground. There you are, up in the air, with no way to get down.

Guide a discussion about the situation with questions like the following:

Can you seesaw when your friend will not let your end of the seesaw down? Why not? How does this make you feel? Why? How would your friend feel if you did this to him? Why? What happens when two people try to do something together, but one person does not do what he is supposed to do?

Choose pairs of students to perform activities that require cooperation. Use activities like the following:

Activity 1 *Turn a long jump rope.*

Activity 2 *Move the teacher's desk.*

Activity 3 *Sweep dust into a dustpan.*

Activity 4 *Open the door while you are carrying an armload of books.*

After all the activities have been performed guide a discussion with questions like the following:

What happened when . . . and . . . tried to turn the jump rope? Could they have turned the jump rope if one of them had tried to turn it one way and the other one had tried to turn it the other way? Why not?

Could . . . move my desk by himself? Why not? Could he do it when . . . helped him? Why? What would have happened if . . . had pulled one way and . . . had pulled the other way? Would they have been able to move the desk? Why not?

What is it called when two people work together to do something? Have you ever cooperated with someone at home? At school? What did you do to cooperate?

Do some things work better when people cooperate? Why? What kinds of things work better when people cooperate? Possible answer: **things that take two or more people to do**

Have the students sing a simple round, such as "Row, Row, Row Your Boat." Discuss why cooperation is necessary in order to sing the round. Ask a student why he would not be able to sing the round by himself.

ADDITIONAL SUGGESTIONS

• Divide the students into groups of two. Have each pair of students sit back to back on the floor. Then have the students try to reach a standing position without using their hands or arms. Point out that this activity cannot be performed without cooperation.

• Have the students run a three-legged race. Use chalk or masking tape to make two lines at least 20 feet apart on the playground or gymnasium. Divide the students into groups of two. Have each pair stand side by side behind the starting line. For each pair, tie the right leg of one student to the left leg of the other student with a piece of rope or cloth. At a starting signal, have the pairs of students walk as quickly as possible to the finish line. The first pair of students to cross the finish line wins the race. After the race is completed, discuss the ways in which the students had to cooperate.

Figure 9-5

Sample Lesson from Social Learning Curriculum

From *Social Learning Curriculum* (Level 1), "Getting Along with Others" (Phase 8) by Dr. Herbert Goldstein, Director of Curriculum Research and Development Center in Mental Retardation at New York University. Copyright© 1974, pp. 28-30, by Charles E. Merrill Publishing Co. Reprinted by permission of Charles E. Merrill Publishing Co.

We recommend the *Social Learning Curriculum* as an excellent program for learning about the self. Throughout the curriculum, the student is guided towards a realistic picture of himself as an acting, reacting, and interacting individual in society.

Toward Affective Development (TAD) (Dupont, Gardner, & Brody, 1974). This instructional kit is an activity-centered program designed to stimulate psychological and affective development. It is intended for use with students ages 8 to 12 (third through sixth grade). TAD is based on the premise that there is an interactive relationship between cognitive processes (classifying, problem solving, reasoning, etc.) and the affective processes (motives, interests, values, feelings, etc.).

The program is divided into five sections comprising 21 units or 191 lessons. The five sections are (1) reaching in and reaching out, (2) your feelings and mine, (3) working together, (4) me: today and tomorrow, and (5) feeling, thinking, doing.

The child's feelings, interests, aspirations, and conflicts are the content focus of TAD. The kit includes discussion pictures, posters, duplicating masters, color chips, a cassette, and a detailed teacher's manual. A lesson from the section on working together is shown in figure 9-6.

TAD lessons, activities, and materials have been planned for integration into the typical classroom schedule. The program authors suggest that all or parts of the program may be used for developmental guidance or as part of a remedial program. They feel strongly that affective learning and development are too significant to a child's entire being to be left to chance.

SUMMARY

We have discussed the social-emotional problems of LD children in this chapter. Following a description of the most prevalent difficulties in this area, various assessment techniques were discussed. Observational procedures, ecological assessment, behavioral checklists and rating scales, and teacher-child interaction techniques were each summarized. A discussion of behavioral strategies for developing social-emotional skills included a description of behavior modification, precision teaching, token economies, and contingency contracting. Interpersonal intervention techniques, along with various commercial programs, were also summarized.

SUGGESTED ACTIVITIES

1. Discuss the available management and instructional alternatives for adolescent LD students with social-emotional problems.

Lesson

132

Purpose:

To encourage students to recall personal problem situations and to think of appropriate ways to help people in those situations.

Space requirement:

Regular classroom setting

Approximate time:

30-45 minutes

Vocabulary:

help   hurt   sad   embarrassed   left out   lost

Activity:

Ask students, **Can you remember a time when you needed help from someone? Maybe you were hurt, sad, embarrassed, disappointed, left out, alone, or lost.** Encourage students to share their experiences and the feelings they had.

Then have each student write or draw a description of a situation in which he or she needed help.

Collect all the papers and redistribute them so that no student receives his or her own paper. Tell students to look at the papers they have received and to write down or draw what they might do to help the person in that situation.

When everyone has finished responding, have students take turns telling about the situations and what they did to be helpful. Some students may want to demonstrate suggested actions. Encourage them to do so.

You may wish to display students' drawings and stories on the bulletin board.

Outcome: Students will recall personal problem situations, and other students will respond with helpful actions for those situations.

Follow-up activity: Have students collect magazine and newspaper pictures and articles which show people in need of help. Have them show these to the class, and have the class suggest appropriate helpful actions.

Figure 9-6
Sample Lesson from TAD Program

From *Toward Affective Development* by H. Dupont, O. S. Gardner, and D. S. Brody. Circle Pines, Minn.: American Guidance Service, 1974. Copyright 1974 by American Guidance Service. Reprinted by permission.

2. Visit a class in which various behavior modification techniques are used in classroom management. Discuss the pros and cons of these techniques with the classroom teacher.

3. Construct an informal checklist or rating scale which might be used in evaluating the social-emotional skills of intermediate grade children.

4. Discuss the various commonalities and differences among the emotionally disturbed and learning disabled.

5. Obtain a copy of a behavioral rating scale discussed in this chapter. Examine the scale and read the accompanying test manual. Arrange to observe administration of the rating scale, and rate various behaviors exhibited by the child.

6. Discuss reasons why social-emotional problems are important considerations in attempting to remediate a child's specific learning disabilities.

7. Locate some of the commercially available instructional materials discussed in this chapter. Evaluate the materials according to their usefulness in teaching various social and emotional skills.

8. Arrange a discussion with the parents or teacher of a LD child exhibiting social-emotional problems. Attempt to discern whether the behavior disorders are the result of frustration caused by the learning disability or because of some other precipitating factor.

References

Adams, G.S. *Measurement in education, psychology, and guidance.* New York: Holt, Rinehart & Winston, 1964.

Baer, P.E. Problems in the differential diagnosis of brain-damaged and childhood schizophrenia. *American Journal of Orthopsychiatry,* 1961, *31,* 728-737.

Bentley, R.R., & Starry, A.R. *The Purdue Teacher Evaluation Scale.* Lafayette, Ind.: Purdue Research Foundation, Purdue University, 1970.

Berkowitz, P., & Rothman, E. *The disturbed child.* New York: New York University Press, 1960.

Blackham, G.J., & Silberman, A. *Modification of child and adolescent behavior* (2nd ed.). Belmont, Calif.: Wadsworth, 1975.

Bower, E. *Early identification of emotionally handicapped children in the school* (2nd ed.). Springfield, Ill.: Charles C. Thomas, 1969.

Bower, E., & Lambert, N. *A Process for In-School Screening of Children with Emotional Handicaps.* Princeton, N.J.: Educational Testing Service, 1962.

Bradfield, R.H., & Criner, J. *Classroom interaction analysis.* San Rafael, Calif.: Academic Therapy Publications, 1973.

Brophy, J.E., & Good, T.L. *Teacher-child dyadic interaction: A manual for coding classroom behavior.* Austin: Research and Development Center for Teacher Education, University of Texas, 1969.

Brown, B.B. Experimentalism in teaching practice. *Journal of Research and Development in Education,* 1970, *4,* 14-22.

Brown, L.L. Teacher strategies for managing classroom behaviors. In D. Hammill & N. Bartel (Eds.), *Teaching children with learning and behavior problems* (2nd ed.). Boston: Allyn & Bacon, 1978.

Bryant, N. Subject variables: Definition, incidence, characteristics, and correlates. In N. Bryant & C. Kass (Eds.), *Leadership training institute in learning disabilities* (Vol. 1). Washington, D.C.: Office of Education, Bureau of Education for the Handicapped, 1972.

Bühler, C. Humanistic psychology as an educational program. *American Psychologist,* 1969, *24,* 736-742.

Burks, H. *Behavior Rating Scales.* Los Angeles: California Association for Neurologically Handicapped Children, 1968, 1969.

Cartwright, C.A., & Cartwright, G.P. *Developing observational skills.* New York: McGraw-Hill, 1974

Chess, S. Hyperactive children: A rational approach to medication. *The Urban Review,* 1972, *5,* 33-35.

Connors, C.K. The effects of dexedrine on rapid discrimination and motor control of hyperactive children under mild stress. *Journal of Nervous and Mental Disease,* 1966, *142,* 429-433.

Connors, C.K., & Eisenberg, L. *The effect of teacher behavior on verbal intelligence in observation of Headstart children.* Baltimore: School of Medicine, Johns Hopkins University, 1966.

Dinkmeyer, D. *Developing understanding of self and others.* Circle Pines, Minn.: American Guidance Service, 1970, 1973.

Dollard, J., Doob, L., Miller, N., Mowrer, O., & Sears, R. *Frustration and aggression.* New Haven: Yale University Press, 1939.

Dupont, H. *Educating emotionally disturbed children: Readings* (2nd ed.). New York: Holt, Rinehart & Winston, 1975.

Dupont, H., Gardner, O.S., & Brody, D.S. *Toward affective development.* Circle Pines, Minn.: American Guidance Service, 1974.

Emmer, E. *Classroom Observational Scales.* Austin: Research and Development Center for Teacher Education, University of Texas, 1971.

Ephron, B. *Emotional difficulties in reading.* New York: Julian Press, 1953.

Fels Institute. *Fels Parent Behavior Scales.* Yellow Springs, Ohio: The Institute, 1949.

Fernald, G. *Remedial techniques in basic school subjects.* New York: McGraw-Hill, 1943.

Fitts, W. *The self-concept and performance.* Nashville, Tenn.: Dede Wallace Center, 1972.

Flanders, N.A. *Flanders' system of interaction analysis.* Reading, Mass.: Addison-Wesley, 1970.

Frostig, M., & Maslow, P. *Learning problems in the classroom.* New York: Grune & Stratton, 1973.

Fuller, F. *Fuller affective interaction records 33.* Austin: Research and Development Center for Teacher Education, University of Texas, 1969.

Gardner, W. *Children with learning and behavior problems: A behavior management approach* (2nd ed.). Boston: Allyn & Bacon, 1978.

Goldstein, H. *Social learning curriculum.* Columbus, Ohio: Charles E. Merrill, 1975.

Hall, R.V. *Behavior modification: Basic principles.* Lawrence, Kans.: H & H Enterprises, 1971.

Harrison, A., & Nadelman, L. Conceptual tempo and inhibition of movement in black preschool children. *Child Development,* 1972, *43,* 657-668.

Havard, J. School problems and allergies. *Journal of Learning Disabilities,* 1973, *6,* 492-494.

Johnson, D., & Myklebust, H. *Learning disabilities: Educational principles and practices.* New York: Grune & Stratton, 1967.

Kagan, J. Reflection-impulsivity and reading ability in primary grade children. *Child Development,* 1965, *36,* 609-628.

Kagan, J. Developmental studies in reflection and analysis. In A.H. Kidd, & J.L. Rivoire (Eds.), *Perceptual development in children.* New York: International University Press, 1966.

Kauffman, J.M. *Characteristics of children's behavior disorders.* Columbus, Ohio: Charles E. Merrill, 1977.

Keogh, B. Hyperactive and learning disorders: Review and speculation. *Exceptional Children,* 1971, *38,* 101-110.

Keogh, B., & McDonion, G. Field dependence, impulsivity, and learning disabilities. *Journal of Learning Disabilities,* 1972, *5,* 331-336.

Laten, S., & Katz, G.A. *A theoretical model for assessment of adolescents: The ecological/behavioral approach.* Madison, Wis.: Madison Public Schools, 1975.

Laufer, M. Medications, learning, and behavior. *Phi Delta Kappan,* 1970, *52,* 160-170.

Lerner, J. *Children with learning disabilities* (2nd ed.). Boston: Houghton Mifflin, 1976.

Lindsley, O. Direct measurement and prosthesis of retarded behavior. *Journal of Education,* 1964, *147,* 62-81.

Lister, J. Personal-emotional-social skills. In R.M. Smith (Ed.), *Teacher diagnosis of educational difficulties.* Columbus, Ohio: Charles E. Merrill, 1969.

Lovaas, O., Freitag, G., Gold, V., & Kassorla, I. Experimental studies in childhood schizophrenia: Analysis of self-destructive behavior. *Journal of Experimental Child Psychology,* 1965, *2,* 67-84.

Lovitt, T. Assessment of children with learning disabilities. *Exceptional Children,* 1967, *34,* 233-239.

Lovitt, T.C. *In spite of my resistance ... I've learned from children.* Columbus, Ohio: Charles E. Merrill, 1977.

Lovitt, T.C. The learning disabled. In N.G. Haring (Ed.), *Behavior of exceptional children* (2nd ed.). Columbus, Ohio: Charles E. Merrill, 1978.

Morse, W. The crisis teacher. In N. Long, W. Morse, & R. Newman (Eds.), *Conflict in the classroom: The education of children with problems* (2nd ed.). Belmont, Calif.: Wadsworth, 1971.

Myers, P.I., & Hammill, D.D. *Methods for learning disorders* (2nd ed.). New York: John Wiley, 1976.

Patterson, C. *Humanistic education.* Englewood Cliffs, N.J.: Prentice-Hall, 1973.

Payne, J., Kauffman, J., Brown, G., & DeMott, R. *Exceptional children in focus.* Columbus, Ohio: Charles E. Merrill, 1974.

Purkey, W. *Self-concept and school achievement.* Englewood Cliffs, N.J.: Prentice-Hall, 1970.

Quay, H.C., & Peterson, D.R. *Manual for the Behavior Problem Checklist.* Champaign, Ill.: Children's Research Center, 1967. Mimeographed.

Redl, F. Strategy and techniques of the life space interview. *American Journal of Orthopsychiatry,* 1959, *29,* 1-18.

Redl, F. The concept of life space interviewing. In N. Long, W. Morse, & R. Newman (Eds.), *Conflict in the classroom* (3rd ed.). Belmont, Calif.: Wadsworth, 1976.

Reichenburg-Hackett, W. Practices, attitudes, and values in nursery group education. *Psychological Reports,* 1962, *10* 151-172.

Reinert, H.R. *Children in conflict: Educational strategies for the emotionally disturbed and behaviorally disordered.* St. Louis: C.V. Mosby, 1976.

Rice, D. *Classroom behaviors from A to Z.* Belmont, Calif.: Lear Siegler/Fearon, 1974.

Sears, R., Maccoby, E., & Levin, H. *Patterns of child rearing.* Evanston, Ill.: Row, Peterson, 1957.

Skinner, B.F. *Science and human behavior.* New York: Free Press, 1953.

Skinner, B.F. *Beyond freedom and dignity.* New York: Knopf, 1971.

Sonstegard, M., & Tseng, M. *Development of criteria for the identification of preschool children with learning problems, Final report.* Morgantown, W.Va.: West Virginia University, n.d.

Strauss, A., & Lehtinen, L. *Psychopathology and education of the brain-injured child* (Vol. 1). New York: Grune & Stratton, 1947.

Tarver, S.G., & Hallahan, D.P. Attention deficits in children with learning disabilities: A review. *Journal of Learning Disabilities,* 1974, *7,* 560-569.

Valett, R.E. *The remediation of learning disabilities.* Palo Alto, Calif.: Fearon, 1967.

Walker, H.M. *Walker Problem Checklist.* Los Angeles: Western Psychological Corp., 1970.

Walker, H.M., & Buckley, N.K. *Token reinforcement techniques.* Eugene, Oreg.: E-B Press, 1974.

Walker, J.E., & Shea, T.M. *Behavior modification: A practical approach for educators.* St. Louis: C.V. Mosby, 1976.

Wallace, G., & Kauffman, J.M. *Teaching children with learning problems* (2nd ed.). Columbus, Ohio: Charles E. Merrill, 1978.

Wallace, G., & Larsen, S.C. *Educational assessment of learning problems: Testing for teaching.* Boston: Allyn & Bacon, 1978.

Walters, R. On the high-magnitude theory of aggression. *Child Development,* 1964, *35,* 303-304.

Wiederholt, J.L., Hammill, D.D., & Brown, J. *The resource teacher: A guide to effective practices.* Boston: Allyn & Bacon, 1978.

Worell, J., & Nelson, C. *Managing instructional problems: A case study workbook.* New York: McGraw-Hill, 1974.

Perceptual-Motor Problems

PREVIEW

The development of perceptual abilities is considered by many professionals to be an essential prerequisite for academic achievement. Many perceptual-motor theories and models have had wide imput in both education and psychology. Hallahan and Cruickshank (1973), for example, note that perceptual programming was the most widely used method of evaluating low-achieving children between 1936 and 1970. In the period of time since 1970, however, there has been very little empirical support for using perceptually oriented tests and training programs in the schools. Most research studies indicate that these training programs do not facilitate academic achievement.

Our introductory discussion in this chapter briefly outlines some recent studies exploring the relationship between measured perceptual skills and various areas of school achievement, particularly reading. Studies investigating the concept of perceptual modality are also summarized.

Various types of perceptual-motor problems are discussed under visual perception deficits, auditory perceptual difficulties, haptic perception deficits, and motor deficiencies. A composite list of subskills within each of these areas is also provided.

Many school districts continue to emphasize the assessment and training of perceptual-motor skills among LD students, even though this practice has been increasingly criticized by many writers. Nonetheless, because of the wide usage in schools, the most common assessment approaches are described in this chapter, along with a complete discussion and evaluation of four representative theories of perceptual-motor development. A discussion of the limitations of perceptual-motor training is also provided at the conclusion of this chapter.

Children with perceptual difficulties, such as B.J., have received a tremendous amount of attention during the early 1960s. Some of this interest is an outgrowth of the perceptual emphasis in the early work of Strauss and Werner (1938) and Strauss and Lehtinen (1947), and the later work of Barsch (1965), Getman (1965), and Kephart (1964). Each of these individuals has proposed a theory of perceptual-motor development that has appeal to people in many different disciplines. Many educators, for example, routinely administer perceptual tests to all LD children, while other teachers systematically utilize perceptual training programs with all children evidencing academic difficulties. Moreover, in some states. the classification *perceptually handicapped* has been used synonymously with learning disabilities.

B.J. is a thin, clumsy boy attending first grade in a private school. His parents initially noticed his awkwardness and extremely poor motor development at the age of 2 when he was unable to walk up and down stairs, jump off the bottom step, or kick a large ball. A pediatric exam at age 4 showed that he was having some difficulty negotiating steps. His parents also pointed out that he was unable to ride a tricycle.

B.J. is still having some difficulty with self-dependence skills such as washing his face, dressing himself, and using eating utensils. The kindergarten teacher reported that B.J. had above average language skills. On the other hand, she also reported that B.J. was noticeably inferior on many tasks requiring fine and gross motor skills. His inability to perform various finger plays (e.g., *The Eensy Weensy Spider*), make simple geometric designs that he could easily differentiate, or use a pair of scissors was observed and reported by the first grade teacher who suggested that B.J. be tested by the LD resource teacher.

The LD specialist, along with the adaptive physical education teacher, observed B.J. in a number of different motor activities. Skill deficiencies were noted in various movement skills, such as running, hopping, jumping, walking, and skipping. In addition, B.J. had some difficulty throwing and catching a ball. The obstacle course, which requires a child to jump in and out of tires along with walking on the rims of some tires, proved to be an extremely difficult activity for B.J.

Nonetheless, increased attention has also been given to the efficacy of perceptual-motor assessment and training. In general, almost all recent studies demonstrate that perceptually oriented tests and training programs do not facilitate academic achievement. Hammill (1978) notes that perception tests do not seem to relate to measures of academic ability to any meaningful degree. He also points out that perceptual training programs have not been demonstrated to produce either better school performance or perceptual motor growth itself.

Basically, the perceptual orientation to understanding learning problems is unsupported by available research (Hammill & Larsen, 1974; Larsen & Hammill, 1975). Increasing numbers of teachers have consequently become dissatisfied with the use of perceptual-motor assessment and training activities because these techniques do not improve a student's performance in any of the basic curricular areas (reading, spelling, arithmetic, written or spoken language).

We have devoted a chapter to this topic because of the widespread use of perceptual-motor tests and training programs in schools throughout this country. We also hope to clarify some of the issues involved in this often emotional topic. However, it is important for us to point out at the onset that we do not recommend the use of these techniques as an alternative to academic skills instruction. A review of the important related research is provided throughout the chapter, along with a presentation of various approaches to perceptual-motor assessment and remediation.

THE PERCEPTUAL PROCESS

Perception usually refers to the cognitive ability of the individual to both recognize and integrate external stimuli. It is a process essentially occurring in the brain. Nonetheless, Travers (1967) asserts that perception remains ill-defined. He comments that "perceptual phenomena are those closely tied to sensory inputs and that the research on perception investigates psychological events near the input end rather than the output end, but beyond that point there is little consensus" (p. 599).

The varying deficits found among children with perceptual disturbances have given rise to the concept of *perceptual modality,* used to refer to a child's preference to learn through a specific modality. It is believed that some children learn best through the visual approach, while others, for example, might learn better through auditory methods. Proponents of this concept, such as Wepman (1967), deHirsch et al. (1966), and Dechant (1966), have argued that knowledge of a child's preferred mode of learning is basic to any instructional program. The development of assessment devices to evaluate modality strengths and weaknesses actually emerged from this emphasis. The Illinois Test of Psycholinguistic Abilities (ITPA) (Kirk, McCarthy, & Kirk, 1968), and the

Learning Methods Test (Mills, 1956) are examples of such assessment tools.

Once modality preferences have been ascertained, Wepman (1967) notes that instructional approaches must be decided upon and implemented. He points out that the teacher is faced with the decision of whether to teach through the intact modality, strengthen the deficient modality, or use a combination approach in which the stronger modality is used initially, with separate lessons being used to build the deficient modality.

Studies that have investigated modality training in reading and other academic skill areas have tended to refute the contention that increased achievement will result from preferred modality training. The work of Bateman (1968), Ringler and Smith (1973), and Waugh (1973) indicates little or no relationship between the preferred learning modality and achievement in reading when the child is taught by the preferred perceptual modality.

In their review of the research on this topic, Tarver and Dawson (1978) found that modality preference has not been demonstrated to interact significantly with methods of teaching reading. They suggest that the modality approach to teaching has been unsuccessful because of the neglect of several important considerations, including the lack of emphasis on (1) task analysis at different stages of learning to read, (2) the roles of reinforcement and repetition in increasing learning rates, and (3) the cognitive aspects of learning to read. It seems that the match between learning style and demands of the task will not be achieved until some of these variables are considered.

TYPES OF PRECEPTUAL-MOTOR PROBLEMS

Visual Perceptual Deficits

Goins (1958) comments that there has been considerable interest in the nature of visual perception since the turn of the century. She mentions that a principal problem that has persisted throughout this time has been that of accurately defining visual perception. Leibowitz (1965) further observes that a universally agreed-upon definition of visual perception simply does not exist. He maintains that part of the reason is that visual perception has interested professionals in many disciplines. Definitions are therefore found in the fields of psychology, philosophy, physiology, physics, and education.

The educational definitions of visual perception have differed according to the point of view of the user of the term. Goins (1958) contends that visual perception is the process by which phenomena are apprehended by the mind through the medium of the eye. Ashlock's (1963) definition is closely related. He defines visual perception as the ability to obtain meaning from visual stimuli. According to Frostig and Horne (1964), the definition of visual perception must be operational so that it describes behavior of the individual.

A number of writers have attempted to define *types* of visual perception difficulties. The work of Frostig (Frostig & Horne, 1964) has been most notable in this regard. Many of the following visual perception components appear on representative lists of subskills.

Figure-Ground Discrimination

This skill involves the ability to focus upon selected figures and screen out irrelevant stimuli in the background. The child with difficulties in this area is often inattentive and very disorganized, since his attention may switch from one distracting stimulus to another. Children with figure-ground disturbances are often unable to sort objects according to shape and size.

Spatial Relationships

The ability to perceive the position of objects in space involves spatial relations. Younger LD children with this difficulty are often unable to reproduce a pattern of beads or a pegboard pattern. The sequencing of letters in a word or words in a sentence is also associated with spatial relationships. The sequencing of steps for completing some arithmetic processes may be an additional area of concern for children with spatial relationship difficulties.

Visual-Motor Integration

This subskill includes the ability to integrate vision with movements of body parts. This skill is one that Kephart (1971) considers important. His theoretical rationale is summarized later in this chapter.

Children with visual-motor deficits usually encounter problems in buttoning, lacing, and/or cutting. Later in school these same children might have writing difficulties. One of the most difficult tasks for children with visual-motor integration problems is copying from the chalkboard.

Form Perception

This ability refers to the perception of shape, size, and positional aspects of an object. Children with form perception problems may not be able to recognize the properties distinguishing a circle from a square or a triangle.

Visual Discrimination

Gillespie and Johnson (1974) suggest that visual discrimination is a component of visual perception that is most often related to beginning reading instruction. They define visual discrimination as "the ability to note differences and likenesses among geometric forms, letters, and words" (p. 64). Since visual discrimination deficits are so closely associated with reading difficulties, detailed discussion of this skill was presented in chapter 6.

Auditory Perceptual Problems

The psychological interpretations of specific auditory perceptual skills vary widely among authors. Hammill (1972) points out that some writers refer to the entire receptive process as perception, others distinguish between sensation and perception, and still others include perception under the cognitive domain. Consequently, definitions of auditory perception vary among writers.

Myklebust (1954) defines auditory perception as the ability to select pertinent sounds out of the environment. Others have used the term to refer to the organization of sensory data that are received through the ear (Lerner, 1976). Some writers (Seymour, 1970), however, have had difficulty differentiating auditory perception and auditory discrimination, while others (Schwalb, Blau, & Blau, 1969) have equated the processes. Chalfant and Scheffelin (1969) refer to auditory perception as the central processing of auditory stimuli. It is important, however, to differentiate auditory perception from auditory acuity, which is an individual's ability to receive sounds physiologically.

A child with auditory perceptual difficulties may hear perfectly well but still be unable to interpret what is heard correctly. Children with these disturbances may be unable to associate what is heard with the sound, to blend isolated sounds into words, or to discriminate between sounds. Other children with auditory perceptual problems may be unable to make any sense of what they hear, or they may have short- or long-term auditory memory deficits.

Different lists of auditory perception subskills are provided by Flower (1968), Chalfant and Scheffelin (1969), and Messing (1968). Many of the following auditory perception components appear on most representative lists of subskills.

Auditory Figure-Ground Association

This ability refers to the skill of selecting and attending to relevant auditory stimuli. Children with this difficulty may have problems focusing their attention on the teacher's directions, for example, in a noisy room. Frostig and Maslow (1973) point out that it is not only important to ignore or screen out distracting auditory stimuli, but the child must also learn to change at will the focus of attention.

Auditory Discrimination

Auditory discrimination refers to "the ability to hear similarities and differences between and among two or more sounds" (Gillespie & Johnson, 1974, p. 65). Many investigators have documented the importance of auditory discrimination for learning various phonics skills. Consequently, this particular skill was discussed earlier in chapter 6.

Auditory Memory

Children with auditory memory deficits may be unable to remember individual letter sounds or the sequences of sounds within a word. Learning other sequential activities such as the days of the week, the months of the year, or the alphabet may also be difficult for the child with auditory memory deficits.

Auditory Blending

Sound, or auditory, blending involves the ability to synthesize component sounds into a word. Many children who experience this difficulty are able to differentiate individual letter sounds in isolation, but they are unable to blend these sounds together to make a complete word.

Haptic Perception Deficits

The haptic perceptual system is the method of acquiring information through the tactile and kinesthetic senses. Chalfant and Scheffelin (1969) suggest that the haptic system is important for obtaining information about object qualities, bodily movements, and their interrelationships.

As a component of haptic perception, tactile perception refers to the sense of touch. Children who are deficient are not able to obtain meaning from the things which they touch (Ayres, 1963). Manipulatory activities do not provide these children with useful data.

Kinesthetic perception, on the other hand, refers to the sense of bodily movements. Children with deficits may have problems with coordination, body image and orientation, and spatial orientation.

Many classroom activities require both movement and touch. Chalfant and Scheffelin (1969, p. 41) outline two major kinds of information provided by the haptic system. The first category includes:

1. geometric information concerning surface area or size, shapes, lines, and angles
2. surface texture
3. qualities of consistency such as hard, soft, resilient, or viscous
4. pain
5. temperature
6. pressure

The second category includes the information obtained through bodily movements, such as:

1. dynamic movement patterns of the trunk, arms, legs, mandible, and tongue
2. static limb positions or postures
3. sensitivity to the direction of linear and rotary movement of the skull, limbs, and entire body

Haptic perceptual disturbances may cause difficulties with the kinds of information in the two lists above. The child with a severe kinesthetic difficulty, for example, may be unable to write because he has little idea of how to move his hand. Similarly, tactile deficits might preclude the use of manipulative materials.

Haptic perception has been a very difficult area for researchers to investigate. Consequently, little information is available in the literature concerning this mode of learning. Chalfant and Scheffelin (1969) believe that research should be conducted in order to determine the feasibility of remedial procedures for haptic perceptual deficits.

Motor Deficiencies

The work of Goldstein (1936, 1939), Werner and Strauss (1939), Strauss and Werner (1942), and Strauss and Lehtinen (1947) contributed to the early emphasis on motor disturbances among LD children. Each of these pioneer investigators studied brain-injured children who demonstrated motor difficulties not unlike the motor deficits of present-day LD children. A number of these motor skills will be briefly discussed.

Gross Motor Skills

Gross motor skill difficulty is sometimes noted in the behavior of LD students. Activities such as walking, running, hopping, skipping, jumping, throwing, catching, and muscular strength, which require larger muscle involvement, are generally considered to be gross motor skills. Kephart (1971) asserts that most children will normally learn these gross motor skills before the more precise fine motor skills.

Learning disabled children with difficulties in these skills have often been described as both clumsy and awkward. The gross motor skills requiring a high degree of motor coordination, such as skipping and jumping, are especially difficult for some LD children to perform. Throwing or catching a ball with any accuracy may also be difficult. Playground games or physical education activities requiring some amount of gross motor skill are often frustrating and embarrassing to the child.

Gross motor deficits contribute to the LD child's inferiority on the playground, in completing tasks, and even in getting from one place to another. Johnson and Myklebust (1967) suggest that "these children know what they should do and they have no paralysis, but they cannot relate the motor patterns that they see to their motor systems" (p. 283).

Various physical fitness exercises are also difficult for the child with gross motor deficits. Touching toes from a standing position, sit-ups, chin-ups, and push-ups are all activities requiring both muscular strength and gross motor ability.

Most corrective programs initiate remediation with the basic skills of walking and running. Activities that require hands, arms, and shoulder movements are usually added after the child has met some success in total body exercises. Specific foot, hand, or arm exercises are usually left until the child increases his muscular strength.

Fine Motor Skills

Fine motor abilities usually include the small muscles, involving eye movements and hand use. According to Kephart (1971), normal class-room activities make greater demands upon fine motor coordination than any other activity. He points out that the highly precise movement of the fingers and hands in coloring, drawing, copying, and writing make very heavy coordination demands upon the child.

If a child exhibits difficulty in fine motor control, gross motor involve-ment should be investigated, because many fine motor skills depend upon gross motor movements.

The LD child with fine motor deficits will often have trouble cutting, fastening snaps, or stringing beads. Meyers, Ball, and Crutchfield (1973) say that this child is slow in learning to tie shoes, button coats, manage zippers, and use scissors. Tracing, paper folding, and fitting puzzles together may also be difficult for the child.

Fine motor deficits usually prove to be a devastating problem for the young child. Most beginning writing skills and many initial reading skills depend upon adequate fine motor ability. Merely holding the pencil properly may be a very difficult task for some children. As the child progresses, he may be unable to copy from the chalkboard, trace stencils, color within an outline, or print various letters. Frostig and Maslow (1973) point out that fine motor coordination is also required for accurate placement of numerals, without which it is impossible to undertake any arithmetic process correctly.

Finally, the fine motor subskill of eye-hand coordination is frequently mentioned in regard to disabled readers (Gillespie & Johnson, 1974). It is a skill that requires the child to coordinate vision with movements of the body and parts of the body. Many problems with writing, copying, and tracing may be due to poor eye-hand coordination.

Balance

Balance is the ability to maintain a position with minimal surface contact (Frostig & Maslow, 1973). It is an important part of such activities as walking, standing, stopping, and pulling (Beter & Cragin, 1972). It has also been noted that a stable relationship to gravity is usually achieved through the motor pattern of balance and posture (Kephart, 1964). Children who do not have this firm relationship to gravity will be unable to develop a spatial structure within the environment.

Balance difficulties may be exhibited in a number of different skills. Some children are unable to perform *static* balance movements requiring them not to move as they stand in a stable position. *Dynamic* balance disturbances are usually associated with a child's inability to maintain a position on a moving surface.

Chaney and Kephart (1968) suggest that equilibrium is the crux of a balance problem. It is therefore not surprising to note that balance beam activities are usually difficult for the child with this kind of problem. The balance beam is actually very useful in attempting to help a child pinpoint his center of gravity. Walking backward, forward, sideways, hopping, and while holding onto something are balance beam activities that prove difficult for some LD children.

Kaluger and Kolson (1978) report the work of Heil, who has researched basic symmetry and balance among children with learning disabilities. Among a number of results, Kaluger and Kolson note that Heil found that LD children appear to listen and/or understand better when they are standing rather than sitting or lying down and that some have difficulty in listening to the request to perform a motor act and consequently following the pattern. These tentative observations seem to have some interesting implications for working with children who have balance problems.

Rhythm

Although much is still unknown about rhythm, it is considered an important phenomenon in movement education. Frostig (1970) refers to rhythm as "flowing, measured, balanced movement" (p. 34). Some children may not be able to perceive rhythms or reproduce them. They might be described as *arhythmic.* For our purposes, rhythmic experiences may be discussed in terms of motor and auditory areas.

Motor rhythm is "the ability to perform a movement or series of movements with a consistent time interval" (Kephart, 1971, p. 177). A child with difficulties in this area would be unable to tap out a pattern or march rhythmically. A jumping jack exercise might also be difficult for this child.

Auditory rhythm activities such as dancing or playing rhythm instruments are usually difficult for children with this problem. Heidmann (1973) suggests that trouble in perceiving similar and dissimilar rhythms or high and low sounds is an indication that a child might have difficulty with differentiating various speech sounds.

Rhythm disturbances among some children have only recently been investigated. Beter and Cragin (1972) believe that rhythm is being increasingly recognized as an important process, even though the extent to which rhythm is involved in human behavior has not been clearly pinpointed.

Laterality

Laterality refers to complete motor awareness of the two sides of the body. Kephart (1971) differentiates laterality from handedness, and from the meaning of right and left, by noting that laterality is an *internal awareness* of the two sides of the body and their differences. He believes that laterality is important for keeping things straight in the world around us. External objects are situated to the *right, left, up, down, near,* or *far* only in relation to our own bodies. Consequently, if a child has not developed the internal concept of left and right, perceptual efficiency in coping with the external environment will be impaired (Beter & Cragin, 1972).

Kephart (1971) describes a child who has not yet established laterality:

> When writing on the chalkboard, this child uses one hand for writing activity while the other hand and arm are noticeably tensed or are making small movements that are mirror images of those being made by the dominant side. Such a child has no need to differentiate the sides because they always perform the same movements. (pp. 87-88)

In addition to the difficulties described by Kephart, some children with laterality difficulties might encounter problems with skipping, balancing on one foot smoothly, or riding a tricycle or bicycle. Older LD children who have not established laterality may have some difficulty using tools with precision or knowing right and left in relation to other people.

Directionality

The ability to know *right* from *left, up* from *down,* and *forward* from *backward* is called directionality. Kephart (1971) points out that directionality depends upon laterality, and the establishment of directionality will be limited and often inaccurate until good laterality has been developed. Thus, if a child has established internal awareness of the distinction between his right and left sides, he will be ready to transfer these concepts of direction to his external world of space. Children learn, for example, that objects are located to their *right,* their *left, up* above them, or *down* below them (Beter & Cragin, 1972).

Children with directionality difficulties usually find commands and instructions such as the following very confusing.

> *Draw a line under the table.*
> *Place the book on top of the desk.*
> *Move backward one step.*
> *Place an X on the girl.*

Most positional words (*in, out, on, under,* etc.) require some explanation for children with directional confusion. In addition, puzzles and mazes are usually difficult to solve.

Very often children who consistently reverse and rotate letters are having directionality problems. Word reversals might also be due to the child's inability to distinguish directional concepts. On the other hand, Gillespie and Johnson (1974) have pointed out that *causal* relationships between directionality and reading reversals have not been completely established, even though directional confusion appears in groups of poor readers.

One other academic area often affected by directionality is handwriting. Jordan (1977) believes that directional confusion often creates "erratic production, with much erasing and writing over" (p. 60). Poor letter formation and a generally messy appearance usually describe the child's written work.

Body Image and Awareness

Body image may be defined as the complete awareness of one's own body and its possibilities of movement and performance (Chaney & Kephart, 1968). A number of writers (Frostig & Maslow, 1973; Guilford, 1959) have emphasized the ultimate importance of body image for both physical and emotional adjustment. Kephart (1971) suggests that only through a consistent body image can the child develop a reliable point of origin for either perceptions or motor responses. The adequate development of body image is actually crucial for all motor movements.

Children with body image and awareness difficulties exhibit diverse difficulties. According to Johnson and Myklebust (1967), some children are unable to identify body parts on command, while others have some difficulty in recognizing their own faces in a mirror. The inability to construct models of human figures may also be a problem. Kephart (1971) also describes the child with body image difficulties:

> Such a child will display this difficulty when asked to select a space on the floor among furniture and other obstacles, which is sufficiently large to permit him to lie down and move his arms and feet freely. He will select a

space that is too small and in which his arms and legs bump into the furniture when he moves them. On the other hand, he may demand more space than he needs for his movements. Either error indicates an imperfect awareness of the space occupied by his body in various positions. (p. 95)

It is important to note the influence of other learning problems on body image disturbances. Consequently, it will be necessary during evaluation to differentiate body image difficulties from auditory comprehension deficits in the case of the child who might not understand directions.

ASSESSING PERCEPTUAL-MOTOR PROBLEMS

An evaluation of the perceptual-motor functioning of children with learning disabilities is often included as one part of the total assessment process. Although this practice has been increasingly criticized by many writers, it is evident that this type of psychological testing is a common practice in many schools (Wallace & Larsen, 1978). Published tests or informal assessment techniques are among the most widely utilized approaches for evaluating perceptual-motor skills. Both of these methods will now be discussed.

Published Tests

Hammill (1978) suggests that published perceptual-motor tests are probably most useful during research projects, when an objective measure of a perceptual trait is required, or during the screening of large numbers of students for perceptual difficulties. In general, most published tests focus upon the evaluation of specific modalities, including visual, auditory, and motor.

Visual Perception Tests

The presumed relationship of visual perceptual ability and early school success if probably partially responsible for the large number of published tests of visual perception. Among their various uses, these tests are often administered to young children as one indicator for predicting school success. Some of the more widely used tests of visual perception are summarized in table 10-1.

Auditory Perception Tests

Tests of auditory perception are not as widely available as published visual perception tests. It is usually concluded that the reason for the lack of auditory perceptual assessment techniques stems from mechan-

During the testing situation, B.J. was talkative, friendly, and very active. He had a tendency to touch and finger all test materials and want to turn pages and hurry on to the next item.

In addition to a number of informal tests, B.J. was administered the *Basic School Skills Inventory* (BSSI) which indicated below average readiness skills. He had some difficulty in accurately holding a pencil, although most items to be copied were duplicated correctly. Capital and lowercase letters were often mixed within words and sentences.

Informal observations verified the teacher's concerns regarding B.J.'s gross motor skills. It was noted that he experienced difficulty in both throwing and catching balls, along with more obvious problems in running, hopping, skipping, and jumping. He performed very poorly with physical education and playground-type activities. The fine motor activities of coloring and writing were also notably deficient. B.J. usually avoided fine motor activities such as solving puzzles and using scissors.

As noted in these photos, B.J. has serious difficulties in walking forward on the balance beam. He also experiences some difficulty walking sideways and backwards on the balance beam. Nonetheless, B.J. seems to enjoy balance beam activities.

Table 10-1
Selected Published Tests of Visual Perception

title	author	number of items	administration time in minutes	age range	norms	group (G) or individual (I)	consumable materials
Bender Visual-Motor Gestalt Test	Bender, L.	9	7-15	4-11	1104	I	No
Chicago Test of Visual Discrimination	Weiner, P. Wepman, J. Morency, A.	9	10-15	6-8	90	G, I	No
Developmental Test of Visual-Motor Integration	Beery, K. Buktenica, N.	24	10-15	2-15	1039	G, I	Yes
Developmental Test of Visual Perception	Frostig, M. Maslow, P. Lefever, D. Whittlesey, J.	72	30-60	4-8	2116	G, I	Yes
Eye-Motor Coordination		16	15-20	4-8	2116	G, I	Yes
Figure-Ground		8	15-20	4-8	2116	G, I	Yes
Form Constancy		32	10	4-8	2116	G, I	Yes
Position in Space		8	5	4-8	2116	G, I	Yes
Spatial Relationships		8	5-10	4-8	2116	G, I	Yes
Illinois Test of Psycholinguistic Abilities	Kirk, S. McCarthy, J. Kirk, W.						
Visual Closure		40	8	2-10	1000	I	Yes
Visual Sequential Memory		25	15-20	2-10	1000	I	No
Memory-for-Designs Test	Graham, F. Kendall, B.	15	5-10	6-80	341	I	No
Metropolitan Readiness Tests	Hildreth, G. Griffiths, N. McGauvran, M.						
Matching		14	5-6	5-6	12231	G	Yes
Copying		14	7	5-6	12231	G	Yes
Motor-Free Visual Perception Test	Colarusso, R. Hammill, D.	36	8-10	4-8	883	I	No

Table 10-1 (cont.)

Perceptual Achievement Forms	Lowder, R.	7	10	6-8	1510	—	No
Primary Visual-Motor Test	Haworth, M.	16	10-15	4-8	500	—	No
Purdue Perceptual-Motor Survey	Roach, E. Kephart, N.	22	60	6-18	200	—	No
Revised Visual Retention Test	Benton, A.	10	5	8-44	600	—	No
Slosson Drawing Coordination Test	Slosson, R.	12	10-15	5-adult	200	G, I	Yes
Wechsler Intelligence Scale for Children	Wechsler, D.						
Total Performance		177	50-60	5-15	2200	—	Yes
Picture Completion		20	10	5-15	2200	—	No
Block Design		7	15	5-15	2200	—	No
Object Assembly		7	12	5-15	2200	—	No
Coding		45 (A) 93 (B)	3 (under 8) 2 (over 8)	5-15	2200	—	Yes
Mazes		8	10	5-15	2200	—	Yes

From "Selecting a Test of Visual Perception" by R.P. Colarusso and S. Gill, *Academic Therapy*, 1975-76, *11*, 157-167. Copyright 1975-76 by Academic Therapy Publications. Reprinted by permission.

ical difficulties in designing reliable and valid test items (Wallace & Larsen, 1978). According to Gillespie and Johnson (1974), the auditory abilities most often measured are auditory discrimination, auditory blending, and auditory sequential memory. Some auditory perception tests are summarized in table 10-2. We do not recommend the administration of these tests as predictors of reading failure or school readiness due to the lack of available research evidence in this regard. The Hammill and Larsen (1974) study reviewed later in this chapter, in fact, suggests that some auditory perceptual skills, as measured, have little to do with the reading process.

Motor Tests

Very few published tests of motor ability are available for use with LD children. Informal techniques are more often utilized in evaluating a student's motor proficiency.

Among the limited number of published motor tests, the Oseretsky scales are used in many schools. These scales were first published in Russia in 1923 and have since been translated and revised in the United States. The Lincoln-Oseretsky Motor Developmental Scale (Sloan, 1954) is the most popular version of the scales. This test consists of a year-by-year scale for children ages 6 to 14. The motor abilities measured include general static coordination, dynamic coordination of the hands, general dynamic coordination, motor speed, simultaneous voluntary movements, and synkinesia (associated involuntary movements). A motor age is calculated based on performance.

The Bruininks-Oseretsky Test of Motor Proficiency (Bruininks, 1977) is the most recent modification of the Oseretsky scales. The Bruininks revision includes standardization information for children from 4 to 18 years of age. Subtests include running speed and agility, balance, bilateral coordination, strength, upper limb coordination, response speed, visual-motor control, and upper limb speed and dexterity. It is an individually administered test with results provided as age equivalents and percentiles for each child's general motor ability.

Informal Techniques

Observational procedures and various informal, teacher-made tests are commonly used for evaluating a child's perceptual-motor skills. Heidmann (1973), for example, notes that systematic observations provide instructionally useful data that might not otherwise be available to the teacher.

In addition to structured physical education classes, recess and free play periods are other common opportunities for observing a child's perceptual-motor skills. During these times, Chaney and Kephart (1968) point out that the teacher should attempt to pinpoint a pattern of

Table 10-2
Selected Published Tests of Auditory Perception

title	skills tested	age range	group or individual
Auditory Discrimination Test (Wepman, 1958)	Sound discrimination	Elementary grades	I
Goldman-Fristoe-Woodcock Auditory Skills Test Battery (Goldman, Fristoe, Woodcock, 1976)	Auditory selective attention, auditory discrimination, auditory memory, and sound-symbol correspondence.	3 yrs. to adult	I
Screening Test for Auditory Perception (Kimmell & Wahl, 1969)	Perceive difference between long & short vowel sounds, initial style consonant sounds and blends, rhyming & non-rhyming words, retaining & identifying rhythmic sequences & words with only subtle phonemic differences	Grades 2-6	G
Test of Auditory Discrimination (Goldman, Fristoe, & Woodcock, 1970)	Speech-sound discrimination under quiet & noisy backgrounds	Preschool to adulthood	I

difficulties rather than trying to isolate various individual problems. Motor skills listed by chronological age, as shown in table 10-3, can be particularly helpful as an observational guideline. The Orpet and Heustis (1971) checklist may also be useful in this regard.

Table 10-3
Informal Guidelines for Motor Development

age	accomplishments involving motor skills
Birth	Little head control. Grasp is a reflex action. Release not possible.
1 month	Reacts with mass motor activity to any stimulation. Hands kept fisted. Startles in response to sudden loud noises.
2 months	Can hold up head for several seconds. Vigorous movements in bath. May smile when caressed. Some babbling.
3 months	If child is held erect, head wobbles slightly. Holds toy for short time. Inspects hands as he moves them about. Picks at clothing. Coos and chuckles.
4 months	Rotates head from side to side while lying on back. Can hold head steadily erect if supported in a sitting position. Moves fingers; scratches. Reaches for toy and grasps it. Turns head toward a sound. Plays with hands or a rattle.
5 months	Can momentarily support large fraction of his weight in standing position. Can roll over by rotating upper part of the body, flexing hips, throwing leg to same side. Rolls from his back to face-down position.
6 months	Holds head erect easily and can rotate it. Supports self on outstretched arms. Can grasp rattle and transfer it from hand to hand. Fingers reflections in a mirror.
7 months	Momentarily can hold trunk erect in a sitting position. Assumes crawl position with weight supported on one or both arms. Dances and bounces when held in upright position. Grasps rattle well with both hands. May inadvertently drop object during hand-to-hand transfer. Reaches out for people.
8 months	Can support entire body weight on feet for short intervals. Pivots about by using arms. Bangs spoon on table in imitation.
9 months	Can hold trunk erect indefinitely in sitting position. Can lean forward and regain sitting position. Can stand on toes. Assumes creeping position on hands and knees. Pokes objects using an index finger.
10 months	Can pull self to knees and can stand with support. May attempt to wave "bye-bye." Drinks from cup when assisted.
11 months	Can go from sitting to face-down to sitting position. Intentional finger release begins.
12 months	Can lower self from standing to sitting by holding onto crib rails, chair, or other support. Cruises or walks about using support. Reaches for objects, not only to grasp them, but also to use them. Rolls or throws ball rolled to him. May attempt to feed self awkwardly.
13 months	Can creep on hands and knees. Has reached good proficiency in releasing or dropping objects.
15 months	Can stand quite independently. Climbs stairs if one hand is held. Opens and closes small boxes.

Table 10-3 (*cont.*)

18 months	Good sitting balance. Can sit without support. Can get into high chair without difficulty, turn around, and sit down. In high chair, if reaching for object, always places opposite hand on table to balance self. Stands with both feet on floor. Toddles about, but turns around poorly. Reaches almost automatically for near objects. Grasps small object with wide-open hand. Opens drawers. Climbs onto chairs and beds. Throws ball. Brings toys on request. Feeds self. Attempts to put on clothing but without success.
20 months	Stands on one foot with help.
21 months	Begins to run. Can walk up flight of three steps alone. Kicks large balls. Scribbles spontaneously.
24 months	Picks up objects from floor. Holds objects without dropping them. May step over chair in seating self. Walks steadily if unhurried. Can imitate clapping, raising arms over head, revolving hands. Begins to hold crayon with fingers. Can turn pages singly.
3 years	Stands with little conscious effort. Stands on one foot momentarily without support. Can walk and run on toes, walk in straight line, and jump off floor with feet together. Can catch large ball with arms extended stiffly. Can ride tricycle with great dexterity. Can sit well, but reaches out somewhat awkwardly. Can pick up small objects with ease. Handles crayons like an adult. Unbuttons front and side buttons of clothes, but has great difficulty in buttoning.
4 years	Carries cup of water without spilling. Takes pleasure in stunts, i.e., whirling, swinging, somersaulting. Can duck-walk. Can catch ball, but uses arms more than hands in receiving the ball. Grasps cube neatly with thumb and middle finger, and smaller objects well with thumb and index finger. Can adjust grasp to brush teeth.
5 years	Keen sense of balance. Marches well in time to music. Less cautious in movements than four-year-old. Performs with greater speed, precision, and confidence than four-year-old. Shows great precision in use of tools (toothbrush, silverware, pencil). Can tie bow knot. Manipulates buttons well. Can lace shoes and can build cube tower well.
6 years	Can stand on each foot alternately with eyes closed. Can bow gracefully. Reaches well. Movements of head, trunk, and arms are smoothly synchronized. Uses great care in building cube tower, and checks frequently on alignment.

From *Motoric Aids to Perceptual Training* by C.M. Chaney and N.C. Kephart. Columbus, Ohio: Charles E. Merrill, 1968. Copyright 1968 by Charles E. Merrill. Reprinted by permission.

The informal use of selected tasks or activities from proficiency tests has also been suggested by Smith (1969). He believes that it is not always necessary to use a test in its entirety. In these cases, the teacher can choose to evaluate only those areas about which information is needed.

Readers who are interested in additional informal techniques for evaluating perceptual-motor skills should consult Valett (1969), Mann and Suiter (1974), Bush & Giles (1977), and Wallace & Larsen (1978).

In addition to a number of very specific teaching suggestions, it was recommended that the movement exploration approach to motor training be used with B.J. The intent of this program is to improve motor efficiency with various gross motor skills. Daily lessons with obstacle courses, training steps, and balance beam activities are included in the program. All of these activities were recommended as necessary parts of any remedial program for B.J.

A very structured program was also recommended for developing fine motor skills.

Picture lacing boards were used to develop finger dexterity, along with activities requiring zippers to be zippered, buckles to be buckled, snaps to be fastened, and bows to be tied. *Pick-up Sticks* and *Jacks* were also recommended for after-school and home play.

The *Write and See* program was used to help B.J. with his handwriting difficulties. This program uses a gradual fading technique for writing letters and numerals so that the child is finally capable of writing the entire letter or word from memory. Use of a salt tray and a sandbox was also recommended for tracing various letters and words.

Many of the teaching activities and materials recommended for B.J. were easily integrated in a primary class curriculum. Consequently, B.J.'s teacher utilized the remedial suggestions for B.J. with small groups of other children who were encountering similar gross motor and fine motor deficiencies.

DEVELOPING PERCEPTUAL-MOTOR SKILLS

The emphasis on perceptual processes and various components of perception has lead to a proliferation of perceptual-motor training programs. However, wholesale adoption of the entire program rather than selecting parts of these approaches has been the target of severe criticism in the professional literature. As mentioned previously, almost all research in this area concludes that improvement in academic skill areas cannot be expected as a result of perceptual-motor training.

Most critics of perceptual-motor training programs caution against the use of such programs with all children in a particular class. On the contrary, it is usually suggested that various parts of these programs be selectively utilized for remedial purposes or in preschool programs. Perceptual-motor activities are *not* recommended as an alternative to instruction in academic skills.

In this section, four representative theories of perceptual-motor development are summarized. An analysis of each theory follows the descriptive presentations. We encourage readers to consult original sources for additional information.

KEPHART: A PERCEPTUAL APPROACH

The perceptual-motor theory of Kephart (1964, 1971) stresses that all parts of the perceptual-motor process operate together as a unit. The theory views the development of the child as being accomplished in a series of stages, each succeeding stage more complex than the preceding one. Most importantly, Kephart believed that all behavior is basically motor and that the prerequisites of any kind of behavior are muscular and motor responses. While drawing a circle, for example, it is not possible to separate what seems like the motor part from the part that seems perceptual. Learning experiences must therefore be designed in terms of the total perceptual-motor process.

Children normally develop and progress through each stage of perceptual-motor development during the preschool years. By the age of 6 or 7, most children have developed sufficient perceptual-motor abilities. Kephart points out that the LD child has failed to develop normally. He suggests that either some perceptual-motor skills have failed to develop or have developed in an atypical or distorted manner. Abnormalities in the developmental sequence may be the result of environmental deprivations, injuries or defects in the organism, or emotional pressures with which the child has been unable to cope. The effects of perceptual-motor deficits may be revealed in the elementary grades through difficulties in learning and low academic achievement.

Kephart believed that basic skills should be taught in their natural order of development. A *motor pattern* is essential for information gathering at a very basic stage of development. A motor pattern consists of coordinated motor behaviors that are combined to serve a purpose. It is a motor generalization allowing for some variability and a much broader purpose. On the other hand, a *motor skill* allows for only limited variation. A motor skill is a motor act that is usually performed with a high degree of precision. The difference between walking as a motor skill and walking as part of a locomotor pattern is often described. The young child who is learning to walk must consider the mechanical aspects of walking (placing one foot in front of the other, etc.) Very little attention is afforded the actual purpose of movement and only limited variation is possible. The locomotor pattern of the child, in contrast, allows the child to walk, run, skip, and so forth. The motor act itself is not attended to as much as the generalization of the process. Extensive variation is possible with motor patterns.

Kephart also refers to the development of *splinter skills* among some LD children. Splinter skills are not part of the sequential development of motor skills. The term is primarily used in reference to behavior existing in isolation or "splintered off" from the remainder of the child's motor activity. The flexibility and utility of splinter skills are very limited. Chaney and Kephart (1968) illustrate a splinter skill by describing a boy who wrote his name on the chalkboard after having memorized the finger movements required for each stroke. The finger movements were not related to other parts of the body, such as the wrist and arm. They suggest that this child must develop a structure of movements by going back to the point where differentiation had departed from the pattern. A sequence of movements must then be reestablished.

Motor Generalizations

A combination of motor patterns leads to *motor generalizations,* an integration of motor patterns that permits extensive exploration of the environment. Kephart lists four motor generalizations as basic to the educational process: (1) balance and maintenance of posture, (2) locomotion, (3) contact, and (4) receipt and propulsion.

Balance and Maintenance of Posture

This is an important and obvious motor generalization that allows the child to maintain his relationship to gravity. A stable relationship to gravity establishes a point of origin for spatial relationships. Balance and posture provide this stability.

Locomotion

Kephart refers to locomotion skills as the motor activities that move the body through space—walking, jumping, running, and so forth. The environment and relationships between objects in the environment are explored through locomotion. Among many slow learning children, locomotion is viewed as not being generalized. Walking may be inflexible and rigid because locomotor skills have not been generalized to a pattern of movements.

Contact

The skills involved in reaching, grasping, and releasing are contact skills. These skills help a child investigate the characteristics of objects through manipulation. The knowledge that the child gains from this experience usually helps in the development of form perception and figure-ground relationships.

Receipt and Propulsion

Receipt skills are described by Kephart as those activities (e.g., catching a ball) by which the child makes contact with a moving object. Propulsion involves those activities (e.g., throwing a ball) by which the child imparts movement to an object.

These four motor generalizations allow the child to investigate relationships in the environment as a base for effective learning. Kephart suggests that some children find it difficult to learn motor patterns. He recommends that these children receive training to learn motor patterns and to learn the more generalized skill of how to gather information.

Perceptual-Motor Match

An important concept discussed by Kephart is a *perceptual-motor match,* the child's ability to combine the motor information that was acquired for perceptual information. The perceptual information is matched to motor information so closely that the two forms of data come to have the same meaning. Kephart suggests many children have difficulties in school because the perceptual-motor match has not yet been completed.

THE KEPHART APPROACH: IN PERSPECTIVE

In addition to developing this particular theory of learning disabilities, Kephart developed a scale called the Purdue Perceptual-Motor Scale (Roach & Kephart, 1966). The scale was summarized previously in this chapter. A series of training suggestions for remedial efforts were also developed. These activities are sequenced from simple to complex. Performance on a specific task is always secondary to teaching the generalization.

Kephart's theory of learning disabilities emphasizes one particular aspect of the problem; that is, the perceptual-motor aspect of learning. The approach has frequently been criticized for its lack of any emphasis upon transition to later academic development. The role of auditory processes and the lack of auditory training is another weakness of the program. Finally, there is little available evidence to suggest any value in perceptual-motor training for LD students (Goodman & Hammill, 1973; Myers & Hammill, 1976.)

BARSCH: A MOVIGENIC THEORY

The theory and curriculum developed by Barsch (1965, 1967, 1968), called a *movigenic* theory, is based upon the belief that movement patterns lead to learning efficiency. Barsch believes that movement is a variable in all learning and that all children need to move. The theory is based upon the following principles:

1. "The fundamental principle underlying the design of the human organism is movement efficiency." Everything that an individual does involves movement.
2. "The primary objective of movement efficiency is to economically promote the survival of the organism." An individual survives in this world by moving. Survival chances are increased if movement is efficient.
3. "Movement efficiency is derived from the information the organism is able to process from an energy surround." Information is an essential of life and the only source of survival. Individuals select and seek information to continue survival.
4. "The human mechanism for transducing energy forms into information is the percept-cognitive system." The sensitivity systems for obtaining data are sight, hearing, touch, feeling, smell, and taste. These organs serve as agents for processing information to the brain.
5. "The terrain of movement is space." Individuals must learn to move in both physical and cognitive space in order to move most efficiently.
6. "Developmental momentum provides a constant forward thrust toward maturity and demands an equilibrium to maintain direction." Individuals move through life with a developmental momentum which usually peaks at middle age.
7. "Movement efficiency is developed in a climate of stress." Stress is viewed as a part of life. Some stress is considered necessary for learning, while other types of stress negatively affect the individual's efficiency.

8. "The adequacy of the feedback system is critical in the development of movement efficiency." An individual's feedback system actually helps him or her to learn more efficiently. Inadequate feedback may result in some type of disorder.
9. "Development of movement efficiency occurs in segments of sequential expansion." Movement efficiency develops from single to more complex, and the rate of learning certain behaviors differs throughout life.
10. "Movement efficiency is symbolically communicated through the visual-spatial phenomenon called language." Movement efficiency is a very important factor in language development (1967, pp. 35-59).

The Movigenic Curriculum

Based upon the 10 principles outlined above, Barsch developed a movigenic curriculum for children with learning problems. The program is intended to improve their motor efficiency over a number of different dimensions. Children should receive instruction in each dimension of the program. Barsch has described the components of the movigenic curriculum as follows:

1. *Muscular strength* is the capacity of the organism to maintain an adequate state of muscle tone, power, and stamina to meet the daily demands appropriate to his body size and chronological age.
2. *Dynamic balance* is the capacity of the organism to activate antigravity muscles in proper relationship to one another against the force of gravitational pull, to maintain alignment, sustain his transport pattern, and aid in recovery.
3. *Spatial awareness* is the capacity of the organism to identify his own position in space relative to his surroundings with constant orientation to surface, elevation, periphery, back, and front.
4. *Body awareness* is the capacity of the organism to achieve a conscious appreciation of the relationship of all body segments to movement, to be able to label body parts, and to appreciate the functional properties of various body parts.
5. *Visual dynamics* is the capacity of the organism to fixate accurately on a target at near, mid, and far points in space, to scan a surround for meaning in the vertical and horizontal planes, to coverge and accommodate, to equalize the use of both visual circuits in a binocular pattern to achieve fusion, and to steer the body in proper alignment for movements through space.
6. *Auditory dynamics* is the capacity of the organism to process information on a receiving and a sending basis for the world of sound and to attach appropriate relationships to the world of sound.
7. *Kinesthesia* is the capacity of the organism to maintain an awareness of position in space and to recall patterns of movement from previous experience for utility in resolving continuing demands.

8. *Tactual dynamics* encompasses the capacity of the organism to gain information from the cutaneous contact of active or passive touching.
9. *Bilaterality* is the capacity of the organism to reciprocally interweave two sides in a balanced relationship of thrusting and counterthrusting patterns around the three coordinates of vertical, horizontal, and depth in proper alignment from initiation to completion of the task.
10. *Rhythm* is the capacity of the organism to synchronize patterns of movement according to situational demands, thus achieving harmony, grace, and use of movement.
11. *Flexibility* is the capacity of the organism to modify or shift patterns of movement appropriate to the situational demand.
12. *Motor planning* is the capacity of the organism to plan a movement pattern prior to execution in order to meet the demands of a task (1965, pp. 15-29)

MOVIGENICS: IN PERSPECTIVE

Barsch's movement and space theory of learning differs little from other perceptual-motor theories. Movigenics is based upon the premise that movement is the basis for learning, and children who experience motor difficulties will subsequently encounter cognitive disturbances. However, no principal studies have documented the effectiveness of this approach. In addition, the movigenic curriculum neglects the important area of language. Transition from movigenic activities to academic skills is also overlooked.

GETMAN: A VISUOMOTOR MODEL

An optometrist by training, Getman developed a visuomotor program based upon the assumption that perceptual skills can be trained and developed. He believes that the development of perceptual skills is related to levels of coordination (Getman, Kane, & McKee, 1968). The Getman model, however, demonstrates his primary interest with visual perception.

The work of Skeffington, also an optometrist, influenced the model finally developed by Getman. Skeffington's theory of perceptual performance included four processes that merged into the emergent vision (Getman, 1965). Getman describes these processes as:

1. *The anti-gravity process,* which is the "total motor system of the organism used for locomotion, exploration, and organization" (p. 52) within the environment.
2. *The centering process,* which is the ability to orient to the environment, including oneself.
3. *The identification process,* which provides a "wholeness" to objects; labeling evolves through manipulation of these objects.
4. *The speech-auditory process,* which permits the use of communication skills unique to the human.

Vision is then "an emergent of all the underlying interrelated processes and modes of performance" (p. 56).

Getman utilized the Skeffington model as a guide for creating his own model that expanded upon the development of the visual process. Getman's model consists of a series of levels.

The first level is called the *innate response system.* The innate responses with which a child is born include the tonic neck reflex, startle reflex, light reflex, grasp reflex, reciprocal reflex, stato-kinetic reflex (readiness to act), and the myostatic reflex (provides the muscles with the information that they have acted). This system is crucial for all learning.

The *general motor system* is the second level of the Getman model. It includes creeping, walking, running, jumping, skipping, and hopping. Getman believes the child who has not mastered these skills will lack coordination.

The third level is an area of more elaborate combinations of the first two systems called *special motor systems.* They include eye-hand coordination, combinations of the two hands, hand-foot relationships, voice, and gesture relationships.

The next level is the *ocular motor system,* which is most concerned with eye movements and coordination. At this level, the following skills are important: (1) fixation, fixating on target; (2) saccadics, eye movements from one target to another; (3) pursuits; both eyes following a moving target; and (4) rotations, freely moving eyes in all diretions.

The fifth level is the *speech motor system.* This level includes babbling, imitative speech, and original speech.

Visualization is the next level in the Getman model, and all systems contribute to this ability. Overt performances may be transformed into covert behavior at this level. An individual who can visualize can visually remember past experiences and preview future events.

Perception and *vision* are used synonymously by Getman. They emerge from all levels of the system. Cognition is represented as the next level of the model, and above this level are both abstractions and elaborations of intellectual development.

Getman, Kane, and McKee (1968) also developed a training program for children that recommends exercises and activities corresponding to each stage of development. The lessons include:

1. Practice in General Coordination
2. Practice in Balance
3. Practice in Eye-Hand Coordination
4. Practice in Eye Movements
5. Practice in Form Perception
6. Practice in Visual Memory

THE VISUOMOTOR MODEL: IN PERSPECTIVE

The Getman approach has been criticized because of the strong visual perception emphasis and the lack of empirical evidence to support this model (Myers & Hammill, 1976). Getman's optometric background must certainly be considered in attempting to explain the dominant role of vision in his model. The similarities to other perceptual-motor approaches, especially that of Barsch, have been frequently noted. Lerner (1976) mentions the weakness of this model in classifying how the individual progresses from motor development to the cognitive stages of learning. Unfortunately, auditory processes are also barely considered in Getman's procedures.

DOMAN-DELACATO: A NEUROLOGICAL ORGANIZATION CONCEPT

The Doman-Delacato concept of neurological organization has been the object of great controversy among professionals, professional organizations, and parental groups since its rise to prominence at the Institute for the Achievement of Human Potential in Philadelphia during the early 1960s.

Doman and Delacato base their theory on the hypothesis that ontogeny recapitulates phylogeny, or that each individual's development progresses through the same stages as did the development of his species. An individual's development is considered logical, orderly, and inextricably bound to his species' anatomical and biological development along the evolutionary scale. In this progress toward full neurological organization, humans develop through the levels common to other species: the spinal cord medulla, the pons, the midbrain, and the early cortical level. Humans add the final stage of cortical hemispheric dominance as an end to the process. The last step is a prerequisite to complete neurological organization.

Delacato (1966) believes, that there are six uniquely human skills. These six skills are walking upright and in cross-pattern, symbolic speech, symbolic writing, reading, understanding human speech, and stereognosis (tactile recognition). These skills are developed fully at maturity when complete neurological organization has been reached.

Doman and Delacato, however, believe that disorganization of the nervous system is the cause of many medically and educationally undiagnosed, and consequently untreated, learning problems in children. Some of the reasons they cite for neurological disorganization include genetic factors, infection during pregnancy, maternal metabolic factors, continuing effect of previous injury, degenerative process, environmental deprivation, and temporal factors related to undetermined causes. Most diagnostic labels are disregarded. The conditions of children who are handicapped are viewed as falling along a single continuum from normalcy to central nervous system disorganization.

Evaluation

An extensive diagnosis is part of the Doman-Delacato procedure. An *index of suspicion,* similar to a case history, is completed on each child.

Neurological examinations are routinely administered. A developmental profile developed by Doman and Delacato is used to evaluate the neurological age of brain-injured children. Six sensory-motor areas, each with seven levels, are assessed. Handedness, footedness, eyedness, and subcortical skills are also measured.

Delacato claims to be able to determine an individual's neurological development in terms of the behaviors he exhibits. The evaluation scale is briefly summarized here.

1. Normal reflex movements in the infant correspond to the spinal cord medulla level.
2. Sleeping positions appropriate for laterality are an indication of development through the pons level.
3. Smooth, rhythmical cross-pattern creeping indicates development through the midbrain level.
4. Cross-pattern walking that is smooth, rhythmical, and with good balance indicates proper development through the early cortex level.
5. Clear dominance of one side of the body indicates cerebral dominance, the highest level of neurological organization.

Delacato points out that the child is studied from the standpoints of etiology, anatomy, pathology, and functional level. Treatment is then initiated at the level of neurological organization indicated by the diagnostic results. McCarthy and McCarthy (1969) point out that "treatment at any level of organization is aimed at reorganizing subsequent disorganized levels" (p. 53).

Treatment

Detailed treatment procedures for each successive level are provided for all children. The method which treats the brain and not the symptoms of brain injury is called *patterning.* Patterning involves precise manipulation of arms, legs, and the head. Myers and Hammill (1976) state that patterning "is based on the theory that all cells in one area of the brain are not usually affected by injury, and that activation of live cells is possible" (p. 343). It is advised that patterning must be carried out for 5 minutes at least four times daily, every day without fail. Lerner (1976) suggests that increased sensory stimulation, breathing exercises, and restrictions of fluids, salt, and sugar may also be prescribed.

Remedial teaching is usually suggested once the premedial patterning treatment has resulted in complete neurological organization. Gillespie and Johnson (1974) have outlined the various requirements of the Doman-Delacato method of teaching reading. They include large crayons, sandpaper letters, the initial reading of whole words, and the subsequent teaching of phonics with consonants taught first. They encourage all work in beginning reading to be done orally.

DOMAN-DELACATO: IN PERSPECTIVE

Few experimentally sound studies have provided positive data concerning the Doman-Delacato approach. On the contrary, the literature has been replete with articles of both a condemning and highly critical nature. In 1968, 10 national medical and educational professional organizations sanctioned an official statement critical of the approach. The statement, as reported in *Archives of Physical Medicine and Rehabilitation* (The Doman-Delacato treatment, 1968), asserts that "the theory is alleged to be of universal applicability (Institutes for the Achievement of Human Potential, 1967, n.d.), but it is largely based upon questionable and oversimplified concepts of hemispheric dominance and the relation of individual sequential development to phylogenesis (Robbins & Glass, 1969)" (as cited in Hallahan & Cruickshank, 1973, p. 95). The statement concludes that "the Institutes for the Achievement of Human Potential appears to differ substantially from other groups treating developmental problems in *(a)* the excessive nature of their undocumented claims for cure and *(b)* the extreme demands placed upon parents in carrying out an unproven technique without fail" (as cited in Hallahan & Cruickshank, 1973, p. 96). This action is an example of the alienation of this approach from educational, medical, psychological, and even some parent groups. The theory must be held in question until more precise data are accumulated under rigid, controlled conditions.

LIMITATIONS OF PERCEPTUAL-MOTOR TRAINING

The motor theories and models summarized in this chapter served as a basis for the subsequent formulation of perceptual-motor remediation programs. The work of Kephart, Barsch, Getman, and Delacato therefore includes perceptual-motor curriculums or teaching suggestions for remedial programs. Perceptual approaches have also been developed by Frostig and Horne (1964), Fairbanks and Robinson (1967), and Semel (1968).

Little empirical evidence is available to validate the usefulness of perceptual-motor assessment or training (Cohen, 1969; Hammill & Wiederholt, 1972; Larsen, Rogers, & Sowell, 1976). For example, the Hammill and Larsen (1974) review of 33 different studies failed to validate the assumption that certain auditory perception skills are necessary for the reading process and that children actually fail to read well because of defects in this area. Similarly, the Larsen and Hammill (1975) review which looked at studies probing the relationship of academic achievement and visual perception development concluded that the time and expense currently devoted to visual perceptual testing and training should be reevaluated seriously if the purpose of their use is to improve academic achievement. In sum, the vast majority of research studies do not support the use of perceptual-motor activities. Therefore, until more substantive research is offered by the supporters of these techniques, we do not recommend using perceptual-motor activities with the vast majority of children in our schools.

SUMMARY

The relationship of perceptual-motor development and learning disabilities was reviewed in this chapter. After considering the concept of perceptual modalities, the various components of visual perception, auditory perception, haptic perception, and motor skills were outlined and discussed. The use of published tests and informal assessment techniques for evaluating perceptual-motor skills was summarized. The perceptual-motor training models proposed by Kephart, Barsch, Getman, and Doman and Delacato were described and evaluated. Finally, the limitations of perceptual-motor assessment and training were reviewed.

SUGGESTED ACTIVITIES

1. Arrange to talk with a physical education teacher about motor development programs for LD students. Observe his or her work with children experiencing specific motor activity difficulties.

2. Design an informal checklist that might be used by preschool teachers to note children with fine and gross motor difficulties.

3. Study one of the original textbook sources of perceptual-motor theories presented in this chapter and evaluate the strengths and weaknesses of the model.

4. Are perceptual-motor programs used in your local school district? Arrange to talk with a LD specialist concerning the types of children with whom these programs are used and the results of such training.

5. Obtain a copy of a published perceptual-motor test discussed in this chapter. Examine the test and arrange to observe the test being administered by a trained examiner.

6. Obtain a copy of the Hammill and Larsen (1974) or Larsen and Hammill (1975) studies discussed in this chapter. Evaluate the procedures used in these studies. How do the results compare to your position regarding perceptual-motor training?

7. Discuss the important factors that should be stressed in most preschool readiness programs. Defend your response.

8. List some instructional activities that might be used with preschool/
kindergarten children who are experiencing fine and gross motor
difficulties.

References

Ashlock, P.R. *Visual perception in children in the primary grades and its relation to reading performance.* Unpublished doctoral dissertation, University of Texas, 1963.

Ayres, J. *A study of perceptual problems.* San Francisco: United Cerebral Palsy Association, 1963.

Barsch, R.H. *A movigenic curriculum* (Bulletin No. 25). Madison Wisc.: Department of Public Instruction, Bureau for the Handicapped, 1965.

Barsch, R.H. *Achieving perceptual-motor efficiency* (Vol. 1). Seattle: Special Child Publications, 1967.

Barsch, R.H. *Enriching perception and cognition* (Vol. 2). Seattle: Special Child Publications, 1968.

Bateman, B. The efficacy of an auditory and a visual method of first grade reading instruction with auditory and visual learners. In H. Smith (Ed.), *Perception and reading.* Newark, Del.: International Reading Association, 1968.

Beery, K.E., & Buktenica, N.A. *Developmental Test of Visual-Motor Integration.* Chicago: Follett, 1967.

Bender, L. *A visual-motor Gestalt test and its clinical use.* New York: American Orthopsychiatric Association, 1938.

Benton, A.L. *Revised Visual Retention Test.* New York: Psychological Corp., 1955.

Beter, T., & Cragin, W. *The mentally retarded child and his motor behavior.* Springfield, Ill.: Charles C Thomas, 1972.

Bruininks, R.H. *Bruininks-Oseretsky Test of Motor Proficiency.* Circle Pines, Minn.: American Guidance Service, 1977.

Bush, W.J., & Giles, M.T. *Aids to psycholinguistic teaching* (2nd ed.). Columbus, Ohio: Charles E. Merrill, 1977.

Chalfant, J.C., & Scheffelin, M.A. *Central processing dysfunctions in children: A review of research* (NINDS Monograph No. 9). Bethesda, Md.: U.S. Department of Health, Education and Welfare, 1969.

Chaney, C.M., & Kephart, N.C. *Motoric aids to perceptual training.* Columbus, Ohio: Charles E. Merrill, 1968.

Cohen, S.A. Studies in visual perception and reading in disadvantaged children. *Journal of Learning Disabilities,* 1969, *2,* 498-503.

Colarusso, R.P., & Gill, S. Selecting a test of visual perception. *Academic Therapy,* 1975-1976, *11,* 157-167.

Colarusso, R.P., & Hammill, D.D. *Motor-Free Visual Perception Test.* San Rafael, Calif.: Academic Therapy Publications, 1972.

Dechant, E. Why an eclectic approach in reading? In J.A. Figurel (Ed.), *Vistas in reading.* Proceedings of the International Reading Association, 1966, *10,* 28-32.

deHirsch, K., Jansky, J., & Langford, W. *Predicting reading failure.* New York: Harper & Row, 1966.

Delacato, C.H. *Neurological organization and reading.* Springfield, Ill.: Charles C Thomas, 1966.

The Doman-Delacato treatment of neurologically handicapped children. Official statement. *Archives of Physical Medicine and Rehabilitation.* 1968, *49,* 183-186.

Fairbanks, J., & Robinson, J. *Fairbanks-Robinson program, Levels 1 and 2.* Boston: Teaching Resources, 1967.

Flower, R.M. The evaluation of auditory abilities in the appraisal of children with reading problems. In H.K. Smith (Ed.), *Perception and reading.* Newark, Del.: International Reading Association, 1968.

Frostig, M. *Movement education: Theory and practice.* Chicago: Follett, 1970.

Frostig, M., & Horne, D. *The Frostig program for the development of visual perception.* Chicago: Follett, 1964.

Frostig, M., & Maslow, P. *Learning problems in the classroom.* New York: Grune & Stratton, 1973.

Frostig, M., Maslow, P., Lefever, W., & Whittlesey, J.R. *Marianne Frostig Developmental Test of Visual Perception.* Palo Alto, Calif.: Consulting Psychologists Press, 1964.

Getman, G. The visuomotor complex in the acquisition in learning skills. In J. Hellmuth (Ed.), *Learning disorders* (Vol. 1). Seattle: Special Child Publications, 1965.

Getman, G.N., Kane, E.R., & McKee, G.W. *Developing learning readiness: A visual-motor tactile skills program.* Manchester, Mo.: McGraw-Hill, 1968.

Gillespie, P.H., & Johnson, L. *Teaching reading to the mildly retarded child.* Columbus, Ohio: Charles E. Merrill, 1974.

Goins, J.T. Visual perceptual abilities and early reading progress. *Supplementary Educational Monographs.* Chicago: University of Chicago Press, 1958.

Goldman, R., Fristoe, N., & Woodcock, R. *Test of auditory discrimination.* Circle Pines, Minn.: American Guidance Service, 1970.

Goldman, R., Fristoe, M., & Woodcock, R. *The Goldman-Fristoe-Woodcock Auditory Skills Test Battery.* Circle Pines, Minn.: American Guidance Service, 1976.

Goldstein, K. The modification of behavior consequent to cerebral lesions. *Psychiatric Quarterly,* 1936, *10,* 586-610.

Goldstein, K. *The organism.* New York: American Book, 1939.

Goodman, L., & Hammill, D.D. The effectiveness of the Kephart-Getman activities in developing perceptual-motor and cognitive skills. *Focus on Exceptional Children,* 1973, *4,* 1-9.

Graham, F.K., & Kendall, B.S. Memory-for-Designs Test. *Perceptual and Motor Skills,* 1960, *11,* 147-190.

Guilford, J. Three faces of intellect. *American Psychologist,* 1959, *14,* 469.

Hallahan, D.P., & Cruickshank, W.M. *Psychoeducational foundations of learning disabilities.* Englewood Cliffs, N.J.: Prentice-Hall, 1973.

Hammill, D.D. Training visual perceptual processes. *Journal of Learning Disabilities,* 1972, *5,* 552-559.

Hammill, D.D., Assessing and training perceptual-motor skills. In D.D. Hammill & N.R. Bartel (Eds.), *Teaching children with learning and behavior problems* (2nd ed.). Boston: Allyn & Bacon, 1978.

Hammill, D.D., & Larsen, S.C. The relationship of selected auditory perceptual skills and reading ability. *Journal of Learning Disabilities,* 1974, *1,* 429-436.

Hammill, D.D., & Wiederholt, J.L. Review of the Frostig Visual Perception Test and the related training program. In L. Mann & D. Sabatino (Eds.), *First review of special education* (Vol. 1). New York: Grune & Stratton, 1972.

Haworth, M.R. *The Primary Visual-Motor Test.* New York: Grune & Stratton, 1970.

Heidmann, M. *The slow learner in the primary grades.* Columbus, Ohio: Charles E. Merrill, 1973.

Hildreth, G.H., Griffiths, M., & McGauvran, M.E. *The Metropolitan Readiness Tests.* New York: Harcourt Brace Jovanovich, 1969.

Institutes for the Achievement of Human Potential. *Bulletin,* 1967, *1.*

Institutes for the Achievement of Human Potential. *Statement of Objectives,* n.d.

Johnson, D.J., & Myklebust, H.R. *Learning disabilities: Educational principles and practices.* New York: Grune & Stratton, 1967.

Jordan, D.R. *Dyslexia in the classroom* (2nd ed.). Columbus, Ohio: Charles E. Merrill, 1977.

Kaluger, G., & Kolson, C.J. *Reading and learning disabilities* (2nd ed.) Columbus, Ohio: Charles E. Merrill, 1978.

Kephart, N.C. Perceptual-motor aspects of learning disabilities. *Exceptional Children,* 1964, *31,* 201-206.

Kephart, N.C. *The slow learner in the classroom* (2nd ed.). Columbus, Ohio: Charles E. Merrill, 1971.

Kimmell, G., & Wahl, J. *Screening Test for Auditory Perception.* San Rafael, Calif.: Academic Therapy Publications, 1969.

Kirk, S., McCarthy, J.P., & Kirk, W. *The Illinois Test of Psycholinguistic Abilities* (Rev. ed.). Urbana, Ill.: University of Illinois Press, 1968.

Larsen, S.C., & Hammill, D.D. The relationship of selected visual skills to school learning. *Journal of Special Education,* 1975, *9,* 281-291.

Larsen, S.C., Rogers, D., & Sowell, V. The usefulness of selected perceptual tests in differentiating between normal and learning disabled children. *Journal of Learning Disabilities,* 1976, *9,* 85-91.

Leibowitz, H.W. *Visual perception.* New York: Macmillan, 1965.

Lerner, J. *Children with learning disabilities* (2nd ed.). Boston: Houghton Mifflin, 1976.

Lowder, R.G. *Perceptual ability and school achievement.* Winter Haven, Fla.: Lions Publications, 1956.

McCarthy, J.J., & McCarthy, J.R. *Learning disabilities.* Boston: Allyn & Bacon, 1969.

Mann, P.H., & Suiter, P. *Handbook on diagnostic teaching.* Boston: Allyn & Bacon, 1974.

Messing, E.S. Auditory perception: What is it? In J. Arena (Ed.), *Successful programming: Many points of view.* Fifth Annual Conference Proceedings, Association of Children with Learning Disabilities. San Rafael, Calif.: Academic Therapy Publications, 1968.

Meyers, E., Ball, H., & Crutchfield, M. *The kindergarten teacher's handbook.* Los Angeles: Gramercy Press, 1973.

Mills, R. *Learning Methods Test.* Fort Lauderdale: Mills Center, 1956.

Myers, P.I., & Hammill, D.D. *Methods for learning disorders* (2nd ed.). New York: Wiley, 1976.

Myklebust, H.R. *Auditory disorders in children: A manual for differential diagnosis.* New York: Grune & Stratton, 1954.

Orpet, R., & Heustis, T. *Move-Grow-Learn Movement Skills Survey.* Chicago: Follett, 1971.

Ringler, L.H., & Smith, I. Learning modality and word recognition of first grade children. *Journal of Learning Disabilities,* 1973, *6,* 307-312.

Roach, C., & Kephart, N. *The Purdue Perceptual-Motor Survey.* Columbus, Ohio: Charles E. Merrill, 1966.

Robbins, M., & Glass, G.V. The Doman-Delacato rationale: A critical analysis. In J. Hellmuth (Ed.), *Educational therapy* (Vol. 2). Seattle: Special Child Publications, 1969.

Schwalb, E., Blau, H., & Blau, H. Child with brain dysfunction. *Journal of Learning Disabilities,* 1969, *2,* 182-188.

Semel, E. *Sound order sense.* Boston: Teaching Resources, 1968.

Seymour, P. What do you mean, "Auditory Perception"? *Education,* 1970, *70,* 175-179.

Sloan, W. *The Lincoln Oseretsky Motor Development Scale.* Chicago: Stoelting, 1954.

Slosson, R.I. *Slosson Drawing Coordination Test.* East Aurora, N.Y.: Slosson Educational Publications, 1967.

Smith, R.M. *Teacher diagnosis of educational difficulties.* Columbus, Ohio: Charles E. Merrill, 1969.

Strauss, A., & Lehtinen, L. *Psychopathology and education of brain-injured children.* New York: Grune & Stratton, 1947.

Strauss, A., & Werner, H. Disorders of conceptual thinking in the brain-injured child. *Journal of Nervous and Mental Disease,* 1938, *96,* 153-172.

Tarver, S.G., & Dawson, M.M. Modality preference and reading: An assessment of the research and theory. *Journal of Learning Disabilities,* 1978, *11,* 5-17.

Travers, R.M. Perceptual learning. *Review of Educational Research,* 1967, *37,* 599-617.

Valett, R.E. *The remediation of learning disabilities.* Palo Alto, Calif.: Fearon, 1969.

Wallace, G., & Larsen, S.C. *Educational assessment of learning problems: Testing for teaching.* Boston: Allyn & Bacon, 1978.

Waugh, R.P. Relationship between modality preference and performance. *Exceptional Children,* 1973, *6,* 465-469.

Wechsler, D. *Wechsler Intelligence Scale for Children.* New York: Psychological Corp., 1949.

Weiner, P.S., Wepman, J.M., & Morency, A.S. A test of visual discrimination. *Elementary School Journal,* 1965, *65,* 330-337.

Wepman, J. *Auditory Discrimination Test.* Chicago: Language Research Associates, 1958.

Wepman, J. The perceptual basis for learning. In C. Frierson & W. Barbe (Eds.), *Educating children with learning disabilities.* New York: Appleton-Century - Crofts, 1967.

Werner, H., & Strauss, A. Types of visuo-motor activity in their relation to low and high performance ages. *Proceedings of the American Association on Mental Deficiency* 1939, *44,* 163-168.

Emerging Directions in Learning Disabilities

Part three of this book is intended to provide you with some indication of the emerging directions in learning disabilities. Variations among the learning disabled in educational needs and learning styles dictate a broad conceptualization of services. Many of these educational provisions are discussed in chapter 11.

The early identification and treatment of LD problems are occurring in a number of ongoing educational programs. Technological and scientific advances in the fields of medicine, psychology, and education have made preventive measures both possible and realistic. The early childhood perspective in learning disabilities is presented in chapter 12.

The recent focus on LD adolescents and adults is discussed in chapter 13. Representative programs and instructional guidelines for the older LD student are described in this chapter.

Parents have been an integral part of the effort for LD children. Their contributions have included assistance in assessment and intervention, and participation in political action programs. Parents and learning disabilities are discussed in chapter 14.

In our previous chapters, we have indicated that the LD field is in a period of transition. Some of the important issues associated with LD in the 1980s are described in chapter 15.

PREVIEW

Children with learning disabilities have the right by law to a free and appropriate education in the least restrictive environment. These provisions of P.L. 94-142 and others shape the service arrangements in schools and other agencies. As we shall discuss, P.L. 94-142 has many implications for state planning, the role of the teacher, and the definition of learning disabilities. We will also suggest some of the key considerations for arranging services.

Service arrangements are based on traditional models of the continuum of services. We are very concerned that misunderstandings of LD have created almost total reliance on placement in resource rooms and/or regular classrooms. The nature, advantages, and disadvantages of different ways to deliver services will be discussed. The LD child in the mainstream will be discussed in particular.

Finally, we think it important to describe the role, training, and background of the LD teacher. Probably the most important factor in LD services, LD teachers and other professionals in learning disabilities have specific challenges they must be equipped to meet.

In order to understand the full significance of *where* an LD student receives services, it is necessary to realize the implications of P.L. 94-142. P.L. 94-142 guarantees that LD children will be served. Its provisions have set into motion an already intense discussion concerning by whom and where LD children will be served. As we discussed in chapters 1 and 2, the LD definition is at the core of assessment and remediation of LD; it is also at the center of an understanding of service arrangements.

Second, the meaning of the principle of "least restrictive environment" must be clarified. Third, P.L. 94-142 has placed particular demands on state departments of education to generate a plan to implement its provision. Finally, we must realize that P.L. 94-142 has had a particular impact on the traditional roles of the LD teacher and the regular class teacher.

P.L. 94-142 AND SERVICE ARRANGEMENTS

P.L. 94-142 guarantees a free and appropriate education for all handicapped children and youth including LD children. By 1980, all LD children between the ages of 3 and 21 must be served. The first priority is to serve LD children not yet being served. Secondly, the most *severe* LD children must be given a high priority. The services available for LD children encompass traditional special education services available in different settings. Special services, like transportation and medical evaluations, are also guaranteed.

Three major principles of P.L. 94-142 are *protective safeguards, least restrictive environment,* and the *individual education plan* (Meyen, 1978). First, the law specifies procedures to be used to insure that the rights of LD children and their parents are not violated. In the past abuses have included inappropriate placement, use of unreliable or invalid diagnostic data, exclusion from school, and so forth. As we discussed in chapter 4, parents have the right to examine all their child's records and to obtain independent evaluations. If parents or guardians are not known or available, surrogate parents must be appointed. Parents or guardians must receive *written* notice in their native language of any change in the identification, evaluation, or placement of their LD child. Finally, parents must be advised of procedures for complaints and/or impartial due process hearings.

The second major aspect of P.L. 94-142 is the concept of least restrictive environment. Simply put, it means that the regular classroom is the preferred base for LD children. Meyen (1978) considers the following elements central to this principle:

> (1) assuming that a handicapped child can best be served through placement with nonhandicapped peers in regular class settings; (2) assigning primary instructional responsibility to regular class teachers; (3) providing support services to the regular class teacher as a means of helping the handicapped child when special assistance is required; (4) providing direct support services on a part-time basis to the handicapped child only if the regular class teacher is unable to provide an appropriate program through assistance from support personnel; (5) reserving assignment to special classes or separate programs as a last alternative; and (6) continually monitoring the child's progress, with the aim of returning the child to the regular class as soon as his or her performance suggests that such placement would be most appropriate. (p. 19)

As we shall see later, this idea of least restrictive environment is having a significant impact on programming for LD children, and in fact, it has been the basis for much misunderstanding.

The third key principle of P.L. 94-142 is the individual education process and plan. We have outlined the IEP procedures in detail in chapter 4. Suffice it to say that IEP represents the core of P.L. 94-142. However, as Meyen (1978) has stated,

> P.L. 94-142 is far more comprehensive than indicated by the discussion presented here. It incorporates provisions which define roles of the federal government, state educational agencies, local educational agencies, and intermediate educational agencies. It includes directives on identification procedures, fiscal responsibilities, application to private agencies, and overall implementation processes. Readers preparing themselves for professional roles in education are encouraged to study the complete rules and regulations. (p. 23)

Learning Disabled vs.
Mildly Handicapped

P.L. 94-142 recognizes learning disabilities as a legitimate type of exceptionality requiring special education (Larsen, 1978). As we indicated in chapter 2, learning disabilities is a designation for *severe* discrepancies in *specific* learning performances. Confusion over these two points makes decisions about educational placement for learning disabilities difficult.

Learning disabilities are considered by some educators to be any *mild* difficulty in learning. Further, *all* learning disabilities are considered mild problems. The natural conclusion is that all LD children should be served in the regular classroom, or at most, through a resource room model.

We must establish early in our discussion of service arrangements these two basic principles of arranging services for LD children; that is, LD children have *severe* learning problems and *specific* disabilities. *They must not be automatically considered mildly handicapped.*

Mildly handicapped is a term used to refer to normal and/or environmentally induced learning problems. As Newcomer (1977) points out, there is a wide range of differences within the concept of normalcy. Many children presently labeled LD are encountering normal and situational problems. The more appropriate service for them should be arranged in the regular classroom, with consultant assistance to the regular teacher.

Mildly handicapped children are also considered the victims of poor learning environment in the classroom, home, and so forth. They are frequently economically and environmentally deprived children as well. There is a great hesitation today to assign them any form of special education label or to place them in educational settings other than the regular classroom. Yet they represent a group of children needing special help.

This unserved population of disadvantaged and frequently culturally different children and youth is therefore included in the concept of mildly handicapped. Furthermore, it is the current feeling in the field that they should not be labeled learning disabled, educable mentally retarded, or emotionally disturbed, as has been the practice. Like other mildly handicapped children who are underachieving, they should be served in the mainstream.

As we also discussed in chapters 2 and 3, the behavioral and environmental perspectives of LD have created a significant shift in defining LD. The previous emphasis was upon inborn, child-centered factors. Now we consider learning disabilities as also environmentally established and maintained. This particular kind of approach has contributed to the effort to serve the mildly handicapped in the mainstream setting, where environmental variables can be modified. Also, there seems to be the tacit assumption that what is environmentally induced is a mild problem.

Needless to say, this environmental and behavioral interpretation of learning disabilities has also contributed to the confusion between the mildly handicapped child and the LD child. Some educators consider LD children as merely products of poor instruction; the best place for them is in the mainstream. The learning environment and teacher behavior should receive the main attention in the remedial effort. However, while many environmental factors contribute to LD, we cannot assume that modification in the mainstream or regular class setting will solve all the problems of LD children. Indeed, we may have to structure special environments for severe cases, perhaps in more restrictive arrangements than we would like.

These misunderstandings of LD are clearly evident in the *noncategorical* or *cross-categorical* movement. Hallahan and Kauffman (1977) have identified historical, conceptual, and practical similarities in the special education services for the learning disabled, mildly retarded, and mildly emotionally disturbed. They argue cogently that *mild* cases of these exceptionalities are sufficiently similar to be grouped together. Specifically, the instructional needs of the children seem quite similar, particularly if perceived from a behavioral approach. In other words, the individual's behaviors in reading, language, social skills, and so forth, are so similar that instruction and service arrangements can be based on the behaviors; the categorical labels offer very little direction in either remediation or arranging services.

In fact Jacobs (1978) and others have noted the prejudicial effect labels have on a teacher's perception of a child. Lilly (1977) has also argued against the usefulness of these labels for these traditional categories. He describes a plan for merging these categories and restructuring the necessary reimbursement system. This emphasis would be upon severe functional learning problems in the school. Decisions about degree of severity for placement would be made at the local level.

This effort to decategorize or cross-categorize designations such as LD, EMR, and ED has obvious implications for service arrangements of LD programs. This movement will encompass the mildly and situationally handicapped children presently served in these arrangements. The most likely service arrangements for them will be a consultant and resource room assistance in the regular classroom. In fact, considering the similarity between learning and behavior-disordered children and children in the regular classroom, the regular classroom may become the site of all programming.

The noncategorical and cross-categorical movement will also better identify children with *severe* learning disabilities, as it will severe retardation and severe emotional distrubance. The needs of LD children with severe academic, language, and social learning deficits will require special service arrangements.

Least Restrictive Environment

P.L. 94-142 explicitly encourages the normalization of LD children and youth. Many educators have taken this mandate to mean that all LD children should be in the regular classroom and/or resource room. Cruickshank (1977), while agreeing with the spirit of this principle, considers some "least" restrictive environments very restrictive. Unselective placement of LD children in regular classrooms may be very restricting, if the classroom teacher has no training or assistance to serve the child. As we shall see, the research on the efficacy of resource rooms is promising but not definitive (Sindelar & Deno, 1978).

Miller and Switzky (1978) find this mandated provision very difficult to implement. First, the administrative environments (e.g., the special class) cannot be automatically considered restrictive. Second, there is much similarity across service arrangements. Third, many other factors (e.g., family life) may be the really restrictive variables affecting the child. Therefore there is a need to carefully define the dimensions of restriction and to recognize the flexibility and interconnections involved in the restriction concept.

Reynolds and Birch (1977) consider this principle of least restrictive environment truly revolutionary. According to past practices, least restrictive environments were those which lacked the special materials, equipment, and personnel to meet the LD child's need. According to current thinking, the very environment (e.g., the home or regular classroom) formerly considered restrictive is now least restrictive. Previously we removed the LD child from his peers to serve him better; today we keep the LD child with his peers to serve him better.

There is a fallacy, however, in reducing the meaning of normalization to *proximity* to peers or to *presence* in naturalized or normal surroundings. As Kauffman and Mona (1978) indicate, the idea of least restrictive environment must be understood in relationship to the other features of P.L. 94-142. The law states that a free and appropriate education for an LD child must be based on objectives and the individual child's needs. LD children are to be educated with normal achieving peers as much as possible; they cannot be removed from the regular classroom without diagnostically based reasons.

The assumptions underlying this approach indicate that *many* service arrangements are possible (Kauffman & Mona, 1978). First, LD children, like other exceptionalities covered in P.L. 94-142, are considered heterogeneous; they may need to be served in different settings. Second, the IEPs discussed in chapter 4 will set forth the goals and objectives for placement; *where* the goals will be accomplished and *by whom* are based on the nature, number, and severity of needs.

Third, a *continuum* of services is implied by P.L. 94-142. Although the legislation stresses normalized environments as ideal settings for LD services, other options based on the child's need are recognized. Finally, the distinction is evident between the methods to be used with LD children (i.e., the *what*) and the delivery system to be used (i.e., the *where* and *by whom).* The past practice of automatically associating a label (LD, MR, ED, etc.) with a placement (special class, resource room, etc.) is no longer functional.

State Planning

The state and local guidelines for compliance with P.L. 94-142 placement procedures are to be present in a state plan. Mayer (1976) reported that only 45 state departments had attempted to develop a comprehensive master plan; only 29 state agencies have printed guidelines. There was considerable variety of content in the plans; however, almost all those states with completed or partially completed state plans included a definition of service components or delivery systems.

P.L. 94-142 (Section 613) has encouraged more specific directives from *all* state departments. The Council for Exceptional Children's *Update* (1978) reports that only 18 state plans are fully approved. Plans from 33 states and territories were partially acceptable according to P.L. 94-142 guidelines. The remaining states had not yet submitted plans that conformed to the regulations.

State agencies must move assertively to develop the necessary base for services. Burrello, Kaye, and Nutter (1978) describe steps taken in Michigan to develop a statewide management network. A peer task force of administrators developed a series of products and procedures to facilitate meeting the needs of LD children and other exceptionalities. This Statewide Technical Assistance Network in Special Education (STANSE) supplied the necessary leadership and communication.

Bradley (1977) has described efforts in Iowa to meet the requirements for identification of LD children. Learning disabilities is defined conceptually; areas of evaluation necessary for LD placement are specified. However, the state rules do not contain arbitrary criteria statements. Furthermore, the definition is in guideline or recommendation format.

These state plans are very instrumental in providing service for LD children. Obviously P.L. 94-142 has required major efforts on the part of state departments to describe their service provisions.

Role Challenges and Conflicts

P.L. 94-142 has had a major impact on the role of LD teachers and others involved with LD children, including the parents. The LD teachers, regular classroom teachers, and speech therapists, among others, must work together in a cooperative fashion. Added responsibilities for meeting the mandates of P.L. 94-142, especially in the areas of assessment and IEP design, have been given to the staff and parents.

As we will discuss later in detail, LD teachers and others are very challenged by these requirements. Hayes and Higgins (1978) have stressed the need for teachers to be very conversant with P.L. 94-142. They will have to clarify the nature and level of their participation in IEP meetings and related activities. The meetings must be conducted in compliance with the law, and an IEP must be written for each child. Furthermore, the LD teacher is likely to see glaring abuses in the system and want to act in an advocate role.

Junkala (1977) found the assessment contributions of *teacher* members of evaluation teams in one state were not clearly evident in the final decisions about placement. In fact, it seemed that IQ scores were more instrumental than what the teachers had to say about appropriate placement. The procedures used by these teams seemed to place more weight on test scores.

LD teachers and other personnel can also anticipate role conflicts that may arise. Newcomer (1977) feels that special educators must assume a broader role than before. They must work with regular classroom teachers to alter learning environments and to share the responsibility for LD children. However, considerable expertise will be necessary to be a consultant to a teacher peer. We cannot assume all special educators have the skills. This is particularly true if the LD teacher was a special class teacher before, a role not necessarily demanding such skills (McLoughlin & Kass, 1978).

The LD definition and P.L. 94-142 are also indicating the overlap of role activities in LD, remedial reading, school psychology, and speech pathology (Wallace, 1976). Interdisciplinary activity in assessment and remediation is mandated by law. As we discuss later, the LD teacher must perform judiciously as the central person in delivering services to the LD child. That task is not easy.

Finally P.L. 94-142 means greater parent involvement in LD programs than ever before (McLoughlin, Edge, & Strenecky, 1978). LD teachers must respond to the needs of parents. They must also actively involve parents in LD programs. We will discuss this challenge in chapter 14.

P.L. 94-142 has affected the foundation of service arrangements for LD children. The definition of LD has been clarified to designate a more severely involved population than before, with specific disabilities. As such, LD children will require a full continuum of services, not merely the regular classroom placement. State plans, the source of guidelines for service arrangements, are beginning to meet these requirements. LD teachers and other personnel are also rising to the challenge.

It is necessary to conceptualize the realities of P.L. 94-142 into a decision-making model. The following discussion will highlight major factors to be considered.

PLACEMENT DECISION-MAKING PROCESS

Level One: The Child's Needs

An educational placement is chosen once a learning disabled child's educational objectives have been identified. In some cases, a child's needs may be so few and mild that a regular classroom teacher can supply the necessary help. On the other extreme, we may find that a child requires a great deal of educational support from a specialist in learning disabilities. Thus the primary and initial consideration for administrative provisions must be the *number, nature, and severity of the child's learning disabilities.* The number, nature, and complexity of the educational objectives for the child will suggest the best setting and personnel to be used.

Once we have identified the *degree* of educational support that the child requires, we must consider two essential factors: the child's chronological *age* and degree of *social development.* Chronological age is important because LD children are usually performing at grade levels much below the levels expected for their age. It is often inappropriate to place them with younger children who are at similar grade levels. Older LD children also react negatively to books and other material that are identified with the primary grades, even though the child may need the basic skills stressed in those materials.

The disruptive behavior and lack of interpersonal skills LD children frequently demonstrate may also make certain settings inappropriate. A regular classroom, with its many demands upon social development, may prove to be a difficult environment for such a child, who often needs to learn to ignore distractions and to function according to different reinforcement systems. We may also have to consider the child's sex, because so many more boys than girls have learning disabilities. Physical needs may have to be considered, too.

The IEP must contain the annual goals and specific objectives arranged in priority order. A child's strengths and weaknesses and learning style must be described and diagnostically documented. Teaching methods and special considerations are to be noted.

Personal attention is still possible in a regular classroom.

Level Two: Availability of LD Personnel

The next factors to be taken into account involve the *training and availability of personnel. Where* a child receives the help is not as important as *who* can help. Personnel who are both willing and trained to help children with learning disabilities must be available. Obviously, some trained individual or individuals must deliver the screening, diagnostic, teaching, and evaluation services, either directly or in-directly. The number, nature, and complexity of the educational objec-tives to be accomplished with a child determine whether there should be a special teacher or other individuals to work with a child on a full- or part-time basis. In either case trained personnel must be available to implement programs for these children.

P.L. 94-142 requires the designation of the individuals who will accomplish the stated goals. The beginning and ending dates of service must be included. LD children require the services of an LD teacher. This specialist may work directly or indirectly with the children depend-ing on the needed service model. While P.L. 94-142 does not explicitly mention LD teachers, it is clear that the certified teacher in LD is to be a member of the IEP team.

Level Three: Availability of Other Personnel and Resources

A school district must also consider the *resources presently available* to meet the educational needs of LD children. We must examine the *existing staff in a school for potential resources,* because there are usually certain staff members who are potentially helpful in accomplish-ing one or more of the educational objectives for a child. Schools may have *regular classroom teachers* who can perform screening, diagnos-tic, and teaching services of a specific kind. Regular classroom teachers are increasingly implementing team teaching and modular instruction with the goal of meeting individual needs. LD children with mild, and perhaps moderate, difficulties can realistically receive assistance from these teachers. *School psychologists* already perform diagnostic ser-vices for schools. Their psychological testing functions can be ex-panded to psychoeducational diagnosis and planning. School *nurses* are capable of assisting in screening and referrals for medical needs. Many *speech therapists,* often concentrating upon articulation difficul-ties, can accomplish goals in language areas. Other potentially useful staff members are *counselors* for social and vocational objectives, *teacher aides, parents,* and even the *academically thriving school child* (Gearheart, 1973).

School districts should consider their *existing special programs* as complementary to the goals of a learning disability program. Various kinds of language enrichment programs (e.g., Head Start), bilingual programs, special education classes, remedial reading programs, speech programs, and vocational career programs already exist in schools. These programs have personnel, curriculum, and materials that could answer at least some of the educational objectives for the LD child. While the administrative patterns, the size of student bodies, and so forth, may prevent the extensive use of these resources, a broader appreciation of common goals and procedures across school system programs may suggest some very real possibilities.

A survey of local and regional resources often uncovers *ancillary support systems* for public school programs. Mental health clinics, guidance clinics, hospital diagnostic facilities, university psychoeducational clinics, and private psychological and educational groups can be called upon for specific aspects of a child's program. Federal and state funds have been used to develop regional centers which disseminate information, perform material searches, offer consultants and training services, and so forth. Unfortunately, these support systems usually continue for a short period of time; then they are discontinued and different projects initiated.

Level Four: Organizational Settings

The specific description and discussion of different delivery systems will be given later. The options include the regular classroom, consultant teacher, itinerant teacher, resource room, special class, special day school, and residential school. Combinations of these different models are also possible.

The key factor to remember is that where or how a LD child gets served is secondary to what is to be done (goals) and by whom (personnel). Lovitt (1978) stresses the need to focus upon the behavioral goals of the child; decisions about placement must be based on them.

Level Five: Possible Resources

An examination of available internal and external resources usually points out the need for *new* personnel, physical arrangements, and the organization of a network of ancillary support personnel such as medical and psychological consultants. Personnel specifically trained in learning disabilities must be hired to deliver services directly to children or to coordinate this delivery through other professionals. Physical arrangements (e.g., classrooms and mobile vans) and materials must be provided. Present *legislation and funding patterns* can often be studied to identify financial resources.

Finally, the *number* of children needing services and the *geographical distribution* of that population will dictate decisions about the best delivery systems to be used. An itinerant service model might be appropriate for large numbers of mild cases. A sufficient number of severe cases might dictate the use of a special class. Usually the number and nature of LD cases found in a school system require a combination of different organizational arrangements.

Table 11-1
Considerations for Educational Provisions

Level I. *The Child's Needs*
    A. Number, nature, and complexity of educational objectives
    B. Chronological age
    C. Social development (behavior problems)
    D. Sex
    E. Physical needs

Level II. *Availability of LD Personnel*
    A. Indirect service
    B. Direct service

Level III. *Availability of Other Personnel and Resources*
    A. Present staff with related skills
    B. Present ongoing programs and projects with complementary goals
    C. Ancillary support systems in the area

Level IV. *Organizational Settings*
    A. Regular classroom
    B. Consultant teacher
    C. Itinerant teacher
    D. Resource room
    E. Special class
    F. Special day school
    G. Residential school

Level V. *Possible Resources*
    A. Legislation and funds for new personnel and physical arrangements
    B. Delivery systems to accommodate population number, severity, and geographical dispersion

This decision-making process is summarized in table 11-1. All of these considerations must be studied before an appropriate educational placement can be made for the child with learning disabilities. In order to supply a comprehensive program for LD children, it is necessary to consider these variables and others.

MODELS OF SERVICES

There are a number of systems or models to delivery services to learning disabled children (Wiederholt, 1972). Deno (1970) and Reynolds (1962) have each graphically represented some of the possible delivery systems for children with special needs (see figure 11-1). The common features of both systems are as follows:

    1. The largest number of children can have their needs met in regular classroom settings or in regular classrooms with support from a special teacher.

2. The need for more complete support systems (e.g., special classes or special schools) is related to the severity of the child's problems.
3. Alternatives to the regular class delivery system must be used cautiously, always with the intent of a return to that system when possible.
4. Departures from the regular classroom model should not be merely techniques to classify or label children.
5. Use of exceptional provisions (e.g., residential schools) should be predicated on the fact that more intensive, if not more distinctive, diagnostic and intervention services will be available.

Reynolds and Birch (1977) and Kauffman and Mona (1978) have described the impact of P.L. 94-142 on the cascade of services model. As we have discussed earlier, the concept of least restrictive environment is a major conceptual shift. Presence in the mainstream and normalized

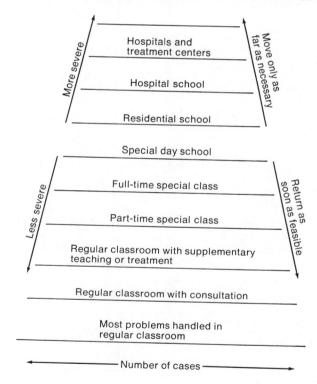

Figure 11-1
Special Education Programs

From "Framework for Considering Some Issues in Special Education" by M. A. Reynolds, *Exceptional Children*, 1962, 7, 368. Copyright 1962 by the Council for Exceptional Children. Reprinted by permission.

environment, proximity to normal peers and others, and the needs of the child define restrictive environment today.

McCarthy (1973) has complemented the Reynolds hierarchy of typical delivery systems by pinpointing the setting and personnel involved in *diagnostic* services. (see figure 11-2). Decisions about the degree of diagnostic service needed depend upon the severity of problems. Few

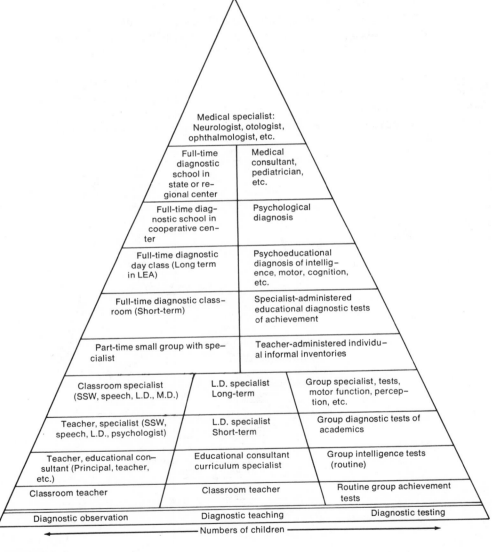

Figure 11-2

Hierarchy of Public School Diagnostic Services

From "Education: The Base of the Triangle" by J. McCarthy, *Annals of the New York Academy of Science,* 1973, *205,* 362-367. Copyright 1973 by the Annals of the New York Academy of Science. Reprinted with permission of the author and publisher. (With adaptations suggested by the author.)

children will require the fully staffed services of diagnostic centers or clinics.

P.L. 94-142 mandates a comprehensive, valid, and reliable assessment upon which to base both placement and programming. The LD teacher, regular classroom teacher, other specialists, and parents are to participate in gathering and analyzing the diagnostic information.

Schworm (1976) has further expanded upon these models by adding the component of form of curriculum (see figures 11-3 and 11-4). Figure 11-3 outlines the basis (horizontal dimension) of placement in certain kinds of programs, materials, and so forth. First, performance in affective, academic, language, and the other areas mentioned in chapter 4 is considered. Then, objectives are established on the basis of this information. Finally, the most appropriate mode or curricular approach (or approaches) is chosen.

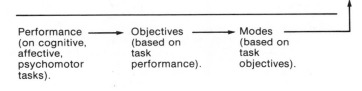

Performance ———▶ Objectives ———▶ Modes
(on cognitive,   (based on   (based on
affective,   task   task
psychomotor   performance).   objectives).
tasks).

Decisions:

1. What goals and how many objectives will student need to reach those goals?
2. How intensive and how extensive will instruction have to be?
3. What teacher(s) and materials are needed by student?

Figure 11-3
Outline of Components for Vertical Placement Decision

From "Models in Special Education: Considerations and Cautions" by R. Schworm, *Journal of Special Education,* 1976, *10,* 181. Copyright 1976 by the Journal of Special Education. Reprinted by permission.

The vertical dimension outlined in figure 11-4 indicates the possible curricula or modes the LD child may require. Curriculum, or mode, is a *composite* of the many approaches, programs, and materials required to meet the goals for the LD child.

Most LD children will not require the specialized, intensive approaches indicated by level D, special instruction and special curriculum. An important point to remember is that the choice of approaches is not based on a diagnostic label. The ultimate choice is the kind of composite curricula and approaches dictated by the LD child's needs.

Many options for delivering services (particularly screening, diagnosis, educational planning, teaching, and evaluation) seem to be available. To avoid the child's unnecessary isolation from peers and from mainstream education, the regular classroom setting should be the *first* consideration.

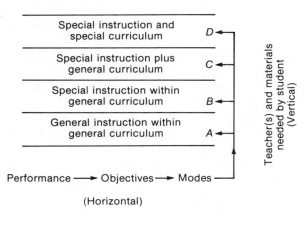

A—Student is placed in general curriculum for all instruction.

B—Student is placed in general curriculum and receives special instruction for certain tasks within that curriculum.

C—Student is placed in the general curriculum and receives special instruction for some tasks that supplement the instruction received in the general curriculum.

D—Student receives a special curriculum for all instruction.

Figure 11-4
Organizational Scheme for Instructional Services

From "Models in Special Education: Considerations and Cautions" by R. Schworm, *Journal of Special Education*, 1976, *10*, 182. Copyright 1976 by the Journal of Special Education. Reprinted by permission.

Regular Classroom Model

The traditional regular classroom setting is presently undergoing some major modifications which make the prospects for children with special needs very promising. Individualized instruction, team teaching, improved and varied curricula (especially in reading), the use of teacher aides, and so on, all offer a climate amenable to meeting the needs of *some* LD children. Preservice and inservice teacher training is increasingly emphasizing screening techniques, informal (even some formal) diagnostic tests, and the use of appropriate methods and materials. Source books, kits, and computerized retrieval systems enable the regular classroom teacher to match the learner's needs with appropriate activities.

It is unrealistic, however, to suppose that *severe* cases of learning disabilities can be managed in the regular classroom (Reger, 1974). Probably the best expectation for this particular delivery system is service for *mild* cases. Regular classroom teachers often need as much support as the child because of the tremendous demands placed upon their time and training. Specialists must assist teachers in developing skills and in supplying activities for the mild cases.

The practice of considering the regular classroom as a realistic service delivery system is also one aspect of the intention to *prevent* learning disabilities. As we have discussed previously, instructional factors may cause or at least compound the learning difficulties of some children. By including the regular classroom setting as one of the key delivery systems, we may be channeling the necessary information and skills where they are most needed.

P.L. 94-142 has placed particular emphasis on maintaining the LD child with his peers as much as possible. As we shall discuss later, many aspects of mainstreamed education must be considered before it can be termed appropriate.

Consultant Model

An increasingly popular model for serving LD children is the consultant model. The LD consultant supports the regular classroom teacher, other staff, and parents in delivering services to the LD child. The role functions of the consultant include assessment, program design, material development and adaptation, demonstration of methods, and program evaluation. The consultant does not directly serve the LD child through instruction.

The model meets the needs of the mildly involved LD child. The consultant can serve more children by supporting the teachers. They can coordinate the many other efforts being made on the child's behalf by parents and other professionals. There is a danger that lack of firsthand teaching experience with the LD child may give a consultant an inaccurate idea of the LD child's difficulties.

Itinerant Model

The use of itinerant teachers for screening, diagnosis, and teaching is not a new system for delivering services. Speech therapists have been supplying services this way for many years. After an initial screening project, itinerant teachers travel from school to school or to some central point to assist children directly. They diagnose, teach, and consult.

After spending a day or series of days in each school, these specialists usually supply the teaching staff with activities and materials for follow-up efforts. Mobile vans are sometimes used to transport the diagnostic and teaching materials.

Some considerations in implementing this model include the number and nature of the child's needs, the number of children requiring assistance, and the willingness of the resident school to implement teaching plans. Mild cases of learning disabilities may only require intermittent attention from a specialist. In some regions, LD children are spread across great distances, making the use of a central delivery system prohibitive. In contrast, a large number of mild LD cases in many schools and a small number of trained personnel suggest this model as a viable alternative, at least in the intial stages of program development.

The itinerant service model has its limitations. The more involved, severely LD children require consistent support. The itinerant teacher may not have a sufficient impact on a particular school because of his or her occasional presence, lack of identification with the staff, and difficulties in transporting necessary materials.

Resource Room Model

This service model seems to be the most attractive and beneficial of all educational provisions (Hammill & Wiederholt, 1972; Reger, 1973, 1974; Reger & Koppmann, 1971; Wiederholt, Hammill, & Brown, 1978). A resident resource teacher, trained specifically in learning disabilities, offers both direct and indirect services to children in their own school. The major part of his or her role is to *teach* children in the resource room, which is usually equipped with necessary materials. During these sessions, the teacher accomplishes objectives which require a one-to-one teacher-student ratio and special methods. Most of the children spend part of the day in the resource room and the rest of the day in the regular classroom.

The LD children who benefit from this model need the daily instruction from the resource teacher (Mayhall & Jenkins, 1977). This feature of regular instruction distinguishes this model from the previous ones.

One-to-one instruction from the LD specialist helps this child in her regular classroom assignments.

Resource teachers often devote some part of each week for screening, diagnosing, planning, and consulting. They consult with regular classroom teachers by supplying activities for the identified population and by maximizing the transfer of skills to the regular classroom. They supply assistance with many other learning problems by observing or assessing children and by making suggestions for curricular modifications and activities.

The resource room system can meet the needs of mild, moderate, and even a few severe cases of learning disabilities. The child with severe learning disabilities, however, may have many complex educational objectives to accomplish. The resource room may not be able to provide the kind and amount of assistance required by the severely handicapped. Still, a resource teacher, through flexible scheduling, can often maintain one or two severe learning disability children. These children would spend the major portion of each school day in the resource room.

The most realistic expectation for this model is service for *general* learning problems and *mild* and *moderate* learning disabilities. Obviously, many more children can receive assistance in this way. The teaching and related functions of the resource teacher in a given school usually allow for the development of a thriving treatment program.

The resource room model also prevents needless labeling of children and maximizes the possibility of mainstreaming. The need to label a child as "mentally retarded," "emotionally disturbed," or "learning disabled" becomes passé and academic *(Journal of Special Education,* 1972). The kind of services provided a child, the amount of attention that the resource teacher gives a child, and the amount of time the child spends away from his peers depend upon the nature and complexity of each youngster's educational needs.

The resource room model can serve as a *diagnostic and experimental teaching filter* to identify the needs of children with very severe learning disabilities. After an initial period of intervention, a resource teacher may discover a few children who need a fuller support system than the resource room. A school system may then establish a special class, with the intention of mainstreaming these children through the resource room model. By perceiving the special class this way, the educational requirements of children with severe learning difficulties may be fulfilled in a more appropriate and sensible way.

Obviously the efficacy of a resource room hinges upon the skills of the teacher. Maturity, teaching experience, and interpersonal skills often dictate how well the model is realized. Ideally, the resource teacher should have some training and teaching experience in the regular classroom. This background usually helps in understanding learning deviancy and allows the resource teacher to make realistic and accurate suggestions for regular classroom teachers. No less important is the increased ability to establish strong interpersonal and interprofessional relationships in a school. The role of the resource teacher may be otherwise unduly limited.

Limits in actualizing the potential of a resource room model may also be established by administrative and staff attitudes and practices (Payne & Murray, 1974). Many schools are familiar with the traditional special class, serving a population labeled "mentally retarded" or "emotionally disturbed." The special teacher who serves these children is often isolated from the rest of the staff. This kind of perception may also be transferred to the resource room model. Changes in teacher role functions, scheduling, and mainstreaming thereby become more difficult.

The past practice of isolation of special education has also created fear, misunderstanding, and feelings of inadequacy within the regular teaching staff. Exposure to the learning characteristics of and educational methodology required by exceptional children has not been part of teacher preparation in colleges and universities. Regular classroom teachers have not been encouraged to visit special classes in their schools. Unfortunately, many educators do not realize that "special education" children are often quite similar to all other children. An opportunity to observe some particularly troublesome children thriving under well planned, and often very simple, intervention procedures might allay the pessimism felt by many educators. This pessimism often prevents many teachers from even contemplating the possibilities available in the resource room model.

Occasionally, children with learning disabilities are transferred to a particular school to receive the services of a resource teacher. Since the administrative and teaching staff at that site must share certain responsibilities for the child, school personnel may resent additional demands placed upon their already heavy schedules.

Obviously, enlightenment is long overdue in regard to educational delivery systems in the public schools. The resource room model may hasten some of this enlightenment, particularly since the resource room can be designated not only for LD children, but also for any child with special needs. Resource rooms should bring about a greater realization of the common needs and teaching strategies across the whole spectrum of education.

McLoughlin and Kass (1978) have expressed concerns over the problems encountered by LD resource teachers. They suggest the use of role analysis to identify troublesome areas. Specific areas needing attention are (1) the label or designation of LD services; (2) the number of students, teacher-student ratio, grade level distribution, and other procedural aspects of the model; (3) the number and kinds of interpersonal and professional relationships; (4) the number and nature of role responsibilities; and (5) the personal qualities and behaviors of the LD teacher.

In spite of the enthusiastic adoption of the resource room model, Sindelar and Deno (1978) have had difficulty in finding empirical evidence that the model is effective. Methodological problems and diversity prevent any clear conclusions. Although academic perfor-

This child enjoys charting his progress in the resource room.

mance seems improved in better-designed research studies of the resource room, social skills of LD children do not seem markedly improved in comparison to children in other settings.

They suggest that future research use observational data, include control groups, study independent factors (e.g., duration and intensity of service, location of school), and use formative (ongoing) evaluation data.

As we indicated earlier, the resource room and/or the regular classroom have been interpreted by some educators as the *only* models permitted by P.L. 94-142. Such short-sighted perspectives of the needs of LD children need to be corrected.

Special Class Model

A smaller number of children with learning disabilities require a full support system through special classes. This alternative is often used after diagnostic and teaching experience with a child in a resource room model. The educational objectives for this child may be numerous and complex. A resource teacher often realizes from diagnostic and teaching efforts that the child requires the full-time attention of one teacher.

A school district usually identifies severe cases of learning disabilities and designates a teacher and classroom for these children. Unlike the previously mentioned models, the self-contained class system provides a full-time, highly specialized service. The special teacher is totally responsible for the child. Drawing upon skills similar to those of the itinerant and resource teacher, he or she offers more intensive and extensive services to children with severe learning disabilities.

It is preferable that the basis for placing a child in a special class be diagnostic and instructional in the resource room model. In this way, the special class system can be used only for the child who needs the most support. Hopefully, after a period in a highly structured environment and under a consistent intervention program, the child can develop communication and social skills to a satisfactory level and be moved back into a less isolated setting.

Children with severe disabilities usually lack skills at the most primary level. Poor reading skills, inability to process stimuli in noisy and busy situations, distractability, poor motivation and work habits, and so forth demand a period of intensive controlled instruction. The educational procedures that are required usually differ in kind and intensity from other service models. The intermittent intervention available in the regular classroom, itinerant service, and resource room is generally not enough for severe cases of learning disabilities.

Children served in the special class need to establish a sound base in written and spoken language, reading, arithmetic, and social skills. A less involved child may merely require assistance in one area, such as handwriting. Many children with learning difficulties lack subskills in a particular area, such as sound blending for word analysis. There are a few children, however, who must begin acquiring almost *all* primary skills in language and social behavior. The special class model is intended for them.

There is the danger that special class placement may become inappropriately *permanent*. Many children have been placed in special classes for their entire school careers. The use of this model should be predicated upon the assumption that, given sufficient progress, the child may be served in less supportive systems. Many children with severe learning disabilities can reach the educational and behavioral competence to be served in resource rooms.

P.L. 94-142's provision for at least yearly evaluation of all placements will guarantee the appropriate use of this model for LD children. This delivery system may be the least restrictive environment for some LD children given the number, nature, and severity of their learning needs.

We indicated earlier that the results of diagnosis and experimental teaching in the resource room should indicate the need for a full support system. A child's departure from mainstream education should be optimistically viewed as temporary. Similarly, we need to regularly examine the progress of a child in a special class. Perhaps his needs will change sufficiently that they can be met in other educational settings.

The self-contained model does not offer some of the advantages of the other systems. The role of the special teacher is limited, the number of children served is smaller, and milder cases go unserved. Also, the teacher in a special class need not perform the full array of functions required of the itinerant and resource teacher. Therefore, the benefits to the general school population—teachers and children—may be considerably less than with other service models.

P.L. 94-142 and the general mood of special educators are definitely against the special class model. Generally it is considered a very restrictive form of service. It is stigmatizing and removes the LD child from his peers.

However, as Kauffman and Mona (1978) and others have pointed out, the research for and against the special class model is mixed. Ribner (1978), for example, has reported that LD children in special classes feel more self-sufficient than their counterparts in regular classes. The implication is clearly that LD children need a continuum of services, including the special class model, which must be used selectively and judiciously.

Special Day School Model

A special day school is another means for providing services. Some school districts designate a particular school as the site for a program in learning disabilities. Children attend the school for a full day or perhaps for part of a day. Local resources of trained personnel and materials are thereby centralized in one school.

Some of the advantages of this option are (1) capacity to serve a large number of moderate and severe cases of learning disabilities; (2) full use of limited resources of trained personnel and space; (3) centralization of diagnostic, teaching, and consulting services; and (4) a means to develop a model program for later replication.

However, as Lerner (1976) points out, many day schools have been *privately* organized and funded in the past. School districts and the general public have been slow in answering the needs of children with learning disabilities. Therefore, parents have often inspired and supported these private service arrangements.

Contrary to popular assumptions, Marver (1976) has found that the private day schools in his survey were reasonable alternative placements. They earned very small profits, did not take unfair advantage of state subsidies, and were not primarily motivated by monetary considerations.

Generally, the day school model is appropriate for large numbers of *severe* cases of learning disabilities or for a cooperative effort among school districts to pool resources for a widely dispersed group of children. With the current development of LD programs in many public schools, the needs of the majority of learning disabled children do not suggest this type of placement. P.L. 94-142 will encourage more local services, in neighborhood schools, for LD children.

Residential School Model

Residential schools for children with learning disabilities generally are used for a few *severely* involved children or in situations where no services are available locally. Since the child must leave his family and peers, this arrangement is usually considered only after all other educational placements have been exhausted.

Many residential facilities have been developed by prominent psychologists and educators. They serve to demonstrate appropriate diagnostic and teaching procedures, to meet the needs of children who cannot be provided for locally, and to satisfy parental desires for alternatives to programs in the public school system.

The disadvantages of the residential school are similar to those of the day school. In addition, the financial expense of residential schools is often prohibitive.

It is very difficult to describe any one of these models as the "least" restrictive. The criteria for that decision are the needs of the LD child. Nonetheless, P.L. 94-142, in fact and in spirit, encourages placement of the LD child in as normal an environment as possible. That generally means the use of the regular classroom, consultant, itinerant, and resource room models.

In table 11-2 we have attempted to summarize this discussion of service arrangements by listing advantages and disadvantages of each model. That task is difficult since some of these models have similar features. Also the needs of the individual LD child form the main criteria for such judgments.

Mainstreaming the LD child particularly highlights the relationships of these different service models. Indeed, as we try to serve the LD child in the least restrictive environment, we often use one or more of these approaches.

THE LD CHILD IN THE REGULAR CLASSROOM

The LD child in the regular classroom is being mainstreamed; his former placement may have been either in the special class totally or in the regular classroom with no special services. Technically, mainstreaming is defined by Kauffman, Gottlieb, Agard, and Kukic (1975) in the following fashion:

> Mainstreaming refers to the temporal, instructional, and social integration of eligible exceptional children with normal peers based on an ongoing, individually determined, educational planning programming process, and requires clarification of responsibility among regular and special eduation administrative, instructional, and supportive personnel. (p. 35)

Under the mainstreaming approach, if the LD child has formerly been in a special class for learning disabilities, his IEP would now indicate his gradual integration into the regular classroom. His IEP would state the percentage of time he was in different service models and the reasons. As Kauffman et al. (1975) note, the goals should also include academic and/or social areas as well as merely time considerations.

Table 11-2

Advantages and Disadvantages of LD Service Models

model	advantages	disadvantages
Regular Classroom Model	Least restrictive setting provides for interaction of handicapped with non-handicapped peers Prevents needless labeling	Instructional factors may compound learning disabilities Large number in class population Teacher not specifically trained Small group or individual instruction often un-available
Consultant Model	Able to reach more teachers Can supply specific instructional methods, programs, and materials Can serve more children Influence environmental learning variables Coordinates comprehensive services for the child	Consultant may not be considered a member of the teaching staff Lacks firsthand knowledge of child that comes from teaching Possible separation of assessment and instruction
Itinerant Model	Aids in screening and diagnosis Some help in area of consulting Part-time services Covers needs of children in different schools or areas Economical ways to serve mild problems	More involved students need consistent support Lack of identification with staff Difficulty in transporting materials Lack of continuity of program Lack of regular follow-up
Resource Room Model	Reduces stigmatization Emphasizes instructional remediation Supplements regular classroom instruction Separates handicapped learner from nonhandi-capped peers for limited periods of the school day Specially trained teacher provides individualized instruction in problem areas Teacher may serve as a consultant to the child's regular teachers Prevents needless labeling Goal is to mainstream the child	Not suited to provide services for the severely learning disabled Scheduling problems Overenrollment Misunderstanding of teacher role Role conflicts No time to observe or consult Little time to assess and plan Questionable efficacy
Special Class Model	Least restrictive setting for severe cases Setting for the implementation of a child's individual education plan	Segregated Permits extremely limited interaction with nonhandi-capped peers Stigmatization

Table 11-2 (*cont.*)
Advantages and Disadvantages of LD Service Models

model	advantages	disadvantages
Special Class Model (cont.)	Provides environmental conditions necessary to meet the needs of LD children with severe problems Individual or small group instruction Maintenance of self-esteem Acceptance of the student Full-time attention of one teacher Provides full-time highly specialized learning conditions	Danger of misplacement Placement may become inappropriately permanent Very restrictive for mild and moderate cases Modeling of inappropriate behaviors Low teacher expectation
Special Day School Model	Full use of limited resources of trained personnel and space A large number of moderate and severe cases of learning disabilities Centralization of diagnostic, teaching, and consulting services Means to develop a model program for later replication Provides special curricula and environment Provides a special environment while permitting a child the advantages of remaining in his or her home and community	Still self-contained Child has no interactions with nonhandicapped peers during the school day Not the least restrictive environment in all cases Sometimes expensive Removes pressures for the development of local services
Residential School Model	Occupational training Attention to diet and necessary medical treatment Provides opportunities for involvement in all facets of normal school life within the school program. Demonstrates appropriate diagnostic and teaching procedures	Segregated from mainstream of society Financial expense Poor staffing Low incidence of exits Not the least restrictive environment Quality control

On the other hand, some LD children who are being mainstreamed have never left the regular classroom (Pasanella & Volkmor, 1977). They are identified and assessed; their IEPs indicate additional ways in which they will be served. These children with learning disabilities may leave the classroom for resource room assistance in reading, arithmetic, and so forth. Otherwise their LD services are administered in the regular classroom.

If the LD teacher is primarily a consultant, it is even possible that the LD child never physically leaves the regular classroom. The regular class teacher, supported by the LD consultant, will meet all the child's needs in the classroom.

Therefore whether the LD child is coming back to the regular classroom or he has never left, the mainstreaming approach is being used. The principles of least restrictive environment and normalization are being used to serve these children. Environments and services are being modified and combined to meet the children's individual needs.

Whichever way we look at it, the goal is to have the LD child in the *regular* classroom. All the other less restrictive models (consultant, itinerant, and resource room) exist in relation to the regular classroom and for that purpose. Indeed, even the special class model, however unappealing it may be, must be considered in this fashion also.

Serving the needs of the LD child in the regular classroom is a challenge. The label *learning disabled* may prejudice the classroom teacher against the child (Jacobs, 1978). Special efforts to speak about the child in behavioral terms are necessary. Strengths must be stressed, weaknesses clarified.

Scheduling of time in the resource room and regular classroom is a problem. The LD teacher must insure adequate time for remediation, yet not deprive the child of experiences in his classroom. Mayhall and Jenkins (1977) stress the importance of this regular and consistent remediation in the resource room for ultimate progress.

Serving LD children in the regular classroom also creates a particular challenge for the LD teacher and regular classroom teacher in the area of methods and materials for these children. Since a child with learning disabilities should be prepared to perform in the mainstream, the LD teacher takes regular classroom programs and materials and uses them with the child. A great deal of adaptation and programming is necessary, but it is generally possible. Also, the LD teacher may need to use a special program or material first, then gradually move the child into the regular methodologies.

One of the ramifications of mainstreaming the LD child is therefore an emphasis on helping him to work with normalized methods and materials. In the past LD teachers concentrated on using very structured programs, quite distinctive from those in the regular classroom. Although such procedures are still used, LD teachers are very aware of the ultimate goal of *transferring* skills to the mainstreamed setting. The LD teacher and regular classroom teacher must work cooperatively to make the necessary modifications in programs and materials.

Some LD children are not accepted well in the regular classroom (Bruininks, 1978; Bryan, 1976). They seem less accepted socially and may be confused about how to relate to other children. LD children may have neither an accurate idea of what others think of them nor have the skills to get along well with other children.

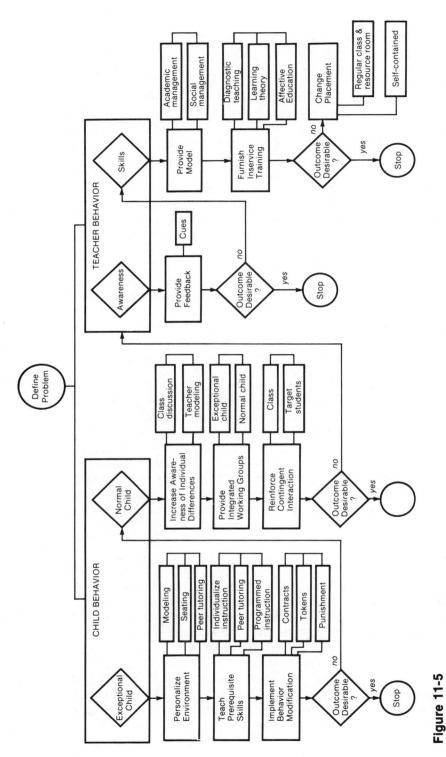

Figure 11-5

The Decision-Making Process

From "Mainstreaming the Mainstreamed Child in the Regular Classroom: The Decision-Making Process" by T. Heron, *Journal of Learning Disabilities*, 1978, *11*, 213. Copyright 1978 by The Professional Press, Inc. Reprinted by special permission of Professional Press, Inc.

The teacher in the regular classroom is also a critical factor in any mainstreaming effort (Gearheart & Weishahn, 1976). How the teacher reacts to the LD child serves as a model for the other children. The teacher's ability to perform informal assessment and modify tasks for the child may mean the difference between success or failure. Regular feedback and positive reinforcement are also important.

As well prepared and as well organized as we may be, the LD child may have problems in the regular classroom. Anticipating that eventuality, Heron (1978) has outlined a process to monitor the progress of the LD child in the least restrictive environment (see figure 11-5).

After the problem has been specifically defined, one may focus upon the LD child, other children in the room, and/or the teacher to solve the problem. As indicated in figure 11-5, there are many things that can be done with either the children or the teacher. First, the LD child may lack prerequisite skills; programmed instruction might help. Second, the other children in the class may pick on the LD child or, at the least, exclude him. Positive reinforcement for playing with the LD child should take care of that problem. Third, the teacher may not know how to reinforce appropriate behavior; assistance from a consultant and inservice training would be helpful.

The following case is a good example of the situation some LD children find themselves in when mainstreamed. The solutions are arrived at in the manner suggested in figure 11-5.

Obviously the LD child in the regular classroom will require much support. The problems and their solutions will involve many factors. As in Sean's case, the LD resource teacher and regular classroom teacher must work together to monitor the mainstreaming approach.

Services for LD children can be arranged through many delivery systems; however, at the center of all these models is the competent LD teacher. The need for a specialist in learning disabilities is particularly evident in mainstreaming programs.

Profile

After being retained a year and served in an LD special class, Sean is being mainstreamed in a regular second-grade classroom. Although 8 years old, he does not appear much bigger than his classmates. He is in the LD resource room 2 hours every morning for reading, spelling, and writing instruction.

Recently Sean has been very restless, not completing tasks and disturbing other children. His problems seemed to result from a combination of things.

The LD teacher and classroom teacher specify the problems as poor initiation and completion of tasks and talking to and disturbing other children. The LD resource teacher observed in the classroom, examined the papers Sean was doing, and did some additional assessments with Sean.

Sean was not understanding the directions for the tasks. While it was known he had a language comprehension problem, he had been able to understand directions on a one-to-one basis in the special class and resource room. However, the LD resource teacher observed that the classroom teacher gave long, verbal directions without many visual cues. The teacher also failed to check if Sean and other children understood the tasks before they began. Here in the regular classroom Sean's receptive language problem was compounded by the teacher's behavior.

The solution: listening comprehension exercises for Sean in the resource room and a demonstration for the teacher of different ways to explain tasks to children.

Many of the unfinished papers that Sean handed in required a good deal of writing ability. Due to lack of time, the classroom and the LD resource teachers had not really discussed the implications of Sean's writing difficulty.

The solution: continued remediation in writing using sample papers from the regular classroom and a demonstration for the teacher of oral game formats to quiz and exercise children in basic skills. Until Sean's writing improves, the teacher will use tapes and oral game formats and avoid heavy demands on written expression.

Finally, it seemed that the other children sitting near Sean were not very friendly toward him. Sean's restlessness and chatter disturbed them. They did not understand and/or particularly like Sean. Sean and they were having a hard time communicating.

The solution: was related to the previous one. A reward for completing work, raising hands, getting high grades, and so forth, was to play the instructional games with Sean. The games supplied Sean with skill exercise, the teacher with evidence of Sean's skills, and the children a chance to have fun with Sean. Everyone was a winner, and Sean was successful in the regular classroom.

THE LEARNING DISABILITY TEACHER

All the considerations we have discussed in connection with educational provisions for LD children can be reduced to one: *the skills of a teacher trained to serve the child.* The basic skills remain the same whether the teacher is serving children through the resource model, the self-contained class, or the residential school. Kass (1970, 1972) and McLoughlin (1973) have each described some essential features of a well-trained teacher of children with learning disabilities.

The Division for Children with Learning Disabilities (DCLD) has developed a code of ethics and a list of competencies. While not a definitive or an empirically based statement of standards, Larsen (1978) considers these efforts as a significant step toward providing quality services for LD children.

Code of Ethics

The code of ethics states that LD professionals must possess the highest qualifications in the field of LD. Second, the best interests of LD children and youth must be promoted in their identification, evaluation, and assessment. This feature of the code forbids any breach of due process procedure or of confidentiality; discriminatory behavior will not be condoned.

Third, LD professionals must engage in research in the best interest of LD children and youth. Both the procedures and publication of the research must reflect competence, fairness, and quality. Finally, LD professionals must work actively to enhance relationships with professionals, parents, and other parties involved in serving LD children.

Competencies

DCLD's standards for competence are *intended to serve as guidelines* for use in teacher training, certification standards, employment criteria, and professional evaluation. Competency statements cover oral language, reading, written expression, spelling, mathematics, cognition, behavioral management, counseling and consulting, career/vocational education, educational operations, and historical-theoretical perspectives. In almost all areas the competencies are divided into categories of general knowledge, assessment, and instruction.

It is not feasible to reproduce the whole list of competencies here. Nor does an outline of the standards reveal much. Therefore, in table 11-3 we have elected to list the competencies involved in just one area, that of reading, to give you an idea of the scope of the competency statements. These competency areas are generally developed in a training program or on a preservice level. They are also the goals of many inservice programs.

Historical, Conceptual, and Affective Perspective

The teacher of LD children needs to have a valid and realistic perspective of his or her role. Knowledge of the characteristics of the target population, assessment and educational techniques, and administrative provisions help the teacher perceive his or her place in the general effort. Past and present procedures used in the schools for referral and program implementation can give important information as can funding and legislative provisions. Exposure to special services in schools, clinics, and institutions assists in the development of this perspective.

Traditionally, teachers enroll in special education survey courses to develop a historical and conceptual perspective. Opportunities to meet disabled learners with different needs help to develop constructive affective attitudes toward these children. On-site visits and active participation offer different models for the prospective teacher. These experiences should assist the teacher in identifying an overall role function. The stage is then set for skill development.

Recognition, Identification, and Screening

The learning disability teacher must obviously be able to recognize children with learning disabilities. A knowledge of normal growth and development and learning theories is essential. Learning disabilities, as well as many other exceptional conditions (visual and hearing impairments, mental retardation, etc.), have an impact on important developmental areas. A teacher can develop a sound understanding of learners' needs by examining the differential effect of learning disabilities and other exceptional conditions on the child's academic, psychological, physical, behavioral/emotional, social, and vocational needs.

Many syndromes, definitions, and models of exceptional learning styles are available to assist the LD teacher to conceptualize the learning problems children face. Knowledge of etiological factors is essential, since their effects may result in many general and specific learning problems.

A major responsibility of the LD teacher is to use various techniques for screening and identifying children with these problems. The teacher learns how to administer inventories and rating scales, apply task analysis, and use behavioral observations in order to identify a target group of LD children. The teacher should have the opportunity to observe children in different settings in order to identify response patterns and learning needs.

Formal and Informal Assessment

Educational diagnosis of children with learning disabilities is a matter of asking *good questions* about the learner's characteristics. The LD teacher must know the *crucial areas* to investigate. Usually these learner characteristics include academic, psychological, physical, emotional, social, and vocational areas (Wallace & Larsen, 1978).

Teachers must know the *sources* of required information. Observation techniques should be emphasized during training. Teachers who rely totally on information from other sources or on test data may develop an inaccurate perception of a child's needs and abilities. The awareness of environmental variables in the classroom will also help the teacher

Table 11-3

LD Teacher Competencies in Reading

I. General Knowledge
  A. Developmental Reading
     The teacher:
     1. understands basic theories related to the field of reading
     2. understands how these theories influence the teaching strategies and the materials used in reading instruction
     3. understands the physical, psychological, and environmental correlates of reading
     4. understands the skills related to reading readiness
     5. understands the sequence of skills leading to the development of the mature reader
     6. understands the components, focus, and approaches associated with developmental reading programs
     7. understands the relationship of developmental reading instruction to corrective and remedial reading instruction
  B. Specialized Reading Instruction
     1. Corrective Reading
        1. understands that corrective reading instruction is as a system for planning and delivering classroom instruction to students who experience minor deficiencies in the elements of developmental reading
        2. understands the type of student who will benefit from such instruction
        3. understands systems that may be used to implement such instruction in the regular classroom on an itinerant basis or in a self-contained classroom
     2. Remedial Reading
        1. understands that remedial reading instruction is as a system for delivering intensive individualized instruction to students who have major reading problems in word recognition, comprehension, and fluency
        2. understands word recognition skills, including:
           2.1 context analysis
           2.2 sight words
           2.3 phonic analysis
           2.4 structural analysis
           2.5 dictionary analysis
           2.6 specialized vocabulary
        3. understands various approaches to reading comprehension; these include:
           3.1 skills (locating main idea, inference, etc.)
           3.2 taxonomy of skills
           3.3 imagery
           3.4 models
           3.5 correlational
           3.6 factor analytic
           3.7 readability

Table 11-3 (*cont.*)
LD Teacher Competencies in Reading

      4. understands comprehension skills, including:
         4.1 vocabulary
         4.2 semantics
         4.3 syntax
         4.4 imagery
         4.5 specific comprehension skills (locating the main idea, following a sequence, inference, noting detail, etc.)
         4.6 critical reading skills
         4.7 meaning in phrases, thought units, sentences, paragraphs, and discourse
      5. understands the skills in reading fluency and reading rate involving both oral and silent reading
      6. understands the interrelationship of reading skills development to other content areas, e.g., written and oral language, spelling, listening
      7. understands the skills associated with problems in structure and syntax
      8. understands the skills associated with problems in reading technical or content specific information

II. Assessment
  A. Screening
      1. has knowledge of appropriate instruments and techniques for general screening for reading
      2. can administer and interpret such instruments and techniques
      3. can identify those students for whom additional assessment and diagnostic evaluations are needed
  B. Evaluation
      1. has knowledge of the appropriate instruments and techniques for specific assessment of the student's level of reading achievement and the areas that warrant specific attention
      2. can administer and interpret such instruments and techniques
  C. Diagnosis
      1. can select and administer formal and informal diagnostic instruments for those specific skills related to reading
      2. can interpret diagnostic data to specify problems in reading
      3. can use the formal and informal data to plan for appropriate reading instructional and intervention programs
  D. Formative/Summative
      1. can develop and use tests to monitor students' ongoing and final level of mastery

III. Instruction
  A. Corrective Reading
      1. can plan and implement instruction for minor problems associated with gaps or deficiencies in the developmental reading process
      2. can use materials to teach the developmental and corrective reading process, e.g., basal reading programs, sight word and phrase cards, specific skill developmental materials

Table 11-3 (*cont.*)

B. Remedial Reading
1. can plan and implement intensive individualized reading instruction in the skill areas associated with remedial reading
2. can use special approaches related to intensive reading instruction
3. can use materials, approaches, and techniques that have application to specific types of reading problems
4. can plan and deliver instruction that will accommodate the development of reading skills in the content areas
5. can deliver instruction in the development of reading skills associated with problems in technical or content specific areas
6. can identify and secure the services of additional appropriate professional resources to meet specific needs
7. can design and deliver an individualized reading program to the student which assures appropriate progress, alterations, goal achievement, etc.
8. can work with others involved in the student's educational program to assure that instruction in reading is integrated into the whole curriculum and that appropriate progress is assured

From *Code of Ethics and Competencies for Teachers of Learning Disabled Children and Youth* by the Division for Children with Learning Disabilities. Copyright 1978 by the DCLD. Reprinted by permission.

compose realistic educational suggestions for classroom implementation.

School records, regular classroom teachers, parents, and support personnel in such fields as medicine, psychology, and speech therapy must be considered as indispensable sources of information. The teacher must have the skills to use these sources. By knowing the kind of information needed, a teacher can direct good questions to appropriate resources. Assessment problems often develop when obvious sources of information have been overlooked. School records, achievement test data, educational histories, and psychological reports offer very special kinds of information. A teacher should consult these records for information but realize their limitations.

The LD teacher must also know what formal and informal *assessment tools* are available. Certain information can be gathered more efficiently by particular techniques. Consequently, how to choose and use interview techniques, observation samples, task analysis, and formal diagnostic instruments in academic, psychological, and social areas should also be known.

Diagnostic information must be gathered systematically, and it must be *synthesized* into a meaningful profile of a learner's characteristics. The LD teacher must be able to identify educationally relevant pieces of information and disregard irrelevant information.

The goal of educational diagnosis is to establish *educational objectives* for the child. The diagnostic effort would therefore concentrate on both strengths and deficits. The teacher must also be able to *communicate* the results of the educational diagnosis to others. He or she has usually cooperated with various people in this process; the ability to transmit the diagnostic information in a sensible fashion to other teachers, parents, and ancillary personnel will often dictate whether a child's needs are met.

The LD teacher must be totally conversant with the provisions of P.L. 94-142. As we discussed in chapter 4, the LD teacher must perform the procedures of the IEP process.

Planning an Instructional Program

An LD teacher plans a program based on the educational objectives identified through diagnostic procedures. The relationship between diagnostic activities and educational planning is essential. We reviewed major programs and materials in part two of this book.

Composing objectives, identifying the appropriate teaching strategies, indicating the necessary materials, and establishing criteria for performance are all involved in designing a program. The LD teacher must also consider which personnel in the program (regular classroom teachers, speech therapists, teacher aides, etc.) would most appropriately accomplish objectives with a child. Certain other objectives may require input and treatment from ancillary personnel in medicine, psychology, counseling, and so forth.

An integral aspect of educational planning is the teacher's working knowledge of *curriculum and remedial methods*. The teacher must know special programs in reading, writing, arithmetic, written and spoken language, social/vocational education, and physical education. A child's needs may dictate the use of a more structured, programmed approach than is available in the regular classroom. Additionally, special *teaching strategies* are often required. Experience with some exceptional children has resulted in the development of very structured teaching approaches. Behavior modification, multisensory approaches, and differential stimuli control represent essential skill areas for LD teachers.

The ability to select and use materials is basic to the role of these teachers. Some LD children require remediation in specific skill areas, such as listening and writing skills. The facility with which the teacher identifies and uses materials, activities suggested in books, and remedial kits usually decides the program's ultimate effectiveness. The use of remedial activities and materials must be based on the teacher's knowledge of skill sequences and curriculum.

LD teachers frequently focus on a *specific skills approach* after they have identified deficit areas through assessment. Based on criterion-referenced assessment, this form of remediation establishes the necessary repertoire of behaviors to perform tasks in reading, arithmetic, and

A special class placement gives LD children intensive help in their academic areas of need.

so forth. However, particular care is taken to transfer these skills to the criterion outcome. As our experience with remediation in perceptual areas taught us, there is a danger of developing splinter skills that do not affect the outcome we want most, e.g., ability to read.

A teacher must know how to use *retrieval systems* (Mann & Suiter, 1974; Valett, 1969; Van Etten & Adamson, 1973) and *references* (Bush & Giles, 1977; Johnson & Myklebust, 1976; Myers & Hammill, 1976; Wallace & Kauffman, 1978). As we discussed in chapter 4, there are many criterion-referenced systems and skill sequences that assist the teacher in designing IEPs.

The learning disability teacher must be able to design a suitable *environment*. Scheduling, arranging learning centers and cubicles, and developing a good clerical system are important skill areas for teachers. In cases where other personnel will deliver assistance to the children, a teacher must be able to identify these people and provide necessary support. Regular classroom teachers, aides, and parents usually require materials and activities to implement remedial suggestions.

Mainstreaming and P.L. 94-142 have added a new perspective to designing instructional programs. Since the goal of instruction is to maintain the LD child in the least restrictive environment, the LD teacher must be conversant with the *curriculum and materials in the regular classroom*. As we have discussed earlier, the emphasis today is to assist the LD child to respond effectively to the procedures used in the mainstream setting. Regular classroom reading materials and other kinds of programs must be adapted and programmed to facilitate that reentry.

Implementing the Instructional Plan

The LD teacher must be able to *teach.* Implementing an instructional program is usually his or her major role. Working on a one-to-one basis and directing many children in individual tasks are required skills, and modeling instructional activities for other teachers and parents is usually necessary.

Many instructional plans fall apart during the actual teaching. The skill to adapt and modify a lesson is necessary. A teacher must have more than instructional objectives, activities, and materials to teach a lesson successfully.

McLoughlin (1973) observed a number of resource teachers in the act of teaching. These teachers demonstrated certain important skills immediately before instruction, during instruction, and immediately following instruction.

Teachers prepared the children for the task by giving explicit directions, reading material before a child proceeded, arousing a child's interest with novelties such as pictures, reviewing or drilling prerequisite skills, warning children of pitfalls in the task, and making realistic demands in view of the child's attitude and mood that day.

During the lesson many teachers exhibited various kinds of skills, including:

1. Directing a child through a task (e.g., with a marker),
2. Directing the student's attention to details (e.g., details of a word),
3. Labeling elements,
4. Shifting tasks regularly,
5. Pointing,
6. Following the student by reading along with him,
7. Modeling for imitation,
8. Timing,
9. Giving answers,
10. Anticipating student mistakes and difficulties,
11. Offering cues,
12. Asking leading questions,
13. Reminding students to use rules and learned materials,
14. Stopping a student in the act of making a mistake,
15. Supplying charts and cards for students references, and
16. Keeping a record of errors for later lessons. (p. 93)

Immediately after a lesson these teachers rehearsed learned material, awarded incentives, sent progress notes to a child's teacher, assisted children in detecting errors, and charted individual performance.

The learning disability teacher must be capable of individualizing instruction in these and other ways. The tone, atmosphere, and pace of a learning session is decided by the teacher's skill in interacting. These teachers must have strategies to react to misbehavior, requests for assistance, student frustration and failure, inattention, and other behaviors.

The LD teacher is accountable for the results of a remedial program—both daily and final evaluation. The original program design should include criteria for performance, as we discussed in chapter 4.

The teacher must know how to perform both *formative* and *summative* evaluation. A regular evaluation, perhaps daily, can be performed by taking short time samples of target behavior. Graphs and charts may even be kept by the children for feedback and motivation.

At least yearly, a teacher is called upon to supply evidence that particular objectives were accomplished. This summative evaluation can take many forms. The teacher usually administers posttests for comparisons with initial baseline data.

Diagnostic-prescriptive reports and suggestions to teachers and parents require follow-up efforts. The learning disability teacher must have the skill to design follow-up projects to assess the effectiveness of his or her input. These teachers also need the skill to compose and transmit progress reports to anyone interested. A data base will help school districts modify or initiate services for children with learning disabilities.

Finally, the learning disability teacher needs to evaluate his or her own teaching ability, perhaps by having someone observe the teaching. Formal and informal rating scales are available for this purpose. The use of videotapes is another possibility. The teacher may then evaluate good teaching techniques during playback sessions.

Liaison-Consultant

Few teacher roles demand such interpersonal and interprofessional skills as that of the LD teacher. Nearly every aspect of this role

These LD children attend a special day school where the requisite instruction is provided.

(screening, diagnosis, etc.) requires an ability to cooperate with other people. The LD teacher is often the central person in channeling services to children and teachers. The abilities of identifying remedial ideas and activities of offering a model for individual instruction, and of coordinating other personnel contribute immensely to the program's effectiveness. The LD teacher can be a major change agent in a school district (Adelman, 1973).

Our description of teacher competencies is not intended to suggest a sequential skill development. Formal and informal assessment techniques and appropriate remedial methodologies may be taught together. Field-based instruction is important throughout a training program (Wiegerink, 1973). An experiential and discovery-learning approach may be ultimately more effective than the traditional didactic training techniques. As Bruininks (1977) notes, there is also a need to blend current teacher-training approaches, such as humanistic and competency-based ones. Blackhurst, McLoughlin and Price (1977) have described another interesting movement in teacher training—cross-categorical.

Finally, we must realize that the LD teacher is apt to have role conflicts with other professionals (Wallace, 1976). Many of the competency areas overlap with the activities of reading specialists, speech and language therapists, and school psychologists: Intensive relationships with teachers in the mainstream will also require study to clarify sensitive areas (McLoughlin & Kass, 1978).

What seems necessary is to appreciate the central role that the LD teacher plays in the *total* program of the LD child. In the training programs of LD teachers and the other professionals involved in the child's program, special emphasis must be placed on working together. P.L. 94-142 and its requirements for cooperative assessment and IEP development make this focus imperative.

In conclusion, there are many ways to deliver services to children with learning disabilities. We need not limit ourselves to the "one teacher-one classroom" model (Deno, 1973). Children with learning disabilities vary in their degree of involvement. A school system should appreciate this continuum of needs and plan accordingly. Multiple arrangements are often necessary.

A survey of in-system and extra-system staff and programs can uncover a variety of potential resources. Although trained learning specialists are required to implement any program, their skills can be utilized in many ways. The children and teachers in a school can benefit immensely by well-conceived service arrangements.

Perhaps the greatest error in the past has been to use microscopic vision in making educational placement decisions. The services that children with varying degrees of disabilities require need not be represented by merely one teacher and one classroom.

These residential school staff members are reviewing the IEP of one of their pupils.

EDUCATIONAL PROVISIONS: IN PERSPECTIVE

Certain assumptions have guided our discussion of providing services to LD children. We should first identify instructional objectives for a child as part of the diagnostic process. Subsequently, an appropriate service model should be chosen.

Secondly, children with learning disabilities have varying degrees of involvement. We must develop multiple arrangements of service models. The regular classroom, perhaps with a support system, should be our first consideration. Severe learning disability cases may require more drastic provisions, such as the special class model.

We must also encourage mainstream education. A network of educational provisions (regular classroom system through the residential school model) should be considered as a continuum of services (Cogen & Ohrtman, 1971). A child with learning disabilities may move through a number of service models, from the resource room model to the special self-contained class, but the ideal is to maintain the child in the service model that permits maximum integration in mainstream education. Much will depend on our ability to identify personnel and program goals that can satisfy a child's needs in the local school and community.

Finally, we assume that we can find a large number of skills and the consequent services in one teacher. The learning disability teacher represents the crux of any plans to provide services to children and teachers in a school or area.

The reality of many situations indicates that we may be overly ambitious. Our efforts to identify and serve children with specific learning disabilities have uncovered many other needs in school systems. We have begun to answer the educational needs of every type of underachievement, developmental lag, and disruptive behavior in the school. The need of regular classroom teachers for training and support systems has begun to drain the limited resources of programs in learning disabilities.

There is the distinct possibility that we have overextended ourselves. The intent of programs in learning disabilities is to serve a specific kind of exceptional child, the child with severe learning problems. The funding and services of these programs seem to be dissipated in many worthy but tangential activities.

Mainstreaming may correct inappropriate placement practices for some groups of children, but we may be straining our resources to widen our province of responsibilities. Thus, there is a definite danger that children with severe learning handicaps will not get sufficient education and training.

Furthermore, most school systems are minimally staffed. Regular classroom teachers, school psychologists, and others are being stretched to the maximum. Staff redistribution, or using the existing staff to meet the special needs of children, may be unrealistic. The present staff in a school system may truly not have the time to implement even the simplest intervention program. Very often we find that one person must perform the diagnostic and teaching services for all children, however mild their problems may be.

The ultimate success of any educational effort to serve LD children is predicated upon the presence of specially trained teachers in a school. One harsh reality is our inability to attract LD specialists to rural and even to some metropolitan areas. There are not and may never be programs in learning disabilities in certain areas of our country, because personnel are simply not available.

When specialists are available, their energies may be drained by services to mild and moderate cases. The smaller proportion of children with *severe* learning disabilities do not get the full support they require. Every extension of the role of the LD teacher (to include consulting, assessment, etc.) means that *direct teaching* of children is lessened. The tragic result is that programs in learning disabilities are weakened.

We must therefore avoid grandiose program designs. The major service which is needed is *teaching* these children in the appropriate environment and with suitable methodology. Furthermore, we must maintain a focus on children with *severe* learning disabilities.

SUMMARY

We have discussed the foundations of decisions about placement of LD children. The provisions of P.L. 94-142 have had a significant impact for children and youth with disabilities.

We organized primary considerations in the decision-making process, taking into account variables that could support a total program for a child. After reviewing various cascades of services models, we described and analyzed each service model, the regular classroom model through the residential school model.

The LD child in the mainstream was discussed briefly, in order to clarify the relationship of these models. Finally, we outlined in detail the role and competencies of the LD teacher, as suggested by the DCLD code of ethics and list of competencies.

SUGGESTED ACTIVITIES

1. Request a copy of the state special education plan from your state department. Read the guidelines for LD placement.

2. Given your state plan, establish how operational the LD definition is. Are specific criteria mentioned? Specific tests?

3. Interview former special class teachers. Find out their impressions of the resource room. Did they have any problems in shifting their role from a special class teacher to a resource teacher?

4. Attend a placement committee meeting. What factors and criteria were most mentioned in the placement decision?

5. Attend a placement committee meeting. Who coordinated the meeting? What input did the following individuals have: regular class teacher, LD teacher, parents, and so forth?

6. Visit an LD resource room. Describe the physical arrangements, schedule, materials, and teacher strategies.

7. Interview an LD child who is being served in the mainstream. Ask him/her about the activities he/she does during the day. Does he/she have any problems being mainstreamed?

8. Visit a school that has an LD resource room. Interview the principal and other staff members. What benefits do they see in the model? What disadvantages?

References

Adelman, H. *Competency-based training in education: A conceptual view* (Special Project Grant No. OEG-0-71-4152 (603). Washington, D.C.: Bureau of Education for the Handicapped, August 1973.

Blackhurst, A.E., McLoughlin, J.A., & Price, L. Issues in the development of programs to prepare teachers of children with learning and behavior disorders. *Journal of Behavioral Disorders*, 1977, *2*, 157-168.

Bradley, C. State education agency considerations in identification of the handicapped. In R.D. Kneedler & S.G. Tarver (Eds.), *Changing perspectives in special education.* Columbus: Charles E. Merrill, 1977.

Bruininks, V. A humanistic competency-based training for teachers of learning disabled students. *Journal of Learning Disabilities*, 1977, *10*, 518-526.

Bruininks, V. Actual and perceived peer status of learning-disabled students in mainstream programs. *Journal of Special Education*, 1978, *12*, 51-58.

Bryan, T. Peer popularity of learning disabled children: A replication. *Journal of Learning Disabilities*, 1976, *9*, 307-311.

Burrello, L., Kaye, N., & Nutter, R. Managing special education statewide: Developing an interdependent management system. *Journal of Special Education*, 1978, *12*, 105-112.

Bush, W.J., & Giles, M. *Aids to psycholinguistic teaching* (2nd ed.). Columbus, Ohio: Charles E. Merrill, 1977.

Cogen, V., & Ohrtman, W. A comprehensive plan for services for the handicapped. *Journal of Special Education*, 1971, *5*, 73-80.

Cruickshank, W. Least-restrictive placement: Administrative wishful thinking. *Journal of Learning Disabilities*, 1977, *10*, 193-194.

Deno, E. Special education as developmental capital. *Exceptional Children*, 1970, *37*, 229-237.

Deno, E. (Ed.). *Instructional alternatives for exceptional children.* Arlington, Va.: Council for Exceptional Children, 1973.

Division for Children with Learning Disabilities. *Code of ethics and competencies for teachers of learning disabled children and youth.* 1978.

Gearheart, B.R. *Learning disabilities in educational strategies.* St. Louis: C.V. Mosby, 1973.

Gearheart, B.R., & Weishahn, M. *The handicapped child in the regular classroom.* St. Louis: C.V. Mosby, 1976.

Hallahan, D., & Kauffman, J. Labels, categories, behaviors: ED, LD, and EMR reconsidered. *Journal of Special Education*, 1977, *11*, 139-150.

Hammill, D., & Wiederholt, J.L. *The resource room: Its rationale and implementation.* Philadelphia: The Journal of Special Education, 1972.

Hayes, J., & Higgins, S.T. Issues regarding the IEP: Teachers on the front line. *Exceptional Children*, 1978, *44*, 267-274.

Heron, T. Maintaining the mainstreamed child in the regular classroom: The decision-making process. *Journal of Learning Disabilities,* 1978, *11,* 210-216.

Jacobs, W. The effect of the learning disability label on classroom teacher's ability objectively to observe and interpret child behavior. *Learning Disability Quarterly,* 1978, *1,* 50-55.

Johnson, D., & Myklebust, H. *Learning disabilities: Educational principles and practices.* New York: Grune & Stratton, 1967.

Journal of Special Education, 1972, *6,* 335-396.

Junkala, J. Teachers' assessments and team decisions. *Exceptional Children,* 1977, *44,* 31-32.

Kass, C. (Ed.). *Final report: Advanced institute for leadership personnel in learning disabilities* (U.S.O.E. Contract No. OEG-0-9-121013-3021 [031]). Tucson: University of Arizona, 1970.

Kass, C. Personnel training practices in learning disabilities. In N.D. Bryant & C. Kass, *Final report: LTI in learning disabilities* (Vol. I) (U.S.O.E. Grant No. OEG-0-71-4425-604, Project No. 127145). Tucson: University of Arizona, 1972.

Kauffman, M.J., Gottlieb, J., Agard, J.A., & Kukic, M.D. Mainstreaming: Toward an explication of a construct. In E. Meyen, G. Vergason, & R. Whelan (Eds.), *Alternatives for teaching exceptional children.* Denver: Love Publishing, 1975.

Kauffman, M., & Mona, L. The least restrictive environment: A major philosophical change. In E. Meyen (Ed.), *Exceptional children and youth.* Denver: Love Publishing, 1978.

Larsen, S. Learning disabilities and the professional educator. *Learning Disability Quarterly,* 1978, *1,* 5-12.

Lerner, J. *Children with learning disabilities: Theories, diagnosis, and teaching strategies* (2nd ed.). Boston: Houghton Mifflin, 1976.

Lilly, M.S. A merger of the categories: Are we finally ready? *Journal of Learning Disabilities,* 1977, *10,* 115-121.

Lovitt, T. The learning disabled. In N. Haring (Ed.), *Behavior of exceptional children* (2nd Ed.). Columbus, Ohio: Charles E. Merrill, 1978.

Mann, P., & Suiter, P. *Handbook in diagnostic teaching.* Boston: Allyn & Bacon, 1974.

Marver, J. The cost of special education in nonpublic schools. *Journal of Learning Disabilities,* 1976, *9,* 651-660.

Mayer, C. State master planning for special education: A national survey of current status. *Journal of Learning Disabilities,* 1976, *9,* 633-637.

Mayhall, W., & Jenkins, J. Scheduling daily or less-than-daily instruction: Implications for resource programs. *Journal of Learning Disabilities,* 1977, *10,* 159-163.

McCarthy, J.M. Education: The basis of the triangle. *Annals of the New York Academy of Science,* 1973, *205,* 362-367.

McLoughlin, J. *Role analysis of resource teachers of children with learning disabilities and educable mental retardation.* Unpublished doctoral dissertation, University of Arizona, 1973.

McLoughlin, J.A., Edge, D., & Strenecky, B. Perspective of parent involvement in the diagnosis and treatment of learning disabled children. *Journal of Learning Disabilities,* 1978, *11,* 291-296.

McLoughlin, J.A., & Kass, C. Resource teachers: Their role. *Learning Disability Quarterly,* 1978, *1,* 56-62.

Meyen, E.L. *Exceptional children and youth.* Denver: Love Publishing, 1978.

Miller, T., & Switzky, H. The least restrictive alternative: Implications for service providers. *Journal of Special Education,* 1978, *12,* 123-132.

Myers, P., & Hammill, D. *Methods for learning disorders* (2nd ed.). New York: Wiley, 1976.

Newcomer, P. Special education services for the "mildly handicapped": Beyond a diagnostic and remedial model. *Journal of Special Education,* 1977, *11,* 153-166.

Pasanella, A., & Volkmor, C. *Coming back . . . Or never leaving.* Columbus, Ohio: Charles E. Merrill, 1977.

Payne, R., & Murray, C. Principals' attitudes toward integration of the handicapped. *Exceptional Children,* 1974, *41,* 123-126.

Reger, R. What is a resource room program? *Journal of Learning Disabilities,* 1973, *6,* 609-614.

Reger, R. What does "mainstreaming" mean? *Journal of Learning Disabilities,* 1974, *7,* 513-515.

Reger, R., & Koppmann, M. The child-oriented resource room program. *Exceptional Children,* 1971, *37,* 460-462.

Reynolds, M. A framework for considering some issues in special education. *Exceptional Children,* 1962, *7,* 367-370.

Reynolds, M., & Birch, J. *Teaching exceptional children in all America's schools.* Reston, Va.: Council for Exceptional Children, 1977.

Ribner, S. The effects of special class placement on the self-concept of exceptional children. *Journal of Learning Disabilities,* 1978, *11,* 319-323.

Schworm, R. Models in special education: Considerations and cautions. *Journal of Special Education,* 1976, *10,* 179-186.

Sindelar, P., & Deno, S. The effectiveness of resource programming. *Journal of Special Education,* 1978, *12,* 17-36.

Update, 1978, *9,* 1. Reston, Va.: Council for Exceptional Children.

Valett, R. *Programming learning disorders.* Palo Alto, Calif.: Fearon, 1969.

Van Etten, C., & Adamson, G. *Select Ed.: Educational descriptor dictionary for prescriptive materials retrieval system.* Olathe, Kans.: Select Ed., 1973.

Wallace, G. Interdisciplinary efforts in learning disabilities: Issues and recommendations. *Journal of Learning Disabilities,* 1976, *9,* 520-532.

Wallace, G., & Kauffman, J. *Teaching children with learning problems* (2nd ed.). Columbus, Ohio: Charles E. Merrill, 1978.

Wallace, G., & Larsen, S. *Educational assessment of learning problems: Testing for teaching.* Boston: Allyn & Bacon, 1978.

Wiederholt, J.L. Administrative and service arrangements in learning disabilities. In N.D. Bryant & C. Kass (Eds.), *Final report: LTI in learning disabilities* (Vol. I) (U.S.O.E. Grant No. OEG-0-71-4425-604, Project No. 127145). Tucson: University of Arizona, 1972.

Wiederholt, J.L., Hammill, D.D., & Brown, V. *The resource teacher.* Boston: Allyn & Bacon, 1978.

Wiegerink, R. An organizational model for preparing future special educators. *Journal of Special Education,* 1973, *7,* 205-216.

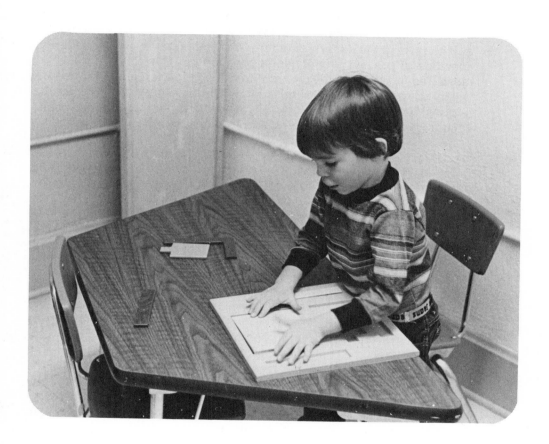

PREVIEW

By now it must be obvious that many aspects of learning disabilities can be prevented. Given that we can identify the LD child early, we should be able to reverse the pattern of failure. In this chapter we will consider the specifics of present identification procedures. The kinds of behaviors measured in tests and the different formats of the screening procedures will indicate the diversity found in identification procedures. We feel that informal procedures, such as teacher ratings and situational observations, are sometimes preferable to formal screening instruments.

We will also consider the different kinds of preschool programs available. Head Start is the frequent setting for existing services for LD children, though some special programs are available. Early childhood educators are struggling to meet the needs of all exceptional children. We feel that the LD child must not be overlooked.

In this chapter we will focus upon the educational components of *preschool* prevention programs. It should be obvious, however, that prevention also involves correction of teaching strategies during the school years. The scope of early intervention programs actually extends from the neonatal stage through the primary grades.

Most prevention programs attempt to stop known factors from causing physical and psychological harm. When we cannot control the variables that ultimately create the "high risk" youngster, we introduce enriching environmental conditions of medical, sociological, and educational natures.

Learning disabilities, as we have described them, are generally the *cumulative* result of many factors. In only rare cases will one factor in a child's development have disastrous consequences on his or her learning ability and learning style. Instead, the educational, environmental, psychological, and physical components interact.

The prevention of learning disabilities is based to a degree upon the elimination of undesirable factors in a child's development. Obviously, a child should not be the victim of inadequate teaching, nor should we discontinue our efforts to prevent sensory, linguistic, and nutritional deprivation.

We may have somewhat less power to guarantee development of psychological and neuropsychological bases of learning. Our ability to deal with the unfolding of perceptual and cognitive functions, as well as the underlying neurological system, is tempered by flaws in our knowledge and technology. The exact nature and contribution of prenatal, perinatal, and postnatal factors in learning disabilities are becoming increasingly apparent.

Patrick is a 4-year-old child who has his parents and day-care teacher concerned. For no obvious reason, he is very active and inattentive at home and at the day-care center. At home it is particularly difficult to get him to follow directions. His teacher at the day-care center complains of his forgetfulness and disruptive behavior.

What is not apparent to Patrick's parents and teacher is the learning disability he has in language. Although his vocabulary and oral expression are good for his age, he has difficulty in understanding what is said to him. He understands names of objects, but gets confused with grammar and other aspects of language.

This language problem became apparent after screening for learning disabilities was done at the day-care center. Patrick was also suffering from allergies and attendant ear infections. The infections were chronic enough to result in a build-up of fluid. As a result, Patrick suffered intermittent hearing loss.

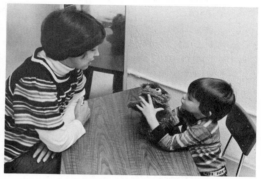

Once his physical and language problems were identified, a conference was held to design a remedial program. The parents, teacher, language specialist, and pediatrician agreed upon goals to accomplish with Patrick. This LD child's program was a multidisciplinary effort.

It was felt that Parick might work best in a quiet area when learning essential skills. He was also given direct instruction in his problem area on a one-to-one or small-group basis. He was able to work with his peers on other kinds of tasks. Once Pat-

rick's disability was corrected, he was able to participate fully in language-oriented activities.

Our desire to prevent learning disabilities is consequently stifled by the nature of the causes that we have previously identified in chapter 3. Some factors are amenable to intervention. Others are so interwoven in a complex network of physical, psychological, cultural, and socioeconomic components that we do not know where to intervene.

Symptoms of learning disabilities must be recognized early and appropriate intervention implemented, if the prevention is to be successful. The necessary research has been difficult to perform, when it has been attempted. Since LD children are a heterogeneous population, very few longitudinal profiles of their development are available. Usually we have reconstructed histories through interviews and case reports.

The result is that we often rely on the predictive ability of certain symptoms, even though the prediction is at best a statistical form of guessing. Learning disabilities take such a variety of forms that it is very difficult to establish a relationship between predictive correlates and subsequent learning behaviors (Bryant, 1972). A child may demonstrate certain early symptoms of learning disabilities, yet ultimately not have any trouble in school. Prediction based on a *single* factor has not proven very successful (Wallace & Larsen, 1978). However, rating scales and situational observations have been used with increasing success to screen for learning disabled children (Colligan, 1977; Glazzard, 1977; Hawthorne & Larsen, 1977; Magliocca, Rinaldi, Crew, & Kunzelmann, 1977).

Furthermore, prevention is not merely a matter of early detection. We must also have appropriate forms of early intervention. Ideally, the nature of the treatment should have maximal transfer to later learning abilities. As McLoughlin and Kershman (1978) point out, well-designed early childhood programs can generate information about successful teaching strategies for LD children. Systematic teaching strategies can be used to program for the preschool LD child.

Preventive measures for learning disabilities should not be considered synonymous with early childhood education. While sometimes taking similar forms, these two efforts to serve early developmental needs of children are motivated and conceptualized differently. Children who demonstrate signs of future learning difficulties require special support and attention. The funds designated for prevention programs for exceptional children must be channeled appropriately (Nazzaro, 1974). The early years of the handicapped child must be occupied with wisely chosen activities, activities which will guarantee a maximal preparation for later learning endeavors. The normally developing child, on the other hand, may profit from a wide variety of activities, none of which would sorely limit his later achievement if omitted.

P.L. 94-142 contains the following provisions for early childhood education (Hayden, 1978).

1. Parents must participate in the establishment of long- and short-term goals for their child; these are Individualized Education Programs (IEPs) for each child.

2. The rights of children and their parents will be protected by confidentiality of all child records, nondiscriminatory testing and due process.
3. Parents must receive written notification in their native language prior to evaluation of their child or any placement change.
4. A comprehensive system of teacher and other professional personnel preparation must be included in state plans and local policies.
5. A special incentive grant to states will be aimed at encouraging the states to provide special education and related services to preschool handicapped children 3 to 5 years old. (p. 35)

Head Start programs have a mandate to integrate the handicapped into their target population; 10% of the group are to be handicapped. Other special preschool programs have also been funded (Hayden, 1978).

Another factor shaping the development of early childhood programs for LD children is the principle of *least restrictive environment*. That is, LD children will be served in the mainstream of the preschool program. With the proper perspective, the early childhood educator can begin to program for children with learning disabilities in major developmental areas.

McLoughlin and Kershman (in press) have identified the following areas of concern for preschool programming of the exceptional child: motor development, verbal comprehension and expression, visual acuity and perception, auditory acuity and perception, cognitive development, and adaptive/self help skills. (See table 12-1 for a list of suggested assessment devices and materials by these areas.) While the LD child may not require specific programming in all of these areas, these domains represent assessment and curricular goals likely to be established in early childhood programs with LD children in them.

With these preliminary thoughts in mind, let us examine our ability to identify potential cases of learning disabilities and the different forms of intervention.

IDENTIFICATION

We have experimented with many forms of early identification and screening of learning disabilities. Our efforts have often been based on profiles of normal development (Bloom, 1964; Freud, 1960; Gesell, 1945; Hunt, 1961; Piaget, 1970). We have also relied upon case history reconstruction of handicapped children's development. Kephart (1971), Frostig and Horne (1965), and Kirk, McCarthy, and Kirk (1968) have also suggested various other conceptualizations of components involved in learning.

Faced with screening large numbers of children, we need to identify highly predictive and meaningful information. However, there is considerable difference of opinion and practice in regard to screening.

Table 12-1

Tests and Materials by Skill Areas for Preschool Handicapped Children

skill areas	tests	materials and/or idea books
Motor Development	*Oseretsky Tests of Motor Proficiency* (Doll, 1946) *Developmental Test of Visual-Motor Integration* (Beery & Buktenica, 1967) *Southern California Perceptual Motor Tests* (Ayres, 1969)	*Move, Grow, Learn* (Frostig & Maslow, 1969) *Dubnoff School Program* (Dubnoff & Chambers, 1968) *Beginning to Learn: Fine Motor Skills* (Thurstone & Lillie, 1970)
Verbal Comprehension and Expression	*Receptive-Expressive Emergent Language Scale* (Bzoch & League, 1971) *Illinois Test of Psycholinguistic Abilities* (Kirk, McCarthy, & Kirk, 1968) *Goldman-Fristoe Test of Articulation* (Goldman & Fristoe, 1969) *Verbal Language Development* Scale (Mecham, 1958) *Test of Language Development* (Newcomer & Hammill, 1977)	Engel (1972) Karnes (1968) *DISTAR Language I* (Engelmann, Osborn, & Engelmann, 1969) *Peabody Language Development Kit: Level P* (Dunn, Horton, & Smith, 1968) *MWM Program for Developing Language Abilities* (Minskoff, Wiseman, & Minskoff, 1973)
Vision: Acuity/Perception	*Home Eye Test for Preschoolers* (National Society for the Prevention of Blindness, 1975) *Marianne Frostig Developmental Test of Visual Perception* (Frostig, Lefever, & Whittlesey, 1964)	*Frostig Remediation Program* (Frostig, Horne, & Maslow, 1973) *Ruth Cheves Program I: Visual-Motor Perception* (Cheves, 1969)
Auditory: Acuity/Perception	*Auditory Discrimination Test* (Wepman, 1958) *Goldman-Fristoe-Woodcock Test of Auditory Discrimination* (Goldman, Fristoe, & Woodcock, 1970) Audiological examination	Zigmond & Cicci (1968) *Sound, Order, Sense* (Semel, 1968) *What's Its Name* (Utley, 1968) *GOAL: Language Development* (Karnes, 1972) *Play It By Ear* (Lowell & Stoner, 1963)
Cognitive	*Boehm Test of Basic Concepts* (Boehm, 1971) *Basic Concept Inventory* (Engelmann, 1967)	*GOAL: Mathematical Concepts* (Karnes, 1973b) *Inquisitive Games: Discovering How To Learn* (Sprigle, 1969).

Table 12-1 (*cont.*)

	Basic School Skills Inventory (Goodman & Hammill, 1975) Leiter International Performance Scale (Leiter, 1948)	Peabody Language Development Kit: Level I (Dunn & Smith 1965)
Adaptive/Self Help	Bayley Scales of Infant Development (Bayley, 1969) Vineland Social Maturity Scale (Doll, 1953) AAMD Adaptive Behavior Scales (Nihira et al., 1969)	DUSO (Dinkmeyer, 1972) Beginning with the Handicapped (Hart, 1974) Project "ME" (Schaeffer, 1972)
Comprehensive	Denver Developmental Screening Test (Frankenburg & Dodds, 1970) Learning Accomplishment Profile (Sanford, 1975) Performance Objectives for Preschool Children (Schirmer, 1974)	Instructional Materials for the Handicapped (Thorum et al., 1976) Portage Guide to Early Education (Bluma et al., 1976) Project Memphis (Quick, Little, & Campbell, 1974) Curriculum Cards for Preschool Children (Schirmer, 1976)

Screening programs have been implemented from the neonatal period through school years. Some of the areas that have been chosen for examination are physical, neurological, psychoneurological, perceptual, linguistic, cognitive, social-emotional, sociocultural, and criterion-referenced academic considerations. Screening devices have been composed of various combinations of predictive tests, checklists, interviews, and observations (see table 12-2).

It is difficult to identify one distinctive, reliable form of early identification of learning disabilities. Consequently, we will identify some of the target variables, child behaviors and other factors, and the techniques used to identify and assess them. We will also discuss guidelines for early identification.

Choice of Target Variables

It would be ideal if we could trace the classroom manifestations of learning disabilities back through a child's earlier development. If

Table 12-2
Screening Tests

name	type	age or grade range	additional references
A Process for In-School Screening of Children with Emotional Handicaps (Bower & Lambert, 1962)	Social-emotional	Grades 1-12	Salvia, Schultz, & Chapin (1974); Hoepfner, Stern, & Nummedal (1971)
A Psychoeducational Inventory of Basic Learning Abilities (Valett, 1968)	Perception, language, conceptual, and social	Ages 5-12	Hoepfner, Stern, & Nummedal (1971)
Basic School Skills Inventory (Goodman & Hammill, 1975)	Basic information, reading readiness, number readiness, self-help, handwriting, oral communication, and classroom behavior	Kindergarten	Hawthorne & Larsen (1977)
Bender Visual-Motor Gestalt Test (Bender, 1938)	Copying test	Ages 5-10	Koppitz (1964, 1968); Norfleet (1973)
Boehm Test of Basic Concepts (Boehm, 1971)	Verbal concepts	Preschool and older (primarily for younger children)	Proger (1970a)
Denver Developmental Screening Test (Frankenburg & Dodds, 1970)	Personal-social, fine motor, language, and gross motor	Ages birth-5 years	Salvia & Ysseldyke (1978)
Detroit Test of Learning Aptitude (Baker & Leland, 1955)	Language, number, social adjustment, auditory attention, motor speed, etc. (19 subtests)	Ages 3-14+	Hoepfner, Stern, & Nummedal (1971)

Table 12-2 (cont.)

Test	Area	Age range	References
Early Detection Inventory (McGahan & McGahan, 1967)	Social-emotional behavior, readiness, motor development, and personal history	Preschool-kindergarten	Proger (1971a)
Evanston Early Identification Scale (Landsman & Dillard, 1967)	Draw-a-person	5-0 yrs.–6-3 yrs.	
First-Grade Screening Test (Pate & Webb, 1969)	Numerous areas	Kindergarten–first grade	
Goldman-Fristoe-Woodcock Test of Auditory Discrimination (Goldman, Fristoe, & Woodcock, 1970)	Factors in auditory discrimination	4 yrs–adult	Finkenbinder (1973); Proger (1970b)
Illinois Test of Psycholinguistic Abilities (Kirk, McCarthy, & Kirk, 1968)	10 areas of information processing	Kindergarten and up (ages 2-10)	Kirk & Kirk (1971); Karnes, Hodgins, & Teska (1969); Burns & Watson (1973); Hammill & Larsen (1974, 1978)
Marianne Frostig Developmental Test of Visual Perception (Frostig, Lefever, & Whittlesey, 1964)	Factors in visual perception	Ages 3-8	Kelly (1970); Hoepfner, Stern, & Nummedal (1971); Hammill & Wiederholt (1972)
Meeting Street School Screening Test (Hainsworth & Siqueland, 1969)	Language, perceptual-motor	Kindergarten–first grade	Denhoff, Hainsworth, & Hainsworth (1971)
Metropolitan Readiness Tests (Hildreth, Griffiths, & McGauran, 1965)	Reading readiness	Kindergarten–first grade	Hoepfner, Stern, & Nummedal (1971)
McCarthy Scales of Children's Abilities (McCarthy, 1972)	Verbal, perceptual-performance, quantitative, general cognitive, memory, and motor	Preschool–first grade	Hoepfner, Stern, & Nummedal (1971)

Table 12-2 (cont.)
Screening Tests

name	type	age or grade range	additional references
Minnesota Preschool Scale (Goodenough, Maurer, & Van Wagenen, 1940)	Vocabulary, comprehension, and numerous other areas	Preschool-first grade	Hoepfner, Stern, & Nummedal (1971)
Preprimary Profile (Schiff, 1966)	Social, language skill development, self-care, and others	Preschool-first grade	Proger (1971a)
Preschool Inventory (Caldwell, 1967)	Numerous areas	Ages 3-6	Hoepfner, Stern, & Nummedal (1971)
Pupil Rating Scale (Myklebust, 1971)	Language, orientation, social, behavior, and motor ability	Grades 3-4 and others	Myklebust & Boshe (1969); Colligan (1977)
Screening Test for the Assignment of Remedial Treatment (Ahr, 1968)	Visual and auditory functions	Ages 4½-6½ yrs	Proger (1972b)
Screening Test for Identifying Children with Specific Language Disabilities (Slingerland, 1962)	Reading, spelling, handwriting, and speaking	Grades 1-4	Hoepfner, Stern, & Nummedal (1970); Proger (1971c); Ansara (1969)
Vineland Social Maturity Scale (Doll, 1963)	Self-sufficiency, occupational, etc.	Ages 3 mths-25 yrs	Hoepfner, Stern, & Nummedal (1971)
Wechsler Preschool and Primary Scale of Intelligence (Wechsler, 1967)	Numerous areas	Ages 4-6½	Hoepfner, Stern, & Nummedal (1971)

developmental patterns of learning disabilities were so identified, school intervention could be introduced confidently and clearly.

It *is* possible to identify a general sequence of skills for reading, computation, handwriting, and so on. These skill sequences, while particularly used for remedial purposes, also have an influence on the content of readiness programs. However, this approach of constructing skill sequence at the readiness level and before to conceptualize critical behaviors needing early attention has some severe limitations. First, the learning of basic school subjects is affected by their interaction and the situation. The learning of reading skills is very likely reinforced by the acquisition of other skills, such as handwriting and spoken language. Furthermore, environmental and situational variables *in* the classroom and outside have a critical impact on the acquisition of competence in written and spoken language and social behavior.

Secondly, an attempt to trace skill development in basic school subjects back to the early foundations falters, particularly at the preschool level. A child comes to school after a number of years experience in learning. Through his environment he has developed in many areas—physical, psychological, linguistic, and social. None of these skills has developed independently of others.

Consequently, the early detection of learning disabilities is very complicated. To focus solely on the physical characteristics or language behaviors of a child seems rather microscopic (Wallace & Larsen, 1978). Professionals from many fields have naturally approached the early identification of learning disabilities from their own scopes of interest and research. Clinical experience with normal and abnormal development alerts them to the significance of certain symptoms and behaviors.

The particular danger in preschool screening and assessment procedures is that teachers may teach to tests. While criterion-referenced assessment techniques are designed for this purpose, most preschool inventories are not so directive. The end result may be the development of useless skills. Such has been the case in the psychomotor domain of tests (Wallace & Larsen, 1978).

Finally, the choice of target behaviors for screening and assessment must be based on ecological and situational perspectives (McLoughlin & Kershman, 1978). Behaviors frequently demonstrated as part of normal development should be focused on. The kinds of tasks that children must perform in preschool, at home, and on the playground should make up the content of these identification devices.

Physical Behaviors

The physical development and general health of young children are of particular interest to medical professionals. The obvious interdependence between physical and psychological development has encouraged a coordinated effort between physicians and developmental psychologists to detect early discrepancies in learning.

Gesell and Amatruda (1947) have supplied norms for physical behaviors at chronological age levels in the Gesell Developmental Schedules. The significance of physical and neurological development is particularly apparent when you consider the outcome of complications during the natal periods of development. Knobloch and Pasamanick (1962) have drawn considerable attention to the significance of birth complications for later learning development. They examined 1,000 normal and abnormal children at age 40 weeks and again at age 3. They found a high correlation between early neurological status and later intellectual potential.

This use of physical and neurological predictors of learning disabilities has been incorporated into a broad prevention system by Denhoff, Hainsworth, and Hainsworth (1971). They have described the use of the Infant Neurological Indices and other instruments for early identification. However, there is still considerable difference of opinion about the significance of physical and neurological symptoms as predictors of later learning problems (Hartlage & Green, 1973; Keogh, 1970).

The factors that Smith and Wilborn (1977) find related to various kinds of learning disabilities are cynanosis; blood incompatibility; difficult delivery; toxemia; prolonged labor; twins; rapid delivery; induced labor; adoption; prematurity; postmaturity; weight; problems during pregnancy; mother's health; type of birth; when the infant crawled, talked, and walked; convulsions; and hand/eye dominance. As we indicated in chapter 3, these kinds of prenatal, perinatal, and developmental patterns may have various kinds of consequences for later learning.

Chronic illness, frequent earaches, allergies, and other health problems are also factors meriting attention (Davis & Silverman, 1965). Even if they do not directly cause a problem in learning, they may affect a young child's hearing, energy level, or attention.

The problems occurring in the early detection of learning disabilities seem similar to those of ascribing significance to physical and neurological correlates of school-age children. Keogh (1970) and Millichap (1977) report that a number of specialists mention the many compounding variables in both the physiological and neurological perspectives.

Perceptual and Perceptual-Motor Behaviors

Many professionals have chosen to concentrate on one or more psychological behaviors in early detection. Generally, their screening devices reflect an appreciation for the integration of physical, neurological, and psychological development.

Getman, Kane, and McKee (1968), Barsch (1965), and Kephart (1971) give particular attention to the integration of visual-motor systems. The activities and behaviors of young children obviously involve the coordinated use of many sensory and perceptual systems. This particular emphasis has also resulted from the apparent problems of school-age LD children in performing tasks requiring visual-motor coordination.

Consequently, a number of perceptual and perceptual-motor tests are used for early detection of learning disabilities. The Bender-Visual-Motor Gestalt Test (Koppitz, 1964), the Marianne Frostig Developmental Test of Visual Perception (Frostig, Lefever, & Whittlesey, 1964), and the Developmental Test of Visual-Motor Integration (Beery & Buktenica, 1967) are three instruments that have been used. Other perceptual and perceptual-motor instruments, with references to their use, are listed in table 12-2. This table also lists a number of other tests that may be used for screening.

The tests just mentioned and all such types of tests have been used with varying degrees of success. Koppitz (1968) used the Bender Visual-Motor Gestalt Test with other measures to predict poor achievement on the Metropolitan Achievement Test at the end of first grade. However, Keogh and Smith (1970) found changes in the predictability of performance on the Bender Visual-Motor Gestalt Test for reading performance in the first through sixth grades. Tauber (1967) found that the Marianne Frostig Developmental Test of Visual Perception was a better predictor of first-grade achievement than the Bender Visual-Motor Gestalt Test.

Attention has also been given to the significance of auditory perception skills. DeHirsch, Jansky, and Langford (1966) found that the Auditory Discrimination Test (Wepman, 1958) was at least a useful predictive device for kindergarten screening. However, Finkenbinder (1973) has suggested certain weaknesses in a similar instrument, the Goldman-Fristoe-Woodcock Test of Auditory Discrimination (Goldman, Fristoe, & Woodcock, 1970).

Most professionals will agree that it is difficult to define and use these behaviors for early screening. Generally, perceptual and perceptual-motor items are included in much broader inventories of behaviors (see table 12-2). This approach is in no small part due to our inability to identify the direct connection between these behaviors and other learning disabilities (Keogh, 1970). We encounter the same problem with perceptual-motor approaches in prevention as we do in later remedial efforts (Wallace & Larsen, 1978).

Cognitive Behaviors

Meier (1976) defines cognitive development as the "uniquely human unfoldment of the ability to think about or reflect upon past, present, or future experiences or thoughts in order to analyze complex and abstract issues, to solve complex problems, and to achieve new syntheses and understandings about oneself and one's milieu" (pp. 91-92).

The work of Piaget (1970) and Bruner (1960) has stimulated interest in the development of cognitive abilities in young children. There is, however, considerable difficulty in accurately assessing the development of thought. According to Mattick and Murphy (1971), many tests do not consider such various forms of cognitive functioning as creativity, problem solving, the process of trial-and-error experimenting, and the subtleties of orientation and cognitive map-making.

Many of the instruments listed in table 12-2 contain items that may be described as "cognitive." The Wechsler Preschool and Primary Scale of Intelligence (Wechsler, 1967) is the most obvious one. Early detection of cognitive factors in learning disabilities is dependent on the practical application of cognitive theories for screening purposes, which Church (1970) indicates is occurring.

Cognitive development has an intrinsic relationship with psychosocial development and language behaviors. Magrab (1976) has described the connection of skill development in cognition and social behavior (see table 12-3).

Wiig and Semel (1976) have outlined the relationship of cognitive and linguistic growth as a matter of *cognitive-semantic processing.* Using Guilford's (1967) cognitive categories, they suggest assessment devices to evaluate cognition and language for the following areas: semantic units (words and concepts), semantic classes (associations between related words and concepts), semantic relations (logical relationships between words and concepts), semantic systems (verbal problems), semantic transformations (redefinitions of words and concepts), and semantic implications (cause-effect relationships).

Language Behaviors

Language ability is inextricably interwoven with all the behaviors mentioned above. Early detection efforts focus particularly on the development and use of language. Every major screening instrument directly, or at least indirectly, taps a child's skills in language. The Illinois Test of Psycholinguistic Abilities (Kirk, McCarthy, & Kirk, 1968) attempts to measure the relationship of language and psychological processing. The Meeting Street School Screening Test (Hainsworth & Siqueland, 1969) and the Minnesota Preschool Scale (Goodenough, Maurer, & Van Wagenen, 1940) also have many language items.

As Wiig and Semel (1976) describe, the LD child may be late in acquiring first words and slow in acquiring knowledge and use of linguistic rules. The child with linguistic learning disabilities may seem slow to respond, confused, impulsive, inattentive, and even obstinate.

We have discussed language disabilities in chapter 5, including key aspects of language development and acquisition. In addition, Wallace and Larsen (1978) suggest the following questions as useful in studying a language disability:

1. When did the child speak his or her first words?
2. Does the child have a history of upper respiratory infections that caused hearing problems?

Table 12-3

Psychosocial Development and Cognitive Determinants

psychosocial development		cognitive skills
Infancy (0-1)	Trust (2, 3)* Attachment (2) Affective expression (1, 2)	1. Movement towards coherent organization of sensory-motor actions 2. Relating actions to specific effects on the environment 3. Simple problem solving
Toddler (1-3)	Autonomy (5,6) Differentiation of emotions (4) Emergence of self-concept (5) Parallel play to interactive play (4)	4. Development of symbolic imagery and genuine representations: words and images distinguished from the thing signified 5. Egocentric thinking 6. Primitive logic based on "centered" thought: attending to only one aspect of the problem at a time, neglecting other important ones; thus distorting the conclusion
Play age (3-6)	Initiating (7, 8, 9) Increased social interaction with adults and children (9) Sex role imitation (9) Personality definition (8, 9) Cooperative play (8) Conscience development (8, 9)	7. Intuitive thought 8. Increased verbal skills to permit verbal mediation and more advanced concept formation 9. More complex representations, thought, and images, including ability to group objects into classes according to perceptions of their similarity
School age (7-11)	Industry (10, 11) Mastery (10, 11) Peer relationships (11) Moral attitudes and values (11) Crystalization of sex role identification (10)	10. Ability to mentally represent a series of actions 11. Development of rules of logical thinking: ability to think in relational terms, ability to reason separately about part of the whole, ability to serialize
Adolescence (12-18)	Social maturation and heterosexual relationships (13, 15) Career choice (13, 14, 15) Emotional control (13) Beliefs and values (12, 13, 15)	12. Ability to deal with abstractions and probabilities 13. Generalized orientation toward problem solving (systematic generation of hypotheses for testing) 14. Deductive reasoning 15. Ability to evaluate the logic and quality of one's own thinking

*Numbers refer to the primary cognitive determinants required for progressing to the designated psychosocial task.

From "Psychosocial Function: Normal Development—Infantile Autism" by P. Magrab. In R. Johnston & P. Magrab (Eds.), *Developmental Disorders*. Baltimore: University Park Press, 1976. Copyright© 1976 by University Park Press. Reprinted by permission.

3. Do siblings also evidence language problems?
4. Has the child's language problem been evaluated previously?
5. When did the parents first notice, if at all, that something was wrong?
6. Were there long periods in the child's life during which no language was used?
7. At what level is the child's social relationship with peers, siblings, and parents? (p. 263)

Social-Emotional Behaviors

Awareness of the significance of emotional and social behaviors is also evident in early identification techniques. However, there has not been the same amount of emphasis placed on these critical behaviors. Experience with preschool education over the past few years has indicated the significance of patterns of interaction between children and the other people in their environment, notably parents (Keogh, 1970). Some of the instruments listed in table 12-2 have items in this area. Wyatt (1971) also incorporates observations of mother-child interactions into screening procedures.

As Dmitriev (1978) points out, disabilities in young children can disrupt the normal development of the parent-child relationship. The quality of the interaction may be affected by parental assumptions about the infant's capabilities (Broussard & Hartman, 1976; Kennedy, 1973). A child's verbal and nonverbal behaviors tend to condition parental interest, proximity, responsiveness, and other factors enhancing social-emotional growth (Gewirtz & Boyd, 1975; Gordon, 1974). If a child's and a parent's behaviors detract from forming a close bond, the basis for psychosocial growth is not established.

Another aspect of development in this area is peer relationship. Bryan (1974b, 1976) has documented the social problems of older LD children. LD children seem to be less popular and rejected more often than normal children by their peers. They use social reinforcement inappropriately and seem to miss subtle interpersonal communication. These social behaviors should receive attention at the preschool level.

Rubin and Balow (1971) studied the success of kindergarten children as they proceeded through school. In spite of adequate readiness for schoolwork, a large percentage of the group was identified as needing special services. It would appear that the school environment puts heavy demands on social-emotional skills, particularly those skills needed to survive in traditional educational settings.

Environmental and Situational Variables

Environmental factors in a child's early and later development are critical. As indicated in chapters 3 and 4, a totally child-focused perspective of learning disabilities is inappropriate.

Economically and otherwise deprived environments signal the possibility that the child's development may be lacking. Over the past few years, prevention programs have been particularly directed at children living in impoverished conditions. The research of Skeels and Dye (1939), Skeels (1966), and Kirk (1958) indicates the possibilities of reversing the development of learning disabilities by improving the environment. *In fact, it seems much easier in some cases to assess the learning environment of a child than to assess the child himself.*

Accumulated research also gives physical (health, safety, etc.), social (family structure, interactional patterns, etc.), and linguistic (communication style, vocabulary, etc.) factors priority status in prevention efforts. As early childhood interventions are established, it is essential to maintain an environmentalist perspective.

McLoughlin and Kershman (1978) underscore the significance of situational analysis in preventive efforts. It seems very microscopic to search for *one* kind of behavior or event or environmental condition. More often than not, we must examine the situation (school, home, playground, etc.) in which the child is frustrated in learning for an explanation of the problem.

Factors that invariably encompass the problem are (1) input (What did we give the child to do?); (2) output (What response did we expect?); (3) sensory information (What kinds of modalities were involved?); (4) kind of learning (How complex was the task?); (5) reinforcement (What encouragement was available?); and (6) distractors (What was going on around the children?). By examining these situational variables, we identify targets for remediation. The need for this association of assessment and remediation cannot be overly stressed.

Identification Techniques

Given the environmentalist perspective, more professionals are examining behaviors directly related to school-age underachievement. Furthermore, screening efforts are relying more on the perceptions of teachers and parents. This approach to early detection is based on an appreciation for the environmental and situational variables that may be precipitating the learning disabilities. Classroom, home, and other *in situ* observations are also very popular.

Batteries of Tests

DeHirsch, Jansky, and Langford (1966) have composed the Predictive Index from a study of many tasks and tests with potential usefulness in kindergarten screening. Some of the variables that ultimately proved predictive were pencil use, the Bender Visual-Motor Gestalt Test, the Auditory Discrimination Test (Wepman, 1958), number of words used in a story, categories, and word matching and recognition tests. Eaves, Kendall, and Crichton (1972) have used the Predictive Index with other tests in their screening project. Perhaps the most interesting aspect of this approach is the resemblance of task items to actual classroom behaviors.

Wyatt (1971) and Smith and Solanto (1971) have drawn upon parental experience with their children in identifying LD children. Wyatt (1971) has used a combination of parent questionnaires, observations of mother-child interactions, and screening tests.

Smith and Solanto (1971) have developed a Preschool Readiness Estimate for Pupils About to Receive Education. The device consists of a parent questionnaire regarding physical development and health information, home-child relationships, play habits, skills, attitudes, and independence; and a formal evaluation of vocabulary skills, number skills, visual-motor skills, intelligence, new learning ability, and psycho-social maturity. A profile was also constructed to indicate below-average, average, and above-average performance. Future kindergarten teachers were subsequently informed of results and taught how to observe and teach the children.

In another study, Ferinden and Jacobsen (1970) asked 10 kindergarten teachers to select potential achievers and underachievers. Sixty-seven kindergarten children were given the Wide Range Achievement Test (Jastak & Jastak, 1965) reading subtest, the Evanston Early Identification Scale (Landsman & Dillard, 1967), the Bender Visual-Motor Gestalt Test, and the Metropolitan Readiness Test. The same battery was administered 4 months into the first grade.

Kindergarten teachers were able to predict potential achievers and underachievers over 80% of the time. The Wide Range and the Evanston Scale were 90% accurate, and the Metropolitan was predictive only for those children who scored below the 30th percentile. The Bender Visual-Motor Gestalt Test was not predictive.

Denhoff, Hainsworth, and Hainsworth (1971) have incorporated a screening device for teachers into an identification system of learning disabilities. The Meeting Street School Screening Test (Hainsworth & Siqueland, 1969) may be used by teachers, psychologists, and lay people. It includes language items and various measures of perception. It is intended for use in kindergarten and first grade.

Rating Scales

Teachers' perceptions and observations are also being used to identify potential learning disabilities. Haring and Ridgway (1967) have found teacher ratings more effective predictors than the results of some test batteries. Ilg and Ames (1964) also obtained a high correlation between kindergarten teacher ratings and sixth-grade achievement. Keogh and Smith (1970) found teachers' ratings consistently significant when correlated with achievement scores in the second through the sixth grades.

Cowgill, Friedland, and Shapiro (1973) examined the anecdotal records composed by kindergarten teachers. Judges used two measures in their analysis of teacher comments on children. They found that anecdotal comments of kindergarten teachers distinguished potential problem learners from normal achievers.

Buchanan, Swap, and Swap (1977) found that preschool teachers were discriminating in identifying hyperactive children. Teachers used more criteria than merely activity level. Compared to a group of merely highly active preschoolers, the hyperactive children demonstrated more resistance to the teacher and engaged in more inappropriate behaviors by themselves and with others. These children also behaved inappropriately without provocation and with and without the teacher's being present.

Glazzard (1977) compared the predictive ability of teacher ratings on the Teacher Estimate of Kindergarten Pupils' Abilities (Kirk, 1966) to performances on a reading readiness test and reading achievement test. The kindergarten teachers rated the following behaviors of the children: reasoning ability, speed of learning, ability to deal with abstract ideas, perceptual discrimination, psychomotor abilities, verbal comprehension, number and space relations, creativity, and verbal expression. The ratings proved highly predictive and efficient.

Other rating scales have also proved useful. The Pupil Rating Scale (Myklebust, 1971) was one of the most reliable screening procedures that resulted from the Myklebust and Boshe screening project in learning disabilities (1969). The rating scale may be used by classroom teachers to identify children with learning disabilities. Colligan (1977) found that this scale correlated highly with criterion measures of kindergarten mastery and academic achievement.

The Basic School Skills Inventory (BSSI) by Goodman and Hammill (1975) is a readiness instrument that blends norm-referenced and criterion-referenced features. Teachers indicate the child's abilities on the basis of observations and/or administration of brief tasks. The seven major areas that first-grade teachers identified as necessary for success in grade 7 were basic information, reading readiness, number readiness, self-help, handwriting, oral communication, and classroom behavior. Hawthorne and Larsen (1977) found that BSSI total score predicted first grade teachers' judgments of children.

Observations

Forness and Esveldt (1975) used direct classroom observation of kindergartners to predict later problems. The child behaviors focused upon were appropriate verbal responses (e.g., recitation), attending (e.g., watching the teacher), not attending (e.g., staring out the window), and disruptions (e.g., hitting classmates). The observations were done at the beginning of kindergarten and later in the year. They compared very favorably to teacher ratings of reading readiness and language development, relationships with other children, and attitude toward classroom rules.

Magliocca, Rinaldi, Crew, and Kunzelmann (1977) designed a screening program for LD children, using classroom observations at the beginning of kindergarten. The children were given a set of tasks each day for a number of days. (See table 12-4 for a description of the tasks.)

Table 12-4
Subtest Selections

subtests	purpose	task	materials	scoring
X's in Circles	Test eye-hand co-ordination when using a pencil	Mark X in each circle	40 ¾-inch circles on grid	Total no. of X's inside circles
XO Pattern	Test ability to produce and imitate a pattern	Continue XO pattern	Paper divided into 88 squares	Total no. of X's and O's in correct pattern
Counting Number Sets	Test ability to count	Count objects on each card	20 cards; Objects 1 to 10	Total no. of correct counts
See-Say Letters	Test ability to name letters	Name letters	Chart with upper and lowercase letters (114)	Total no. of letters named
Matching Colors	Test ability to match colors	Match colored blocks to colored boxes	46 blocks and 6 matching boxes	Total no. of blocks matched
Naming Pictures	Test ability to name picture symbols of objects	Name pictures of objects	77 pictures mounted on a chart	Total no. of pictures named
Hear-Touch (body parts)	Test auditory discrimination and locating body parts	Touch body parts named	Audiotape with 40 cues	Total no. of responses
See-Write Letters	Test ability to reproduce letters	Reproduce letters underneath samples	Paper with upper case letters	Total no. of letters copied
See-Say Numbers	Test ability to name numbers	Name random numbers from 1 to 20	78 numbers on a chart	Total no. of numbers named

Time = 60 seconds.

From "Early Identification of Handicapped Children Through a Frequency Sampling Technique" by L. Magliocca, R. Rinaldi, J. Crew, & H. Kunzelmann, *Exceptional Children*, 1977, 7, 417. Copyright 1977 by The Council for Exceptional Children. Reprinted by permission.

The results of this continuous measurement procedure were compared to kindergarten teacher ratings at the end of the school year. The relationship was very high, indicating excellent predictive ability for the observational procedures. The two most significant factors were see-write letters and see-say numbers.

Ultimately, early childhood educators will identify a suitable combination of identification procedures. Teacher ratings obviously have proven very useful. However, as Forness and Esveldt (1975) have pointed out, the hope is that classroom observations can have as much predictive power. To use teacher ratings at the beginning of an educational effort may encourage the development of binding teacher expectations and consequently a self-fulfilling prophecy.

Guidelines

A useful tool for those attempting to select a screening instrument is the study of Hoepfner, Stern, and Nummedal (1971). An analysis of screening instruments used in early detection was investigated in this study. After identifying a broad array of objectives for preschool education, the authors question the ability of some tests to probe these behaviors accurately, efficiently, and reliably. Some of the screening instruments listed in table 12-2 were examined.

Keogh and Becker (1973) have suggested a number of guidelines for early detection and treatment of learning problems. These suggestions are motivated by the questionable validity of certain identification techniques, the tenuous relationship between diagnostic procedures and recommended remedial programs, and possible negative effects on expectations for the child.

First, screening measures which are close to the criterion or outcome measures in both *content* and *time* should be used. If we want to insure that a child will have successful experience in kindergarten or first grade, we should identify the skills necessary to achieve in that particular setting. We can identify these prerequisites for use in screening devices through the task analysis process. The more removed from the target behaviors in terms of content and time our identification criteria are, the more likely we are to fail to prepare a child adequately.

We must also identify a child's *competencies* as well as his deficits. Typically, a child with learning disabilities demonstrates a profile of strengths and weaknesses. We can capitalize upon his strong skills while training his deficit skills. This intraindividual analysis is imperative.

A third guideline is to consider the *task* components and *situation* variables in screening. Speaking, reading, writing, and so forth, require different skills. Furthermore, as a child progresses from kindergarten through senior high school, increasingly more complex demands are placed upon him.

There is also the danger that our choice of screening data may be too narrow. A standardized test battery approach may *screen out* very important variables. Keogh and Becker (1973) suggest the use of a more process-oriented behavioral approach. "How a child approaches a learning task, his strategies for solutions, his sensitivity to various kinds of reinforcers, and his ability to sustain attention and persist may all be important indicators of his likelihood of success in school" (p. 9).

Finally, the use of standardized tests rather than behavioral analyses may not be sufficiently directive for educational intervention. Certain instruments reflect hypotheses about prereadiness skills for academic achievement. The more narrow and removed components are from the actual skill areas needed in the classroom, the less likely it is that we will teach the child the information he needs to succeed.

Early detection of learning disabilities is only the first step. Programs and curricula are also required for successful child development.

FORMS OF INTERVENTION

Prevention programs for LD children take many different forms; however, all early intervention efforts to guarantee a child's later success in learning have a similar goal: *to prevent later learning problems by providing early habilitative support.* Sometimes the target population might have physical and psychological constitutions that are particularly liable to environmental neglect. These children require sufficient, if not enriched, support during their early years.

Diverse Forms

Prevention programs vary along a number of different dimensions. The screening criteria and identification techniques may indicate the kind of intervention thought most necessary. Perceptual-motor advocates may focus upon visual, auditory, and motor perception in screening and treatment. Linguistic proponents might examine language development deviations and introduce various language enrichment experiences. Others choose to identify deficiencies in the cultural and socioeconomic milieu of the child and to correct the physical, psychological, and emotional support systems in families and communities. Usually we see a combination of these emphases in prevention programs.

There is considerable difference of opinion concerning which kinds of early learning experiences will best prevent later learning problems. Confidence in developmental and readiness interventions is not universally shared. There is an increasing emphasis upon early learning experiences which directly resemble the activities of school years (Keogh & Becker, 1973). Goodman and Hammill (1975) and Sanford (1975) have developed more criterion-referenced procedures upon which to base programming.

The amount and kind of structure vary among intervention formats (Gallagher, 1973). A nondirective preschool experience may be characterized by a loosely structured, bombardment approach. Experiential discovery learning opportunities may be available in another program. Highly directive and reinforcing teachers may emphasize strenuous labeling activities in language and other school-related areas. Dmitriev (1978) has generally found that degree of structure and environmental conditions arranged to attain specific objectives distinguish preschool programs for normal and exceptional children.

Although there are differences across prevention programs in conceptual basis and screening criteria, they have similar curricular areas. Most programs include activities which develop physical, perceptual, cognitive, language, and social behavior. Lillie and Trohanis (1976) have found that early childhood programs for preschool children are home-based, school or center-based, or some combination of them. Parent involvement is highly encouraged.

Target Population

Early intervention programs seem to serve a heterogeneous population. Many programs seem to be directed at children from socioeconomically deprived environments. The other target population, which often overlaps the first group, consists of exceptional children. These youngsters vary along a continuum from the severely physically and mentally deficient to the extremely gifted. Needless to say, there are also preschool programs for children that maintain constitutional and environmental integrity.

Children with learning disabilities are presently being served in many kinds of early intervention programs. Because of the dearth of preschool programs in general, LD children share programs with youngsters lacking environmental support and those suffering from physical and mental deficiencies. By definition we exclude physical, sensory, mental, and environmental deficiencies from the description of learning disabilities. However, we should not be surprised at the heterogeneity of the population in prevention programs.

Unfortunately, there are very few preschool programs to prevent later learning problems in children. Except for economically affluent segments of our society, there are comparatively fewer programs to equip the economically and environmentally deprived or the handicapped child in his early development. Some steps have been taken to remedy this situation (Hayden, 1974; Nazarro, 1974). The programs and projects to be described in the following section represent a combined effort to identify and provide for the successful development of LD children, together with other youngsters who may otherwise falter in their schooling (Gallagher, 1973).

P.L. 94-142's incentives for early childhood programs for LD children and other exceptional children will increase the numbers of opportunities. Given the principle of least restrictive environment, the general model will be a mainstreaming one (Meisels, 1977). This practice is consistent with the hesitancy of early childhood educators and other LD professionals to label young children.

INTERVENTION PROGRAMS

Emphases

Bereiter and Engelmann (1966) have particularly emphasized language development and academic skills in preschool programs. The Direct Instructional System to Teach Arithmetic and Reading (DISTAR) programs in language, reading, and arithmetic represent an effort to prevent later underachievement among disadvantaged preschoolers through structured intervention. Emphasizing a more rote than discovery learning approach, teachers are very directive and consistently reinforcing. Specific, academically oriented goals are set for the children in the program. Bereiter and Engelmann have found this structured approach very useful.

The effects of various forms of early intervention programs were compared by Karnes, Hodgins, and Teska (1969). They generally found highly structured programs more beneficial in developing intellectual functioning, language abilities, perceptual development, and school readiness. Five models were compared, controlling for sex, race, and intelligence. The models included:

1. The traditional nursery school program modeled after a university child development program and focusing on informal instruction of children.
2. A community-integrated program where disadvantaged children were placed in existing preschool programs, with the notion that such a placement would enhance their opportunities to acquire language from adult and peer models.
3. A Montessori approach with little stress on language acquisition.
4. A game-oriented activity for learning, or the GOAL curriculum, based on the ITPA clinical model, stressing the acquisition of special information-processing skills. Using a game format, children were taught in small groups through three structured periods of 20 minutes each. Directive play, art, and music made up the rest of the day. The goal of this program was to prepare the children for successful participation in the standard school curriculum.
5. The Bereiter and Engelmann (1966) program consisted of intensive oral drill and verbal and logic patterns with 20-minute structured periods in which language, arithmetic, and reading were taught.

The two structured programs, the GOAL program and the Bereiter-Engelmann program, yielded the greater gains in IQ over a year's time. Superior performances of children in these programs were noted on various tests, including the ITPA.

Weikart (1972) also compared three curricular models: the traditional nursery school, a Piaget-based curriculum, and the Bereiter-Engelmann approach. All groups gained in intelligence test scores, with no difference between groups. Weikart suggests that the important point is *how well* the program is used and not necessarily the *kind* of curriculum.

Head Start

Head Start programs have been the site of much of the early childhood programming for the LD child. Of the children served in Head Start programs, 10% must be exceptional learners. These programs have undergone considerable study in attempting to identify effective and ineffective interventions (Ensher, Blatt, & Winschel, 1977; Payne & Mercer, 1974).

The Westinghouse Report (Cicirelli, 1969), which evaluated 104 centers, found no significant difference between experimental and control groups in grades 1 through 3 on measures of language development, learning readiness, and academic achievement.

Payne, Mercer, Payne, and Davidson (1973) summarized five points from this study:

1. Summer Head Start programs did not produce early cognitive and affective gains that continued in the first grade and beyond.
2. Full-year programs produced marginal cognitive gains which continued through the first three grades, but no affective gains were made.
3. Programs worked best in black centers, in some urban areas, and in the Southeast region of the nation.
4. Project children were below national norms on the Illinois Test of Psycholinguistic Abilities and the Stanford Achievement tests, although Metropolitan Readiness Test scores approahed national norms.
5. Parents liked the program and took an active part in it. (pp. 93-94)

Certain models have been developed to supply a better conceptual basis and direction for these programs (Payne & Mercer, 1974). Some of the components of these models include: programmed instruction and behavior modification, Piagetian-based curriculum, academically oriented activities, use of parents as teacher aides in the home and classroom, and environments that encourage healthy self-concept and sense of responsibility in children.

Ensher, Blatt, and Winschel (1977) have found that Head Start programs may be overidentifying and overlabeling children as handicapped, particularly the visually, hearing, physically, and other health impaired. Although LD children are included in the traditional "other health impaired" group it would appear that LD children are not being identified at a level commensurate with prevalence figures. Head Start programs seem better able to identify the more obvious exceptionalities. There is also some indication that LD children may be merely integrated with the general preschool population without formal identification.

These early childhood programs particularly struggle to meet the 10% mandate and yet to avoid overlabeling. Recruitment is a problem, particularly because of competition for the children from other community agencies. Although very apparent in the case of the severely handicapped child, Head Start programs and the public schools have not generally developed continuity of programming. The public schools usually admit mildly and moderately handicapped children, but they do not necessarily welcome them. Finally, preschool teachers and staffs do not feel capable of meeting the needs of the exceptional children.

Ensher, Blatt, and Winschel (1977) make a number of recommendations that would enhance early childhood opportunities for LD children in Head Start programs. First, the 10% mandate should be reexamined for its appropriateness for serving *all* exceptional children. Second, segregated settings should be avoided. Third, better cooperation with the public schools and related community agencies must be developed to improve identification and transfer of exceptional children. Fourth, parent involvement and staff training should be priority goals.

Infant Programs

Two programs which have particularly emphasized infant intervention involving parents and the home are the Milwaukee project (Garber & Heber, 1973; Strickland, 1971) and the Ypsilanti-Carnegie infant education project (Lambie & Weikart, 1970).

The Milwaukee project is a longitudinal study of maternal rehabilitation and infant stimulation. Identified in deprived urban communities, mothers receive vocational, child-rearing, and homemaking training. Beginning before 6 months of age, the infant is stimulated on a one-to-one basis; gradually the stimulation is administered in small groups. The stimulation program is directed at language and cognitive development. The children receiving the intervention have tended to score better on physical and developmental measures, intelligence tests, language, and other tests than a control group.

The Ypsilanti-Carnegie project is similar to the Milwaukee program. Beginning in the child's preschool years, a public school teacher works in the home with mothers and children. Besides the usefulness and convenience of the educational intervention, this home-based approach develops a healthy relationship between the family and the school.

Parent Programs

The involvement of parents and others is necessary for successful early intervention programs. Quick, Little, and Campbell (1973) have described a training program for foster parents of exceptional children.

Furthermore, the shortage of personnel has encouraged the training and use of paraprofessionals to assist parents and children. Schortinghuis and Frohman (1974) found paraprofessionals to be as effective as professionals in their program.

Lillie and Trohanis (1976) have described many ways in which parents can participate in early childhood programs. The models used have ranged from home-centered programs in which parents are the primary teachers to center-based programs in which parents play more supportive roles.

P.L. 94-142 and research in special education have inspired greater parent involvement. Early childhood educators working with LD children should support this participation. As we discuss in chapter 14, parents of LD children can assume many roles if given support and training (McLoughlin, Edge, & Strenecky, 1978).

McLoughlin (1978) has identified potential roles for parents of children with learning disabilities. These responsibilities encompass home, school, and community action on behalf of their children. To perform these activities parents will need certain skills. They may possess the skills, but in some cases training may be necessary. (See table 12-5 for a list of skills needed for major roles.)

Personnel Preparation

Hirshoren and Umansky (1977) surveyed the status of teacher certification in preschool special education. Teacher certification to work with preschool handicapped children was offered in 12 states; 5 states were in the process of developing such a program. Many states were not planning any separate training requirements. Ironically, training programs were available in some of the states without this kind of teacher certification.

McLoughlin and Kershman (in press) have identified the following areas for training: (1) identifying handicapping conditions; (2) recognizing individual learning styles and rates; (3) adapting activities and materials; (4) using special assessment devices and methods; (5) involving parents; and (6) communicating with fellow teachers and support personnel. The need for trained preschool personnel will probably be met by a combination of preservice and inservice training programs.

The possible forms and scope of early intervention programs are numerous. Consequently, community agencies and school systems are experimenting with many different ways to identify and treat the needs of children with learning disabilities and other problems (Holliday & Olswang, 1974); Schleichkorn, 1972).

GUIDELINES

According to Karnes (1973a), a number of guidelines must be followed for successful intervention programs. First, the approach should be

roles	Parenting	Homemaking	Assertiveness training	Informed Person	Communication skills	Community awareness	Political awareness	Organizational and administrative skills	Teaching skills	Behavior Management	Special educational procedures	Team person
1. Warm/loving fan	X	X										
2. Family energizer	X	X										
3. Parent	X	X										
4. Social skill developer	X	X			X				X	X	X	
5. Academic skill developer	X	X			X				X		X	
6. Language developer	X	X			X				X		X	
7. Advocate/lobbyist			X	X	X	X	X	X			X	X
8. Organizer			X	X	X		X	X				X
9. Advisor			X								X	X
10. Resource person				X	X	X	X				X	X
11. Classroom volunteer/aide					X				X	X	X	X
12. Assessor					X				X	X	X	X
13. Program planner			X	X	X				X	X	X	X
14. Tutor					X				X	X	X	X
15. Evaluator				X	X						X	X

Table 12-5
Roles and Skills of Parents
From "Roles and Practices of Parents of Children with Learning and Behavior Problems" by J. McLoughlin. In D. Edge, B. Strenecky, & S. Mour (Eds.), *Training Parents of Learning Problem Children: An Educator's Perspective.* Columbus, Ohio: The Ohio State University Press, 1978. Copyright 1978 by The Ohio State University Press. Reprinted by permission.

carefully defined and have a strong theoretical basis. Second, there should be ample provisions for continuous inservice training, curriculum development, daily planning and critiquing of instruction, and a small teacher-student ratio and supervisory support.

The curriculum should attend to many areas of development. The more obvious ones include cognition, language, motivation to learn, self-concept, social skills, motor skills, and information processing.

Finally, family involvement greatly enhances any early intervention effort. Bronfenbrenner (1975) and Gallagher (1973) also present support for this aspect of early intervention programs. Lillie and Trohanis (1976) supply many examples of how it can be done.

Gallagher (1976) stresses the need for techniques in program planning and evaluation to guarantee more quality control. Specifically, he suggests the use of a strategy containing the following steps: (1) define the scope of the problem, (2) identify alternative strategies, (3) establish criteria for strategy choice, (4) identify needed resources, (5) identify technical assistance and consultants, and (6) establish an evaluation system. Many problems in budget, program modification, and so forth, can be avoided.

Finally, it is important to maintain a mainstreaming attitude in preschool programs for LD children. Experience and research support this general approach for early childhood programs. Peterson, Peterson, and Scriven (1977) were concerned that nonhandicapped preschoolers would imitate the inappropriate behaviors of the exceptional children. They found that both groups of children would imitate one another, but also tended to imitate nonhandicapped peers more. Parental apprehensions about normal children's reactions to the handicapped seem unfounded.

Progress in the development of assessment and methods for use in the regular preschool classroom also facilitates the use of the principle of least restrictive environment. The diagnostic and programming ideas that we have discussed indicate a mainstreaming direction. As McLoughlin and Kershman (1978) point out, the use of similar procedures and practices for all children conveys the strong acceptance of individual differences, including those of the LD child.

EARLY CHILDHOOD LEARNING DISABILITIES: IN PERSPECTIVE

The review of etiological factors in learning disabilities (see chapter 3) should encourage us to remove the scarring factors that seem to contribute to learning disabilities. The descriptions of the various forms that learning disabilities can take (see part two) should suggest some educational interventions to prevent the poor development of learning foundations.

However, any serious effort to intervene in the early development of potential learning problems must be broad in form and scope. Children with learning disabilities require attention to their physical, psychological, sociological, and educational needs (Denhoff, Hainsworth, & Hainsworth, 1971; Hayden, 1974).

Such a massive effort requires cooperation among medical personnel, social workers, and educators. The organization of alternative service delivery systems on a preschool basis is as important as the educational provisions suggested in chapter 11 for school-age programming. Depending upon our ability, we must consider children from birth through the first grade in our screening and treatment programs.

Hayden (1974) has noted the legislative support for a system of early intervention. A survey of existing community agencies may suggest the development of a cooperative network among medical services, social-action projects, and early childhood programs.

Denhoff, Hainsworth, and Hainsworth (1971) have suggested one form that such a program could take. Equipped with the necessary measurement devices and treatment programs, personnel from various professions can identify and treat children's early needs. Pediatricians, educators, and parents can effectively prevent many learning problems from occurring, or at least supply the child and his or her teachers with an accurate plan for later education.

There are many problems inherent in prevention programming. As we have noted previously, screening techniques have not always been reliable (Gallagher & Bradley, 1972). Furthermore, there is a danger that highly predictive factors may become the object of instruction. The instruction of such behaviors does not yield the ultimate transfer effect to other learning behaviors (Silberberg, Silberberg, & Iversen, 1972).

We also do a considerable disservice to handicapped children if massive screening programs are not followed by well-conceptualized intervention programs (Frankenburg, 1973). As we explained in chapter 4, there is a critical relationship between screening and diagnostic procedures and subsequent educational planning (McLoughlin & Kershman, in press).

Therefore, recent trends in educational screening and programming seem highly justified (Karnes, 1973a; Keogh & Becker, 1973). An examination of a wide range of early learning behaviors seems necessary. Task analysis of the learning behaviors and situation variables present in school settings should be considered in developing screening instruments and preschool activities. Observation can identify many important variables in a child's learning development (Bryan, 1974a; Magliocca et al., 1977). Furthermore, teachers are excellent sources of information for early intervention. Our ability to train teachers to recognize and treat the early learning needs of children with learning disabilities is particularly critical.

Another problem area is the possible intrusion upon the family life of LD children (Honig, 1972). We must have confidence in detection technology and intervention strategies before we prematurely involve parents and their children. Training of professionals and paraprofessionals should include an appreciation for family integrity. While we have become keenly aware of the importance of familial cooperation (DeLacey et al., 1973), we must proceed cautiously so that early *intervention* does not become *intrusion*.

Certain administrative and funding considerations create problems of labeling children as "learning disabled," "emotionally disturbed," and so forth (Nazzaro, 1974). The directive to include handicapped children in Head Start programs has resulted in considerable confusion about the definitions of handicapping conditions at the preschool level (Ensher et al., 1977). LD professionals have a responsibility to implement the provisions of P.L. 94-142 at the preschool level. Services seem to be more directed toward other exceptionalities, particularly the more obvious disabilities.

We are not encouraging the unnecessary labeling and isolation of LD children at the preschool level. On the contrary, we support a policy of mainstreaming and nonlabeling. However, LD professionals and parents must make sure that LD children are not neglected, mistreated, or mistaught because of lack of understanding of their learning disabilities. P.L. 94-142 guarantees services for *all* handicapped children, including LD children. As Clay (1977) points out, the legacy of well-organized early education programs for LD children will be better understanding of teaching strategies that work with the LD child.

Finally, there is a danger that some children with learning disabilities may be neglected in early intervention programs. Most prevention programs have arisen to correct socioeconomic and environmental deprivation. The definition of "learning disabilities" implies that there are some youngsters who are raised in optimal environments who are learning disabled. These children still falter in school achievement even though they are raised in environments conducive to the development of physical and psychological bases for later learning. Low socioeconomic status and cultural diversity must be considered in identifying children for early intervention programs, but we must also be attentive to children reared with environmental advantages. Supposedly sound familial and community environments may contain subtle, harmful features. Unrealistic demands for early development in language and other skills may place undue pressure on the LD child.

Children with learning disabilities present a profile of delayed and differential development in basic skill areas. They are misunderstood in school because they do not display the more obvious factors in underachievement—sensory and physical handicaps, mental retardation, and environmental and educational deprivation. We would be terribly negligent if we did not attend to the unfolding of this pattern early. Children with learning disabilities are easily accused of being "slow, naughty, and inattentive" at an early age.

It seems necessary to subject the "advantaged" environment of children to as much scrutiny as the "disadvantaged" environment. The pressures of successful, achievement-oriented, and compulsive segments of our society may prove as difficult for some youngsters as a disadvantaged environment for other children. All the trappings of environmental support may disguise the absence of healthy psychological and educational experiences.

Hayden (1978) perceives much promise in emerging directions of early childhood education for the handicapped. There is an increasing awareness of individual differences. Systematic observations of children in early childhood settings will clarify special needs. Parental and multidisciplinary involvement guarantees a more comprehensive program for the child. Lastly, the infant and early intervention components in certain programs will do much to prevent learning disabilities.

Therefore, prevention of learning disabilities must be considered a cooperative and multidimensional effort. Considering the present state of preschool programs for the handicapped and disadvantaged, it is unrealistic to expect or want a categorical program specifically for children with learning disabilities. The essential factor at this time is that legislative mandates and funds intended for handicapped children be realized in prevention programs. Children with learning disabilities will surely benefit.

SUMMARY

We have discussed some major considerations in the prevention of learning disabilities in this chapter. Screening techniques and guidelines for screening were discussed. Various intervention programs were described, and target populations for these programs reviewed. Guidelines for intervention programs were suggested. Finally, some of the problems inherent in prevention programs were indicated.

SUGGESTED ACTIVITIES

1. Choose one of the tests or materials in table 12-1 or 12-2. Critique it for relevancy to regular classroom instruction.

2. Examine one of the preschool screening tests. Identify the items that measure different kinds of critical behavior (for example, language, social behavior). Were some kinds of behaviors unmeasured? Did some overlap.

3. Interview parents of a LD child who is in elementary school. Ask them about the early indications of their child's learning disability.

4. Using the questions suggested by McLoughlin and Kershman (1978) on page 411, analyze the learning problems of a preschool child. Were you able to identify some factors needing modification?

5. Ask first grade teachers for a dozen behaviors necessary for achieving in their classroom. Compare what they say to the content of the tests mentioned in this chapter.

6. Observe young children in a preschool setting. Discuss with the teacher some cues he or she feels are indicative of potential learning problems. What assessment and methods does he or she use?

7. Interview a pediatrician. Discuss the indicators he or she uses for early identification of learning disabilities.
8. Survey early childhood programs in your area. Find out how many of the children served by these programs are exceptional. What kinds of exceptionalities are served? Are special personnel available?

References

Ahr, E. *Screening test for the assignment of remedial treatment.* Skokie, Ill.: Priority Innovations, 1968.

Ansara, A. *Classroom screening for learning disabilities in the primary grades: Utilization of the Slingerland Screening Test.* (ERIC Document Reproduction Service No. ED 029 761)

Ayres, B. *Southern California Perceptual Motor Tests.* Los Angeles: Western Psychological Services, 1969.

Baker, H., & Leland, B. *Detroit Tests of Learning Aptitude.* Indianapolis: Bobbs-Merrill, 1955.

Barsch, R.H. *A movigenic curriculum.* Madison, Wis.: Department of Public Instruction, Bureau for the Handicapped, 1965.

Bayley, N. *Bayley Scales of Infant Development.* New York: Psychological Corp., 1969.

Beery, K.E., & Buktenica, N.A. *Developmental Test of Visual-Motor Integration.* Chicago: Follett, 1967.

Bender, L. *Bender Visual-motor Gestalt Test and its clinical use.* New York: American Orthopsychiatric Association, 1938.

Bereiter, C., & Engelmann, S. *Teaching disadvantaged children in the preschool.* Englewood Cliffs, N.J.: Prentice-Hall, 1966.

Bloom, B.S. *Stability and change in human characteristics.* New York: Wiley, 1964.

Bluma, S., Shearer, M., Frohman, A., & Hilliard, J. *Portage guide to early education* (Rev. ed.). Portage, Wis.: Cooperative Educational Service Agency Number 12, 1976.

Boehm, A. *Boehm Test of Basic Concepts.* New York: Psychological Corp., 1971.

Bower, E.M., & Lambert, N.M. *A Process for In-School Screening of Children with Emotional Handicaps.* Princeton, N.J.: Educational Testing Service, 1962.

Bronfenbrenner, U. Is early intervention effective? In B.L. Friedlander, G. Sterrett, & G. Kirk (Eds.), *Exceptional infant* (Vol. III). New York: Brunner/Mazel, 1975.

Broussard, E.R., & Hartman, M.S. Further considerations regarding maternal perception of the first born. In J. Hellmuth (Ed.), *Exceptional infant: Studies in abnormalities* (Vol. II). New York: Brunner/Mazel, 1976.

Bruner, J.S. *The process of education.* New York: Vintage, 1960.

Bryan, T. An observational analysis of classroom behaviors of children with learning disabilities. *Journal of Learning Disabilities,* 1974, *7,* 26-34. (a)

Bryan, T. Peer popularity of learning disabled children. *Journal of Learning Disabilities,* 1974, *7,* 261-268. (b)

Bryan, T. Peer popularity of learning disabled children: A replication. *Journal of Learning Disabilities,* 1976, *9,* 307-311.

Bryant, N.D. Subject variables: Definition, incidence, characteristics, and correlates. In N.D. Bryant & C. Kass (Eds.) *Final report: LTI in learning disabilities* (Vol. I). Tucson: University of Arizona, 1972.

Buchanan, B., Swap, S., & Swap, W. Teacher identification of hyperactive children in preschool settings. *Exceptional Children,* 1977, *43,* 314-315.

Burns, G., & Watson, B. Factor analysis of the revised ITPA with underachieving children. *Journal of Learning Disabilities,* 1973, *6,* 371-376.

Bzoch, K., & League, R. *Receptive-Expressive Emergent Language Scale.* Gainesville, Fla.: Tree-of-Life, 1971.

Caldwell, B.M. *Preschool inventory* (Rev. ed.). Princeton, N.J.: Educational Testing Service, 1967.

Cheves, R. *Ruth Cheves Program I: Visual-Motor Perception.* Boston: Teaching Resources, 1969.

Church, J. Techniques for the differential study of cognition in early children. In J. Hellmuth (Ed.), *Cognitive studies* (Vol. I). New York: Brunner/Mazel, 1970.

Cicirelli, V.G. *The impact of Head Start: An evaluation of the effects of Head Start on children's cognitive and affective development* (Vol. I). Springfield, Va.: Clearinghouse, 1969.

Clay, M.M. An emphasis on prevention. *Journal of Special Education,* 1977, *11,* 183-188.

Colligan, R. Concurrent validity of the Myklebust Pupil Rating Scale in a kindergarten population. *Journal of Learning Disabilities,* 1977, *10,* 317-320.

Cowgill, M., Friedland, S., & Shapiro, R. Predicting learning disabilities from kindergarten reports. *Journal of Learning Disabilities,* 1973, *6,* 577-582.

Davis, H., & Silverman, S.R. (Eds.). *Hearing and deafness.* N.Y.: Holt, Rinehart & Winston, 1965.

DeHirsch, K., Jansky, J.J., & Langford, W.S. *Predicting reading failure.* New York: Harper & Row, 1966.

DeLacey, P.R., Nurcombe, B., Taylor, L.J., & Moffitt, P. Effects of enrichment preschooling: An Australian follow-up study. *Exceptional Children,* 1973, *40,* 171-177.

Denhoff, E., Hainsworth, P., & Hainsworth, M. Learning disabilities and early childhood education: An information-processing approach. In H. Myklebust (Ed.), *Progress in learning disabilities* (Vol. II). New York: Grune & Stratton, 1971.

Dinkmeyer, D. *Developing Understanding of Self and Others (DUSO).* Circle Pines, Minn.: American Guidance Service, 1972.

Dmitriev, V. Normal and delayed development in young children. In N. Haring (Ed.), *Behavior of exceptional children* (2nd ed.). Columbus, Ohio: Charles E. Merrill, 1978.

Doll, E.A. *Oseretsky Tests of Motor Proficiency.* Circle Pines, Minn.: American Guidance Service, 1946.

Doll, E.A. *Vineland Social Maturity Scale.* Vineland, N.J.: The Training School, 1953.

Dubnoff, B., & Chambers, I. *Dubnoff School Program I: Perceptual-Motor Exercises, Level III.* Boston, Mass.: Teaching Resources, 1968.

Dunn, L., Horton, R., & Smith, J. (Eds.). *Peabody Language Development Kit: Level P.* Circle Pines, Minn.: American Guidance Service, 1968.

Dunn, L., & Smith, J. (Eds.). *Peabody Language Development Kit: Level I.* Circle Pines, Minn.: American Guidance Service, 1965.

Eaves, L., Kendall, D.C., & Crichton, M.B. The early detection of minimal brain dysfunction. *Journal of Learning Disabilities,* 1972, *5,* 454-462.

Engel, R. *Language motivating experiences for young children.* Sherman Oaks, Calif.: Rose Engel, 1972.

Engelmann, S. *Basic Concept Inventory.* Chicago: Follett, 1967.

Engelmann, S., Osborn, J., & Engelmann, F. *DISTAR Language 1.* Chicago: Science Research Associates, 1969.

Ensher, G.L., Blatt, B., & Winschel, J.F. Head Start for the handicapped: An audit of the Congressional mandate. *Exceptional Chidren,* 1977, *43,* 202-213.

Ferinden, W.E., & Jacobsen, S. Early identification of learning disabilities. *Journal of Learning Disabilities,* 1970, *3,* 589-593.

Finkenbinder, R. A descriptive study of the Goldman-Fristoe-Woodcock Test of Auditory Discrimination and selected reading variables with primary school children. *Journal of Special Education,* 1973, *7,* 125-132.

Forness, S.R., & Esveldt, K.C. Prediction of high-risk kindergarten children through classroom observation. *Journal of Special Education,* 1975, *9,* 375-388.

Frankenburg, W. Increasing the lead time for the preschool age handicapped child. In M. Karnes (Ed.), *Not all little wagons are red.* Arlington, Va.: Council for Exceptional Children, 1973.

Frankenburg, W., & Dodds, J. *Denver Developmental Screening Test.* Denver: University of Colorado Medical Center, 1970.

Freud, S. *A general introduction to psychoanalysis.* New York: Washington Square Press, 1960.

Frostig, M., & Horne, D. An approach to the treatment of children with learning disorders. In J. Hellmuth (Ed.), *Learning disorders* (Vol. I). Seattle: Special Child Publications, 1965.

Frostig, M., Horne, D., & Maslow, P. *Frostig Remediation Program.* Chicago: Follett, 1973.

Frostig, M., Lefever, W., & Whittlesey, J.R. *Marianne Frostig Developmental Test of Visual Perception.* Palo Alto, Calif.: Consulting Psychologists Press, 1964.

Frostig, M., & Maslow, P. *Move-grow-learn.* Chicago: Follett, 1969.

Gallagher, J. Preventive intervention. *The Pediatric Clinics of North America,* 1973, *20,* 681-693.

Gallagher, J. Planning for early childhood programs for exceptional children. *Journal of Special Education,* 1976, *10,* 171-178.

Gallagher, J.J., & Bradley, R. Early identification of developmental difficulties. In I. Gordon (Ed.), *Early Childhood Education.* Yearbook, National Society for the Study of Education, 1972, *7,* Part II.

Garber, H., & Heber, R. *The Milwaukee project: Early intervention as a technique to prevent mental retardation.* Storrs, Conn.: University of Connecticut Technical Paper, 1973.

Gesell, A. *The embryology of behavior: The beginning of the human mind.* New York: Harper & Row, 1945.

Gesell, A., & Amatruda, C.S. *Gesell Developmental Schedules.* New York: Hoeber-Harper, 1947.

Getman, G.N., Kane, E.R., & McKee, G.W. *Developing learning readiness programs.* Manchester, Mo.: McGraw-Hill, 1968.

Gewirtz, J.L., & Boyd, E.F. *The infant conditions his mother: Experiments on directions of influence in mother-infant interaction.* (ERIC Document Reproduction Service No. ED 114 299)

Glazzard, M. The effectiveness of three kindergarten predictors for first-grade achievement. *Journal of Learning Disabilities,* 1977, *10,* 95-99.

Goldman, R., & Fristoe, M. *Goldman-Fristoe Test of Articulation.* Circle Pines, Minn.: American Guidance Service, 1969.

Goldman, R., Fristoe, M., & Woodcock, R. *Goldman-Fristoe-Woodcock Test of Auditory Discrimination.* Circle Pines, Minn.: American Guidance Service, 1970.

Goodenough, F., Maurer, K., & Van Wagenen, M.J. *Minnesota Preschool Scale.* Minneapolis: Educational Test Bureau, 1940.

Goodman, L., & Hammill, D. *Basic School Skills Inventory.* Chicago: Follett, 1975.

Gordon, I.J. An investigation into the social roots of competence. Final Report to National Institute of Mental Health, Department of Health, Education, and Welfare, October 1974. (ERIC Document Reproduction Service No. ED 113 428)

Guilford, J.P. *The nature of intelligence.* New York: McGraw-Hill, 1967.

Hainsworth, P.K., & Siqueland, J.L. *Early identification of children with learning disabilities: The Meeting Street School Screening Test.* Providence, R.I.: Crippled Children and Adults of Rhode Island, 1969.

Hammill, D.D., & Larsen, S. The effectiveness of psycholinguistic training. *Exceptional Children,* 1974, *41,* 5-15.

Hammill, D.D., & Larsen, S.C. The effectiveness of psycholinguistic training: A reaffirmation of position. *Exceptional Children,* 1978, *44,* 402-418.

Hammill, D.D., & Wiederholt, J.L. Review of the Frostig visual perception test and the related training program. In L. Mann & D. Sabatino (Eds.), *The first review of special education* (Vol. I). Philadelphia: JSE Press, Grune & Stratton, 1972.

Haring, N.G., & Ridgway, R.W. Early identification of children with learning disabilities. *Exceptional Children,* 1967, *33,* 387-395.

Hart, V. *Beginning with the handicapped.* Springfield, Ill.: Charles C Thomas, 1974.

Hartlage, L., & Green, J. The EEG as a predictor of intellective and academic performance. *Journal of Learning Disabilities,* 1973, *6,* 239-242.

Hawthorne, L., & Larsen, S. The predictive validity and reliability of the Basic School Skills Inventory. *Journal of Learning Disabilities,* 1977, *10,* 44-50.

Hayden, A. Perspectives of early childhood education in special education. In N. Haring (Ed.), *Behavior of exceptional children: An introduction to special education.* Columbus, Ohio: Charles E. Merrill, 1974.

Hayden, A. Special education for young children. In N. Haring (Ed.), *Behavior of exceptional children* (2nd ed.). Columbus, Ohio: Charles E. Merrill, 1978.

Hildreth, G., Griffiths, N., & McGauvran, M. *Metropolitan Readiness Tests.* New York: Harcourt Brace Jovanovich, 1965.

Hirshoren, A., & Umansky, W. Certification of teachers of preschool handicapped children. *Exceptional Children,* 1977, *44,* 191-196.

Hoepfner, R., Stern, C., & Nummedal, S. *CSE elementary school test evaluations.* Palo Alto, Calif.: Consulting Psychologists Press, 1970.

Hoepfner, R., Stern, C., & Nummedal, S. *CSE-ECRC preschool/kindergarten test evaluations.* Palo Alto, Calif.: Consulting Psychologists Press, 1971.

Holliday, F., & Olswang, L. *School-community program in early childhood development.* Evanston, III.: Miller School, PECD, 1974.

Honig, A. *Infant development research: Problems in intervention* (EDRS Acquisition No. ED062008, PS005593).

Hunt, J. McV. *Intelligence and experience.* New York: Ronald Press, 1961.

Ilg, F.L., & Ames, L.B. *School readiness: Behavior tests used at the Gesell Institute.* New York: Harper & Row, 1964.

Jastak, J.F., & Jastak, S.R. *Wide Range Achievement Test* (Rev. ed.). Wilmington, Del.: Guidance Associates, 1965.

Karnes, M. *Helping young children develop language skills.* Reston, Va.: Council for Exceptional Children, 1968.

Karnes, M. *GOAL: Language Development.* East Long Meadow, Mass.: Milton Bradley, 1972.

Karnes, M. Evaluation and implications of research with young handicapped and low-income children. In J.C. Stanley (Ed.), *Compensatory education, ages 2-8: Recent studies of educational intervention.* Baltimore: Johns Hopkins University Press, 1973.(a)

Karnes, M. *GOAL: Mathematical Concepts.* East Long Meadow, Mass.: Milton Bradley, 1973. (b)

Karnes, M., Hodgins, A., & Teska, J. The effects of preschool interventions: Evaluations over two years. In M.B. Karnes et al., *Investigations of classroom and at-home interventions: Research and development program on preschool disadvantaged* (Final Report, Vol. 1). Washington, D.C.: Office of Education, Bureau of Research, 1969.

Kaufman, A.S., & Kaufman, N.L. Research on the McCarthy Scales and its implications for assessment. *Journal of Learning Disabilities,* 1977, *10,* 284-291.

Kelly, G. Group perceptual screening at first grade level. *Journal of Learning Disabilities,* 1970, *3,* 640-644.

Kennedy, J.C. The high risk maternal-infant acquaintance process. *Nursing Clinics of North America,* 1973, *8,* 849-856.

Keogh, B. (Ed.). Early identification of children with potential learning problems. *Journal of Special Education,* 1970, *4,* 307-366.

Keogh, B., & Becker, L. Early detection of learning problems: Questions, cautions, and guidelines. *Exceptional Children,* 1973, *40,* 5-12.

Keogh, B.K., & Smith, C.E. Early identification of educationally high potential and high risk children. *Journal of School Psychology,* 1970, *8,* 285-290.

Kephart, N. *The slow learner in the classroom* (2nd ed.). Columbus, Ohio: Charles E. Merrill, 1971.

Kirk, S.A. *Early education of the mentally retarded: An experimental study.* Urbana: University of Illinois Press, 1958.

Kirk, S.A., & Kirk, W.D. *Psycholinguistic learning disabilities: Diagnosis and remediation.* Chicago: University of Illinois Press, 1971.

Kirk, S.A., McCarthy, J.J., & Kirk, W.D. *Illinois Test of Psycholinguistic Abilities* (Rev. ed.). Urbana: University of Illinois Press, 1968.

Kirk, W.D. A tentative screening procedure for selection of bright and slow children in kindergarten. *Exceptional Children,* 1966, *32,* 235-241.

Knoblock, H., & Pasamanick, B. The developmental behavioral approach to the neurologic examination in infancy. *Child Development,* 1962, *33,* 181-198.

Koppitz, E.M. *The Bender-Gestalt test for young children.* New York: Grune & Stratton, 1964.

Koppitz, E.M. *Psychological evaluation of children's human figure drawings.* New York: Grune & Stratton, 1968.

Lambie, D.Z., & Weikart, D.P. Ypsilanti-Carnegie infant education project. In J. Hellmuth (Ed.), *Disadvantaged child* (Vol. 3). New York: Brunner/Mazel, 1970.

Landsman, A.L., & Dillard, H. *Evanston Early Identification Scale.* Chicago: Follett, 1967.

Leiter, R.G. *Leiter International Performance Scale.* Los Angeles: Western Psychological Services, 1948.

Lillie, D., & Trohanis, P. *Teaching parents to teach.* New York: Walker, 1976.

Lowell, E.L., & Stoner, M. *Play it By Ear: Auditory Training Games.* Los Angeles, Calif.: John Tracy Clinic, 1963.

Magliocca, L., Rinaldi, R., Crew, J., & Kunzelmann, H. Early identification of handicapped children through a frequency sampling technique. *Exceptional Children,* 1977, *7,* 414-423.

Magrab, P. Psychosocial function: Normal development—Infantile autism. In R. Johnson & P. Magrab (Eds.), *Developmental disorders.* Baltimore: University Park Press, 1976.

Mattick, I., & Murphy, L.B. Cognitive disturbances in young children. In J. Hellmuth (Ed.), *Cognitive studies: Deficits in cognition* (Vol. II). New York: Brunner/Mazel, 1971.

McCarthy, D. *McCarthy Scales of Children's Abilities.* New York: Psychological Corp., 1972.

McGahan, F., & McGahan, C. *Early Detection Inventory.* Chicago: Follett, 1967.

McLoughlin, J.A. Roles and practices of parents of children with learning and behavior problems. In D. Edge, B. Strenecky, & S. Mour (Eds.), *Training parents of learning problem children: An educator's perspective.* Columbus, Ohio: Ohio State University Press, 1978.

McLoughlin, J.A., Edge, D., & Strenecky, B. Perspective on parent involvement in the diagnosis and treatment of learning disabled children. *Journal of Learning Disabilities,* 1978, *11,* 291-296.

McLoughlin, J.A., & Kershman, S. Including the handicapped. *Behavioral Disorders,* 1978, *4,* 31-35.

McLoughlin, J.A., & Kershman, S. Mainstreaming in the preschool: Strategies and resources for including the handicapped. *Young Children,* in press.

Mecham, M.J. *Verbal Language Development Scale.* Circle Pines, Minn.: American Guidance Service, 1958.

Meier, J.H. Cognitive function: Normal development—mental retardation. In R. Johnston & P. Magrab (Eds.), *Developmental disorders.* Baltimore: University Park Press, 1976.

Meisels, S.J. First steps in mainstreaming. *Young Children,* 1977, *33,* 4-13.

Millichap, J.G. (Ed.). *Learning disabilities and related disorders.* Chicago: Year Book Medical Publishers, 1977.

Minskoff, E., Wiseman, D., & Minskoff, G. *The MWM Program for Developing Language Abilities.* Ridgefield, N.J.: Educational Performance Associates, 1973.

Myklebust, H. *Pupil rating scale: Screening for learning disabilities.* New York: Grune & Stratton, 1971.

Myklebust, H., & Boshe, B. *Final report: Minimal brain damage in children* (U.S. Public Health Service Contract 108-65-142). Evanston, Ill.: Northwestern University Publications, 1969.

National Society for the Prevention of Blindness. *Home Eye Test for Preschoolers.* New York: National Society for the Prevention of Blindness, 1975.

Nazzaro, J. Head Start for the handicapped—What's been accomplished? *Exceptional Children,* 1974, *21,* 103-108.

Newcomer, P., & Hammill, D. *Test of Language Development.* Austin, Tex.: Empiric Press, 1977.

Nihira, K., Foster, R., Shellhaas, M., & Leland, H. *AAMD Adaptive Behavior Scales.* Washington, D.C.: American Association on Mental Deficiency, 1969.

Norfleet, M. The Bender-Gestalt as a group screening instrument for first grade reading potential. *Journal of Learning Disabilities,* 1973, *6,* 48-53.

Pate, J.E., & Webb, W.W. *First grade screening test manual.* Circle Pines, Minn.: American Guidance Service, 1969.

Payne, J.S., & Mercer, C.D. Head Start. In S.E. Goodman (Ed.), *Handbook on contemporary education.* Princeton, N.J.: Bowker, 1974.

Payne, J.S., Mercer, C.D., Payne, R.A., & Davidson, R.G. *Head Start: A tragicomedy with epilogue.* New York: Behavioral Publications, 1973.

Peterson, C., Peterson, J., & Scriven, G. Peer imitation by nonhandicapped and handicapped preschoolers. *Exceptional Children,* 1977, *43,* 223-224.

Piaget, J. *Science of education and the psychology of the child.* New York: Viking, 1970.

Proger, B. Test review no. 2: The Boehm test of basic concepts. *Journal of Special Education,* 1970, *4,* 249-252. (a)

Proger, B. Test review no. 3: Goldman-Fristoe-Woodcock Test of Auditory Discrimination. *Journal of Special Education,* 1970, *4,* 367-374. (b)

Proger, B. Test review no. 5: Three informal preschool evaluation scales: Preprimary profile. *Journal of Special Education,* 1971, *5,* 85-92. (a)

Proger, B. Test review no. 6: Screening test for the assignment of remedial treatment. *Journal of Special Education,* 1971, *5,* 191-198. (b)

Proger, B. Test review no. 7: Screening tests for identifying children with specific language disability. *Journal of Special Education,* 1971, *5,* 293-299. (c)

Quick, A., Little, T., & Campbell, A. Early childhood education for exceptional foster children and training of foster parents. *Exceptional Children,* 1973, *40,* 205-207.

Quick, A., Little, T., & Campbell, A. *Project Memphis: Enhancing developmental progress in preschool exceptional children.* Belmont, Calif.: Lear Siegler, Fearon Publishers, 1974.

Rubin, R., & Balow, B. Learning and behavioral disorders: A longitudinal study. *Exceptional Children,* 1971, *38,* 293-298.

Salvia, J., Schultz, E., & Chapin, N.S. Reliability of Bower scale for screening of children with emotional handicaps. *Exceptional Children,* 1974, *41,* 117-118.

Salvia, J., & Ysseldyke, J. *Assessment in special and remedial education.* Boston: Houghton Mifflin, 1978.

Sanford, A. *Learning Accomplishment Profile.* Winston-Salem, N.C.: Kaplan School Supply, 1975.

Schaeffer, F. *Project "me."* Glendale, Calif.: Bowmar, 1972.

Schiff, H. *Preprimary profile.* Chicago: Science Research Associates, 1966.

Schirmer, G. *Performance objectives for preschool children.* Sioux Falls, S.D.: Adapt Press, 1974.

Schirmer, G. (Ed.), *Curriculum cards for preschool children.* Sioux Falls, S.D.: Adapt Press, 1976.

Schleichkorn, J. The teacher and recognition of problems in children. *Journal of Learning Disabilities,* 1972, *5,* 501-502.

Schortinghuis, N., & Frohman, A. A comparison of paraprofessional and professional success with preschool children. *Journal of Learning Disabilities,* 1974, *7,* 245-247.

Semel, E. *Sound, Order, Sense.* Boston, Mass.: Teaching Resources, 1968.

Silberberg, N., Silberberg, M., & Iversen, I. The effects of kindergarten instruction in alphabet and numbers on first grade reading. *Journal of Learning Disabilities,* 1972, *5,* 254-261.

Skeels, H.M. Adult status of children with contrasting early life experiences. *Monographs of the Society for Research in Child Development,* 1966, *3,* 31.

Skeels, H.M., & Dye, H.B. A study of the effects of differential stimulation on mentally retarded children. *Convention Proceedings American Association of Mental Deficiency,* 1939, *44,* 114-136.

Slingerland, B. *Screening tests for identifying children with specific language disabilities.* Cambridge, Mass.: Educators Publishing Services, 1962.

Smith, D., & Wilborn, B. Specific predictors of learning difficulties. *Academic Therapy,* 1977, *12,* 471-477.

Smith, S., & Solanto, J. An approach to preschool evaluation. *Psychology in the Schools,* 1971, *8,* 142.

Sprigle, H. *Inquisitive games: Discovering how to learn.* Chicago: Science Research Associates, 1969.

Strickland, S.P. Can slum children learn? *American Education,* 1971, *7,* 3-7.

Tauber, R. Identification of potential learning disabilities. *Academic Therapy,* 1967, *2,* 66-67.

Thorum, A.R., Stearns, E.C., Harms, K.L., Van Vliet, D., & Martinez, G. *Instructional materials for the handicapped: Birth through early childhood.* Salt Lake City, Utah: Olympus Publishing, 1976.

Thurstone, T., & Lillie, D. *Beginning to learn: Fine motor skills.* Chicago: Science Research Associates, 1970.

Utley, J. *What's Its Name: A Guide to Speech and Hearing Development.* Urbana: University of Illinois Press, 1968.

Valett, R.E. *A psychoeducational inventory of basic learning abilities.* Palo Alto, Calif.: Fearon, 1968.

Wallace, G., & Larsen, S. *Educational assessment of learning problems: Testing for teaching.* Boston: Allyn & Bacon, 1978.

Wechsler, D. *Wechsler Preschool and Primary Scale of Intelligence.* New York: Psychological Corp., 1967.

Weikart, D.P. Relationship of curriculum, teaching, and learning in preschool education. In J.C. Stanley (Ed.), *Preschool programs for the disadvantaged: Five experimental approaches to early childhood education.* Baltimore: Johns Hopkins University Press, 1972.

Wepman, J. *Auditory Discrimination Test.* Chicago: Language Research Associates, 1958.

Wiig, E.H., & Semel, E.M. *Language disabilities in children and adolescents.* Columbus, Ohio: Charles E. Merrill, 1976.

Wyatt, G. *Early identification and remediation of developmental deficits.* Wellesley, Mass.: Wellesley Public Schools, 1971.

Zigmond, N., & Cicci, R. *Auditory learning.* San Rafael, Calif.: Dimensions Publishing, 1968.

Adolescents and Adults with Learning Disabilities

PREVIEW

LD children grow up, frequently still struggling with their learning problems. Some of these children received services in the elementary schools; others did not. Whatever the case, adolescents with learning disabilities are beginning to be served in the secondary schools. As we shall see, the kinds of available programs vary in format and focus. We concur with the judicious and calculated fashion in which the characteristics, assessment, and methodological features of secondary LD programs are being formulated by specialists in the field. There are indications that a broad array of services for secondary LD students are being developed, including career-vocational services and counseling. We will also consider adulthood and learning disabilities.

Programs for adolescents with LD are a new emphasis in the public schools. Scranton and Downs (1975) surveyed state directors of special education concerning the availability of elementary and secondary programs for LD children. Of the 37 states that reported on a per district basis, 40% of the districts reported elementary programs; only 9% of the districts had secondary LD programs. This gap has gained the attention of many parents and professionals interested in learning disabilities.

Secondary programming for LD adolescents has been a cautious endeavor. The effort has been shaped by the difficulties of implementing LD programs at the elementary school level. Problems with definition, assessment, and methodologies with younger children prevent generalizations to older students. The questionable usefulness of labeling has caused many professionals to hesitate in launching massive secondary LD programs. Awareness of the complexities of the secondary school structure and of the psychology of adolescents has also affected the directions taken in secondary LD programming.

PAST AND PRESENT STATUS

The past history and status of secondary LD programs are sparse and discouraging. Occasional criticisms and demands for such interventions appeared in the literature (Kline, 1972). The few classes that were started were staffed frequently by LD teachers with preparation and orientation toward younger children. The models used were essentially an adaptation of the structure of services for the retarded. In fact, the relationship among services for the retarded, vocational education, and career education seemed confused.

Bill is 15 years old and a fortunate LD adolescent. Unlike many of his peers with learning disabilities around the country, he is receiving individual assistance in his junior high school from an LD specialist. Bill has struggled with severe reading and spelling disabilities throughout his years in school. His performance level in these skills areas is significantly below his present grade level.

What is a surprise to many people is how someone as clever and amiable as Bill can struggle so through a reading passage. Teachers, relatives, and friends are also horrified by the misspellings in Bill's papers and letters. Bill tries to ignore what he knows they say about him.

Bill is not the product of neglect. He was identified as having a learning disability in grade 2 and received assistance from an LD teacher throughout elementary school. Individualized instruction from the LD teacher and helpful classroom teachers enabled Bill to develop some basic word attack and comprehension skills in reading and spelling.

When Bill reached junior high school, an LD program had recently been developed. His skills were assessed, and an individually designed academic program was developed for him. Bill's affability and oral language skills help him cope with tasks that demand a great deal of reading and spelling. Although he cannot read his history and science books well aloud, he is able to figure out the material well enough to answer test questions. Trying to follow the lectures and discussions also helps. His teachers are generally lenient with his written spelling on content area tasks.

Periodically the LD teacher, Bill's parents, and his other teachers meet to discuss the program plan and Bill's progress. Bill has been included in these meetings, in order to have him share his own thoughts and feelings. This opportunity to participate in the decision-making process about his school program has been reinforcing to Bill.

A central figure in Bill's LD program is the career counselor. Bill and his parents are concerned about the future and recognize the realities of making a living. The school program includes many experiences designed to clarify career goals and to develop

preliminary vocational skills.

A comprehensive LD program also accounts for Bill's social and emotional growth. Mainstreamed with his peers for appropriate activities, Bill has the opportunity to develop the communication and interpersonal skills necessary for life. His LD teacher, other teachers, counselors,

and parents must assist Bill is social skill development as well as in language, academic, and vocational skill development.

In spite of the present state of affairs, Bill, his teachers, and parents have some real concerns. The LD program is not available in the senior high school, and the individualized support will be gone.

Secondary LD programs have quickly become a major priority. The Association for Children with Learning Disabilities has given particular support to the effort through conference programming and project funding. ACLD has supported special projects on the relationship of LD and juvenile delinquency and other topics. A large percentage of the Title VI-G model demonstration centers in learning disabilities include secondary-age students in their projects (Goodman, 1978). P.L. 94-142 and regulations in the individual states guarantee that these services will be developed. However, as Zigmond (1978) points out, we must analyze the proposed procedures lest our interventions merely serve to correct the mistakes of the elementary LD programs or to substitute for more effective individualized secondary-level programs for all children.

There are several reasons for the slow initiation of programs for secondary LD students (Goodman & Mann, 1976). Total orientation toward the primary and elementary years is reflected in the kinds of tests, materials, and literature produced since the mid 1960s. Second, many professionals set out to cure the learning disability early. Third, the focus of most LD procedures is on basic skills; that is, reading, arithmetic, language, and so forth. Finally, the LD adolescents seem to have the ability to mask or cope with their learning problems, at least enough to manage in the secondary school.

These explanations of the poorly developed state of LD programs at this level also serve to indicate the genesis for many of the procedures presently being used. Thus there are skill-oriented programs, basically reviewing the fundamental skill areas. Other emphases are on compensatory programs that teach coping and survival skills, since the LD adolescent did not seem to respond to remediation.

Proposed Models

Wiederholt (1978) suggests that secondary schools should anticipate the need for a broad range of services. Thus the needs of LD adolescents may require (1) noneducational services (medical welfare), (2) residential schools, (3) full-time special classes, (4) resource programs, and (5) consultation to teachers of handicapped students in regular education programs. By and large, the more popular models are the resource room programs and the LD teacher-consultant.

Goodman (1978) concluded from her review of existing secondary LD programs that a modification of the regular secondary program is preferred to a resource room or self-contained classroom, the latter being least implemented. The guiding principle seems to be the minimal disruption and alteration of the student's regular school placement and schedule. However, severely disabled students may benefit from a self-contained or a semicontained model (Wiederholt, 1978).

Kinds of Programs

Goodman (1978), Goodman and Mann (1976), Zigmond (1978) and others have described specific secondary LD projects. Deshler, Lowrey, and Alley (1979) have analyzed these programs and others and have characterized them by certain categories (see table 13-1). According to teachers' responses, very few programs followed one model entirely; however, there seemed to be some bias toward one approach more than others.

An *academic elementary* model was the most popular. Like the elementary LD programs, this model stresses basic academic and language skill areas. Reading decoding, reading comprehension, arithmetic computation, and problem solving are the primary target behaviors being taught. The major responsibility for the school curriculum rests with the regular class teachers. The LD teacher performs assessment and basic skill instruction. The categorical resource room is frequently the delivery system. Many professionals are concerned that it is shortsighted to emphasize basic skills to the exclusion of other areas of development. In fact, it would be misleading to assume that this approach is preferable because most of the surveyed programs use it.

The *tutorial* model mainly involves adaptation of the regular curriculum for students. The LD teacher supplies instruction in deficient content areas (i.e., history, language arts, and mathematics). The regular classroom curriculum is valued and serves as the focal point of the model. However, such an approach is short term, represents a shift in responsibility from the regular classroom teacher to the LD teacher, and may create confusion concerning grades and schedules.

In a *functional* model, a new curriculum is composed because the regular curriculum is considered inappropriate. The LD teacher as-

Table 13-1
Results of a Nationwide Survey of Secondary LD Programs

model	percentage of programs reporting
Academic Elementary	49%
Tutorial	24%
Functional	11%
Work-Study Model	5%
Statue of Liberty	5%
Learning Strategies	4%
Elementary Process	2%
Total	100%

Based on a study reported in "Programming Alternatives for LD Adolescents: A Nationwide Survey," by D. Deshler, N. Lowrey, and G. Alley, *Academic Therapy*, 1979, *14*, 8–12.

sumes primary instructional responsibility, generally in a self-contained classroom. The emphasis is upon the development of survival skills in consumerism, employment, health, and so forth. Language arts and mathematics skills also receive attention.

The major problem with this approach is that the demands of society change; preparation in certain skills (e.g., writing checks) may be useless in 10 years. Total application of this kind of program may also ignore the strengths of some LD adolescents. There is also a tendency for this approach to use the self-contained classroom model exclusively.

The *work-study* approach is another popular format, though a less frequently used one. Under this system an LD student attends classes part of the day and works part of the day. Career-vocational material is emphasized, in addition to job-supportive academics. This approach seems to be used primarily in senior high schools.

Difficulties arise when the special educator, and not the more qualified vocational educator, makes the job placement. As a result, the work opportunities are frequently menial. Furthermore, commercial enterprises have low tolerance for mistakes in higher echelon functions; LD students quickly get relegated to more menial activities when they err.

The well-meaning LD teacher who is willing to do anything and everything to maintain the LD adolescent in the mainstream can be characterized as using the *statue of liberty* approach. The resource room model is used to serve a large number of students with assorted needs. Multidisciplinary services are offered, with academic assistance being predominant. LD teachers using this approach are challenged by the multiplication of demands and requests for individual programming.

Fewer secondary LD programs use the *learning strategies* approach. In this approach, emphasis is placed upon teaching the LD student efficient means to perform tasks and learn. Although instruction is mainly directed to academic content, emphasis is placed on study skills and their relationship to the task to be learned; the inquiry method is used. Since many LD adolescents have problems with symbolic tasks, this approach identifies and teaches techniques, principles, and rules for performing symbolic tasks. Thus, students are actively involved in selecting materials, directing activities, and analyzing results. This approach relies heavily on the cooperative planning between the LD resource teacher and other teachers.

The *elementary process* approach is the least frequently used one. Processing skills such as auditory discrimination are taught. Tutoring and academic remediation are also involved.

None of these models is appropriate for all LD secondary students. Some students might be ripe for a rigorous *basic skills* approach, if they never had a full exposure to one. Other students who failed to respond to such approaches may benefit more from a combination of the *learning strategies* approach and the *functional* model. Research is necessary to establish the substance of various approaches and their appropriateness for LD students.

TARGET POPULATION

Before we hastily begin to organize programs at the secondary level for adolescents with learning disabilities, we must consider the characteristics of our target group. Hammill (1978) considers the National Advisory Committee on Handicapped Children (NACHC) definition acceptable, if the word *student* is substituted for *children*. Wiederholt (1975) has abstracted the following characteristics of LD adolescents from the literature: severe underachievement, major cognitive deficits, excessive daydreaming, high distractibility, inflexibility toward ideas and activities, perceptual confusions, hyperactivity, short attention span, general body or motoric awkwardness, inadequacy in dealing with symbols, secondary emotional problems, immaturity, smaller than peers, frustration with self, inner rage, passive or active aggression, feelings of inadequacy, alienation from their families, delinquency, truancy, persistent confusion, poor development of logical reasoning and abstract-thinking abilities, difficulty in generalizing from experience, problems in modifying behavior, difficulty in choosing from alternatives, problems in anticipating the behavior of others, few established principles or ideals, makes snap decisions and judgments, and yields quickly to immediate pressure.

Caution must be exercised in using one or more of such characteristics since they represent the limitations of clinical perception and sampling practices. Like so many traits, they lack the kind of empirical validation necessary to use them to identify LD adolescents.

Deshler (1978) suggests a partial profile of the adolescent with learning disabilities is beginning to emerge. First, the LD adolescent demonstrates distinctive strengths and weaknesses. Second, the LD adolescent is still deficit in prerequisite skill areas like reading and arithmetic. Third, prolonged failure in schools has created poor self-concept and reduced motivation. Fourth, childhood traits like hyperactivity and incoordination seem manifested more subtly.

Deshler (1978) also strikes a note of caution. The presence of any given characteristic is neither conclusive proof of a learning disability nor a requirement. Indeed, the characteristics often are closely related. If learning disabilities persist into adolescence, then we must be prepared for different manifestations. Finally, we must be concerned about nonacademic characteristics as well as academic skills since the adolescent encounters social demands and career expectations.

ASSESSMENT

As with younger LD students, there are two major concerns in assessment for LD adolescents: placement and programming. In both cases we must grapple with the same problems of assessment format, reliability, validity, and so forth. In addition, we are faced with a dearth of individual secondary assessment techniques.

The National Learning Disabilities Assistance Project (1976) indicated the tests used in model learning disabilities centers. Of the 29 centers, 7 serve LD adolescents exclusively. Marsh, Gearheart, and Gearheart (1978) indicate that certain tests were used by these 7 centers (see table 13-2). From their analysis they conclude that no standard battery seems to be in use. The tests used also neglected the topic of vocational training and were not often suited for older students.

It is obvious that the academic deficits of LD adolescents need assessment. However we must decide if the aptitude, psychological processes, and other such variables can be or should be assessed in the secondary school context. Ysseldyke (1978) has strongly questioned our ability and the appropriateness of assessing and remediating psychological processes or abilities. He suggests instructional analysis, learning-task analysis, and job-task analysis as alternatives.

Another suggestion for LD secondary assessment has been the use of student interviews. The Title VI-G Project staff in Ohio (Moorehead & Meeth, 1976) developed a format for such an interview (see table 13-3). This procedure encourages the participation of LD students in the planning of their programs.

Ensminger (1976), in a handbook developed by participants in a Seminar on Secondary Programs for Adolescents with LD, stressed the role of the classroom teacher in the identification and assessment process. A screening device was developed as a means toward that end (see table 13-4, p. 448). Like most screening devices, it mentions behaviors exhibited by any child. No one or all of these traits can be considered sufficient to establish a learning disability (Deshler, 1978). Further research must be done to verify the significance of these behaviors and others. In the meantime, such efforts as represented by this device must be encouraged; this information should be combined with other assessment data to substantiate the existence of a learning disability.

In addition to teacher referrals and student interview, secondary LD personnel can use the traditionally administered group achievement tests to identify severe underachievers (Wiederholt, 1975). While of little or no use in educational programming, such tests as the *California Achievement Tests* (Tiegs & Clark, 1963) and the *Iowa Tests of Basic Skills* (Lindquist & Hieronymous, 1956) may assist in the screening process. Lists of appropriate other tests have been developed by Goodman and Mann (1976, pp. 48-55).

Lerner (1978) has considered the analysis of the learning disabilities of adolescents in three contexts: the student, the curriculum content and environmental conditions. Student analysis is not advisable because of the inappropriateness of applying concepts and tests designed for younger children to older students. Further, the reliability and

Table 13-2

Tests Used in Secondary LD Programs

Auditory Discrimination Test (revised edition)
Bender Visual Motor Gestalt Test
Benton Visual Retention
California Achievement Test
Columbia Test of Mental Maturity
Detroit Tests of Learning Aptitude
Developmental Test of Visual Perception (3rd edition)
Diagnostic Reading Scales (revised edition)
Durrell Analysis of Reading Difficulty
Gates-MacGinitie Reading Tests
Gates-McKillop Reading Diagnostic Tests
Goldman-Fristoe-Woodcock Auditory Skills Test Battery
Gray Oral Reading Test
Hiskey-Nebraska Test of Learning Aptitude
Illinois Test of Psycholinguistic Abilities
Jesness
Key Math Diagnostic Arithmetic Test
Leiter International Scale
McCall-Crabbs Standard Test Lessons in Reading
Metropolitan Achievement Tests (revised edition)
Minnesota Percepto-Diagnostic Test (revised edition)
Ohio Vocational Interest Survey
Peabody Individual Achievement Test
Peabody Picture Vocabulary Test
Perceptual Forms Test
Piers-Harris
Roswell-Chall Auditory Blending Test
Roswell-Chall Diagnostic Reading Test of Word Analysis Skills
Slosson Intelligence Test
Slosson Oral Reading Test
SRA Achievement Series
Stanford Achievement Test: Reading Tests
Stanford-Binet Intelligence Scale
Stanford Diagnostic Tests
Survey of Study Habits and Attitudes
Tennessee Self-Concept Scale
Test of Visual-Motor Integration
Wepman Auditory Discrimination Test
Wide Range Achievement Test
WISC-R
Woodcock Reading Mastery Tests

From "National Learning Disabilities Project," *Catalogue of Child Service Demonstration Centers 1975-76.* Merrimac, Mass. 1976.

Table 13-3
Student Interview Form

Name _____ Date _____ Age _____

Present Grade Level _____ Interview _____

I. Current Course Schedule and Grades:
   a. Based on the above, why does the student feel he needs the services of this program?

II. Work Experiences:
   a. Has the student ever had a job? How long? Any problems?
   b. Would the student like to work, if he isn't presently employed? Any preference of jobs? Any skills?
   c. What job would the student like to prepare himself to do upon graduation?

III. Personal Goals:
   a. Does the student feel he gets along in school? With his friends? With teachers? What would he like to change?
   b. Does the student feel satisfied with his accomplishments (grades, sports, clubs, activities, etc.) in school? What would he like to change?
   c. Does the student feel like he is doing what he knows best? If not, why not?

IV. Educational Goals:
   a. What does this student hope to accomplish in high school? (list his goals)
   b. What courses are necessary to help the student accomplish this goal? (outline these courses)

FOUR YEAR PLAN (Course Requirements)

FRESHMAN YEAR:

SOPHOMORE YEAR:

JUNIOR YEAR:

SENIOR YEAR:

From *A Handbook: Development of Program Alternatives for Educating Secondary Learning Disabled Students* by S. Moorehead and D. Meeth. Title VI-G Project, Worthington, Ohio, 1976. Reprinted by permission.

validity of cognitive-processing, sequential-stages-of-development approaches and test-related approaches are questionable.

However the focus on curriculum and environmental conditions seems promising. In particular the use of criterion-referenced assessment, task analysis, and applied behavioral analysis represent sound assessment bases.

MATERIALS AND METHODS

Brown (1975b) identified student-related characteristics and school-related characteristics that influence goals as well as curriculum and

Table 13-4

Sample Checklist of Behavioral Characteristics

The classroom teacher is afforded an excellent opportunity to note slight deviations in the behavior of children which may be the precursors of greater problems. A checklist can be of help to the teacher in selecting the child who warrants further study. It is imperative that no assumptions be made on the basis of a checklist alone; however, it may serve as the initial screening device.

Sample Checklist of Behavioral Characteristics

This checklist is composed of the following broad classifications: General Behavior, Coordination and Motor Activities, Perception, Auditory Responses, Verbal Communication, General Classroom Performance, and the Content Areas.

CODE: FRE — Frequently observed in the student; OCC — Occasionally observed in the student; NO — Not a problem

I. *General Behavior*

FRE   OCC   NO

____ ____ ____ 1. Becomes frustrated easily

____ ____ ____ 2. Poor concept of time

____ ____ ____ 3. Cannot tolerate changes in routine

____ ____ ____ 4. Forgetful

____ ____ ____ 5. Lacks emotional control

____ ____ ____ 6. Appears hostile

____ ____ ____ 7. Appears disorganized in activities

____ ____ ____ 8. Distractable

____ ____ ____ 9. Daydreams

____ ____ ____ 10. Generally excluded by peers

____ ____ ____ 11. Impulsive

____ ____ ____ 12. Anxious

____ ____ ____ 13. Exhibits moods of unhappiness

FRE   OCC   NO

____ ____ ____ 14. Poor social judgment

____ ____ ____ 15. Continues activity beyond appropriate point

____ ____ ____ 16. Unable to concentrate on task

____ ____ ____ 17. Poor self concept

____ ____ ____ 18. Avoids new tasks

____ ____ ____ 19. Short "academic" attention span

____ ____ ____ 20. Resists help

Table 13-4 (*cont.*)

II. *Coordination and Motor Activities*

—— —— —— 1. Hyperactive

—— —— —— 2. Fatigues easily

—— —— —— 3. Clumsy

III. *Perception*

—— —— —— 1. Unable to focus on one item

—— —— —— 2. Disorganized

—— —— —— 3. Short attention span

IV. *Responses (Listening)*

—— —— —— 1. Repeats what is told before he acts or responds

—— —— —— 2. Asks the same question repeatedly

—— —— —— 3. Tends to forget what is heard

—— —— —— 4. Requests directions time and time again

V. *Communication (Verbal)*

—— —— —— 1. Omits word endings

—— —— —— 2. Unable to vocalize thoughts

—— —— —— 3. Makes irrelevant remarks

—— —— —— 4. Poor articulation

—— —— —— 5. Poor enunciation

—— —— —— 6. Speaks in incomplete sentences

VI. *General Classroom Performance*

—— —— —— 1. Discrepancy between oral discussions and written work

—— —— —— 2. Inability to follow through sequential steps

—— —— —— 3. Appears lazy

—— —— —— 4. May feign illness or frequent absences

—— —— —— 5. Difficulty or delay in formulating a response

—— —— —— 6. Unequal performance in content areas

VII. *Reading*

—— —— —— 1. Mechanical oral reading without expression

—— —— —— 2. Many mistakes on small words; omissions and substitutions

—— —— —— 3. Reads fast orally; ignores punctuation and phrasing

—— —— —— 4. Lip movements, head movements during silent readings

Table 13-4 (*cont.*)
Sample Checklist of Behavioral Characteristics

VII. Reading (*cont.*)

_____ _____ _____ 5. Two or more grade levels behind in reading

_____ _____ _____ 6. Cannot spell words he can read

_____ _____ _____ 7. Knows isolated sounds, but cannot sound out words

_____ _____ _____ 8. Poor blending ability

_____ _____ _____ 9. Word reversals (e.g., saw - was)

VIII. *Written Expression*

_____ _____ _____ 1. Cannot organize ideas into sentences

_____ _____ _____ 2. Uses little or no punctuation

_____ _____ _____ 3. Reverses sequences of letters

_____ _____ _____ 4. Cannot copy

_____ _____ _____ 5. Writes fast or carelessly

_____ _____ _____ 6. Writes slowly, painstakingly

_____ _____ _____ 7. Poor spelling

_____ _____ _____ 8. Cannot stay on lines or hold to margin

_____ _____ _____ 9. Has many erasures

IX. *Math*

_____ _____ _____ 1. Cannot reason abstractly

_____ _____ _____ 2. Has severe problems with place value and carrying

_____ _____ _____ 3. Poor computation skills

_____ _____ _____ 4. Does not know math facts automatically

_____ _____ _____ 5. Poor application of arithmetic processes

_____ _____ _____ 6. Poor concept of measure; unable to tell time

From *Handbook on Secondary Programs for the Learning Disabled: Some Guidelines* by G. Ensminger (Ed.). Atlanta: Georgia State University, 1976. Reprinted by permission.

materials. Secondary LD students are more independent, mobile, and experienced; they are under pressure to make occupational and life decisions and engage in complex social relationships. Therefore, they may not be very excited about working on short vowels!

The secondary schools, on the other hand, have structures and requirements that may hamper sound practices for LD students. Grading systems, schedules, and program options and alternatives are real considerations. The traditional content orientation must be shifted to a student orientation.

A hasty scramble for kits and materials or the development of a special LD curriculum is not the answer.

Instead, the program should be based upon as honest an appraisal as possible of the community, and of the scope and quality of the existing secondary program school philosophy, and a description of what constitutes a favorable educational milieu for students. The selection or development of curricula will follow from intervention. (Brown, 1975b, p. 178)

Goodman and Mann (1976) suggest the adaptation of existing programs and materials from regular education. They further encourage the identification of core and supplemental materials in priority areas like reading, mathematics, spelling, and written communication skills. The criteria they use for curriculum development are as follows:

1. The curriculum will include a comprehensive, structured, developmental sequence of the subject matter content,
2. The appearance and format of the program should be appealing to the older student.
3. The scope and sequence of the program should be clearly delineated and preferably presented in a behaviorally objective format.
4. The program should have an accompanying curriculum management evaluation system.
5. The program should focus on mastery of basic skills. (p. 134)

A list of secondary materials has been developed by core and supplemental categories for the following areas: career education, reading, language arts, spelling, math, social studies, consumer education, science and health (Goodman et al., 1976).

Materials must be adapted in many ways to meet the needs of LD adolescents. Morrissey (1976) suggests considerations for material modification (see figure 13-1). An LD teacher can modify quantitative or qualitative features of the material. The spacing or time requirements can be changed. Depending upon the LD student's disability, different modes of presentation and response can be used, for example, demonstrations, tapes, and printed material.

Various cueing techniques can also be used to highlight features of material, such as color. Finally, an educational material may offer only one feedback system; that is, the right answer. Other alternative checks for accuracy could be stating the rule for getting the answer or an example of the answer.

Wiederholt and McNutt (1977) suggest two forms of material evaluation for secondary students: static and dynamic. Static evaluation will establish the relevancy, readability level, language features, and prerequisites of the material. Dynamic evaluation will supply information about the use and effects of the material through pretesting and posttesting, observation, analytic teaching, and interviews. Other considerations for material evaluation have been made by Bleil (1975) and Brown (1975a).

	Factor	No. of Units			Repetitions		
QUANTI-TATIVE	Spacing Time	per page seconds/minutes			per page per minutes		
QUALITATIVE	Modes Presentation Mode Response Mode	Demo. x x	Typed x	Taped x x	Printed x	Written x	Calculator x
	Cueing Position Saliency	Numbering x x	Color Coding x x	Blocking x x	Questions who, when, how what, where, why	Listening x	
	Feedback Terminal Adaptive	Binary x	Answer x	State Rule x	Give Example x		

Figure 13-1

Factors To Be Considered in Materials Adaption

From "For Secondary Teachers: An Individualized Intervention Model for Programming for Learning Disabled Children" by P. Morrissey, *Association of Special Education Technology Report*, 1976, *1*, 28-31. Reprinted by permission.

CAREER AND VOCATIONAL PREPARATION

In addition to attention to basic skill instruction and curriculum modification, secondary LD teachers are giving particular attention to career and vocational preparation. Adolescents with LD must be oriented to the future, particularly to the reality of gainful employment.

As in the cases (program models, assessment, and methods) mentioned before, schools and society must demonstrate considerably more flexibility in order to serve secondary LD students. Marsh, Gearheart, & Gearheart (1978) point out the resistance of schools to any deviation from a strictly academic program. Culture and society seem to associate who you *are* with what you *do.* Such attitudes are not conducive to the development of other vocational and career options than college-bound activities.

Career education is a promising educational movement in this regard (Williamson, 1975). Not synonymous with vocational education, career education permeates all grade levels and the total school experience. It highlights the relationship of the world of work to all school topics.

Previous school failure and the attendant poor self-concept may adversely affect the LD adolescent's career attitudes. Bingham (1978) studied secondary students and their feelings concerning involvement in the career-choice process, orientation toward work, independence in decision making, preference for career choice factors, and conceptions of the career choice process. LD students were much less mature in their responses to demands associated with career choice and the necessary planning. Problems in organizing and sequencing may appear in this area of endeavor as they did in academics.

Increased federal support for vocational training has included provisions for handicapped students. The Vocational Education Act of 1963 was amended in 1968 to require that 10% of federal funds for vocational education be used for the handicapped. Unfortunately, such provisions have not necessarily meant that handicapped students receive quality training programs (Irvine, Goodman, & Mann, 1978). Much depends on the enlightenment of vocational educators and the working relationship between special and vocational educators.

Two pieces of federal legislation should guarantee more quality vocational outlets for LD students. The Vocational Rehabilitation Act of 1973 provides for equal opportunity for handicapped persons where federal contracts and grants are involved. This measure may encourage more interest and effort toward training the handicapped for a vocation. P.L. 94-142 (1975) will also bolster the vocational cause of LD adolescents. By its extension of services to the age of 21 and its specific inclusion of LD students, this federal law may clarify the appropriateness of including LD students in vocational programs. There has been some question in the past if LD adolescents are sufficiently handicapped to merit such services.

Irvine et al. (1978) and Washburn (1975) have described in detail programming ideas for career and vocational training. Some critical concepts are (1) matching a student's occupational strengths to job requirements, (2) fostering communication between the vocational and academic skill instructors, and (3) offering a broad array of occupational possibilities.

COUNSELING

A critical service for LD adolescents is counseling. Their frustrations with academics, social-emotional areas, and career and vocational choices must be dealt with. Trained counselors can support LD students in such areas of development as well as coping with lingering learning disabilities. Teachers, counselors, and parents must work together to supply a supportive emotional base for LD adolescents as the students cope with the effects of their learning problems.

Kelly (1971) describes adolescence as a particularly challenging time for secondary students and their parents. There are the natural feelings of alienation of generation groups, struggles for independence and self-sufficiency, and anxiety over social-sexual development. The natural stress of this period may be intensified by both the LD adolescent's inability to cope adequately or the types of parents' responses. After prolonged struggles by parents to assist their children in learning academic skills, parents may approach the adolescent's learning needs in a similar fashion. The result may be a strained relationship, not a helping one.

There is also the possibility that the LD adolescent's position in the family may become undesirable. LD adolescents may be regarded as burdens for their families and/or as reasons for family problems. Abrams and Kaslow (1977) suggest the need for a continuum of services to meet both the needs of the LD student and his family. In the case of LD adolescents, some form of counseling and/or tutoring may be advisable. The deciding factors would be the state of the family dynamics and the learning needs of the LD secondary student.

ADULTHOOD

Concern is also being expressed about the ramifications of learning disabilities for adults. Learning problems in reading, mathematics, language, and so forth, can have implications in career and vocational areas, family dynamics, future academic pursuits, and social relationships.

Silberberg and Silberberg (1978) argue that reading and other language requirements for many jobs are so minimal that a reading emphasis in vocational training may be inappropriate. They suggest that special educators, vocational educators, and employers make the work world more accessible to the LD adult.

LD adults are also being found in responsible positions in various professions. Specific strengths in such areas as verbal expression or social relations enable individuals to perform the essential functions in certain fields. Persons with learning disabilities seem to develop considerable coping ability, searching out alternative ways to do things or merely avoiding certain situations (Baker, 1975; Schwartz, Gilroy, & Lynn, 1976). One organization, *Time Out to Enjoy, Inc.* (113 Garfield St., Oak Park, Ill.), is attempting to identify and support such individuals.

Unfortunately, the strain of coping on some LD adults may be considerable. These individuals may be fearful and anxious about being labeled as disabled or different. In an effort to hide their problems, they may be driven to overcompensate (Schwartz, Gilroy, & Lynn, 1976). They may use elaborate mnemonic devices, avoid certain situations, or overaccentuate certain abilities.

Prolonged problems with learning can affect the adult's self-concept adversely. Such a condition may in turn take its toll on married life and parenthood. Lenkowsky and Saposnek (1978) describe the disruption of a family because of the severe reading disorder of the father. The father became dependent on his wife and children to read and write for him. He had to struggle with feelings of inadequacy, guilt, and embarrassment. His family felt imposed upon, burdened with unwanted responsibilities, and fearful of his impulsive temper. The role relationships of the family were totally confused.

Hallahan and Kauffman (1976) have reviewed the kinds of problems that LD individuals have in the development of social skills, moral judgment, and so forth. The implication for the LD parent with learning disabilities is obvious. The parents' attempts to transmit cultural mores in a clear and consistent fashion may be thwarted by their own behaviors and social misconceptions. LD adults may not be able to offer appropriate models for their children.

Young adults with learning disabilities may also be challenged if they want to pursue college studies. Vandivier and Vandivier (1977) lament the implication that learning disabilities preclude a college education for LD adults. Their prospects for college are clouded by a dearth of quality college programs.

Moss (1971, 1975), Fielding (1975), and Goodman and Mann (1976) have compiled lists and descriptions of LD college programs. However, Marsh, Gearheart, & Gearheart (1978) have been discouraged by the lack of real provisions for LD adults, even at schools professing to have special programs. It is necessary to discriminate among colleges that offer merely admission, provide some special services, and/or have trained personnel available.

The needs of the LD college students are for special provisions in reading, testing, study skills, organization of effort, and so forth. Colleges with LD programs may offer taped textbooks, readers, and tutorial assistance. Regular meetings with LD students are necessary to help them plan their activities, troubleshoot problems, and offer individual counseling. Trained LD personnel can support instructors who are willing to cooperate in matters such as alternative ways of testing and provisions for note taking in class. With student motivation and maturity, much can be done for LD adults by an enlightened college faculty and staff (Herbert & Czerniejewski, 1976).

ADOLESCENTS AND ADULTS: IN PERSPECTIVE

Professionals and parents interested in supporting LD adolescents and adults are faced by quite a challenge. Teachers and other professionals must be prepared to work with such individuals. Zigmond, Silverman, and Laurie (1978) strongly suggest the development of competency-based teacher education programs. Secondary LD teachers must be competent to offer direct services (diagnostic-prescriptive teaching, group meetings, and career exploration) and indirect services (consultation services to mainstream educators and parent education).

Research must also be performed with some priority areas. What has happened to the secondary students who received no follow-up LD services? How have LD adults fared in society? What are the characteristics of LD adolescents? What are the characteristics of learning and other kinds of environments in which LD adolescents fail and succeed? How cooperative are employers, unions, colleges, and so forth, in meeting the challenge posed by these individuals?

Program development is also necessary. Materials and curriculum must be adapted, and some special materials must be developed. Assessment techniques must be perfected to validly and reliably gather useful information for placement and programming decisions. Particular pains should be taken to avoid negative and stigmatizing program arrangement. Russell (1974) stresses the need to make the program as invisible as possible. Undue attention should not be focused only on the LD person. The environment, interactional patterns, and so forth, should also receive scrutiny. Institutions such as schools and industry should be tested for their flexibility and malleability.

The biggest danger in secondary LD programming is to superimpose the academic-basic skills approach at a higher level. The exit concerns of the LD adolescent population include many more areas than merely academic and language behaviors. Thus, structured learning experiences in career and vocational options, recreation and leisure time, and family living are essential. The relationship of learning disabilities to juvenile delinquency needs special study.

As more and more states study the issue of minimal competencies for high school graduation, the plight of the LD adolescent becomes intensified. Intelligent discourse is imperative among parents and the many professionals involved with the LD adolescent.

SUMMARY

In this chapter we reviewed the past and present status of LD secondary programs. The present direction of thinking in the areas of definition, assessment, and methods was described. The need for career and vocational services and counseling support was also mentioned. Finally, we described challenges faced by the LD adult.

SUGGESTED ACTIVITIES

1. Review state guidelines for placement and programming provisions for LD adolescents.

2. Interview an LD secondary teacher about the program. Compare it to the categories developed by Deshler, Lowrey, and Alley (1979).
3. Survey secondary teachers and counselors about their knowledge of learning disabilities.
4. Survey the reading and written language requirements of local jobs.
5. Review the following films on LD adolescents:
   a. *Adolescence and Learning Disabilities*
   b. *If A Boy Can't Learn*

   Rental and/or purchase information is available from Lawren Productions, Inc., P.O. Box 1542, Burlingame, Calif. 94010, (415) 697-2558.
6. Examine some assessment procedures, including standardized tests, for their appropriateness for LD students in secondary schools.
7. Choose one regular classroom curriculum or material used at the secondary level. Using Morrissey's suggestions (1976), identify ways to modify it.
8. Read the articles on material evaluation by Wiederholt and McNutt (1977), Bleil (1975), or Brown (1975b). Choose one material currently in use in a secondary LD program. Using the suggested considerations, evaluate it.

References

Abrams, J., & Kaslow, F. Family systems and the learning disabled child: Intervention and treatment. *Journal of Learning Disabilities*, 1977, *10*, 86-90.

Baker, L. I am me. *Bulletin of the Orton Society*, 1975, *25*, 185-198.

Bingham, G. Career attitudes among boys with and without specific learning disabilities. *Exceptional Children*, 1978, *44*, 341-342.

Bleil, G.B. Evaluating instructional materials. *Journal of Learning Disabilities*, 1975, *8*, 12-24.

Brown, V. A basic Q-Sheet for analyzing and comparing curriculum materials and proposals. *Journal of Learning Disabilities*, 1975, *8*, 407-416. (a)

Brown, V. *Curriculum and materials for secondary level learning disabilities programs: What we have and what we need.* Paper presented at the LD Secondary School Conference, Montgomery County Intermediate Unit 23, Penn.: March 1975. (b)

Deshler, D.D. Psychoeducational aspects of learning-disabled adolescents. In L. Mann, L. Goodman, & J.L. Wiederholt (Eds.), *Teaching the learning disabled adolescent.* Boston: Houghton Mifflin, 1978.

Deshler, D., Lowrey, N., & Alley, G. Programming alternatives for LD adolescents: A nationwide survey. *Academic Therapy*, 1979, *14*, 8-12.

Ensminger, G. *Handbook on secondary programs for the learning disabled: Some guidelines.* Atlanta: Georgia State University, 1976.

Fielding, P. *A national directory of four-year colleges, two year colleges, and post-high school training programs for young people with LD.* Tulsa, Okla.: Partners in Publishing, 1975.

Goodman, L. Educational programming: A survey of current practice. In L. Mann, L. Goodman, & J.L. Wiederholt (Eds.), *Teaching the learning disabled adolescent.* Boston: Houghton Mifflin, 1978.

Goodman, L. & Mann, L. *Learning disabilities in the secondary school.* New York: Grune & Stratton, 1976.

Goodman, L. & Mann, L. *Learning disabilities in the secondary school: A review of the literature* [Title III, E.S.E.A. Report, Project No. 74-74006H-46-23-01-13 (1)]. Montgomery County Intermediate Unit 23, Penn., 1975.

Goodman, L., Stitt, M., Ness, J., & Eells, J. *Curricular materials for secondary learning disabilities programs* [Title III, E.S.E.A. Report, Project No. 74-74006H-46-23-01-13 (1)]. Montgomery County Intermediate Unit 23, Penn., 1976.

Hallahan, D.P., & Kauffman, J.M. *Introduction to learning disabilities: A psycho-behavioral approach.* Englewood Cliffs, N.J.: Prentice-Hall, 1976.

Hammill, D. Adolescents with specific learning disabilities: Definition, identification and incidence. In L. Mann, L. Goodman, & J.L. Wiederholt (Eds.), *Teaching the learning disabled adolescent*. Boston: Houghton Mifflin, 1978.

Herbert, M., & Czerniejewski, C. Language and learning therapy in a community college. *Bulletin of the Orton Society*, 1976, *26*, 96-106.

Irvine, P., Goodman, L., & Mann, L. Occupational education. In L. Mann, L. Goodman, & J.L. Wiederholt (Eds.), *Teaching the learning disabled adolescent*. Boston: Houghton Mifflin, 1978.

Kelly, E. *Common sense in child raising*. Denver: Love Publishing, 1971.

Kline, C.L. Adolescents with learning problems: How long must they wait? *Journal of Learning Disabilities*, 1972, *5*, 262-271.

Lenkowsky, L.K., & Saposnek, D.T. Family consequences of parental dyslexia. *Journal of Learning Disabilities*, 1978, *11*, 47-53.

Lerner, J. Instructional strategies: A classification schema. In L. Mann, L. Goodman, & J.L. Wiederholt (Eds.), *Teaching the learning disabled adolescent*. Boston: Houghton Mifflin, 1978.

Lindquist, E., & Hieronymous, A. *Iowa Test of Basic Skills*. New York: Harcourt, Brace & World, 1956.

Marsh, II, G.E., Gearheart, C., & Gearheart, B. *The learning disabled adolescent*. St. Louis: Mosby, 1978.

Moorehead, S., & Meeth, D. *A handbook: Development of program alternatives for educating secondary learning disabled students*. Title VI-G Project, Worthington, Ohio, 1976.

Morrissey, P. For secondary teachers: An individualized intervention model for programming for learning disabled students. *ASET Report*, 1976, *1*, 28-31.

Moss, J.R. (Ch.) *A national directory of four year colleges, two year colleges and post high school training programs for young people with learning disabilities*. Compiled for the Membership Committee of ACLD. Commerce, Texas: East Texas State University, 1971, 1975.

National Learning Disabilities Assistance Project. *Catalogue of child service demonstration centers, 1975-76*. Merrimac, Mass., 1976.

Russell, R. The dilemma of the handicapped adolescent. In R. Weber (Ed.), *Handbook on learning disabilities*. Englewood Cliffs, N.J.: Prentice-Hall, 1974.

Schwartz, M.L., Gilroy, J., & Lynn, G. Neuro-psychological and psychosocial implications of spelling deficit in adulthood: A case report. *Journal of Learning Disabilities*, 1976, *9*, 144-148.

Scranton, T.R., & Downs, M.L. Elementary and secondary LD programs in the U.S.: A survey. *Journal of Learning Disabilities*, 1975, *8*, 394-399.

Silberberg, N.E., & Silberberg, M.C. And the adult who reads poorly? *Journal of Learning Disabilities*, 1978, *11*, 3-4.

Tiegs, E.W., & Clark, W.W. *California Achievement Test*. Los Angeles: California Test Bureau, 1963.

Vandivier, P., & Vandivier, S. Letter to Editor. *Journal of Learning Disabilities*, 1977, *10*, 547-548.

Washburn, W.Y. Where to go in voc-ed for secondary LD students. *Academic Therapy*, 1975, *11*, 31-35.

Wiederholt, J.L. *A report on secondary school programs for the learning disabled.* [Final report (Project No. H12-7145B, Grant No. OEG-0-714425).]

Wiederholt, J.L. Adolescents with LD: The problem in perspective. In L. Mann, L. Goodman, & J.L. Wiederholt (Eds.), *Teaching the learning disabled adolescent.* Boston: Houghton Mifflin, 1978.

Wiederholt, J.L., & McNutt, G. Evaluating materials for handicapped adolescents. *Journal of Learning Disabilities,* 1977, *10,* 132-140.

Williamson, A.P. Career education: Implications for secondary LD student. *Academic Therapy,* 1975, *10,* 193-200.

Ysseldyke, J.E. Remediation of ability deficits: Some major questions. In L. Mann et al. (Eds.), *Teaching the learning disabled adolescent.* Boston: Houghton Mifflin, 1978.

Zigmond, N. A prototype of comprehensive services for secondary students with learning disabilities. *Learning Disability Quarterly,* 1978, *1,* 39-49.

Zigmond, N., Silverman, R., & Laurie, T. Competencies for teachers. In L. Mann, L. Goodman, & J.L. Wiederholt (Eds.), *Teaching the learning disabled adolescent.* Boston: Houghton Mifflin, 1978.

Parents and Learning Disabilities

PREVIEW

We have considered many aspects of learning disabilities and programs that suggest areas for parent involvement. Indeed, as we will point out, parents of children with learning disabilities have been very instrumental in developing these programs. P.L. 94-142 has been particularly effective in identifying programming areas in which parents and LD teachers can cooperate. We encourage active parent participation in screening, assessment, planning, implementation, and evaluation activities. We also will discuss parent advocacy and parent training as areas for this parent/professional partnership.

Parents have always played an essential role in providing services to children with learning disabilities. They have often been the first people to voice concern about their children's learning development. Their search for assistance from public schools and other agencies has been energetic. Parent groups such as the Association for Children with Learning Disabilities (ACLD) have provided a forum for information dissemination and political action. Political lobbies by parents and others have resulted in federal and state legislation and funds to support services for children with learning disabilities.

Parents play a vital role in the early detection and habilitation of learning disabilities. Consequently, parents have cooperated with teachers and other professionals in intervention programs and follow-up activities. Their encouragement and support have created a cooperative atmosphere among all those concerned with LD children. The initial development and expansion of services for the learning disabled have been predicated upon active, intelligent participation by parents.

P.L. 94-142 has literally vindicated many parents of LD children who have struggled to obtain services for their children. Although previous legislation established the basis for funding LD programs (Marsh, Gearheart & Gearheart, 1978), parents still had to struggle to be treated as mature participants in the assessment and remedial services of their children. As we saw in chapter 4, P.L. 94-142 has guaranteed a new level of participation for parents.

AREAS OF PARTICIPATION

Parents of LD children can be involved in services for their children in many ways. P.L. 94-142 expressly states certain guarantees and rights for their children. Parents must be notified of referrals for special education; give written consent for testing; participate in the group deciding on placement and programming goals; agree to any recommendations for placement and goals; and have at least an annual review of the child's program. LD parents have the right to appeal any aspect of this process and seek any additional diagnostic opinions.

While the letter of the law mentions the main features of the program, the spirit of the law suggests a wide variety of possibilities for parent involvement (see table 14-1) (McLoughlin, Edge, & Strenecky, 1978). It is well to conceptualize parental involvement as a cooperative venture, in concert with professional activity. As we shall see, parents can participate quite actively. LD teachers, however, must be willing to encourage their activity.

PARENTAL SCREENING

By virtue of their regular and intensive contact with their children, LD parents often notice early indications that their children are not learning well. While the school environment precipitates the surfacing of certain learning disabilities, the home environment also places considerable demands for performance upon a child. A parent may therefore notice developmental lags or problems in motor, linguistic, and social skills.

A survey conducted by the California Association for Neurologically Handicapped Children (CANHC) indicated that mothers were often credited with first noticing their child's problem (Tarnopol, 1969). School personnel were credited with the identification of 18% of the cases, pediatricians with 14%. The median age at which the problem was initially discovered was 4 years. However, in more than 30% of the cases, the problem was not discovered until the child began attending school.

Some parents are not capable of or willing to admit to and deal with their children's learning disabilities. Barsh (1961), for example, has estimated that as many as half of the parents of handicapped children are not actively involved in parent organizations. Whatever their reasons for not joining, many of these parents are at a decided disadvantage in not knowing either the characteristics of learning disabilities or the services available for their children.

If teacher perceptions have proven useful indicators of children needing special services (Keogh & Becker, 1973), it is equally plausible that parents can notice learning problems early. The various sources of information that parents usually rely on for their screening efforts include comparison to siblings, information from other parents, popular press and media, and knowledge of the behaviors expected in school.

Parent-child interactions usually decide the quality of a child's early learning experiences. Development of language, mental set, social attachments, and so forth, is predicated upon intelligent, loving support by parents (Kagan, 1970).

Table 14-1
Parental Activities

stages	parental activities	professional facilitation
Identification	Be alert to early warning signs Be aware of etiology Be aware of services Refer child to proper service Talk to other parents	Be aware of community resources Use public service media Make information available Offer parent education groups Assure adequate funding Make services available

Assessment	Maintain a developmental log
	Respond to interview questions
	  and written questionnaires
	Cooperate with teachers and
	  other professionals
	Be a team member
	Agree to assessment
	Attend committee conferences
	Supply relevant information
	  from previous evaluations
		Avoid jargon
		Be interdisciplinary
		Conduct conferences slowly
		  and clearly
		Be realistic
		Be positive
		Supply samples of a child's work
		Write understandable reports
		Supply assessment reports

Programming	Consider appropriate place-
	  ment options and program
	  goals
	Choose a placement site and
	  program goals cooperatively
	Identify and choose goals for
	  own use
	Attend committee conferences
	Visit classrooms
	Read parents' literature
	Review materials
		Encourage classroom
		  observation
		Explain educational curriculum
		Demonstrate strategies and
		  materials
		Design and supply parent
		  activities
		Explain placement alternatives
		Point out goals for parents
		  (if advisable)

Implementation	Be a classroom aide
	Join parent organizations (PTA,
	  ACLD, etc.)
	Support efforts of professionals
	Model good attitude toward
	  program
	Be a tutor
	Reinforce child's skills at home
		Supply parent education groups
		Support parents' organizations
		Supply discussion groups
		Maintain home programs
		Design materials and activities
		  for parent use
		Design formal parent intervention
		  programs in school and home

Evaluation	Hold professionals accountable
	Be accountable
	Supply feedback to
	  professionals
	Help evaluate educational plans
	Serve on parent advisory boards
	Support parent activism (ACLD)
		Supply parent training programs
		Establish parent advisory boards
		Support parents' organizations
		Include parents' contributions in
		  evaluation procedures
		Facilitate communication with
		  parents

From "Perspective on Parent Involvement in the Diagnosis and Treatment of Learning Disabled Children" by J.A. McLoughlin, D. Edge, & B. Strenecky, *Journal of Learning Disabilities*, 1978, *11*, 295. Copyright 1978 by Professional Press, Inc. Reprinted by permission.

Informed parents, with support from professionals in the field, can usually improve environmental conditions for their children. Education of parents can also emphasize appropriate parent behaviors needed in developing basic skills in children. The education of many young adults for future parenthood seems to be an important consideration for the prevention of learning disabilities. Knowledge of the importance of maternal health, diet, and so forth may help young adults avoid inadvertently harming their own offspring. As discussed in chapter 3, medical research and information from other fields are helping identify increasingly greater numbers of factors related to the birth and rearing of high-risk children.

Parents and the general public must be aware of the needs and services available for the young child with possible learning disorders. Hayden (1974) suggests the following considerations for prevention efforts: (1) early education for parenthood, (2) resources for genetic counseling, (3) good prenatal, natal, and postnatal care, (4) good nutrition for mother and child, (5) regular health checks for children, (6) early assessment services to identify learning problems, (7) accident prevention, (8) child advocacy groups, (9) regular evaluation of a child's progress, and (10) future research.

Among the preschool behaviors which receive parental attention, alertness and activity levels, language, motor ability, and social behavior all rank high. Once a child enters school, parents usually attend to basic skill achievement, particularly in reading. School behavior problems and hyperactivity are additional concerns of parents of school-age LD children.

Criteria for recognizing and understanding learning disabilities have also become available to parents. Minde (1971) emphasizes the problem of hyperactivity and appropriate management techniques. Hayes (1975) has composed a set of activities for parents to simulate the experience of having learning disabilities. Other useful sources for parents are contained in table 14-2.

Literature for parents about learning disabilities is generally written cautiously. If the uninformed parent is at a disadvantage, so too is the inaccurately informed parent. The key to the problem, of course, is mutual respect and communication between parents and the professionals working with their children.

PARENTAL ASSESSMENT AND PLANNING

Parental involvement in the entire IEP process is guaranteed by P.L. 94-142 (see chap. 4). However, it is possible that LD parents will still be ignored as useful sources of information and advisors in assessment and program planning activities. Reluctant professionals neglect to use interviews and conferences with parents effectively.

Table 14-2
Parent Information Sources

Brutten, Milton, Richardson, Sylvia, & Mangel, Charles. *Something's wrong with my child.* New York: Harcourt, Brace & World, 1973. This book contains practical advice on identification, sources of help, and a discussion of problems of the older LD child.

Clarke, Louise. *Can't read, can't write, can't talk too good either: How to recognize and overcome dyslexia in your child.* New York: Walker & Co., 1973. This book is an account of a long search for diagnostic and teaching services for a child with severe language disabilities. The success story traces the family's efforts in understanding and effectively coping with the learning problem.

Cohen, Martin. *Bets wishz doc.* New York: Arthur Fields, 1974. A director of a school for children with learning disabilities describes his students, their problems before entering the school, the remedial program, and so forth.

Ellingson, Careth. *The shadow children.* New York: Taplinger Publishing Co., 1967. The author explains learning disabilities in nontechnical language.

Ellingson, Careth. *Speaking of children: Their learning abilities/disabilities.* New York: Harper & Row, 1975. The author reveiws problems that the LD child has in the schools. The book also covers developmental milestones and information on evaluation and remedial techniques.

Hart, Jane, & Jones, Beverly. *Where's Hannah? A handbook for parents and teachers with learning disorders.* New York: Hart Publishing Co., 1968. This book is an account of the struggle for services and the remedial work that helped a learning disabled child. The parent and teacher of Hannah wrote the book.

Weber, Robert (Ed.). *Handbook on learning disabilities: A prognosis for the child, the adolescent, the adult.* Englewood Cliffs, N.J.: Prentice-Hall, 1974. This book is a collection of articles covering LD children at different ages and problems they encounter.

Interviewing LD parents can be very useful. Kroth (1975) suggests many topics to discuss with parents, including the child's medical background, leisure time activities, and so forth. However, the LD teacher must exercise caution and sensitivity in interviews; questions must be judged as appropriate only if they directly affect the LD child's instructional needs.

Sloman and Webster (1978) have identified a number of useful questions to ask LD parents (see table 14-3). The responses to such questions should clarify child management strategies and other aspects of parent-child interaction. An LD teacher who wishes to establish a consistent management system between school and home can use this information for the child's benefit.

Parents participate in informal and formal conferences with the LD teacher. Informal encounters outside the school building, phone calls, and note exchanges make up a broad category of contacts between the

A home-based program for the LD child augments the instruction received in school.

LD teacher and parents. However, formal conferences are the most frequently used method of parent participation.

The formal meetings demanded by P.L. 94-142 allow for a level of parental involvement beyond mere acquiescence. The LD teacher should be prepared to explain diagnostic data to parents in a meaningful way. Samples of the child's work and other graphic indicators of the child's learning disability should be provided. Parents should also be encouraged to establish goals for themselves in order to support their child's efforts. These goals would be included in the IEP.

At subsequent conferences the LD teacher must recognize parents as partners in the educational process. Materials and methods should be described to the parents. Parents should also receive regular reports on their child's progress.

In addition, LD teachers should be aware of the need to make physical arrangements for conferences, for example, arranging for a place free of distractions. Kroth and Simpson (1977) and Losen and Diament (1978) make many excellent suggestions about conferencing with parents.

PARENTAL INTERVENTION AND EVALUATION

Many parents participate in educational and other forms of intervention for LD children. In addition to supplying vital information to physicians, psychologists, and educators for assessment purposes, many parents subject their home environment to close scrutiny. This self-examination, while sometimes painful, has often resulted in the identification of crucial variables for intervention strategies.

Table 14-3

Interview Questions

1. Are there any activities that you particularly enjoy doing with
   _____ ? (child's name)

2. What do you feel are some of _____ 's greatest problems?

3. Are there any ways in which you have been able to help him with this?

4. Do you feel that this approach has helped?

5. How do you come to try this?

6. Inquire specifically about areas that have not been covered (i.e., physical, social, language, academic).

7. Do you feel that it is important for a child to learn to do things and to manage on his own? Give examples of things _____ does on his own? Give examples of things _____ does on his own at home. How often during the day do you find yourself helping _____ with something?

8. When you think about _____ , do you ever feel that he grew up too fast, or not fast enough?

9. Does _____ give up easily with things he finds difficult to do? Give an example of the type of thing he might give up on.

10. Do you feel that _____ needs a lot of praise and encouragement? Give examples of situations where you would give him this.

11. Is _____ very affectionate with you?

12. In what ways does _____ express his affection? Physically? Verbally? How often?

13. Are there any ways in which _____ gives you more pleasure that your other children? Or are there any little things about _____ that you especially enjoy? Give examples.

14. Are there any ways in which _____ is more difficult to enjoy than your other children? Give examples.

15. When during the day does _____ place the most demands on you?

16. Does _____ ever become annoyed when you try to help him with something? Give an example.

17. When do you become most annoyed with _____ ? How frequently do you end up feeling irritated and angry with _____?

18. When is _____ the easiest to manage? When is _____ the most difficult to manage?

19. Give an example of a recent situation where _____ really wanted to do something that you didn't want him to do. What happened?

20. When during the day do you feel that you place the most demands on _____ ?

Table 14-3 (*cont.*)

21. Do you have any special rules for _____ in your home? Do these apply to your other children as well?

22. Are there ever situations that are likely to end up with both you and _____ feeling angry or frustrated with each other? Give an example.

23. Can you give me a recent example of a situation where you lost your temper with _____ ? What did _____ do? What did you do?

24. How do you usually express your affection for _____ ? Verbally? Physically? Special privileges or presents?

25. Do you feel you more often show your affection when _____ has achieved something?

26. Are there ever times when you show your affection for no special reasons?

27. Are there any particular situations when you are more apt to show your affection for _____ ? Give examples.

_____

Each of the five dimensions can be most readily derived from the parent's answer to certain specific questions. The relevant questions are as follows: evaluation, 1 to 6; autonomy, 7 to 10; affection, 11-14 and 24 to 27; hostility, 15 to 18, 22 and 23; pressuring, 19 to 21.

All ratings are comprehensive and based on the interview as a whole.

The possible consequences of parental attitudes on efforts to help LD children have been suggested by Brown (1969). Usually a child's self-concept is affected by parental reactions to his learning disabilities. Parents may reject, accept, or overcompensate for a child's difficulties.

Wetter (1972) compared the attitudes of parents of children diagnosed as having a learning disorder to the attitudes of parents of children without learning disorders. He concluded that parental attitudes toward children with learning disorders were distinctive. These parents showed more overindulgence and rejection, though they were not overprotective in their attitudes. Parents with LD children disagreed more about their children's overall adjustment. Wetter suggested the need for early identification of parental attitudes and appropriate counseling.

Brown (1969) has also described some of the possible reactions to a child's handicap, such as guilt and anger, with which many parents must deal. Stewart (1978) considers the LD parents' situation unique because the learning disability is generally unapparent to others and confusing to themselves. Thus LD parents must discriminate constantly between the effects of a learning disability and other factors affecting their child's learning and social problems. This inextricable bond between the child's learning disability and parental feelings suggests the need for a link between the child's educational remediation and counseling (Abrams & Kaslow, 1977).

Parents have played essential roles in medical and educational intervention projects. Physicians rely upon parents to supply feedback on the behavioral consequences of medication treatment. Educators, too, depend upon the cooperation of parents for the reinforcement of newly learned behaviors outside the classroom. Academic skills and social behaviors are usually taught under structured, highly reinforcing conditions in the classroom. Once made aware of the target behaviors, parents can facilitate their development by encouraging them at home.

Parents can also formally assist in the educational instruction of children with learning disabilities (Stott, 1972). Some may work with their children at home or in the classroom. This practice seems feasible in view of the obvious educational role many parents have played throughout a child's preschool years.

Strenecky, McLoughlin, and Edge (in press) have identified key considerations in the development of parent tutor programs in the schools. First, parents should receive orientation and training for their duties. Second, administrative, parental, and staff support must be evident. Third, parents should not teach their own children in the school. Fourth, parent tutors must be carefully supervised.

In consultation with involved educators and other professionals, parents often use materials and activities suggested by the child's teacher and published in guides for parents. Two such guides were written by Valett (1969) and Behrman and Millman (1973). An annotated list of additional guides is provided in table 14-4.

The use of parents for after-school phonics tutoring was reported by Coe (1971). The teacher supplied the parents with a list of the children's reading errors each week, as well as appropriate activities and materials.

Behavioral analysis techniques and behavior modification are skills parents may use effectively to encourage basic skills. Parents usually learn a simple observational record-keeping procedure to identify the number and dimensions of a particularly important behavior. With the assistance of a teacher, the parents then identify appropriate responses for the development of the target skill. In this regard, Galloway and Galloway (1971) taught precision teaching skills to parents to supply them with a better understanding of their child's behavior and practical ability to change it. Parents were given the responsibility to maintain and accelerate those behaviors taught in school. They had the ultimate responsibility to choose the behaviors, consequences, and other aspects of the approach. The authors indicated that the skills made the parents more effective as change agents, as well as generally improving their attitude about the child's handicap.

Table 14-4
Parent Activity Guides

Blanchet, Eileen. *When your child can't read: A do it yourself program.* San Rafael, Calif.: Academic Therapy Publications, 1972. A mother, motivated by her own experience in teaching her learning disabled child, offers various activities for helping children learn.

Edington, Ruth. *Helping children with reading disability.* Chicago: Developmental Learning Materials, 1968. This book is intended for parents helping their children with reading disabilities. The book describes specific activities in eight areas, including general suggestions for the study period, hand-eye coordination activities, phonics training, ear training, reading, relaxation activities, muscle memory, writing, and spelling. Thirteen approaches to methods of teaching are specified. The appendix lists instructional materials, including commercial work, textbooks and programs, and 27 illustrated aids.

Flowers, Ann M. *Helping the child with a learning disability: Suggestions for parents.* Danville, Ill.: Interstate Printers & Publishers, 1969. Written for parents of children with learning disabilities, the booklet provides information on the nature of learning and suggests activities which parents may use to help children become more aware of their environments and to stimulate their learning.

Granowsky, A., Middleton, F., & Mumford, J. *A guide for better reading.* Asheville, N.C.: Tarmac, 1977. Designed to foster parental reading instruction at home, the booklet contains suggested tests and activities. The teacher performs the necessary assessment and shows the parent how to follow-up at home.

Kronick, Doreen. *They too can succeed: A practical guide for PARENTS of learning disabled children.* San Rafael, Calif.: Academic Therapy Publications, 1969. Written for parents of children with learning disabilities, the text offers practical hints for the solution of recurring educational, physical, and social problems.

Miele, Norma, & Smith, Sara, E. *Help for parents and teachers: A handbook to enhance learning potential.* Ridgefield, N.J.: Educational Performance Associates, 1974. This booklet contains useful suggestions for parents about activities to carry out at home.

Miller, Julano. *Helping your learning disabled child at home.* San Rafael, Calif.: Academic Therapy Publications, 1973. This booklet contains activities to develop various learning skills. Suggestions are grouped by general age level.

Weiss, Helen, & Weiss, Martin. *A parents' and teachers' guide to learning disabilities.* Great Barrington, Mass.: Treehouse Associates, 1973. This booklet contains general guidelines for better understanding of a child's unique learning style, with specific suggestions for teaching activities at home and at school.

Some LD children are inattentive, distractible, and so forth. These behaviors are a concern at home as well as in school. Parents can use the skills of applied behavioral analysis for managing such behaviors. Becker (1971), Patterson (1971), Smith and Smith (1976), and Cooper and Edge (1978) have written excellent guides for parents and teachers.

A program for foster parents and their children has been described by Quick, Little, and Campbell (1973). The diagnostic-prescriptive program includes gross motor, fine motor, personal-social, language, and perceptual-cognitive areas. The parents observe the clinical instruction of the child once a week, perform the activities with their child under supervision, and continue the tasks at home.

Latham and Hofmeister (1974) outlined the effective use of multimedia training packages for parents of preschool mentally retarded and physically handicapped children. In this program, a public health nurse utilized a slide-sound presentation, workbooks, and other materials. Through this mode of instruction, parents were taught skills in behavioral control and in training their children's self-care, or self-help skills. Parents of LD children might be taught skills similarly through such packaged materials.

In addition to involvement in the implementation of the individual education plans, parents can assist in the evaluation of the IEP and other aspects of the LD program. As indicated in chapter 4, Hudson and Graham (1978) have identified questions that parents can use to evaluate the implementation of the due process procedures.

Kroth (1975) encourages regular communication between teachers and parents concerning child progress. Through the use of attractive and brief forms, the LD teacher indicates to the parent progress on

By observing each other's techniques in working with an LD child, the parent and teacher can insure consistency.

The teacher can explain diagnostic data to a parent.

certain behaviors. Upon receiving a form, parents praise the child accordingly, sign and return it to the teacher. Such a procedure has been used with varying numbers of students.

Ryan and Ryan (1973) have also found that parents of exceptional children like getting written report cards with more information than traditional grades. Two evaluation procedures that will facilitate reporting progress to parents are criterion-referenced assessment and precision measurement. In the former case, the LD teacher can develop a report card of subject skills and merely indicate skills learned, skills in progress of being learned, and skills unlearned. Beginning and ending dates of learning achievement might also be interesting to parents.

The latter procedure involves the development and maintenance of a graph of a particular behavior, for example, the number of correct and incorrect words read orally in particular materials. After the LD teacher has the child read each day, the teacher or child can mark the graph for that day. Parents can be shown the graph on a regular basis. Worell and Nelson (1974), Cooper and Edge (1978), and Lovitt (1977) explain these procedures in detail.

The need for individualization in meeting the needs and concerns of parents has been emphasized by Karnes and Zehrbach (1972). To involve parents effectively, a teacher must have a positive attitude toward them and develop individualized and realistic activities for them to perform. Karnes and Zehrback suggest guidelines for parent meetings and teaching through parents. Parent meetings are more successful if parents are involved in the planning, babysitting is provided at the site, dynamic speakers and visual aids are used, and so forth. The actual training is more effective if teachers model procedures and offer opportunity for practice.

Shearer (1976) suggests the following considerations for involvement of parents in the actual program, either at home or in the school. First, set regular goals that can be reasonably accomplished in a week or so. Second, show parents what to do and how to do it. Third, have parents practice teaching a skill. Fourth, reinforce the parents for their achievements. Fifth, individualize as necessary to encourage and instruct parents. Sixth, involve the parents in planning.

On the other hand, the indiscriminate use of parents in home instructional programs may have some unfortunate consequences. Neifert and Gayton (1973) have indicated that certain variables in a family structure may adversely affect the success of some home programs. When a mother and father disagree about the significance of the child's learning problem, an actual power struggle may develop between the parents. Other families may already be experiencing multiple problems (e.g., marital, financial, health). These problems may require added attention and make home instruction difficult. The psychological problems of some parents may suggest that another way be found to assist the children. Large families, with busy schedules and a premium on space and parental attention, may also make parental involvement difficult.

PARENT ADVOCACY

Many parents have had unfortunate experiences when they sought diagnostic and remedial assistance for their children. Before educators and other professionals became aware of learning disabilities, parents encountered confusing diagnostic conclusions, a dearth of public school services, and few concrete suggestions concerning intervention.

Tarnopol (1969) and Hennessey (1965) have found that parents were generally dissatisfied with traditional medical and psychological case reports. Parents have also often been prevented from reading the evaluations of their children's performances (Munsey, 1973). Gorham (1975) captured the feeling and experience of many LD parents when she wrote:

> Although I have learned much, I am clearly one of the lost generation of parents of handicapped children. We are parents who are either intimidated by professionals or angry with them, or both; parents who are unreasonably awed by them; parents who intuitively know that we know our children better than the experts of any discipline and yet we persistently assume that the professionals know best; parents who carry so much attitudinal and emotional baggage around with us that we are unable to engage in any real dialogue with professionals—teachers, principals, physicians, or psychologists—about our children. (p. 521)

The other major stumbling block previously encountered by many parents was the scarcity of trained teachers and classes for children with learning disabilities. This is still a major concern in some parts of the United States.

Some of these problems led parents and interested professionals to form coalitions to develop adequate services for children with learning disabilities (Hallahan & Cruickshank, 1973). The Association for Children with Learning Disabilities (ACLD) was officially formed in 1964. While some local groups preceded this parent organization, ACLD represented the first major concerted effort by parents to participate in the development of services for LD children.

ACLD was instrumental in the adoption of the term *learning disabilities* as a viable alternative to more organically and etiologically based terminology (e.g., minimal brain dysfunction). It lobbied for the passage of the Learning Disabilities Act of 1969 (Part G, Title 6) which established federal aid to states for model programs, teacher training, information dissemination, and research.

On the state and local level, ACLD has cooperated with school systems and other agencies to develop services for children with learning disabilities. Conferences have been held at various levels to encourage dissemination of information about learning disabilities and to supply a forum for parental and professional interaction.

In many ways parents are in a better position than professionals to encourage the development of new services for LD children (Tarnopol, 1969). Administrators and teachers often find it difficult to make the necessary changes in school districts (Biklen, 1976). Parents seem to be in a better position to exert the necessary political pressure for legislative changes. In some cases, parents have even been forced to resort to the courts for publicly supported services for children with learning disabilities and other learning problems (Abeson, 1972, 1974; Kuriloff, True, Kirp, & Buss, 1974).

In addition to these services, some parents have also had to use legal action for (1) local screening projects to identify children with handicaps, (2) access to the cumulative folders and diagnostic reports on their children, (3) the opportunity to have their cases heard and to appeal placement decisions, and (4) regular evaluations of the progress of children in special education placements.

P.L. 94-142 has of course made the picture much brighter for LD parents. Continued support for services, safeguards against due process violations, mandates for the identification of LD children, and so forth, erase many of the abuses of the past.

However, new challenges exist for parents of children and adolescents with learning disabilities. There is a dearth of teacher training and school programs in the area of learning disabilities among adolescents. The career, vocational, and college prospects of these young people must be clarified.

The relationship of juvenile delinquency and learning disabilities must also be given attention. Parents must also meet the challenge of nonexistent or inadequate preschool education for their children. These problems are only a few which will attract the energies of strong parent advocacy groups.

PARENT-PROFESSIONAL PARTNERSHIP

As we indicated earlier, the LD teacher can do much to support parent involvement (see table 14-1). Professionals in learning disabilities recognize that parents foster a cooperative atmosphere among people from many fields concerned with the LD child. Parental involvement in habilitative and rehabilitative programs is a necessary condition for an effective program (Kelly, 1974).

Many parents are presently members of the advisory boards for professional organizations, school systems, and teacher-training institutions. They provide a perspective of the whole child for professionals who, by necessity, may consider only some aspects of behavior. P.L. 94-142 has placed particular attention upon the importance and significance of parental input for decision making.

This cooperative effort usually provides parents with accurate knowledge about their child's learning ability, an awareness of the necessary interaction strategies, and an opportunity to help other LD children. In addition, most professionals usually enjoy the benefits accrued from parental encouragement of the behaviors taught in clinical and classroom situations.

The school team can involve the parent in the decision-making process.

Parents and professionals involved in learning disabilities are also working together to develop parent training programs. There are at least four major areas to consider in planning these programs: supporting parents emotionally, exchanging information with parents, improving parent-child interactions, and encouraging parent participation in the program (Lillie, 1976). Initially, a needs assessment must be performed to identify parents' concerns. The LD teacher and cooperating parents can subsequently identify objectives for parent meetings.

There are infinite numbers of topics for parent meetings (Kroth, 1975). LD teachers with the attitude that they can share information about learning disabilities and their LD program with parents will find many interesting ideas for parent education sessions. Other kinds of topics include community resources for medical care and recreation, relationships with professionals and others, and so forth (Kelly, 1974). The LD teacher should be prepared to bring in consultants whenever necessary. Cooper and Edge (1978) discuss problems and solutions for organizing parent education programs.

The efforts of one community in coordinating their efforts to develop awareness and procedures for LD children have been described by Oberst (1973). Physicians, educators, and parents were involved in an impressive series of educational and program planning sessions.

McWhirter (1976) developed a parent education program in learning disabilities. LD definitions, laterality and directionality, visual and auditory perceptual problems, and perceptual-motor difficulties were the topics. Experiential activities were used to help the parents experience the world of the learning disabled.

Finally, many parents have found the journal *Exceptional Parents* helpful in living and working with their learning disabled child. This journal offers articles written by parents and professionals on topics of interest to parents of handicapped children. Other sources of information are ACLD's *Newsbriefs, Closer Look, Journal of Learning Disabilities,* and state departments of education. Moore and Morton (1976) have compiled a guide to these sources and others.

PARENTAL INVOLVEMENT: IN PERSPECTIVE

Professionals certainly carry a tremendous responsibility for encouraging intelligent parental involvement. Recent changes in traditional diagnostic procedures have begun to remove the devastating impact of labels and perfunctory clinical conclusions. Educationally relevant assessment and accompanying practical suggestions should clarify the necessary goals and strategies for all LD children. The astute clinician can also cooperatively identify reasonable objectives and activities for parental involvement.

P.L. 94-142 mandates many activities for LD parents. The LD teachers have the responsibility to support parent participation. Professionals must learn to relate to parents on levels different than the ones they are used to; they can involve parents actively in the assessment and remedial aspects of their child's program.

LD teachers must also become sensitive to the needs and concerns of parents. Sometimes there are communication problems (Kroth, 1975). Professionals need skills such as active listening and other techniques to clarify parental concerns. Then and only then can parents and teachers develop a coordinated program for LD children.

LD teachers must also begin to develop various kinds of parent education programs. Through these experiences parents can be equipped to perform the many responsibilities suggested by P.L. 94-142.

Professionals in learning disabilities must expect half-heartedness and even resistance to parent participation in school programs from administrators and teachers. General education has not fostered as much parent involvement as it could. LD teachers, in cooperation with parents, will have to move intelligently and cautiously in order to provide the necessary parent programs.

We must broaden our perspective of educational settings to include the home and playground. Teachers and other professionals desire the transfer of learned behaviors to settings other than the classroom. Parents will be helpful in this regard.

It is also our belief that parent-child interactions and other dimensions of the home environment should be a research priority. Studies should include all socioeconomic, cultural, and social classes. Middle-class and upper-class homes should be as closely scrutinized as lower socio-economic homes have been previously.

Fathers and siblings need also be considered more in planning for parental involvement. Mothers seem to take the major role in home instruction and other efforts to help their children. *Family* involvement should be the emphasis, rather than *maternal* involvement.

Additional study and use of parents as tutors is warranted and justified. Many youngsters require individual tutoring to review and practice deficient skills. Willing parents can be enlisted to help the increasing numbers of children with mild learning disabilities. This practice can prevent unnecessary labeling practices and free special teachers to spend more time with severely disabled children.

Parents should also be encouraged to continue their zealous pursuit of improved services for LD children. Their influence and support is something that no professional group could possibly supply.

However, special education services and teacher training practices are undergoing profound changes. The current trend to delabel and decategorize these services suggests that all parent groups interested in various handicapping conditions should cooperatively plan for special education services.

Finally, professionals in all fields have the ethical responsibility to suggest only well-proven assessment and treatment procedures to parents of children with learning disabilities. Driven by anxiety and frustration, parents may be prone to accept the latest fad. Physicians, educators, and other professionals must be confident in their procedures, lest parents establish unrealistic expectations.

SUMMARY

In this chapter we have described the impact of P.L. 94-142 on the role of parents of LD children. There are many actual and possible parental activities in different aspects of the LD child's program. They must be involved in screening, assessment, planning, implementation, and evaluation. Parental advocacy and training must be supported by professionals. In cooperation with professionals, parents can develop a familial and educational support system needed by LD children.

SUGGESTED ACTIVITIES

1. Interview parents of an LD child about their experience in obtaining diagnostic and remedial services for their child. Develop a directory of local resources from what they tell you.
2. Ask parents to evaluate their experiences at a placement conference. Were they satisfied? Use the questions suggested by Hudson and Graham (1978).
3. Review the activities suggested for parents in table 14-1. Identify the skills that parents would need to perform the functions. How would you get them the training?
4. Ask an LD parent and a parent of a child with another kind of disability (e.g., physical, hearing, etc.) about their reactions to their child's handicap. Are the responses different? If so, why?
5. Attend an ACLD meeting. If a chapter of the ACLD does not exist in your area, assist parents in organizing one.
6. Organize a parent volunteer group for a school. Develop the necessary plans for training, role descriptions, schedule, and so forth.
7. Prepare a brief presentation about LD for the PTA. Stress techniques for identification and referral.
8. Interview a principal and teachers about their feelings concerning parent involvement. Identify the critical obstacles posed by their views.

References

Abeson, A. Movement and momentum: Government and the education of handicapped children—I. *Exceptional Children,* 1972, *39,* 63-66.

Abeson, A. Movement and momentum: Government and the education of handicapped children—II. *Exceptional Children,* 1974, *41,* 109-116.

Abrams, J. & Kaslow, F. Family systems and the learning disabled child: Intervention and treatment. *Journal of Learning Disabilities,* 1977, *10,* 86-90.

ACLD Newsbriefs. Association for Children with Learning Disabilities, 4156 Library Road, Pittsburgh, Pa., 15236.

Barsh, R. Counseling the parent of the brain-injured child. *Journal of Rehabilitation,* 1961, *27,* 26.

Becker, W.C. *Parents and teachers.* Champaign, Ill.: Research Press, 1971.

Behrman, P., & Millman, J. *EXCEL—Experience for children in learning.* Cambridge, Mass.: Educators Publishing Service, 1973.

Biklen, D. Advocacy comes of age. *Exceptional Children,* 1976, *42,* 308-314.

Brown, G.W. Suggestions for parents. *Journal of Learning Disabilities,* 1969, *2,* 40-47.

Bryant, J.E. Parent-child relationships: Their effect on rehabilitation. *Journal of Learning Disabilities,* 1971, *4,* 325-329.

Coe, Sr. M.A. Parent involvement in remedial reading instruction. *Academic Therapy,* 1971, *6,* 407-410.

Closer Look. National Information Center for the Handicapped, Box 1492, Washington, D.C., 20013.

Cooper, J.O., & Edge, D. *Parenting: Strategies and educational methods.* Columbus, Ohio: Charles E. Merrill, 1978.

Exceptional Parent. Psy-Ed Corp., 262 Beacon Street, Boston, Mass., 02116.

Galloway, C., & Galloway, K.C. Parent classes in precise behavior management. *Teaching Exceptional Children,* 1971, *3,* 120-128.

Gorham, K. A lost generation of parents. *Exceptional Children,* 1975, *41,* 521-526.

Hallahan, D., & Cruickshank, W. *Psychoeducational foundations of learning disabilities.* Englewood Cliffs, N.J.: Prentice-Hall, 1973.

Hayden, A. Perspectives of early childhood education in special education. In N. Haring (Ed.), *Behavior of exceptional children.* Columbus, Ohio: Charles E. Merrill, 1974.

Hayes, M. *Oh Dear, Somebody said, "Learning disabilities." A book for teachers and parents.* San Rafael, Calif.: Academic Therapy Publications, 1975.

Hennessey, E. A study of diagnostic services for brain-injured children. Bethesda, Md.: 1965. (ERIC Document Reproduction Service No. ED018886).

Hudson, F., & Graham, S. An approach to operationalizing the I.E.P. *Learning Disability Quarterly,* 1978, *1,* 13-32.

Journal of Learning Disabilities. The Professional Press, Inc., 101 E. Ontario St., Chicago, Ill., 60611.

Kagan, J. On class differences and early development. In V.H. Deneberg (Ed.), *Education of the infant and young child.* New York: Academic Press, 1970.

Karnes, M.B., & Zehrbach, R.R. Flexibility in getting parents involved in school. *Teaching Exceptional Children,* 1972, *5,* 6-18.

Kelly, E.J. *Parent-teacher interaction.* Seattle, Wash.: Special Child Publications, 1974.

Keogh, B., & Becker, L. Early detection of learning problems: Questions, cautions, and guidelines. *Exceptional Children,* 1973, *40,* 5-12.

Kroth, R.L. *Communicating with parents of exceptional children.* Denver: Love Publishing, 1975.

Kroth, R.L., & Simpson, R.L. *Parent conferences as a teaching strategy.* Denver: Love Publishing, 1977.

Kuriloff, P., True, R., Kirp, D., & Buss, W. Legal reform and educational change: The Pennsylvania case. *Exceptional Children,* 1974, *41,* 35-42.

Latham, G., & Hofmeister, A. A mediated training program for parents of the preschool mentally retarded. *Exceptional Children,* 1974, *41,* 35-42.

Lillie, D. An overview to parent programs. In D. Lillie & P. Trohanis (Eds.), *Teaching parents to teach.* New York: Walker and Co., 1976.

Losen, S.M., & Diament, B. *Parent conference in the schools.* Boston: Allyn & Bacon, 1978.

Lovitt, T. *In spite of my resistance . . . I've learned from children.* Columbus, Ohio: Charles E. Merrill, 1977.

Marsh, II, G.E., Gearheart, C.Z., & Gearheart, B.R. *The learning disabled adolescent.* St. Louis: Mosby, 1978.

McLoughlin, J.A., Edge, D., & Strenecky, B. Perspective on parent involvement in the diagnosis and treatment of learning disabled children. *Journal of Learning Disabilities,* 1978, *13,* 295-300.

McWhirter, J.J. A parent education group in learning disabilities. *Journal of Learning Disabilities,* 1976, *9,* 16-20.

Minde, K. *A parent's guide to hyperactivity.* Quebec, Canada: Quebec Association for Children with Learning Disabilities, 1971.

Moore, C.B., & Morton, K.G. *A reader's guide for parents of children with mental, physical or emotional disabilities.* DHEW Publication No. (HSA) 77-5290. Rockville, Md.: HEW, Bureau of Community Health Services, 1976.

Munsey, B. The parent's right to read. *Journal of Learning Disabilities,* 1973, *6,* 392-394.

Neifert, J.T., & Gayton, W.F. Parents and the home program approach in the remediation of learning disabilities. *Journal of Learning Disabilities,* 1973, *6,* 85-89.

Oberst, B.B. A community approach to a specific learning disability: The Omaha "Starr" Project. *Journal of Learning Disabilities,* 1973, *6,* 421-429.

Patterson, R.R. *Families*. Champaign, Ill.: Research Press, 1971.

Quick, A.D., Little, T.L., & Campbell, A.A. Early childhood education for exceptional foster children and training of foster parents. *Exceptional Children*, 1973, *40*, 206-207.

Ryan, S.B., & Ryan, R.E. Report cards? Why not ask the parents? *Teaching Exceptional Children*, 1973, *6*, 34-37.

Shearer, M.S. A home-based parent training model. In D. Lillie & P. Trohanis (Eds.), *Teaching parents to teach*. New York: Walker & Co., 1976.

Sloman, L., & Webster, C. Assessing the parents of the learning disabled child: A semistructured interview procedure. *Journal of Learning Disabilities*, 1978, *11*, 73-79.

Smith, J.M., & Smith, D.E.P. *Child management: A program for parents and teachers*. Champaign, Ill.: Research Press Co., 1976.

Stewart, J.C. *Counseling parents of exceptional children*. Columbus, Ohio: Charles E. Merrill, 1978.

Stott, D.H. *The parent as teacher*. Toronto, Canada: New Press, 1972.

Strenecky, B., McLoughlin, J.A., & Edge, D. Parent involvement: A consumer perspective—in the schools. *Education and Training of the Mentally Retarded*, in press.

Tarnopol, L. Parent and professional relations. In L. Tarnopol (Ed.), *Learning disabilities*. Springfield, Ill.: Charles C Thomas, 1969.

Valett, R.E. *Modifying children's behavior: A guide for parents and professionals*. Palo Alto, Calif.: Fearon, 1969.

Wetter, J. Parents' attitudes toward learning disability. *Exceptional Children*, 1972, *38*, 490.

Worell, J., & Nelson, C. *Managing instructional problems*. New York: McGraw-Hill, 1974.

Issues in Learning Disabilities

PREVIEW

Learning disabilities as a self-conscious discipline is a phenomenon of the 1960s and 70s. The proliferation of services for LD students during this period of time is both unique and unparalleled in the history of services to handicapped children. The implementation of a full range of public school programs for LD children and youth and the establishment of professional organizations, journals, and certification standards are reflective of the surge of both public and professional interest (Wallace, 1976). Nevertheless, a number of important issues in this field remain essentially unresolved. Some of these issues serve as the focus of this chapter.

Confusion regarding definitions of LD has been a persistently perplexing issue for special educators. The lack of consensus among professionals concerning what specifically constitutes a learning disability is a problem basic to many other issues. In this chapter, we discuss some reasons why LD has been difficult to define. A number of suggestions are also offered for helping to resolve this crucial issue.

Another important issue involves the controversial therapies offered through the medical profession. Some of these medical treatments are discussed and evaluated.

The issue of where to educate the LD student is another problem which has persisted throughout the years. Moreover, P.L. 94-142 guidelines have added the mainstreaming variable as another factor that must be considered in placing the LD student in the most appropriate educational environment. Interdisciplinary concerns, too, must also be considered an outgrowth of P.L. 94-142 guidelines. Both of these issues are discussed in terms of past problems and recommendations for the future.

A currently debated topic in learning disabilities is the issue of process training. We summarize the important components of this debate as gleaned from current research. We also share our opinion in regard to this controversial topic.

In describing the major concepts and characteristics of learning disabilities, we have reflected on past and present practices in this constantly developing area of interest. However, our discussion throughout the book has also been organized so as to suggest a number of important issues in this field. In particular, we tried to explain traditional perceptions of the major aspects in the LD concept. The "in perspective" sections were intended to appraise some prevalent practices realistically, but only after fair and accurate images of these practices were presented.

The discussion of *definition* indicated a directional change in the concept of learning disabilities. The prevalent mood among educators in learning disabilities toward *causative* considerations suggested that a number of very controversial therapies were being considered very cautiously. The presentation of *diagnosis* and *assessment* procedures suggested a shift from diagnosis for placement to assessment for teaching and the inclusion of teacher input throughout the appraisal process.

The descriptions of learning problems, assessment techniques, and methodologies in part two reflected a wide assortment of influences. It was sometimes difficult to suggest the appropriateness of one methodology over another. However, the format of discussion suggested emerging techniques to encourage children *how* to learn and *what* to learn.

Part three has reflected a similar readjustment in the areas of educational provision, early childhood education, adolescence and adults, and parental involvement. The emergence of a broader concept of educational and other service provisions was indicated. Efforts in early childhood education and adult education highlighted the need for a broad support system in learning disabilities. Finally, the preceding chapter illustrated how involved parents have been and will continue to be in the total development of their children.

In this concluding chapter, we intend to develop further what may have been suggested throughout various chapters of this book. Some of the important issues to which the learning disabilities field must address itself in the next few years are listed and discussed in this chapter. Each of these issues is involved in a gradually emerging literature which we have identified and which promises to refute or validate many of these issues in the future.

DEFINITIONAL CONSIDERATIONS

Learning disabled, by definition, describes a *specific* population of handicapped children. The term is *not* intended to be used as a broad classification for all children experiencing learning problems in our schools. However, throughout the relatively brief history of this field, the definitional problem has been a persistently crucial issue which is still hotly debated by many professionals.

As mentioned throughout this book and specifically discussed in chapters 1 and 2, we believe it is a mistake to label anywhere from 5% to 30% of a given school population as learning disabled. This practice is a gross misconception of what actually constitutes a learning disability and unfortunately detracts from the provision of services to students who exhibit severe LD problems (Larsen, 1978).

It has been suggested that a large number of students who are referred for learning disabilities placement have IQs in the 80 to 90 range. Ames (1977) points out that this group of children suffers and struggles and often fails. She believes that these students are usually too intelligent for a class of retarded children, but yet they are not able to keep up with the regular class. Larsen (1978) also points out that many of these children are simply unmotivated, poorly taught, or come from home environments where scholastic success is not highly valued.

Other groups of children who are often mistakenly identified as learning disabled include students who are simply academically over-placed, those with uneven abilities, and the tremendous number of boys and girls who suffer from minor physical difficulties such as poor vision or hearing, an inadequate behavior chemistry, or allergies (Ames, 1977).

The Kirk and Elkins (1975) study also lends support to the notion that many children are inappropriately classified as being learning disabled. The purpose of this project was to study the characteristics of over 3,000 children enrolled in the federally-funded Child Service Demonstration Centers for Learning Disabilities in 21 states. The results revealed that many children served by the projects were simply underachieving students and that the distribution of IQs contained a larger proportion with below average ability than is found in the general population of children.

It should also be noted that the differences among various states in defining learning disabilities have contributed to the confusion and misunderstandings in this area. In some states, children with behavioral problems are considered eligible for LD programs, while other states specifically exclude these children from the learning disabilities category. The Mercer, Forgnone, and Wolking (1976) study of 42 state departments of education, for example, attempted to operationalize the LD definitions used by each state. Their analysis of the state definitions reflected the tremendously diverse nature of the term *learning disabilities*. Table 15-1 provides the exact number and percentage breakdown for each of the definitional components analyzed in this study.

We find the continual expansion of the learning disabilities classification to be particularly distressing. We also find it regrettable that solutions to this problem are almost nonexistent even though some writers have recommended a number of excellent suggestions. Lovitt (1978), for example, feels that attempts to define LD will continue to be useless until intelligence and achievement tests are no longer used as the primary means for classifying children. He believes that direct, daily measurements should replace intelligence and achievement tests since these tests do not reveal an index of learning, nor are they frequent or direct measures of identified behavior.

Myers and Hammill (1976) suggest that the parameters of the LD population must be at least operationally defined. They recommend that a new definition

Table 15-1

Number of states and respective percentages of various components included in state LD definitions

components	no. of states	percent
Definition		
NACHC only	9	21.4%
NACHC with variations	15	35.7%
Different	16	38.1%
None	2	4.8%
Intelligence		
Average and above	11	26.2%
Above mental retardation	8	19.1%
Not stated	23	54.8%
Process		
Process disorder	36	85.7%
Language disorder	35	83.3%
Academic		
Reading	31	73.8%
Writing	31	73.8%
Spelling	31	73.8%
Arithmetic	31	73.8%
Exclusion—primary		
Visual impairment	26	61.9%
Auditory impairment	26	61.9%
Motor impairment	23	54.8%
Mental retardation	21	50.0%
Emotional disturbance	25	59.5%
Environmental dis-advantaged	23	54.8%
Exclusion—primary & secondary		
Visual impairment	3	7.1%
Auditory impairment	3	7.1%
Motor impairment	2	4.8%
Mental retardation	11	26.2%
Emotional disturbance	1	2.4%
Environmental dis-advantaged	1	2.4%
Neurological Impairment		
Included	4	9.5%
Not included	0	.0%
Possible	26	61.9%
Not stated	12	28.6%

Table 15-1 (*cont.*)

components	no. of states	percent
Affective		
Includes emotionally disturbed	4	9.5%
Includes socially maladjusted	6	14.3%
Miscellaneous		
Attention deficits	5	11.9%
Motor deficits	7	16.7%
Thinking deficits	30	71.4%
Discrepancy component	12	28.6%
Special education required	14	33.3%
Intraindividual differences	4	9.5%
Prevalence	2	4.8%
Chronological age	4	9.5%

From "Definitions of Learning Disabilities Used in the United States" by C.D. Mercer, C. Forgnone, and W.D. Wolking, *Journal of Learning Disabilities*, 1976, *9*, 381. Copyright 1976 by Professional Press, Inc. Reprinted by permission.

embody the fundamental intuitions of the old ones, be practical enough for use in the schools, be specific enough to permit the identification of research samples, be clear and straightforward in wording, be educational in focus, and be brief in length. (p. 10)

On the other hand, Senf (1977) believes that no definition of learning disabilities formulated at either the federal or state levels can be responsive to the diverse theoretical perspectives of either research or practice. He recommends that multiple means of operationally defining LD be fostered for research purposes and that these definitions be empirically replicable by other investigators.

It is our hope that the P.L. 94-142 definition of learning disabilities (see chap. 2) helps to foster some uniformity and consistency among state and local educational agencies. In the meantime, we believe that specific criteria must be developed in order to provide guidelines for determining the boundaries of the learning disability classification. Learning disabilities specialists must also guard against the continual expansion of the LD category. We believe that professional educators must take an activist role in protecting the integrity of the LD field. Otherwise, as noted by Larsen (1976), the professional talents of the LD specialist will be misused and, in many cases, essentially wasted.

CONTROVERSIAL THERAPIES

Various therapies and treatments for remediating a student's specific learning disabilities have been recommended by individuals from a wide variety of fields, and many of these approaches have recently been subjected to vigorous investigation by researchers. Some of the most controversial treatments are discussed in this section.

Medication

The administration of various drugs to control the "hyperkinetic" behavior of LD children has certainly been a widely debated topic in recent years. Some believe that all children with suggested "minimal brain dysfunction" should be given medication on at least a trial basis (Wender, 1971), while other professionals urge caution in prescribing drugs to children (Kornetsky, 1975).

The most widely used drugs have been the chemical stimulant drugs such as Ritalin and amphetamines, which have been generally regarded as most effective for providing a calming effect on very active children. Ritalin is probably the most frequently prescribed drug for helping to control hyperactivity. Generally, according to Quinn (1976), it is thought that the stimulant drugs increase attention, increase the speed of response, decrease the amount of motor behavior, and increase motivation.

Nonetheless, efficacy studies of drug therapy with LD students are actually very rare. In this regard, the Sroufe (1975) article, as reviewed by Kauffman (1977), includes the following major points:

1. Studies of drug effects have been almost exclusively short-term assays. Practically nothing is known about the long-term effects of drugs on children's behavior.
2. Even the short-term physical side effects of drugs (e.g., loss of appetite, insomnia) have been inadequately researched. There are no research data on the possible long-term physical side effects (e.g., effects on linear growth or weight gain).
3. Little or nothing is known about the effects of drugs on conceptual abilities.
4. How particular types of children will respond to specific medications cannot be predicted with much accuracy or confidence.
5. Placebo effects (i.e., effects attributable to the fact that the child is receiving a "pill" of some kind, whether it contains the active drug ingredient or not) have not been adequately researched. The expectation set for the child when he is given the drug and the environment in which the child lives during drug treatment may have a profound effect on the outcome.
6. Behavior modification or educational intervention may often eliminate the need for drugs or considerably reduce disruptive behavior. At

present there is little evidence that medication is superior to behavior modification or tutoring or that drugs enhance the effects of other methods of behavioral control. Drug effects must be considered within the context of reinforcement and other environmental manipulation.

7. More research is needed to assess the possible relationship between medication prescribed for the control of young children's behavior and later drug abuse or the availability of drugs to individuals for whom they are not intended.

8. Drug treatment may offer so facile a "solution" to behavioral difficulties that improvement of the child's home or school environment is over-looked. Drugs may be used as an excuse for avoiding professional commitment to the needs of children. (p. 151)

In sum, it seems apparent that additional research is needed before more definite conclusions can be made regarding the efficacy of drug therapy with LD students. In addition to improving methodological deficiencies and problems of definition, we believe that long-term studies should be a priority for future investigations.

Food Additives

A number of hypotheses consider food additives to be the major cause of hyperactivity and learning disabilities. According to Sieben (1977), all foods containing additives, dyes, or natural salicylates are to be excluded from the diet of hyperactive LD students. The theoretical basis for the hypothesis was proposed by Feingold (1975). A diet, known as the Kaiser-Permanente diet (K-P diet), is usually prescribed for the child who follows this treatment. The K-P diet eliminates all chemical additives (see chap. 3).

It is generally recommended that the food additive hypothesis be considered as still in the developmental stages. Additional controlled research is needed before general acceptance (Lerner, 1976). In fact, Spring and Sandoval (1976) recommend a moratorium on further public advocacy of the Feingold hypothesis until the efficacy of the diet for a defined population is firmly established by controlled investigations.

Megavitamins

Megavitamin therapy refers to the use of vitamins in quantities up to one thousand times the usual daily requirement for treatment of a wide range of problems including autism, hyperactivity, and learning disabilities (Sieben, 1977). Cott (1971) is generally attributed with introducing the megavitamin therapy to the LD population. He reports that the treatment is an effective approach for the learning disabled. However, many physicians question the claims of megavitamin theorists and the lack of empirical data to support the observations made by the advocates of this approach. The American Academy of Pediatrics Committee on Nutrition published a statement (1976) which concluded that mega-vitamin therapy is not justified as a treatment for learning disabilities in children.

Finally, we believe that it is important to point out that the burden of proof for each of these treatments should rest with the advocates of these theories. We agree with Sieben (1977) who suggests that the promoter of each theory should perform studies which test the validity of each hypothesis. In sum, he believes that it is a tremendous disservice to the individual child and the public at large to promote a hypothesis as fact without first submitting it to the rigors of meaningful scientific scrutiny.

EDUCATIONAL PROVISIONS

Many school districts provide a variety of educational provisions for LD students due to the varying degrees of involvement usually found among this group of children. Generally, however, most children with learning disabilities receive their special instruction in the regular class, the resource room, or in special classes. According to Myers and Hammill (1976), the regular class usually accommodates the mild to moderate cases, the resource room handles moderately involved youngsters, and special class placement is most often reserved for the moderately to severely impaired LD student.

This issue of instructional placement, nevertheless, is a topic which continues to be debated by many professional educators. Larsen (1978), for example, notes that some state education agencies and local school districts regard resource rooms as the *only* appropriate educational provision for LD students. He argues that the arrangement is woefully lacking in the intense and long-term educational programming that is absolutely essential for many severely handicapped LD students.

On the other hand, Lovitt (1978) points out that arguments over the location for instructing the learning disabled may have been decided by P.L. 94-142, which provides for the *least restrictive* educational environment. He believes this provision will be interpreted to mean that most LD students should be assigned to regular classes and that few of the learning disabled will be educated in self-contained classes.

The mainstreaming process, however, has not been without its critics. For example, Cruikshank (1974) notes his concerns regarding the handicapped child who is not fully accepted by the regular educator and the handicapped students who stand out as different from their non-handicapped peers. Additional concerns have been voiced by Lovitt (1978) who believes that the mainstreaming movement has progressed too rapidly and with little research support. Also, very few regular teachers have generally been consulted about the feasibility of this approach.

We believe that the mainstreaming concept is a viable instructional alternative for some LD students. However, it must be considered to be part of a continuum of services, and one which will be rarely used with many learning disabled students due to their severe and pervasive academic disorders. As noted by Larsen (1978), "pupils whose problems are moderate to severe in intensity will require an educational arrangement where their needs can be addressed on a full-day basis until skills and abilities are elevated to a level where successful matriculation into the regular classroom is a definite possibility" (p. 10).

In addition to the increased development of educational services for all age groups of LD children and youth, we recommend that provisions for LD students will also need to develop in every area, including physical and mental health, socioeconomic development, academics, and career education. School systems will obviously need to expand service delivery systems to meet all of the needs of individual children. Lastly, while the age range of 2 to 21 is usually mentioned for educational services, our discussion in chapter 13 indicates that adults over 21 may also benefit from this trend.

In conclusion, we would like to reiterate a point we discussed in chapter 11. As mentioned, we regret every extension of the LD specialist's role (e.g., consulting, in-service teaching) because direct teaching of children is lessened, and LD programs become increasingly diluted. We believe *teaching* these children in the appropriate environment with suitable methodology should continue to be the focus of our professional efforts.

PROCESS TRAINING

The field of special education and, in particular, the area of learning disabilities have been plagued by a variety of philosophies of treatment that are associated with questionable assessment and remedial procedures (Vellutino, Steger, Moyer, Harding, & Niles, 1977). The *process approach* is an example of a popular and widely accepted theory which recently has been seriously questioned in the professional literature.

The process approach in education is specifically associated with the varied models and theories of psychological processes that were developed to describe numerous mental operations such as reception, memory, association, perception, and so forth (Newcomer, 1975). Some of the most popular process approaches have included the tests and materials based on the models proposed by Frostig, Getman, and Kirk-Osgood. Tests representing these models include The Marianne Frostig Developmental Test of Visual Perception (Frostig, Lefever, & Whittlesey, 1964), the Illinois Test of Psycholinguistic Abilities (ITPA) (Kirk, McCarthy, & Kirk, 1968), and the Auditory Discrimination Test (Wepman, 1958). A number of widely used instructional activities and programs based upon a process approach have also been developed by Frostig & Horne (1964), Minskoff, Wiseman, and Minskoff (1972), and Bush and Giles (1977).

Although the basic assumptions underlying training are the same, some individuals prefer making reference to specific types of process training (i.e., *perceptual* training or *psycholinguistic* training). Nevertheless, according to Newcomer (1975), those individuals who utilize a process-oriented approach all assume the following:

(a) the particular theoretical premises which they adopt constitute a valid model for learning;

(b) the manner in which they operationalize these tenets for the purpose of diagnosing learning disabilities has prevailing value in education; and

(c) it is efficacious to train psychological processes. (p. 6)

In regard to the first assumption, we believe our discussion of various perceptual-motor theories in chapter 10 clearly suggests that they lack any sound theoretical basis. Similarly, the basic theoretical tenets of psycholinguistic models have been criticized in the literature (Hammill & Larsen, 1974; Newcomer, Larsen, & Hammill, 1975).

Regarding the second and third assumptions listed for those advocating a process approach in education, our discussion of the efficacy of perceptual-motor assessment and training (see chap. 10) questions the lack of an empirical foundation for either testing or training in this area. In addition, some recent evidence indicates that the effectiveness of psycholinguistic training is essentially nonvalidated.

The apparent genesis of the debate regarding the efficacy of psycholinguistic training began with the Hammill and Larsen (1974) study which concluded that the effectiveness of psycholinguistic training had not been definitely demonstrated. The Hammill and Larsen article reviewed 38 studies which attempted to train children in psycholinguistic skills using the ITPA as the criterion for improvement. Approximately two-thirds of the studies were reexamined by Lund, Foster, and McCall-Perez (1978) who indicated that some of the original 38 studies had been inaccurately reported, inappropriately categorized, and/or misinterpreted. These changes were responded to by Hammill and Larsen (1978) in an article essentially reaffirming their position that psycholinguistic training remains nonvalidated.

In our opinion, the lack of any clearcut experimental data verifying psycholinguistic approaches leads us to strongly question the use of training programs based upon the psycholinguistic model. We are skeptical of these approaches for many of the same reasons we dispute the use of perceptual-motor programs. As noted by Hammill and Larsen (1978), the burden of documenting the essential value of these approaches rests with the individuals who produce and/or advocate their usage in our schools.

In conclusion, we would like to strongly recommend the assessment and treatment principles offered by Vellutino and his colleagues (1977). We wholeheartedly endorse their suggestions that testing and training procedures should:

1. Focus upon performance and task variables in units that most closely approximate the skill to be learned,
2. Emphasize direct instruction rather than discovery methods of learning,
3. Ascertain and capitalize upon competencies already possessed by the learner,
4. Incorporate no assumptions about the learner's ability to acquire a specific skill—as a result of tenuous or ill-founded etiological theories, or prior to attempts at teaching him that skill, and
5. Facilitate development of individualized programs. (p. 383)

INTERDISCIPLINARY CONCERNS

Professionals from many different disciplines have, for much longer than generally assumed, provided supplementary educational assistance for students who now comprise the LD population (Maitland, 1976). Remedial reading teachers, for example, have been assisting students experiencing reading failure for many years. Similarly, speech and language clinicians have had a continuing concern for the language problems exhibited by scores of LD children. Consequently, the vested interest in the disabled learner, recently exhibited by various professional groups, is not unexpected in view of the long history of involvement with this type of child by different disciplines (Wallace, 1976).

Recently, professional disputes have arisen as to which groups are best qualified to instruct the LD child. The problems associated with the issue have been referred to as the *territorial rights* issue (Larsen, 1976). For the most part, according to Myers and Hammill (1976), the jurisdictional problems exist between the LD specialist and

(a) those who up to now have been exclusively responsible for conducting educational assessment, for example, the school psychologist and the educational diagnostician,
(b) those who have been providing remedial reading and arithmetic services, and
(c) those who have been managing the speech and language problems of children. (pp. 108-109)

It has been noted that the territorial rights problems might be due to any or all of the following reasons: maintaining handicapped children in regular classes, increasing the number of resource and consultant programs in public schools, and providing services for exceptional children under traditional special education categories (Wiederholt, 1975). In addition, Lovitt (1978) believes that the lack of professional consensus regarding a definition of the learning disabled, varying state regulations, and differential professional training programs might also account for the confusion, jealousy, and suspicion among various professionals.

There is no doubt that the problems associated with territorial rights are both varied and exceedingly complex. Unfortunately, many competent professionals are being denied the opportunity of working with disabled students due to misunderstandings regarding terminology, faulty certification regulations, and discriminating funding.

Terminology and Definition

We believe that the lack of consensus among professionals concerning what specifically constitutes a learning disability is a central problem in the issue of territorial rights. According to Lovitt (1978), each discipline seems to have its own definition for handicapped students. Sartain (1976), for example, notes that the term *reading disability* is commonly used in the schools even though there is no universally accepted definition. Other professionals utilize the classification of learning disabled for all children not learning in school, or for those children who are merely underachieving in one academic subject. Under these circumstances, it has often become impossible to implement educational programs because of the resulting confusion of who it is these programs should serve and which professionals should be involved (Wallace, 1976).

The definition of learning disabilities included in P.L. 94-142 (see chaps. 1 and 2) might help to alleviate some of the confusion regarding definition and terminology since this definition deals specifically with children and youth who have very *severe* and *specific* learning disabilities. Broader groups of children with more general learning problems are not intended to be included in this definition. How this definition is operationalized by various school districts will, of course, become the essential variable in the months and years ahead. Nonetheless, it is our belief that there is little chance that problems associated with who should teach will ever be settled if there is disagreement on who should be taught.

Professional Training and Certification

According to Stick (1976), the majority of institutions of higher learning in this country have not modified existing training programs to reflect recent trends and needs, but instead continue to prepare teachers in a manner similar to that of over two decades ago. Moreover, there is usually very little communication across the disciplines when it comes to professional training. Jacupcak's (1975) description of his study, for example, "noted both the absence of LD coursework in descriptions of training provided by reading specialists and few courses in corrective or remedial reading in the training of LD graduates" (p. 156).

The lack of uniform certification standards across the country can certainly be considered a part of the problem. Lovitt (1978) points out that there is little consistency from one state to another in certifying LD specialists or remedial reading teachers. For example, 32 states have no specific coursework requirements in developmental or remedial reading for LD certification (Lewandowski, 1977). Very few states require learning disability coursework for remedial reading teachers or speech and language clinicians, even though 47 states mention the category of learning disabilities in their administrative guidelines (Larsen, 1976).

Although certification standards have been of concern to professionals for some period of time, very little cooperation has been noted among states in this regard. From our vantage point, it seems that *national* professional organizations might be the key element for any future national rules and regulations for certification. We believe that various professional organizations (e.g., Division for Children with Learning Disabilities) must attempt to establish some sort of national consistency for certification regulations by proposing a number of appropriate standards. The recently published *Code of Ethics and Competencies for Teachers of Learning Disabled Children and Youth* by DCLD (1978) must certainly be considered an excellent initiative in this regard.

State and Federal Funding

It has been noted that the issue of state and federal funding of so-called LD projects seems to have contributed to further separation of professionals involved with LD children (Wallace, 1976). Because funds have been more readily available for initiating programs in this area, school districts have sometimes implemented questionable LD programs. Similarly, Lovitt (1978) contends that when monies became scarce for reading and speech programs and when their personnel were cut, they found a possible source of revenue in LD funds. The Kirk and Elkins (1975) study, for example, showed that approximately two-thirds of the cases identified as LD in the federally funded Title VI-G projects in the country were essentially reading problems. Sartain (1976) points out the potential tragedy in this situation when some school districts, because of discriminatory funding, dismiss their remedial reading teachers and turn all of the remedial pupils over to LD teachers.

As mentioned throughout this book, we believe that all children with learning disabilities must be individually judged. Not all LD children will require the services of a speech and language clinician, nor will they require a psychiatric examination. Consequently, many writers have begun to question the usefulness and relevance of an interdisciplinary approach for all children. Maitland (1976) points out that the most common concerns include: (a) the arbitrary referral of children for a full range of evaluation procedures without regard for individual needs; *(b)* the detrimental effects of professional prejudices that often interfere with successful programming; and *(c)* the lack of follow through in regard to program implementation. Nevertheless, we believe that co-operative efforts among professionals are possible, for example, in establishing funding priorities, or in revising local, state, and federal regulations concerned with certification standards. Moreover, Larsen (1976) provides what we consider to be the most reasonable approach for solving the issue of who should work with the LD child when he suggests that the individual with the demonstrated skills corresponding to the needs of the student should take responsibility for carrying out an appropriate educational plan for the LD pupil.

SUMMARY

Some of the most important issues in learning disabilities were discussed in this chapter: definitional considerations, controversial therapies, educational provisions, process training, and interdisciplinary concerns. The background of each issue was briefly described, and our impressions and opinions concerning each issue were outlined.

SUGGESTED ACTIVITIES

1. List some additional issues in learning disabilities to which the field must address itself in the next few years.
2. Upon your completion of this book, write another definition of learning disabilities and compare it to the definition written after you completed reading the first chapter.
3. List and discuss some common misconceptions about learning disabilities. How have your conceptions of this field changed since reading this book?
4. Arrange a visit with an LD specialist in your local school district and ask the specialist to discuss the issues which he or she feels are important to the LD field.
5. Debate the pros and cons of the issues discussed in this chapter and discuss your own opinion of each issue.
6. Arrange to visit a physician in your community who is knowledgeable about learning disabilities. Discuss his opinion of the controversial therapies (medication, food additives, and megavitamins) discussed in this chapter.

7. Review the Hammill and Larsen (1974, 1978) and Lund, Foster, and McCall-Perez (1978) articles discussed in this chapter. Formulate your own impression of psycholinguistic training after reading these articles.

8. Discuss the pros and cons of each of the educational provisions discussed in this chapter. List the characteristics of the child for whom each provision is most applicable.

References

American Academy of Pediatrics Committee on Nutrition. Megavitamin therapy for childhood psychoses and learning disabilities. *Pediatrics*, 1976, *58*, 910-912.

Ames, L.B. Learning disabilities: Time to check our roadmaps? *Journal of Learning Disabilities*, 1977, *10*, 328-330.

Bush, W.J., & Giles, M.T. *Aids to psycholinguistic teaching* (2nd ed.). Columbus, Ohio: Charles E. Merrill, 1976.

Cott, A. Orthomolecular approach to the treatment of learning disabilities. *Schizophrenia*, 1971, *3*, 95.

Cruickshank, W.M. The false hope of integration. *The Australian Journal on the Education of Backward Children*, 1974, *21*, 70-72.

Division for Children with Learning Disabilities, *Code of Ethics and Competencies for Teachers of Learning Disabled Children and Youth*. Kansas City, Kans: DCLD, University of Kansas Medical Center, 1978.

Feingold, B.F. *Why your child is hyperactive.* New York: Random House, 1975.

Frostig, M., & Horne, D. *The Frostig program for the development of visual perception.* Chicago: Follett, 1964.

Frostig, M., Lefever, D., & Whittlesey, J. *The Marianne Frostig Developmental Test of Visual Perception.* Palo Alto, Calif.: Consulting Psychologists Press, 1964.

Hammill, D.D., & Larsen, S.C. The effectiveness of psycholinguistic training. *Exceptional Children*, 1974, *41*, 5-14.

Hammill, D.D., & Larsen, S.C. The effectiveness of psycholinguistic training: A reaffirmation of position. *Exceptional Children*, 1978, *44*, 402-414.

Jakupak, M.J. Areas of congruence in remedial reading and learning disabilities. *Journal of Special Education*, 1975, *9*, 155-157.

Kauffman, J.M. *Characteristics of children's behavior disorders.* Columbus, Ohio: Charles E. Merrill, 1977.

Kirk, S.A., & Elkins, J. Characteristics of children enrolled in the child service demonstration centers. *Journal of Learning Disabilities*, 1975, *8*, 630-637.

Kirk, S., McCarthy, J., & Kirk, W. *Illinois Test of Psycholinguistic Abilities.* Urbana, Ill.: University of Illinois Press, 1968.

Kornetsky, C. Minimal brain dysfunction and drugs. In W. Cruickshank and D. Hallahan (Eds.), *Perceptual and Learning Disabilities in Children* (Vol. 2). Syracuse, N.Y.: Syracuse University Press, 1975.

Larsen, S.C. The learning disabilities specialist: Role and responsibilities. *Journal of Learning Disabilities*, 1976, *9*, 498-508.

Larsen, S.C. Learning disabilities and the professional educator. *Learning Disability Quarterly*, 1978, *1*, 5-12.

Lerner, J. *Children with learning disabilities* (2nd ed.). Boston: Houghton Mifflin, 1976.

Lewandowski, G. Learning disabilities certification: A needed revision. *The Reading Teacher,* 1977, *31,* 132-133.

Lovitt, T.C. The learning disabled. In N.G. Haring (Ed.), *Behavior of exceptional children* (2nd ed.). Columbus, Ohio: Charles E. Merrill, 1978.

Lund, K.A., Foster, G.E., & McCall-Perez, F.C. The effectiveness of psycholinguistic training: A reevaluation. *Exceptional Children,* 1978, *44,* 310-319.

Maitland, G. Who's child is he—yours, mine, or ours? *Journal of Childhood Communication Disorders,* 1976, *8,* 15-26.

Mercer, C.D., Forgnone, C., & Wolking, W.D. Definitions of learning disabilities used in the United States. *Journal of Learning Disabilities,* 1976, *9,* 376-386.

Minskoff, E.H., Wiseman, D.E., & Minskoff, J.G. *The MWM program for developing language abilities.* Ridgefield, N.J.: Educational Performance Associates, 1972.

Myers, P.I., and Hammill, D.D. *Methods for learning disorders* (2nd ed.). New York: John Wiley, 1976.

Newcomer, P.L. *The process approach: A non-advocacy position.* Paper presented at the Council for Exceptional Children International Conference, Los Angeles, April 1975.

Newcomer, P., Larsen, S.C., & Hammill, D.D. A response. *Exceptional Children,* 1975, *42,* 144-148.

Quinn, J. The efficacy of drug therapy for children with learning disabilities. Unpublished manuscript, 1976. (Available from Department of Special Education, University of Virginia, Charlottesville, Va.)

Sartain, H.W. Instruction of disabled learners: A reading perspective. *Journal of Learning Disabilities,* 1976, *9,* 489-497.

Senf, G.M. Needed—A new perspective on our learning disabilities definitions. *Journal of Learning Disabilities,* 1977, *10,* 537-539.

Sieben, R.I. Controversial medical treatments of learning disabilities. *Academic Therapy,* 1977, *13,* 133-147.

Spring, C., & Sandoval, J. Food additives and hyperkinesis: A critical evaluation of the evidence. *Journal of Learning Disabilities,* 1976, *9,* 560-569.

Stick, S. The speech pathologist and handicapped learners. *Journal of Learning Disabilities,* 1976, *9,* 509-519.

Sroufe, L.A. Drug treatment of children with behavior problems. In F.D. Horowitz (Ed.), *Review of child development research* (Vol. 4). Chicago: University of Chicago Press, 1975.

Vellutino, F.R., Steger, B.M., Moyer, S.C., Harding, C.J., & Niles, J.A. Has the perceptual deficit hypothesis led us astray? *Journal of Learning Disabilities,* 1977, *10,* 375-385.

Wallace, G. Interdisciplinary efforts in learning disabilities: Issues and recommendations. *Journal of Learning Disabilities,* 1976, *9,* 520-526.

Wender, P.H. *Minimal brain dysfunction in children.* New York: John Wiley, 1971.

Wepman, J. *Auditory Discrimination Test.* Chicago: Language Research Associates, 1958.

Wiederholt, J.L. Introduction to remedial reading and learning disabilities: Are they the same or different? *Journal of Special Education,* 1975, *9,* 117-119.

SUBJECT INDEX

NAME INDEX